Discovering Christ

In

The Gospel Of Mark

Discovering Christ
In
The Gospel Of Mark

Donald S. Fortner

Go *publications*

Go Publications
The Cairn, Hill Top, Eggleston, Co. Durham, DL12 0AU, ENGLAND

© Go Publications 2011
First Published 2011

British Library Cataloguing in Publication Data available

ISBN 978-095486249-7

Printed and bound in Great Britain
By Lightning Source UK Ltd.

Publisher's Dedication

This book is dedicated to Stewart Boyd,
a fellowlabourer in the gospel.

Contents

Foreword

I will never forget the first time I heard Pastor Don Fortner preach from his pulpit at Grace Baptist Church of Danville, Kentucky. The sermon was titled *"Ye Are Complete in Christ"*. The text for that sermon was taken from Colossians 2:10. To this day, I can still hear those glorious words being thundered by his boisterous voice, "Ye are complete in Christ!" What good news that sermon brought to this ruined sinner!

Since then, I have noted that every sermon and book preached or published by my dear friend contains as its theme the substance of that first sermon. It is the theme of all Scripture. It is the theme that fuels the flame of hope in all of God's people. It is the theme that the reader will find throughout the seventy-eight short chapters of this book.

I know Pastor Don Fortner personally and I know why he wrote this book. This book was written for one purpose. It was written to illuminate Jehovah's Righteous Servant, the Lord Jesus Christ, to men who have no righteousness of their own or in themselves. This Righteous Servant, as He is set forth in the Gospel of Mark, was sent into this world of sin and death to fulfill all righteousness for His chosen people. These chosen people are now made complete by this Righteous Servant.

It will not take the reader very long to discover that this book was not written for theologians, but for sinners. It was not written for righteous men and women, but for poor and needy souls. It was not written for those of high intellect, but for those of us who often struggle in finding the Christ of holy scripture presented clearly in plain and simple language.

As you read this book, I pray that God the Holy Spirit will reveal His Righteous Servant to your heart, that you too might know "Ye are complete in Christ!"

Anthony Moody
Kingsport, Tennessee

Introduction

Christ The Servant

The words of our Saviour in Mark 10:45 give us a clear summary of Mark's Gospel. Remember, Mark's object is to present our Saviour in his character as Jehovah's righteous Servant; and that is exactly how our Lord describes himself. "For even the Son of man came not to be ministered unto, but to minister, and to give his life a ransom for many".

Distinct Purpose

Each of the four gospel narratives is distinct. Each one presents our Saviour in a specific character. It is a mistake to read Matthew, Mark, Luke, and John as four biographies of the Lord Jesus. They are not biographies at all. They are biographical character sketches. Each is intended to be different from the other. Each presents our Saviour from a distinctly different point of view. The four Gospels give us four distinct views of our Lord and of his work.

The Gospel of Matthew is written to present Christ as the King. The Gospel of Mark presents his character as Jehovah's Servant. The Gospel of Luke presents him as the Son of man. The Gospel of John presents him as the Son of God.

No Genealogy

Have you ever wondered why there is no record of our Lord's ascension in Matthew and John, and why there is no record of his genealogy in Mark? Luke gives his own record of our Lord's genealogy as a man; but John gives us neither a record of his genealogy nor his ascension. Why? The answer is obvious when you remember the distinct purpose of each.

Matthew presents Christ as the King, and Luke presents him as the man promised in the Old Testament. In both cases a genealogical record is needed. Because Christ is the King from eternity, a record of his ascension in

Matthew's case would be redundant. John presents the Saviour as the incarnate God, that One who is immutably God over all and blessed forever. In his case, a record of our Lord's genealogy or his ascension would be contrary to his purpose. Mark only mentions the ascension, because his intent is to show us that as Jehovah's Servant, our Saviour's mission is complete, successful, and accepted by the Father. Having finished his work, he sat down on the right hand of the Majesty on High (Hebrews 1:1-3; 10:10-14).

Christ The Servant

Mark's Gospel narrative is "a joyful account of the ministry, miracles, actions, and sufferings of Christ" says John Gill. It is all about the obedience of our Saviour to the will of God. He tells us nothing about the birth and early life of our Lord. He gives us very few details about our Master's sermons. Yet he gives greater details than others about his miracles. Mark's is the shortest of the four Gospels. Yet it is not in any way less significant. Mark used greater brevity than the others; but his narrative is just as important. Those who suggest that Mark simply copied down some facts from Matthew, or that he wrote what Peter told him to write both miss the purpose of Mark's work and undermine the inspiration and authority of holy scripture. Without question, he got information from those men who taught him the gospel; but he wrote by divine inspiration.

J. C. Ryle very properly observed that Mark's Gospel is "The independent narrative of an independent witness, who was inspired to write a history of our Lord's works, rather than of his words ... Like all the rest of scripture, every word of St Mark is 'given by inspiration of God' and every word is 'profitable.'"

Mark Himself

The man God used to give us this inspired narrative of our Saviour's obedience as our Representative, as the One who worked out righteousness for us, was a man like us, not always dependable, a sinner saved by grace, just like we are.

In other places he is called John Mark. He was the man who accompanied Paul on his first missionary journey and proved himself at that time an unfaithful servant. He could not take the pressure of the work: the constant opposition, the thankless labour, and the relentless long, lonely hours. So he ran back home to momma. This is not the only time we see Mark displaying such weakness.

If you want to meet Bro. Mark turn to chapter 14. There is an unnamed young man here, who is probably Mark himself. I say that because Mark does not give us the man's name and because this is the only time this incident is mentioned in scripture. After our Lord's arrest in Gethsemane, we are told that the disciples forsook him. But Mark adds what is found in verses 51 and 52. "And there followed him a certain young man, having a linen cloth cast about his naked body; and the young men laid hold on him: And he left the linen cloth, and fled from them naked".

Yet, this is the man God chose to use to give us this portion of his Word. A less than dependable servant, a man who was at times very weak, was chosen to record for us the perfect faithfulness of that Servant of God of whom it is written, "He shall not fail", the Lord Jesus Christ. I am thankful for that fact. Aren't you? If the Lord used one failure, maybe he will use another (1 Corinthians 1:26-29).

Peter's Influence

Mark was Peter's son in the faith (1 Peter 5:13). He was converted under the influence of Peter's ministry and taught by Peter. He was, as well he should have been, greatly influenced by his pastor, Peter. His Gospel narrative naturally reflects the teachings and viewpoints we see in Peter.

In fact, if you will look at Acts 10:38, you will see that Peter gives us a very brief summary of all that is recorded for us in the Gospel of Mark. Speaking in the house of Cornelius, we read that Peter stood among them and told them exactly what Mark tells us in these 16 chapters. "How God anointed Jesus of Nazareth with the Holy Ghost and with power: who went about doing good, and healing all that were oppressed of the devil; for God was with him".

Matthew and John, like Peter and Paul, were apostles of Christ. As such, they learned the gospel from the Master himself. Neither Mark nor Luke was an apostle. What they learned of Christ, they learned, like us, through the preaching of others by the teaching of the Holy Spirit through the preached Word (Romans 10:17).

Profitable Mark

The human author of this Gospel narrative was John Mark, the son of Barnabas' sister, Mary (Acts 12:12, 25; Colossians 4:12). Paul and Barnabas eventually had a falling out because Paul refused to take Mark with them on his second missionary journey (Acts 15:36-41). But that is not the end of the story. At some point, Paul and Mark did some fence-mending, and in his latter days the old man Paul found Mark to be one of few who were loyal to the gospel. As he was awaiting execution, he wrote to Timothy and said, "Take Mark, and bring him with thee: for he is profitable to me for the ministry" (2 Timothy 4:11).

Mark's Message

Instead of opening with a record of our Lord's incarnation and birth, instead of telling us about his youth and early years, as one might imagine, Mark begins at once with his ministry. Look at verse 1 of chapter 1. "The beginning of the gospel of Jesus Christ, the Son of God". This is the beginning, but not the end, for there is no end to the story Mark tells. He is telling us the God-story of redemption, grace, and salvation by God's Servant, "Jesus Christ, the Son of God".

Our Lord tells us that the story will go on forever, even in eternity. This is too wondrous to grasp; but our Lord tells us that in that great day called "eternity", "he shall gird himself and make (us) to sit down to meat, and will come forth and serve (us)" (Luke 12:37). We will never come to the end of the story. The gospel of Jesus Christ, the Son of God, is everlasting.

Time Fulfilled

After describing the ministry of John the Baptist and our Lord's baptism by him (1:2-13), Mark gives a very brief description of the wilderness temptation (vv. 12, 13). Yet, even in his brevity, Mark adds some things that show the greatness of that trial by which the faithfulness of Jehovah's Servant was proved.

Matthew and Luke tell us that our Lord was "led" of the Spirit into the wilderness. Mark's words are stronger. "The Spirit driveth him into the wilderness". It is Mark who tells us the temptation of the Lord Jesus lasted forty days, and that the Son of God was "with the wild beasts" in the wilderness.

Then, he begins to describe our Lord's earthly ministry in verses 14 and 15 of chapter 1. "Now after that John was put in prison, Jesus came into Galilee, preaching the gospel of the kingdom of God, And saying, The time is fulfilled, and the kingdom of God is at hand: repent ye, and believe the gospel".

Mark tells us that our Lord stepped onto the scene of history and declared that the time God had promised for the accomplishment of his promises of redemption were fulfilled. That meant that the kingdom of God was now in the midst of men. If we enter into that kingdom, we must enter in by faith's door, believing on the Lord Jesus Christ. In due time, Christ came here to die for the ungodly (Romans 5:6; Galatians 4:4, 5). Paul writes, "When the fulness of the time was come, God sent forth his Son, made of a woman, made under the law, to redeem them that were under the law, that we might receive the adoption of sons". He came here as Jehovah's Servant (Philippians 2:5-8).

First Disciples

Immediately after announcing our Lord's appearance in Galilee, calling sinners to repentance, Mark shows us what is meant by that. In verses 16-18 we are told how that the Lord Jesus called his first disciples, Simon and Andrew, James and John. Those who repent and believe, those who come to and follow Christ, those who are born into his kingdom are called by him. And those who are called by him forsake all and follow him.

Full Of Activity

The Gospel of Mark is a book full of activity. He moves rapidly from one place to another and from one miracle to another. The words 'immediately', 'forthwith', 'anon', and 'straightway' meet us constantly in these 16 chapters. Many of the chapters begin with the word "And". If Mark were telling us his story orally, we might say, "Slow down. You're moving too fast". That is exactly the sense the Holy Spirit intends to give us in this book. Mark is describing God's faithful Servant, our all-glorious Christ, whose meat and drink it was to do the will of his Father. He had nothing to call his own, not even his time. O Lord, my God, give me grace to be such a servant!

Mark moves like lightning as he declares our Lord's works in Galilee, casting out demons and healing the sick (1:21-3:12; 5:25-34; 6:53-56; 7:24-37). He gives us display after display of our Lord's power and authority as that Servant into whose hands the Father has given all things. After giving us four kingdom parables in chapter 4, he calmed the raging sea and the troubled hearts of his disciples with his mere word (4:35-41). He cast demons out of the poor Gadarene (5:1-20). A woman was healed of her twelve-year issue of blood by the touch of his garment (5:25-34). He raised Jairus' twelve year old daughter from the dead (5:35-43). He fed hungry multitudes by miraculously multiplying little (6:34-44; 8:1-9). Twice we read of him giving sight to the blind. Repeatedly, we read of our tender Saviour having "compassion" upon needy souls.

Pictures Of Grace

These miracles were intended to display our Saviour's power and authority as that man who is Jehovah's Servant, that man who is God, to show that he has power and authority by virtue of who he is and by virtue of the sacrifice he made in eternity and was about to make at Calvary, to forgive sins (2:9, 10).

It is therefore obvious that these miracles were intended to be pictures of his wondrous works of grace in saving lost sinners. Like the leper, saved sinners have been made whole by Christ, the Priest, who touched us and made himself unclean to make us clean. We are made whole by the omnipotent touch of his grace. Like the woman with that twelve-year issue of blood, who had spent all she had on physicians of no value, we are made whole by virtue we get from touching him. Like the Syrophenician woman, we who have no claim on the children's bread have obtained mercy by faith in Christ. Like the Gadarene, we have been made whole and set free by the Master's word of grace. Like the blind men, our Lord has given us eyes to see him and to see "every man clearly" (8:25). Like Jairus' daughter, the Lord Jesus Christ raised us up from the dead.

Determination To Die

Beginning in chapter 8 (v. 31), we see a marked determination in our Saviour, Jehovah's Servant. He set his face like a flint to go up to Jerusalem, to suffer all the wrath of God as our Substitute (Isaiah 50:5-7). "And he began to teach them, that the Son of man must suffer many things, and be rejected of the elders, and of the chief priests, and scribes, and be killed, and after three days rise again".

The Lord Jesus did not come here hoping that the Jews would allow him to be their king, sitting on a physical throne in Jerusalem. He came here as the King to suffer and die, rise again the third day, and ascend to his throne to give eternal life to his elect by the virtue and efficacy of his blood atonement. He came here to do the will of his Father, suffering death as our Substitute at Jerusalem, and nothing could deter or hinder him from accomplishing his purpose.

Peter's Reaction

Look at Peter's response to the Lord's declared purpose (8:32). "Peter took him, and began to rebuke him". Matthew gives a fuller quotation of Peter's words. "Then Peter took him, and began to rebuke him, saying, Be it far from thee, Lord: this shall not be unto thee" (Matthew 16:22). Peter said, "Spare yourself of this, Lord".

That is always the response of the flesh to trouble. "Spare yourself." Then the Master sternly rebuked Peter, saying, "Get thee behind me, Satan: for thou savourest not the things that be of God, but the things that be of men" (v. 23).

John Gill suggests, I think accurately, that, "the Lord rebuked him in a very severe, though just manner; being touched in his most tender part, and dissuaded from that which his heart was set upon, and he came into the world for; whose keen resentment is seen by using a phrase he never did but to the devil himself". The Master knew the source and cause of Peter's comments. The flesh, like Satan, is always opposed to the will of God. The flesh always chooses that which is easiest on, and most appealing to, the flesh.

That this is the meaning of this conversation between Christ and his errant disciple is obvious because of what follows in verses 34-38. If we would follow the Lord Jesus Christ, if we would be his disciples, if we would be God's servants – that is what it is to be a believer – we must give up our will to his will. We must surrender the rule of our lives to the rule of God our Saviour. That is what Jehovah's righteous Servant did in the example he left us in the rest of Mark's Gospel (1 Peter 2:21).

Transfiguration

In chapter 9 we have Mark's account of the Transfiguration. "And he said unto them, Verily I say unto you, That there be some of them that stand here, which shall not taste of death, till they have seen the kingdom of God come with power" (v. 1). Then the Lord Jesus led Peter, James, and John up on the mountain and they literally did not taste of death till they saw the King coming in glory. Peter refers to this in 2 Peter 1:16-18.

"For we have not followed cunningly devised fables, when we made known unto you the power and coming of our Lord Jesus Christ, but were eyewitnesses of his majesty. For he received from God the Father honour and glory, when there came such a voice to him from the excellent glory, This is my beloved Son, in whom I am well pleased. And this voice which came from heaven we heard, when we were with him in the holy mount."

The suggestion is that God's purpose for his elect and the purpose of Christ's redemptive work is that we should not taste of death. He came to deliver us from the awful taste of death. Our all-glorious Saviour tasted death for everyone he came to save that we might never taste it (Hebrews 2:9), that we might ever behold and be the recipients of his glory as Jehovah's righteous Servant (John 17:22-26).

Then he identifies his family, those who shall behold and enjoy his glory forever, his children, the citizens and heirs of his kingdom. They are those who, in this world, cast all their care on him (9:17-24), becoming as little children taken into his omnipotent arms, trusting him as Lord and Saviour (vv. 36, 37), and blessed in and by him. Mark alone tells us that he took the little children up in his arms when he blessed them (10:13-16).

Money Changers

Our Lord's last week on earth before the crucifixion begins in chapter 11. Here again Mark tells us about a very significant event the other Gospel writers were not inspired to record. "And they come to Jerusalem: and Jesus went into the temple, and began to cast out them that sold and bought in the temple, and overthrew the tables of the moneychangers, and the seats of them that sold doves; and would not suffer that any man should carry any vessel through the temple" (vv. 15, 16).

This is not the same event John spoke of in John 2:13-16. That event took place at the beginning of our Lord's ministry. That which Mark records took place at the end of his ministry. For the second time, the Lord Jesus overthrows the tables of the money-changers, and cleanses the temple. Mark says, he "would not suffer that any man should carry any vessel through the temple".

According to the Mosaic law, it was the responsibility of the priests to catch the blood of the sacrifices on the brazen altar in the outer court and carry it into the holy place before the altar. Once each year the high priest would go into the Holy of Holies and sprinkle that blood upon the mercy seat. All of this was highly symbolic of Christ's sin-atoning work.

He of whom the priests and the sacrifices were types had come to put an end to all this. He would not allow any man to carry anything through the temple. In other words, he ended the sacrifices. He is the end of the law (Romans 10:4). In this act our Lord was saying, "The Lamb of God has come to put away sin by the sacrifice of himself".

More Questions
Mark chapters 10-13 are primarily concerned with the questions people asked the Saviour. In chapter 10 he answers the Pharisees questions about divorce, the rich young ruler's question, the disciples' question about salvation, and James and John's question about greatness. He tells the Pharisees that marriage is forever. He told the rich young ruler that the way to eternal life is by faith alone, the faith that surrenders all to Christ as Lord and God. When the disciples heard the conversation between Christ and the rich young ruler, and heard the Master's explanation of why that man so rich in material property and religious morality did not believe, they said, "Who then can be saved?" The Master answered, "With men it is impossible, but not with God: for with God all things are possible".

In chapter 11 he answers the questions of the priests, the scribes, and the elders who come out of hatred for him and try to trap him with their questions about his authority to purge the temple. He answered them by refusing to answer them.

In chapter 12 the Pharisees, Herodians, Sadducees, and a scribe tried to trap him with their questions. The Lord Jesus saw through their hypocrisy and answered them accordingly. The Pharisees and Herodians were trying to get him to say something that could be used to accuse him of stirring insurrection against Caesar. The Sadducees tried to trick him into saying something that might be twisted into a denial of the resurrection. Then a scribe tried to trick him into speaking a word against the law.

In chapter 13, as they sat on the Mount of Olives, Peter, James, John, and Andrew ask the Lord Jesus what he meant when he spoke of the destruction of the temple. They said, "Tell us, when shall these things be? and what shall be the sign when all these things shall be fulfilled" (v. 4). The rest of the chapter is taken up with our Saviour's answer, warning them and us of the great danger of following false christs.

A Good Work

Multitudes talk about good works. Usually their intent is to defend their pretended good works of self-righteousness. In chapter 14 Mark shows us an event that displays what a good work is. "There came a woman having an alabaster box of ointment of spikenard very precious; and she brake the box, and poured it on his head" (v. 3). Others, including the disciples, sharply criticized her.

"And Jesus said, Let her alone; why trouble ye her? she hath wrought a good work on me. For ye have the poor with you always, and whensoever ye will ye may do them good: but me ye have not always. She hath done what she could: she is come aforehand to anoint my body to the burying. Verily I say unto you, Wheresoever this gospel shall be preached throughout the whole world, this also that she hath done shall be spoken of for a memorial of her" (14:6-9).

The Master said, "She hath wrought a good work on me". That is the only time in the Bible anything done by a sinful human being is specifically called "a good work" by our Lord. That fact is very instructive. Good works are not what most imagine they are. A good work is a work of faith. This dear lady seems to have been the only person who understood and believed what the Lord had said about his death and resurrection. A good work involves personal sacrifice. It is always costly. A good work is a work of spontaneous love wrought for Christ. A good work is doing what you can for the Saviour. A good work is a work that God our Saviour never forgets.

The Crucifixion

Beginning with chapter 15, we have the account of the crucifixion. Mark describes this as an act of horrible brutality done in the name of justice and righteousness. The Lord Jesus appears to be a defeated man, a tragic failure, and his cause hopelessly lost. He is hounded, bludgeoned and spat upon. Finally, he is crucified upon the cursed tree between two thieves. Is this Jehovah's Servant?

No wonder the high priests, as they saw him hanging naked, upon the tree, covered in his own blood and the excrement of men, laughed and said, "He saved others; himself cannot save" (v. 31).

That is a strange statement. Yet it is one of the most remarkable statements of gospel truth ever to fall from the lips of men. It shows that God is able to make even his enemies praise him.

Three Things

As we read this account, we see three things that they could not make our Lord do. First, they could not make our Lord speak. "And Pilate asked him again, saying, Answerest thou nothing? behold how many things they witness against thee" (v. 4). He could have called twelve legions of angels to deliver him; but the Master said nothing, and Pilate wondered.

Second, they could not make him drink. "And they gave him to drink wine mingled with myrrh: but he received it not" (v. 23). Why not? The mixture offered him would have relieved our Lord of some of the agony he endured. Had he drunk what they gave him, he would have saved himself the effect of the agony of the cross and the weight of the burden of all hell and all the wrath of God pressing upon him; but he would not. He would not spare himself.

Then, third, they could not make him die. "And Jesus cried with a loud voice, and gave up the ghost" (v. 37). "He unspirited himself". He dismissed his spirit. He did not die at the hands of the Jews or the Romans. He died at the hand of God, by his own voluntary will, as Jehovah's Righteous Servant (John 10:17, 18).

"And being found in fashion as a man, he humbled himself, and became obedient unto death, even the death of the cross. Wherefore God also hath highly exalted him, and given him a name which is above every name: that at the name of Jesus every knee should bow, of things in heaven, and things in earth, and things under the earth and that every tongue should confess that Jesus Christ is Lord, to the glory of God the Father" (Philippians 2:8-11).

The Resurrection

When we get to the last chapter and the resurrection of our Lord, we see his reason. He was silent and refused to appeal to Pilate or the crowd, because he was laying the basis for a coming day, when in resurrection power and glory every knee will bow and every tongue will confess that Jesus Christ is Lord to the glory of God the Father.

He would not drink to dull his senses, because he was laying a basis upon which even those who stood around the cross might enter into a life eternal. He was laying the foundation upon which God can be just and the Justifier of all who believe. He was determined to die, that he might be exalted as Lord of all, to give eternal life to as many as the Father had given him.

He would not let men take his life; but he voluntarily laid it down himself in order that he might overcome our greatest enemy, death, and forever deliver all who would believe in him from the power and awful sting of death. That is the Gospel. He saved others, but himself he could not save. That is Mark's story.

My Favourite Verse

Before we conclude this introduction, let me give you my favourite verse in Mark's Gospel. It is not surprising to me that it is Mark and Mark alone who says what he does here (16:7). In this verse, he who was himself a disciple who had been unfaithful, speaks a word about his beloved friend and father in the faith, his pastor, Peter. He tells us that the young man who stood by the tomb of the risen Lord said to Mary Magdalene and Mary the mother of James, "Go your way, tell his disciples and Peter that he goeth before you into Galilee: there shall ye see him, as he said unto you".

It is as though he was reminding Peter, and all of us who are like Peter – weak, faltering, failing, sinful followers of Christ, that God's forgiveness of our sins in Christ is full, absolute, and complete. Christ died for our sins. That means, between us and our God and Saviour, everything is all right!

The book of Mark began with the words "the beginning of the gospel of Jesus Christ, the Son of God". In the last two verses of chapter 16 we have the continuation. The Lord Jesus Christ, Jehovah's Servant, is still carrying on his work, working in and through the preaching of the gospel by his church. "So then, after the Lord had spoken unto them, he was received up into the heaven, and sat on the right hand of God. And they went forth, and preached everywhere, the Lord working with them, and confirming the word with signs following".

"The beginning of the gospel of Jesus Christ, the Son of God; As it is written in the prophets, Behold, I send my messenger before thy face, which shall prepare thy way before thee. The voice of one crying in the wilderness, Prepare ye the way of the Lord, make his paths straight. John did baptize in the wilderness, and preach the baptism of repentance for the remission of sins. And there went out unto him all the land of Judaea, and they of Jerusalem, and were all baptized of him in the river of Jordan, confessing their sins. And John was clothed with camel's hair, and with a girdle of a skin about his loins; and he did eat locusts and wild honey; And preached, saying, There cometh one mightier than I after me, the latchet of whose shoes I am not worthy to stoop down and unloose. I indeed have baptized you with water: but he shall baptize you with the Holy Ghost".

(Mark 1:1-8)

Chapter 1

"The Beginning Of The Gospel"

There is much speculation about the evangelist Mark and his gospel. For our part we shall leave the speculation to the people who are interested in chasing rabbits and be content with what is revealed. The book we are studying is called, "The Gospel According To St Mark". John Gill calls it "a joyful account of the ministry, miracles, actions, and sufferings of Christ".

The human author of this gospel narrative was John Mark, the son of Barnabas' sister, Mary (Acts 12:12, 25; Colossians 4:12). He is probably the same Mark whom Peter describes as his son in the faith (1 Peter 5:13).

Mark's Gospel is somewhat different from the other three. He tells us nothing about the birth and early life of our Lord. He gives us very few details about our Lord's sermons. Yet he gives greater details than others about his miracles. Of the four inspired histories of our Saviour, Mark's is the shortest. Yet it is not in any way less significant. Mark used greater brevity than the others; but his narrative is just as important. As we saw in the *Introduction*, those who suggest that Mark simply copied down some facts from Matthew, or that he wrote what Peter told him to write both miss the purpose of Mark's work and undermine the inspiration and authority of holy scripture. J. C. Ryle very properly observed that Mark's gospel is, "The independent narrative of an independent witness, who was inspired to write a history of our Lord's works, rather than of his words."

As we go through these sixteen chapters, I hope we will read every word with reverence and that God the Holy Spirit will give us understanding in the things written in them. I quote Ryle again, "Like all the rest of scripture, every word of St. Mark is 'given by inspiration of God', and every word is 'profitable'."

Passing by the incarnation, birth, and early life of our Saviour, Mark begins his gospel narrative by telling us who Jesus Christ is, and his starting point is the ministry of John the Baptist, when the Lord Jesus was about thirty years old.

The Beginning

"The beginning of the gospel of Jesus Christ" (v. 1). Obviously, Mark does not mean for us to understand that the gospel began at this time, or that he was the first to preach it. There are a few religious imposters like that around; but Mark was not one of them. The gospel of Christ began back in eternity, in the mind and purpose of God almighty, when Christ was in his decree "The Lamb slain from the foundation of the world" (Revelation 13:8). It was preached by God himself to our fallen parents in the garden (Genesis 3:15). It was preached to, believed by, and then preached by Job, Noah, Abraham, and the prophets of God throughout the days of the Old Testament.

By these opening words of Mark's Gospel, the Holy Spirit simply means for us to understand that this gospel age, this dispensation of grace, began with the ministry of John the Baptist, which was introductory to and one with the ministry of the Lord Jesus Christ. John's ministry announced the end of the legal dispensation, the fulfilment and termination of the law by Christ, and the dawn of this day of grace. This is not a guess, but exactly what the scriptures state (Matthew 11:13; Luke 16:16).

The gospel revealed in holy scripture, the gospel by which the Word of God is preached and expounded to sinners is here called "the gospel of Jesus Christ". It is not the Baptist gospel, the Protestant gospel, the Catholic gospel, the Arminian gospel, or even the Calvinist gospel. It is "the gospel of Jesus Christ". The gospel is not a theological system, a denominational creed, or a religious practice. The gospel is a Person. Mark calls it; no, the Holy Spirit calls it, "the gospel of Jesus Christ".

Jesus Christ is the gospel. Do you see that? Very few people do. He is the Author of it, the great Preacher of it, the Substance of it, and the Message of it. The gospel is God's good word, faithful and true, about his Son, Jesus Christ. The gospel is the revelation and proclamation of Jesus Christ, who he is and what he has done. You cannot separate Christ and the gospel. Christ is the gospel; and the gospel is Christ.

It is God's revelation and declaration that his Son is Jesus, the Redeemer and Saviour of lost sinners, the Christ, the Messiah, who was promised in the Old Testament, the Mediator between God and men, the Prophet who has declared all the mind and will of God, the Great High Priest who has offered himself a sacrifice for his people's sins, made peace, procured pardon, brought in everlasting righteousness, obtained eternal redemption, and now lives to make intercession for us according to the will of God, and the King of Glory who reigns over all things to save, defend, protect, provide for, and preserve his redeemed ones.

26

That is the commencement of the gospel. It began with, and has its beginning in our hearts with the coming, the revelation, and the knowledge of Jesus Christ.

The Claim Of Christianity
Look at verse one again. "The beginning of the gospel of Jesus Christ, the Son of God". That is the unique, foundational, essential, basic claim of Christianity. Jesus Christ is himself God the eternal Son. Those who deny the eternal deity and godhead of the man Christ Jesus, either openly and directly, or by inference of their teachings, are not Christians.

When Mark asserts that Jesus Christ is "the Son of God", he makes no effort to prove his claim. He simply states it as a matter of well-known, commonly received fact, because among Christians, it is a well-known, commonly received fact.

The man Jesus Christ is God the eternal Son, in every way one with and equal with the Father and the Spirit, of the same nature and essence, possessing the same perfections and the same glory. He is "over all God, blessed forever". In him "dwelleth all the fulness of the godhead bodily". The whole of the gospel stands or falls here. Christianity stands or falls here. The satisfaction of Christ is of infinite merit and efficacy because he is God. His death upon the cross is of infinite value to God and infinitely effectual for sinners because he is God. The death of Christ was not the death of a mere man, but the death of a man who is God. That means He cannot fail. Those for whom he died must and shall be saved. Those who deny the efficacy of Christ's atonement, in effect, deny the deity of his Person, for if his blood is not effectual, his sacrifice is worthless! John Gill wrote:

> Matthew began his Gospel with the humanity, Mark with the divinity of Christ. The one calls him the Son of David, the other the Son of God. Both (are) true. Christ is the Son of David according to his human nature, (and) the Son of God according to his divine nature. So a testimony is borne to the truth of both his natures, which are united in one person.

The Unity Of Holy Scripture
"As it is written in the prophets, Behold, I send my messenger before thy face, which shall prepare thy way before thee. The voice of one crying in the wilderness, Prepare ye the way of the Lord, make his paths straight" (vv. 2, 3).

27

Matthew Henry observed that, "The gospel of Jesus Christ begins, and goes on, just as it is written in the prophets; for it saith no other things than those which the prophets and Moses said should come" (Acts 26:22). The gospel of Christ is the fulfilment of the Old Testament scriptures. From Genesis through to Malachi we see the event foretold again and again with constantly increasing clarity. The promise was made to Adam, renewed to the patriarchs, and repeated to the prophets that the Redeemer would come. His birth, his character, his life of obedience, his sin-atoning death, his resurrection, even his forerunner, were prophesied and typified hundreds of years before he came. Our Saviour's great work of redemption was accomplished in every detail exactly as the Old Testament scriptures declared it must be. That is what Paul preached to the Jews at Antioch. "And when they had fulfilled all that was written of him, they took him down from the tree, and laid him in a sepulchre" (Acts 13:29).

In this passage Mark quotes from both Malachi (3:1) and Isaiah (40:3), two Old Testament prophets who lived three hundred years or more apart, telling us that both wrote of the coming of Christ and redemption by him. In doing so he tells us three things about John the Baptist, and really about every true gospel preacher.

As John was God's messenger sent ahead of Christ, so every true gospel preacher is God's messenger sent to those to whom he shall send his Son in saving grace.

As John the Baptist was sent to prepare the way for Christ, so God's servants are sent to prepare the way for Christ by the preaching of the gospel.

As John's was "the voice of one crying in the wilderness", so gospel preachers are voices crying in a spiritually dark, empty, desolate wilderness, "Prepare ye the way of the Lord, make his paths straight". That means, "Prepare to meet thy God". The only way any sinner can prepare to meet God is to turn to him in genuine repentance, believing on the Lord Jesus Christ.

We have read the Old Testament with absolutely no spiritual profit, with no profit to our souls, if we have only observed its historical facts, moral laws, supernatural events, and fulfilled prophecies. The message of the Old Testament is Christ. Our Lord was referring to the Old Testament when he said, "These are they which testify of me" (John 5:39). The Old Testament and the New Testament is one revelation of God. We do not have two Bibles, just one; and its theme is "Jesus Christ and him crucified".

Believer's Baptism

"John did baptize in the wilderness, and preach the baptism of repentance for the remission of sins. And there went out unto him all the land of Judaea, and they of Jerusalem, and were all baptized of him in the river of Jordan, confessing their sins" (vv. 4, 5).

We must not make more of baptism than the New Testament makes of it. Yet, we dare not make less of it than the New Testament does. Baptism has absolutely no saving merit or efficacy; but it is not a matter of indifference. It is not an optional, insignificant religious ritual. Baptism is not a sacrament by which grace is conferred or even received; but it is an ordinance of divine worship, by which we confess our faith in and allegiance to the Lord Jesus Christ, by whose blood we have the remission of sins. Taking John the Baptist as our example, three things are clearly revealed in these verses about the gospel ordinance of baptism.

Baptism Is And Must Be By Immersion
We read, "John did baptize in the wilderness". We do not read that he sprinkled, or that he poured, but that he baptized (dipped, plunged, immersed) those who came to him. The word translated "baptize" in the New Testament cannot, with honesty, be made to mean "sprinkle" or "pour". The word means, "dip, plunge, or immerse". Immersion is not a mode of baptism. Immersion is baptism.

Baptism Has Reference To Redemption
John preached "the baptism of repentance for (unto or because of) the remission of sins". He did not preach that baptism washes away or remits our sins, but that it symbolizes and portrays the washing away and remission of our sins by the blood of Christ, the Lamb of God (John 1:29). Baptism does not represent regeneration, or conversion, or sanctification; and it certainly does not represent circumcision! Baptism represents the remission of sins by the sin-atoning death of our great Substitute, the Lord Jesus Christ. That is why it is always described as a burial. Believers are buried with Christ in the watery grave of baptism symbolizing our death, burial, and resurrection with him representatively as our Substitute (Romans 6:3-6; Colossians 2:10-12).

Baptism Is For Believers Only
Those who were baptized by John came to him. They were not brought to him. They were baptized in the river, not with a teacup. And when they were baptized, they personally confessed their sins by the symbolic act of water baptism. That is to say, they confessed their need of a Saviour because of their sins, their faith in Christ by whose blood their sins were (in the decree of God and soon would be by the actual shedding of his blood) put away, and their allegiance to him who would put away their sins by the sacrifice of himself. Throughout the New Testament, the one pre-requisite for baptism is

personal faith in Christ. This is one reason why we reject the practice of infant baptism (Acts 8:35-39).

There is absolutely no precedent for infant baptism or for sprinkling in the place of baptism in the Word of God. Those things are nothing but remnants of papacy in Protestant churches. There is no reason to practice sprinkling, except to make it convenient to baptize babies; and there is no reason to baptize babies, unless you think there is some spiritual, saving efficacy in doing so. Thus, in reality, infant baptism is as much a denial of the gospel of salvation by grace alone as the corrupt Roman Catholic doctrine of indulgences.

Another fact that is displayed in John's ministry is that outward success and popularity is never to be depended upon or used as the measure of a preacher's usefulness. We read in verse 5 that "there went out unto him all the land of Judaea, and they of Jerusalem, and were all baptized of him in the river of Jordan, confessing their sins". Large crowds are always pleasing to see and encouraging; but we must never forget that very few of those who heard John and were baptized by him were truly converted. John the Baptist stirred things up. People were scared, emotionally excited, and greatly moved by his preaching; but few heard his message. It is not enough to hear and approve of popular preachers. We must hear Christ. It is not enough to follow the crowd, even when the crowd is right. We must follow Christ. We must never judge the success or failure of a ministry by the things we can see. It is not enough to be baptized in water. We must be baptized into Christ. "For as many of you as have been baptized into Christ have put on Christ" (Galatians 3:27).

A True Prophet

"And John was clothed with camel's hair, and with a girdle of a skin about his loins; and he did eat locusts and wild honey; And preached, saying, There cometh one mightier than I after me, the latchet of whose shoes I am not worthy to stoop down and unloose. I indeed have baptized you with water: but he shall baptize you with the Holy Ghost" (vv. 6-8).

John did not live delicately in luxury. He was not much concerned about the brand of clothes he wore or the ratings of the restaurants in which he ate. His concern was for the kingdom of God, the gospel of God, the truth of God, the glory of God, and the Son of God. He never tried to please men, and never sought the approval of men. John the Baptist was a prophet, a man sent from God with a message from God, a message that eternity bound sinners must hear and obey. He really was not very concerned about anything else. John was a prophet.

30

That which John preached is exactly what every prophet of God in every generation is sent of God to preach. Let me show you seven things about the preaching of John the Baptist. If these seven things do not characterize me, and my preaching, I am not God's servant, I have no business claiming to be a preacher, and no human being should hear me preach or read anything I write. The same is true of every other man to whom the term "preacher" is applied.

John preached the remission of sins by the blood atonement accomplished by the sacrificial death of Christ, the Lamb of God.

He preached repentance because of the remission of sins. We do not preach repentance to get your sins forgiven, but because of sin's forgiveness experienced in the soul (Zechariah 12:10).

John preached Jesus Christ and him crucified. Matthew Henry wrote, "The preaching of Christ is pure gospel preaching, and that was John Baptist's preaching". I say to myself and to every man who dares speak to eternity bound sinners in the name of God, preach Christ or preach nothing!

John preached Christ's great pre-eminence. He had such high views of Christ and such low views of himself that he felt totally unfit to serve his Saviour in the lowest, most menial, insignificant way, unfit to stoop down and untie his shoes.

He preached the great power of Christ. Men thought he was something and somebody. He said, "No, I'm nothing and nobody; but I have come to tell you about one who is mighty, the mighty God who is mighty to save.

John preached the effectual, saving operations of Christ. "He shall baptize you with the Holy Ghost". The Word of God nowhere talks about the Holy Spirit baptizing us into Christ; but it does talk about Christ baptizing chosen, redeemed sinners into the Holy Spirit. Christ baptized his church into the Spirit on the day of Pentecost in Acts 2. The Kingdom of God was then immersed in the Spirit. It ceased to be a carnal, family kingdom, and became a spiritual kingdom. In a sense, believers are baptized by Christ into the Holy Spirit in the new birth. That is to say, when a person is born again he is translated from the kingdom of darkness into the kingdom of light. He is taken from being in the flesh to being in the Spirit (Romans 8:1-14).

John the Baptist was a man who preached with genuine humility. He thought of himself as nothing but a voice, unworthy of and unfit for the least service to God, but willing to be used by God, and hoping God would be pleased to use him (2 Corinthians 4:7).

This was John's attitude. I pray that it is mine and that it is yours. "He must increase, but I must decrease" (John 3:30).

"And it came to pass in those days, that Jesus came from Nazareth of Galilee, and was baptized of John in Jordan. And straightway coming up out of the water, he saw the heavens opened, and the Spirit like a dove descending upon him: And there came a voice from heaven, saying, Thou art my beloved Son, in whom I am well pleased. And immediately the Spirit driveth him into the wilderness. And he was there in the wilderness forty days, tempted of Satan; and was with the wild beasts; and the angels ministered unto him. Now after that John was put in prison, Jesus came into Galilee, preaching the gospel of the kingdom of God, And saying, The time is fulfilled, and the kingdom of God is at hand: repent ye, and believe the gospel. Now as he walked by the sea of Galilee, he saw Simon and Andrew his brother casting a net into the sea: for they were fishers. And Jesus said unto them, Come ye after me, and I will make you to become fishers of men. And straightway they forsook their nets, and followed him. And when he had gone a little farther thence, he saw James the son of Zebedee, and John his brother, who also were in the ship mending their nets. And straightway he called them: and they left their father Zebedee in the ship with the hired servants, and went after him".

(Mark 1:9-20)

Chapter 2

Our Saviour's Baptism, His Temptation, And His First Disciples

These few verses are typical of Mark's writing. They cover a great amount of matter in a very brief amount of space. Within the scope of these twelve verses, Mark relates a brief account of the baptism of our Lord, his temptation in the wilderness, his earliest preaching, and the calling of his first disciples. We will look at each of these things in the order in which they are given.

Our Lord's Baptism

This paragraph opens with a record of our Lord's baptism. "And it came to pass in those days, that Jesus came from Nazareth of Galilee, and was baptized of John in Jordan. And straightway coming up out of the water, he saw the heavens opened, and the Spirit like a dove descending upon him: And there came a voice from heaven, saying, Thou art my beloved Son, in whom I am well pleased" (vv. 9-11).

Our Lord's public, earthly ministry began with him submitting to baptism at the hands of John the Baptist, that he might symbolically fulfil all righteousness and justify God. Baptism was not considered a light, insignificant thing by the Son of God. He walked all the way from Nazareth of Galilee to Jerusalem to be baptized by John. Why? I can give one very good reason, and only one. He knew it was his Father's will. It was not convenient; but it was his Father's will. It might not be understood by his family and friends; but it was his Father's will. He might be ridiculed as a fanatic; but none of that mattered to him. It was his Father's will for him to be baptized by John. So he came to John at Jerusalem to be baptized. There is much to be learned from our Master's baptism. Let me direct your attention to just four things concerning it.

His Baptism Was An Act Of Humility
Remember, this is the Son of God, the Lord of glory. He came to be baptized in that same river that Naaman despised. Not only did he submit to the ordinance; but he came to John to observe it. He did not call for John to come to him. He came to John.

Our Saviour's Baptism Was An Act Of Obedience
He had come into this world to do his Father's will; and part of that will was this act by which, at the very outset of his public ministry, he identified himself with God's prophet, his message, and his people.

There are many reasons for the practice of believer's baptism. It is the answer of a good conscience toward God. It is a picture of the gospel. It identifies us with Christ, his people, and the gospel of his grace. But there is no reason more noble than this: The Lord commands it. Baptism is the believer's first act of obedience to Christ as his Lord. And nothing is nobler in a servant than implicit obedience to his master.

Our Lord's Baptism Was A Very Meaningful, Significant Act
Baptism is not an empty, meaningless religious ritual. It is now and has been from its inception a highly symbolic act. Though Mark does not give the details, both Matthew and Luke tell us the meaning and significance of baptism. Our Master's baptism meant exactly the same thing that our baptism means.

Matthew tells us that our Saviour insisted on being baptized "to fulfil all righteousness" (Matthew 3:13-15). Obviously, baptism did not make the Son of God righteous. But it did signify the means by which he must establish and bring in righteousness for his people. As our Substitute, the Lord Jesus brought in and fulfilled all righteousness as Man by his perfect obedience unto death (Philippians 2:5-11; Hebrews 10:5-14).

Having perfectly obeyed the law of God, he was made sin for us, who knew no sin, that we might be made the righteousness of God in him. When he was made sin for us, he was slaughtered under the fury of God's unmitigated wrath. When he was slain as our Substitute, he was buried in the earth. After he had been in the earth for three days, to prove that he had indeed fulfilled all righteousness and had by his sacrifice put away our sins, he was raised from the dead. That is exactly what was pictured in his baptism; and that is exactly what is pictured in believer's baptism today (Romans 6:3-6).

Luke records our Lord's later explanation of his baptism by John to have been an act by which he "justified God" (Luke 7:29, 30). We know that baptism does nothing to make God just; but it is the symbolic confession that our God is and must be just. His justice must be satisfied; and our Saviour, by his baptism, confessed that he would satisfy the justice of God by dying under the wrath of God as our Substitute.

We come to the waters of baptism for exactly the same reason: To confess our sins and to confess our faith in him by whose blood God can be both "a just God and a Saviour".

Our Lord's Baptism Was An Honourable Act

It was an act by which he was publicly owned to be the Son of God, in whom God the Father is well pleased. At his baptism, God the Father publicly announced his full, complete acceptance of Christ's sacrifice as our Mediator, Surety, and Substitute.

There is a great wealth of spiritual instruction in these words: "Thou art my beloved Son, in whom I am well pleased". The text does not say, *with whom*, but *in whom* I am well pleased. That means that the Father is well pleased with all his people in his Son, by virtue of his obedience unto death, by virtue of his sin atoning sacrifice.

> With His spotless garments on,
> I am as holy as God's Son!

Let every believer find comfort and assurance here. God looks on us in Christ. Looking on us in Christ, he sees no spot in us (Song of Solomon 4:7). He beholds us in Christ as being clothed from head to foot with the garments of salvation, his robe of perfect righteousness, invested with his perfect merit, "accepted in the Beloved", and a people with whom he is "well pleased".

It is at our baptism that believers are honoured and publicly owned as the sons of God. Baptism does not make us the sons of God. But in the watery grave of baptism, as we there own our God when we are buried with Christ, so we are owned of God as his sons and daughters in Christ. "For as many of you as have been baptized into Christ have put on Christ" (Galatians 3:27).

Our Saviour's Temptation

Second, Mark gives us a brief description of our Saviour's temptation in the wilderness. "And immediately the Spirit driveth him into the wilderness. And he was there in the wilderness forty days, tempted of Satan; and was with the wild beasts; and the angels ministered unto him" (vv. 12, 13).

When trials, troubles, and temptations come upon you, do not imagine that some strange thing has happened to you. The Son of God was also tempted in all points like as we are, yet without sin (1 Corinthians 10:13;

Hebrews 2:17, 18; 4:15, 16). Here are four things in Mark 1:12, 13 that are of tremendous importance. As they were true concerning our Lord, so they are true concerning every child of God. May God be pleased to inscribe these four things upon every believing heart. You may not need them now, but as sure as you belong to and follow Christ, you will soon need to know these things.

> Though he was tempted of the devil, he was still the Son of God and the Spirit of God was with him.
> Though he was the Son of God, his temptations were many, they were real, and they lasted a long time.
> Though he was among wild beasts in the wilderness of temptation, he was under special divine protection, and the angels of God ministered to him.
> Though he was tempted for forty days, tempted in all points of human weakness, and tempted among wild beasts, his temptations did come to an end.

When trials, temptations, or sorrows come to us, rather than asking, "Why do God's people suffer?", we should be asking, "Why shouldn't we suffer?" After all, we are sinners, like all other people. Our Lord Jesus suffered as no man ever suffered, in order to redeem us from sin and save us. If he who knew no sin was in this world a "man of sorrows", why should not we have sorrows to endure? Yet, it is not altogether wrong for us to ask, "Why?", when sorrows come to us, as long as our questions arise from submissive, believing hearts.

When believers suffer, it is because it is the will of God, our heavenly Father. Satan could not touch Job, but by the will of God. And sorrow does not come to your house or mine, in any form, but by the will of God. It is written, "All things are of God". Nothing happens by "chance" in a world controlled by God (Romans 11:36).

Sorrow is intended to wean us of this world. God says to his saints, "Give me thine heart". And he graciously sees to it that we give him our hearts. He will never allow his own to be completely content with life in this world.

God visits his saints with affliction to correct us for sin and cause us to call upon him. Read Psalm 107 and learn the mystery of providence. Blessed is that sorrow that turns our hearts to Christ in firmer faith, greater gratitude, and more loyal love.

"Who knoweth what is good for a man's life?" (Ecclesiastes 6:12). Is it better for me to be wealthy or poor? Is it better for me to be healthy or sick?

Is it better for me to be strong or weak? The fact is, only God knows. Wealth, health, and strength of life may be a great blessing or a great curse. Poverty, sickness, and weakness, the things all men seek to avoid, may be tremendous blessings from God. All these things come from him (Isaiah 45:7; Romans 11:36).

This much I know: Whatever it takes for God to get my attention is good for me. Whatever makes me wake up and think upon my sin, my immortal soul, the brevity of life, the certainty of God's judgment, and the eternality of heaven and hell; whatever God uses to drive me to my knees, to force me to call upon him for mercy is good for me. Whatever it takes to reconcile this rebel's heart to God and bring me to Jesus Christ in faith, to wean me from this world and keep me looking to Christ is good for me. "There hath no temptation taken you but such as is common to man: but God is faithful, who will not suffer you to be tempted above that ye are able; but will with the temptation also make a way to escape, that ye may be able to bear it" (1 Corinthians 10:13).

Christ's Preaching
In verses 14 and 15 Mark describes the preaching of our Lord Jesus Christ. "Now after that John was put in prison, Jesus came into Galilee, preaching the gospel of the kingdom of God, And saying, The time is fulfilled, and the kingdom of God is at hand: repent ye, and believe the gospel".

After John the Baptist was cast into prison for his bold preaching, the Lord Jesus came into Galilee preaching the very same thing that John had preached before him and his apostles preached after him. It is the message every gospel preacher is commanded of God to preach.

"Jesus came preaching the gospel of the kingdom of God". The long and short of that is this: Our Lord came pressing upon men the claims of God as their rightful sovereign, as their Lord and King, demanding that all who heard him submit and surrender to his dominion over them (Matthew 10:39; 16:25; Mark 8:35; Luke 9:24; 17:33; John 12:25).

Our Saviour proclaimed, "The time is fulfilled, the kingdom of God is at hand". The fulness of time had now come (Romans 5:6-8; Galatians 4:4, 5). The King of grace had now come and the Kingdom of God was at hand. The kingdom of God is that spiritual kingdom which is the church of God, the kingdom in which God rules by his Son through his Word.

The Lord Jesus commanded all who heard him, saying, "Repent ye, and believe the gospel". This is what God requires of all: repentance and faith. The two always go hand in hand. You cannot have one without the other. This is what Noah preached in his generation, and what Paul preached in his (Acts 20:21). Repentance and faith were the foundation stones of Christ's ministry. J. C. Ryle wrote, "Repentance and faith must always be the main subjects of every faithful minister's instruction".

We must repent. We must believe the gospel. It is only by repentance toward God and faith in Christ that we obtain peace. Church membership will not bring us to God. Baptism will not bring us to God. The priestly pronouncement of some man that our sins are absolved will not give us peace. The only way to peace is repentance toward God and faith in our Lord Jesus Christ. These things are not one time acts, but a continual way of life. Believers turn to God with willing hearts, surrendering themselves to him in all things, looking to Christ alone for acceptance with him.

The First Disciples
The last thing to which Mark directs our attention in this passage is the calling of our Lord's first disciples. This is a matter to which the Lord gave careful attention.

"Now as he walked by the sea of Galilee, he saw Simon and Andrew his brother casting a net into the sea: for they were fishers. And Jesus said unto them, Come ye after me, and I will make you to become fishers of men. And straightway they forsook their nets, and followed him. And when he had gone a little farther thence, he saw James the son of Zebedee, and John his brother, who also were in the ship mending their nets. And straightway he called them: and they left their father Zebedee in the ship with the hired servants, and went after him" (vv. 16-20).

Mark does not describe the salvation of these men. Our text is not talking about the effectual call of grace, but about the call of believing men to the work of the ministry. Let me point out three things in these verses about our Lord's first disciples.

First, our Lord Jesus did not choose the great, the mighty, and the noble to be his disciples. The church of God began with a few, simple fishermen, not with rich, well-educated, influential men (Zechariah 4:6; 1 Corinthians 1:26-29). There is an abhorrent notion among men that there is something noble about being rich and something shameful about being poor. We must never subscribe to that folly. Plain, ordinary, blue collar, working men were the men chosen of God to turn the world upside down. It is a disgrace to be proud, to be covetous, to be a drunk, a cheat, or a thief; but it is no disgrace to be poor.

Second, those who were called to the work of the ministry were occupied with and were faithfully pursuing honourable careers when the Lord called them. The trend in religion is for a man to announce his call to preach and then go about figuring out a way to put himself in the ministry. That is totally wrong. God finds his preachers in the field tending sheep like Moses, or ploughing corn like Elisha, or thrashing wheat like Gideon, or by the seaside mending nets. He never finds them sitting in a pew or Bible college waiting for a church to open up!

Third, those who are called by Christ to be his servants are called to be "fishers of men", men who fish for the souls of men. Fishermen have a purpose. They go out to catch fish. Fishermen must be very diligent. And fishermen must be very patient. I ask all who read these lines to pray for me and for every faithful, gospel preacher you are privileged to know. "Who is sufficient for these things?" Yet, we know that "Our sufficiency is of God". "Finally, brethren, pray for us, that the word of the Lord may have free course, and be glorified, even as it is with you" (2 Thessalonians 3:1).

"And they went into Capernaum; and straightway on the sabbath day he entered into the synagogue, and taught. And they were astonished at his doctrine: for he taught them as one that had authority, and not as the scribes. And there was in their synagogue a man with an unclean spirit; and he cried out, Saying, Let us alone; what have we to do with thee, thou Jesus of Nazareth? art thou come to destroy us? I know thee who thou art, the Holy One of God. And Jesus rebuked him, saying, Hold thy peace, and come out of him. And when the unclean spirit had torn him, and cried with a loud voice, he came out of him. And they were all amazed, insomuch that they questioned among themselves, saying, What thing is this? what new doctrine is this? for with authority commandeth he even the unclean spirits, and they do obey him. And immediately his fame spread abroad throughout all the region round about Galilee. And forthwith, when they were come out of the synagogue, they entered into the house of Simon and Andrew, with James and John. But Simon's wife's mother lay sick of a fever, and anon they tell him of her. And he came and took her by the hand, and lifted her up; and immediately the fever left her, and she ministered unto them. And at even, when the sun did set, they brought unto him all that were diseased, and them that were possessed with devils. And all the city was gathered together at the door. And he healed many that were sick of divers diseases, and cast out many devils; and suffered not the devils to speak, because they knew him".

(Mark 1:21-34)

Chapter 3

Lessons From A Day Of Miracles

This passage is the beginning of a long list of miracles recorded by Mark. As I read it, I cannot avoid noticing how much our Saviour crammed into one day. Our Lord seems to have rested little. He was always about his Father's business, either preaching the good news of salvation by the grace of God or performing good works of mercy by the power of his grace as God.

We recognize, of course, that the days of visible, demonstrative miracles being performed ended with the completion of holy scripture. There have been none with the gift and ability to do those things by the Spirit of God since the days of the apostles. Those who yet pretend to possess such supernatural gift are just pretenders. They are not the servants of Christ. Our Lord still performs miracles, but not in a public, demonstrative way.

However, he did perform great miracles of mercy upon the bodies of men and women and for the benefit of their lives while he lived upon the earth. He did so, and gave his apostles power to do so, to confirm in a public manner his claims as the Messiah.

In the passage before us, we begin on Saturday morning, the sabbath day, with our Lord and his disciples in the synagogue at Capernaum. There he taught with authority the Word of God and cast a demon out of a man. Then he healed Simon Peter's mother-in-law of a fever. The news of his power and mercy spread like wildfire through the town. By nightfall "all the city was gathered at the door. And he healed many that were sick of divers diseases, and cast out many devils". These miracles performed by our Master are instructive pictures of his grace and power, and are here recorded by Divine inspiration to teach us about him, his grace, and his salvation.

False Doctrine
The first thing we learn from this passage is that it is right, and sometimes necessary, to correct false doctrine. "And they went into Capernaum; and straightway on the sabbath day he entered into the synagogue, and taught. And they were astonished at his doctrine: for he taught them as one that had authority, and not as the scribes" (vv. 21, 22).

Our Lord and his disciples went into the synagogue because that was the place where men and women met in the name of God, claiming to worship God. There he opened the Word of God and taught them as one having authority. He spoke boldly and plainly. He spoke the truth of God in such unmistakable terms that those who heard him were astonished by his doctrine.

I am sometimes told, when I am asked to preach in churches and places where people do not believe the gospel of God's free and sovereign grace in Christ, I ought to be careful not to offend. That means, "Be careful not to preach the gospel. Let men go to hell with a Bible in their hands. Do not cause a disturbance just because people are lost, Christ is blasphemed, and the truth of God is perverted".

God's servants are not such self-serving creatures. Faithful men are faithful to the souls of men, faithful to the truth of holy scripture, and faithful to the glory of God. They who have a word from God speak the word of the Lord clearly and distinctly, regardless of cost or consequence. Only a hireling courts the favour of his hearers or fears their frowns.

Heart Faith

The second thing we see in these verse is the necessity of heart faith. We are specifically told twice that the demons knew the Lord Jesus. "And there was in their synagogue a man with an unclean spirit; and he cried out, Saying, Let us alone; what have we to do with thee, thou Jesus of Nazareth? art thou come to destroy us? I know thee who thou art, the Holy One of God" (vv. 23, 24). "And he healed many that were sick of divers diseases, and cast out many devils; and suffered not the devils to speak, because they knew him" (v. 34).

The Scribes did not know him. The Pharisees did not know him or acknowledge the truthfulness of his doctrine. The religious leaders of the day denounced Jesus Christ, the Son of God, as a false prophet and a deceiver. But those demons knew both who he was and the truthfulness of all that he taught. Yet, they were not saved. Why? Because their knowledge was not unto salvation.

We should lay this to heart. The mere belief and acknowledgment of Bible facts and Bible doctrine is not salvation. I realize that there is no salvation apart from the knowledge of gospel truth. But merely having your head full of facts is not salvation. That kind of faith is no better than the faith of devils.

They all believe and know that Jesus is the Christ, the Son of God. The demons all know that he died at Calvary as the victorious, effectual, sin-atoning substitute for God's elect. They all know that he is seated upon his throne in heaven. And all the demons know that he is coming again in judgment and will cast them, along with all the wicked, into everlasting hell. The demons of hell know a heap sight more than most preachers and most professing Christians. There is no infidelity among them.

But saving faith is no more an act of the head than it is an act of man's imaginary free will. Saving faith is a matter of the heart (James 2:19; Romans 10:9, 10). Heart faith is more than information in the head. It is the transformation of the life, from the inside out. Heart faith is more than knowing about Christ. It is trusting him, loving him, rejoicing in him, commitment to him, and cleaving to him.

Martin Luther once wrote, "Christianity consists of personal pronouns". It is one thing to say, "Christ alone is Saviour". It is another thing altogether to lift your heart to heaven and say, "Christ alone is my Saviour". The demons of hell acknowledge the first. Only a child of God can truthfully state the last.

Salvation is not a reformed life or a reformed creed. Salvation is the personal knowledge of Jesus Christ revealed in your heart by the Holy Spirit. It is not information in you, but Christ in you, which is the hope of glory (Colossians 1:27).

Simplicity In Prayer
The third thing we have set before us the simplicity of true prayer. Faith, worship, and prayer are simple, unadorned, unpretentious things. Where they are true and sincere, there is nothing about them that even resembles show, formality, ceremony, or hypocrisy. Far too often, particularly in acts of public worship and prayer, I fear that most of what is said and done is said and done to be heard and seen of men.

Carefully observe the simplicity of everything in these three verses. When we are in trouble, when we have heavy burdens and cares, we ought to follow the example of simplicity we see here. The best remedy for our troubles, the best cure for our cares is the simple prayer of faith.

When Peter's mother-in-law was sick, "they told him (the Lord Jesus) of her". This is the first and best thing to be done in all cases. When trouble comes, cry out to him who is touched with the feeling of our infirmities. No one else is so compassionate and willing to help as he is. No one else is so powerful and able to help as he is.

When Jacob was in trouble, he turned to the Lord for help. He cried, "Deliver me, I pray thee, from the hand of Esau" (Genesis 32:11). When Hezekiah was in trouble, he spread Sennacherib's letter before the Lord, and said, "I beseech thee, save thou us out of his hand" (2 Kings 19:19). When Lazarus was sick, Martha and Mary sent a message to the Lord Jesus, saying, "Lord, he whom thou lovest is sick" (John 11:3).

We ought always to do the same. When sicknesses, bereavements, sorrows, trials, and troubles come, let us act in the simplicity of faith and tell him who is able and willing to help.

> Are you weary, are you heavy hearted?
> Are you grieving over joys departed?
> Do you fear the gathering clouds of sorrow?
> Are you anxious what shall be tomorrow?
> Tell it to Jesus, tell it to Jesus;
> He is a Friend that's well-known;
> You've no other such a friend or brother,
> Tell it to Jesus alone.

This is the counsel we are given in holy scripture. "Cast thy burden upon the LORD, and he shall sustain thee: he shall never suffer the righteous to be moved" (Psalm 55:22). "Be careful for nothing; but in every thing by prayer and supplication with thanksgiving let your requests be made known unto God" (Philippians 4:6) "Casting all your care upon him; for he careth for you" (1 Peter 5:7). There are three more facts set before us by the Spirit of God in verses 29-31.

Simon Peter Was A Married Man
I mention this fact simply because the church of Rome has historically claimed Peter as the first pope, while at the same time teaching the necessity of clerical celibacy, as though celibacy is somehow more spiritual than marriage. They are wrong on all counts. Peter was never a papist. He was a married man. It is hard to have a mother-in-law without being married! And celibacy and spirituality have nothing to do with one another.

Believers Get Sick
Though Peter's mother-in-law appears to have been a believer, a true, faithful servant of the Lord, she got very sick. Peter's relationship to Christ did not exempt his family from trouble. His mother-in-law's relationship with the Saviour did not keep her from trouble. The fact is, God's children suffer in this world just as other people do. As long as we live in this world of woe, we will have trials, troubles, sicknesses, bereavements, and sorrows.

Use Proper Means
When we have troubles of different kinds, it is both prudent and proper to use the means at our disposal by God's providence. There is no contradiction

between faith and the diligent use of means. When you get sick, go to the doctor. If you have legal problems, hire a lawyer. When you need help, turn to your family and friends; and say, "I need help". But be sure you do not fail to recognize this:

Christ's Perfect Work

In verse 31 we are given a picture of our great Saviour's work. It is always perfect. "And he came and took her by the hand, and lifted her up; and immediately the fever left her, and she ministered unto them".

When the Son of God heals, he heals. One minute this woman was lying in bed, sick with a fever. The Master took her by the hand, lifted her up, and immediately the fever left her. The next minute she is serving him. Such a fever, even after it is broken, usually leaves a person very, very weak; but when our Saviour works a work, he leaves nothing undone.

This is certainly a picture of the way he deals with sin-sick souls. He who redeemed us with his blood, when he comes in saving grace to our souls in the power of his Spirit, gives us everything we need to make us completely whole. He who chose us redeemed us. He who redeemed us justified us. He who justified us calls us. He who calls us gives us faith. He who paid our debt gives us grace. He who obtained eternal redemption with his blood gives life to all his redeemed ones. He who gives us life gives us faith. He who gives us faith gives us power to become the sons of God. He who washed away our sins with his blood cleanses us by his Spirit in regenerating grace. He who justified us also sanctifies us. He who sanctifies us will also glorify us. He who has saved us also gives us the grace and strength to serve and minister unto him.

The sin-sick soul is not merely cured, and then left to itself. It is also supplied with a new heart and a right spirit, and grace and strength sufficient for all that is required of it. Whatever God demands, he gives.

Here is encouragement and comfort for those who are reluctant to publicly confess faith in Christ and identify themselves with him. Some fear that if they come forward and take up their cross to follow him, they may not be able to continue, that they will in time fall away. That was one of the things with which I struggled greatly, as Satan tried to keep me from confessing my Redeemer in believer's baptism. The fact is, if you come in your own strength, trusting yourself, you will soon fall. But if Christ calls you, Christ will keep you. There are no half-cured cases with the Son of God! He leaves nothing unfinished. Every pardoned soul shall be preserved unto the end and perfected at last. It is written, "Faithful is he that calleth you, who also will do it" (1 Thessalonians 5:24). "He which hath begun a good work in you will perform it until the day of Jesus Christ" (Philippians 1:6).

Here is comfort to those who are serving the Saviour, but cast down by the sense of their own weakness and insufficiency. As your days demand shall your strength ever be. The difficulties you fear shall vanish before you. The lion that roars before you, as you walk in the path set before you, has no teeth, and no claws, and is on a chain; and the one holding the chain is our Redeemer. The lion cannot hurt you! The very worst he can do is make a lot of noise. He who gives you grace will also give you glory.

Christ's Dominion And Grace

We are assured of these things just in proportion as we grasp the fifth thing taught in these verses; and that is the totality of our Saviour's dominion, particularly in the exercise of his saving grace. In this portion of holy scripture we see that our Saviour, the Lord Jesus Christ, truly is "God over all". Sickness and disease, Satan and the demons of hell, sin and death all flee at his word. "With authority commandeth he even the unclean spirits, and they do obey him."

"For this purpose the Son of God was manifested, that he might destroy the works of the devil" (1 John 3:8). And here we see our Redeemer, the Holy One of God, destroying the works of the devil in the life of a chosen sinner by his omnipotent grace. That poor soul in the synagogue aptly portrays fallen man under the dominion of Satan. God's elect, like all others, are by nature "children of wrath" and vassals of the devil.

Yet, on the sabbath day, this poor soul came to the house of God. There he sat, as Satan's helpless captive, until the Lord Jesus met him in his house and delivered him by his almighty grace, fulfilling Isaiah's prophecy (Isaiah 49:24-28).

At the very approach of our Saviour, the unclean spirit in that poor wretch trembled, knowing that the Lord Jesus possesses all power and authority, even over Satan himself, as "the Holy One of God". What confidence believing souls ought to have in such a Saviour! No weapon formed against us can prosper (Isaiah 54:17). No temptation can destroy us (1 Corinthians 10:13). And the God of peace shall bruise Satan under our heels shortly (Romans 16:20).

He who loved us and gave himself for us is the absolute, sovereign Monarch of the universe. We may safely trust him. He is too wise to err, too good to do wrong, and too strong to fail.

Lessons From A Day Of Miracles

"And in the morning, rising up a great while before day, he went out, and departed into a solitary place, and there prayed. And Simon and they that were with him followed after him. And when they had found him, they said unto him, All men seek for thee. And he said unto them, Let us go into the next towns, that I may preach there also: for therefore came I forth. And he preached in their synagogues throughout all Galilee, and cast out devils".

Mark 1:35-39

Chapter 4

A Sunday With The Saviour

Every event in our Lord's earthly life, every word he spoke, every act he performed ought to be regarded by us as matters of immense importance and deep interest. In all that he said, in all that he did, in all that he refused to do our Saviour is both our Example and our Teacher, showing us both what we are to believe and how we are to live in this world for the glory of God.

On Saturday, the sabbath day, the Lord Jesus crammed as much into the day as possible for the glory of God and the good of men. He taught in the synagogue at Capernaum, cast out devils, and healed Peter's mother-in-law and many in the city who were sick. In this passage, after an exhausting sabbath day, we see our Saviour rising early for prayer on Sunday morning. Mark records the events of that day for our learning. May God the Holy Spirit be our Teacher as we seek to learn from the things which transpired on that Sunday that Mark describes in these five verses.

Diligence In Prayer
First, I want us to take notice of and learn from our Saviour's diligence in prayer. "And in the morning, rising up a great while before day, he went out, and departed into a solitary place, and there prayed" (v. 35).

Remember, Mark is telling us about the incarnate God. This is not a weak, sinful, fallen, and needy man. This man is God. Yet, as a man, he placed great importance upon the matter of prayer, especially private prayer. Throughout the days of his humiliation, we find our Master engaged in prayer. We do not often see him engaging in public prayer. He seems to have avoided, as much as possible, any public show or display of devotion; but private prayer, private worship was another matter. Most do just the opposite. Most people make a great show of devotion publicly, but greatly neglect private prayer, private worship, and private communion with God.

Our Saviour seems never to have begun anything, he seems never to have made a decision, without prayer. When he was baptized, Luke tells us he was "praying" (Luke 3:21). When he was transfigured upon the mount, we read that, "as he prayed, the fashion of his face was altered" (Luke 9:29). Before choosing his apostles, our Saviour "continued all night in prayer" (Luke

6:12). When all men spoke well of him, and wanted to make him a king, Matthew tells us, "He went up into a mountain apart to pray" (Matthew 14:23). When he was assaulted by Satan in Gethsemane, our Lord Jesus said to his disciples, "Sit ye here, while I shall pray" (Mark 14:32).

Our Saviour prayed always and did not faint. Though he was sinless, he prayed as sinner never prayed. He diligently sought to maintain communion with God his Father as a man, giving us an example. His eternal godhead did not cause him to live independent of God's ordained means of ministering to men. Here is the God to whom we pray, as a man, showing us the necessity of prayer. The Son of God, as a man, never considered himself strong enough, wise enough, or spiritual enough to live in this world without private prayer and public worship. "In the days of his flesh, when he had offered up prayers and supplications with strong crying and tears unto him that was able to save him from death, and was heard in that he feared" (Hebrews 5:7). "We ought to see in all this", wrote J. C. Ryle, "the immense importance of private devotion". If the Son of God felt it important to pray, how much more important it is for us to pray. If he who is holy, sinless, and always pleasing to God spent much time in private prayer, how much more important it is for us to do so. Our Saviour never neglected the worship of God, neither the public worship of God nor private worship. Let us follow his example.

What does this tell us about men and women who do not pray, who wilfully neglect the worship of God? There are multitudes who, while professing to be believers, exercise no diligence at all in the matter of worship. Their profession is a delusion. Prayerless people are not the servants of this praying Saviour. Prayerless souls are Christless souls. The Spirit of adoption always causes adopted children to call upon their Father in prayer.

"Let us therefore come boldly unto the throne of grace, that we may obtain mercy, and find grace to help in time of need" (Hebrews 4:16). Let all who know, trust, and worship the Lord Jesus Christ always be watchful over their souls in this matter. Prayer is the pulse of spiritual life. With believers, this is not a duty. Yet, it must be dutifully maintained. Prayer is not an act of life, but a way of life. Those who do not pray are yet without life before God. Do we pray? The disciples knew Saul of Tarsus had experienced grace when they were told, "Behold, he prayeth".

We are urged by God the Holy Spirit to diligently maintain the use of every means of grace. Our engagement in prayer and worship is not the cause of grace. Without doubt, many who carefully keep up the exercise of both private and public prayer are lost. Their religion is all form and formality. But anyone who altogether despises and neglects worship and prayer is altogether without life and grace before God (Hebrews 10:24-26).

Christ's Sovereignty

Second, Mark sets before us an example of our precious Saviour's divine sovereignty.

"And Simon and they that were with him followed after him. And when they had found him, they said unto him, All men seek for thee. And he said unto them, Let us go into the next towns, that I may preach there also: for therefore came I forth" (vv. 36-38).

We are all far too much inclined to judge the blessings of God by the outward response of men to what we are doing. This is nowhere more common and nowhere more foolish than in the matter of preaching. Our Lord's disciples were very excited because he was so popularly received in their hometown. They thought this was a sure evidence that he would give a repeat performance; but they were mistaken. Instead, our Lord gave a clear, unmistakable display of his total sovereignty in the exercise of his mercy, grace, and saving power. Though there were many in Capernaum who sought him, he turned from them.

The fact is there are many who seek the Lord today who never find him, who never obtain mercy from him, many who seek him from whom he hides himself. Without question, all who seek the Lord spiritually, all who truly seek him in faith, all who seek him because they need him and want him shall find him (Jeremiah 29:12-14). Yet, Mark here tells us of a great multitude who sought the Lord Jesus from whom he withdrew and hid himself. Why?

They sought him in the wrong way and for the wrong reason. These people of Capernaum sought him physically, not spiritually. They sought him with their words and deeds, but not with their hearts. And they sought him for the wrong reasons. They sought nothing from him but carnal things. They did not seek him. They sought what he could do for them! Many seek Christ, but not by faith. Like the Jews described by Paul, they seek him upon the merit and in the strength of the flesh (Romans 9:30-33; 10:1-4).

Not only did those at Capernaum seek the Lord Jesus carnally, they sought him too late. The Saviour passed through Capernaum the day before. He would not go back now. They did not seek him when he was to be found. It is written, "Seek ye the LORD while he may be found, call ye upon him while he is near" (Isaiah 55:6). Our Lord Jesus refused to go back to Capernaum, the larger, more populated city, and carried his grace to the smaller towns and villages surrounding it, because he has mercy on whom he will have mercy.

We need to learn this. No one dictates to God almighty. He does what he will. He is gracious to whom he will be gracious. The sooner we learn this, the better! God always displays his sovereignty in every aspect of grace. He chose to save fallen men, but not fallen angels. He chose some, and passed by others. He redeemed some, but not all. He sends the gospel to some, and hides it from others. He calls some who hear the gospel, and leaves others in darkness, death, and condemnation (Matthew 11:20-30).

Christ The Preacher

Third, Mark directs us to our Master's chosen occupation. "And he said unto them, Let us go into the next towns, that I may preach there also: for therefore came I forth. And he preached in their synagogues throughout all Galilee, and cast out devils" (vv. 38, 39). When the Son of God came into this world, he purposefully chose to be a gospel preacher. He came here to be a preacher of the gospel. He came to fulfil the scriptures by coming as a prophet, the prophet greater than Moses, foretold by Moses himself (Deuteronomy 13:15).

What a high, high honour the Son of God put upon the office and work of the gospel preacher. He might have chosen to come as a ceremonial priest, like Aaron. He could have worn a crown like David. But he chose to be a preacher. The Son of God left the glory which he had with the Father before the worlds were made to do the work of an evangelist, to be a street preacher. He came down here not only to establish peace, but to preach it, not only to bring in righteousness, but to preach it, not only to obtain eternal redemption by the shedding of his blood, but to peach it! Jesus Christ came preaching the gospel, proclaiming deliverance to the captive, the recovering of sight to the blind, and peace to them that were far off (Isaiah 61:1-3).

I stress this fact with very good reason. In our day men and women everywhere have decided that preaching is out-of-date. It is no longer accepted in intellectual circles for a man to stand in a pulpit and preach the gospel to men. Many have given up preaching because it is not popular. They have become spiritual counsellors. Rather than preaching to sinners, they engage in dialogue. We have cantatas, plays, ceremonies, celebrations, and candlelight services! What nonsense! The Son of God came here as a preacher. The church of Christ was originally gathered by preaching. Throughout history her health, strength, and prosperity have been promoted and maintained by preaching. It is by the preaching of the gospel that sinners are saved, saints are edified, and the kingdom of God is built up.

Take care that you never despise or lightly esteem this great, God honoured, God ordained service. "Despise not prophesyings" (1 Thessalonians 5:20). The preacher may be very learned or very plain, very deep or very simple, very polished or very rough, but if he is the messenger of God to your soul, treat him as the angel of God, the messenger of God to your soul; and teach your children to do the same.

May God the Holy Spirit graciously enable us to remember the things set before us in this passage of scripture and apply them effectually to our hearts. Nothing is more important than the worship of our God. We "ought always to pray, and not to faint" (Luke 18:1), "praying always with all prayer and supplication in the Spirit, and watching thereunto with all perseverance and supplication for all saints" (Ephesians 6:18). "Watch ye therefore, and pray always, that ye may be accounted worthy" (Luke 21:36).

Our God is always sovereign in the operations of his grace. Let us ever seek his will and bow to his will. He has mercy on whom he will. And, as he is sovereign in all his works of grace, he is effectual. He will save his people from their sins. And the means by which he has chosen to do so is the preaching of the gospel. Gospel preaching is the one thing that is called "the power of God unto salvation to everyone that believeth ... For therein is the righteousness of God revealed" (Romans 1:16, 17). It is God's ordained instrument of spiritual blessing and benefit to the souls of men (compare Isaiah 52:7; 1 Thessalonians 5:12, 13; Hebrews 13:7, 17).

Mark speaks of "the beginning of the gospel of Jesus Christ, the Son of God" in direct connection with the preaching of John the Baptist (Mark 1:1-4), because God makes known the good news of redemption and grace, salvation and eternal life in Christ by sending preachers to proclaim it in the power of the Holy Spirit.

Yet, the means itself is of no benefit to our souls without the power and grace of God the Holy Spirit. It is only by the Spirit of God that the preached Word of God can make us wise unto salvation through the faith that is in Jesus Christ. To use the words of Robert Hawker, "May the Holy Three, which bear record in heaven, grant to us such sweet testimonies in our hearts and consciences of the truth as it is in Jesus, that we may enjoy that life eternal, to know the Lord Jehovah, Father, Son, and Spirit, to be the only true God, and Jesus Christ whom he hath sent".

The gospel of Jesus Christ, the Son of God, which began before the worlds were made, has its beginning in the hearts of chosen sinners as it "is now made manifest by the appearing of our Saviour Jesus Christ, who hath abolished death, and hath brought life and immortality to light through the gospel" (2 Timothy 1:10). "For the preaching of the cross is to them that perish foolishness; but unto us which are saved it is the power of God ... For after that in the wisdom of God the world by wisdom knew not God, it pleased God by the foolishness of preaching to save them that believe" (1 Corinthians 1:18, 21), "to the intent that now unto the principalities and powers in heavenly places might be known by the church the manifold wisdom of God" (Ephesians 3:10).

"And there came a leper to him, beseeching him, and kneeling down to him, and saying unto him, If thou wilt, thou canst make me clean. And Jesus, moved with compassion, put forth his hand, and touched him, and saith unto him, I will; be thou clean. And as soon as he had spoken, immediately the leprosy departed from him, and he was cleansed. And he straitly charged him, and forthwith sent him away; And saith unto him, See thou say nothing to any man: but go thy way, shew thyself to the priest, and offer for thy cleansing those things which Moses commanded, for a testimony unto them. But he went out, and began to publish it much, and to blaze abroad the matter, insomuch that Jesus could no more openly enter into the city, but was without in desert places: and they came to him from every quarter".

(Mark 1:40-45)

Chapter 5

How Can A Sinner Obtain Mercy?

Here is an unclean leper seeking mercy from the hands of Christ. And he obtained mercy. The Lord made him whole. If there is a sinner, like the leper, unclean, hopeless, helpless, friendless, and alone who reads these lines, I want you to know that there is hope for sinners like you in Christ. The man who writes them is such a sinner; and when I read about this leper and the mercy he obtained from the Lord Jesus, I think to myself, "If one has been made whole, why not another? Does God forgive sin, then why not my sin? Does God justify the ungodly, then why not me? Does Christ receive sinners, then why not me? Is there mercy with the Lord for the guilty, then why not for me? Did Christ die for sinners, then why not for me? Does God save the unrighteous, then why not me?"

If we would obtain mercy, we must seek mercy like this poor leper, from the hands of the Lord Jesus Christ. Let every saved sinner, as he reads again of God's free, saving grace in Christ, remember and rejoice in what the Lord has done for him by his matchless, free, and sovereign grace in Christ Jesus. Let every poor, lost soul, whose uncleanness before God causes him to crave the cleansing that Christ alone can give, look to the Son of God by faith.

Deep Sense Of Need
This poor wretch came to the Lord Jesus with a deep sense of his need. We do not read anything else in the Bible about the history of this man. We do not know who his parents were, where he was from, how old he was, or what became of him. He seems to be set before us for one reason – he shows us how a sinner must come to the Lord, if he would have mercy. And the first thing is this: If you would obtain mercy from Christ, you must come to him because you need him. No sinner will ever come to Christ in faith until God the Holy Spirit creates in him a sense of his need. No one seeks mercy until he needs mercy.

We are all familiar with what leprosy is and what it represents. Leprosy was a loathsome disease, common during the days of our Lord's earthly ministry. It was a disease so peculiar that it was always considered a mark of divine displeasure on those who were afflicted with it (Numbers 12:10; 2

Kings 5:27; 2 Chronicles 26:19). Because they were ceremonially unclean, lepers were not allowed to walk in the company of others, or come into the house of God.

Leprosy fitly represents the plague of sin with which sons of Adam are diseased. It is to the body what sin is to the soul. Mr Thomson in his famous work, *The Land and the Book* describes lepers in Israel like this: "The hair falls from the head and eyebrows. The nails loosen, decay, and drop off. Joint after joint of the fingers and toes shrink up and slowly fall away. The gums are absorbed, and the teeth disappear. The nose, the eyes, the tongue, and the palate are slowly consumed". The leper was a miserable, outcast creature. He was walking death.

Leprosy, like sin, was a loathsome, unclean disease. Leprosy, like sin, was (by human means) an incurable disease. Leprosy, like sin, was a consuming disease. Leprosy, like sin, was the sure forerunner of death.

The man here held before us by the Spirit of God had a keen sense of his desperate need. Here is a man whose body was covered from head to toe with leprosy. His disease was always before him. There was no hiding it. His body was covered with ulcers oozing with a liquid of sickening smell. His body was wracked with pain. Luke tells us that he was "full of leprosy". He knew that he needed help. He needed supernatural, merciful, divine help. He needed the help of God. Without it, he would surely die.

This is the very reason men and women do not come to Christ. They do not have any sense of need. They do not know their need of Christ. But when the plague of sin in a man's heart causes his very soul to burn with fever, when the sinner knows he is lost, helpless, unclean, and doomed, that without Christ he must surely die, he seeks him.

Christ alone has power to heal our souls. This was portrayed in the ceremonial law (Leviticus 14). But the cleansing of grace is found only in Christ (Ezekiel 36:25; 1 John 7-9). His blood alone can cleanse the leprous soul. His mercy alone can save. Christ alone can make the unclean clean and righteous before God.

Hymn writer Joseph Hart grasped beautifully how those who know their need of mercy will soon obtain mercy.

> All the fitness he requireth
> Is to feel your need of Him.

And it is the work of God the Holy Spirit that makes us know our need of Christ. Robert Hawker wrote, "This poor creature, which came to Jesus, is the representative of every poor sinner, when convinced of the leprosy of sin, from the teaching of God the Holy Ghost. Such an one is convinced of Christ's ability, because God the Spirit hath taught him who Christ is, and what Christ is able to perform". Joseph Hart gives us the same thing in one of his great hymns:

What comfort can a Saviour bring
To those who never felt their woe?
A sinner is a sacred thing;
The Holy Ghost hath made him so.
New life from Him we must receive,
Before for sin we rightly grieve.

This faithful saying let us own,
Well worthy 'tis to be believed,
That Christ into the world came down,
That sinners might by Him be saved.
Sinners are high in His esteem.
And sinners highly value Him.

Utter Humiliation
This leper came to the Lord Jesus in utter humiliation. Matthew tells us he came "worshipping". Luke says that, "Seeing Jesus, he fell on his face". Mark tells us that he came "kneeling". That is just the way sinners must come to the Saviour, kneeling and falling on their face at his feet, worshipping! The sinner must come down, down from his pride, down from his self-righteousness, down from his self-sufficiency! He must come down in his own eyes, down, down, down, all the way down to the feet of Christ (Luke 18:9-14).

If ever we see who and what we are, we will come down. We are poor sons and daughters of Adam, full of uncleanness, cursed, condemned, and ready to die. If ever we see who Christ is and what he is, we will come down. He is holy, righteous, and true. He is God full of mercy, love, and compassion. He is God able and willing to save. He is a Fountain opened for cleansing. He is God, whose glory it is to forgive sin.

God knows how to bring sinners down to the feet of his Son. Psalm 107 is a song of praise to God for his wondrous work of providence, by which he brings chosen sinners down. But providence alone will not cause sinners to seek the Lord. God brings sinners down by causing his holy law to enter their hearts, exposing their sin, pronouncing their uncleanness, and declaring their guilt (Romans 7:9). God brings sinners down by the gospel, by revealing

Christ to them and in them (Zechariah 12:10; Galatians 1:15, 16). Sinner, do you feel your desperate need of Christ? Has your heart been thoroughly broken and humbled at the feet of Christ? Are you sweetly compelled, like Job, to cry, "I have heard of thee by the hearing of the ear: but now mine eye seeth thee. Wherefore I abhor myself, and repent in dust and ashes" (Job 42:5, 6)?

Great And Weak Faith

This poor leper came to the Lord Jesus in very weak faith, but faith that obtained great grace. And that makes the weakest faith great faith (Hebrews 11:6). I do not know how he came to have faith in Christ. Perhaps he had heard our Lord preach. Perhaps he was familiar with the Old Testament prophets. Perhaps he had heard the fame of our Lord from others. But this much is certain: He knew who Christ was. He believed his claims. And he came to the Saviour in faith, because God the Holy Spirit had given him faith in Christ (Ephesians 2:8; Colossians 1:12).

The leper came to the Lord by himself. Others had been led to Christ by one of his disciples, but not this man. Others had been picked up and brought to the Lord, but not the leper. Others, who could not come and were not brought, were blessed by a visit from the Lord himself, but not this leper. Everyone had given this poor man up as a hopeless case. He was a lonely, isolated man. No man cared for his soul. No one could or would take him to the Saviour. But it is our Lord's delight to save the hopeless, the helpless, and the friendless.

This leper came to the Lord against many obstacles. He had no precedent to follow. No leper had come to the Lord Jesus before him. He had no promise of cure. He was not invited to come. He had no legal right to come. Yet, the leper came to Christ confessing faith in him. He worshipped the Lord Jesus as God. It appears he believed him to be the very God by whom others like him were healed in days of old. He bowed and worshipped Christ as his Lord. He knew the Christ had it in his power to make him clean and whole. He confessed faith in Christ in his own words. In all those things this man's faith appears to be great and remarkable. Truly, it was. Yet, he displayed a great weakness of faith. Though he had no doubt that the Lord Jesus was able to heal him, he doubted whether he would heal *him*. He said, to the Lord Jesus, "If thou wilt, thou canst make me clean".

All God's children know, by experience, what it is to come to the Lord Jesus with such weakness of faith. Where is the saved sinner who has not come to the throne of grace, seeking mercy and grace in time of need, while greatly in doubt that God would give the mercy and grace needed? God forgive our unbelief! It was in such weakness of faith that this poor leper came to the Saviour. But such is the greatness of our Saviour's grace and the character of our God "who delighteth in mercy", that the weakness of our faith does not restrain his arm of grace! "Jesus, moved with compassion, put forth his hand, and touched him, and saith unto him, I will; be thou clean" (v. 41).

Total Submission

This leper came to the Lord Jesus Christ, knowing his need of him, in great humiliation, and in faith. And he came to the Saviour in total submission. He recognized that the whole issue was in the hands of Christ. He cried, "Lord, if thou wilt, thou canst make me clean". He understood what few understand. Grace is God's prerogative alone. Salvation depends entirely upon the will of the Lord our God, who has mercy on whom he will have mercy. Christ alone has the right to save and the power to save; and the whole matter of salvation is according to his sovereign will (Romans 9:16, 18). Recognizing the sovereignty of Christ's power and the sovereignty of his will, the leper submitted to the Lord with joyful hope. He simply threw himself upon Christ. We must do the same. "Lord, if you will you can save me".

Yet, he had hope. The Lord had never refused such a request before. And there is hope for us. God never has yet turned away one seeking, believing, submissive sinner. It seems likely, then, that he will not turn any away now.

> Perhaps he will admit my plea,
> Perhaps will hear my prayer;
> But if I perish, I will pray,
> And perish only there.
>
> I can but perish if I go,
> I am resolved to try;
> For if I stay away I know,
> I must forever die.
>
> But if I die with mercy sought,
> When I the king have tried;
> This were to die (delightful thought!)
> As sinner never died.

The leper could not be worse off, even if he had been rejected. And if it were to happen that you sued for mercy and obtained it not, what would be your loss?

Mercy Obtained

But that was not the case. This poor leper obtained the mercy he desperately needed. "Jesus, moved with compassion, put forth his hand, and touched him, and saith unto him, I will; be thou clean". The Lord Jesus was moved with compassion toward him. And being moved with compassion toward him, he healed him immediately and completely.

Yet, there is more. The Lord Jesus healed this poor leper by touching him. Imagine that! Infinite, spotless purity reached down and touched utter corruption! The spotless Lamb of God took into union with himself our nature. He became one of us that he might save us poor, leprous sinners from our sin and make us clean by the sacrifice of himself. Upon the cursed tree, our Lord Jesus Christ was made sin for us (2 Corinthians 5:21). He who is altogether holy and pure, clean and righteous was made unclean before his own holy law, just as the priest who burned the red heifer with her dung was made unclean by the sacrifice required in Numbers 19:7. The Lord Jesus was made sin for us, that we might be made the righteousness of God in him. He died for his elect, the just for the unjust, because there was no other way he could make us just!

An Important Lesson

When we read the last three verses of this passage, we will find a very important lesson taught by our Master.

"And he straitly charged him, and forthwith sent him away; And saith unto him, See thou say nothing to any man: but go thy way, show thyself to the priest, and offer for thy cleansing those things which Moses commanded, for a testimony unto them. But he went out, and began to publish it much, and to blaze abroad the matter, insomuch that Jesus could no more openly enter into the city, but was without in desert places: and they came to him from every quarter" (vv. 43-45).

This cured leper's disobedience to the Saviour's express command is here recorded by divine inspiration for a reason. The Holy Spirit is here showing us that there is a time to be silent about the things of God as well as a time to speak (Ecclesiastes 3:7). Our Saviour says, "Give not that which is holy unto the dogs, neither cast ye your pearls before swine, lest they trample them under their feet, and turn again and rend you" (Matthew 7:6).

I realize that this is a matter to be dealt with carefully; but sometimes we serve the cause of Christ better by silence than by speech. It is best for us to be silent when the cause of Christ cannot be served by us speaking. We do not serve the cause of Christ by trying to cram our doctrine down the throats of those who oppose it. It is best to leave such people alone, until God opens the door to minister to them. It is best for us to be silent when those around us have no interest in hearing the good news of God's grace. It is best for us to be silent when those around us only quibble and scoff at the things of God. And it is certainly best for us to be silent when we are supposed to be doing something else. It is a rare thing for an employer to pay a man wages to teach others the things of God.

No doubt, this man was sincere, and blazed the matter abroad because he wanted all around him to know what great grace he had experienced. But the result was "that Jesus could no more openly enter into the city". There is a zeal which is "not according to knowledge". Such zeal causes much harm. I would not attempt to prescribe to any when he should be silent and when he should "blaze abroad" the things of God. Yet, I do know that there are times when we serve our Saviour and the interests of his kingdom far more effectively in silence than in other way. Commenting on this passage, J. C. Ryle cautions, "The subject is a delicate and difficult one, without doubt. Unquestionably the majority of Christians are far more inclined to be silent about their glorious Master than to confess Him before men and do not need the bridle so much as the spur. But still it is undeniable that there is a time for all things; and to know the time should be one great aim of a Christian. There are good men who have more zeal than discretion, and even help the enemy of truth by unseasonable acts and words."

May God give us the Spirit of wisdom, that we may serve and not hinder his cause in this world, that we may serve our Saviour with good sense. We must never be fearful to confess Christ before Pharaoh as Moses did, or before Herod as John the Baptist did. Yet, we must not cast the pearls of his grace before swine to be trampled beneath their feet with contempt.

Still, there is more. Not only did the Saviour command this man, "See that thou say nothing to any man", he also said, "Go thy way, shew thyself to the priest, and offer for thy cleansing those things which Moses commanded, for a testimony unto them". He told him to go and show himself to the priest, specifically "for a testimony unto them". He was told to go to the priest, so that the priest would pronounce him clean, as a testimony to the priests, either a convincing testimony to them that the Lord Jesus was the Son of God and true Messiah, or a standing testimony against them forever.

Certainly there is still more in this command. For all grace and mercy we should, first and foremost, show ourselves to the Lord Jesus Christ, our great High Priest and Almighty Saviour, the Author and Giver of all. He is to be eyed and acknowledged first in all things. In all things let us live before him and unto him, not before men and unto men. As Paul puts it, "Do I seek to please men? for if I yet pleased men, I should not be the servant of Christ" (Galatians 1:10).

"And again he entered into Capernaum after some days; and it was noised that he was in the house. And straightway many were gathered together, insomuch that there was no room to receive them, no, not so much as about the door: and he preached the word unto them. And they come unto him, bringing one sick of the palsy, which was borne of four. And when they could not come nigh unto him for the press, they uncovered the roof where he was: and when they had broken it up, they let down the bed wherein the sick of the palsy lay. When Jesus saw their faith, he said unto the sick of the palsy, Son, thy sins be forgiven thee. But there were certain of the scribes sitting there, and reasoning in their hearts, Why doth this man thus speak blasphemies? who can forgive sins but God only? And immediately when Jesus perceived in his spirit that they so reasoned within themselves, he said unto them, Why reason ye these things in your hearts? Whether is it easier to say to the sick of the palsy, Thy sins be forgiven thee; or to say, Arise, and take up thy bed, and walk? But that ye may know that the Son of man hath power on earth to forgive sins, (he saith to the sick of the palsy,) I say unto thee, Arise, and take up thy bed, and go thy way into thine house. And immediately he arose, took up the bed, and went forth before them all; insomuch that they were all amazed, and glorified God, saying, We never saw it on this fashion".

(Mark 2:1-12)

Chapter 6

Four Of The Most Important Men In The Bible

May God the Holy Spirit, whose words these are, be our Teacher as we study this passage. May he be pleased to take the things of Christ revealed here and show them to us, effectually applying them to our hearts, that we may be instructed in the gospel of his grace.

Gospel Hardened
The first obvious lesson to be learned from these verses is that those who live under but do not believe the gospel are the greatest and most blameworthy of all sinners in the world. This is a truth that is strikingly illustrated by the history of Capernaum. No other place in Palestine enjoyed so many displays of our Lord's miraculous power, so much of his presence, or so many words of instruction from his lips as the city of Capernaum. After he left Nazareth, our Master dwelt at Capernaum (Matthew 4:13). Capernaum was the headquarters of his ministry. His sermons were often heard there. His miracles were performed there. He was both well known and very popular there. The people of Capernaum gathered in great crowds to see him and to hear him. They were astonished at his power, dazzled by his words, and awed by his Person.

"And again he entered into Capernaum after some days; and it was noised that he was in the house. And straightway many were gathered together, insomuch that there was no room to receive them, no, not so much as about the door: and he preached the word unto them" (vv. 1, 2).

The opening words of this chapter would be very delightful to read were it not for one sad, sad fact: Nothing that our Master said or did seems to have had any lasting, spiritual effect upon the hearts of the people at Capernaum.

Is not that amazing? The men and women of Capernaum lived under the bright, dazzling, noonday brilliance of the Sun of Righteousness. Yet, they were unconverted. Rather than being melted to repentance, they were hardened against Christ by their spiritually barren familiarity with him. It was against this city that our Lord Jesus pronounced his heaviest curse and condemnation (Matthew 11:23, 24).

Capernaum stands before our eyes as a beacon of warning. Never was there a people so highly favoured as the men and women of Capernaum. Never was there a people more hardened against the gospel. Never was there a people more severely condemned by our God. Let us beware of walking in their steps!

The same gospel, which is a savour of life unto life to those who believe it, is a savour of death unto death to those who believe it not. The same fire that melts the wax hardens the clay. None are so hardened as those who are gospel hardened. From such hardness may God be pleased to keep us by his grace.

Blessings In Disguise

The paralyzed man in our text shows us a second very important lesson. Great afflictions, trials, and sorrows are often the forerunners of great blessings.

"And they come unto him, bringing one sick of the palsy, which was borne of four. And when they could not come nigh unto him for the press, they uncovered the roof where he was: and when they had broken it up, they let down the bed wherein the sick of the palsy lay. When Jesus saw their faith, he said unto the sick of the palsy, Son, thy sins be forgiven thee" (vv. 3-5).

I suspect this poor, impotent man spent many hours every day of his miserable life asking, "Why did God do this to me? If there is a God in heaven, if he is good and wise and gracious, why did he give me these wasted legs and mangled feet?" And I do not doubt for a moment that, from this day forward, he never ceased to thank God for that lifelong trouble which at last brought him to Christ and brought the forgiveness of sin to his soul! He would never have been brought by his friends to the Master had he not been in such a miserably helpless condition.

William Cowper wrote:

> God moves in a mysterious way,
> His wonders to perform.
> He plants His footsteps in the sea,
> And rides upon the storm.
>
> Deep in unfathomable mines,
> Of never failing skill,
> He treasures up His bright designs,
> And works His sovereign will.

Ye fearful saints, fresh courage take;
The clouds ye so much dread,
Are big with mercy, and shall break,
In blessings on your head.

Judge not the Lord by feeble sense;
But trust Him for His grace.
Behind the frowning providence,
He hides a smiling face.

His purposes will ripen fast,
Unfolding every hour.
The bud may have a bitter taste;
But sweet will be the flower.

Blind unbelief is sure to err,
And scan His work in vain.
God is His own interpreter,
And He will make it plain.

Let every child of God understand that the paths of our lives are well ordered; for they are ordered by our heavenly Father, who is too wise to err, too strong to fail, and too good to do wrong.

The Use Of Means

Third, we learn from the behaviour of this man's friends that faith in a mighty God and Saviour produces diligence in the use of means.

"And they come unto him, bringing one sick of the palsy, which was borne of four. And when they could not come nigh unto him for the press, they uncovered the roof where he was: and when they had broken it up, they let down the bed wherein the sick of the palsy lay. When Jesus saw their faith, he said unto the sick of the palsy, Son, thy sins be forgiven thee".

The Holy Spirit does not tell us who these men were, where they lived, or what their occupations were. We know absolutely nothing about them except these five things: They had a friend who was in need of mercy. They believed that the Lord Jesus Christ could heal their friend of his terrible paralysis. They brought their needy friend to the place where Christ was working miracles of mercy. They were not deterred by obstacles, hindered by difficulties, or put off by problems. They saw their friend saved by the Son of God.

These four men, Bros. Faithful Fred, Witnessing Willie, Praying Perry, and Diligent Dan, got what they wanted. Their friend was cured, both physically and spiritually. God honoured their labours of love, which were the fruit of their faith. "When Jesus saw their faith, he said unto the sick of the palsy, Son, thy sins be forgiven thee".

As far as we know, not one of these men was a preacher. None of them wrote a word of inspiration. These four men were not prophets or apostles. They appear to have been insignificant, if not totally unknown among their peers. The names, ages, and birth places of these four men are not mentioned anywhere in the Word of God. Yet, these four men rank among the most important men in the Bible.

These four, unknown nobodies were instruments by which God brought one of his elect sheep to Christ. These four men had a friend who was paralyzed, both physically and spiritually; and they brought their friend to Christ, and Christ both healed their friend and forgave his sin. The story of their remarkable faith and zeal is recorded in Matthew, Mark, and Luke. Never in all the world did any mortal perform a more important work than these four men. Because of their labours a sinner was saved and God was glorified.

Try to picture the scene. It is a truly remarkable story of hope, persistence and faith. These four men knew who Christ is; and they knew the power of his grace. They knew a man who needed Christ. They knew where the Lord was. They resolved together to bring their friend to the Saviour. And, by thoughtful pain, labour, and perseverance, they succeeded in getting their friend to the Lord Jesus.

The work required much pain, trouble, time, and diligence. But they were in dead earnest. They knew that Christ had the power to save their friend; and they knew that their friend needed his grace. They were determined to let nothing stand in their way. They were determined to get their friend to Christ. They could not heal his disease. They could not save his soul. They could not forgive his sin. And they did not know whether or not the Lord would do these things for him. But they could get their friend to Christ. And what they could do they were determined to do. And, as a direct result of their diligent labours, a sinner was saved and God was glorified. Nothing in all the world could be more important. When the Lord Jesus saw their faith, he forgave that man's sin.

These four men are held before us as examples for us to follow. They show us the importance and the necessity of those who know the Saviour bringing needy souls to him. I know that "salvation is of the Lord". No man can save himself; and we cannot save other men. It is not possible for us to create a new heart in another person. We cannot give them repentance and faith in Christ. We cannot reveal Christ to a man's heart. But there are some things we can do; and what we can, we must do. These five facts are plainly revealed in the Word of God.

All men by nature are totally depraved, helplessly lost, and spiritually dead. No man will ever, of his own accord, by his own, imaginary, free-will, seek the Lord and come to Christ (Romans 3:10-12). Sinners cannot save themselves, nor can they make any contribution to their salvation, or even make themselves more likely to be saved.

God has an elect people in this world whom he has chosen for himself in eternal love and determined to save; and they must and shall be saved (Romans 8:29, 30). The Lord Jesus has redeemed God's elect by his own precious blood; and all for whom he shed his blood he shall bring into the bliss and glory of eternal life in heaven (Isaiah 53:9-11). God the Holy Spirit shall effectually quicken, regenerate, and preserve all of those who were chosen by God the Father and redeemed by God the Son, calling them to faith in Christ by irresistible grace (Psalms 65:4; 110:3). And God always uses men to reach the hearts of men with the gospel (1 Corinthians 1:18-29; Romans 10:14-17; 1 Peter 1:23-25).

If these facts, clearly revealed in scripture, mar our theological system, our theological system needs to be marred. It is God's good pleasure to use sinful men to proclaim the gospel to sinful men. He could use angels. He could speak to men directly. He could even preach the gospel to dead sinners by the mouths of asses, were that his pleasure. But he has chosen to speak to men through men. This is no limitation to God's sovereignty. It is the marvel of his sovereign grace that he is pleased to use the men he uses to communicate the message of life to dead sinners (1 Corinthians 1:26-29).

Only One
The fourth lesson taught in this passage is the fact that there is one man, and only one man, in all the universe, who has power on the earth to forgive sins and speak peace to the hearts of men. Blessed be his name, Christ Jesus, the God-man, can forgive sin.

"But there were certain of the scribes sitting there, and reasoning in their hearts, Why doth this man thus speak blasphemies? who can forgive sins but God only? And immediately when Jesus perceived in his spirit that they so reasoned within themselves, he said unto them, Why reason ye these things in your hearts? Whether is it easier to say to the sick of the palsy, Thy sins be forgiven thee; or to say, Arise, and take up thy bed, and walk? But that ye may know that the Son of man hath power on earth to forgive sins, (he saith to the sick of the palsy,) I say unto thee, Arise, and take up thy bed, and go thy way into thine house. And immediately he arose, took up the bed, and went forth before them all; insomuch that they were all amazed, and glorified God, saying, We never saw it on this fashion" (vv. 6-12).

The Son of Man, our Lord Jesus Christ, has power on earth to forgive sins, because he who is the Son of man is also God the Son. No mere man can absolve the guilty. No church or denomination can pardon the guilty. Not even God himself can forgive sins apart from Christ. Only the God-man could obtain the forgiveness of sins for us and grant forgiveness to us.

The reasoning of the Scribes and Pharisees was but the venting of their malice toward Christ and their enmity against God; yet, it was precisely the doctrine of holy scripture. None but God can forgive sins. When the man Christ Jesus publicly exercised this divine prerogative, he publicly asserted that he is himself God; and, as if to confirm that claim, he healed the sick man's body, visibly demonstrating his sovereign power over all things.

Christ is the Fountain opened for cleansing from sin. We point sinners to the Fountain; but we cannot forgive sin or even pronounce forgiveness. Only Christ can do that. We must go to Christ, go directly to Christ, and go to Christ alone for absolution. He is our only Priest, our only Mediator, our only Advocate, our only Way to the Father. God's justice demands satisfaction. Only Christ could give it. God's holiness demands perfect righteousness. Only Christ could give it. Our guilty consciences demand the same, both righteousness and satisfaction. Only Christ can quieten the guilty conscience.

Spiritual Palsy

The palsy with which this man's body was afflicted is a vivid picture of the palsy of every man's soul by nature. What a crippled, helpless creature we are since the fall of our father Adam! This poor, needy creature had no ability to come to Christ. So it is with all the fallen children of Adam (John 6:44). But his friends brought him to the Saviour with earnestness. They refused to allow the crowd, or the obstructions before them to stop them. If the only way they could accomplish their desire was to tear up the house-top, they did not hesitate to tear it apart. Robert Hawker wrote:

> Oh! that the Lord's people, who know, in their own cases, the blessedness of Jesus' grace, would feel somewhat of the same earnestness for the salvation of others. Methinks I would bring to ordinances, and also in private approaches, to the mercy seat, the whole of my carnal, graceless relations; and do as they did by this man, lay them down before the presence of Jesus. More than this I am not able to do; but thus far I am encouraged to do. And that compassionate Lord, who hath healed my crippled soul, can cure theirs.

As is ever the case, the Lord Jesus did indescribably more than they desired. They brought their friend to be healed of his physical palsy; but the Son of God, in his great mercy, healed both the palsy of his body and of his soul. He said, "Son, thy sins are forgiven thee".

He identified this man as one of the many children the Father gave to him before the world was made, one of those of whom he spoke as a covenant Surety in eternity (Isaiah 8:18), and of whom he will say at the last day, when presenting his church "faultless before the presence of his glory with exceeding joy" (Jude 24), "Behold I and the children which God hath given me" (Hebrews 2:13).

Until the Lord Jesus spoke this word of grace to this poor soul, he was completely unaware of his eternal adoption and the covenant relationship which he had with Christ from eternity. So it is with all God's elect, until called by the omnipotent grace and power of God the Holy Spirit. Though they are Christ's people, the people he came to save, children of God by eternal adoption, and given to Christ in covenant grace, they are, in their own minds, "children of wrath even as other" (Ephesians 2:3).

"And he went forth again by the sea side; and all the multitude resorted unto him, and he taught them. And as he passed by, he saw Levi the son of Alphaeus sitting at the receipt of custom, and said unto him, Follow me. And he arose and followed him. And it came to pass, that, as Jesus sat at meat in his house, many publicans and sinners sat also together with Jesus and his disciples: for there were many, and they followed him. And when the scribes and Pharisees saw him eat with publicans and sinners, they said unto his disciples, How is it that he eateth and drinketh with publicans and sinners? When Jesus heard it, he saith unto them, They that are whole have no need of the physician, but they that are sick: I came not to call the righteous, but sinners to repentance. And the disciples of John and of the Pharisees used to fast: and they come and say unto him, Why do the disciples of John and of the Pharisees fast, but thy disciples fast not? And Jesus said unto them, Can the children of the bridechamber fast, while the bridegroom is with them? as long as they have the bridegroom with them, they cannot fast. But the days will come, when the bridegroom shall be taken away from them, and then shall they fast in those days. No man also seweth a piece of new cloth on an old garment: else the new piece that filled it up taketh away from the old, and the rent is made worse. And no man putteth new wine into old bottles: else the new wine doth burst the bottles, and the wine is spilled, and the bottles will be marred: but new wine must be put into new bottles."

(Mark 2:13-22)

Chapter 7

New Wine In Old Bottles

This passage is almost identical with the account given by Matthew in Matthew 9:9-17. Yet, there are slight differences in the two accounts of these events. The differences are no more accidental than the similarities. Though there are no contradictions between Matthew and Mark, the differences in these accounts, light as they are, are instruments by which unbelievers are tripped up and stumble because God has made Christ a stone of stumbling to them. When rebels will not bow to Christ, when they will not believe the Word of God, God gives them that which in their minds justifies their rebellion and unbelief.

The slight differences between the way Matthew tells a thing and the way Mark, or Luke, or John tell the same thing demonstrates the sovereignty and wisdom of God the Holy Spirit. He used these men as instruments in his hand, as a man would use a pen or a typewriter, to write the very words he inspired, exactly as he wanted them written. Yet, he allows the contrasting personalities of those men to shine through their writings.

You have probably read this passage many times, just as I have, passing over the things recorded here very casually. When reading the Word of God, that is always a mistake. The things written here were written by Divine inspiration and written specifically for our edification, consolation, and instruction in the things of God. This brief narrative of a brief segment of our Lord's earthly life contains important, spiritual lessons we need to learn and lay to heart. May God the Holy Spirit, who inspired these words, apply them to our hearts by his grace and power, for Christ's sake.

Unlikely Servants
The first lesson set before us is the fact that the Lord Jesus Christ often calls the most unlikely men to be his servants.

"And he went forth again by the sea side; and all the multitude resorted unto him, and he taught them. And as he passed by, he saw Levi the son of Alphaeus sitting at the receipt of custom, and said unto him, Follow me. And he arose and followed him" (vv. 13, 14).

The man called Levi here, and in Luke's account, is the same person who is called Matthew in the gospel narrative bearing his name. What we have before us is the early history and remarkable conversion and transformation by the grace of God of a base publican named Matthew. This man was transformed in an instant by the almighty, irresistible call of the Son of God. The publican became a disciple, then an Apostle, and an Evangelist, because the Son of God passed his way one day and said, "Levi, follow me". Three things should be obvious as we read these two verses.

First, Matthew was called at a specific time. The Lord Jesus called him "as he passed by". Salvation comes to chosen redeemed sinners at the appointed "time of love", when he comes to them in grace (Ezekiel 16:6-8).

Second, this was the call of a specific person. Levi, Matthew, a publican, a tax collector. This is one of the many illustrations of our Saviour's sovereign, distinguishing grace. He passed by the Scribes and Pharisees, leaving them to themselves, and called Matthew. Matthew was not seeking the Lord. He was sought of the Lord.

Third, the call of Christ to Matthew was an irresistible, effectual call. The Master said, "Follow me ... And he arose and followed him"! So it is "that the purpose of God, according to election, might stand; not of works, but of him that calleth ... So then it is not of him that willeth, nor of him that runneth, but of God that sheweth mercy" (Romans 9:11-16).

Matthew, Mary Magdalene, the thief on the cross, and multitudes of others have found Christ who sought him not (Isaiah 65:1), while "Israel hath not obtained that which he seeketh for; but the election hath obtained it, and the rest were blinded" (Romans 11:7). Every saved sinner, like Matthew, is a trophy of God's distinguishing grace. We should never despair of anyone's salvation. Our Lord can take a money-loving taxman, like Matthew, and make a saint and an evangelist by the mere call of his almighty, irresistible grace. We never know who is elected, until they are called. And once they are called, God's elect are usually surprising (1 Corinthians 1:26-29).

Great Physician
In verses 15-17 we see that our Lord Jesus Christ is the Great Physician of sin-sick souls. "And it came to pass, that, as Jesus sat at meat in his house, many publicans and sinners sat also together with Jesus and his disciples: for there were many, and they followed him. And when the scribes and Pharisees saw him eat with publicans and sinners, they said unto his disciples, How is it that he eateth and drinketh with publicans and sinners? When Jesus heard it, he saith unto them, They that are whole have no need of the physician, but they that are sick: I came not to call the righteous, but sinners to repentance".

The Scribes and Pharisees were highly offended by the fact that the Lord Jesus was comfortable in the company of publicans and sinners, and that they were comfortable in his company. The murmuring of the Pharisees is exactly what we might expect from them. It is the identifying mark of Pharisees in all ages. When the Lord Jesus heard the report of their insinuating gossip, he told them plainly that he had come into the world specifically to save sinners (1 Timothy 1:15; Matthew 1:21). Robert Hawker wrote:

> As Jesus opened Matthew's heart to receive him, Matthew opens his house to welcome Jesus. Neither is this all. For as this one Publican had found mercy from the Lord, Matthew invited other Publicans to come and find mercy also. There is enough in Christ for all. What a lovely view to behold the Great Redeemer, encircled at Matthew's table, with Publicans and Sinners!

The very character of Christ, the Great Physician, led him to the place where sin-sick souls were found, that he might exercise his healing power upon them. Our Saviour's name is Jehovah-rophe, "the Lord that healeth thee" (Exodus 15:26).

Our Lord Jesus performed many mighty miracles on the bodies of men. And I have no doubt that he still does. I know what it is to experience his marvellous intervention, when medical help seems futile. Yet, his miracles of mercy, love, and grace were and still are indescribably more glorious. The bodies he healed were soon to sicken again and die. But the souls he heals are healed forever. The physical healings were intended only to demonstrate that he has the right and the power to heal the soul and save his people.

Our great and glorious Saviour saves sinners by three mighty acts of free and sovereign grace, which he alone can perform: by blood redemption, by sovereign regeneration, and, ultimately, by glorious resurrection. And he heals every sin-sick soul that comes to him for healing (Luke 9:11). No sinner ever came to the Son of God for mercy who did not obtain mercy. How encouraging that ought to be to poor, lost sinners!

Confused Believers
The question of John the Baptist's disciples (v. 18) about fasting illustrates another lesson we need to learn. Sometimes true believers become sidetracked and confused by meaningless things and fall under the influence of religious hypocrites. "And the disciples of John and of the Pharisees used to fast: and they come and say unto him, Why do the disciples of John and of the Pharisees fast, but thy disciples fast not?"

Christ's sheep will not follow a stranger (John 10:5). God's saints have an unction from the Holy One and cannot be deceived with regard to the gospel (1 John 2:17, 27). Still, God's saints in this world are only frail, fickle, sinful men and women of flesh and blood. They often fall under the influence of wicked men, thinking that they are doing good. Sometimes by bad influence from people they think are sincere, they get sidetracked by meaningless issues.

That is exactly what happened here with John's disciples. They got to listening to the Pharisees, with whom they had in common the practice of religious, ceremonial fasting. Ignoring the indescribably greater issues of redemption, grace, and forgiveness, they joined the Pharisees, carping and criticizing the Lord Jesus and his disciples because they did not fast.

Let no one be mistaken. John's disciples were true believers (John 1:29-37). They are called John's disciples simply because it was John the Baptist who had instructed them in the gospel of Christ. Yet, these true disciples, men who were taught by a faithful man, fell under the influence of the Pharisees and erred greatly, both in doctrine and in practice. These believing men fell into the horribly evil tendency of our proud nature. They set themselves up as the judges of others, making themselves the standard of righteousness and true godliness. The fasts they kept were fasts of their own appointing. Yet, they considered them acts of godliness, and looked upon our Lord's disciples as behaving in an ungodly way because they did not observe their fasts. How sad. Yet, how common such behaviour is among true believers. The fourteenth chapter of Romans was written specifically for such believers.

How sad it is to see brethren fighting against brethren, as though they are enemies. God save us from such evil.

Our Bridegroom
Set before us in verses 19 and 20 is the blessed fact that the Lord Jesus Christ is our Bridegroom and we are his chosen bride.

"And Jesus said unto them, Can the children of the bridechamber fast, while the bridegroom is with them? as long as they have the bridegroom with them, they cannot fast. But the days will come, when the bridegroom shall be taken away from them, and then shall they fast in those days".

How sweet it is to see the Lord Jesus taking up the cause of his disciples, defending his beloved bride from the accusations raised against her. That is exactly what he does for us still at the Father's right hand as our Advocate in heaven (1 John 2:1, 2).

As John's disciples were Christ's disciples, too. They were as much a part of the bride (the church) as the others. In their weakness, and without the guidance of their pastor who had been imprisoned, they were seduced with the leaven of the Pharisees. And in their weakness and fault, the Lord Jesus here deals with them gently, giving us an example to follow. At the same time, he defends those who were accused by them.

What the bridegroom is to the bride, Christ is to his people. He loves us with an everlasting love. He has taken us into union with himself. We are one with him, "For we are members of his body, of his flesh, and of his bones" (Ephesians 5:30). He paid all our debt. He supplies all our needs. He sympathizes with us in all our troubles. He bears all our infirmities, forgives all our sins, and supplies us with grace sufficient to make up for all our weaknesses. The glory he has received from his Father, he has given to us. And where he is, there we shall soon be. These are the privileges of all believers. We are the Lamb's wife (Revelation 19:7). God has joined our poor, sinful souls to Christ as our precious Husband. And those whom God has joined together with his Son shall never be put asunder.

The disciples of John the Baptist, like their leader, were ascetics. Like the Pharisees, they kept many religious fasts. Apparently, they had been scandalized by their association with Christ and his disciples, who were seen at the feast in Matthew's house and did not fast. Therefore, they raised the question, with the Pharisees, "Why do thy disciples fast not?"

The Lord Jesus gently answers by declaring that he is "the Bridegroom" who had come to his bride. He said, "As long as I am with my bride she cannot fast." He is the Bridegroom of whom Solomon sang. Why should we fast while he is near? The marriage of the bride and Bridegroom is a time for feasting and rejoicing. John had taught his disciples this (John 3:29). The Bridegroom rejoices over the bride (Isaiah 62:5), and his rejoicing over her causes her to rejoice in him.

But the Lord Jesus would soon be separated from his bride. He said, "The Bridegroom shall be taken away from them." No doubt, he was talking about his death. When their Beloved was gone, then his disciples would fast. And that is exactly what happened. What sorrows fell upon them after the Saviour's crucifixion! C. H. Spurgeon wrote, "It is the same with us. Our Lord is our joy: his presence makes our banquet, his absence is our fast, black and bitter." All ritualistic, ceremonial fasting is the husk that swine eat.

Our Lord Jesus is not teaching us here that we ought to practice fasting. The reality of fasting is known only to the children of the bridechamber when their Lord's presence is not known. Religious people, like the Pharisees, talk a good bit about fasting, though they know nothing about it. Our Lord Jesus intends for us to understand the mere abstinence from food is not a fasting of the soul before God. "The kingdom of God is not meat and drink, but righteousness and peace, and joy in the Holy Ghost" (Romans 14:17). "Meat commendeth us not to God, for neither if we eat are we the better, neither if we eat not are we the worse" (1 Corinthians 8:8).

It is an astonishing indication of the pride and corruption of our sinful hearts and vile nature that inclines us (as is so constantly the case) to substitute physical acts in the place of vital godliness and heart worship. This inclination is strong among all the fallen sons and daughters of Adam, because that which we do gratifies the flesh. Our proud flesh will bring anything to God but Christ, trust anything but Christ, and find consolation and hope in anything but Christ.

To trust the person, work, and finished salvation of the Lord Jesus none will ever do, except those who are taught of God the Holy Spirit and made willing to do so by the power of his grace. All outward shows of godliness, devotion, and spirituality the Spirit of God declares are nothing but "a show of wisdom in will-worship, and humility, and neglecting the body" (Colossians 2:23). Instead of directing us to Christ, they lead us away from him into everlasting ruin (Colossians 2:16-23).

In times of great strain and trial, Moses, Elijah, and the Lord Jesus all fasted. But with the Pharisees fasting had become a common, publicly advertised ceremony. It was an outward show of holiness, piety, and devotion. John's disciples seem to have placed great emphasis upon this religious custom. But our Lord always dealt with it as an insignificant thing and insisted that when men do fast they must do so in utter privacy (Matthew 6:16-18). We are never to make a show of religion!

No Mixture
The next lesson is found in the parable given by our Lord in verses 21 and 22. In spiritual matters we must never attempt to mix things that differ. We must never put new wine in old bottles.

"No man also seweth a piece of new cloth on an old garment: else the new piece that filled it up taketh away from the old, and the rent is made worse. And no man putteth new wine into old bottles: else the new wine doth burst the bottles, and the wine is spilled, and the bottles will be marred: but new wine must be put into new bottles".

Our Saviour delivered this parable in response to the question raised by John's disciples and the Pharisees about fasting. It may have been proper, our Lord says to John's disciples, for the friend of the Bridegroom and his disciples to fast. But to require the Bridegroom and his disciples to fast was as ludicrous as sewing a piece of new cloth in an old garment, or putting new wine into old bottles or wineskins.

Actually the parables here given were simply proverbial sayings that may be applied to many things. But essentially their meaning is simply this: We must never try to mix things that do not mix. Many great evils that have arisen in the church could have been avoided if the lesson of these parables had simply been heeded. And many of the evils exiting in the church today could be corrected if this lesson was followed.

In spiritual matters we must never attempt to mix things that differ. Just as under the Mosaic law the mixture of linen and wool and the ploughing of an ox and an ass together were prohibited, so in this age, we cannot mix and must never try to mix law and grace, flesh and spirit, Christ and the world, or carnal ordinances with spiritual worship.

The problem at Galatia was that they tried to put the old wine of Mosaic laws and ceremonies into the new bottle of grace. The Judaizers at Galatia tried to mix Judaism and Christianity. They tried to hold both to the law and the gospel. They wanted both Moses and Christ. They tried to mix physical circumcision with spiritual circumcision. Such mixture can never take place. Either we are under the law, or we are free from the law. It cannot be both (Galatians 5:1, 2, 4).

In the early church many tried to mix the philosophies and religious customs of a pagan world with the gospel of Christ, just as they do today. Nothing is new under the sun. In the earliest days after the apostles, and even while the apostles were living there were those who attempted to make the gospel palatable to the world by mixing the religious customs, traditions, and opinions of paganism with the gospel of Christ. The result was disastrous then and shall be now. In those days compromise paved the road to Romanism. Today men are laying the road back to Romanism as fast as possible. We simply cannot mix flesh and spirit or works and grace in the worship and service of our God. "For we are the circumcision, which worship God in the spirit, and rejoice in Christ Jesus, and have no confidence in the flesh" (Philippians 3:3). We cannot worship God in the Spirit while kneeling before crosses and pieces of idolatry. We cannot rest in Christ as our Sabbath while observing sabbath days.

Many professing Christians today constantly attempt to stitch Christ and the world together. How many there are who seem determined to prove our Lord wrong, who try to serve both God and mammon. They wear the name of Christ in profession, but serve the world. They want to enjoy the new wine of Christ, but they want to drink it from the old bottle of the world. They will not utterly despise the new garment of discipleship, but they want it without cost or cross. So they try to sew it to the old garments of pleasures, covetousness, and love of the world. They will find one day soon that they have attempted that which cannot be done.

How fond fallen humanity is of carnal religion and religious rituals! Fallen man will substitute anything for Christ. He prefers anything to real godliness. Ceremonial fasts, benevolent alms for the poor, and costly religious ceremonies are things dearly loved by our fallen nature. Man looks to them, performs them, and vigorously defends them, because these are the things trusted by men for pardon, peace, and acceptance with God. But they are all as damning to those who trust them as the blasphemies of the most abominable reprobate.

Religious ceremony is nothing but the dressing of the old creature in a new piece of cloth, not the renewing of the Holy Ghost. Our Saviour used these two parabolic statements to show the folly of such. You may sew new cloth into an old garment, but the two will never become one. The new will soon rip away from the old, and the rip will be an obvious gaping hole. If (as in the days when wine was stored in bottles made from animal skins) you put new wine into an old wineskin, the fermenting wine will soon burst the old wineskin.

Robert Hawker says:

> In cases where the outward ministry of the word is heard and received into the old unrenewed heart of the Adam-nature, as the fermentation of new wine burst the old dried skins into which it is put, so men, unrenewed by the Holy Ghost, will burst with hatred, both against Christ and his people. Perhaps no hatred is equal to that which the carnal mind fosters against the people of God. And not simply the carnal, but the professor, in whose heart no saving work of grace hath been wrought. It is painful to flesh and blood, sometimes, to meet the malice of the ungodly and openly avowed profane. But the professors of godliness, in the Pharisees and self-righteous, under the cover of sanctity, comes with deeper malignity.

Our Lord's doctrine is just this. The new robe of Christ's perfect righteousness cannot be patched to our filthy rags; and the new wine of the gospel cannot be held in the old wineskin of our fallen nature. But when God the Holy Spirit makes us new creatures in regeneration, when he makes all things new in the experience of saving grace, Christ's righteousness is made to us a completely new robe of salvation; and the blood of Christ poured into our souls as the new wine of grace makes glad the heart of man (Psalm 104:15; Isaiah 61:10).

New Wine In Old Bottles

"And it came to pass, that he went through the corn fields on the sabbath day; and his disciples began, as they went, to pluck the ears of corn. And the Pharisees said unto him, Behold, why do they on the sabbath day that which is not lawful? And he said unto them, Have ye never read what David did, when he had need, and was an hungred, he, and they that were with him? How he went into the house of God in the days of Abiathar the high priest, and did eat the shewbread, which is not lawful to eat but for the priests, and gave also to them which were with him? And he said unto them, The sabbath was made for man, and not man for the sabbath: Therefore the Son of man is Lord also of the sabbath".

(Mark 2:23-28)

Chapter 8

The Lord Of The Sabbath

We have before us a remarkable scene in the earthly life and ministry of our Lord Jesus Christ. It was early in the morning on Saturday, the sabbath day, the appointed day of worship for the Jews in the Old Testament.[1] Our Lord Jesus and his disciples were, in all likelihood, on their way to a place of public worship. As they walked to the place of worship, they passed through a field of corn. As they walked along, the disciples began to pick a few ears of corn. They rubbed the corn in their hands, I presume to get the grain out and soften it up a little.

To them, it was a totally insignificant thing. They made no attempt to hide or cover their actions because they never gave the matter a thought. But when the Pharisees saw the Lord's disciples picking corn on the sabbath day, they jumped on them like ducks on June-bugs. Immediately, they accused them to the Lord, as if they had committed some terribly evil moral offence.

"Why do they on the sabbath day that which is not lawful?" The answer our Master gave to these self-righteous, work mongers is full of wise instruction for our souls. We should study the passage with care and lay its teachings to heart.

---

[1] We observe the sabbath of faith, a spiritual sabbath rest in Christ, and live in the hope and anticipation of a glorious, eternal sabbath rest with Christ (Hebrews 4:3-9); but there is absolutely no sense in which we keep a carnal, legal sabbath day in this age of grace. The New Testament clearly forbids the observance of such sabbath days, which were but *"a shadow of things to come"* (Colossians 2:16, 17). Believers commonly gather in the house of God and worship on Sunday, which is called *"the Lord's day"* (Revelation 1:10), because our Saviour arose on the first day of the week; but Sunday is not the Sabbath.

Why are we so insistent and dogmatic about this? Because Christ, who is the Lord of the sabbath, is Christ our Sabbath. For us to go back to keeping a sabbath day, as the Jews did in the Old Testament, or for us to put on the yoke of legal religion, is to say that Christ fulfilled nothing. Legalism is, in its essence, a denial of Christ's finished work as the sinners' Substitute. That was the reason for Paul's strong denunciation of Peter's behaviour at Antioch.

Fault Finders

The first thing that is obvious in these verses is the fact that self-righteous, religious legalists are always quick to spot and point the faults of others.

"And it came to pass, that he went through the corn fields on the sabbath day; and his disciples began, as they went, to pluck the ears of corn. And the Pharisees said unto him, Behold, why do they on the sabbath day that which is not lawful?" (vv. 23, 24)

These Pharisees represent the very worst of religious men. They were mere ceremonialists and legalists. They cherished the outward shell and show of religion. They loved it so much that they added laws to the laws given by God to Moses and ceremonies to God's appointed symbolic and typical ceremonies. Their godliness was all form and formality, creed and custom. For them washings and fastings, tithings and forms of prayers, pageantry and ceremonies were holiness. Their godliness was all bodily exercise and will-worship. They knew absolutely nothing of repentance, faith, and mercy. People who have obtained mercy are merciful. Those who have experienced forgiveness are forgiving. Those who know grace are gracious.

Our Lord plainly told the Pharisees that if they had known anything of true godliness, they would not have condemned the guiltless. "But if ye had known what this meaneth, I will have mercy, and not sacrifice, ye would not have condemned the guiltless" (Matthew 12:7).

But the disciples had done nothing wrong. The Saviour said they were guiltless in doing what they did. The Pharisees simply presumed that since it was commonly thought to be wrong, since it broke their traditions, it was horribly wrong. Let us watch and pray, lest we fall into the wickedness of the Pharisees. The leaven of the Pharisees, which our Lord warned us to beware of, is that subtle self-righteousness that makes sinners think they are righteous because of what they do and do not do. Only self-righteous Pharisees and legalists spy on one another. Only self-righteous Pharisees and legalists are quick to point out the faults and offences of others. Only self-righteous Pharisees and legalists seek to regulate the lives of others.

Bible Doctrine

The second thing I want us to see is that, as believers, we should always be able to defend our doctrine and our behaviour from the Word of God. If our doctrine is not Bible doctrine it is false doctrine. Our Lord's reply to these carping Pharisees was taken directly from the Word of God. He was thoroughly familiar with holy scriptures. I realize that he is the Author as well as the Subject of this Book. Yet, his example, as always, is a pattern for us. He defended his disciples and their behaviour from the Word of God.

"And he said unto them, Have ye never read what David did, when he had need, and was an hungred, he, and they that were with him? How he went into the house of God in the days of Abiathar the high priest, and did eat the shewbread, which is not lawful to eat but for the priests, and gave also to them which were with him?" (vv. 25, 26)

In spiritual and doctrinal matters nothing is so powerful a defence, nothing is so powerful a weapon to stop the mouths of gainsayers as the plain texts of scripture, where the meaning is so obvious that it cannot be mistaken.

In all points of doctrine and behaviour our only authority, our only basis of conduct is the inspired Word of God. In spiritual matters we have no right to believe or do anything for which we are not able to point to the Word of God and say, "This is why"! We ought to be able to comfortably show from the Word of God the reason of our hope, the reason for our doctrine, and the reason for our ordinances.

The only way we will be able to use the Word of God this way is by making ourselves personally acquainted with its contents. Do not be content with second-hand knowledge and second-hand religion. Study the Word of God for yourself. Read it diligently, perseveringly, and prayerfully, carefully comparing scripture with scripture (John 5:39; 2 Timothy 2:15). J. C. Ryle rightly observed: "There is no royal road to the knowledge of the Bible. It does not come to man by intuition. The book must be studied, pondered, prayed over, searched into, and not left always lying on a shelf, or carelessly looked at now and then."

Our Saviour's allusion to the hunger of David and his companions in eating the shewbread opens a blessed spiritual application before us. This gospel day in which we live is day of our High Priest, of whom Abiathar and his days were but a shadow. And the Lord Jesus has made all his redeemed both kings and priests unto the Father (Revelation 1:6). On the Lord's day, or any day, when hungry souls gather in the house of God seeking Christ, the true Shewbread (the Bread of Life), the Master's servants are to always spread the gospel feast. Where else should the hungry soul go for spiritual sustenance, but to the house of God? When our Lord Jesus, of whom David was a type, comes to his house with two or three gathered in his name (Matthew 18:20), he spreads a feast of fat things before them and says, "Eat, O friends; drink, yea, drink abundantly, O beloved" (Song of Solomon 5:1). Then the hungry soul is fed from the Master's table.

Apparent Discrepancies

A third thing that may be observed from this passage is the fact that apparent discrepancies in the Word of God are easily cleared when thoughtfully considered. Though you may have missed the fact that, while Mark identifies the High Priest in David's day as a man named Abiathar, in the book of 1 Samuel he is called Ahimelech (1 Samuel 21:6). Others have pointed to this as one of many things they see as discrepancies in the Bible. Believers do not quickly spot such apparent discrepancies in the blessed Book, because we do not look for them. But many look for an excuse for their scepticism. They point to this text and say, "There, you see, Mark messed up. How can you say the Bible is the inspired, inerrant Word of God, when it contains such errors?"

Let me assure you first that such apparent discrepancies in the Word of God are not accidental. This Word of God is deliberately written to confuse rebels who will not bow to Christ. For those who are determined to go to hell, who are too smart to live by faith, who are too sophisticated to trust a crucified Substitute, God has put plenty of stumbling stones in the road to keep them tripped up. When God sends blindness, he sends complete and total blindness.

Yet, that which seems a discrepancy to the infidel is easily cleared for the believer. There are two very likely reasons why Mark and Samuel may have used different names in their accounts of David going into the house of the High Priest and eating the shewbread. First, there may have been, as was sometimes the case, two men serving as the High Priest at that time (2 Samuel 8:17). If that were the case, both may well have acted together in providing the shewbread to David and his men; and it would be altogether proper, when describing the matter, to use either name. Second, and in my opinion most likely, Ahimelech had a second name, by which he was commonly called, Abiathar.

Lord Of The Sabbath

The fourth thing revealed in this passage is the fact that Christ our Saviour is the Lord of the sabbath. "And he said unto them, The sabbath was made for man, and not man for the sabbath: Therefore the Son of man is Lord also of the sabbath" (vv. 27, 28). There is a great depth of spiritual truth in these two verses, truths that simply must be understood and remembered by us. They are set before us in three, crystal clear, simple statements. I do not doubt that neither the Pharisees nor the Lord's disciples understood them at the time. But there is no reason for confusion in these matters today. The Holy Spirit has now taken the things of Christ and shown their meaning in the Apostolic Epistles. Let's look at these three statements, one by one.

"The Sabbath Was Made For Man"

Theologians, commentators, and preachers labour, and dig, and study, and work very hard to make that statement seem confusing. It is not confusing at all. When God established the sabbath day, he established it for the benefit of man. It was made to help, not to hurt, man. God instituted the sabbath observance of the Old Testament for exactly the same reason he instituted the temple, the priesthood, and the sacrifices of that typical age. He did it to portray to man the way of salvation and life by faith in Christ.

The sabbath was made for man. It was made to be a day of rest, pointing to the blessed rest of faith we find in Christ, who is our Rest, our Sabbath (Isaiah 28:12; Psalm 116:7). "There remaineth therefore a rest to the people of God" (Hebrews 4:9); and Christ is that Rest. Just as a man, keeping the sabbath, ceased from his works, trusting God to provide everything he needed, so we come to Christ, ceasing from our own works, trusting him alone for everything. Resting in him, we keep the sabbath of faith (Matthew 11:28-30; Hebrews 4:7-10).

When our Lord says the sabbath was made for man, we must never imagine that it was made for all men. The scriptures are explicitly clear in telling us that the sabbath was made for the Jews of the Mosaic dispensation, who were the typical people of God. It was never given to or required of Gentiles (Exodus 31:16, 17). Not only did the ancient Jews never require Gentiles to keep the sabbath, they positively forbade sabbath day observance by Gentiles.[2] And our Lord is the Sabbath Rest made for the Israel of God.

Man Was Not Made For The Sabbath
Though the Lord God himself kept a sabbath of rest, after creating the heavens and the earth, he never required sabbath-keeping of anyone until the law was given to Moses and the children of Israel at Sinai. Understand the meaning of this. Men and women worshipped and served God for hundreds, even thousands of years, without being under laws of sabbath-keeping, or any other form of law for that matter. Enoch walked with God; but he never kept a sabbath day. Noah was a righteous man; but he never observed a sabbath. Abraham was the friend of God; but he never kept a sabbath day.

Christ Is The Lord Of The Sabbath
"Therefore the Son of man is Lord also of the sabbath" (2:28). The simple, clear, and obvious meaning of this sentence is that he who is the Christ of God instituted the sabbath, fulfilled the sabbath, dispensed with the sabbath, and abrogated the sabbath in exactly the same way and to exactly the same degree as he did all the other carnal ordinances, rituals, and ceremonies of the legal dispensation.

---

[2] The Jerusalem Council's recommendations said nothing about sabbath day observance (Acts 15). If ever the practice of sabbath-keeping was to be imposed upon Gentiles that is the place where it would have been done.

You may be thinking, "If that is the case, then we ought never keep a legal, ceremonial sabbath day." If so, you are exactly right. Sabbath day observance is expressly and positively forbidden in the New Testament, just as much so as Passover observance (Galatians 4:10, 11; Colossians 2:16, 17).

Sabbath observance was never binding upon Gentiles. "And believers in Christ", wrote John Gill, "be they who they will are by no means obliged to it, nor ought they to observe it. Should it be imposed upon them, they ought to reject it. Should they be judged, censored, and condemned for so doing, they ought not to mind it".

Christ, who is the Lord of the sabbath is himself our Sabbath. We keep no Sabbath, but the sabbath of faith. We do so because this is what our God requires of us. Not only are we free from the law in Christ, it is our responsibility to live as free men and women in him. To do otherwise is to deny his finished work as our Substitute, Redeemer, and Saviour (Romans 10:4; Galatians 5:1-4).

The sabbath day, that day of rest,
Was sanctified and blest,
To point us to our Saviour Christ,
In whom alone is rest.

That legal sabbath ended when,
Christ died and rose again.
Yet, there's a sabbath that remains,
A rest that's found in Him.

"Come unto Me", the Saviour said,
"And I will give you rest."
O weary sinners, cease from works,
Trust Christ and find sweet rest.

Ah, sweet refreshment for my soul,
The rest of faith is rest!
Ceasing from works, I trust God's Son,
Christ is my Sabbath Rest!

The Lord Of The Sabbath

"And he entered again into the synagogue; and there was a man there which had a withered hand. And they watched him, whether he would heal him on the sabbath day; that they might accuse him ... And he looked round about on them which sat about him, and said, Behold my mother and my brethren! For whosoever shall do the will of God, the same is my brother, and my sister, and mother".

(Mark 3:1-35)

Chapter 9

Watch Him

In this chapter Mark was inspired by God the Holy Spirit to link five things together, almost as though they were one, so that we might see the connection between them and learn from it. In verse two Mark describes the conduct of the Pharisees in the synagogue with these words: "They watched him". They watched him, ready to seize any word or action by which they might slander his name and accuse him of evil. Let us watch him, not to accuse him, or merely to gratify our curiosity, but to worship him and learn from him, that we may both imitate him and honour him as we make our pilgrimage through this world. Let us watch the Son of God, our Saviour, as he moves in and out among men in different circumstances and conditions.

Watch Him In The Synagogue

"And he entered again into the synagogue; and there was a man there which had a withered hand. And they watched him, whether he would heal him on the sabbath day; that they might accuse him. And he saith unto the man which had the withered hand, Stand forth. And he saith unto them, Is it lawful to do good on the sabbath days, or to do evil? to save life, or to kill? (But they held their peace.) And when he had looked round about on them with anger, being grieved for the hardness of their hearts, he saith unto the man, Stretch forth thine hand. And he stretched it out: and his hand was restored whole as the other. And the Pharisees went forth, and straightway took counsel with the Herodians against him, how they might destroy him" (vv. 1-6).

Our Lord Jesus came to the synagogue that day on an errand of mercy for the benefit of one specific man. A man, whose hand was withered, was about to be made whole. In verses three and five the Saviour singled out this needy soul. "And he saith unto the man which had the withered hand, Stand forth". Then, in verse five, "he saith unto the man, Stretch forth thine hand. And he stretched it out: and his hand was restored whole as the other".

That is a beautiful picture of God's saving operations of grace in the salvation of sinners. An election was made and a commandment was given.

The Lord Jesus sovereignly singled out one man. He chose to be gracious to one among many. Then he issued a command. "Stretch forth thine hand". This man was commanded to do what he absolutely could not do. Yet, being commanded to do it, he was enabled to do it. Even so, when sinners are called to life and faith in the Lord Jesus Christ, by the omnipotent mercy and irresistible grace of his Spirit, they are made alive in Christ and enabled to believe on him, though it is absolutely impossible for them to do so otherwise.

After the Lord's command an act of faith was performed. "And he stretched it out: and his hand was restored whole as the other". With the commandment came the ability to obey. And when God the Holy Spirit calls a sinner to life and faith in Christ, he gives that sinner life; he gives him the will to obey; and he gives him the gift of faith. Thus it is written, "Thy people shall be willing in the day of thy power".

Mark tells us, in verse two, that these pompous, self-righteous, tithing, sabbath-keeping, Pharisees watched the Saviour's every word and movement. They did not watch to learn. "They watched ... him that they might accuse him"! Here they are in the house of God, pretending to worship God, pretending to keep the sabbath day, pretending to be holy, pretending to be lovers of God and lovers of men. But they were nothing but hardhearted hypocrites. These men would not break the sabbath day for anything; but they did not hesitate gathering with the Herodians on the sabbath day in a church discipline committee to plot the murder of the Son of God!

The Pharisees and Herodians hated one another passionately; but their religion was the same (Proverbs 14:12; 16:25). It was the religion of man, the religion of the beast, the way of Cain. Both the Pharisees and the Herodians were self-righteous legalists, pretending to honour God, flattering themselves with the delusion that they were holy, while using religion for their own advantage. When the Lord Jesus and the gospel he reveals exposed their hypocrisy, they gladly embraced one another to oppose him. Nothing has changed. Legalism always produces hardness. Those who watch others in the name of "brotherly love" that they might accuse them to others do so because of a hardness of heart that comes only from self-righteousness.

Any religion that produces such hardness of heart is not of God. The grace of God does not produce mean-spirited legalism. The grace of God does not produce gossiping, slandering, backbiting hypocrites. Grace makes people gracious. Forgiveness makes men forgiving. The knowledge of Christ and the experience of his grace in the soul makes a person loving, kind, tender, forbearing, and patient with others.

Our Lord knew the Pharisees were watching him; but he made no effort to impress them or prevent their slanders. When Paul admonishes us to "abstain from all appearance of evil", he is not telling us to live in a way that will prevent carping religionists from speaking evil of us. He is telling us to abstain from every form of doctrine that is evil, every form that has the smell of free will, works religion, every form of self-righteous legality!

I hear people say, "We ought to live so that the world will see Christ in us". The world did not see Christ in Christ. How do you think the world is going to see Christ in you? Do not try to impress the world with your godliness. The world (secular or religious) does not have the slightest idea what godliness is. Live for the glory of Christ, to do the will of God, and serve the interests of men's souls, and ignore the world.

Verse five tells us that our Lord Jesus looked around the room, glaring at these pompous religionists "with anger, being grieved for the hardness of their hearts". Everyone in the room could plainly see the fire in his eyes. There is an anger that is sinful and to be avoided. Personal vengeance, sensual wrath, the anger of jealousy and envy, all those things are horribly evil. But anger at hard, self-righteous, legalistic, damning religion, anger in the cause of God's glory is a just anger. Anger at a backbiting tongue is altogether proper. "The north wind driveth away rain: so doth an angry countenance a backbiting tongue" (Proverbs 25:23; Psalm 139:19-22).

Watch Him At The Seashore
"But Jesus withdrew himself with his disciples to the sea: and a great multitude from Galilee followed him, and from Judaea, And from Jerusalem, and from Idumaea, and from beyond Jordan; and they about Tyre and Sidon, a great multitude, when they had heard what great things he did, came unto him. And he spake to his disciples, that a small ship should wait on him because of the multitude, lest they should throng him. For he had healed many; insomuch that they pressed upon him for to touch him, as many as had plagues. And unclean spirits, when they saw him, fell down before him, and cried, saying, Thou art the Son of God. And he straitly charged them that they should not make him known" (vv. 7-12).

Here is another picture of God's saving operations of grace. In the case of the man with the withered hand, we saw a picture of the effectual call and of God's omnipotent grace in that call. Here we see a demonstration of God's method of grace. Do not imagine that God is in any way limited. He is not. Yet, there are some specific things which are always involved in the conversion of chosen sinners. Here are three things always involved in the experience of grace.

First, a message was heard. When our Lord and his disciples gathered at the seashore, great multitudes came from everywhere, "when they heard what great things he did".

Second, they did not hear just any message. They heard a message about him. They did not hear about what he wanted to do, or tried to do, or even would do. There is no gospel in that kind of preaching. "They heard what great things he did"! Gospel preaching is all about him. It is all about Jesus Christ. Gospel preaching declares what great things he has done. He has brought in everlasting righteousness. He has satisfied divine justice. He has put away sin by the sacrifice of himself. He has accomplished redemption, obtaining eternal redemption by the merit of his blood for his people.

Third, gospel preaching is absolutely indispensable in God's method of salvation and grace (Romans 10:17; 1 Corinthians 1:18-23; 1 Peter 1:23-25). It is the catalyst God has chosen to employ in saving his elect.

A catalyst is an agent of action. If a chemist desires to unite two substances to create another, in many cases, a catalyst is necessary. The catalyst does not cause the union and never enters into the union of those substances. But without the presence of that specific catalyst, the union would never take place and could not continue. That is exactly what the preaching of the gospel is in God's saving operations.

Were it his pleasure to do so, God almighty could have chosen to save sinners without the use of any means or agency of any kind. Had he chosen to do so, he could have sent angels to pull us into heaven by our noses, once atonement was made for us. But that is not his pleasure. The Lord God has chosen to regenerate and call redeemed sinners through the agency of gospel preaching, because God has so ordained it. That makes the preaching of the gospel the catalyst necessary for the communication of his powerful saving grace.

Some cry out against this and say, "That limits God's sovereignty. That makes salvation depend upon man." Do not be so foolish as to be found fighting against God. We must never force the scriptures to mean what we want them to mean. We must never bend the Word of God to our doctrinal notions and theological system. Rather, we bow to God's Word. We cannot extol and honour God if we refuse to submit our reason to his Revelation.

Carefully read the scriptures once more. It is impossible to read the following passages in their context without concluding that regeneration and faith in Christ, gifts of God the Holy Spirit and operations of his irresistible grace, are communicated to chosen sinners through the instrumentality of gospel preaching (Romans 1:15-17; 10:13-17; 1 Corinthians 1:21; Ephesians 1:13; 1 Timothy 4:12-16; Hebrews 4:12; James 1:18; 1 Peter 1:23-25). In each of those passages the Lord God plainly declares that it is his purpose and pleasure to save his elect through the preaching of the gospel.

Perhaps you think, "What if one of God's elect is in a remote barbarian tribe in the jungles of New Guinea where no gospel preacher has ever been?"

I can see how that would create a problem, except for one thing: there are no problems with God! He knows exactly how to get his prophet to the people to whom he has purposed to show his mercy. Just ask Jonah!

We preach the gospel with a sense of urgency, knowing that sinners cannot believe on Christ until Christ is preached to them. Yet, we preach with confidence of success, knowing that our labour is not in vain in the Lord (1 Corinthians 15:58). God's Word will not return to him void. It will accomplish his will and prosper in the thing it is sent to do (Isaiah 55:11). Every chosen, redeemed sinner must be regenerated and called by the Holy Spirit. That work will be accomplished through the preaching of the gospel.

The Saviour was touched. Hearing what great things the Lord Jesus had done, these poor, needy souls thronged around the Son of God, like the woman with the issue of blood, in hope of touching him. Granted, their hope, like hers, may have been shaky, maybe even desperate. But, like her, Christ was all the hope they had. And when Christ is all you have, Christ is enough! In their great need, they touched him. If we can, with the hand of hope and faith touch him, we shall be made whole. Like the publican in the temple, we will receive complete justification from God. God help you to touch him.

Christ was confessed. "And unclean spirits, when they saw him, fell down before him, and cried, saying, Thou art the Son of God" (v. 11). When those who were possessed of demons were delivered from the powers of hell by the grace of God, they who had experienced his power fell before him and confessed, "Thou art the Son of God"! That is how God saves his elect. 1. He causes them to hear the gospel of grace. 2. He gives them the hope of grace, causing them to come to Christ in faith. 3. He causes them to confess Christ as their God and Saviour.

Watch Him On The Mountain
"And he goeth up into a mountain, and calleth unto him whom he would: and they came unto him. And he ordained twelve, that they should be with him, and that he might send them forth to preach, And to have power to heal sicknesses, and to cast out devils: And Simon he surnamed Peter; And James the son of Zebedee, and John the brother of James; and he surnamed them Boanerges, which is, The sons of thunder: And Andrew, and Philip, and Bartholomew, and Matthew, and Thomas, and James the son of Alphaeus, and Thaddaeus, and Simon the Canaanite, And Judas Iscariot, which also betrayed him: and they went into an house" (vv. 13-19).

There are things here that need to be thoughtfully and prayerfully studied and things that are so obvious they grab our attention as we read them. Here is a display of our Saviour's sovereignty. Our Lord Jesus called whom he would (v. 13) and all whom he was pleased to call came to him. Here is a description of gospel preachers. "And he ordained twelve, that they should be with him, and that he might send them forth to preach, And to have power to heal sicknesses, and to cast out devils" (vv. 14, 15).

That which Mark tells us in verse fourteen about the original apostles may be applied to every man in every age who is called of God to preach the gospel of Christ. The gospel preacher is a man chosen and ordained of God. He is a man who is with the Lord, and more importantly, with whom the Lord is. The stars of the churches are in his right hand. The gospel preacher is a man sent of God. God sends his servants where he wants them, and puts them there at the time he has ordained. The preacher is a man sent to preach. God's messengers are all preachers. They are men with a message. And their message is Jesus Christ crucified. And they are men accompanied with God-given power to perform the work to which they are sent.

Here is a fraud numbered among the apostles of our Lord. "Judas Iscariot, which also betrayed him" (v. 19). I am thankful that Judas is listed here among those the Lord Jesus sent out as his apostles. Remember, the Lord sovereignty called to him "whom he would". Judas was not there by accident but by divine purpose, just as much as Peter was. Though he was a wicked, reprobate man, he was an instrument in the hands of the sovereign Lord God, by which his eternal purpose was accomplished. Our Lord Jesus Christ is Lord (absolute despot) still over the false prophets who deny him (2 Peter 2:1).

Watch Him Among Unbelievers

"And the multitude cometh together again, so that they could not so much as eat bread. And when his friends heard of it, they went out to lay hold on him: for they said, He is beside himself" (vv. 20, 21). If you have a marginal reference in your Bible, you will see that "friends" might be translated, "kinsmen". Our Lord's unbelieving kinsmen pitied him as a madman. His family apparently tried not to show open hostility to him; but they were obviously embarrassed by the fact that he was a relative. Mark tells us they tried to take him by the arms and lead him out of the streets, saying to the crowds, "Do not pay any attention to him, the poor man has lost his mind"!

"And the scribes which came down from Jerusalem said, He hath Beelzebub, and by the prince of the devils casteth he out devils" (v. 22). When confronted with the doctrine of Christ, and his undeniable power as the Son of God, rather than bowing to him, they ascribed everything he did to the devil. Our Lord responded to the "courteous" unbelief of his pretended friends and the open blasphemy of the Pharisees in exactly the same way.

"And he called them unto him, and said unto them in parables, How can Satan cast out Satan? And if a kingdom be divided against itself, that kingdom cannot stand. And if a house be divided against itself, that house cannot stand. And if Satan rise up against himself, and be divided, he cannot stand, but hath an end" (vv. 23-26). He asserts his sovereignty over the powers of hell. "No man can enter into a strong man's house, and spoil his goods, except he will first bind the strong man; and then he will spoil his house" (v. 27). Next, he assures us of the forgiveness of sins. "Verily I say unto you, All sins shall be forgiven unto the sons of men, and blasphemies wherewith soever they shall blaspheme" (v. 28). Then, he warns us of the danger of wilful unbelief. "But he that shall blaspheme against the Holy Ghost hath never forgiveness, but is in danger of eternal damnation" (v. 29).

Any man who dares thumb his nose at God almighty and his darling Son is courting eternal reprobation. There comes a time when men and women cannot be saved, when God will not show mercy. I do not know when that time comes. I do not know where God has drawn that line but I do know he has. Any who cross that line in obstinate rebellion and unbelief cannot be saved. They are as surely damned as if they were already in hell (Proverbs 1:23-33). When that happens, God leaves them alone. His people have no ability to pray for them. God's servants are not able to speak to their hearts. There is no gentle wooing of the Spirit tugging at their hearts. The Lord God himself declares, "My Spirit shall not always strive with man" (Genesis 6:3). Men can make of that whatever they will, or make nothing of it if they dare. Wilful unbelief is a dangerous thing.

Watch Him Among His Real Family
"There came then his brethren and his mother, and, standing without, sent unto him, calling him. And the multitude sat about him, and they said unto him, Behold, thy mother and thy brethren without seek for thee. And he answered them, saying, Who is my mother, or my brethren? And he looked round about on them which sat about him, and said, Behold my mother and my brethren! For whosoever shall do the will of God, the same is my brother, and my sister, and mother" (vv. 31-35). It appears that those brethren who tried to get him to go with them to the insane asylum went to his mother, hoping to use her influence to put an end to the family's embarrassment. But our Lord describes his family, the family of God, as being made up of chosen, redeemed, called sinners who "do the will of God".

We do not have to guess or speculate as to what the will of God is. He tells us plainly in his Word. "And this is his commandment, That we should believe on the name of his Son Jesus Christ, and love one another, as he gave us commandment" (1 John 3:23). The only way sinners can get into his family is by adoption (Galatians 4:4-7; 1 John 3:1-3). The evidence of adoption is faith in Christ. (Romans 8:14-16).

"And he entered again into the synagogue; and there was a man there which had a withered hand. And they watched him, whether he would heal him on the sabbath day; that they might accuse him. And he saith unto the man which had the withered hand, Stand forth. And he saith unto them, Is it lawful to do good on the sabbath days, or to do evil? to save life, or to kill? But they held their peace. And when he had looked round about on them with anger, being grieved for the hardness of their hearts, he saith unto the man, Stretch forth thine hand. And he stretched it out: and his hand was restored whole as the other. And the Pharisees went forth, and straightway took counsel with the Herodians against him, how they might destroy him. But Jesus withdrew himself with his disciples to the sea: and a great multitude from Galilee followed him, and from Judaea, And from Jerusalem, and from Idumaea, and from beyond Jordan; and they about Tyre and Sidon, a great multitude, when they had heard what great things he did, came unto him. And he spake to his disciples, that a small ship should wait on him because of the multitude, lest they should throng him. For he had healed many; insomuch that they pressed upon him for to touch him, as many as had plagues. And unclean spirits, when they saw him, fell down before him, and cried, saying, Thou art the Son of God. And he straitly charged them that they should not make him known".

(Mark 3:1-12)

Chapter 10

"They Watched Him"

When the Lord God told Eli that he was going to kill his sons, take the priesthood from his family, and destroy his family because he indulged his sons in their wickedness, he said, "And I will raise me up a faithful priest, that shall do according to that which is in mine heart and in my mind: and I will build him a sure house; and he shall walk before mine anointed for ever. And it shall come to pass, that every one that is left in thine house shall come and crouch to him" (1 Samuel 2:35, 36). God has fulfilled his Word in sending his Son to be a merciful, faithful, obedient High Priest over the house of God, before whom everyone and everything in heaven, earth, and hell must bow.

The third chapter of Mark opens with our Lord Jesus in his Father's house doing his Father's business, according to his Father's will. Here, while the Pharisees watched him so that they might accuse him, our Lord Jesus healed in the synagogue on the sabbath day "a man there which had a withered hand".

While he walked upon this earth, our Lord Jesus was always about his Father's business, always doing good. In the sight of his enemies and in the sight of his friends he did that which he knew to be his Father's will, whether men approved or disapproved mattered little to him. He was concerned about the will of God and the welfare of men, the glory of God and doing good to men. That was the daily tenor of our Lord's earthly life and ministry. Thus, he left us an example that we should follow his steps (1 Peter 2:21). Blessed are those men and women who, believing on Christ as Lord and Saviour, seek to imitate their Master, striving to walk in his steps and follow his example.

A Place Of Hope

First, I want to remind you that the house of God is a place of hope. "And he entered again into the synagogue; and there was a man there which had a withered hand" (v. 1). We have no way of knowing whether this man came to the synagogue as one who regularly attended the worship of God, or because he knew that Christ was going to be there that day and came hoping to be healed by him. What his reasons were we are not told; but our Saviour's reason for being there is obvious. He came on an errand of mercy to heal this man by the power of his omnipotent grace.

This man no more knew what the purpose of God was than we do. He did not know whether the Lord would be gracious to him or not; but he knew he had a withered arm. I suspect that he knew that Christ had power to heal his withered arm. Perhaps he knew that on the appointed day of worship Christ would be in the place of worship. Therefore, he came to the synagogue. It was to him the place of hope.

I do not know for sure that that was the case; but I do know for sure that the church of God, the gathering of God's saints in public worship, is the place of hope for needy sinners. This is the place where God meets with men (Matthew 18:20; 1 Corinthians 3:16). And this is the place where God sends forth his Word and his power for the healing of men's souls.

Many who profess to believe God make public worship an insignificant matter. If you are determined to do so, you have no difficulty in finding a way to justify absenting yourself from the house of God and the ministry of the Word. But God has promised to meet sinners nowhere else. And those who need mercy will be found in the place of hope. Those who need no mercy may be found anywhere. But sick people are found in the hospital. Hungry people are found in the soup kitchen. And needy sinners are found in the house of God, the place of hope.

God Hating Religionists
Second, the Pharisees in the synagogue, watching our Saviour that they might accuse him, are held before us as a representation of God hating, self-righteous religionists. "And they watched him, whether he would heal him on the sabbath day; that they might accuse him" (v. 2). If you read Matthew's account (Matthew 12:10), you will notice that they first ask the Lord Jesus in a pretence of piety, "Is it lawful to heal on the sabbath days?" But their only motive was to lay a trap for him. What a shameful display these men are of the depravity and deceitfulness of the human heart. Carnal men still watch Christ's disciples, hoping to catch them doing or saying something that can be used against them.

These things happened on the sabbath day. They did not take place in a bar room, or a back alley, but in the house of God! Men who were assembled in the name of God, supposedly to hear the Word of God and worship God, plotted to destroy the Son of God! These men who pretended to be so strict, so sanctimonious, so very precise about the things of God, sat in the house Of God with malicious hearts, plotting murder! It is no surprise that the Lord Jesus looked round about upon them with anger.

As these Pharisees watched our Saviour that they might accuse him, so men and women today, especially self-righteous religionists, watch God's saints, that they might accuse them. The servant is not above his Master, nor the disciple above his Lord. We must never expect to fare better among men than our Saviour did if we walk in his steps. God's saints are marked people in a godless world. They are watched by everyone. They do nothing without the world noticing.

The Pharisees watched the Lord Jesus, not to adore him for his grace and mercy, but "that they might accuse him". And as soon as our Saviour manifested his tender mercy toward this poor man, they took counsel to kill him. Robert Hawker's comments on John 8:43-47 concerning the conduct of these wretched creatures are instructive:

> Do not overlook these things: for very awful as they are, they become precious testimonies to the truth as it is in Jesus. The Lord himself hath explained the same. For while he saith, 'My sheep hear my voice; and I know them and they follow me: and I give unto them eternal life' (John 10:27, 28), he saith to those that are not his sheep: 'Why do ye not understand my speech? even, because ye cannot hear my word. Ye are of your father the devil, and the lusts of your father ye will do'.

No wonder Jesus "looked round about upon them with anger". The seed of the woman, and the children of the wicked one, can never agree. And let it be remembered that the destruction of the enemies of Christ forms a part of Christ's mission as much as the salvation of his chosen. The hour of decision will come when Jesus will "gather out of his kingdom all things that offend" and, while the redeemed shall "shine forth as the sun in the kingdom of their Father", the Lord will cast them that do iniquity into "the furnace of fire, where is wailing and gnashing of teeth" (Isaiah 63:4; Matthew 13:36-43, 15:31 ff.).

That which is true concerning believers in general is doubly true concerning gospel preachers. Their dress, their use of their time, their recreations, the cars they drive, the restaurants they eat in, every relationship of their lives, every word they speak, and everything they do is rigidly observed, closely scrutinized, and noted by men and women, especially religious men and women, who are hoping to catch them in some error that can be magnified and used against them.

That being the case, what should we do? Should we live like hermits, wear simple, unadorned attire like the Amish, and take great care never to do anything with which anyone can find fault? That is impossible. If you live like a hermit, someone will say, "He is so unfriendly. He thinks he is better than anyone else." If you are warm and friendly, and you happen to be a lady, your gossiping sisters will say, "Look at her. She is such a flirt. Doesn't she care what people think?" If you wear plain, simple clothes, people will say you do not pay enough attention to your appearance. If you wear stylish clothes, they will say you are a show-off. And if you should happen to say, or do something that really is bad, something that is totally out of character for you, they will jump on that like fleas on a dog, and say, "Well, I always was suspicious. Sooner or later, the truth will come out."

What are we to do? How are we to live before such people? Do exactly what your Lord did here. He knew what the Pharisees thought and what they would say and do in response to his actions; but he paid absolutely no attention to them. He simply did what he knew was his Father's will, for the glory of his Father's name and the benefit of other men. He looked upon the Pharisees and their opinions about what he did and did not do with absolute, utter contempt.

Let me give you a few, simple guidelines for day by day behaviour, as you attempt to follow Christ in this world: Seek in all things to do the will of God and to live for the glory of God. Try never to give the enemies of our God occasion to blaspheme. Do nothing that violates the law of God or principles of righteousness. Always seek to do that which is good for and never injurious to others. In all things, seek to be governed by love for Christ and his people. In a word, live as God the Holy Spirit has told us to live in this world.

"This I say therefore, and testify in the Lord, that ye henceforth walk not as other Gentiles walk, in the vanity of their mind, Having the understanding darkened, being alienated from the life of God through the ignorance that is in them, because of the blindness of their heart: Who being past feeling have given themselves over unto lasciviousness, to work all uncleanness with greediness. But ye have not so learned Christ; If so be that ye have heard him, and have been taught by him, as the truth is in Jesus: That ye put off concerning the former conversation the old man, which is corrupt according to the deceitful lusts; And be renewed in the spirit of your mind; And that ye put on the new man, which after God is created in righteousness and true holiness. Wherefore putting away lying, speak every man truth with his neighbour: for we are members one of another. Be ye angry, and sin not: let not the sun go down upon your wrath: Neither give place to the devil. Let him that stole steal no more: but rather let him labour, working with his hands the thing which is good, that he may have to give to him that needeth. Let no corrupt communication proceed out of your mouth, but that which is good to the use of edifying, that it may minister grace unto the hearers. And grieve not the holy Spirit of God, whereby ye are sealed unto the day of redemption. Let all bitterness, and wrath, and anger, and clamour, and evil speaking, be put away from you, with all malice: And be ye kind one to another, tenderhearted, forgiving one another, even as God for Christ's sake hath forgiven you. Be ye therefore followers of God, as dear children; And walk in love, as Christ also hath loved us, and hath given himself for us an offering and a sacrifice to God for a sweetsmelling savour. But fornication, and all uncleanness, or covetousness, let it not be once named among you, as becometh saints; Neither filthiness, nor foolish talking, nor jesting, which are not convenient: but rather giving of thanks. For this ye know, that no whoremonger, nor unclean person, nor covetous man, who is an idolater, hath any inheritance in the kingdom of Christ and of God" (Ephesians 4:17-5:5).

Omnipotent Mercy

Third, in verses 3-6 we see a display of our Saviour's omnipotent mercy. Our Lord Jesus had come to the synagogue on an errand of mercy. He was not about to let these Pharisees turn him aside from his mission. There is much in these verses deserving serious contemplation.

A command was given to the helpless soul. "And he saith unto the man which had the withered hand, Stand forth" (v. 3). In light of the fact that the Pharisees had already challenged the lawfulness of a man being healed on the sabbath day (Matthew 12:10), it required considerable courage for this man to stand forth, considerable courage or great need and great faith. Those two things, great need and great faith, always produce great courage.

"And he saith unto them, Is it lawful to do good on the sabbath days, or to do evil? to save life, or to kill? But they held their peace" (v. 4). Not to do good when there is opportunity is to do evil. Passive wickedness is just as evil as the performance of evil (Revelation 2:4, 14, 20; 3:4,15,16).

With this poor soul standing before them and before the entire congregation, these Pharisees, who would not hesitate to pull an ox out of a ditch on the Sabbath, could hardly say it is wrong to heal on the sabbath. They held their silence; but they were not happy. The Lord had embarrassed them; and embarrassed men are angry men.

"And when he had looked round about on them with anger, being grieved for the hardness of their hearts" (v. 5). Our Lord was filled with anger, but it was not an anger of personal revenge. We see that by the fact that his anger toward these men was the anger of one who was grieved, not the anger of one who was enraged. He looked upon their behaviour with contempt. He looked upon their hypocrisy with anger. He looked upon their hearts with grief.

"He saith unto the man, Stretch forth thine hand. And he stretched it out: and his hand was restored whole as the other". Here is a display of the saving power of our Saviour's irresistible grace. When our Lord called the man to stretch forth his hand, he gave him the power to do what he otherwise could not do. When he called Lazarus to come forth from the dead, with his call came the power for the dead to come forth. So it is with the call of God the Holy Spirit. He does not merely nudge dead sinners toward life by his call. With his call comes the power that gives life to the dead. He does not merely call us to grace, but "into the grace of our Lord Jesus Christ" (Galatians 1:6). He does not merely call dead sinners to live, but calls the dead unto life in Christ (2 Timothy 6:12).

As soon as the Saviour showed his tender mercy in healing this needy soul, the Pharisees and Herodians conspired to murder the Lord Jesus. "And the Pharisees went forth, and straightway took counsel with the Herodians against him, how they might destroy him" (v. 6). The Pharisees had what they wanted, a pretence of grounds upon which to justify the murder of the Lord of glory. They hated the Herodians. They had nothing in common with the Herodians. Yet, they did not hesitate to unite with the Herodians, when it served their ends. It cannot be ignored that these "good" men did this on the sabbath day!

Hope Inspired
Fourth, we see in verses 7-10 thronging crowds of needy souls rushing to the Saviour, inspired with hope.

"But Jesus withdrew himself with his disciples to the sea: and a great multitude from Galilee followed him, and from Judaea, And from Jerusalem, and from Idumaea, and from beyond Jordan; and they about Tyre and Sidon, a great multitude, when they had heard what great things he did, came unto him. And he spake to his disciples, that a small ship should wait on him because of the multitude, lest they should throng him. For he had healed many; insomuch that they pressed upon him for to touch him, as many as had plagues".

The Lord withdrew himself from the Pharisees. Multitudes heard about his power and grace. These needy souls came to the Lord Jesus with the prospect of being healed. They were inspired with the hope of mercy by the fact that "he had healed many". They seem to have thought within themselves, "If he healed Leper Larry, he can surely heal me, if he will"! And those who needed healing spared no effort in coming to him who was their only hope of being healed. They came not with the promise that they would be healed, only with the hope that the Son of God might do for them what he had done for the man with the withered arm, and with the faith that he could, if he would, heal them too. That is the way for sinners to come to Christ.

Hell Defeated

Fifth, in verses 11 and 12 we see hell defeated and prostrate before the Lord Jesus Christ. "And unclean spirits, when they saw him, fell down before him, and cried, saying, Thou art the Son of God. And he straitly charged them that they should not make him known". Here is a picture of what will happen in the last day. These unclean spirits were compelled by God our Saviour to give open testimony to his eternal Godhead and sovereignty over them as God the Son. So it shall be with every creature. Hell itself shall bow to Christ (Philippians 2:8-11). Satan, the fallen angels, and all the damned shall see Christ in his glory, confess him as God and Lord, and shrink away from his presence into everlasting torment.

The destruction of Christ's enemies and ours is as much a part of his mission as our Mediator and Jehovah's Servant as the salvation of God's elect. The hour will soon come when he will gather out of his kingdom all things that offend. In that day the redeemed of the Lord shall "shine forth as the sun in the kingdom of their Father", and "death and hell ... the fearful, and unbelieving, and the abominable, and murderers, and whoremongers, and sorcerers, and idolaters, and all liars, shall have their part in the lake which burneth with fire and brimstone: which is the second death". The Lord Jesus shall cast all his foes and ours into "the furnace of fire, where is wailing and gnashing of teeth" (Isaiah 63:4; Matthew 13:36-43; 15:31; Revelation 20:14; 21:18).

"And he goeth up into a mountain, and calleth unto him whom he would: and they came unto him. And he ordained twelve, that they should be with him, and that he might send them forth to preach, And to have power to heal sicknesses, and to cast out devils: And Simon he surnamed Peter; And James the son of Zebedee, and John the brother of James; and he surnamed them Boanerges, which is, The sons of thunder: And Andrew, and Philip, and Bartholomew, and Matthew, and Thomas, and James the son of Alphaeus, and Thaddaeus, and Simon the Canaanite, And Judas Iscariot, which also betrayed him: and they went into an house. And the multitude cometh together again, so that they could not so much as eat bread. And when his friends heard of it, they went out to lay hold on him: for they said, He is beside himself."

(Mark 3:13-21)

Chapter 11

The First Twelve Preachers

Here the Holy Spirit describes the calling of the twelve Apostles by our Lord Jesus Christ. This is an event, which ought to always be remembered and studied with deep gratitude. No twelve men in history have been so important as these twelve. None have done so much good. None have been of such benefit to us. J. C. Ryle wrote: "What a vast amount of benefit these few men have conferred upon the world! The names of a few Jewish fishermen are known and loved by millions all over the globe, while the names of many kings and rich men are lost and forgotten."

These apostles were a special order of men. The apostolic office was in existence for only a very brief period of time, during which the canon of holy scripture was completed. They had distinct gifts of healing, tongues, and inspiration, which no one has possessed since the Apostolic Era. They were men specifically chosen, gifted, and ordained by our Lord Jesus Christ to preach the gospel during the earliest days of Christianity and to write the New Testament, explaining by divine inspiration the teachings of our Lord Jesus Christ. They had no successors, when the Apostles died their office died, and all the gifts and signs accompanying apostleship died as well.

Twelve Men

Here are twelve men called and commissioned to be the first preachers of the gospel in this dispensation: Peter and Andrew, James and John the sons of Zebedee, Philip, Bartholomew, Thomas, Matthew, Simon the Canaanite, Jude the brother of James, James the son of Alphaeus, and Judas the Traitor.

The number of the apostles was twelve. That is significant. There were twelve tribes in the nation of Israel. The church is represented by twelve stars (Revelation 12:1). John saw twelve foundations in the New Jerusalem (Revelation 21:12-14). And the Lord Jesus spoke of the twelve apostles sitting upon thrones to judge the twelve tribes of Israel (Luke 22:30).

Judas' betrayal of our Saviour made a vacancy in the apostolic office, leaving only eleven. You will recall that in Acts 2 Peter mistakenly concluded from Psalm 69:25 that it was the responsibility of the church to fill the vacancy left by Judas' apostasy, and to choose Matthias to take his place. It was true; the Lord's intention was for his church to have twelve apostles, twelve and only twelve. David's prophecy must be fulfilled. Another apostle was needed to take Judas' place. But, like the others, he must be personally chosen and ordained to the office by Christ himself. The Lord had not chosen Matthias for this office. He had chosen Paul (1 Corinthians 15:8).

Just as the call of these twelve men was the evidence that Christ had chosen them to this high office, so it is the call of God that evidences every believer's election by God in eternity and his redemption by Christ at Calvary. That faith which is given us in effectual calling is our God-given evidence that we are his (Hebrews 11:1). Those who are called are justified (Romans 8:30). Those whom the Son of God has saved by his blood he will call by his Spirit (2 Timothy 1:9).

The same thing is true regarding those men whom the Lord God has chosen to be gospel preachers. Those who are sent by him are men chosen and called by him. And the evidence of their call is the fruit of their labour. Those preachers he has not sent forth as his messengers may preach truth; but they do so with no authority, because they have no authority from God. Those who are men chosen, called, and sent of God have, by the Word they proclaim, power over unclean spirits, and are used to heal the diseases and sicknesses of immortal souls in Christ's name and power.

These twelve men are held before us as patterns and examples of what is required and what is to be expected of those men who are called of God to preach the gospel of his free and sovereign grace in Christ. It is my intention to use them in just that way in this study. It would be of no benefit to your soul for me to write about an office that no longer exists. But it will, if blessed of God, be of great benefit to your soul for me to tell you who these men were, what the Lord did for them, and what they, by the power and grace of God, did for others as the first twelve preachers of this gospel age. Here the Holy Spirit shows us by example how preachers are made, what they must do, and what may be reasonably expected from them.

The Lord's Choice
It is a sad commentary upon our deluded society that I should have to call your attention to the fact that the apostles, these first twelve preachers, were all men. There is not a woman named among them. That is not an accident. A preaching woman is an abomination! God never called a woman to be a preacher or a missionary. Women are commanded of God to keep silence in the churches, never to teach or usurp authority over a man, and to learn in subjection. I cannot think of anything more obnoxious than effeminate men, except pushy, domineering women; and among them none are so abhorrent as female preachers!

Having said that, let me show you seven things about those men who are called and gifted of God to preach the gospel of his free and sovereign grace in Christ. What I have to say here applies to every man who is called of God. It matters not where he was educated, what his denominational affiliation is, or what his physical appearance is. If a man is called of God to the work of the gospel ministry, he must be like these first preachers in these seven areas.

Converted Men
Those who are called of God to preach the gospel are converted men. I know Judas was not a converted man. And I know that our Lord Jesus knew Judas was unconverted. I will deal with those things later. But Judas professed to be a converted man, as well as Peter, James, and John. That is the important point here. A call to the ministry is always preceded by a call to discipleship. You cannot lead men to follow Christ unless you are a follower of Christ.

We must never attempt to raise men up for the ministry. We must never entice young men to dedicate themselves to the work of the ministry by glamorizing it. It is our responsibility to simply preach the gospel, pray for God to make it effectual, pray for him to send forth labourers into his vineyard, and wait for him to work. As soon as we start glamorizing the work and start trying to get men to go into the ministry, we will send men who are not called of God, (That would be disastrous!), worse than that, we would send men who are not even converted!

An unconverted man is as unfit for the ministry as an elephant is for flying. How can he talk about grace who has never tasted that the Lord is gracious? How can he point sinners to the Saviour who does not know the Saviour? How can he urge sinners to flee to Christ who has not fled to Christ himself? No one does so much injury to the cause of Christ as lost, unconverted preachers. They promote infidelity. They are co-labourers with the evil one and an offence to God.

Chosen Men
Gospel preachers are divinely chosen men. The Lord called to him "whom he would"! He did not call the tallest, most handsome, smartest, most appealing, or most eloquent. The longer I live the more I think Bro. B. B. Caldwell was right when he told a bunch of Bible college boys, "God never called any of you pretty boys to be a preacher"! Gospel preachers are not chosen by us, or even as we would choose them. The Lord Jesus calls to him whom he will.

Called Men
First, they are chosen. Then they are called. And all who are called by our God to preach the gospel are found preaching the gospel. No man has been

called to preach the gospel who is not preaching the gospel. The call of our God is always effectual. Those whom he has chosen as his messengers he makes willing to be his messengers.

This is a picture of our Lord's effectual, irresistible grace in salvation. All the chosen are at God's appointed time called. All the called are made willing in the day of the power of his grace. God's works are effectual. God never tried to do anything. God's election is effectual election. Christ's atonement is effectual atonement. The Spirit's call is an effectual call.

Communing Men

Every man chosen, called, gifted, and sent of God to preach the gospel is a man in communion with Christ. Mark tells us in verse fourteen that these men were called to him "that they should be with him". Like the apostles, faithful gospel preachers live with the Son of God, fellowship with him, abide with him, and, like Mary, sit at his feet to hear his word. As these men went up into the mountain of prayer with Christ and went home with Christ, God's servant must live at home with the Son of God in prayer, dwelling with him, seeking his Spirit, walking in his steps, studying him, copying him, so that when he steps into the pulpit, he can honestly say what John said to the saints in his day.

"That which was from the beginning, which we have heard, which we have seen with our eyes, which we have looked upon, and our hands have handled, of the Word of life; (For the life was manifested, and we have seen it, and bear witness, and show unto you that eternal life, which was with the Father, and was manifested unto us;) That which we have seen and heard declare we unto you, that ye also may have fellowship with us: and truly our fellowship is with the Father, and with his Son Jesus Christ" (1 John 1:1-3).

Consecrated Men

Gospel preachers are consecrated to Christ. These were men who literally left all and followed Christ. They were not self-serving merchandisers of men's souls. They served the souls of men. "And the multitude cometh together again, so that they could not so much as eat bread" (v. 20). While there was work to be done and opportunity to do it, for the good of men and the glory of God, they did not even stop to eat. Matthew Henry was exactly right in his observation. "They whose hearts are enlarged in the work of God can easily bear with inconveniences to themselves in the prosecution of it".

Caring Men

God's servants are caring men. They care for those trusted to their care. In verse fifteen we are told that these men were given "power to heal sicknesses and to cast out devils". And that which the Lord gave them the power to do, they did with all their might. You can mark this down. It applies to anything and everything. It is particularly applicable to the work of the ministry. Consecrated men are caring men; and caring men, truly caring men, are consecrated men.

Commissioned Men

And every man sent of God to preach the gospel goes forth with a divine commission. "And he ordained twelve, that they should be with him, and that he might send them forth to preach". They have a divine mandate. They are sent forth to preach. All who are called of God into the work of the gospel ministry are first and foremost preachers, gospel preacher! They are not counsellors, baby-sitters, social workers, or denominational promoters. God's servants are preachers; faithful, gospel preachers (Romans 1:15-17; 1 Corinthians 9:16; 2 Corinthians 5:18-21). Nothing in all the world is more utterly useless than a pastor who wastes his time on other things. Such a man is as useless as a lighthouse without a light.

A Reasonable Expectation

What should we expect to find among gospel preachers? What should we expect from men who are the servants of Jesus Christ, men who are God's ambassadors to our souls? Let me be crystal clear. When I speak of gospel "preachers" and "God's ambassadors", I do not have in mind Arminians, free-willers, and work-mongers. Gospel preachers are gospel preachers!

Taking these first twelve men as the standard, it is reasonable that we should expect God's servant to be a steady, steadfast, rock of strength, faithfulness and courage, like Peter, though a mere man, who will sometimes be very disappointing. The gospel preacher ought to be a bold, courageous son of thunder like James and John, though just a man, who will sometimes seek to promote their own interests above others. The man who speaks for God ought to be a Thomas who is willing to go with Christ to Jerusalem to die with him, though but a weak man, who will sometimes be weak and doubtful. He should be a Bartholomew (Nathaniel) in whom there is no guile, an honest man, yet a man who knows himself by nature to be full of guile. The faithful servant of God may be a faithful Matthew, Andrew, Philip, James, or Simon, about whom very little is known, but a man with God's message, without whom much would be lost.

There is no greater burden and no more awesome responsibility in the world than the work of preaching the gospel. Those who faithfully labour to preach the gospel need your prayers constantly. No wonder Paul says so often, "Brethren, pray for us"!

Why Judas?

Yet, among those who are doctrinally sound and orthodox, who preach the letter of the Word in truth, we find an occasional self-serving Judas, who gives the enemies of God occasion to blaspheme.

Have you ever wondered, "Why did the Lord pick Judas and put him among the Apostles?" I have. Let me tell you at least part of the reason why he did it. Without question, he chose Judas to fulfil the purpose of God and the prophecy of the Old Testament. Our Lord Jesus chose the betrayer that he might use him to bring on his death and accomplish the redemption of our souls. And I am confident that he chose the son of perdition that he might be a stumbling block to the unbelieving.

Judas did not pop on the scene as an unexpected surprise to God. He was as much a part of God's purpose as Peter and Paul. And when Judas was gone, no harm had been done. His betrayal of the Master and his suicide were simply the means God used to accomplish his purpose of grace toward his elect and make room for the Apostle to the Gentiles to step into place at precisely the time God had ordained.

Crowds Mean Nothing

In verse 20 Mark directs our attention to the constant crowds ever pressing around our Redeemer. "And the multitude cometh together again, so that they could not so much as eat bread". Everywhere he went, our Lord Jesus drew huge crowds around him. What a great sight it must have been to see huge crowds gathered in the presence of the incarnate God! But we have something indescribably better. You and I have the privilege of gathering at his throne every day, with the ever swelling, innumerable crowd of his elect around the world and in heaven, for the constant healing of our souls in the boundless supply of his grace (Psalm 100:4, 5; Hebrews 12:22, 23).

But great crowds mean nothing. During his earthly ministry, the crowds that constantly pressed our Saviour, for the most part, did not attend his ministry because they believed him and worshipped him. They pressed around him hoping to get something from him, to be fed by him, to see some miracle performed by him, or to have a miracle performed upon their bodies.

Our Lord Jesus Christ was a perfect preacher. He never had to pause and look for words. He never had to think of an illustration. He always preached with power. More than that, he healed multitudes, performed miracles, and even raised the dead. Yet, very, very few were converted under his ministry. Multitudes heard his words and felt the power of his words as he preached; but few heard his message and believed him.

How sadly true that is to this day! What multitudes use religion for nothing more than the gratification of the flesh; and self-serving preachers, churches and religious leaders are all too happy to supply unregenerate men with religious entertainment as they run to hell. Sunday after Sunday, churches are packed with crowds to see and perform plays, engage in contests, debate issues, rally support for some politician or political cause, enjoy a concert, and play countless games. Those places in which needy souls gather to hear the gospel preached, sing hymns of praise to our God, read his Word, and seek him in prayer are few and far between. Rarely are they packed with crowds.

Crowds mean nothing. They are no indication that Christ is present or honoured. He is present and honoured wherever two are three are gathered by his grace in his name to worship him in spirit and in truth. It is our responsibility to prayerfully and faithfully preach the gospel to eternity bound sinners, and leave the results entirely in his sovereign purpose of grace.

Family And Friends

The Spirit of God directs our attention in verse 21 to some of our Lord's family and friends, who were utterly embarrassed by him. "And when his friends heard of it, they went out to lay hold on him: for they said, He is beside himself". These friends were his kinsmen (John 7:5). They were members of his family, relatives who were embarrassed by his gospel and his devotion, and were scared to death of what the Scribes and Pharisees might think of them because of him.

There is nothing here that should be of any surprise to anyone. The prophet who came to anoint Jehu was called a "mad fellow" (2 Kings 9:11). Festus told Paul that he was a madman. I can think of very little that more fully displays the corruption of the human nature than man's utter inability to understand devotion and consecration to God.

If a person is a loyal fan for a football team, he is honoured for his fanaticism. If a man is zealous about money, science, business, sports, or even war, he is applauded as a man of discipline. If he injures his own health because of his consuming passion in any of these areas, he is admired for his sacrifice. But zeal for Christ, devotion to the glory of God, the consecration of a redeemed sinner saved by grace to his God and Saviour is looked upon by the wiseacres of the world as a sign of a weak mind. The world has not changed. The things of the Spirit are now, as they always have been and always will be, foolishness to the natural man (1 Corinthians 2:14).

When you have to drink the bitter cup of being misunderstood and misrepresented by family and friends who do not know God, do not allow their folly to shake your faith or cause you to turn on them in retaliation.

"And the scribes which came down from Jerusalem said, He hath Beelzebub, and by the prince of the devils casteth he out devils. And he called them unto him, and said unto them in parables, How can Satan cast out Satan? And if a kingdom be divided against itself, that kingdom cannot stand. And if a house be divided against itself, that house cannot stand. And if Satan rise up against himself, and be divided, he cannot stand, but hath an end. No man can enter into a strong man's house, and spoil his goods, except he will first bind the strong man; and then he will spoil his house. Verily I say unto you, All sins shall be forgiven unto the sons of men, and blasphemies wherewith soever they shall blaspheme: But he that shall blaspheme against the Holy Ghost hath never forgiveness, but is in danger of eternal damnation: Because they said, He hath an unclean spirit."

(Mark 3:22-30)

Chapter 12

The Glory Of The Gospel:
The Danger Of Unbelief

The Scribes came down from Jerusalem specifically to slander the Son of God. They saw the miracles he performed and could not deny their reality. They heard his doctrine and could not refute it. Yet, they would not bow to the Lord Jesus as their Lord, acknowledging him to be the Christ of God. They would not repent of their sins and believe on the Son of God. Instead they accused him of being in league with the devil. They said, "He hath Beelzebub, and by the prince of devils casteth he out devils"!

Throughout his life on this earth, our Master was misunderstood by his family and friends, and deliberately misrepresented by his enemies. This was a trial he had to endure from his childhood until his death as our Substitute upon the cursed tree. While he was most humble, he was thought to be most arrogant. When he went about his Father's business, he was thought to be negligent and irresponsible. Though he was perfectly righteous, he was thought to be altogether sinful.

We must not expect better treatment in this world. As we endeavour to live for Christ, as we seek the glory of God, as we try to walk in obedience to the will of God, others will judge us to be self-serving, self-promoting, rebels and antinomians. Unbelieving friends and relatives will not understand us. Enemies will deliberately misrepresent our actions and accuse us of being ruled by the most vile and base motives imaginable. Our Lord Jesus told us plainly that these things must come to pass (Matthew 10:16-26).

Our Saviour's kinsmen said, "He is beside himself"! The Pharisees called him a glutton, a drunk, and a sinner. The Scribes said, "He hath Beelzebub, and by the prince of devils casteth he out devils". We will be wise to expect and be prepared for the same treatment, because "the world knoweth us not", even as "it knew him not". Yet, even these base actions of wicked men were turned by our sovereign Master into an occasion for good to his chosen. He took their evil works and words and used them to teach us much needed spiritual lessons that we would be wise always to remember. The things taught in these verses deserve special attention. They are recorded here by divine inspiration for our learning and admonition.

Slandering Scribes
Lost, self-righteous, religious people, while pretending to be loving, benevolent, and gracious are never reluctant to slander the names of others to promote themselves. "But", as John Trapp observed, "envy never regards how true, but how mischievous." The lying heart is manifest by the lying tongue. The Scribes who had come down from Jerusalem, seeking to find some accusation against the Lord Jesus, when they saw, or were informed that he had cast out unclean spirits, said, "He hath Beelzebub, and by the prince of the devils casteth he out devils" (v. 22). Sometimes they called him Beelzebub (Satan), the prince of devils (Matthew 10:25). At other times they said our Saviour's work of mercy and grace was the work of the devil.

They were filled and guided by enmity and envy toward the Son of God. These men knew that he was not insane. And they knew that he had exercised power that only God possesses, healing the bodies of men and casting out devils; but that, they refused to acknowledge. In their malice and envy they attributed to Satan the power and work of God, hoping by their slander to defame him whose doctrine they could not refute and whose work they could not deny.

The Scribes were trying to protect themselves, to guard their religious turf, and protect their position of influence. They had no concern for either the souls of men, the truth of God, or the glory of God. They were moved by nothing more noble than envy. If they owned the Saviour's work to be of God, their religious importance, their occupation, and their gain would be gone. The proud, self-serving religionists, claiming to be God's servants, were the slaves of Satan. As such, they blasphemed the Son of God.

Let all be warned. Such deceitful workers are present and highly esteemed throughout the religious world in all ages, "transforming themselves into the apostles of Christ ... as the ministers of righteousness" (2 Corinthians 11:13-15). "And many shall follow their pernicious ways; by reason of whom the way of truth shall be evil spoken of" (2 Peter 2:2).

The Parable
Our Lord Jesus responded to the Scribes' accusation by a parable (vv. 23-26). In the parable he clearly shows the absurdity of their accusation against him. Any fool knows that "a kingdom divided against itself cannot stand".

"And he called them unto him, and said unto them in parables, How can Satan cast out Satan? And if a kingdom be divided against itself, that kingdom cannot stand. And if a house be divided against itself, that house cannot stand. And if Satan rise up against himself, and be divided, he cannot stand, but hath an end".

There are many things that may be properly taught from this parable. However, that which is, in my opinion, the most important lesson to be drawn from these words of our Redeemer is the one thing most often overlooked. This parable shows us the shameful sinfulness of strife and division among those who are supposed to be friends and allies in the same cause.

I realize that wicked men, men who would utterly destroy the gospel of Christ, promote peace at all cost. There are many who tell us that we must never oppose anything or anyone. Such traitors to Christ and his gospel must not be heard. Yet, there is a form of strife and division that is evil, always evil, and only evil. It is to be avoided by us at all cost. It is our responsibility to seek, pray for, and promote the peace of Jerusalem, the unity and harmony of God's church and kingdom in this world (Ephesians 4:1-6, 30-32; 5:1, 2). We should, as much as possible, avoid needless differences, disputes, and debates about spiritual things.

Nothing so weakens the arms of the church as the carnal strife which divides it. Needless disputes absorb thought, energy, time, and effort that should be spent in the furtherance of the gospel. They furnish infidels with weapons to use against us. The divisions that exist among God's true people in this world, no matter how justified we think we are in maintaining them, are but taking sides with the devil against ourselves.

Satan is the one who initiates them, the one who maintains them, and the one who profits by them. If he cannot extinguish the kingdom of God, he labours tirelessly to divide the soldiers of Christ's kingdom into combating armies, fighting each other. The crafty old serpent knows by long experience that "to divide is to conquer".

We must and should be zealous for the glory of God and the truths of the gospel. I utterly abhor that sentimentality that is willing to sacrifice the truth and glory of God upon the altar of what men call love and peace. We cannot be too jealous about the truths of the gospel and the glory of our God. Divine sovereignty, total depravity, eternal election, effectual atonement, almighty grace, and the preservation of God's elect are matters vital to truth, vital to the glory of God, and vital to the souls of men. With regard to these things, we must never budge an inch for anyone. But the method of church government, the kind of musical instruments employed in worship, and whether the congregation concludes the sermon by saying, "Amen", or saying nothing are matters totally insignificant.

We should never make a fuss about trifles. Far too many are morbidly scrupulous about pointing out, calling attention to, and debating differences with others about the most minute details. They are far more anxious to point out insignificant differences and magnify them than they are to lock arms with their brethren and promote truth for the glory of Christ.

Nothing can ever justify such behaviour. Nothing! There is something more important than you and me, something more important than our opinion, our name, or our desires. The truth of God, the glory of God, and the kingdom of God are infinitely more important. The fact is, all debate is wicked. It is of the flesh, does nothing for God's glory, accomplishes no good, and only gratifies the flesh. Debate is always listed in the Word of God with envy, wrath, strife, whisperings, backbiting, slander, and murder (Romans 1:29; 2 Corinthians 12:20).

As we ought to scrupulously avoid needless strife about words and promote the unity of the church and kingdom of God throughout the world, let every child of God be doubly scrupulous in protecting and promoting the peace, harmony, and unity of the local church to which God has joined him (1 Corinthians 1:9-13). Love one another. Be kind and thoughtful toward one another. Speak well to and of one another. Forgive one another. Be patient, forbearing, and longsuffering with one another (James 3:13-18; 4:1-3).

Great Grace

"No man can enter into a strong man's house, and spoil his goods, except he will first bind the strong man; and then he will spoil his house" (v. 27).

Here our Saviour speaks of his great, omnipotent, saving grace. There seems to be a direct connection between these words and the prophetic words of Isaiah concerning our most glorious Lord Jesus Christ and his almighty, gracious, saving operations in and upon chosen, redeemed sinners.

"Shall the prey be taken from the mighty, or the lawful captive delivered? But thus saith the Lord, Even the captives of the mighty shall be taken away, and the prey of the terrible shall be delivered: for I will contend with him that contendeth with thee, and I will save thy children. And I will feed them that oppress thee with their own flesh; and they shall be drunken with their own blood, as with sweet wine: and all flesh shall know that I the Lord am thy Saviour and thy Redeemer, the mighty One of Jacob" (Isaiah 49:24-26).

We are all, by nature, sinners under the dominion of Satan. Our hearts are his house and palace. His tyrannical rule and dominion over us is so great that we are his willing servants. We could never free ourselves from his dominion if we would, and would not if we could. Salvation comes when the Lord Jesus Christ invades the city of Mansoul by the sovereign power of his omnipotent grace. He breaks in, casts Satan out, and takes possession of our lives, planting his throne where once Satan reigned, in the very core of our hearts.

The Lord of glory is not a pathetic little Jesus, knocking at the sinner's heart's door, waiting for the dead sinner, by an act of his will, to open the door and let him in! He who is our Saviour is the sovereign Son of God, omnipotent in mercy and irresistible in grace. When he knocks at the heart's door, he knocks the door in, bolt and bar. He comes in, takes possession of the soul and brings his welcome with him! The first time the heaven-born soul is aware of his presence is when he begins to cast the devil out!

Every chosen, redeemed sinner shall be set free by the power of God's omnipotent grace at God's appointed time. Our glorious Christ regenerates and gives eternal life to dead sinners by the irresistible power and grace of his sovereign Spirit. And awakened, regenerate sinners come to Christ with willing hearts, because he gives them faith and causes them to come to him (Psalms 65:4; 110:3). All who are saved by the grace of Christ willingly bow to him as their only and rightful Lord. Believers are his willing bond-slaves, men and women who stoop down before him and slip under his yoke.

Great Forgiveness

"Verily I say unto you, All sins shall be forgiven unto the sons of men, and blasphemies wherewith soever they shall blaspheme" (v. 28).

What a great, glorious declaration this is! He who delights in mercy declares, "All sins shall be forgiven unto the sons of men, and blasphemies wherewith soever they shall blaspheme"! That may appear to be a trifling matter to some. But to that person who has tasted his sin, who knows the corruptions of his own heart, whose soul burns with the very fires of hell tormenting his conscience, this is the greatest thing ever heard. "All sins shall be forgiven unto the sons of men, and blasphemies wherewith soever they shall blaspheme"! The sins of my youth and the sins of my old age, the sins of my heart and the sins of my hand, the sins of my mind and the sins of my mouth, open sins and secret sins, past sins, present sins and future sins, my sins as an infidel and my sins as a believer he has freely, fully and forever forgiven! The sins of persecutors like Saul, the sins of idolaters like Manasseh, and the sins of harlots like Rahab are forgiven by the Son of God.

"All sins shall be forgiven unto the sons of men, and blasphemies wherewith soever they shall blaspheme"! What a magnificently broad proclamation of God's infinite mercy! The blood of Christ cleanses us from all sin (Acts 13:39; 1 John 1:7, 9; 2:1, 2). The righteousness of Christ covers all iniquity. The intercession of Christ prevails over all transgressions. "This", J. C. Ryle said, "is the glory of the Gospel. The very first thing it proposes to man is free pardon, full forgiveness, complete remission, without money and without price."

Lay hold of this thing, which is the very glory of the gospel. Often we faint, falter, and fail. We rightly feel ourselves altogether unworthy before our God. We are cast down in our souls. And Satan harasses us with our countless sins. But this is a fact beyond all dispute. If we trust Christ alone as our Lord and Saviour, if we trust his blood alone to atone for our sins and his righteousness alone to give us acceptance with God, then our God has cast our sins, all our sins behind his back forever. He will never remember them against us.

Eternal Damnation

It has become acceptable, and even popular, in many circles today for men, while claiming to believe the Bible, while claiming to preach the gospel, to deny the reality of hell and eternal punishment; but in verses 29 and 30 the Son of God speaks about "eternal damnation"!

"But he that shall blaspheme against the Holy Ghost hath never forgiveness, but is in danger of eternal damnation: Because they said, He hath an unclean spirit". Terrible as this truth is, it is true. We must not shut our eyes to it or fail to declare it. Sin is an infinitely evil thing. It required an infinite sacrifice and atonement to satisfy the justice of God for our sins. And if God finds sin upon any in the day of judgment, he will pour out upon that soul his infinite wrath, without mercy in "everlasting damnation"!

Let it ever be ours to preach the gospel of free, full forgiveness by the blood of Christ, calling and urging eternity bound sinners everywhere to flee from the wrath of God. Come take refuge for your soul in the City of Refuge. Never rest until you rest in him who is the Rock of Ages. You and I will spend eternity either under the blackness and darkness of the terror and torment of everlasting hell, or in the bliss, glory, and delight of heaven. Where will you spend eternity? We must soon meet the holy, eternal God in judgment. What will you plea for acceptance with him? The sinner's only hope is Christ; and, oh, what blessed hope believing sinners have in him by the gospel!

> In Christ I now believe, and trusting in His name,
> Redemption through His blood I have! Complete in Him I am!
>
> This hope my soul uplifts, when sin and Satan press:
> Unchanging are my Father's gifts, who promises to bless.
>
> My sins, my sins, my sins, are blotted out, each one!
> No cause for wrath on me remains! God sees me in His Son!
>
> So, come to me what may, it must, I know, be blest.
> God, who for me His Son did slay, will do for me what's best!

The Unpardonable Sin

In verse twenty-nine the Son of God states emphatically, "He that shall blaspheme against the Holy Ghost hath never forgiveness". There is such a thing as the unpardonable sin. This is not a matter of speculation. It may not fit well with our theological systems; but it is a matter of divine revelation. It is plainly stated in holy scripture and undeniable (Hebrews 6:4-6; 10:26; 1 John 5:16, 17).

What is the unpardonable sin? I fully recognize that caution must be used here. The scriptures clearly reveal the fact that there is an unpardonable sin; but they do not expressly tell us what it is. However, the Word of God does hold these Scribes and their cohorts, the Pharisees (Matthew 12:31, 32), as examples of men who committed it.

The unpardonable sin appears to be the wilful rejection of Christ and his gospel, a deliberate, persistent refusal to bow to the claims of Christ as Lord. It seems to be a combination of a clear intellectual knowledge of the gospel and a deliberate rejection of it, a knowledge of Christ in the head and a hatred of Christ in the heart (Proverbs 1:23-33). Though Saul of Tarsus was a persecutor and a blasphemer, he obtained mercy because he did it ignorantly (1 Timothy 1:12, 13).

Many of God's children in this world have been greatly distressed with this, fearful that they may have committed the unpardonable sin. I understand their fear. I have had the same fear. It is a fear with which Satan often buffets the soul brought low with the knowledge of his sin. Of this much I am certain, the blasphemy our Lord speaks of here, this sin that is unpardonable, whatever it is, none of God's elect can commit it.

The sinner who trusts Christ alone for all grace, salvation, forgiveness, righteousness, eternal life, and acceptance with God has not and cannot commit it. Those fearful, timid, tempted souls who are most fearful they may have committed it before they trusted Christ, have unfounded fears. If you believe on the Son of God, you have not committed this blasphemy; and you can never be in danger of committing it.

Yet, some are in danger of committing this unpardonable crime. Those who trifle with the gospel, trifle with their souls! There is forgiveness with God for all sin through the blood of Christ. "If we confess our sins, he is faithful and just to forgive us our sins, and to cleanse us from all unrighteousness" (1 John 1:9). But, for every unbelieving soul "is in danger of eternal damnation". "Seek ye the LORD while he may be found, call ye upon him while he is near" (Isaiah 55:6).

119

"There came then his brethren and his mother, and, standing without, sent unto him, calling him. And the multitude sat about him, and they said unto him, Behold, thy mother and thy brethren without seek for thee. And he answered them, saying, Who is my mother, or my brethren? And he looked round about on them which sat about him, and said, Behold my mother and my brethren! For whosoever shall do the will of God, the same is my brother, and my sister, and mother".

(Mark 3:31-35)

Chapter 13

The Master's Family

In the previous verses (vv. 22-30) we saw our all-glorious Saviour accused by pompous, self-righteous religionists of being in league with the devil. They said, "He hath Beelzebub, and by the prince of devils casteth he out devils". But the absurd charges and scandalous accusations of the Scribes were not the only trials our Lord had to endure at this time.

In these last verses of chapter 3 we are told that, "His brethren and his mother came, and standing without, sent unto him, calling him". In these five verses the Son of God identifies himself with his disciples and owns his disciples as his true family. Our Master's earthly family did not understand the beauty of his life, the necessity of his obedience, and the purpose for which he had come into the world.

I do not doubt that they loved him as a brother. I have no doubt that they were, at least somewhat, concerned for his physical welfare. They must have been concerned about him over-exerting himself, not getting enough rest, exposing himself to too much danger. They understood very little, or gave little regard to those words spoken by the Lord Jesus when he was just a boy of twelve years old, "Wist ye not that I must be about my Father's business?" (Luke 2:49) They probably did not understand the implications of their actions recorded in this passage. But these things are written for our learning.

Mary The Sinner
The words of this passage, and the many other passages in the gospel narratives, which identify Mary's sinfulness and weaknesses in the flesh, were intended by God the Holy Spirit to prevent the idolatrous worship of Mary, which is so much a part of popish idolatry. We recognize, and the scriptures clearly teach, that our Saviour's human body was conceived in Mary's virgin womb by the Holy Spirit. But the papists would have us believe that Mary herself was immaculately conceived and that she had no sin. Nothing could be further from the truth.

No doubt, Mary was a woman of honourable character. But she was no more spiritual and holy by nature than Rahab, or you, or me. Mary was the sinful daughter of sinful parents. She was made holy and honourable by the free grace of God in Christ, whom she herself worshipped as her Saviour and Lord (Luke 1:46-48).

Mary is to be called "blessed", because she was and is blessed of God in Christ and for Christ's sake. But we must never look upon her as being blessed in any way, or to any degree, except as she was and is blessed of God in Christ in exactly the same way as all chosen sinners are blessed, eternally and immutably blessed, in Christ and for Christ's sake (Ephesians 1:3). Mary was a sinner loved and chosen of God the Father, redeemed by the precious blood of Christ the Son, and justified, regenerated, called and sanctified by the Holy Spirit in exactly the same way we are. She was a sinner saved by grace.

Papists also assert, contrary to the plain statements of holy scripture, that Mary's virginity was perpetual. But this reference to our Saviour's brothers tells us that other sons of Joseph and Mary were born after the Lord Jesus. His younger brothers are named in Matthew 13:55. The papists' doctrine of Mary's perpetual virginity, like most of Rome's teaching, is nothing but religious superstition.

There is no religious practice more completely destitute of biblical foundation than the exaltation and adulation of Mary. The blasphemous practice of offering prayers to Mary are as foolish and idolatrous as offering prayers to me! The only sinless human being ever to live in this world is the sinless Son of God, our Saviour. The only Mediator between God and men, by whom and through whom sinners may come to God, is the God-man, the Lord Jesus Christ, our Saviour. The only human being to whom prayer is to be made and through whom we may hope for grace is that Man who is God, the Lord Jesus Christ, our Saviour.

Family Hindrance

Here we see a clear example of the fact that even the best intentions of flesh and blood may often hinder us, as we seek to do the will of God. Regarding spiritual matters, particularly matters of obedience to the will of God, family and friends are never safe guides.

As noted, our Saviour's family appears to have been concerned for his health and well-being. Perhaps they feared that he was needlessly exposing himself to danger. They must have been aware of the plots of the Scribes, Pharisees, and Herodians to kill him. So they sent a messenger to fetch the Lord home. Some read into their words suggestions of impertinence and disrespect. But that does not appear to have been the case, especially on Mary's part. She was, at times, a weak believer; but there is no doubt that she was a genuine believer.

Still, though Mary, and probably our Master's other family members as well, had only the best of intentions and desiring only what they thought was best for him, they were in no position to make that judgment. This incident is not recorded here by accident. It is written for our learning. Do not miss the lesson. In spiritual matters we must not confer with flesh and blood (Galatians 1:16). If we would know the state of our souls, we must not be satisfied with the good opinions of others. If we would know and do the will of God, we must not take into account the desires of our own flesh, the desires of our families, or the counsel of human wisdom.

No one knows the will of God for you in any given area of your life, but you. It is your responsibility to do what you know the Lord would have you to do. If he had consulted with Sarah, Abraham would never have taken Isaac up to Mount Moriah. Had Moses listened to Zipporah, the Lord would have killed him before he ever got back to Egypt. Nathan would never have taken God's word to David, if he had sat down to consider with his family what the consequences might have been.

Faithfulness Required

In this passage our Lord Jesus exemplifies the fact that the one thing required in all true servants of God is faithfulness. In the face of constant opposition from his enemies and the misguided concerns of those people who were by nature dearest to him, our Saviour's resolve was firm and unrelenting. He had set his face like a flint. He had a baptism to be baptized with and was straitened until it was accomplished. He was determined to fulfil his Father's will, to finish his work of establishing perfect righteousness for his people, and to drink the cup of wrath as our Substitute upon the cursed tree to satisfy the justice of God for us.

May God give us grace as his people and his servants to be like minded. Let nothing turn you from the narrow way. Have you put your hand to the plough? Let nothing persuade you to look back. Have you entered the race? Look not to the right hand, nor to the left. Look only to the Lord Jesus Christ, the Author and Finisher of our faith. If well meaning friends would dissuade you, reply like Nehemiah of old, "I am doing a great work, and I cannot come down" (Nehemiah 6:3). If those who truly love you and truly love Christ would unknowingly turn you aside from doing that which you know to be the will of God, respond as Paul did to his friends, "None of these things move me, neither count I my life dear unto myself, so that I might finish my course with joy, and the ministry, which I have received of the Lord Jesus, to testify the gospel of the grace of God" (Acts 20:24). "What mean ye to weep and to break mine heart? for I am ready not to be bound only, but also to die for the name of the Lord Jesus" (Acts 21:13). Keep the eyes of your heart, the eyes of your soul focused upon the Lord Jesus Christ, and the great host of men and women who have gone before us into heaven who were found faithful even unto death (Hebrews 12:1-4).

The Lord our God requires only one thing of us. And the one thing he requires of us is the very least that we can give. Yet, it is the best we can give. God requires faithfulness. May he give us grace to give it. "Moreover it is required in stewards, that a man be found faithful" (1 Corinthians 4:2).

Christ's Family

The Lord Jesus tells us plainly in verses 33-35 that all who are truly his disciples, and only they, are the members of his family.

Who can imagine the depth of love our Saviour had for his physical family as a man? Who can imagine how he loved that woman who nursed and nurtured him as a baby? Who can imagine how he must have loved his brothers and sisters, those who were born from the same womb as he was? No mortal has ever come close to knowing the affection of Christ's heart as a man for his aunts, uncles, and cousins. Yet, in comparison to his chosen, in comparison to you and me who believe on his name, our Lord Jesus gave no regard to the desires of his own family and dearest kinsmen.

There is great comfort to be found in the things recorded here for every true believer. There is One in heaven, who is both God and man, One who is both bone of our bone and flesh of our flesh, who knows us, loves us, cares for us, and counts us to be his own family. We may be poorer than dirt; but we have no cause to be ashamed. We are the brothers and sisters of the Son of God! We may be persecuted and mistreated, even in our own families, because of our faith in him. If that is the case with you, take David's words for your own, "When my father and mother forsake me, the Lord will take me up" (Psalm 27:10). To be numbered among those who are in this family is to be the object of God's constant care, the beneficiary of God's special providence, and an heir of God and joint-heir with Christ.

"Behold, what manner of love the Father hath bestowed upon us, that we should be called the sons of God: therefore the world knoweth us not, because it knew him not. Beloved, now are we the sons of God, and it doth not yet appear what we shall be: but we know that, when he shall appear, we shall be like him; for we shall see him as he is. And every man that hath this hope in him purifieth himself, even as he is pure" (1 John 3:1-3).

Solemn Warning

This passage also contains a solemn warning for the persecutors of God's saints. All who abuse, harass, and persecute the children of God have reason to tremble. If you are inclined to slander, abuse, malign, or persecute one of God's children, or one of God's servants, you would be wise to remember, they are the sons and daughters of God almighty. Those who are the objects of your scorn are the true blood-kin of the Son of God. This is the family of him who is King of kings and Lord of lords.

We have a mighty, mighty Friend, who has sworn that he will avenge his own elect in all things. Our Redeemer is mighty; and he will plead our cause (Proverbs 23:11). The Lord Jesus Christ in heaven always pleads our cause. Let us ever be found faithful in his cause.

"And he began again to teach by the sea side: and there was gathered unto him a great multitude, so that he entered into a ship, and sat in the sea; and the whole multitude was by the sea on the land. And he taught them many things by parables, and said unto them in his doctrine, Hearken; Behold, there went out a sower to sow: And it came to pass, as he sowed, some fell by the way side, and the fowls of the air came and devoured it up. And some fell on stony ground, where it had not much earth; and immediately it sprang up, because it had no depth of earth: But when the sun was up, it was scorched; and because it had no root, it withered away. And some fell among thorns, and the thorns grew up, and choked it, and it yielded no fruit. And other fell on good ground, and did yield fruit that sprang up and increased; and brought forth, some thirty, and some sixty, and some an hundred. And he said unto them, He that hath ears to hear, let him hear. And when he was alone, they that were about him with the twelve asked of him the parable. And he said unto them, Unto you it is given to know the mystery of the kingdom of God: but unto them that are without, all these things are done in parables: That seeing they may see, and not perceive; and hearing they may hear, and not understand; lest at any time they should be converted, and their sins should be forgiven them. And he said unto them, Know ye not this parable? and how then will ye know all parables? The sower soweth the word. And these are they by the way side, where the word is sown; but when they have heard, Satan cometh immediately, and taketh away the word that was sown in their hearts. And these are they likewise which are sown on stony ground; who, when they have heard the word, immediately receive it with gladness; And have no root in themselves, and so endure but for a time: afterward, when affliction or persecution ariseth for the word's sake, immediately they are offended. And these are they which are sown among thorns; such as hear the word, And the cares of this world, and the deceitfulness of riches, and the lusts of other things entering in, choke the word, and it becometh unfruitful. And these are they which are sown on good ground; such as hear the word, and receive it, and bring forth fruit, some thirtyfold, some sixty, and some an hundred".

(Mark 4:1-20)

Chapter 14

The Parable Of The Sower

Of all the parables spoken by our Lord during his earthly ministry, none is so widely known and so little heeded as the parable of the sower. The parable itself is easily comprehended.[3] Everyone is familiar with the work of a

---

[3] Robert Hawker's comments on this same parable and our Saviour's explanation of it in Matthew 13:3-23 are so helpful that I give them to you in their entirety.

"Very happily for the Lord's people, Jesus hath not left this parable of the sower to our interpretation, but hath given it himself, and which therefore supersedes all the labours of his servants. And so plain and clear is our Lord's explanation of it, that a little child, under grace, may understand it. I detain not the Reader to add to what Jesus hath here said, but only to observe upon it what a beautiful vein of instruction runs through the whole of it.

When the Lord Jesus compares himself to a Sower, and the seed he soweth to the Gospel of his kingdom, we enter at once into the blessedness of apprehension concerning the whole purport of salvation. But when Jesus speaks of the devil, under the figure of the fowls of the air, catching away that which was sown in the heart, it should be remembered, that it is the ministry of the word, and not the grace of the Lord Jesus that is thus rendered unprofitable. The heart is sometimes put for the memory; as in the instance of *Mary. And she kept all these sayings in her heart; that is, in her memory (Luke 2:51). So that by the devil's catching away the word from them that understand it not, (see also what is meant in scripture of the want of understanding, Job 28:28) means not that he taketh away what was sown of grace in the heart, for grace implanted by the Lord can never be taken away, but that he causeth the *graceless* hearers to forget what they heard. In them, as well as all others of the unprofitable hearers, as children *not* of the kingdom, is fulfilled that striking prophecy of *Isaiah,* which, from its vast importance, is quoted no less than six times in the New Testament; namely, in this Chapter, verses 14, 15; Mark 4:1; Luke 8:10; John 12:40; Acts 28:26; Romans 9:8.

In like manner, concerning the sun arising on the stony-ground hearers, we are not to suppose that our Lord meant the Sun of righteousness, for he ariseth not to scorch, but to warm, and with healing in his wings. But by the sun being up, is meant the sun of persecution, the drying, scorching heat of what the Church complained of, Song 1:6, the anger of men.

The persons here spoken of were never rooted in Christ, and therefore no dews of heaven to water them; and moreover the seed is said not to have fallen *into* the ground, but *upon* stony ground. And those men who, from hence, have argued of the possibility of falling *from* grace, should first have observed, that they never were *in*

farmer. He ploughs his fields, sows his seeds, tends his plants, and gathers in his crop. And every farmer knows that much of the seed sown is lost forever, bears no fruit, and is profitable for nothing. Yet, very few people appear to understand the spiritual implications of this well-known parable.

This parable is of universal application. So long as the Kingdom of God is in this world, and sinners gather as local churches to worship God in the name of Christ, this parable will be applicable. In it our Lord Jesus Christ teaches us plainly that the vast majority of those who hear the gospel of the grace of God preached, even the vast majority of those who profess faith in him after hearing the gospel, are unregenerate, lost, and perish under the wrath of God. "He that hath ears to hear, let him hear" the parable of the sower.

The Sower

The sower is the gospel preacher. Gospel preachers are like farmers sowing wheat. They broadcast the Word of God upon the ground, upon the hearts of eternity bound men and women. This is not a careless, thoughtless process. The preacher, if he is a faithful, gospel preacher, has his heart in his work. He is not indifferent to those to whom he preaches, or indifferent to their response. God's servants care for the souls of men. They sow in hope of harvest (Psalm 126:5; Ecclesiastes 11:1; Isaiah 55:11). The sower is the servant of God, sowing the seed of the gospel, expecting a great harvest.

---

grace. It is impossible to lose *that* we never had. An union *with* Christ, brings after it a communion *in* Christ. These stony-ground hearers never had root, and, as such, could not do otherwise than wither away.

To the same purport is what is said concerning *the seed sown among thorns*. It is not supposed that the characters here alluded to are the openly profane, and such as are inattentive to divine things, but rather such as make much profession. They have received conviction in the head, of the importance of salvation, but from never having felt it in their heart, and no saving grace having passed upon them, this world's riches are preferred to the riches of eternity, and their hearts, like ground over-run with thorns, and wholly unfruitful.

By the *good ground,* into which the seed is cast, is meant an heart renewed, and made good by sovereign grace, for every man's heart by nature is evil. And the different product from hence, is also wholly from the same grace, and not man's improvement. But it is blessed for the soul of that man, whose increase is but of the lowest kind, that all is of the same *quality,* though not of the same *quantity.* The drop of dew on the blade of grass is as truly water as the ocean. And an union with Christ makes the blessed, the humblest soul as much as the highest. For it is all *of* Jesus, *and from* Jesus, and *to* Jesus, all the glory."

The Seed

The seed sown is the Word of God, the gospel of the grace of God revealed in holy scripture. "The sower soweth the word" (v. 14). We recognize, preach, and rejoice in the glorious sovereignty of our God, especially in the salvation of his elect. Yet, we recognize that God almighty has chosen to use specific means for the accomplishment of his purposes. "It pleased God, by the foolishness of preaching, to save them that believe". "Faith cometh by hearing, and hearing by the Word of God". That is Bible language. God declares that he saves sinners through the utility of the Word (James 1:18; 1 Peter 1:23-25).

God has chosen to save his elect through, or by means of, the faithful exposition of the scriptures. And the Word of God is faithfully expounded and preached only when the gospel of Christ is faithfully expounded and preached. Roland Hill was right when he said, "Any sermon that does not contain the 'Three R's' (Ruin by the fall, Redemption by the blood, and Regeneration by the Holy Spirit) ought never to have been preached."

God's servants are not just preachers. They are gospel preachers. They do not just preach. They preach the gospel. The sower is the gospel preacher. The seed is the Word of God, the gospel of Christ.

The Results

The results of gospel preaching are always exactly according to the purpose of God. We randomly preach the gospel to all who will hear us; but the results are not random. When God almighty sends forth his Word, his Word always accomplishes his purpose (Isaiah 55:11). It either produces life and faith in Christ, or it produces judicial blindness and hardness of heart (2 Corinthians 2:14-16).

"And he said unto them, Unto you it is given to know the mystery of the kingdom of God: but unto them that are without, all these things are done in parables: That seeing they may see, and not perceive; and hearing they may hear, and not understand; lest at any time they should be converted, and their sins should be forgiven them" (vv. 11, 12).

Here, the Lord Jesus is quoting from the prophecy of Isaiah.

"And he said, Go, and tell this people, Hear ye indeed, but understand not; and see ye indeed, but perceive not. Make the heart of this people fat, and make their ears heavy, and shut their eyes; lest they see with their eyes, and hear with their ears, and understand with their heart, and convert, and be healed" (Isaiah 6:9, 10).

The apostle Paul tells us essentially the same thing in 2 Corinthians 2:14-16. Man's unbelief does not in any way, or to even the slightest degree alter the purpose of God. Rather, even the wilful unbelief of the reprobate fulfils God's sovereign purpose

"For what if some did not believe? shall their unbelief make the faith of God without effect? God forbid: yea, let God be true, but every man a liar; as it is written, That thou mightest be justified in thy sayings, and mightest overcome when thou art judged" (Romans 3:3, 4).

"Now thanks be unto God, which always causeth us to triumph in Christ, and maketh manifest the savour of his knowledge by us in every place. For we are unto God a sweet savour of Christ, in them that are saved, and in them that perish: To the one we are the savour of death unto death; and to the other the savour of life unto life. And who is sufficient for these things?" (2 Corinthians 2:14-16).

Faith in Christ is the gift of God. The seeing eye, the hearing ear, and the believing heart are from the Lord. Faith is not something men muster from within. Faith is the gift and operation of God's free grace in Christ. If you believe, it is because "unto you it is given in the behalf of Christ to believe on his name".

To those who will not believe, the Word of God is both blinding and binding. None are so blind as those who will not see. And none are so hardened as those who are gospel hardened. When men and women wilfully despise the gospel of the grace of God, when they resolutely harden themselves to the Word preached, the very Word, which they despise, becomes the instrument by which they are bound over to everlasting judgment (Proverbs 1:23-33).

Wayside Hearers
Some who hear the gospel receive it as seed sown by the wayside. "And these are they by the way side, where the word is sown; but when they have heard, Satan cometh immediately, and taketh away the word that was sown in their hearts" (v. 15).

Some come to the house of God and hear the gospel preached with no concern for their souls, glory of God, or eternity. They go to church because they have to, because it is the respectable thing to do, or because they think it is their duty to do so. But they really have no interest in what is going on there. They try their best not to hear a word the preacher says, or at least not to be bothered by what he says. All the time he is preaching, they try to think about something else. Unless God intervenes and does something for them, the gospel they hear will profit them nothing. Before they get out the door, the old black crow of hell will have snatched away the seed from their hard hearts. They are wayside hearers.

Stony Ground Hearers

Others are described by the Lord Jesus as stony ground hearers.

There are many stony ground hearers. The preaching of the gospel makes very quick, but only temporary, impressions upon them. Their religion is all superficial, just a flash in the pan, nothing else. Like burning briars in a fire, they may crackle and pop, and make a lot of noise, but they produce nothing. They appear enthusiastic. They talk a good game. They are sometimes moved to tears. They may even speak about inward conflicts, hopes, desires, struggles, and fears. But they lack one thing. They have no root. The root of the matter is not in them. Like seed sown in unprepared soil, the Word of God takes no root in them, because there is no work of the Holy Spirit in their hearts. No conviction. No repentance. No faith in Christ.

The stony ground hearer may endure for a while; but he will not last. His religion is like Jonah's gourd. It springs up in a night and is gone in a night. He is like cut flowers that look pretty and smell nice for a while, but soon wither and die. He has no root. Christ is not in him, and he is not in Christ. A little trial, affliction, or temptation will be too great for the stony ground hearer to endure. Any persecution or opposition because of the offence of the gospel will destroy him.

John Trapp said of the stony ground hearers, "They stumble at the cross, and fall backwards. These are prosperity proselytes, holy day servants, political professors, and passive Christians."

Thorny Ground Hearers

Others are described in this parable as thorny ground hearers.

As we have seen, the wayside hearer has no interest at all in the things of God. He could not care less who Christ is and what he did. Likewise, the stony ground hearer is more impressionable and his responsiveness is more impressive. He makes a big splash, but does not last very long. The thorny ground hearer is something else.

The thorny ground hearer assents to the gospel, approves of it, and is moved by it. He appears to make a good start and appears to go a long way in religion. He feels much, experiences much, and may even do much that appears to be truly spiritual. He may even know much; but he has a basic, fundamental, underlying problem. It is a problem that may lie under the surface, hidden from every eye but God's. It may even be hidden from his own eyes. But it will eventually destroy him. The problem is worldliness. The world still holds his heart. He loves the world.

Yet, it is written, "If any man love the world, the love of the Father is not in him" (1 John 2:15). Sooner or later those who love the world will choose the world. The sad fact is that though they wilfully choose the world and turn from Christ, they are so thoroughly justified in their own minds that what they are doing is right they never even realize they have done it, until they wake up in hell. If you are one of these thorny ground hearers, the Lord Jesus plainly warns you that one of three things will eventually destroy your soul: Either "the cares of this world" (even legitimate cares), or "the deceitfulness of riches" (materialism), or "the lusts of other things" (fame, recognition, acceptance, power, sensuality, pleasure) will eventually choke out the influence of the Word of God, by which you are now restrained.

Beware of religion without Christ! You may think, "All is well with my soul. No one could ever feel what I feel and experience what I have experienced and yet be lost." You ought to think again! False faith is a strong delusion, a delusion by which many who profess faith in Christ are dragged down to hell! Reader, beware, nothing is so hardening and so damning as false faith.

False faith may be greatly enlightened and knowledgeable of the gospel (Hebrews 6:4). False faith may greatly reform the outward life, as it did the lives of the Pharisees. False faith may speak very well of Christ, as the Jews did. False faith may confess personal sin like King Saul. False faith may humble itself in sackcloth and ashes with Ahab. False faith may repent in tears with Esau and Judas. False faith may diligently perform religious works with Saul of Tarsus. False faith may be very generous and charitable, like Ananias and Sapphira. False faith may tremble under the Word with Felix. False faith may experience great things in religion (Hebrews 6:1-4). False faith may enjoy great religious privileges with Lot's wife. False faith may preach, perform miracles, and cast out devils, like those mentioned by our Lord. False faith may attain high office in the church like Diotrephes. False faith may walk with great preachers like Demas. False faith may even be peaceful and carnally secure to the end, like the five foolish virgins.

Good Ground Hearers

The true believer is that person who receives the gospel as seed sown in good ground. "And these are they which are sown on good ground; such as hear the word, and receive it, and bring forth fruit, some thirtyfold, some sixty, and some an hundred" (v. 20).

The good ground is a regenerate heart, a heart prepared by God the Holy Spirit to receive the Word of grace. The fallow ground of the heart has been broken up by the deep cutting, sharp plough of the law. The hard clods have been broken by the heavy harrow of conviction, beaten to pieces by the thunderous rain of God's wrath, and at last softened by the sweet dew of heaven.

The Word of God sown in the regenerate heart prepared by the power of God to receive it, brings forth fruit unto God. Some bear fruit more rapidly and more plentifully than others; but all bear fruit from God. The fruit they bear is the fruit of the Spirit, not the works of self-righteousness, the works of the flesh (Galatians 5:16-23).

What kind of hearer are you? What kind of hearer am I? A wayside hearer? A stony ground hearer? A thorny ground hearer? A good ground hearer?

"And he said unto them, Is a candle brought to be put under a bushel, or under a bed? and not to be set on a candlestick? For there is nothing hid, which shall not be manifested; neither was any thing kept secret, but that it should come abroad. If any man have ears to hear, let him hear. And he said unto them, Take heed what ye hear: with what measure ye mete, it shall be measured to you: and unto you that hear shall more be given. For he that hath, to him shall be given: and he that hath not, from him shall be taken even that which he hath".

(Mark 4:21-25)

Chapter 15

Some Matters Of Personal Responsibility

Salvation is the work of God's free grace in Christ. Every gift and blessing we enjoy now and hope to enjoy in heaven's glory, is the result of grace. All spiritual blessings are gifts of pure, free, sovereign grace.

Yet, the Word of God also teaches that every one of us is responsible for his own soul. You are responsible for what you are, what you do, and what you fail to do. I am responsible for what I am, what I do, and what I fail to do. That is exactly what our Lord Jesus teaches us in Mark 4:21-25.

These sobering, pithy statements, given immediately following our Lord's parable about the sower, are to be understood in that context. They are short, pointed, barbed arrows designed to pierce the heart. Our Saviour is warning us, particularly all who profess to be his disciples, to make certain that our faith is true faith, and not the spurious faith of an unregenerate religionist.

Any casual reader of the New Testament is aware of the fact that our Lord Jesus in his preaching ministry frequently repeated himself. Numerous attempts have been made over the years to harmonize the different accounts of his ministry by the gospel writers. But most of these efforts raise more questions than they answer, and confuse rather than clarify. The fact is the best preacher who ever lived, the Son of God, showed us that spiritual truths need to be repeated and pressed upon the consciences of men. Our Lord preached about not putting the candlestick under a bushel, that "nothing is hidden that shall not be revealed", that "with what measure ye mete, it shall be measured unto you", and the danger of false religion. He made no apology for preaching the same sermon many times, even to the same people, because the truth of God never changes, though it is always fresh and new. The best message is the oldest message, the one most repeated, and the one most constantly needed. It is the message preached to fallen Adam in the garden and the message preached to the fallen sons of Adam today, the message of redemption and salvation by Christ, the last Adam.

The Responsibility Of Light
First, in verses 21 and 22 our Lord teaches us that it is the privilege of all who have the light of the gospel to spread that light, the responsibility of all who know the gospel to make the gospel known to others. Our Lord's

language is not difficult to understand. No one with good sense lights a candle and then covers it up. The purpose for lighting the candle is that it may give off light. If you turn on a light it is to dispel darkness.

The meaning is this: If God almighty has been so gracious and good to us as to give us the light of the gospel of his free grace in Christ, he intends us to hold forth that light in this world of darkness and death. The Lord did not give us the light of the gospel for our own benefit alone. He did not teach us the truth merely for our personal gratification. If God has taught us, it is our responsibility to teach others. All who know Christ are responsible to make the gospel of Christ known to their own generation. This is not the work of preachers alone, but the work of all who know the Lord. If you have received the gift of grace, it is your responsibility to carry that gift to others. "As every man hath received the gift, even so minister the same one to another, as good stewards of the manifold grace of God" (1 Peter 4:10).

We would be worse than barbarians if we had discovered a cure for a devastating disease but did not tell our neighbours, politely excusing ourselves, saying to ourselves, "They wouldn't understand. They would just think I am a fanatic. I would not want them to think I was proselytizing." Nonsense! That is exactly what we are supposed to do. We have been placed where we are in this world by God's providence to make proselytes out of every heretic who we can influence by the Spirit of God.

It is no accident that our Lord here refers to us as candles. "The spirit of man is the candle of the LORD, searching all the inward parts of the belly" (Proverbs 20:27). Regenerate men and women are the candles of God in this world of darkness, lit by the Father of lights. Yet, the brightest candles are but candles, very poor, dim lights, compared with the Sun of righteousness. Matthew Henry wrote, "A candle gives light but a little way, and but a little while, and is easily blown out, and continually burning down and wasting."

Many who claim to be candles, lit by grace, put the light they say God has given them under a basket. They seem to manifest very little grace and minister even less grace to others. They have plenty, but do little with it. In fact, though there are exceptions to the rule, as a general rule, I have observed that those who have the most and have the most ability to do good, do the least for others.

I know many wealthy people who profess to know Christ, who seem very content to watch a brother or sister endure hardship without a thought of helping. Those who seem to be in the strongest health, possess the greatest wealth, and have the greatest abilities usually do the least for others. They may think they are very spiritual, but no one is better off because of them. They are like candles burning in a basket. They burn for themselves.

If we belong to God, it is our great privilege and responsibility to be his witnesses in this world. Every believer is Christ's missionary. Our mission field is the world in which we live and the people our lives touch (Isaiah 44:1-8; Acts 1:8). Those who are lit as candles should set themselves on a candlestick. We should seize every opportunity for doing good, as those that were made for the glory of God and the service of others. We were not born for ourselves. We are born of God and born for God, for the service of God, to make known the light of the gospel of the glory of God. We have the light of the gospel that we may give the light of the gospel to others.

Our Lord tells us plainly that though the gospel was hidden from the nations of the world in ages past, it must be proclaimed everywhere, to all men in this generation of grace. "For there is nothing hid, which shall not be manifested; neither was any thing kept secret, but that it should come abroad" (v. 22). Everything revealed in the Book of God was revealed to be taught and preached publicly. It is the responsibility of every gospel preacher to faithfully preach to eternity bound sinners all the counsel of God revealed in holy scripture, keeping back nothing that is profitable for their souls.

To the heaven-born soul there is nothing hidden. Our Saviour has declared, "All things that I have heard of my Father I have made known unto you" (John 15:15). There is nothing in the covenant of grace and the eternal purpose of God that we need to know that is hidden from us. And it is the responsibility of every heaven-born soul to make manifest to others the treasure of grace the Spirit of God has hidden in his soul.

The Responsibility Of Hearing

Second, our Redeemer teaches us our responsibility to avail ourselves of the means of grace afforded us by the providence and grace of God. Nothing in this world is so needful, important, and beneficial to your soul as the ministry of the gospel. Our Saviour says, "If any man have ears, let him hear". You may think, "That is talking about spiritual ears and spiritual hearing." You are right. But I ask, "How you are going to hear the gospel spiritually, if you do not hear it physically?"

No one will ever be saved, no one will ever trust Christ, who does not first hear the Word of truth, the gospel of their salvation accomplished by Christ. That is what Paul said to the Ephesians (Ephesians 1:13). That is God's appointed means of grace for the saving of chosen, redeemed sinners (Romans 10:17; James 1:18; 1 Peter 1:23-25). In this day when men everywhere decry the preaching of the gospel as an antiquated thing, let us remember Paul's words: "Despise not prophesyings" (1 Thessalonians 5:20). His dying charge to Timothy, and to every gospel preacher in this world was, "Preach the word" (2 Timothy 4:2). It is by the preaching of the gospel that the glory of God is revealed. Through preaching, chosen, redeemed sinners are regenerated and called by God the Holy Spirit, believers are instructed in the gospel, edified, built up in the faith and sustained in this world, and our lives are moulded into the will of God in conformity to Christ.

Not only is it vital that we attend the worship of God in the public assembly of his saints, it is also vital that we "take heed what we hear". I frequently meet people, and regularly hear from people all over the world, who wilfully put themselves and their families under the influence of pagan, Arminian, free-will, works religion. They try to justify themselves, saying, "We have to go to church somewhere. We must not forsake the assembly of the saints." "The preacher says some good things." "I don't pay any attention to what they teach." To all such people, I repeat our Saviour's warning: "Take heed what ye hear"! Our Lord was not beating the air when he said that. Mark was not filling up space when he wrote it (1 John 4:1; 2 John 7-10). If you care for your soul and for the souls of those under your influence, do not subject them to Arminian, free will, works religion to any degree, for any reason. If you care for your soul and care for those under your influence, if you care for the worship and glory of God, addict yourself to the ministry of the gospel, to the preaching of God's free and sovereign grace in Christ.

The Responsibility Of Measure
Third, we are taught in verses 24 and 25 that it is our responsibility to grow in the grace and knowledge of our Lord Jesus Christ. In these two statements our Saviour tells us plainly that every one of us is responsible for his own soul. You can back off from these two statements and say, "That cannot mean what it seems to mean. That is not consistent with good Calvinism." You can do that, if you dare so trifle with the Word of God. For my part, I want to hear what our Lord is saying. Look at these two statements carefully.

"With what measure ye mete, it shall be measured to you: and unto you that hear shall more be given". Our Lord is telling us that God measures out his grace to us in proportion as we measure it out to ourselves by the use of the means he has given us. As I stated earlier, we know that salvation is altogether by the grace of God. We know that both grace and our growth in grace is God's work. Yet, just as no man will be saved without hearing and believing the gospel, no believer will grow in the grace and knowledge of Christ except as he applies himself to the use of the means of grace, the ministry of the gospel. The wise words of Solomon are applicable. "The soul of the sluggard desireth, and hath nothing: but the soul of the diligent shall be made fat" (Proverbs 13:4). "Slothfulness casteth into a deep sleep; and an idle soul shall suffer hunger" (Proverbs 19:15).

All who grow in grace and in the knowledge of Christ are diligent, diligent in prayer, diligent in reading, diligent in hearing the Word of God. And the man who is diligent in these things is usually diligent in other things. Yet, when he thinks of himself, he would never describe himself in such terms. Regarding this matter of growing in grace, we generally sow what we reap. We are commanded to do it, because it is something we are responsible to do. "Grow in grace, and in the knowledge of our Lord and Saviour Jesus Christ. To him be glory both now and for ever" (2 Peter 3:18).

"For he that hath, to him shall be given: and he that hath not, from him shall be taken even that which he hath". John Gill wrote, concerning these words that fell from the lips of our Saviour: "He that has Gospel light and knowledge, and makes a proper use of it, shall have more. His path shall be as the path of the just, which shines more and more to the perfect day. The means of grace and knowledge shall be blessed to him. Attending constantly thereon he shall ... come to the measure of the stature of the fulness of Christ, shall grow up to maturity, and be a man in understanding."

That is exactly what our Lord is teaching us here. Those who have the grace of God in truth shall have the grace of God in abundance. Though the beginnings of grace in the soul are small, and keep a saved sinner humble, in the end, the glory of grace shall be indescribable. As we exercise faith in Christ and learn of him, we grow in the grace and knowledge of our blessed Saviour by the power and grace of his Spirit. We do not get more holy, or make ourselves more holy; but God's saints do grow in grace. That is to say, being taught of God continually, believers grow in faith, in love for Christ, in love for one another, and in consecration to their Redeemer.

This last statement, "For he that hath, to him shall be given: and he that hath not, from him shall be taken even that which he hath", also means that those who profess faith in Christ, but do not possess the grace of Christ shall in the end lose what they thought they possessed. Perhaps there is a reference here to Judas. Certainly, there is here a warning to all who have nothing but a profession of faith, without the possession of grace.

He that has only a speculative notion of the gospel and is without any experience of it will sooner or later lose everything. In course of time his candle will be put out. His light will be made darkness. He will drop and deny the truths he once held and relinquish the profession he once made. He that has only counterfeit grace, a pretence of faith, a false hope, and lip love, will, in due time, be discovered for what he really is: Nothing but a hypocrite! True grace can never be lost. But all pretensions of grace and faith shall be an everlasting embarrassment and torment to the hypocrite.

"And he said, So is the kingdom of God, as if a man should cast seed into the ground; And should sleep, and rise night and day, and the seed should spring and grow up, he knoweth not how. For the earth bringeth forth fruit of herself; first the blade, then the ear, after that the full corn in the ear. But when the fruit is brought forth, immediately he putteth in the sickle, because the harvest is come".

(Mark 4:26-29)

Chapter 16

Spiritual Growth

In these verses Mark records one of our Lord's parables that none of the other gospel writers was inspired to record. It was delivered by our Master shortly after the parable of the sower, just before the parable of the mustard seed. This parable about spiritual growth was delivered immediately after our Lord said, "With what measure ye mete, it shall be measured to you". If we have reason to hope we are Christians, we ought to be very interested in the teachings of our Lord in this parable. It is deeply instructive. "It summons us", wrote J. C. Ryle, "to an examination of our experience in divine things." This parable, though very short, is just as sweet and instructive as our Lord's other parables. It sets before us a history of God's work of grace in chosen sinners. John Newton wrote:

> I asked the Lord that I might grow,
> In faith, and love, and every grace;
> Might more of His salvation know,
> And seek more earnestly His face.
>
> 'Twas He who taught me thus to pray,
> And He, I trust, has answered prayer;
> But it has been in such a way,
> As almost drove me to despair.
>
> I hoped that in some favoured hour,
> At once He'd answer my request;
> And, by His love's constraining power,
> Subdue my sins and give me rest.
>
> Instead of this, He made me feel,
> The hidden evils of my heart,
> And let the angry powers of hell,
> Assault my soul in every part.

Yea, more, with His own hand He seemed
Intent to aggravate my woe;
Crossed all the fair designs I schemed,
Blasted my gourds, and laid me low.

"Lord, why is this?" I trembling cried;
"Wilt Thou pursue Thy worm to death?"
"'Tis in this way", the Lord replied,
"I answer prayer for grace and faith."

"These inward trials I employ,
From self and pride to set thee free;
And break thy schemes of earthly joy,
That thou mayest seek thine all in Me."

Our Lord here uses the growth of a grain of a tiny seed into a strong and fruitful plant to teach us four specific lessons about every believer's growth in grace. "So is the kingdom of God." Let's look at these four lessons together, praying that God the Holy Spirit, who inspired Mark to record this parable, will be our Teacher.

The Sower
First, as the growth of corn requires that someone sow the seed, in God's work of grace in his kingdom there must be a sower to sow the precious seed of the gospel. "And he said, So is the kingdom of God, as if a man should cast seed into the ground" (v. 26).

The earth never brings forth corn on its own. Left to itself, since the sin and fall of our father Adam, this sin-cursed earth brings forth nothing but weeds, and briars, and thorns. It produces weeds, but never wheat, thorns, but never corn. The hard earth must be broken up by the farmer's plough and harrow. The seed must be sown by the hand of man. Otherwise, there will be no harvest.

So it is with the heart of man. No man left to himself would ever turn to God in repentance, believe on the Lord Jesus Christ, and obey the Word of God. The heart of man is totally depraved, void of all that is spiritual, good, righteous, and gracious. Man, by nature, is dead in trespasses and in sins, spiritually dead. The heart of man is enmity against God. No sinner is capable of any righteous, spiritual activity. A dead man can do nothing for himself. His condition is altogether and utterly helpless.

The Son of God must break up the fallow ground of the depraved heart by his Spirit. He must sow the seed of life by his power, as his servants scatter the precious seed, and he must create life in the dead sinner. Otherwise, the lovely plant of grace will never spring to life. Grace in the heart of man is an exotic plant. It is an altogether new thing. It comes down from heaven. Left to himself, no man would ever even know his need of Christ, much less seek him. Grace and by it, spiritual life, is the work of God alone.

Yet, in this parable, and throughout the New Testament, our Lord teaches us that in communicating grace, God works by appointed means: the preaching of the gospel! Those who despise the appointed means and yet hope to obtain God's grace might just as well expect to see a field of corn grow in an uncultivated jungle where no seed has been sown.

The man in this parable is a gospel preacher, one sent by Christ, bearing precious seed. Robert Hawker rightly observed, "The man who is said to cast seed into the ground, cannot mean our Lord Jesus Christ, for he neither slumbereth nor sleepeth; neither can it be ever said of him, that his seed springeth, and groweth he knoweth not how" (Psalm 121:4: Isaiah 27:2, 3).

The Seed

The Seed sown is the Word of God, the gospel of God's free and sovereign grace in Christ, the incorruptible seed that lives and abides forever (1 Peter 1:23-25). "It is", John Gill wrote,

> so called for its smallness, the diminutive character it bears, and contempt it is had in by some; and for its choiceness and excellency in itself, and in the account of others; and for its generative virtue under a divine influence. The gospel is like the manna, which was a small round thing, as a coriander seed; and as that was contemptible in the eyes of the Israelites, so the preaching of the gospel is, to them that perish, foolishness. And yet it is choice and precious seed in itself, and to those who know the value of it, by whom it is preferred to thousands of gold and silver. As worthless and unpromising as it may seem to be, it has a divine virtue put into it; and, under the influence of powerful and efficacious grace, it is the means of regenerating souls, and produces fruit in them, which will remain unto everlasting life. Yet, as the seed is of no use this way, unless it is sown in the earth, and covered there, so is the gospel of no use for regeneration, unless it is by the power of God let into the heart, and received there, where, through that power, it works effectually.

Casting the seed into the earth is the preaching of the gospel. Faithful gospel preachers do not spread divers and strange doctrines. Their ministry is one. They all see eye to eye (Isaiah 52:7, 8). They always sow the same precious seed, without any mixture of the tares of free will, works religion. God's servants do not deal out the truths of the gospel in a narrow and niggardly way. They do not restrain and conceal any part of holy scripture. They proclaim pure gospel truth from the housetop and set before their hearers the whole counsel of God.

I quote John Gill again:

> Though there may be many discouragements (that) attend them, many temptations arise to put off from sowing the word; the weather bad, storms and tempests arise, reproaches and persecutions come thick and fast, still they go on; using all that heavenly skill, prudence, and discretion God has given them, preaching the word in season, and out of season; and when they have done, they leave their work with the Lord, knowing that Paul may plant, and Apollos water, but it is God only that gives the increase.

The ground into which the Seed is cast are the different hearers of the Word. In this parable our Lord is describing those who hear and receive the gospel as seed sown in good ground. Those whose hearts are broken up by the Spirit of God, the stoniness of them taken away, are made receptive hearers of the good Word of God.

The Growth

Second, in growing corn and in the work of grace is much that is beyond man's comprehension and control. "And should sleep, and rise night and day, and the seed should spring and grow up, he knoweth not how" (v. 27).

The sleep mentioned here is not a natural sleep. Our Lord is teaching spiritual lessons, not natural lessons. God's servant ministers to his people (Galatians 3:5). Yet, as the seed of the gospel takes root in the hearts of sinners and grows, he readily acknowledges that, "he knoweth not how". Though every faithful gospel preacher watches over the garden of God, soaking the Word sown with tears and prayers, the fruit is brought forth as they sleep. I am confident that our Saviour did not use the word "sleep" here to refer to slothfulness on the part of faithful men, though faithful men know their own slothfulness. The sleep mentioned here may refer either to the sleep of death or to the confidence of faith.

Our Lord may be talking here about the sleep of death. Frequently, the fruitfulness of a faithful man's labour is not known until after he sleeps in his Master's arms. The churches and people among whom and for whom he has faithfully laboured bring forth fruit after he has been taken from the scene. As Robert Hawker puts it:

> The harvest arrives not, to their consciousness, in the fields of their labours in numberless instances, until they themselves have fallen asleep in Jesus. Many a seed time, and many a day's labour, followed up with prayer, do faithful ministers of Jesus leave behind them, which are answered, when their poor bodies are mouldering in the grave.

Perhaps our Lord's words refer to the confidence of faith in which faithful men labour. Faithful men believe God. They labour with confidence and satisfaction, leaving the work in God's hands. They are confident that God who sent his Word will make his Word fruitful. Thus, when the day is done, they sit down with the confidence of faith, with the satisfying security that their labour will be fruitful in the souls of men, in the kingdom of God and for the glory of God. God's servants do not despair of success. They know that they shall be successful (Isaiah 55:11; 1 Corinthians 15:58; 2 Corinthians 2:14-17).

Like diligent farmers, faithful, Christ-honouring pastors "rise night and day". They understand the importance of their calling and constantly attend to their work. It is a responsibility that is always on their minds. It is a weight in their souls and a burden in their hearts. It never leaves them. Nevertheless, they know, too, that it is God alone who gives the increase; and they wait for him to do so.

Whether he knows it or not, every good farmer exemplifies faith in and resignation to the sovereign will of God. He labours with great diligence, sows his seed with great care, and waits for God to give the increase. Though he labours with great care, the seed springs to life and grows up, "he knoweth not how". He sows good seed, and plenty of it, in good ground. Yet, no farmer can command the grain to grow, keep the crows from stealing it, or even tell you exactly what corn is in all of its components, though he knows corn when he sees it. He cannot tell you exactly when the corn sprang to life; but he knows whether the seed has sprung to life. He cannot define what life is; but he can discern it.

So it is in the works of grace in the hearts of chosen sinners. The greatest abilities, the most powerful preaching, and the most diligent labours cannot command success. Only God can give life to dead sinners (John 3:8). Yet we labour with confidence, knowing that our only work is to sow the seed. God alone can and will, as he sees fit, cause the Seed sown to spring forth into life. "God giveth the increase"!

Mysterious as nature is, grace is indescribably more mysterious. We sow good seed under the clods of the earth. There, the seed dies before it springs to life, grows, and brings forth fruit. In God's mighty operations of grace, the gospel, planted in the heart by the Holy Spirit, becomes the engrafted Word. But no man can know when or how God's saving grace is, by this means, implanted in the heart (John 3:8). These things are not even known to the sinner who experiences them, let alone to others. Suddenly, the sinner, who could not believe on the Lord Jesus Christ, finds himself trusting the Son of God and rejoicing in his salvation; but he cannot tell how it happened. This marvellous, wondrous work of grace, this mighty operation of God is done secretly and powerfully, under the influence of divine grace, without their knowledge.

Particularly, our Lord here teaches us that it is accomplished without the knowledge of the instrument God uses to perform the work. Though God uses men as instruments to sow the Seed, it springs to life and grows up "he knoweth not how", in the night as he sleeps. Though the sowing and planting are the preacher's responsibility, all the increase is God's work alone. The earth (the regenerate heart) is said to bring forth fruit, as the man who sowed the seed sleeps night and day, while the seed is growing without his knowledge, because God's work in the heart is "Not by might, nor by power, but by my spirit, saith the Lord" (Zechariah 4:6). "Salvation is of the Lord"!

Gradual Growth

Third, in both the cultivation of corn and in the work of grace life is made manifest gradually by degrees. "For the earth bringeth forth fruit of herself; first the blade, then the ear, after that the full corn in the ear" (v. 28). Two things are set before us in this verse.

"The earth bringeth forth fruit of herself". Once the seed is sown, and watered, and fertilized, the farmer's work is over. And, similarly, once the gospel is preached, watered, and fertilized by prayer, the preacher's work is over. As the fruitfulness of the earth is God's production and God's work, so the fruitfulness of the Word is God's production and God's grace (Romans 9:16).

No one would imagine that our Lord means for us to understand that the earth actually produces life. Yet, many would have us believe that man himself brings forth fruit unto everlasting life by his own will! Nothing could be further from the truth. The whole work of grace is God's work.

Repentance is the gift of God (Romans 2:4; Acts 5:30, 31). Faith is the gift and operation of grace (Ephesians 2:8, 9; Colossians 2:12). Love is the fruit of the Spirit. Joy is the result of God's work in us. Peace is the product of grace (Galatians 5:22, 23). Sanctification is God's work for us and in us, not our work for God (Hebrews 10:10-14; Jude 1). Commenting on our Lord's words here, John Gill wrote:

> All these things are owing to the Spirit, power, and grace of God. Men are regenerated according to the abundant mercy of God, of water and of the Spirit, by the word of truth, through the sovereign will and pleasure of God. They are quickened, who before were dead in trespasses and sins, and were as dry bones, by the Spirit of God breathing upon them.
>
> Conversion in the first production, is the Lord's work; 'turn thou me, and I shall be turned'. Faith in Christ is not of ourselves; it is the gift of God; and so is repentance unto life. Love is one of the fruits of the Spirit. In short, the whole work of grace is not by might, nor by power of man, but by the Spirit of the Lord of hosts; who begins and carries on, and performs it until the day of Christ.
>
> The work of sanctification is therefore called the sanctification of the Spirit. It is through him the deeds of the body are mortified. Indeed, without Christ, believers themselves can do nothing at all; even cannot perform good works, or do any action that is truly and spiritually good.
>
> The design is to show, that as the earth without human power, without the husbandman, under the influence of the heavens, brings forth fruit. So without human power, without the gospel minister, the Word having taken root under divine influence, through the Sun of Righteousness, the dews of divine grace, and operations of the blessed Spirit, it rises up and brings forth fruit.

God's works of grace in us are gradual works. Nothing in nature grows suddenly except weeds. The same thing is true in the kingdom of God. The seed does not burst forth into life as soon as it is sown. The ripe corn does not appear the day after the first green blade shoots out of the ground. It takes a while. The plant goes through many stages of growth before it is ready for harvest, "first the blade, then the ear, after that the full corn in the ear". Yet, the plant is living.

In the kingdom of God things are exactly the same. God's works of grace in the hearts of his elect proceed by degrees. None of the Lord's children are born full grown. None of them are born with mature and perfect faith, hope, knowledge, and love. Our beginning is a "day of small things". We see in part and know in part. We see our sinfulness, but only in small measure. We see Christ's fulness, but only in small measure. We know that God's grace is sufficient, but have no idea how sufficient it will prove to be!

Yet, wherever there is faith, even as a grain of mustard seed, there is life. Without question, there is weakness and infirmity; but still there is life. The seed of grace has come up in the heart, though perhaps only as a tender plant, a tiny blade shooting out of the ground.

There is much instruction here. He that is wise will lay it to heart. The strongest man was a helpless baby once. Everything must have a beginning. We must never despise the day of small things. We must never look upon, or treat, a brother or sister in Christ as though they are unregenerate because they are babes in grace or weak in faith. As it is in nature, so it is in grace. The child, though perfect in all its parts, must grow from the babe to the young man, and at length to the father.

And, as Hawker wrote,

> when grace is ripened for glory, like the fruit ripe for harvest, Jesus takes home his redeemed to him, to his harvest in heaven. The seed cast in the renewed heart, made so by grace, is the sure earnest of the harvest. Though men sleep, and know not how the advance is made, Jesus both knows, gives the needed supply, and watches over the whole plantation. To you, to me, things may at times appear, as in a wintry dispensation. But to Jesus the progress is advancing. The promise is absolute from God the Father. 'I will pour my spirit upon thy seed, and my blessing upon Mine offspring' (Isaiah 44:3; 59:21). And a soul renewed in Christ, must be separated from Christ, before those promises can fail (Romans 8:39). Blessedly, therefore, the Apostle sings, to the full assurance of faith, when he saith, 'Now he that hath wrought us for the selfsame thing is God, who hath also given unto us the earnest of the Spirit' (2 Corinthians 5:5).

Seedtime And Harvest

Fourth, in the cultivation of corn and the kingdom of God there is both seedtime and a time for harvest. "But when the fruit is brought forth, immediately he putteth in the sickle, because the harvest is come" (v. 29). There is a time appointed for the harvest. No farmer thinks of cutting his wheat while it is green, or gathering his corn before the ears are formed. He waits for the sun and rain, the heat and cold to do their work. Then, when the golden grain bows and the ears are full, but not until then, he puts in his sickle and reaps the harvest. Things are exactly the same in the kingdom of God.

God never gathers his people out of this world until they are ripe for harvest. He never takes his chosen until grace has made them ready. He never removes his elect until their work is done. God's children always die at precisely the right time. The great Husbandman never cuts the corn early or late.

> So now the future holds no fear,
> God guards the work begun;
> And mortals are immortal here,
> Until their work is done.

And our blessed Saviour, the Lord Jesus Christ, will come at exactly the right time to gather his harvest out of the world. When all things are ready, when everything has been done that God purposed to do, when all the elect are saved, then the Lord will come again and gather in his harvest. He is gathering his harvest by gospel preachers today. He gathers his harvest by his holy angels as he calls his elect up to heaven at death. He shall gather his harvest personally in resurrection glory at the last day.

May God the Holy Spirit enable us to carry the teachings and the comfort of this small, but instructive parable in our hearts. The next time a brother or sister is taken in death, remember this parable. Our Lord only gathers his harvest at the right time. There are no chances, accidents, or mistakes with our God. He knows best what to do in his own garden and with his own wheat.

It is our responsibility to sow the good seed of the Word. God will give the increase as he sees fit, when he sees fit. Wherever there is life there is growth. The growth is gradual, but sure; and it is God's work. At his appointed time, the harvest will come.

"And he said, Whereunto shall we liken the kingdom of God? or with what comparison shall we compare it? It is like a grain of mustard seed, which, when it is sown in the earth, is less than all the seeds that be in the earth: But when it is sown, it groweth up, and becometh greater than all herbs, and shooteth out great branches; so that the fowls of the air may lodge under the shadow of it. And with many such parables spake he the word unto them, as they were able to hear it. But without a parable spake he not unto them: and when they were alone, he expounded all things to his disciples".

(Mark 4:30-34)

Chapter 17

The Parable Of Mustard Seed

Here our Saviour employs another of his parables to teach us spiritual truth. It is the same parable recorded by Matthew (13:31) and Luke (13:19). Remember, parables are common, familiar earthly illustrations of spiritual, heavenly truths. In this case the parable is drawn from a commonly used proverbial expression during the days of our Lord's earthly ministry.

Faith Illustrated
Though not mentioned in the Old Testament, many varieties of mustard plants grew in Palestine. Some grew in the wild. Others were cultivated for various purposes. In the New Testament it is mentioned only by our Saviour. In two other places he compares true faith to a grain of mustard seed (Matthew 17:14-21; Luke 17:3-6). In both of these places our Lord uses mustard seed to illustrate faith. Our Saviour's use of mustard seed to illustrate faith teaches us four specific things about the character of true faith.

True, saving faith begins as a very small thing; like a grain of mustard seed. True believers always recognize that their faith is a small, a very small thing. We often look upon our brothers and sisters in Christ as being men and women of great faith; but anyone who thinks he has great faith probably has no faith at all. It is not the greatness of our faith, but the greatness of our God and Saviour, the object of our faith, that gives it merit, power, and efficacy.

Far too many have faith in their faith; which is to say they have faith in themselves. We must never imagine there is some mystical power to faith. The power of our faith is Christ. It is not our faith that moves the mountain of our sins or plucks up the sycamore tree of trouble; but the blood of Christ and the power of Christ. The question is not, "How much faith do I have?" but, "What is the object of my faith?" Great faith in an idol is useless but faith in the God of glory, even as small in size as a grain of mustard seed is mighty, effectual, saving faith.

With God, nothing is impossible; and therefore, "Jesus said unto him, If thou canst believe, all things are possible to him that believeth" (Mark 9:23).

Nothing can stand in the way of, hinder, or defeat that man and those people who, being called of God, believe him. It was impossible for Egypt to destroy Israel because Moses believed God. It was impossible for the Red Sea to stop the march of God's elect because Moses believed God. The walls of Jericho had to fall. Joshua believed God. The land of Canaan had to be possessed. Caleb believed God. The Philistine giant had to die because David, defending the cause of God's glory and his people, believed God. Jairus' daughter had to live. He believed God. The centurion's servant had to rise. That centurion believed God. Our Saviour was not lying when he said, "If thou canst believe, all things are possible to him that believeth". "If thou wouldest believe, thou shouldest see the glory of God".

Yet, nothing is more abominably wretched than the paralyzing effect of unbelief. When the Lord Jesus came into his own land, among his own people, we read, "He did not many mighty works there because of their unbelief" (Matthew 13:58). Just in proportion as we believe God, we experience his power and grace. Just in proportion as we believe him, we see his glory. Nothing is as costly as unbelief (Isaiah 48:16-19).

The Purpose
The purpose of the parable is to assure us of the certain growth and blessedness of Christ's church and kingdom in this world.

Robert Hawker's brief summary of the parable is excellent and worth reading in full.

> These verses are so many different similitudes, to illustrate the progressive work of grace in the soul. A child of God is apt to make false conclusions, in forming his view of such scriptures, by what passeth in his own experience. He feels at times such a deadness to divine things, that he is at a loss to ascertain any growth in the divine life. But the truth is, the growth he is looking for is to be found in the reverse of what he expects to find. He supposes to find himself more holy: whereas, the holiness the Holy Ghost is ripening him in, is in Christ. He doth indeed make great progress, when, from making every day more discoveries of his own unholiness, he becomes more and more longing for the holiness in Jesus. When a sense of the remains of indwelling sin makes him more out of love with himself and more in love with Christ. This is indeed, from small beginnings, to arise to large attainments, because, as it begins in Christ, so it ends in Christ. And Christ is the Tree of Life, under whose branches his people find both a banquet and a shadow (Song of Solomon 2:3, 4).

The Veracity Of Holy Scripture

Ignorant men who think themselves wise, reprobate men who think themselves spiritual, pass judgment upon the Word of God. They claim to be Christians, to be people of faith, and claim to honour Christ, while denying the veracity of the Bible. In this day of spiritual darkness and perversion there is almost a universal abandonment of belief in the verbal, plenary inspiration of God's holy, inerrant Word. Rejecting the veracity and, consequently, the authority of holy scripture, men and women everywhere are turning to necromancy, astrology, and sorcery for spiritual counsel and aid. Isaiah specifically addressed such evil (Isaiah 8:19, 20). John Hazelton warned, "Satan assumes the garb of an angel of light and his deceptions in this disguise are deadly."

Frequently, those who think they are smarter than God point to this parable to show that our Saviour was either ignorant or misinformed, because he spoke of the mustard seed as the smallest of all seeds and of the mustard plant as a tree. However, those who make such judgments are themselves ignorant and misinformed.

When our Lord said that the mustard seed is "the smallest of all seeds in the earth", he was not talking about all seeds without exception, but all the seeds a man sows in his garden. Though we usually think of mustard plants as bushy, leafy plants, there is a variety of mustard that grows into a good size, tree-like plant, similar to a banana tree in size.

We must never allow men, with their imaginary proofs of inaccuracies in the Bible, shake our faith in the Word of God. "All scripture is given by inspiration of God, and is profitable for doctrine, for reproof, for correction, for instruction in righteousness: That the man of God may be perfect, thoroughly furnished unto all good works" (2 Timothy 3:16, 17).

The Growth Of God's Kingdom

Like faith in the heart, the church and kingdom of God in this world began as a very small thing. The expression, "as a grain of mustard seed", was a common, proverbial saying among the Jews, referring to anything small and insignificant. As a rule, God's works in the world are always looked upon by men as trivial and insignificant. Certainly, that is the way it was with the Church of the New Testament.

Those who were chosen to be the foundational apostles of Christ's kingdom were poor, unlettered fishermen. He who is the Lord and Master of this Church, the King of this Kingdom, was a despised Nazarene, a crucified Jew. The doctrine proclaimed by this Church, the doctrine, which they preached everywhere, was the doctrine of grace, life, and eternal salvation by the merit and efficacy of a crucified Substitute. In the eyes of men, nothing could have been less likely of success, nothing more despicable, nothing more offensive. Yet, this is God's work, God's Church, and God's Kingdom. Once planted, this Church and Kingdom grew into a great Kingdom.

Our Lord's parable here was prophetic. He was telling his disciples not to despise the "day of small things". Though it appeared small, like mustard seed, the Lord promised his Church would be a great, large Kingdom. He said, "As the mustard plant grows to be the greatest of all herbs, so shall my church grow to be the greatest of all kingdoms." So it has come to pass. It began to grow on the day of Pentecost. Three thousand were born into his Kingdom on that day. The Church grew so rapidly, that nothing can account for it except the finger of God. A few days after Pentecost, thousands were added to the Church at once. Wherever God's servants went preaching the gospel, it proved to be the power of God unto salvation (Romans 1:14-17).

Today the Church of God is the greatest Empire the world has ever known and our God still employs the same means today as he did in the beginning for the building of his Church, the preaching of the gospel (1 Corinthians 1:21-31; Matthew 16:18). As J. C. Ryle put it, "In spite of all the predictions of Voltaire and Payne, in spite of foes without and treachery within, the visible Church progresses, the mustard plant still grows"!

As Hawker observed in his summary of this parable, that which is true of the Church as a whole is true of each member of it. The beginnings of grace in the life of a believer are very small; but where there is life there is growth; and those who are born of God are grown by God. The more they grow, the smaller they appear in their own eyes. Yet, when God is finished with us, we shall at last be transformed into the very likeness of the Son of God.

The Sanctifying Influence Of The Church

Though no one in the world knows it, and few in the Kingdom of God realize it, the Church and Kingdom of God has a deep sanctifying effect upon the rest of society. That is, at least in part, what is meant by the birds of the air flocking to and nesting in the mustard plant. The Church and Kingdom of God, like a great tree, shelters the world and influences it for good. We have an example of this in 1 Corinthians 7:14. "For the unbelieving husband is sanctified by the wife, and the unbelieving wife is sanctified by the husband: else were your children unclean; but now are they holy".

As in a home, the unbelieving are sanctified by the believing in a moral sense, so in the world. Read your history books. Education did nothing to improve the moral condition of the Greek and Roman worlds. Plato and Aristotle secured no moral good. That which has improved every society, culture, family, and relationship under its influence is the gospel of Christ.

The Mixed Inhabitants Of Zion

The fowls of the air also represent the mixed multitude in the visible Church and Kingdom of God in this world. The visible Church has always been inhabited by both the clean and the unclean. There is no perfect Church in this world. Every true Church has within both goats and sheep. It is a nesting place for birds, clean and unclean. It is a garden enclosed, but a garden with wheat and tares growing side by side. What are we to do about this? Nothing! Do not try to scare off the crows. If you do, you will drive away all the birds. Do not try to pull up the tares. If you do, you will pull up wheat every time. Never try to separate sheep from goats. We are not equipped for it. Only the Lord God himself is able to distinguish the true from the false. It is his work and prerogative alone to do the separating.

The Method Of Our Lord's Teaching

When the Lord Jesus preached, he always preached in the plainest, simplest manner imaginable. He who is the embodiment of wisdom and knowledge never used complicated words and phrases. He never once referred to the original language, or even defined a word. He did not use words that required definition. Instead, he told stories and illustrated the truths he taught by parables. "And with many such parables spake he the word unto them, as they were able to hear it. But without a parable spake he not unto them: and when they were alone, he expounded all things to his disciples" (vv. 33, 34).

Our Lord's example speaks volumes. He preached in such a way that people understood what he preached. He never tried to impress his hearers with how smart a man he was, or with how much he knew. He did not display knowledge. He taught knowledge. There is a huge difference. Those who follow the Master's example do not try to impress men. They instruct men.

Our Master taught with plainness and simplicity. He did not preach what he could not illustrate; and when he was finished, the people who heard him understood what he had said. Our Saviour taught with knowledge and understanding. He knew exactly what they needed, and what they could bear, and taught them accordingly. And every pastor called and gifted of God preaches as he did (Jeremiah 3:15). The Son of God expounded all things to his disciples. He kept back nothing from them. He expounded to them all the Word of God. Faithful men follow his example. The parable of the mustard seed teaches us that we should never despise the "day of small things". God is building his Church, gathering in his elect, and establishing his Kingdom. "The Lord GOD which gathereth the outcasts of Israel saith, Yet will I gather others to him, beside those that are gathered unto him" (Isaiah 56:8).

"And the same day, when the even was come, he saith unto them, Let us pass over unto the other side. And when they had sent away the multitude, they took him even as he was in the ship. And there were also with him other little ships. And there arose a great storm of wind, and the waves beat into the ship, so that it was now full. And he was in the hinder part of the ship, asleep on a pillow: and they awake him, and say unto him, Master, carest thou not that we perish? And he arose, and rebuked the wind, and said unto the sea, Peace, be still. And the wind ceased, and there was a great calm. And he said unto them, Why are ye so fearful? how is it that ye have no faith? And they feared exceedingly, and said one to another, What manner of man is this, that even the wind and the sea obey him?"

(Mark 4:35-41)

Chapter 18

A Parable Of Every Believer's Life

As our Lord Jesus and his disciples were crossing the Sea of Galilee, a terrible storm arose. The disciples, in the panic of their terror, were filled with unbelief. When they cried out, "Master, carest thou not that we perish", the Lord Jesus arose, calmly rebuked their unbelief, and, by the mere power of his word, calmed the sea and the storm.

Few, if any, of our Lord's miracles were so likely to leave his disciples with such an unforgettable, convincing demonstration of his divine omnipotence. At least four of these men were professional fishermen and skilled seamen. In all likelihood, Peter, Andrew, James, and John were very familiar with the Sea of Galilee. They had probably been exposed to its devastating and often fatal storms from their youth. Never, not even in the greatest of our Lord's other miracles, had they seen such power as he demonstrated here. By the word of his mouth, our Saviour stopped the storm!

Lessons
Faith in and obedience to Christ do not exempt God's saints from the storms that other people face. That our Lord was weary and required sleep shows he was a real man. That the wind and sea obeyed him shows our Redeemer's complete deity. This Man is the omnipotent God! The wind and sea knew the voice of their Creator! Only One who is both God and man could redeem us and save us from our sins. The greatest saints in this world are still sinners; and the strongest believers are sometimes filled with unbelief. Our Lord Jesus Christ is a tender, compassionate, forgiving Saviour. He is kind, gentle, and gracious, even in the rebuke of his disciples. "Why are ye so fearful? How is it that ye have no faith?"

Our Saviour's reason for all he does is the salvation of his elect. He went to the other side of the sea because there was a lost Gadarene on the other side, for whom the fulness of time had come. All who are in the good ship Grace with Christ are safe as they pass through the stormy seas of this world.

Parable Of Life
Those seven lessons are lessons frequently taught in holy scripture. They should be frequently taught to God's people. They are lessons we all need to

be reminded of frequently. Yet, as I read these verses, I see a parable that portrays every believer's life as he makes his pilgrimage through this world.

When the Son of God enters the hearts of chosen sinners in his sovereign, saving power, he brings us with himself into the church and kingdom of God, he brings us with himself into the ship of grace and salvation. As he does, he casts his eyes and ours across the waters of time to the other side of the sea of life, and says, as he did to his disciples in our text, "Let us pass over unto the other side". Read again Psalm 107:23-31 and you will see that we have a good, biblical basis for using this parable as a parable of our lives in this world.

A Voyage

First, every believer's life is a voyage. It is a voyage across a troubled sea to our "desired haven" on the other side. As we embark on this voyage, the Son of God takes us into the good ship Grace and says, "Let us pass over unto the other side". Death is often spoken of poetically as a passing over, the crossing of a sea or a river. We sing, "He will keep me 'til the river rolls its waters at my feet. Then He'll bear me safely over, where my loved ones I shall meet." However, this passing over the sea is not something we shall do someday. It is something we do every day. Living in this world, we are passing over the sea of time unto the other side. We are walking through the valley of the shadow of death.

The sea is a fit emblem for our passage and all the varied circumstances of our lives in this world. How quickly we pass across the sea. "What is your life? It is even a vapour, that appeareth for a little time, and then vanisheth away" (James 4:14). "My days are swifter than a weaver's shuttle, and are spent without hope" (Job 7:6). "Now my days are swifter than a post: they flee away, they see no good. They are passed away as the swift ships: as the eagle that hasteth to the prey" (Job 9:25, 26).

I have watched a lot of people die. As I look into the faces of eternity bound sinners day after day, as I am about to preach the gospel to them, I think to myself, "There go the ships, not painted ships upon a painted sea, but immortal souls, rising and falling upon the billows of time, disappearing one by one over the horizon of time into eternity." Soon, we must all pass over that horizon.

Perhaps, the horizon seems very far away to you. Do not be so foolish. Soon, you will pass from this changing world of time into the unchanging world of eternity. Here all things are temporal and changing. There all things are eternal and unchanging. How will it be for you in that day? How will it be for you in the swelling of the Jordan?

A Parable Of Every Believer's Life

A Voyage Across A Stormy Sea
Second, life in this world is not only comparable to a voyage, but it is a voyage across a stormy sea. "And there arose a great storm of wind, and the waves beat into the ship, so that it was now full" (v. 37). We must often sail into the tempests of sorrow, affliction, adversity, and grief; but Christ's presence assures us of safety no matter what the storm may be.

These disciples followed the Master into the ship at his command. It is important to note that fact, because we need to recognize that loyalty and obedience to Christ is often the surest course to trouble. The path of faithfulness is always right through the eye of the storm. Though our storms are many and varied, basically, all our trials and troubles in this world arise from two sources: the contrary winds of our circumstances without, and the waves of sin and unbelief within (Romans 7:14-24; Psalm 73:1-3, 21-28).

A Voyage With Christ
Third, our life in this world is a voyage with Christ. A voyage, yes. A voyage through stormy seas, yes. But, blessed be God, it is a voyage in the company and constant presence, protection, and care of the Son of God, our Saviour.

The Lord Jesus does not say, "Go over to the other side and I will meet you there." He said, "Let us pass over unto the other side". And, though "there arose a great storm, and the waves beat into the ship, so that it was full", we read that the Lord Jesus "was in the hinder part of the ship". He was silent; but he was there. So it is with us. Our Lord may appear to be asleep. He may be silent. It may even appear at times, to our feeble, sinful hearts, that He does not care if we perish. But He is always with us!

How I pray that God will teach me and teach you to believe him. Did not our Saviour say, "Lo, I am with you alway"? Did He not promise, "I will never leave thee" (Hebrews 13:5)? Read also Isaiah 41:10, 43:2 and Philippians 4:4-7 and see the promises of Christ's presence for yourself.

A Voyage Marked By Miracles
Fourth, ours is a voyage marked by miracles. "And he arose, and rebuked the wind, and said unto the sea, Peace, be still. And the wind ceased, and there was a great calm" (v. 39). The charismatics talk about miracles. We experience them. They put on a show of sham tomfoolery; but God's saints are men and women whose biographies are histories of God's miraculous works. The redemption of our souls was accomplished by the miracle of God the Son assuming our nature, being made sin for us, dying in our place, and rising from the dead as our Surety. The new birth is a wonder of miraculous grace, accomplished by Christ himself invading our spiritually dead souls by his Spirit and taking up permanent residence in our hearts.

159

Soon, our blessed Saviour will perform another miracle, the resurrection. "Behold, I shew you a mystery; We shall not all sleep, but we shall all be changed, In a moment, in the twinkling of an eye, at the last trump: for the trumpet shall sound, and the dead shall be raised incorruptible, and we shall be changed. For this corruptible must put on incorruption, and this mortal must put on immortality. So when this corruptible shall have put on incorruption, and this mortal shall have put on immortality, then shall be brought to pass the saying that is written, Death is swallowed up in victory. O death, where is thy sting? O grave, where is thy victory? The sting of death is sin; and the strength of sin is the law. But thanks be to God, which giveth us the victory through our Lord Jesus Christ. Therefore, my beloved brethren, be ye stedfast, unmoveable, always abounding in the work of the Lord, forasmuch as ye know that your labour is not in vain in the Lord" (1 Corinthians 15:51-58).

Still, there is more to consider. It is upon the dark background of our great troubles that our Lord most clearly displays his wondrous power and grace. It is in the fiery furnace of adversity that we know the preserving power of His presence. It is only in the lions' den that we see the Lord's dominion over the lions. The Lord God who is with us and for us is the God who is able to deliver us. He is God alone. He is God indeed!

A Voyage Free Of Fear
Fifth, our voyage with Christ across the stormy sea of life ought to be free of fear. The voyage we are on is a perfectly safe voyage. "And he said unto them, Why are ye so fearful? how is it that ye have no faith?" (v. 40).

The disciples' fear arose from their unbelief. Fear is the rank weed of nature that grows wild in the soil of unbelief. These poor disciples were so much like us. They should have been perfectly calm. They were on the Master's business. They were in the Master's presence. They had repeatedly seen and experienced the Master's power. They should have most reasonably looked to Christ; but they did not. Instead of looking to the Lord God omnipotent, they looked at the terrible storm, their own weakness, and the apparent frailty of their ship.

Let us take the Lord's gentle rebuke personally. I try to apply it to myself and I hope God will enable you to do the same. Our greatest difficulties, our greatest temptations, our greatest falls and failures are always the result of unbelief. Yet, unbelief on the part of one who has experienced the saving power and grace of God in Christ is the most absurd and unreasonable thing in the world.

"Why are we so fearful? How is it that we have no faith?' Our Saviour is the sovereign God of providence; wise, good, and omnipotent. He is in the boat with us. Yes, the Son of God is in the little boat of your heart and mine (Colossians 1:27; 1 John 4:4). He is in the boat of his Church (Deuteronomy 23:14; Psalm 46:5; Revelation 2:1). The Church of God, the true Church, is safe. She will pass over this sea and be brought to her desired haven. She will reach the other side. No one aboard the good ship Grace will be lost at sea.

Our Lord Jesus Christ is in the boat of holy scripture. His Word is forever settled in heaven. It cannot be broken. All the shifting winds of pseudo-science and waves of unscholarly criticism will not sink the Vessel. We have no reason to fear the carping of reprobate men. The Word of God abides forever. When their laughter is turned to weeping and their criticisms burn as fire in their souls, the Word of God will still be forever settled in heaven!

Our Lord Jesus Christ is in the boat of Providence. Not only is He in the boat, He is at the helm. We do not trust providence, or worship providence, we are not Deists; but the Lord God almighty whom we do trust and worship is the God of providence; and we rejoice to know it. The Lord Jesus Christ, who is with us, has the whole world in His hands. All power in heaven and earth is given unto him. He holds the reins of universal dominion. This omnipotent God bids us cast our care upon him with these assuring words, "For he careth for you"! He says to us, "Be not afraid, only believe".

A Call To Faith

Are you yet without Christ? Has God brought you into deep waters and begun to cause you to lurch by reason of your soul's trouble? Is the storm of God's wrath beating your little boat? May the Spirit of God make this parable a call to faith in your soul. Cry out from your soul to Christ, the Master. Appeal to his great compassion, "Carest thou not that I perish?"

"They that go down to the sea in ships, that do business in great waters; These see the works of the LORD, and his wonders in the deep. For he commandeth, and raiseth the stormy wind, which lifteth up the waves thereof. They mount up to the heaven, they go down again to the depths: their soul is melted because of trouble. They reel to and fro, and stagger like a drunken man, and are at their wit's end. Then they cry unto the LORD in their trouble, and he bringeth them out of their distresses. He maketh the storm a calm, so that the waves thereof are still. Then are they glad because they be quiet; so he bringeth them unto their desired haven. Oh that men would praise the LORD for his goodness, and for his wonderful works to the children of men! ... The righteous shall see it, and rejoice: and all iniquity shall stop her mouth. Whoso is wise, and will observe these things, even they shall understand the lovingkindness of the LORD" (Psalm 107:23-31, 42, 43).

Believe him, believe him, and you will see the glory of God (John 11:40).

"And they came over unto the other side of the sea, into the country of the Gadarenes. And when he was come out of the ship, immediately there met him out of the tombs a man with an unclean spirit, Who had his dwelling among the tombs; and no man could bind him, no, not with chains: Because that he had been often bound with fetters and chains, and the chains had been plucked asunder by him, and the fetters broken in pieces: neither could any man tame him. And always, night and day, he was in the mountains, and in the tombs, crying, and cutting himself with stones. But when he saw Jesus afar off, he ran and worshipped him, And cried with a loud voice, and said, What have I to do with thee, Jesus, thou Son of the most high God? I adjure thee by God, that thou torment me not. For he said unto him, Come out of the man, thou unclean spirit. And he asked him, What is thy name? And he answered, saying, My name is Legion: for we are many. And he besought him much that he would not send them away out of the country. Now there was there nigh unto the mountains a great herd of swine feeding. And all the devils besought him, saying, Send us into the swine, that we may enter into them. And forthwith Jesus gave them leave. And the unclean spirits went out, and entered into the swine: and the herd ran violently down a steep place into the sea, (they were about two thousand;) and were choked in the sea. And they that fed the swine fled, and told it in the city, and in the country. And they went out to see what it was that was done. And they come to Jesus, and see him that was possessed with the devil, and had the legion, sitting, and clothed, and in his right mind: and they were afraid. And they that saw it told them how it befell to him that was possessed with the devil, and also concerning the swine. And they began to pray him to depart out of their coasts. And when he was come into the ship, he that had been possessed with the devil prayed him that he might be with him. Howbeit Jesus suffered him not, but saith unto him, Go home to thy friends, and tell them how great things the Lord hath done for thee, and hath had compassion on thee. And he departed, and began to publish in Decapolis how great things Jesus had done for him: and all men did marvel".

(Mark 5:1-20)

Chapter 19

A Madman Who Lived Among The Dead

I read the story recorded in these verses with great personal interest, because no other person mentioned in the pages of holy scripture more fully exemplifies my experience of God's amazing, free, sovereign, almighty, irresistible, saving grace in Christ than the maniac of Gadara. Forty years ago I was a madman, running wild in the darkness of my own depravity among the tombs of the dead. Every attempt to restrain me was futile. Many tried, but none could bind me. Many tried, but none could tame me. Though I did not know it, I was hell bent on my own destruction. Like the maniac of whom these verses speak, I was a madman who lived among the dead. Then something happened. The Son of God stepped into my life, cast Satan out, took possession of my heart, and saved me by his almighty grace. That which Christ did for the madman of Gadara, and that which he has done for me, he still does for sinners today. The Lord Jesus Christ saves by his almighty grace!

The Saviour Of Sinners

"And they came over unto the other side of the sea, into the country of the Gadarenes". The Lord Jesus had just come from the other side of the Sea of Galilee to the shores of Gadara. When he set sail for Gadara, he knew that he was sailing directly into a storm. Yet, he set sail willingly. He was on an errand of mercy. He was going to Gadara to save one chosen sinner, for whom the time of love had come. The Lord Jesus came through the storm, across the sea, with willing heart to save the chosen sinner, when the fulness of time had come. When he had delivered the object of his grace, he returned to the other side of the sea, from whence he came.

This is exactly what our Redeemer did for all his people. He left his lofty throne in heaven, came across the sea of time and mortality, suffered the horrible storm of God's wrath as our Substitute to save us, and, when he had done that mighty work by which his chosen must be saved, when he had satisfied the law and justice of God and put away our sins by the sacrifice of himself, he went back to the other side again (Matthew 1:21; Luke 19:10; 1 Timothy 1:15; Romans 5:8; 1 John 3:5; Hebrews 10:10-14).

He came to save the least likely of the Gadarenes, a wild man, a maniac, one who was entirely possessed of the devil. In fact, a legion of demons resided in his poor soul. However, as we shall see, this man would be the instrument of mercy by whom God would bring his grace and salvation to many others in days to come (1 Corinthians 1:26-29).

The Son of God came to Gadara to dispossess Satan of one of his captives, to bind the strong man, take his house, and spoil him of his goods; and he did not leave until he had done what he came to do. The Lord Jesus Christ, the Son of God, is the Saviour of sinners.

A Miserable Wretch
"And when he was come out of the ship, immediately there met him out of the tombs a man with an unclean spirit, Who had his dwelling among the tombs; and no man could bind him, no, not with chains: Because that he had been often bound with fetters and chains, and the chains had been plucked asunder by him, and the fetters broken in pieces: neither could any man tame him. And always, night and day, he was in the mountains, and in the tombs, crying, and cutting himself with stones" (vv. 2-5).

Matthew in his account tells us that there were two mad, demon possessed Gadarenes who met the Master on the shores of Gadara. Some point to that fact and say, "There, you see, the Bible is full of contradictions." I fail to see their brilliance. If there were two, there had to be one; and Mark was inspired of God to write about one, giving far more detail than Matthew did in his description of the two. Apparently, the man described by Mark was the more notoriously wicked of the two. Look at what the Holy Spirit tells us about this sinner. What a sad, sad picture it is.

This poor Gadarene was a miserable wretch. Though the picture falls far short of the thing portrayed by it, the distressing circumstances of the poor demoniac vividly portray the terrible consequences of the fall of our father Adam, and the utter ruin of our race in the fall. Every descendent of Adam is, by nature, under the full sway and influence of an unclean spirit. We are all, by nature, ruled by our own depraved, corrupt hearts and wills, and are taken captive by Satan at his will (Romans 3:10-19; 1 John 3:8; 2 Timothy 2:26). Robert Hawker rightly observed, "Were it not for restraining grace, of which the sinner is wholly unconscious, what tremendous evils, in ten thousand times ten thousand instances, would take place"! We are, because of the fall and Satan's conquest of our nature, in bondage to sin with all its dreadful consequences. The flesh with its lusts and passions, the world with its deceits, and Satan with his devices rule the fallen sons of Adam with absolute sway.

In addition to all this, we are justly condemned by the law and justice of God threatening us with everlasting torment, and by the accusations of our own consciences. This is the state and condition of every fallen son and daughter of Adam, which causes all to live all their life time in the fear of death (Hebrews 2:14, 15).

An Unclean Spirit

Like this poor Gadarene, we all have an unclean spirit by nature. Yes, this man was possessed of the devil; but the devil could never have possessed him had he not been unclean by nature. Even so, the wicked, who opposing God oppose themselves, are this day "taken captive by Satan at his will" (2 Timothy 2:26). Isaiah declares that we are all as an unclean thing. Our hearts are deceitful above all things and desperately wicked. Out of our hearts come forth every abominable evil that exists in this world. Oh, if only we knew the evil of our hearts, the shocking horror of that wickedness that resides in us would prevent us from ever again saying, with regard of any vile act of a man, "How could a man do such a thing?"

Living Among The Dead

This poor, mad, depraved soul lived among the dead, "dwelling among the tombs" (v. 3). Dead sinners, dead in trespasses and sins, live among dead sinners, like themselves. Is that the case with you? You who live without Christ live among the dead, for you are dead. This man was not dead physically, but he was dead spiritually. Therefore, he was most comfortable among the dead. That is where I was when the Lord found me; and that is where you are by nature (Ephesians 2:1-4).

Could Not Be Bound

This poor, wild man could not be bound with the fetters and chains that bind other men. The fetters of society, social acceptance, peer approval, social advantage, family pressure, reputation, and concern for the opinions of others, those things that bind most men and make them behave with an outward form of decency, simply have no effect on some. The law of God has no influence upon most. They refuse to acknowledge its power, and cannot be bound by it. Night and day they run to destruction in a life of mad behaviour that will inevitably bring them to hell, except the grace of God intervene.

I say it to my shame, but that was my condition. Like the maniac of Gadara, social fetters could not bind me; and the fetters and chains of religion were no more effectual. I knew something of the terror of God's law. The wrath of God, the terrors of judgment, hell, and endless death tormented my soul, sometimes for months on end. Those terrors would sometimes appear effectual; but those fetters were also easily cast off. The fear of hell never changes a sinner's heart.

Could Not Be Tamed

No man could tame this madman. When society sees that chains and fetters cannot bind a man and make him better, it tries by refinement, education, reward, and gentle persuasion to tame him into moral respectability. The Lord Jesus does not bind or tame. He renews, regenerates, and breaks! And when he gets done, the broken sinner rejoices to be broken.

This poor maniac, like me, like some who read these lines, was hell bent on the destruction of his own soul. He was "always, night and day, in the mountains, and in the tombs, crying, and cutting himself with stones". Imagine the terror that this man wreaked upon others as they passed by this place, especially at night. Imagine yourself living near such a man. You would put iron bars around your windows and doors, and sleep with a gun under your bed every night. Whenever you saw him coming down the street, you would nod politely to keep from incurring his fury; but you would hurry away and try every way possible to protect your family from the influence of his madness.

But, can you imagine what misery such a person is in himself? His wickedness is his own doing; and it is inexcusable. But I also know the misery of his soul. I have been there among the tombs, moaning, groaning, crying, and cutting myself, always playing with death, yet always terrified of dying, despising loneliness and isolation, yet always doing that which of necessity brought me into greater loneliness and isolation.

Are you like this poor wretch? Were you once like him? If you are now in Christ, saved by his omnipotent mercy and infinite grace, you know that you were once unconscious of such mercy and grace. If you are yet without Christ, you are in the bondage of sin, Satan, and death, though you are completely unconscious of your lost and ruined condition.

A Worshipping Devil

"But when he saw Jesus afar off, he ran and worshipped him, And cried with a loud voice, and said, What have I to do with thee, Jesus, thou Son of the most high God? I adjure thee by God, that thou torment me not" (vv. 6, 7).

Here is the confession of a demon spirit. I do not know much about demons and demonology, and I do not want to know much. But I do know this: Demons are real! You will be wise to stay as far away from the occult, spiritism, witchcraft, and Satanism as you can.

Here the devil pretends to be a worshipper of Christ. He does not hesitate to assume the character of an angel of light, when it serves his purpose. I have seen him at work often. He makes people religious, and think they have become worshippers of God, though there is no worship in their hearts. What a cunning, crafty adversary Satan is! Many serve the devil best when they pretend to be worshippers of Christ! Worship from the teeth outward is not worship, but blasphemy! Many there are on the road to hell who have nothing but the faith of devils. They know that the Lord God is the most high God, and that Jesus Christ is the Son of God, but there is no commitment of heart to him as God. John Owen wrote,

> Of all the poison which at this day is diffused in the minds of men, corrupting them from the mystery of the gospel, there is no part that is more pernicious than this one perverse imagination, that to 'believe in Christ' is nothing at all but to 'believe the doctrine of the gospel!'

Run To Christ

Yet, these two verses also show us a picture of a poor, lost sinner coming to Christ. I cannot pass this without pointing out the fact that our great Saviour sovereignly and graciously used the very devils who would destroy the Gadarene to bring him to him for mercy!

Look at this man. He was "afar off"! So are we by nature. He was afar off from Christ, and the Lord Jesus was afar off from him. In character he was afar off. This man and the God-man had nothing in common. In knowledge he was afar off. The demoniac knew who Christ was, but did not know him. In possessions he was afar off. This man had nothing to offer Christ, no good feelings, no repentance, no good thoughts, no holy desires. He cried, "What have to do with thee?" The poor demoniac was utterly helpless and hopeless.

If you are yet without Christ, no words can paint the picture of your desperate need. You are so far off from God that you cannot and will not, of your own accord and by your own ability, return to him.

Though he was afar off, the Lord Jesus came to him, and he saw him coming! How he knew, I do not know; but this poor sinner knew some things about the One coming to him. I suspect he knew, because whenever Christ comes to a sinner in saving mercy, he makes himself known as the God of mercy and the Saviour through whom mercy comes. He saw that the Lord our God is God almighty, the most high God. He saw that the man Christ Jesus is God the Son. He saw that this great Saviour has total, sovereign power over all things, even the devils who possessed him. And he saw that if he would, he could deliver him from the devils and from himself.

"He ran and worshipped him". The poor soul was in a terrible mess. He was torn by powerful influences. Here is the Son of God, who has come to save him. Yet, there is within him a legion of devils bent on destroying him. He loves the evil that is destroying him; yet, he has grown to hate it because it is destroying him. He did the only thing he could do. In utter despair he ran to the only One who could help him, prostrated himself before his sovereign majesty, and worshipped him. C. H. Spurgeon said:

"A needle will move towards a magnet when once a magnet has moved near to it. Our heart manifests a sweet willingness towards salvation and holiness when the great and glorious good will of the Lord operates upon it. It is ours to run to Jesus as if all the runnings were ours; but the secret truth is that our Lord runs towards us, and this is the very heart of the business".

Do you need the mercy and grace of God? Run to Christ! With nothing but sin within you, with time fleeing from you, with eternity pressing upon you, with hell gaping beneath you, with heaven above you, O sinner, run, run to Christ! If you would have forgiveness, peace, pardon, and eternal life, run to Christ! This I know, if you do, you will find God your Father running to you in saving mercy, love, and grace! When sinners need mercy, they run to get it and God runs to give it!

What a blessed picture we are given of this in Luke 15:20. When the poor prodigal came to himself, as he was coming to his father with overwhelming shame, we are told that, "when he was yet a great way off, his father saw him, and had compassion, and ran, and fell on his neck, and kissed him". What a picture that is! The only time in the Bible we have any indication of the eternal God ever being in a hurry, it is here, hurrying to welcome his darling, chosen prodigal home!

In a sermon preached almost 400 years ago Tobias Crisp made the following comments on Luke 15:20. The quote is lengthy, but too precious and needful to be omitted or edited.

> His father sees him first. He spies him afar off. He stands ready to welcome a sinner, so soon as his heart looks but towards him. He that will draw nigh to them that are afar off will certainly draw nigh to them that draw near to him (Jeremiah 31:18). Nay, the father had compassion on him. His bowels yearn towards him, whilst he is afar off. Nay, he runs to meet him. He prevents a sinner with speed; mercy comes not on a foot-pace, but runs; it comes upon wings, as David speaks, 'He rides on the cherubs, he did fly; yea, he did fly on the

wings of the wind' (Psalm 18:9, 10) ... The son's pace is slow. He arose and came. The father's is swift. He ran. Though the son had most need to run, bowels moving with mercy out-pace bowels pinched with want. God makes more haste to shew mercy, than we to receive. Whilst misery walks, mercy flies; nay, He falls on his son's neck, hugging and embracing him.

Oh! The depth of grace! Who would not have loathed such a person to touch or come near him, whilst he smells of the swine he kept? Could a man come near him without stopping his nose? Would it not make a man almost rid his stomach, to smell his nastiness? Yet, behold, the Father of sinners falls upon the neck of such filthy wretches! Mercy and grace are not squeamish. The prodigal comes like a rogue. Yet the father clips him like a bride. He falls a kissing of him, even those lips that had lately been lapping in the hog trough and had kissed baggage harlots. A man would have thought he should rather have kicked him than kissed him. Yet this token of reconciliation and grace he gives him, with this seal he confirms his compassion. Nay, he calls for the best robe, and kills the fatted calf for him. The son's ambition was to be but as a hired servant, and lo, he is feasted in the best robes. God will do far better for a sinner than he can imagine, above all he is able either to ask or think. How then do poverty, nakedness, emptiness pinch thee, because of thy riot? Canst thou see enough in thy father's house, and therefore begin to pant in heart after him? Wouldest thou then have admittance? The Father of mercy is ready to deal thus with thee. Therefore object not unworthiness; for who more unworthy than such a son?

I say, again, run to Christ for mercy, and you will find the God of heaven running to you with mercy, infinite, overwhelming, saving mercy. Oh! That every poor sinner God the Father has given to his Son, whose redemption Christ has purchased with his own precious blood, may be led by God the Holy Spirit to flee to Christ, as this Gadarene demoniac was for deliverance.

Christ Is Lord
"For he said unto him, Come out of the man, thou unclean spirit. And he asked him, What is thy name? And he answered, saying, My name is Legion: for we are many. And he besought him much that he would not send them

away out of the country. Now there was there nigh unto the mountains a great herd of swine feeding. And all the devils besought him, saying, Send us into the swine, that we may enter into them. And forthwith Jesus gave them leave. And the unclean spirits went out, and entered into the swine: and the herd ran violently down a steep place into the sea, (they were about two thousand;) and were choked in the sea" (vv. 8-13).

Our Lord Jesus Christ is absolute Monarch of the universe. These demons, a legion, were compelled to Christ's feet like a dog to its master. They sought permission to enter into the herd of swine, for they must receive leave of our Saviour to do anything. I can think of at least two good reasons for our Lord allowing the demons to enter into, then slaughter the herd of hogs, (1) he wanted this poor Gadarene to know and remember what these demons of hell would have done to him, had it not been for his divine, saving intervention, and (2) he wanted to get the attention of the people of the city.

Our Lord's purpose of grace was toward many others in Gadara, others for whom the time of love would soon come. In order to prepare them for what he had in store for them he demonstrated both his awesome, sovereign power over the demons of hell and the creatures of his hand, and his awesome, saving grace in this man who had once been the terror of the city.

"What is thy name?" Our Saviour asked this question and compelled the demon to answer him audibly, not for his own information, but for the benefit of his disciples, both those then present and all who shall be his disciples to the end of time. The enemy of our souls is truly a legion. Multitudes of his soldiers reside within us, in the lust of our flesh, and are at his command. But such is the greatness of Christ's power and grace that he has made us more than conquerors in himself (Romans 8:37), and says to his redeemed, "Fear not, thou worm Jacob, and ye men of Israel; I will help thee, saith the Lord, and thy redeemer, the Holy One of Israel ... Fear not: for I have redeemed thee, I have called thee by thy name; thou art mine" (Isaiah 41:14; 43:1).

A Heaven-born Sinner

"And they that fed the swine fled, and told it in the city, and in the country. And they went out to see what it was that was done. And they come to Jesus, and see him that was possessed with the devil, and had the legion, sitting, and clothed, and in his right mind: and they were afraid" (vv. 14, 15).

What a change! It was a change everyone in town could see. This terror of a man had been born again. He who had been possessed of the devil was now possessed by the Son of God. He who was before uncontrollably wild and wicked was sitting before his Master. He who once roamed about half naked, or totally naked was clothed.

We were by nature naked before God. Now we are clothed with the very righteousness of God in Christ. Like the prodigal, our Father has placed upon us the family robe of Christ's righteousness, the family ring of everlasting covenant love, the family shoes of gospel peace, and feeds us at the family buffet upon the sacrifice of Christ!

He who was before a madman was now in his right mind. Someone said, "Every man is out of his mind until he has the mind of Christ."

But those who saw what had happened, but had not experienced it, were afraid. When God saves a sinner, others who thought they were all right are terrified by it, especially if the saved man was once one of them. These poor souls were terrified in the presence of almighty mercy, omnipotent love, and saving grace. Why? Because they knew nothing about it. They still lived in bondage. The only difference between them and the demoniac was that they were held by fetters and chains, and tamed by society. They mistook their fetters for righteousness and their tameness for goodness.

Some have asked, "Why did Christ permit the devils to possess the swine?" He did not do so merely to gratify the devils. Rather, he permitted them to possess the herd of swine to fulfil his own purpose. As Satan obtained permission to tempt Job, our Lord Jesus gave this legion of devils permission to enter into and destroy this herd of swine for the good of his own elect, the glory of his own name, and Satan's confusion. Just as Job's trial brought him great benefit and joy, and Satan's confusion, so it shall be with all the works the devil is permitted to perform in this world (Job 1:8-12; Romans 8:28-30).

Christ Despised

"And they that saw it told them how it befell to him that was possessed with the devil, and also concerning the swine. And they began to pray him to depart out of their coasts" (vv. 16, 17).

I cannot imagine reading sadder words than these. Here stands in the midst of a congregation of eternity bound sinners the Saviour of the world. He has just demonstrated his saving power and grace. Yet, their hearts are so full of the world that they fear he may cost them their living. So they pray; but it was a very strange prayer. They prayed for him to leave them; and he did! Matthew tells us that the whole city was united in urging the Son of God to depart from them (Matthew 8:34). As long as this poor Gadarene was possessed of the devil, he was a terror to them all. Yet, they preferred to have the devil raging among them, to having the Lord Jesus manifesting his grace and mercy!

Do we not observe the same behaviour day by day? Multitudes, who hear the gospel of Christ, like these Gadarenes, by their unbelief, say to the Son of

God, "Depart from us"! Once, we did the same. Are we now sitting at the Saviour's feet, clothed and in our right mind? Let us ever pray, "Blessed Saviour, do not go away, and never let me depart from you."

Request Denied

"And when he was come into the ship, he that had been possessed with the devil prayed him that he might be with him. Howbeit Jesus suffered him not, but saith unto him, Go home to thy friends, and tell them how great things the Lord hath done for thee, and hath had compassion on thee. And he departed, and began to publish in Decapolis how great things Jesus had done for him: and all men did marvel" (vv. 18-20).

This young convert wanted to go immediately with Christ and become a preacher; but the Lord would not allow it. How many there are who have mistaken a desire to be a preacher for a call to the ministry. It is not. The Lord Jesus sent him home to his family and friends with a message to deliver to them.

The Master would not allow him to go where he wanted to go or do what he wanted to do; but he was given something far better, far more useful to do. God made him a witness to his own community. Now, that's a preacher! The Lord told him exactly what to tell those to whom he would be a witness. He was sent to tell his family and friends what great things the Lord had done for him and how he had compassion on him.

And this sinner, saved by the grace of God, did what the Lord told him to do. "And he departed, and began to publish in Decapolis how great things Jesus had done for him: and all men did marvel". Notice the language here. He was told to publish what great things the Lord had done. So he told everyone what great things Jesus had done. He knew that Jesus is Lord. He learned it by experience from the Lord himself.

The Lord Jesus graciously used this man in Decapolis for the good of many. The next time the Saviour came into the region, he was readily received. Many came to him. Many were healed by him. Multitudes were fed by his hand (Mark 7:31- 8:1). Mercy came to many, because one sinner saved by grace faithfully told other sinners what great things the Lord had done for him!

Something Better

What a wonderful change grace had wrought in the Gadarene! He who was a madman, possessed of the devil, was immediately so transformed by the saving grace of Christ that he desired never to leave his Lord's side. Is this not the case with every child of God, when delivered from the power of darkness and translated from the cruel bondage of sin and death into the kingdom of God's dear Son? Once we have tasted that the Lord is gracious, we cannot but long to be "absent from the body, and present with the Lord". But this must not immediately be the case. "To abide in the flesh is more needful". Saved sinners are to go home to their lost families and friends, and proclaim "the praises of him who hath called us out of darkness into his marvellous light".

Christ has, by his saving grace, made us members of his church upon earth. In this capacity we are to serve him and the souls of eternity bound sinners, until the time comes he has appointed to take us home. None of us will live here beyond that appointed time. And that appointed time cannot be too long, if God our Saviour will be pleased to employ us for the welfare of his chosen. Mr Hawker wrote, "Let this make us happy in waiting 'all the days of our appointed time, until our change come.'" Until then, may God give us grace to make it our lives' business to tell our family and friends, and all who will hear us, "what great things the Lord hath done for us, and hath had compassion on us".

"And when Jesus was passed over again by ship unto the other side, much people gathered unto him: and he was nigh unto the sea. And, behold, there cometh one of the rulers of the synagogue, Jairus by name; and when he saw him, he fell at his feet, And besought him greatly, saying, My little daughter lieth at the point of death: I pray thee, come and lay thy hands on her, that she may be healed; and she shall live. And Jesus went with him; and much people followed him, and thronged him. And a certain woman, which had an issue of blood twelve years, And had suffered many things of many physicians, and had spent all that she had, and was nothing bettered, but rather grew worse, When she had heard of Jesus, came in the press behind, and touched his garment. For she said, If I may touch but his clothes, I shall be whole. And straightway the fountain of her blood was dried up; and she felt in her body that she was healed of that plague. And Jesus, immediately knowing in himself that virtue had gone out of him, turned him about in the press, and said, Who touched my clothes? And his disciples said unto him, Thou seest the multitude thronging thee, and sayest thou, Who touched me? And he looked round about to see her that had done this thing. But the woman fearing and trembling, knowing what was done in her, came and fell down before him, and told him all the truth. And he said unto her, Daughter, thy faith hath made thee whole; go in peace, and be whole of thy plague".

(Mark 5:21-34)

Chapter 20

"Who Touched Me?"

Our Lord Jesus was on his way to Jairus' house to perform a miracle of mercy upon his daughter, who was at the point of death. No doubt, word had gotten around in a hurry about what the Saviour had done in Gadara. Therefore, Jairus ran to the Master, fell down at his feet, and begged him to come to his house and heal his daughter. As they went along the crowds began to gather. You can imagine the commotion.

"And when Jesus was passed over again by ship unto the other side, much people gathered unto him: and he was nigh unto the sea. And, behold, there cometh one of the rulers of the synagogue, Jairus by name; and when he saw him, he fell at his feet, And besought him greatly, saying, My little daughter lieth at the point of death: I pray thee, come and lay thy hands on her, that she may be healed; and she shall live" (vv. 21-23).

Excitement filled the air. Here was a man, who claimed to be God's Messiah, the Christ, God incarnate. Everyone knew his claim; but he had begun to back it up and substantiate it by doing things that no one else could possibly do. In Gadara the devils themselves were constrained to publicly acknowledge him as the Lord their God, who had absolute power over them. Now, he is going to heal a young girl, whose father was a very prominent citizen in the community. This little girl was at the point of death. Everybody wanted to see the miracle. They followed the Lord as closely as possible, pressing him as he walked along. Everyone was excited. Everyone was curious. Everyone was filled with anticipation.

As they moved along, a poor, stooped, anaemic woman, a woman who had been plagued with an issue of blood for twelve, long, tormenting years, made her way through the crowd. I can almost see her. She is trying to remain hidden. She is unclean! She has no right by law to even be in the streets; but she is dying. She has heard about the Lord Jesus. No one else could help her. She had tried everything imaginable. Yet, she believed that Jesus of Nazareth was indeed the Christ, the Son of God. She said, "If I could just touch the hem of his garment, I am sure, he would make me whole." So she crawled through the thronging crowds until she got close. Then, weak and trembling, she stretched out her hand in faith and touched the Lord Jesus.

As soon as she touched him, the Lord Jesus stopped dead in his tracks. He felt virtue, power, and efficacy go out of him. Therefore, he turned around and said, "Who touched me?" The disciples said, "You've got to be kidding. With all these people around, you are asking, 'Who touched me?'" Then, the Master said, "Somebody touched me" (Luke 8:46). As this poor woman was immediately healed of her plague when she touched the Lord Jesus, so sinners are healed of the plague of their hearts, freed from the curse of the law and the guilt of sin just as soon as they touch the Lord Jesus Christ by faith.

The Curse

"And a certain woman, which had an issue of blood twelve years, And had suffered many things of many physicians, and had spent all that she had, and was nothing bettered, but rather grew worse" (vv. 25, 26).

There is no greater evidence of the total depravity of all human beings by nature than the fact that we all incur disease, get sick, and die. All sickness, disease, and death are the result of sin and the curse of God upon the human race because of sin. This woman's sickness was a specific example of sin and the curse of God's law upon us all by nature. Her sickness, her unceasing issue of blood was something that made her ceremonially unclean. So it is with us all by nature. We are plagued with sin. The plague of sin makes us unclean. Being unclean, we are cursed and barred from the holy Lord God. Look at what the Holy Spirit tells us about this woman.

She "had an issue of blood twelve years". She was ceremonially unclean (Leviticus 15:25) because of a disabling sickness that was killing her. This poor soul "had suffered many things of many physicians". She had been to every doctor in town, including the quacks, the charlatans, the snake oil herbalists, and the faith healers. There are countless "physicians of no value" (Job 13:4) to the souls of men.

Dr Decision tells sinners that they can be saved if they will simply make their decision for Jesus. Dr B. Good exhorts the sinner to reform his life. Dr Freewill admonishes the sinner to will himself into life. Dr Ceremony urges the poor soul to observe religious ordinances and sacraments to get the grace he needs. Dr Right-Church tells poor souls that they can be made whole if they get into the right church. Dr Excitement urges the sin-sick soul to seek a miracle, speak in tongues, pray through, and wrestle with God until he gets God to save him. Dr Emotion prescribes introspection, urging dead sinners to look within themselves for feelings of repentance and sorrow, or longings and affections for the Lord Jesus Christ, by which they may know they are fit to be saved.

Next, we are told that the poor dying woman "spent all that she had". Like those described in Isaiah 46:6 lavishing out everything for the help of idols, though she spent everything she had seeking help from "physicians of no value", she "was nothing bettered, but rather grew worse". Religion without Christ is of no value to lost sinners. It never helps. Rather, it only makes the sinner's condition worse. The practice of religion without Christ is but eating and drinking damnation (1 Corinthians 11:29). Oh, that sinners crippled with sin, instead of looking to "physicians of no value" in tears and attempted reforms in their own strength, might, like this woman, be brought to Christ!

The Crowd

"And Jesus went with him; and much people followed him, and thronged him. And a certain woman, which had an issue of blood twelve years, And had suffered many things of many physicians, and had spent all that she had, and was nothing bettered, but rather grew worse, When she had heard of Jesus, came in the press behind, and touched his garment" (vv. 24-27).

Like the crowds that pressed the Lord, people come to church, profess faith, and claim to follow him for many reasons. Some come being stirred by religious excitement, following the crowd. Some take up a profession because of peer pressure. Many do so because they fear going to hell.

The crowds of people thronged our Lord; but only one person gained any benefit. Only one person came from behind and touched him. Only one person in this great crowd needed him. Only one person believed the Lord Jesus could actually cure her of her plague. Believing him, she touched him. Be wise and follow her example.

The Cure

"When she had heard of Jesus, came in the press behind, and touched his garment. For she said, If I may touch but his clothes, I shall be whole. And straightway the fountain of her blood was dried up; and she felt in her body that she was healed of that plague. And Jesus, immediately knowing in himself that virtue had gone out of him, turned him about in the press, and said, Who touched my clothes? And he said unto her, Daughter, thy faith hath made thee whole; go in peace, and be whole of thy plague" (vv. 27-30, 34).

There are several things here, which ought to catch our attention. Many reading this story miss the most important aspects of it. They put all the emphasis upon the woman. Inspiration puts the emphasis on the woman only as the recipient of mercy and benefactor of grace. But, insofar as the act of mercy and the work of grace are concerned, the emphasis must be placed upon the Saviour. This woman was made whole in exactly the same way every sinner saved by the grace of God is made whole. She was made whole by a fivefold work of God almighty.

A Work Of Providence

Her sickness was not an accident, but a work of God for her soul to bring her to Christ. That which was the destruction and death of others was for her the instrument of mercy. By his wise, gracious, and good providence, the God of all grace brought the chosen sinner and the appointed Saviour together at the time of love.

A Work Of The Word

She came to Christ in faith "when she had heard of Jesus" (v. 27), not before. No one is ever saved apart from the hearing of Christ, the hearing of the gospel (Romans 10:17; James 1:18; 1 Peter 1:23-25). God never bypasses the appointed means of grace. There is no need for him to do so.

A Work Of Grace

The grace of God is not verbally mentioned in the text; but it is written all over it. Grace had chosen "a certain woman". Grace brought the Lord Jesus to pass her way. Grace caused her to hear about him. And grace gave her faith and wrought faith in her (Ephesians 1:19; 2:8; Philippians 1:29; Colossians 2:12).

A Work Of Faith

This woman's faith, like all true faith, was the gift of God. Yet, it was her faith. She chose to come to Christ. She chose to believe on the Son of God. She was made willing in the day of his power; but she was willing. She was caused to come by the sweet constraint of grace; but she did come.

A Work Of Omnipotence

The arm of God's omnipotent, almighty, irresistible power brought this thing to pass exactly according to his everlasting purpose of love and grace toward this chosen sinner. The virtue that went out of the Saviour to this woman was his own omnipotent grace.

The Confession

"And Jesus, immediately knowing in himself that virtue had gone out of him, turned him about in the press, and said, Who touched my clothes? And his disciples said unto him, Thou seest the multitude thronging thee, and sayest thou, Who touched me? And he looked round about to see her that had done this thing. But the woman fearing and trembling, knowing what was done in her, came and fell down before him, and told him all the truth" (vv. 30-33).

Our Saviour did not ask, "Who touched me?" because he needed to learn who had done this, but because we need to learn the necessity of confessing

Christ before men. "With the mouth confession is made unto salvation". This woman came and told the Saviour publicly, "all the truth". She told the Lord Jesus all about her plague, the power of his grace she experienced within, and the cure his omnipotent mercy had wrought.

"In the greatest throng, as well as in the secret place", Robert Hawker wrote, "Jesus sees all, knows all, and both appoints and will sanctify all ... We never can sufficiently admire the abundant tenderness the Lord Jesus manifested upon this occasion, to this poor woman. She wished the cure to be in secret: but no! Jesus will have her faith in him made public. His grace to poor sinners shall be proclaimed thereby; and, her trust in him shall make her history illustrious through endless generations."

It is not needful for us to blow the trumpet in the streets and force others to hear us when they choose not to listen. However, it is required that we identify ourselves with Christ and his gospel publicly. We must not be ashamed to confess Christ before men, both in believer's baptism and as his witnesses.

This woman's confession did not cause her to be healed any more than the believer's confession of Christ causes him to be saved. Our confession of faith in Christ is not a confession made that we might be saved, but a confession made of salvation granted. With our mouths we make confession with reference to the salvation Christ has bestowed.

The Commendation

"And he said unto her, Daughter, thy faith hath made thee whole; go in peace, and be whole of thy plague" (v. 34). Here, our Lord Jesus commends faith, that great work of grace of which he is himself both the Object and the Author. Nothing brings such glory to Christ as that faith which looks to Christ for everything. Nothing is so useful to our souls as faith in Christ. The believer's life is a life of faith in Christ. We begin in faith, live by faith, stand in faith, walk by faith, have peace with God by faith, see the glory of God by faith, and die in faith. Nothing is so important as this "Dost thou believe on the Son of God?"

Yet, the primary object of this miracle is not the woman's great faith, but our blessed Saviour's great grace. Though at the time unknown to her, the faith she had in him was faith he had given her and had wrought in her by his Spirit (Colossians 2:12). Obviously, the poor soul thought she had escaped the notice of all; as soon as she touched him, the Master let her know that he both knew her need and performed her cure.

While he yet spake, there came from the ruler of the synagogue's house certain which said, Thy daughter is dead: why troublest thou the Master any further? As soon as Jesus heard the word that was spoken, he saith unto the ruler of the synagogue, Be not afraid, only believe. And he suffered no man to follow him, save Peter, and James, and John the brother of James. And he cometh to the house of the ruler of the synagogue, and seeth the tumult, and them that wept and wailed greatly. And when he was come in, he saith unto them, Why make ye this ado, and weep? the damsel is not dead, but sleepeth. And they laughed him to scorn. But when he had put them all out, he taketh the father and the mother of the damsel, and them that were with him, and entereth in where the damsel was lying. And he took the damsel by the hand, and said unto her, Talitha cumi; which is, being interpreted, Damsel, I say unto thee, arise. And straightway the damsel arose, and walked; for she was of the age of twelve years. And they were astonished with a great astonishment. And he charged them straitly that no man should know it; and commanded that something should be given her to eat".

(Mark 5:35-43)

Chapter 21

Talitha Cumi

Two Complementary Miracles
The two miracles described in Mark 5:21-43 are deliberately blended together by the Spirit of God for our learning and consolation. Who can imagine what a great trial it must have been to Jairus' faith to see the Lord Jesus stopped by the woman? What fears must have risen in his heart! His need was urgent. His daughter was dying. He must have been completely distraught. Yet, the Lord Jesus stopped to heal a poor woman before going to heal his dying child. Often, that is exactly what the Lord Jesus does with us. He seldom answers our prayers immediately or in the way we expect. He requires us to trust him to do what is best. Jairus did just that. What compassion he showed! What patience he exercised! What self-denial he exemplified! What faith he practised!

I do not doubt that all the time the events recorded in verses 25-34 were going on, Jairus was thinking about his dying child. Yet, he said nothing. He just waited patiently before the Lord Jesus, trusting that he who had moved toward his daughter would heal his daughter in his time. Then, while the Lord Jesus was still talking to the woman, "there came from the ruler of the synagogue's house certain which said, Thy daughter is dead: why troublest thou the Master any further?"

Yet, Jairus continued to look to the Lord Jesus. What a great miracle of mercy, love, and grace the Master performed for this needy soul who believed him! His dead daughter was raised to life by the power of the Saviour's word. Death is called "The King of Terrors". But here is One who is mightier than the king of terrors. The Son of God, our Lord Jesus Christ is he who has the keys of death and hell in his hands. He who is the Resurrection and the Life by his own death and resurrection vanquished death for us as our Substitute. Soon, he will "swallow up death in victory" (Isaiah 25:8); and, just as he raised this young girl from death to life, he will raise all the hosts of God's elect from death and the grave to everlasting life in resurrection glory.

Vanity

The first thing demonstrated most clearly in this passage is the utter vanity of all earthly, material things. "Vanity of vanities, all is vanity! saith the preacher". Those are not the words of a frustrated, grumpy old man, but the words of the wisest, mere mortal man ever to walk the face of God's earth. When Solomon considered all the things a man can possess and enjoy in this world of time and space, in this present state of things, he said, all earthly, material things are utterly vain and meaningless.

Jairus was, in all likelihood, a man of tremendous political power and influence, and of considerable wealth. He was "one of the rulers of the synagogue". Yet, his daughter, his only daughter, as Luke tells us, lay dying. The apple of his eye, the darling of his heart was dying; and she was only twelve years old. Go ask Jairus, "How important is money? How useful is power, influence, and fame? If the world were yours for the asking, what would you want now?" He would tell you, I want only one thing. I want the Son of God. I want him to come under my roof, to visit my family, to have mercy upon my only dear, dying daughter. Nothing else matters.

I wonder if we will ever learn that nothing here is really of any value, significance, or importance. "The things which are seen are temporal"! Everything here is temporal. Be wise. "Set your affection on things above, not on things on the earth". Let us ever beware of the "cares of this world, the deceitfulness of riches, and the lusts of other things"! Let us value nothing in this world more highly now than we will value it when we stand before God.

Death

This passage also demonstrates the certainty and universality of sorrow, sickness, and death. Jairus' daughter was only twelve years old. Yet, she became ill and died. Sickness, sorrow and death are common things that believers must suffer, just as all other people do. Jairus was a believer. Yet, his young, darling daughter was dying when he left home to seek the Lord's help; she died while he was seeking that help that Christ alone could give.

Like Jairus' daughter, each of us must soon die. We will all die at the time appointed by the means appointed in the place appointed. For believers, death is a blessed rest. Our Lord said, concerning Jairus' daughter, "The damsel is not dead, but sleepeth" (v. 39). That is the same thing he said regarding Lazarus. In reality, God's elect never die. Did not the Son of God say, "Whosoever liveth and believeth in me shall never die" (John 11:26)? Those who die in the Lord sleep in the arms of Jesus. Their bodies sleep in the earth; but they have entered into heavenly rest. For the unbeliever death is the beginning of sorrow and everlasting woe.

Prayer

In verses 22 and 23 we learn something about the nature of true prayer.

"And, behold, there cometh one of the rulers of the synagogue, Jairus by name; and when he saw him, he fell at his feet, And besought him greatly, saying, My little daughter lieth at the point of death: I pray thee, come and lay thy hands on her, that she may be healed; and she shall live".

I do not pretend to know very much about prayer; but I know that wherever there is true prayer in the heart of a man or woman before God, it has these five characteristics: Prayer arises from a knowledge of the Lord Jesus Christ. Jairus "saw him!' Prayer bows to and worships Christ. Jairus "fell at his feet". True prayer is persevering and importunate. We read that Jairus "besought him greatly"! True prayer is always importunate and persevering, because it arises from a heartfelt, desperate need. "My little daughter lieth at the point of death". True prayer arises from a heart of faith in the Son of God. "I pray thee, come and lay thy hands on her, that she may be healed; and she shall live".

I know this, too. None of us knows "what we should pray for as we ought" (Romans 8:26). We like to think otherwise but we never know what is best. None of us knows what is best for the glory of God, the good of our own souls, or the accomplishment of God's purpose of grace in Christ. Because we do not know what is best, we do not know how to pray for anything as we ought.

Prayer is not for the gratification of our carnal lusts. It is not the means by which we obtain what we want from the Lord. Prayer, true prayer, involves submission to the will of God. It is the cry of the believer's heart to his heavenly Father to do what is right and best. If I am God's child, if truly I know him and trust him, I want what he has purposed. I bow to him, surrendering my will to his will, my desires to his purpose, my pleasure to his glory, knowing that his will is best. Therefore, when we pray (in our ignorance), the Holy Spirit cleans up our prayers and presents to the Father the true groanings of our hearts (Romans 8:26).

Jairus demonstrates this spirit and attitude in this passage. He had come to the Lord Jesus seeking that his daughter might not die. When he heard that she had died, he continued trusting the Saviour, bowing to his will.

God's Requirement

Verses 35 and 36 show us what our God requires of us. The one thing that God requires and demands of us is faith. I am fully aware that faith is the gift of God and the operation of his grace in us. Yet, faith is what he requires of us. He requires that we "only believe".

"While he yet spake, there came from the ruler of the synagogue's house certain which said, Thy daughter is dead: why troublest thou the Master any further? As soon as Jesus heard the word that was spoken, he saith unto the ruler of the synagogue, Be not afraid, only believe".

If we would be saved, the Lord Jesus says, "only believe". If we would honour God, his command is "only believe". If we would see the Lord God work, he says, "only believe". If we would see the glory of God, we must "only believe". In John 11:40 we read, "If thou wouldest believe, thou shouldest see the glory of God".

In all our exercises of faith, when the Lord seems to give no gracious answers to prayer, when he brings us into trials and difficulties, when our hearts appear to be cold and dead and our spirits are languishing, let us remember Jairus, and look still to our blessed Saviour. It is one thing to trust the Son of God when things appear hopeful; but it is something else to trust him when everything appears hopeless.

With regard to our own selves, when we most feel and know our own impotence before God, the depravity of our hearts, and the corruption of our souls, when we feel utterly dead before him, it is a good thing to have "the sentence of death in ourselves, that we should not trust in ourselves, but in God which raiseth the dead" (1 Corinthians 1:9). In such times let us rejoice to trust him who says to our souls, "I am the resurrection, and the life: he that believeth in me, though he were dead, yet shall he live: And whosoever liveth and believeth in me shall never die" (John 11:25, 26).

Omnipotent Christ

Surely, the Holy Spirit inspired Mark to record this incident to remind us that our Lord Jesus Christ is the omnipotent God to whom "belong the issues from death" (Psalm 68:20).

"He took the damsel by the hand, and said unto her, Talitha cumi; which is, being interpreted, Damsel, I say unto thee, arise. And straightway the damsel arose, and walked; for she was of the age of twelve years. And they were astonished with a great astonishment" (vv. 41, 42).

In this glorious miracle we are once more shown what Christ can do for dead sinners and how he does it. When God our Saviour saves a sinner, when he calls a sinner from spiritual death to life and faith by the power of his omnipotent grace, he secretly, sovereignly touches the dead soul by the hand of his irresistible mercy. He calls the chosen sinner by the power of his Spirit through his Word. The dead, being called by omnipotence, arise and come to Christ. All who see it are astonished. The living sinner is astonished, the observant saints are astonished and the confused religionists are astonished.

Christ's Provision
In verse 43 the Lord Jesus "commanded that something should be given her to eat". He said to those who stood by, "Give her something to eat." Our blessed Saviour has provided and continually provides food for the souls of his children in this world, by which he sustains us in life and causes us to grow in his grace. To this end he has given his church pastors according to his own heart, called and gifted by his Spirit, to feed his people by the preaching of the gospel with knowledge and understanding (Jeremiah 3:15; Ephesians 4:8-16).

Resurrection
The resurrection of Jairus' daughter stands before us in the Book of God as a remarkable pledge of our own resurrection in the last day. As our Lord Jesus came to Jairus' house and raised his daughter from death to life, soon he shall come again to this earth and raise us up to glory (1 Corinthians 15:51-58; 1 Thessalonians 4:13-18).

"And he went out from thence, and came into his own country; and his disciples follow him. And when the sabbath day was come, he began to teach in the synagogue: and many hearing him were astonished, saying, From whence hath this man these things? and what wisdom is this which is given unto him, that even such mighty works are wrought by his hands? Is not this the carpenter, the son of Mary, the brother of James, and Joses, and of Juda, and Simon? and are not his sisters here with us? And they were offended at him. But Jesus said unto them, A prophet is not without honour, but in his own country, and among his own kin, and in his own house. And he could there do no mighty work, save that he laid his hands upon a few sick folk, and healed them. And he marvelled because of their unbelief. And he went round about the villages, teaching".

(Mark 6:1-6)

Chapter 22

"Is Not This The Carpenter?"

In these six verses of Inspiration we are given a sad, bleak illustration of the wickedness of the human heart. Our Lord Jesus Christ returned from Capernaum to Nazareth, his hometown. He had performed notable miracles which would have made him the town hero except for one thing. This One who had done such miracles taught the gospel of God's free, sovereign, saving grace, contrary to their religious traditions. Rather than believing him, receiving him, and honouring him as the Christ of God, his countrymen refused to believe him, despised him, and held him in contempt. "He came unto his own, and his own received him not" (John 1:11). These verses call for our special attention. Look at them carefully, line by line. As we do, I will direct your attention to five very important things revealed in them.

True Christianity
"And he went out from thence, and came into his own country; and his disciples follow him" (v. 1). First, note that true disciples follow their Master. That fact should be obvious. Marxists are followers of Marx and Leninists are followers of Lenin, so Christians are followers of Christ. The disciples at Antioch were such ardent followers of the Lord Jesus that those who observed their doctrine and behaviour called them "Christians". Understand what I am saying. A Christian is not a person who says he is a Christian, or the person who professes the right doctrine. A Christian is a person who follows Christ. Our following Christ is not the basis of our hope or the ground of our assurance before God. It is Christ's obedience unto death, not our obedience, that gives us hope with God and assurance of his grace. Yet, if we do not follow Christ, whatever hope and assurance we have is a delusion.

We read here, "His disciples follow him". The Word of God does not teach that his disciples follow him perfectly. It does teach that all true believers follow Christ as their Lord and Master in the tenor of their lives. All who are saved by the grace of God bow to Christ as their Lord, take up their cross and follow him. The Word of God identifies Christians as people who follow Christ. "These are they which follow the Lamb whithersoever he goeth" (Revelation 14:4). Christians are followers of Christ. They follow him in believer's baptism. They follow his doctrine, believing that which he has revealed. And they follow his example, loving and serving one another.

Public Worship

The second lesson to be learned from this passage is the fact that all who follow Christ addict themselves to the worship of God. When our Lord and his disciples came to Nazareth, or to any town or village, at the appointed time of worship they were found in the house of God. In verse 2 we read, "And when the sabbath day was come, he began to teach in the synagogue: and many hearing him were astonished, saying, From whence hath this man these things? and what wisdom is this which is given unto him, that even such mighty works are wrought by his hands?"

It is the great privilege and responsibility of God's people to addict themselves to the worship of God in the public assembly of his saints and to the ministry of the Word (Hebrews 10:25). In those days the appointed place of worship was the synagogue of the Jews. The appointed day of worship was Saturday, the Jewish sabbath day. Though the Jews and the synagogues had long since forsaken the oracles and worship of God, and had replaced the commandments of God with the traditions of men, they still professed to worship the Lord God and professed to reverence his Word.

We ought never to be found in churches where the gospel is not preached and our God is not worshipped. Yet, we must not forsake the assembly of God's saints in worship. Sheep are social creatures. Unless they are very sick or utterly lost, you will never find them alone. We must not allow any earthly care or social concern to keep us from the house of God. This is the place where Christ has promised to meet with his people (Matthew 18:20). This is the place where God sends forth his Word. It is here that God speaks to men. This is the place where we find food for our souls. This is the place where God is worshipped.

When our Lord came to the house of God, he taught the Word of God. There are many aspects of public worship which must never be neglected. The reading of holy scripture, the praise of God in song and public prayer, and the observance of baptism and the Lord's Supper are matters of immense importance. However, that which is and always must be paramount in the house of God is the preaching of the gospel, the teaching of the Word of God.

We do not need to guess what the Saviour preached in the synagogue. He expounded the law and the prophets, just as he had done the last time he was there, preaching the gospel to all who would hear him (Luke 4:16-32). He preached himself as the only Saviour of sinners (vv. 18, 19), the fulfilment of all the scriptures (v. 21), and the glorious sovereignty of God in the exercise of his saving grace (vv. 25-27). I have no hesitancy in asserting these things, because God the Holy Spirit tells us plainly that there is no preaching of the Word of God apart from the preaching of the gospel (1 Peter 1:23-25).

There is no room in the house of God for religious entertainment, political propaganda, social crusades, psychological analysis, and religious dialogue. What we need and must have in the house of God is preaching, plain, forthright, dogmatic, decisive, gospel preaching! As before, those who heard Christ preach were astonished by his wisdom and power, and offended by his doctrine (vv. 2, 3). Though they acknowledged what they could not deny, his wisdom and power, they were offended by his gospel.

Nothing has changed. The offence of the cross has not ceased. Those who preach the gospel of Christ will always find that natural, unregenerate, lost religious people are offended by it. The gospel of God's free grace in Christ will never be palatable to men who do not know God. Total depravity offends man's pride. Unconditional election offends man's self-righteousness. Limited atonement offends men who will not submit themselves entirely to the merits of Christ or salvation. Irresistible grace offends man's sense of personal superiority and dignity. The sure preservation of God's elect offends man's sense of religious fairness and righteousness.

Christ's Humiliation
Third, the Spirit of God here reminds us again of the great humiliation of our Lord Jesus Christ. "Is not this the carpenter, the son of Mary, the brother of James, and Joses, and of Juda, and Simon? and are not his sisters here with us? And they were offended at him" (v. 3). "Is not this the carpenter?" This particular expression is found nowhere else in the Bible. Its implications are significant and far reaching. In order to redeem and save us the Son of God condescended to become a man, and, being found in fashion as a man, humbled himself in all things relating to manhood (2 Corinthians 8:9; Philippians 2:5-8; Hebrews 2:14-18). Robert Hawker says:

In Christ becoming a curse for his redeemed, it behoved him to undergo that curse in all its branches. The tenor of the curse pronounced at the fall, ran in those words: In the sweat of thy face shalt thou eat bread; meaning toil and labour. Had not Jesus therefore toiled and laboured for his bread, this part of the curse could not have lighted upon him.

And J. C. Ryle adds:

He who made heaven, and earth, and sea, and all that therein is, He, without whom nothing was made that was made, the Son of God Himself, took on Him the form of a servant, and in the sweat of His face ate bread, as a working man. This is

189

indeed that 'love of Christ which passeth knowledge'. Though He was rich, yet for our sakes He became poor. Both in life and death, He humbled himself, that through Him sinners might live and reign for evermore.

Living and working as an ordinary carpenter, our dear Saviour taught us by example the honour of diligent labour and the dishonour of laziness, idleness, and slothfulness. Every honourable man is a working man. We ought to abhor idleness and teach our children to abhor it. Nothing is more repugnant than a man who claims to be a follower of Christ who will not work and provide for his own (Ephesians 4:27, 28; 2 Thessalonians 3:10; 1 Timothy 5:8). By assuming the work and trade of a carpenter, our Redeemer placed great honour upon working people, that class of society commonly disdained by those who consider themselves the nobler part of society. The only things that might be more repugnant than lazy, loitering people are those who snub their noses at others whom they consider beneath them. Pride of place, pride of race, and pride of grace are utterly despicable!

Blessings Despised

"But Jesus said unto them, A prophet is not without honour, but in his own country, and among his own kin, and in his own house" (v. 4). It is ever the tendency of our fallen, depraved nature to undervalue and disregard those things with which we are most familiar. The people of Nazareth were offended at our Lord. They did not think it possible that one who had lived among them for thirty years, whose family they knew well, one who was reared and trained as nothing but a carpenter could be worthy of such reverence, esteem, and adulation as many heaped upon this man. They certainly did not believe him to be a prophet of God, and most particularly, did not believe it remotely possible that he could be the Christ of God, as he claimed. Though the Son of God dwelt among them for thirty years, they looked upon him with utter contempt. Why? Because it is ever the tendency of flesh and blood to disregard and even despise those things with which we are most familiar, even when those things are more valuable than silver and gold and vital to the welfare of our souls.

The Word of God, the preaching of the gospel, the ordinances of divine worship, when readily and abundantly available, are rarely truly cherished as things which are vital and more precious than all earthly things. It is more true with regard to these things than with anything else, that familiarity breeds contempt. Be warned. Such contempt will not go unnoticed by God (2 Chronicles 36:15, 16; Matthew 23:37, 38).

The Greatest Evil

"And he could there do no mighty work, save that he laid his hands upon a few sick folk, and healed them. And he marvelled because of their unbelief. And he went round about the villages, teaching" (vv. 5, 6).

The greatest, most astonishing evil in the world is the sin of unbelief. There are two statements in these two verses that must not be glossed over. First, we are told that our Lord could do no mighty work in Nazareth. Matthew tells us that the reason why he could do no mighty work there was the glaring, obstinate unbelief of the people who lived there (Matthew 13:58).

Our Lord could have done at Nazareth anything he desired to do. Do not imagine that the arm of omnipotence is halted or hindered by the unbelief of man! He could have given these people faith as easily as he has given us faith. The fact is these people did not so much as ask a favour of him. Thus, they received no favour from him. Because of their unbelief in the face of his manifest wisdom and power they were not given the grace and favour of the Lord working his wonders among them.

Our Lord "marvelled because of their unbelief". Twice we are told the Son of God marvelled. Only two things seem to have made an impression upon the God-man. He marvelled at the faith of those from whom no one would expect faith: the centurion and the Canaanite woman (Matthew 8:7-15, 15:21-28) and here Mark says, he "marvelled because of their unbelief". He marvelled at the unbelief of those in whom we might most naturally expect to find faith. Here are people who had been all their lives, from generation to generation, favoured with God's Word, the oracles of divine worship, even with the presence of the Son of God. Yet, they believed not on him!

The unbelief of those who enjoy and are favoured with the means of grace and the manifest saving power of Christ is truly as amazing as it is inexcusable. Unbelief is the oldest of all sins, the most common of all sins, the most inexcusable of all sins, and the most ruinous of all sins. Unbelief is blasphemy. Unbelief is the bold, brazen, suicidal assertion that God is a liar, the Son of God is a fake, and the Spirit of God is a delusion! Unbelief will be forever damning to the wicked!

It is not the lack of evidence that makes men and women unbelievers, nor the difficulties of Christian doctrine, nor the want of godliness, love, and mercy among believers, but their own unwillingness to trust the Lord of glory. Men and women vainly point at this and that as the reason for their unbelief. But the will not to believe on the Son of God arises from their love of sin, love of the world, and spiritual blindness. Yet, I hasten to add, the root of unbelief is never destroyed, even in God's saints, so long as we live in this world. "Lord, increase our faith ... I believe. Help thou mine unbelief"!

"And he called unto him the twelve, and began to send them forth by two and two; and gave them power over unclean spirits; And commanded them that they should take nothing for their journey, save a staff only; no scrip, no bread, no money in their purse: But be shod with sandals; and not put on two coats. And he said unto them, In what place soever ye enter into an house, there abide till ye depart from that place. And whosoever shall not receive you, nor hear you, when ye depart thence, shake off the dust under your feet for a testimony against them. Verily I say unto you, It shall be more tolerable for Sodom and Gomorrha in the day of judgment, than for that city. And they went out, and preached that men should repent. And they cast out many devils, and anointed with oil many that were sick, and healed them".

(Mark 6:7-13)

Chapter 23

The Calling Of The Twelve

All true gospel preachers, all who are called, gifted, and sent of God to preach the gospel are, like the Lord's chosen apostles, his messengers. God's servants are not just men who went off to Bible College or seminary and learned how to study, preach, and exercise the political savvy it takes to avoid ruffling the feathers of the wrong people. God's servants are messengers. They are men with a message from God. I want you to understand what I mean. One Sunday night, I said to our congregation:

"I am not here tonight merely to give you the facts recorded in this text. Any honest man, woman or child here who studies the passage carefully can give you the facts revealed and the doctrine taught in these verses. I have been studying this passage this week, seeking a message for your souls from God. I believe the Holy Spirit has given me a message to deliver to you."

Perhaps you are thinking, "Pastor, what is the difference between giving out a sermon, factually expounding a text or a doctrine, and delivering a message?" Let me tell you. If all I have is a sermon I have prepared, it really does not matter whether you are here to hear it or not. But, if I have come here with a message from God, a message fresh from God's heart, to my heart, for your heart, and you miss that, you've missed something! You have missed something that can never be repeated. You have lost something you can never regain. Tapes will not make up for it. You can put my words on tape; but you simply cannot put the Spirit of God on tape!

Do you understand what I am talking about? God's servants are messengers. This is what Paul said to the Corinthians, "Now then we are ambassadors for Christ, as though God did beseech you by us: we pray you in Christ's stead, be ye reconciled to God" (2 Corinthians 5:20). Our Lord Jesus is called "the Messenger of the Covenant" because he was commissioned by God the Father to fulfil the covenant as our Surety. He came into the world with a commission from God, with a specific work assigned to him as Jehovah's Servant. He came to save his people from their sins; and he did it.

Even so, every man who is called and sent of God into the work of the gospel has a commission from God, a work to do, a work which no other man can do, a unique work which he must do. He has a divine messianic mandate.

A commission is a mandate. A commission from God is a mandate from God almighty. I cannot imagine a nobler work or a greater and weightier burden of responsibility! Mark 6:7-13 describes the commissioning of the Apostles by our Lord Jesus Christ as his messengers. As our Lord Jesus, the King of Glory, sent out messengers (Apostles) from the beginning, so today he sends out messengers of mercy, calling sinners to repentance and rebels to surrender, with the promise of grace, salvation, and eternal life to all who obey the gospel they preach.

What Christ Did
First, look at and carefully consider what the Lord Jesus did, as the Holy Spirit describes it in this passage. Whenever we think about men and God, our Saviour and us, what we do and what he does, we would be wise first to find out what he has done. We cannot really understand what we do under his influence and for his glory until we understand something about what he has done and is doing for us, in us, and with us. So Mark first describes what the Lord Jesus Christ did for, in, and with these men, before telling us what they did for him.

He called his messengers. "And he called unto him the twelve". You will notice that Mark does not here name the twelve Apostles, as Matthew did in his account. That may be because he is giving a shorter account of the same event and had already listed the names in chapter three; or it may be that Mark is describing a different account of the sending out of the disciples. Be that as it may, I want you to notice this one thing. Men who are God's messengers to your soul, God's servants in this world, God's preachers are men who have been specifically called by Christ. Every true gospel preacher has a twofold call from Christ.

First, these men were called to Christ himself, as their Saviour and Lord (Mark 3:13-19). When first he called them to be his Apostles, these men had first been called into union and fellowship with the Lord himself. They must know him before they can make him known. They must sit at his feet before they can run on his errands. They must walk with him before they can represent him.

Before a man can be a preacher, he must be a believer. Before a man can be a leader of others, he must prove his faithfulness as a disciple. Before a man can teach, he must be taught. Before a man can be a messenger, he must get a message.

Then, after they had been some time in the Lord's company, the Lord Jesus called these men to be his Apostles, his messengers. As the prophetic office ceased with John the Baptist, so too, the apostolic office began and ceased with the twelve Apostles. There are no inspired prophets or apostles in

194

our day. We have the complete Revelation of God in his Word. Yet, every true gospel preacher is both a prophet, that is, a proclaimer of the gospel and an apostle, that is, a messenger of God.

Therefore, the things revealed in Mark 6:7-13 are in every detail applicable to us today, and specifically identify those men who are sent of God to preach the gospel.

This business of gospel preaching is not a chosen career, or a vocation for which a man volunteers his services, though every man called to the work chooses to do so and volunteers most willingly, counting such a call to be a great honour put upon him by God (Ephesians 3:8; 1 Timothy 1:12-17).

God's call upon a man is made manifest by the fact that the Lord God has put him into the ministry. There is no way a man can know that he has been called to Christ until he is brought to Christ. And there is no way a man can know that he is called to the work of the ministry until God puts him in the ministry. More often than not, those who wear the name "preacher" have simply assumed the name. They have entered their office untried, unproved, inexperienced, and uncalled. They have run without being sent. They have no message, no mandate from God. Therefore, they soon tire of the work, become over-burdened, get ulcers, have nervous breakdowns, burn out, and find something else to do.

Those men who are called of God to preach the gospel, to pastor a local church, or serve as a missionary are gifted for the work to which they are called. By the gift of God the Holy Spirit, they are "apt to teach". If a man is not gifted to teach the scriptures, he is not called to be a preacher. Those who are called are qualified by the grace of the Spirit for the work to which they are called (Jeremiah 3:15; 1 Timothy 3:1-7; Titus 1:1-9). If a man is not qualified for the work, he has not been called and gifted to perform the work of the gospel ministry.

Set Apart
And any man who is called of God to preach the gospel and pastor his people is doing the work. No man has been called of God to be a preacher who is not a preacher. No man has been called to be a missionary who is not a missionary. And no man has been called to be a pastor who is not a pastor. As my first pastor used to say to young men who presumed that God had called them into the work of the ministry, "God never made a possum that he didn't make a persimmon tree; and he never made a preacher that he didn't make a pulpit." Those who are called of the Lord to preach the gospel are sent by him. They are not waiting to be sent. They are sent. When the Master called these men, "He began to send them forth by two and two".

195

The word "send" that is used here is the verb form of the word "apostle". It means, to set apart, to send out on a mission, (not just to send out, but to send out on a mission), to send away, send forth, or set at liberty. God's servants are men who have been set apart for the work of the gospel by God's decree and God's call, sent out on a mission for God himself, sent away into the world as God's ambassadors, and set at liberty in their souls by the call and power of God residing in and upon them. They have been separated unto the gospel by God's call; and they separate themselves unto the gospel continually (Romans 1:1).

Two By Two
Mark was inspired to tell us specifically that our Master sent his disciples out in pairs of two. He sent them forth "by two and two". Neither Matthew nor Luke make mention of this fact; but the Holy Spirit inspired Mark to record it for us to teach us, no doubt, the advantages of serving Christ in the company of others. The wise man had a good reason for telling us that, "two are better than one" (Ecclesiastes 4:9). In most labours two men working together can do much more than one man alone, or two men working separately. Two men together assist one another in judgment and make fewer mistakes. They aid one another in difficulties, uphold one another in temptations, encourage one another in trials, and arouse one another in times of languishing. Two men together comfort one another and are less likely to be cast down.

It seems obvious to me that our Lord is teaching us a principle. God's servants are not free-lance, self-appointed apostles, who are answerable to no one. While a church is under the pastoral direction of one man, the work of the ministry is not one man's work. It is the work of the entire assembly. Moreover, it is our privilege and responsibility to, as much as possible, work together with other gospel churches and other gospel preachers.

The Apostle's words to the Hebrew Christians are applicable to us all: pastors, elders, deacons, teachers, and all believers. "Let us consider one another to provoke unto love and to good works: Not forsaking the assembling of ourselves together, as the manner of some is; but exhorting one another: and so much the more, as ye see the day approaching" (Hebrews 10:24, 25).

Power And Provision
Every man called by Christ to the work of the ministry is sent by Christ into his vineyard. Next we are told that our Lord gave power to his messengers. He "gave them power over unclean spirits". These men were commissioned to attack Satan's kingdom in the name of Christ. Therefore, they were equipped with the God given power that was necessary to do their work.

Their miraculous, apostolic power to cast demons out of men's bodies was an emblem and sign of the power of Christ and his gospel, which we preach, to bind the strong man armed in the City of Mansoul and cast him out. The gospel of Christ, the doctrine of the cross is "the power of God unto salvation".

In verses 8 and 9 the Lord Jesus expressly commanded his messengers to take nothing for their journey. To many, this seems to be insignificant and relatively meaningless. But nothing in this passage is more important, more instructive, or more needed than the instruction given to gospel preachers in these two verses.

"And commanded them that they should take nothing for their journey, save a staff only; no scrip, no bread, no money in their purse: But be shod with sandals; and not put on two coats".

There is no discrepancy in the fact that in Matthew we are told that our Lord forbade his servants from taking staves for their journey and that here Mark tells us he told them to "take nothing for their journey save a staff only". That which seems to be a contradiction to some is explained very easily in two ways: first, they were not allowed to carry two staves, which would be a needless encumbrance; but it was perfectly proper to carry one staff, which might be a very useful instrument. Second, though they might not be allowed to carry staves for their protection and defence, they were allowed to carry a staff for their assistance in walking.

The doctrine taught in verses 8 and 9 needs to be taught with emphatic clarity in our day. The doctrine of these two verses is as plain as the nose on your face. There is nothing mysterious about it. Yet, it is almost universally ignored by churches and preachers. Three things are here taught; and these three things are taught throughout the Word of God.

Gospel preachers must take great care not to be, or appear to be, covetous, self-serving, worldly men, men who enrich themselves by the ministry.

Gospel preachers are not to provide for their own livelihood, or entangle themselves with the affairs of this life, but to give themselves wholly and entirely to the business of study, prayer, and preaching.

Gospel preachers are to be provided for by those to whom they minister, provided for by local churches in a manner comfortable enough to keep them from the mundane concerns of feeding, clothing, educating, and properly caring for their families.

John Gill was exactly right in his exposition of these verses. He wrote:

> A minister of the Gospel ought not to be a worldly minded
> man, (a man) that minds earth and earthly things, and seeks to
> amass wealth and riches to himself, and preaches for filthy

lucre's sake. Neither should he be a sensual and voluptuous man, serving his own belly, and not the Lord Jesus Christ, feeding himself, and not the flock. Nor should he be filled with worldly cares, overwhelmed in worldly business, and entangled with the affairs of this life. He ought to have his mind free from all solicitude and anxious concern, about a subsistence for himself and his, so that he may with greater and more close application attend to his ministry, to preparations for it, and the performance of it; and give up himself entirely to the Word and prayer, and not have his mind distracted with other things. Upon which account it is highly necessary, that the people to whom he ministers should take care, that a sufficient provision be made for him; that he may live without any anxious care and thought about such things, and his mind be more intent about the work he is called unto. This is what our Lord chiefly designs by all this, who has ordained that they that preach the Gospel, should be comfortably provided for, and live of it; and which, as it makes for the peace of their minds that minister, it issues in the advantage of those who are ministered to.

In verse 10 the Lord Jesus specifically told these first gospel preachers how they were to be provided for as they served him. "And he said unto them, In what place soever ye enter into an house, there abide till ye depart from that place". As they went about from place to place, they were, according to Matthew, forbidden to ask anyone for anything. They were not to go from house to house. God's servants are not grovelling beggars! They are the servants of the most high God, the King of glory! Not only does our Lord forbid begging, he commands his servants not to provide anything for themselves. Yet, he tells them, as they serve him, to live, and expect to live upon the generosity and hospitality of those to whom they preach the gospel.

Proud men do not like to live upon the generosity of others. And miserly men do not like to generously provide for others. But gospel preachers are to be comfortably supported in their labours by the generous, voluntary, free gifts of those whose souls are served by them. "If we have sown unto you spiritual things, is it a great thing if we shall reap your carnal things?" (1 Corinthians 9:11). "Even so hath the Lord ordained that they which preach the gospel should live of the gospel" (1 Corinthians 9:14). "Let him that is taught in the word communicate unto him that teacheth in all good things" (Galatians 6:6).

God's servants ought to be, and faithful men will be, content to live upon the provision God supplies through the generosity of his people.

While these apostles were in a house, as long as they were there, they lived according to the ability of the household to provide for them. That is the idea conveyed by our Lord's words. If a man pastors poor people, he should not seek to live above the people he serves. If there are ten families in a congregation who are willing to support a pastor and give of their means no more than a tithe, the pastor and his family ought to be able to live on what those other families live on. If a man pastors a wealthier congregation, they ought to provide more comfortably for him; but he should never take more than he needs. In either case there is no need for the gospel preacher to maintain a side job and give himself "part-time" to the work of the ministry. Our God deserves better than our left over time!

It is true, when the Apostle Paul preached at Corinth, and among other Gentiles, he made tents to support himself and his companions. But a few things need to be remembered about that. Paul did not make tents to enrich himself, but to provide for his expenses and the expenses of those preachers travelling with him. The fact that Paul laboured with his hands was a fact for which the Church at Corinth ought to have been embarrassed and ashamed. It is the Apostle Paul, more than any writer in the entire Bible, who deals with and insists upon the necessity of pastors and missionaries being supported by God's people. This much is certain: If God almighty sends a man out as his ambassador, he will more than sufficiently provide for him and his household (Luke 22:35).

A Great Responsibility

In verse 11 our Lord shows us what an awesome thing it is to be privileged to hear the gospel. "And whosoever shall not receive you, nor hear you, when ye depart thence, shake off the dust under your feet for a testimony against them. Verily I say unto you, It shall be more tolerable for Sodom and Gomorrha in the day of judgment, than for that city".

To receive an ambassador is to receive the king who sent him, the king he represents. To reject an ambassador is to reject the king who sent him. This is our Lord's teaching, not mine (Matthew 10:40-42). To receive Christ's servant and the gospel of the grace of God which he preaches is to receive Christ himself. But to reject, despise, or ignore God's servant and his message is to reject, despise, and ignore God himself! That is the most horrible crime and offence against God in the universe. Not even the wickedness of Sodom and Gomorrah rivals the wickedness of wilful unbelief!

199

Commenting on verse eleven, J. C. Ryle said, "One of the greatest sins a man can commit in the sight of God is to hear the Gospel of Christ and not believe it ... To reject the Gospel will sink a man to the lowest place in hell". That is exactly what the Apostle Paul stated in 2 Corinthians 2:14-16.

"Now thanks be unto God, which always causeth us to triumph in Christ, and maketh manifest the savour of his knowledge by us in every place. For we are unto God a sweet savour of Christ, in them that are saved, and in them that perish: To the one we are the savour of death unto death; and to the other the savour of life unto life. And who is sufficient for these things?"

What The Disciples Did
Now, look at verses 12 and 13, and see what the disciples did. "And they went out, and preached that men should repent. And they cast out many devils, and anointed with oil many that were sick, and healed them".

Matthew Henry wrote, "Though they were conscious to themselves of great weakness, and expected no secular advantage by it, yet, in obedience to their Master's order, and in dependence upon his strength, they went out as Abraham, not knowing whither they went." These men, like all God's messengers today, went out into the world preaching exactly what they had experienced, what they had been taught, and what the Master himself preached, namely, repentance. Repentance is a change of mind about myself, my sin, that is, my nature; my sins, that is, my wicked acts, and my righteousnesses or those filthy rags by which lost sinners hope to win God's favour. Repentance is a change of masters and a change of motives. It is the turning of our hearts to Christ.

True repentance is inseparably connected with a proper view of God, a revelation and knowledge of the person and work of the Lord Jesus Christ; his eternal deity, his glorious humanity, his effectual accomplishments; right views about holiness; right views about sin; and right views about justice. Repentance is the gift of God, the result of the new birth (Jeremiah 31:19). It is the fruit of faith's look at the crucified Son of God (Zechariah 12:10).

The Apostles anointed with oil many that were sick. They did not anoint all who were sick, but many. Oil, as you know, throughout the scriptures, is a symbol of God the Holy Spirit, who was yet to be given in his office capacity. While the ceremony of anointing with oil may not be practiced by faithful men today, the thing symbolized is keenly understood by them all. Without the blessing, unction, and anointing of God the Holy Spirit, our labour is utterly vain and meaningless. Only God the Holy Spirit can make the labour of his servants in the gospel effectual to the healing of sin-sick souls.

We must not fail to see that all who were anointed with oil were also healed. So it is now. All who are anointed by and given the unction of God the Holy Spirit in regeneration are effectually healed by God's sovereign grace, by the application of Christ's sin-atoning blood and his saving power. Christ is that sweet Balm of Gilead, by whom our souls are healed.

Have you repented? Our Saviour declares, "Except ye repent, ye shall all likewise perish"! It is not enough to have our creed right. Our hearts must be right. It is not enough to know truth. It must be experienced. Behold the crucified Son of God, now risen from the dead and seated upon the right hand of the majesty on high, and repent (Lamentations 1:12; 2 Corinthians 5:20, 21). May God grant you repentance, for Christ's sake!

"And king Herod heard of him; (for his name was spread abroad:) and he said, That John the Baptist was risen from the dead, and therefore mighty works do shew forth themselves in him. Others said, That it is Elias. And others said, That it is a prophet, or as one of the prophets. But when Herod heard thereof, he said, It is John, whom I beheaded: he is risen from the dead. For Herod himself had sent forth and laid hold upon John, and bound him in prison for Herodias' sake, his brother Philip's wife: for he had married her. For John had said unto Herod, It is not lawful for thee to have thy brother's wife. Therefore Herodias had a quarrel against him, and would have killed him; but she could not: For Herod feared John, knowing that he was a just man and an holy, and observed him; and when he heard him, he did many things, and heard him gladly. And when a convenient day was come, that Herod on his birthday made a supper to his lords, high captains, and chief estates of Galilee; And when the daughter of the said Herodias came in, and danced, and pleased Herod and them that sat with him, the king said unto the damsel, Ask of me whatsoever thou wilt, and I will give it thee. And he sware unto her, Whatsoever thou shalt ask of me, I will give it thee, unto the half of my kingdom. And she went forth, and said unto her mother, What shall I ask? And she said, The head of John the Baptist. And she came in straightway with haste unto the king, and asked, saying, I will that thou give me by and by in a charger the head of John the Baptist. And the king was exceeding sorry; yet for his oath's sake, and for their sakes which sat with him, he would not reject her. And immediately the king sent an executioner, and commanded his head to be brought: and he went and beheaded him in the prison, And brought his head in a charger, and gave it to the damsel: and the damsel gave it to her mother. And when his disciples heard of it, they came and took up his corpse, and laid it in a tomb"

(Mark 6:14-29)

Chapter 24

John The Baptist Beheaded

We have before us Mark's divinely inspired account of the cruel, barbaric murder of God's faithful servant, John the Baptist. I have never understood why so many seem to be ashamed to wear the name Baptist, when it was so honourably worn by John, the first Baptist. I count it an honour to wear the name he wore and pray for grace to walk in his steps until my work on this earth is done. Mark tells the melancholy story of John's slaughter by Herod in greater detail than either Matthew or Luke. Always read it with the reverence it deserves, praying that God the Holy Spirit will graciously seal to our hearts the lessons it contains.

Human Depravity

Here we are given a very plain display of humanity. As we read these verses, we cannot avoid the fact that the human race is fallen, sinful, and utterly depraved. We do not like to acknowledge that fact, because such an acknowledgement forces us to acknowledge our own depravity. Yet, the wickedness of Herod, Herodias, and her daughter is the wickedness of your heart and mine (Matthew 15:19, 20). How savage, cruel, and barbaric proud man is! Rather than lose face before men, Herod had a man he knew to be innocent of any crime, a man he believed to be the servant of God, beheaded! And the evil one man is capable of performing every man is capable of performing. I hope we truly recognize that fact. Robert Hawker rightly observed, "Until this is feelingly known in the heart, never will the infinitely precious redemption by the Lord Jesus Christ be understood or valued." The seeds of sin are the same in every heart, because of the sin and fall of our father Adam. Until the Spirit of God convinces us of that fact, we will never know and acknowledge that it is Christ alone who puts a difference between Israel and Egypt, between his chosen and the world (1 Corinthians 4:7).

Man's Conscience

Herod's conscience was so tormenting to him, after the murder of John the Baptist, that when he heard about the miracles the Lord Jesus performed, he was terrified at the thought that John had come back from the dead to destroy him. How completely unimaginable the everlasting torments of the damned must be in hell, where the gnawing worm of a guilty conscience never dies!

God has not left himself without a witness, even in the depraved hearts of fallen men. A sinner's conscience is an amazing thing. Like the rest of our nature, our consciences are depraved and sinful. Yet, truth has an amazing power over the consciences of men. King Herod was afraid of John the Baptist, in life and even after he had been dead for some time, the memory of the Baptist preacher and the sound of his voice tormented him still.

Herod feared John the Baptist. Felix trembled as he listened to Paul preach the gospel. Agrippa was "almost persuaded", as the imprisoned preacher reasoned with him about the things of God. Fallen and depraved as man is there is within him a voice called conscience, a voice that either accuses or excuses him, a persistent voice that cannot be silenced, a voice that can make even great and powerful kings tremble. This voice, the conscience, is one of many things that distinguish men from beasts. The conscience is, or is at least the reflection and result of the law of God written upon the hearts of all men by their Creator. The conscience may be temporarily quietened by many things. But the only thing that can purge a guilty conscience is the blood of Christ. What it takes to speak peace to the troubled conscience it takes to satisfy the law of God, the sin-atoning sacrifice of God's dear Son.

Herod was a vile and wicked man. Luke tells us that John reproved him for all the wickedness he had done, though Matthew and Mark mention only the two most notable, obvious, commonly known things practised by the king. Herod was guilty of incest and adultery. He had taken his brother Philip's wife, divorcing his own, and publicly flaunted his sordid behaviour.

According to Josephus, the Jewish historian, and quoted by John Gill, the situation was this: "Herod being sent for to Rome, called at his brother Philip's by the way, where he fell into an amorous intrigue with his wife, and agreed, upon his return, to take her with him and marry her; as he accordingly did, and divorced his own wife, who was daughter of Aretas, king of Arabia Petraea; which occasioned a war between Herod and his wife's father, in which the former was beaten".

God's Faithful Servant

For these public disgraces, these public displays of contempt for God's holy law, John publicly reproved the king. "For John had said unto Herod, It is not lawful for thee to have thy brother's wife". In doing so, this faithful man stands as an example and pattern for every gospel preacher to follow. In this day and age, when everyone, from the White House to the wash house, is advocating and promoting homosexuality, lesbianism, fornication, and adultery, those things are still brazen, contemptuous violations of God's law, "for which things' sake the wrath of God cometh upon the children of disobedience". Those who live in such debauchery not only bring upon themselves the wrath of God, they continually demoralize society, teaching all who are under their influence to disregard God. They wreck families for generations to come.

John the Baptist, when called to preach in the king's court, spoke to Herod, Herodias, and the assembled crowd, with the courage and boldness of a lion pursuing a lamb. He did not smooth his words, soften his language, or try to find a way to get out of telling Herod what God required him to say.

Many men, like Balaam, try to serve both God and their own bellies. They do not exactly lie to men. They do not exactly deny Christ and the gospel of his grace. However, they try to make the gospel palatable to unregenerate men by stating things very carefully so that they do not offend their hearers. Some men call such behaviour wisdom. I call it compromise and treason. That man who serves Christ, that man who is led by and filled with the Holy Spirit carefully words his message to expose man's sin and enmity against God, probe his conscience, and demand that he acknowledge and bow to the truth of God (Acts 4:5-12).

God's servant, John the Baptist, was faithful in his preaching and faithful in his behaviour. Herod knew that "he was a just man and an holy, and observed him; and when he heard him, he did many things, and heard him gladly". The Spirit of God tells us, "A bishop then must be blameless, the husband of one wife, vigilant, sober, of good behaviour, given to hospitality, apt to teach" (1 Timothy 1:2). God's servants must, for the gospel's sake, live as blameless men in a crooked and perverse generation. I do not mean that God's servants are perfect in their behaviour. They are not. They do not claim to be. Neither do I suggest that wicked men will acknowledge and wilfully honour faithful preachers. They seldom do. However, God requires that those men who preach the gospel behave in such a manner as not to give men a reason to hold them in contempt, or give God's enemies occasion to blaspheme. Herod did not repent of his sin, but he knew that John the Baptist was God's man; blameless in his behaviour, just and holy.

Point of Rebellion
Herod also demonstrates the fact that God always meets sinners at their point of rebellion and demands surrender. People may go far and do much in the exercise of religion and yet miss Christ and his salvation, because they refuse to yield at their point of rebellion. Herod went further than many. We are told that he "feared John". He "observed" him and "knew that he was a just man and holy". He "heard him gladly" and was moved in response to his preaching. However, there was one thing Herod would not do. He would not give up Herodias. He would not give up his adultery. He is in hell today.

Let all be warned. We will either bow to Christ at our point of rebellion, or we will perish in our sins under the wrath of God. Christ demands surrender. Naaman had to dip in the Jordan seven times, or die as a leper. Herod had to give up Herodias or perish. And you and I will either surrender to Christ as Lord at that very spot where we most ardently desire to have our own way, or we will perish in hell.

We must keep back nothing. It is better far to cut off your right arm and pluck out your right eye, and enter into the kingdom of God halt and blind than to go to hell with them. It is not enough that a person admire his favourite preacher and hear him gladly. Christ demands the surrender of our hearts and lives to his dominion as our Lord (Luke 14:25-33).

Often Despised
Another thing displayed in this passage is the fact that those who will not hear God's messenger often become his implacable enemy. As Herodias sat beside Herod and heard John, she was seething. No doubt, she hid her anger, smiled politely, and may have even said, as John greeted her at the door, "You sure stepped on our toes today". But from that moment, she was John's resolved enemy, determined to destroy him if she could. Like a cat watching a bird, she waited for her opportunity to kill him.

We must never be surprised when faithful men are vilified by those who hate God. Elijah was accused of being the cause of Israel's troubles. Ahab hated Micaiah, because he never prophesied good things to him, but only evil. And Herodias hated John the Baptist, because he exposed her adultery.

You can mark it down as a matter of certainty, when a man or woman suddenly turns against a preacher, though he or she may not know how, when, or where it happened, that preacher has, by his faithful preaching of the gospel, stuck his finger right in the sore spot of their hearts and exposed their sin.

It is no disgrace to a preacher to be unpopular, disliked, and evil spoken of by men. It is not an honour, but a dishonour for a preacher to be applauded by the community. Our Lord said to his disciples, "Woe unto you when all men speak well of you"! We must never forget it.

Dangerous Revelling
Herod threw a big birthday party for himself. Everybody who was anybody was there. The place was crowded with people, eating, drinking, dancing, and having a good time in "harmless" fun. But when the "harmless" fun was over, lying in the queen's lap was the head of John the Baptist on a silver platter!

Herodias and her daughter knew what a weakness Herod had for women. So the queen sent her daughter in to do a striptease act before Herod. When his passions were hot, in a moment of unguarded excitement, the king made a ridiculous oath publicly. He promised the stripper anything she requested, up to half his kingdom. Now, she had him where she wanted him. Herod was backed into a corner from which he could not extricate himself without embarrassment. And, rather than shame himself before all those important people, he did something that haunted him until his last breath, something that continues to torment soul in hell today. On a whim he murdered John the Baptist, a just and holy man who had been faithful to his soul!

Perhaps you are thinking, "What's the point?" The point is just this: People sometimes do things at times of great revelling when passions are high that they normally would not do. Things they regret for the rest of their lives. We would be wise always to avoid giving space to the devil. We would be wise never to willingly put ourselves in the place of temptation. Mischief and misery often follow the "harmless" pleasures of this world.

Young people often wonder why their parents refuse to allow them to go to the parties all their friends get to attend, why they refuse to let them run around all hours of the night, why they do not seem to trust them to always do what is right. It is because they know what can happen when passions are high. None of us knows what we are capable of doing. Mischief and misery often follow the "harmless" pleasures of this world.

A Better World

Our best things are yet to come. We must never look for good in or from this world. John the Baptist was beheaded. Stephen was stoned to death. The apostles were imprisoned, tortured, and cruelly murdered. This was the world's "thank you" to those faithful men, of whom the world was not worthy, for their labours. The histories of these men are meant to remind us that our reward is not here. Our rest, our crown, our wages, our reward is on the other side of the grave. "If in this life only we have hope in Christ, we are of all men most miserable"!

There is a day of retribution, a time of reaping. There is a glorious harvest yet to come. The value of Christianity is not to be measured by the things of this world, of time, or that are seen. We are moving rapidly to a better world; and Heaven will make amends for all! "For I reckon that the sufferings of this present time are not worthy to be compared with the glory which shall be revealed in us". "As it is written, Eye hath not seen, nor ear heard, neither have entered into the heart of man, the things which God hath prepared for them that love him". "For our light affliction, which is but for a moment, worketh for us a far more exceeding and eternal weight of glory".

"And the apostles gathered themselves together unto Jesus, and told him all things, both what they had done, and what they had taught. And he said unto them, Come ye yourselves apart into a desert place, and rest a while: for there were many coming and going, and they had no leisure so much as to eat. And they departed into a desert place by ship privately. And the people saw them departing, and many knew him, and ran afoot thither out of all cities, and outwent them, and came together unto him. And Jesus, when he came out, saw much people, and was moved with compassion toward them, because they were as sheep not having a shepherd: and he began to teach them many things. And when the day was now far spent, his disciples came unto him, and said, This is a desert place, and now the time is far passed: Send them away, that they may go into the country round about, and into the villages, and buy themselves bread: for they have nothing to eat. He answered and said unto them, Give ye them to eat. And they say unto him, Shall we go and buy two hundred pennyworth of bread, and give them to eat? He saith unto them, How many loaves have ye? go and see. And when they knew, they say, Five, and two fishes. And he commanded them to make all sit down by companies upon the green grass. And they sat down in ranks, by hundreds, and by fifties. And when he had taken the five loaves and the two fishes, he looked up to heaven, and blessed, and brake the loaves, and gave them to his disciples to set before them; and the two fishes divided he among them all. And they did all eat, and were filled. And they took up twelve baskets full of the fragments, and of the fishes. And they that did eat of the loaves were about five thousand men. And straightway he constrained his disciples to get into the ship, and to go to the other side before unto Bethsaida, while he sent away the people. And when he had sent them away, he departed into a mountain to pray".

(Mark 6:30-46)

Chapter 25

"They Have Nothing To Eat"

In verse 36 we are told of this great multitude, "They have nothing to eat". That is a good description of us. Hungry sinners come to Christ with nothing to eat. We have nothing. We can provide nothing for ourselves. We have tried to feed our souls on the swine husks of materialism, ritualism, ceremonialism, and even licentiousness, but found nothing to satisfy our souls! So we come to Christ, hungry and thirsty, having nothing to eat.

Yet, before the day was over, we read that five thousand men (not including women and children), "did all eat, and were filled". Not only did the Son of God feed five thousand men with five loaves and two fish, when everyone had eaten all he wanted, the disciples took up twelve baskets full of fragments! May God the Holy Spirit teach us the meaning of this great miracle and the lessons contained in this passage. Christ alone is able to feed and satisfy immortal souls. May we ever be fed by him and fed upon him, who is the Bread of Life, fed to the satisfaction of our souls.

Christ's Servants

First, Mark was inspired to describe the conduct of Christ's servants when they returned from their first preaching mission. "And the apostles gathered themselves together unto Jesus, and told him all things, both what they had done, and what they had taught" (v. 30). These are instructive words. Every servant of God should do exactly what these Apostles did. When preparing to preach, they must seek a message from the Master. While preaching, they must seek the Lord's power, wisdom, grace, and strength. When the message is done, they must report back to the Master, tell him all they have done and taught in his name, and seek his Spirit to make their labours effectual.

In the work of the ministry nothing is so important as prayer. Prayer moves him who moves heaven and earth. Prayer displays faith in and dependence upon Christ. Let every gospel preacher be diligent in study, devoted in labour, and ardent in preaching. But the secret of power in the pulpit is prayer. Blessed is that church with a praying pastor, who knows he cannot preach without the power of God's Spirit, who cries with Ezekiel, "Come from the four winds, O breath, and breathe upon these slain, that they may live" (Ezekiel 37:9). He is a faithful pastor, he is a faithful servant of God who gives himself to "prayer and the ministry of the Word" (Acts 6:4).

Christ's Instruction

Second, I want to show you Christ's instruction to these faithful disciples who had been ministering to the souls of men. "And he said unto them, Come ye yourselves apart into a desert place, and rest a while: for there were many coming and going, and they had no leisure so much as to eat. And they departed into a desert place by ship privately" (vv. 31, 32).

I realize that there are very few who need instruction about the necessity of rest and relaxation. There are very few who are so zealously devoted to the work of the gospel that they do not even have time to sit down for a meal. Yet, for those few who are so devoted, our Lord's words here are very needful. It is said, "We must come apart for a while, or we will come apart".

The work of the ministry is, to a faithful man, a matter of tremendous labour. It is a labour of the heart and mind, involving the entire life of a man (Romans 1:1; 2 Corinthians 11:28). Yet, while constantly ministering to the souls of others, faithful men are in great danger of neglecting their own souls (Song of Solomon 1:6).

J. C. Ryle wrote, "The prosperity of a man's ministry and public work is intimately bound up with the prosperity of his own soul." Our Lord knows that we carry the treasure of his gospel in earthen vessels. He knows that we are only weak, frail mortals compassed with many infirmities. If it is not abused, occasional times of rest, reflection, relaxation, and recuperation are very useful and beneficial. We must never become so encumbered with doing things for Christ and serving him that we fail to take the time to sit quietly at his feet and hear his Word. Our loving Master does not require more than we can do. It is better to do little and do it well than to do much and do it haphazardly.

Christ's Compassion

Third, in verses 33 and 34 we are given a glimpse of Christ's compassion. "And the people saw them departing, and many knew him, and ran afoot thither out of all cities, and outwent them, and came together unto him. And Jesus, when he came out, saw much people, and was moved with compassion toward them, because they were as sheep not having a shepherd: and he began to teach them many things".

Our dear Saviour was moved with compassion as he beheld the multitudes. Thousands stood before him "as sheep not having a shepherd". They had plenty of priests, but not from God. They had preachers, but none after God's own heart, to feed them with knowledge and understanding. They had prophets in abundance; but they were prophets of deceit. They had religious forms and ceremonies, traditions and customs, devotion and zeal; but "they had nothing to eat". Their form of godliness was empty and meaningless. They knew nothing of the power of godliness, nothing of the gospel. Their religion was all husk. Thousands of immortal souls stood before our Lord Jesus, ignorant, helpless, needy and on the high road to hell. Angry as he was when denouncing the Scribes and Pharisees who should have taught the people the way of life, when our Lord beheld the perishing multitudes, he was ever "moved with compassion toward them". How often we read that our Saviour was "moved with compassion" toward those who stood before him as he walked through the earth (Matthew 9:36; 14:14; 15:32; 20:34; Mark 1:41; 5:19; 8:2; Luke 7:13; 10:33; 15:20).

When our Lord saw the sick, "he was moved with compassion toward them, and healed them". When he saw these thousands of people out in a desert place, ready to faint for hunger, he was moved with compassion for them and fed them. This great feature in our Lord's character can never be remembered too often, esteemed too highly, or declared too frequently. The movement of his heart toward the sick and needy before him shows us how tender and affectionate our Saviour was and is. How often we read of our Saviour's compassion toward men! These words are not given to fill up space. They are written in the Book of God because the Lord God intends for us to understand that he who is our God is a God full of compassion! God the Holy Spirit intends for us to know and be assured of the tenderness of Christ's love to his own. His are the mercies and compassions of a man who is himself God. The tender mercies of the eternal God flow to chosen sinners through the God-man Christ Jesus.

The mercies and compassions of our God and Saviour are the mercies and compassions of God, for he is "over all, God blessed for ever". But they are no less the mercies and compassions of the Man Christ Jesus, for, "verily, He took not on him the nature of Angels, but he took on him the seed of Abraham, that he might be a merciful and faithful High Priest in things pertaining to God, to make reconciliation for the sins of the people". In Christ Jesus, the God-man, our Saviour, there is both an infinite fulness of mercy and a tenderness of feeling (the tenderness of perfect manhood) toward his redeemed. Being full of compassion, he forgives our iniquity and destroys us not, turns away his anger, and stirs not up all his wrath (Psalm 78:38).

The word, "compassion", is very expressive. It means, as Spurgeon put it, "His whole being was stirred to its lowest depth, and therefore he proceeded at once to work miracles of mercy among them". He knew that many in the crowd had no faith in him and no love for him. They followed him because of curiosity, because the crowds went after him, or because they wanted to see a miracle. Yet, our Master pitied them. All were fed. All were relieved. All were filled.

Let no one ever question the gracious character of our God and Saviour (Exodus 34:6). He "delighteth in mercy" (Micah 7:18). Let all who profess to be followers of Christ follow him in his example of mercy and compassion (John 13:25; Galatians 6:1, 2; Ephesians 4:32-5:1; James 1:27). J. C. Ryle rightly urges, "Let us never forget that our Lord is the same yesterday, today, and forever. He never changes. High in heaven, at God's right hand, He still looks with compassion on the children of men. He still pities the ignorant, and them that are gone out of the way."

Being "moved with compassion toward them", our Saviour not only healed the sick and fed them, but also "began to teach them many things". I have no doubt at all what he taught them. He taught these people the same, blessed gospel he taught everywhere else: their need of grace, the necessity and nature of the new birth, the purpose of his coming, the wonders of redemption by his blood, and the blessedness of repentance and faith.

Here is a place for personal examination. We must not attempt to examine and judge one another; but we must examine and judge ourselves, lest we be judged with the world. Am I like my Saviour, tenderly concerned for and moved with compassion toward perishing sinners? Do I really care for eternity bound men and women? Am I willing and ready to meet and minister to the needs of those around me? These are serious questions. Do not answer them in haste. We ought to look upon ourselves as Paul did, as debtors to all men. We ought to use every means to preach the gospel to eternity bound men and women. We ought to give willingly for the spread of the gospel throughout the world. If the definition of a Christian is one who is Christ-like, it must be concluded that anyone who is not moved with compassion toward the souls of men is not a Christian.

Christ's Patience

Verses 35 and 36 give us another display of Christ's patience. "And when the day was now far spent, his disciples came unto him, and said, This is a desert place, and now the time is far passed: Send them away, that they may go into the country round about, and into the villages, and buy themselves bread: for they have nothing to eat".

These disciples were so much like us! Rather than trusting the Lord to do what was best, they presumed they knew best. They judged by what they could see; it was well past the time for supper, the people had nothing to eat, they were a long way from town, and the crowd was hungry. They said to the Lord Jesus, "Send them away to get something to eat." They leaned on their own understanding, rather than trusting the Lord. Yet, the Lord Jesus was so patient! How much like them we are! Yet, the Lord Jesus is patient!

212

Christ's Power

Christ's power as God is manifestly displayed in the miracle recorded in verses 37-44. Our Lord Jesus fed five thousand men, besides women and children, with five loaves and two fish. We are distinctly told that the crowd had nothing to eat. There was one boy in the bunch who had just these five loaves and two small fish with him. These were put into the Master's hands. With them, the Lord Jesus fed many thousand people. Then after dinner the disciples took up twelve baskets full of fragments. What a banquet! We would be wise to store up the facts here revealed in our hearts and minds, so that we may remember them in times of need.

He who is our Saviour is also God our Creator, one whose power to protect and provide for us is the power of omnipotence. He does not need us to do anything; but he graciously condescends to use such things as we are in the accomplishment of his miracles of mercy.

Those five loaves and two small fish were insignificant. Such a little could never feed such a crowd, but it did! That boy's lunch was insignificant until it was put in the hands of the Son of God. The lad could never have dreamed of feeding a multitude that day, perhaps numbering twenty thousand people, but he did!

What is given to Christ is never wasted, lost or even diminished, but only increases. That which was given was very little, but what was done with it was very great. The lad did not give much; but he gave what he could. He gave all he had at the time; and God honoured his gift. There are lessons to be learned here about giving. "Honour the LORD with thy substance, and with the firstfruits of all thine increase: So shall thy barns be filled with plenty, and thy presses shall burst out with new wine" (Proverbs 3:9, 10).

"This I say, He which soweth sparingly shall reap also sparingly; and he which soweth bountifully shall reap also bountifully. Every man according as he purposeth in his heart, so let him give; not grudgingly, or of necessity: for God loveth a cheerful giver. And God is able to make all grace abound toward you; that ye, always having all sufficiency in all things, may abound to every good work: (As it is written, He hath dispersed abroad; he hath given to the poor: his righteousness remaineth for ever. Now he that ministereth seed to the sower both minister bread for your food, and multiply your seed sown, and increase the fruits of your righteousness;) Being enriched in every thing to all bountifulness, which causeth through us thanksgiving to God" (2 Corinthians 9:6-11). "Let him that is taught in the word communicate unto him that teacheth in all good things. Be not deceived; God is not mocked: for whatsoever a man soweth, that shall he also reap. For he that soweth to his flesh shall of the flesh reap corruption; but he that soweth to the Spirit shall of the Spirit reap life everlasting. And let us not be weary in well doing: for in due season we shall reap, if we faint not. As we have therefore opportunity, let us do good unto all men, especially unto them who are of the household of faith" (Galatians 6:6-10). "Give, and it shall be given unto you; good measure, pressed down, and shaken together, and running over, shall men give into your bosom. For with the same measure that ye mete withal it shall be measured to you again" (Luke 6:38).

Christ's Provision
In verse 42 we are given an example of Christ's provision. "And they did all eat, and were filled". I am told the Jews did not consider it a meal unless everyone had all he wanted, and looked upon it as a shameful embarrassment if there was not a good amount left over after everyone had eaten his fill.

Be that as it may, this is certain: All who feed at Christ's banqueting table are well fed! His provisions of grace are infinitely bountiful. His redemption is "plenteous redemption". His righteousness is righteousness enough for our souls. His forgiveness is infinite forgiveness. His peace is "peace that passeth understanding". The life he gives is abundant, eternal life. His grace is super-abounding grace! Like his grace, our Saviour's provisions of providence are overflowing with goodness. Robert Hawker wrote:

> If from a few loaves and fishes the Lord Christ made such a supply for so great a multitude, and left such an over plus, think, what infinite resources are with our God, for every occasion, to both the spiritual, and temporal necessities of his chosen? Very blessed is the apostle's conclusion on this point, when he saith; 'But my God shall supply all your need, according to his riches in glory by Christ Jesus.'

Those who drink at his well always find it full. Those who feed from his barrel of meal find bread enough and to spare. Those who dip their cups in his supply of oil have their vessels filled. The only empty vessel is the vessel not brought to him (Psalms 34:7-10; 37:23-25; Luke 22:35). That has been my experience. I have lacked nothing. Have you?

Christ's Conduct
Our Lord constrained his disciples to take a ship to Bethsaida, knowing full well that he was sending them into the eye of a terrible storm. "And straightway he constrained his disciples to get into the ship, and to go to the other side before unto Bethsaida, while he sent away the people. And when he had sent them away, he departed into a mountain to pray" (vv. 45, 46). He

214

sent his beloved disciples into the storm deliberately. Then, he came to them and made himself known, in the storm, in a way that they could not have known him otherwise. He brought them safely through the storm.

When he had sent his disciples away, the Lord Jesus went up into a mountain to pray. What a picture that is! Child of God, your Saviour, your Master, your Lord has sent you through many a storm and will yet send you through many more. Sometimes he acts as if he will pass you by and leave you in the storm; but he never does. He who sent you into the storm has gone up into the high mountain of heaven. There he prays for you and makes intercession on your behalf before the throne of God (John 17:6-19, 25, 26).

The Gospel

This miracle serves as a beautiful and clear allegory of the gospel of God's grace. We must never attempt to make allegories where the Holy Spirit does not make them. We must never try to make the scriptures say what they obviously do not say. But just as Paul used Sarah and Hagar as an allegory to teach the distinction between law and grace (Galatians 4), so the Holy Spirit has given us these recorded miracles to teach us spiritual, gospel truths.

This hungry multitude in a desert place is a good representation of lost mankind in this world. All the sons of Adam are an assembly of perishing souls, lost, helpless, starving, and upon the verge of eternal ruin, without the gospel of Christ. There is but a breath between them and everlasting ruin. Their only hope of salvation is the gospel of Christ (Romans 1:15, 16). The loaves and fishes, despised as inadequate to meet the needs of so many, might well be looked upon as representing the preaching of the gospel, Jesus Christ and him crucified, which God has ordained for the saving of his elect (1 Corinthians 1:21-23; John 6:33). Like the loaves and fish, the preaching of the cross of Christ meets all the spiritual needs of sinners in this world.

The disciples' passing out the loaves and fishes to the crowd shows us the sphere of human instrumentality. I cannot make loaves and fish; but I can bring my lunch to the Master. I cannot multiply the loaves and fish; but I can pass them out. I cannot save anyone or do anything to help anyone get saved; but I can preach the gospel to eternity bound sinners. And what I can do, and have the opportunity and means to do, I am responsible to do. And the same is true of you. Bring your lunch to Christ and watch him work! The satisfaction of all the crowd and the full baskets leftover, appear to me to be a beautiful representation of the fulness of grace to be found in the Lord Jesus Christ. He freely gives all to all who trust him. All who come to him have all they want and need. Finding all in him, we find satisfaction for our souls. Drinking the water he gives, we never thirst again. The storehouse of grace is never diminished. In our Father's house is "bread enough and to spare"!

"And when even was come, the ship was in the midst of the sea, and he alone on the land. And he saw them toiling in rowing; for the wind was contrary unto them: and about the fourth watch of the night he cometh unto them, walking upon the sea, and would have passed by them. But when they saw him walking upon the sea, they supposed it had been a spirit, and cried out: For they all saw him, and were troubled. And immediately he talked with them, and saith unto them, Be of good cheer: it is I; be not afraid. And he went up unto them into the ship; and the wind ceased: and they were sore amazed in themselves beyond measure, and wondered. For they considered not the miracle of the loaves: for their heart was hardened. And when they had passed over, they came into the land of Gennesaret, and drew to the shore. And when they were come out of the ship, straightway they knew him, And ran through that whole region round about, and began to carry about in beds those that were sick, where they heard he was. And whithersoever he entered, into villages, or cities, or country, they laid the sick in the streets, and besought him that they might touch if it were but the border of his garment: and as many as touched him were made whole".

(Mark 6:47-56)

Chapter 26

Five Reasons For Good Cheer

Every step in the earthly life of the incarnate God, our Lord Jesus Christ, is full of deep meaning and spiritual significance. It is impossible for us to grasp the full meaning of his words and deeds until we see him face to face. Yet, it is easy to see that the events recorded in this passage of holy scripture have a very wide range of instruction.

These verses clearly show us a picture of every believer's position in this world and the hopeful prospect of our Lord's glorious second advent. Like the disciples in their little boat, we are often tossed to and fro by many storms and contrary winds. Like these disciples, we are frequently without the enjoyment of Christ's manifest presence in this world. Yet, we shall see our Lord face to face. This is our joyful hope. Christ will come again and receive us unto himself.

Like these disciples tossed about upon the stormy sea, soon we shall see things changed for the better. When our Master comes, we will no longer be tossed about. Our storms will be over. All that is contrary to our happiness will come to an end. We will enter into a great eternal calm. Knowing this, let us focus our attention on our Master's words in verse 50. He said to his disciples, and he says to you and me, in all the storms and contrary winds we must endure in this world, "Be of good cheer: it is I; be not afraid". I want to use the story recorded in these verses to give you five reasons for good cheer.

Before I proceed, I realize that some who read these lines have absolutely no reason for good cheer. The wrath of God is upon you. You are hovering over the very brink of hell. You are but a breath away from everlasting torment. Unless and until you flee to Christ for refuge, unless and until you bow to the Son of God in repentance and faith, trusting Christ alone as your Lord and Saviour, you have no reason to rejoice in anything. Every breath you take in rebellion against God will increase your misery in the world to come! I plead with you in Christ's stead, "Be ye reconciled to God"!

However, for you who believe God, though you may be required for now to sail through stormy seas and be tossed about by contrary winds, there are found in these few verses of inspiration five reasons for good cheer. As I call your attention to them, I pray that God the Holy Spirit will seal them to your heart and to my own, for Christ's sake.

Providence Of God

All who believe God have, at all times, in all circumstances, reasons for good cheer. If I believe God, I ought always to find a reason for good cheer in the wise and good providence of God, my heavenly Father. Divine providence is God's rule, government, dominion over, and disposition of all things for the good of his elect and the glory of his great name. Read again carefully the verses before us and you will see it was no accident that these disciples came into this storm and experienced the great distress recorded. They were compelled and constrained by the Lord Jesus Christ himself to sail into this storm. "And straightway he constrained his disciples to get into the ship, and to go to the other side before unto Bethsaida, while he sent away the people" (v. 45).

Listen to the words of the Apostle, Paul, "And we know that all things work together for good to them that love God, to them who are the called according to his purpose" (Romans 8:28).

"O the depth of the riches both of the wisdom and knowledge of God! how unsearchable are his judgments, and his ways past finding out! For who hath known the mind of the Lord? or who hath been his counsellor? Or who hath first given to him, and it shall be recompensed unto him again? For of him, and through him, and to him, are all things: to whom be glory for ever. Amen" (Romans 11:33-36).

No matter what storm I am compelled to endure, no matter what contrary winds I must face, I am given two key assurances in the Word of God. First, my life and all the affairs of it are ordained and ordered by God my Saviour. Second, my Lord will come to me and make himself known upon the raging billows in such a way as I could not otherwise know him.

I will sail through the storm and reach the other side of the sea, by God's grace and in God's appointed time.

> When peace, like a river, attendeth my way,
> When sorrows, like sea billows, roll,
> Whatever my lot, Thou hast taught me to say,
> "It is well, it is well with my soul."

Presence Of God

Not only are we assured of the universal providence of God over all things, we are assured of and should be of good cheer in the awareness of the presence of God our Saviour at all times and in all circumstances. We are not always aware of him; but he is always aware of us. We do not always know his presence; but we are always in the immediate presence of God our

Saviour. "And he saw them toiling in rowing; for the wind was contrary unto them: and about the fourth watch of the night he cometh unto them, walking upon the sea, and would have passed by them" (v. 48).

With those words the Holy Spirit tells us several things. The Lord Jesus saw his disciples in the storm, though they could not see him. We are never beyond the reach of his eye. Our way is never hidden from him. He knows the path we take. Wherever we are, whatever our circumstances may be, the Son of God sees us. Alone or in a crowd, in sickness or in health, in perils at sea, in perils upon the shore, and in perils in the wilderness, his eye is upon us! The same eye that watched the tempest tossed disciples watches us. Our darkness is light before him. There are many times when we cannot see him; but there are no times when he does not see us.

The Lord Jesus came to his disciples in the midst of their great trouble and distress. He came to them in the fourth watch of the night, after a long night of great distress. He came to them in a supernatural, unexpected, unexplainable way, "walking upon the sea", the raging sea that terrified them! He came to them when they were in desperate need, after they had toiled all night in rowing. And though he was coming to them, it appeared as though he would have passed them by. Nothing could have been further from his mind, but he appeared to be entirely unaware of and totally unconcerned for his disciples. Yet, he was right there with them.

He who walked upon the water never changes! He always comes to us at the right time. He always comes when we most need him and are made to know that we need him, in the fourth watch of the night, after we have toiled long and hard and accomplished nothing by our toiling. When it appears that he would pass us by and cares nothing for us, the Lord is at hand.

"Rejoice in the Lord alway: and again I say, Rejoice. Let your moderation be known unto all men. The Lord is at hand. Be careful for nothing; but in every thing by prayer and supplication with thanksgiving let your requests be made known unto God. And the peace of God, which passeth all understanding, shall keep your hearts and minds through Christ Jesus". (Philippians 4:4-7)

Power Of God
We who believe should always be of good cheer because of the providence of God, the presence of God, and, third, because of the power of God. I can never make up my mind which is more comforting to my soul: the omniscience of God, the omnipresence of God, or the omnipotence of God (Psalm 139:1-18). "And he went up unto them into the ship; and the wind ceased: and they were sore amazed in themselves beyond measure, and wondered" (v. 51).

As soon as our Lord stepped on board their little boat, the storm ceased. What power he possesses! What power there is with him! Even the winds and storms obey his will. Everything in God's universe is completely, totally, and constantly under his dominion and subservient to his will. "The Lord God omnipotent reigneth"!

The fact that the disciples "were sore amazed in themselves beyond measure, and wondered" should not surprise us. How often we have experienced such amazement at our Saviour's intervention in our lives. Like these disciples, we do not doubt for a moment our Redeemer's divine omnipotence. Yet, like these disciples, we rarely expect it to be displayed; and when it is, we are filled with astonishment.

Pity Of God
Fourth, believing God, we should ever be of good cheer, realizing the great pity of God our Saviour toward us.

"But he, being full of compassion, forgave their iniquity, and destroyed them not: yea, many a time turned he his anger away, and did not stir up all his wrath. For he remembered that they were but flesh; a wind that passeth away, and cometh not again". (Psalm 78:38, 39)

"Like as a father pitieth his children, so the LORD pitieth them that fear him. For he knoweth our frame; he remembereth that we are dust". (Psalm 103:13, 14)

Look at the disciples' behaviour in verses 49 to 52, and remember that God our Saviour is God who has compassion upon chosen sinners and pities us in our weak, sinful condition in this world.

"But when they saw him walking upon the sea, they supposed it had been a spirit, and cried out: For they all saw him, and were troubled. And immediately he talked with them, and saith unto them, Be of good cheer: it is I; be not afraid. And he went up unto them into the ship; and the wind ceased: and they were sore amazed in themselves beyond measure, and wondered. For they considered not the miracle of the loaves: for their heart was hardened".

Their behaviour is a fair, accurate, faithful representation of us all. We should never be proud, heady, and high minded. We should never be too harsh in our judgment of these men or of other believers who behave as they did. These men were the Lord's disciples, faithful men, gospel preachers. Yet, when they saw the Lord walking on the water, they thought they had seen a ghost, and were terrified! They forgot the miracles they had just witnessed and experienced. And their hearts were hardened in unbelief. Yet, their hardness and unbelief did not prevent Christ from coming to them, delivering them, and using them.

Path To God

Fifth, we should ever be of good cheer because Christ is the path to God (vv. 53-56).

"And when they had passed over, they came into the land of Gennesaret, and drew to the shore. And when they were come out of the ship, straightway they knew him, And ran through that whole region round about, and began to carry about in beds those that were sick, where they heard he was. And whithersoever he entered, into villages, or cities, or country, they laid the sick in the streets, and besought him that they might touch if it were but the border of his garment: and as many as touched him were made whole".

Commenting on these four verses Robert Hawker wrote:

> I would appeal to the common sense and history of all mankind, whether the imagination can furnish a portrait so beautiful, so affectionate, and interesting, as is here drawn of our Lord Jesus Christ. The Prophet, ages before had said, 'Behold, your God will come and save you! Then the eyes of the blind shall be opened, and the ears of the deaf be unstopped. Then shall the lame man leap as an hart, and the tongue of the dumb sing' (Isaiah 35:4-6). And here we behold God indeed in the person of his dear Son, surrounded by the sick and diseased of every description and character, while as many as touched him were made whole. Oh! for grace, to come to Him now by faith; for surely, none whom God the Holy Ghost shall lead to Jesus, will the Lord send empty away.

As those mentioned here brought needy souls to the Saviour, you and I are responsible to tell other eternity bound sinners who Christ is, what he has done for us, and where he may be found. The place of mercy is the place where Christ is, where his Word is preached, his name is honoured, and his power is manifest. Bring the needy to his house, bring them to the Saviour himself in prayer, lay them before him, and seek the grace of his Spirit for them, that they might touch him in faith and be made whole by him. The only path to God is Christ, faith in Christ. "As many as touched him were made whole"! It is still true. As many as touch him are made whole.

"Then came together unto him the Pharisees, and certain of the scribes, which came from Jerusalem. And when they saw some of his disciples eat bread with defiled, that is to say, with unwashen, hands, they found fault. For the Pharisees, and all the Jews, except they wash their hands oft, eat not, holding the tradition of the elders. And when they come from the market, except they wash, they eat not. And many other things there be, which they have received to hold, as the washing of cups, and pots, brasen vessels, and of tables. Then the Pharisees and scribes asked him, Why walk not thy disciples according to the tradition of the elders, but eat bread with unwashen hands? He answered and said unto them, Well hath Esaias prophesied of you hypocrites, as it is written, This people honoureth me with their lips, but their heart is far from me. Howbeit in vain do they worship me, teaching for doctrines the commandments of men. For laying aside the commandment of God, ye hold the tradition of men, as the washing of pots and cups: and many other such like things ye do. And he said unto them, Full well ye reject the commandment of God, that ye may keep your own tradition. For Moses said, Honour thy father and thy mother; and, Whoso curseth father or mother, let him die the death: But ye say, If a man shall say to his father or mother, It is Corban, that is to say, a gift, by whatsoever thou mightest be profited by me; he shall be free. And ye suffer him no more to do ought for his father or his mother; Making the word of God of none effect through your tradition, which ye have delivered: and many such like things do ye".

(Mark 7:1-13)

Chapter 27

The Religion Of The Pharisees

As our Lord Jesus warns us elsewhere to "beware of false prophets", he warns us here to beware of false religion. Nothing is more dangerous to the souls of men, and nothing more deadly than false prophets and false religion.

The Apostle Paul warns us that those who eat and drink the bread and wine of the Lord's Table without faith in Christ eat and drink damnation to themselves. What he says about the Lord's Table is true of and applicable to all other religious practices without faith in Christ. To profess faith without faith, to claim an interest in Christ without an interest in Christ, to be baptized without being born of God, to pretend to be a child of God while you are yet a child of the devil, all these things are eating and drinking damnation to yourself.

Our Lord Jesus warns us again and again to, "beware of the leaven of the Pharisees". The warning is repeated often because it is needed often. Here he explains exactly what he meant by the leaven of the Pharisees. When our Lord warns us to beware of the leaven of the Pharisees, he is talking about the doctrine, or the religion of the Pharisees.

What a humbling picture we have before us of apostate, human religion. Here we see, to some extent, what man is capable of doing in the perversion of truth, while clinging to the name of God. These well read, highly educated, greatly respected religious men really thought God was impressed by watching them meticulously wash their hands and their dishes in religious ceremony! There are multitudes exactly like them today. In fact, the religion of the Pharisees is the natural religion of the carnal heart. All men, by nature gravitate to it. Yet, the religion of the Pharisees, though it is naturally appealing to and universally approved of by all men, is deadly to a man's soul and an utter abomination in the sight of God. The religion of the Pharisees is both the most ancient and the newest of all religions. In this study I will call your attention to seven things that characterize the religion of the Pharisees. As we look at these seven characteristics of it, let us ask ourselves this question: Is my religion the religion of Christ or the religion of the Pharisees?

The religion of the Pharisees makes people self-righteous, critical, and judgmental.

"Then came together unto him the Pharisees, and certain of the scribes, which came from Jerusalem. And when they saw some of his disciples eat bread with defiled, that is to say, with unwashen, hands, they found fault" (vv. 1, 2).

The Pharisees were always watching other people, inspecting the behaviour of other people, finding fault with other people. They had a keen eye for what others did, or failed to do. Such critics and fault-finders are a penny a dozen. If you do something, anything, before you sit down, someone who never does anything will come along and find something wrong with what you have done. In natural things this is annoying; but in spiritual things it reveals a proud, unregenerate, self-righteousness, which is always the result of legalistic, works religion.

These Pharisees really thought they could tell, by observing the outward conduct of men in their daily routine of life, who was spiritual and who was carnal. We have many like them in our day. Self-righteous religionists in our day, like the Pharisees of our Lord's day, ever justify themselves in their own minds, before others, and before God, proudly asserting, "I am not as other men" (Luke 18:11).

Pharisees always justify themselves by comparing themselves with people they consider more sinful than they are. "I am not as this publican". Their claim to holiness is based upon what they do and what they do not do, not upon the work of Christ's gift of God's grace in him. Though they talk much above love, they despise others. That is manifest by their treatment of others. They are professional critics of men, who love to point out the weaknesses of others.

Here, the Pharisees and Scribes seized the opportunity to point out what they thought was a terrible evil in our Lord and his disciples. They saw them eating in public without ceremonially washing their hands beforehand. That was a breach of their religious traditions that was simply unpardonable! John Trapp tells us that, "the Pharisees deemed it as great a sin to eat with unwashen hands, as to commit fornication."

The complaint of the Scribes and Pharisees against the disciples was not that they were evil, corrupt, covetous men, but that they did not, in keeping with Jewish traditions, wash their hands before they ate! Obviously, it is always good to wash your hands, the more often the better, as a matter of personal hygiene. But the practice of always washing one's hands before eating, as a show of religious devotion, had become a religious tradition with them, a tradition they would never dare to break, at least not in public. They washed their hands, whether they needed washing or not, because they vainly imagined that in doing so they showed spirituality and devotion to God. Our Lord's disciples, following his example and instruction, felt no compulsion to obey religious tradition. "They washed not their hands when they ate bread"! Why should they wash them if they were clean? Tradition had no power over their consciences.

You may think, "What does that have to do with me? How does this apply to anyone today?" There are multitudes who do much of what they do purely out of religious tradition, only to be seen of men, so that they will appear to others to be true Christians, spiritually minded, and devoted to Christ. How often have you heard people say, or said yourself, "I do that to show people that I am a Christian. I want people to know that I love the Lord"? The one thing our Lord Jesus tells us plainly that we are never to do is to try, by our dress, our public appearance, or our public behaviour, to show that we are Christians. Read Matthew 6:3-18. You may say, "But I want people to see Jesus in me". Lost, unbelieving people did not see Jesus in Jesus. They certainly are not going to see him in you and me.

Let us take care that we live as men and women who trust and worship the Lord Jesus Christ in honesty, in labour, in conversation, in modesty, in love, and in patience. "Adorn the doctrine of God our Saviour" (Titus 2:10). But do nothing to be seen of men. Several years ago, I was in the company of several pastors in a restaurant. When his meal was served, the senior pastor among us began eating his meal without bowing to give thanks first (without publicly washing his hands). One of the younger men objected to his conduct, saying, "I could never do that. I always give thanks before I eat, especially in a public place". When my older friend asked, "Why?", he said, "I want people to know I'm a Christian." The older, wiser pastor smiled and said, "If you want people to know you're a Christian, leave the waitress a good tip."

No man has any more right to institute a new religious duty in the kingdom of God than to neglect an old one. The issuing of commands is for the King alone. Yet these religionists wanted to know why the Lord's disciples broke a law, which was never established by God as a law. Lost religionists in all ages love to invent traditions and then rest their souls upon them. Going about to establish their own righteousness, they refuse to submit themselves to the righteousness of God in Christ. They refuse to trust Christ alone for righteousness before God. They have a form of godliness, which they cherish, but deny the power of true godliness, which is the gospel of God's free, saving grace in Christ (Romans 1:16, 17). That which our Saviour said to the Pharisees of his day is yet true. "Ye are they which justify yourselves before men; but God knoweth your hearts: for that which is highly esteemed among men is abomination in the sight of God" (Luke 16:15).

The washing of hands, like all other religious tradition, is nothing. "Faith which worketh by love" is everything. "The blood of Jesus Christ cleanseth us from all sin". All those things that men do to make themselves righteous in will worship "is abomination in the sight of God".

The religion of the Pharisees is a religion which has apostatized and departed from the Word of God.

"For the Pharisees, and all the Jews, except they wash their hands oft, eat not, holding the tradition of the elders. And when they come from the market, except they wash, they eat not. And many other things there be, which they have received to hold, as the washing of cups, and pots, brasen vessels, and of tables. Then the Pharisees and scribes asked him, Why walk not thy disciples according to the tradition of the elders, but eat bread with unwashen hands? He answered and said unto them, Well hath Esaias prophesied of you hypocrites, as it is written, This people honoureth me with their lips, but their heart is far from me. Howbeit in vain do they worship me, teaching for doctrines the commandments of men. For laying aside the commandment of God, ye hold the tradition of men, as the washing of pots and cups: and many other such like things ye do. And he said unto them, Full well ye reject the commandment of God, that ye may keep your own tradition" (vv. 7:3-9).

Never was there a nation of men raised so high and fallen so low as the nation of Israel. Never was there a people given such great privileges and opportunities, only to cast them aside, as the Jews. Israel was the nation to whom God gave his law, his ordinances, his priests, his tabernacle, his temple, his altar, his mercy-seat, and his prophets. These are the people to whom Moses, Samuel, and Isaiah prophesied. This is the people who sprung from Abraham's lions, who descended from David's kingdom, and wore Israel's name.

These are the people who once trembled before the ark of the covenant. How they have fallen! Here are Abraham's sons. Here are men who claim Moses' name, though they had long ago rejected his doctrine, who consider the ceremonial washing of hands, cups, saucers, and pots and pans an evidence of spirituality! In their opinion, the person who paid the most rigid attention to the external observance of man-made religious customs was the most holy among them.

Let us be warned. Once a church, a denomination, or an individual leaves the King's highway of truth, we must not be surprised to see them washing pots and calling it godliness! Multitudes today are just like the Pharisees. They wear the names of God's prophets and claim identification with them; but have long since forsaken the truth of God's Word in utter apostasy. Today's religion places great emphasis on getting people into church, but none on getting them into Christ. Multitudes who pass by the doctrine of the cross proudly wear a cross around their necks. In churches everywhere, people sing "Amazing Grace", though they despise the doctrine of grace.

People everywhere make a big show of outward religion, but ignore righteousness, peace, and joy in the Holy Ghost. They have a form of godliness, but despise the gospel of Christ, which is the power of God. Pharisees in all generations are great washers of the outside. But formal, ritualistic, ceremonial, outward religion, without heart faith, is empty, useless religion.

The Pharisees' religion is outward, lip-service religion.

"He answered and said unto them, Well hath Esaias prophesied of you hypocrites, as it is written, This people honoureth me with their lips, but their heart is far from me" (v. 6).

The passage our Lord referred to is Isaiah 29:13. I wonder if we will ever learn that God Almighty is not impressed with the way we comb our hair, the clothes we wear, the food we eat, or the show we make in our pretence of piety and godliness. "The Lord looketh on the heart"! God says, "My son, give me thine heart". "Keep thy heart with all diligence". Let us remember the heart is the principle thing in faith, in private worship, in public worship, at the Lord's Table, in prayer, and in all things spiritual.

The heart is the principle thing in the relationship of a husband and wife, parents and children, friend and friend. And in our relationship with, service to, and worship of our God the matter of chief concern is our hearts (Isaiah 29:13; Ezekiel 33:31; Romans 10:13; 14:17).

What must we have to be saved? A New Heart! What sacrifice does God require from us? A Broken and Contrite Heart! What is true circumcision? Heart Circumcision! What does God call for from his sons? "My son, give me thine heart"! Where does Christ dwell? In Our Hearts!

J. C. Ryle wrote, "The bended knee, the bowed head, the loud Amen, the daily chapter, the regular attendance at the Lord's Table, are all useless and unprofitable, so long as our affections are nailed to sin, or pleasure, or money or the world."

The religion of the Pharisee is a religion which uses the pretence of piety as a covering and excuse for irresponsibility.

"For Moses said, Honour thy father and thy mother; and, Whoso curseth father or mother, let him die the death: But ye say, If a man shall say to his father or mother, It is Corban, that is to say, a gift, by whatsoever thou mightest be profited by me; he shall be free. And ye suffer him no more to do ought for his father or his mother" (vv. 10-12).

While true religion, true spirituality is a very practical thing. False, empty religion will allow a man or woman to neglect and despise the most common duties of life. True religion, true Christianity causes people to cherish and faithfully perform the most common duties of everyday life for the glory of God.

The Lord Jesus declares (Matthew 15:5-8) that if a person refuses to take care of his parents, trying to excuse his selfishness, by saying that the only money he possesses has been devoted as a gift to God, he nullifies the Word of God, and proves himself a religious hypocrite. The worship of God causes a believer to honour his parents, causes a father and husband to provide for his family, causes a believer to be a diligent employee, causes a Christian to be a faithful employer, and causes a woman to be a good wife and mother. Rowland Hill once said, "When a man comes to know the Lord, even his dog and cat and farm animals will be the better for it." It was William Jay who wrote, "A person, when he comes to Christ, will be better in every relationship. He is a better husband, father, master, worker, and friend than before or else his religion is not genuine."

The religion of the Pharisee is a religion which rejects and makes of none effect the Word of God, supplanting it with the customs, creeds, and confessions of men.

Three times our Lord lays this charge at the feet of these pompous, self-content, self-righteous religionists. You lay aside the Word of God, holding the traditions of men (v. 8). "Full well ye reject the commandment of God, that ye may keep your own tradition" (v. 9). You make the Word of God of none effect through your tradition (v. 13). First, they added their traditions to the scriptures. Next, they made their traditions equal with the Word of God. In the end, they rejected the Word of God altogether and held to their traditions!

The religion of the Pharisees is religion that supplants the Word of God with the doctrines and traditions of men. Instead of teaching the doctrine of holy scripture, the gospel of Christ, salvation by his blood, righteousness, and grace alone, it teaches religious morality. Instead of teaching people to observe our Saviour's ordinances of worship, believer's immersion and the Lord's Supper, it teaches duties and ceremonies of purely human invention, the sprinkling of infants, the observance of Lent, and religious pageantry. Such religion, though practised with great devotion and ceremonial gaudiness, is an utterly vain thing, an empty show void of life, power, and spirituality. It is unacceptable to God and of no benefit to man. The practice of it is eating and drinking damnation to one's own soul!

The religion of the Pharisee is a religion of legalism, works, and asceticism. It is far removed from the simple gospel of the New Testament, the witness of the apostles and the teaching of the Lord Jesus Christ.

The Pharisees thought they would defile themselves by touching or using things and people they considered unclean. Multitudes today follow their example. Entire systems of works based religion have been established and gained popular acceptance by inventing extra-biblical taboos for "Christians".

Adventism is a classic example. All men by nature are legalists and love legal religion, any religion that gives them something to do or not to do, by which they can distinguish themselves from others and make themselves "holier" than others. That religion which says, "touch not, taste not, handle not", no matter what denominational name it wears, is nothing but "a show of wisdom in will-worship" (Colossians 2:21-23). I personally know people who question the spirituality of anyone who enjoys boxing, horse races, baseball, basketball, or football, of anyone who eats pork, red meat, or catfish, and of anyone who drinks coffee, tea, or Coca-Cola! I am not exaggerating. I really do know such people.

Every servant of God, each child of God stands or falls before his own Master. We have absolutely no business in trying to govern the lives of God's children. That is the work of God the Holy Spirit. Perhaps you are thinking – "If we do not, by some means, try to regulate people's lives, what is there to prevent them from drunkenness, lasciviousness, fornication, and adultery?" That is the thinking of every legalist. Because he must be governed by rules, he presumes that everyone else must be. The believer is governed and constrained by the love of Christ, seeks to honour God in all things, and endeavours to mould his life to the Word of God.

Our energies and efforts would be far better spent if we would seek to love and serve one another, rather than rule and judge one another. I ask the reader to weigh these thoughts by only one criteria: Are they or are they not in total compliance with both the spirit and the letter of the New Testament?

In its essence, at its core, the religion of the Pharisee is a religion that denies the need of grace and redemption, because it denies the utter, total depravity of man (vv. 14-23).

"And when he had called all the people unto him, he said unto them, Hearken unto me every one of you, and understand: There is nothing from without a man, that entering into him can defile him: but the things which come out of him, those are they that defile the man. If any man have ears to hear, let him hear. And when he was entered into the house from the people, his disciples asked him concerning the parable. And he saith unto them, Are ye so without understanding also? Do ye not perceive, that whatsoever thing from without entereth into the man, it cannot defile him; Because it entereth not into his heart, but into the belly, and goeth out into the draught, purging all meats? And he said, That which cometh out of the man, that defileth the man. For from within, out of the heart of men, proceed evil thoughts, adulteries, fornications, murders, Thefts, covetousness, wickedness, deceit, lasciviousness, an evil eye, blasphemy, pride, foolishness: All these evil things come from within, and defile the man" (vv. 14-23).

All human religion, like the religion of the Pharisees, operates on the assumption that the defilement and corruption of a person's soul comes from without, from the things we come into contact with in this world. But the Lord Jesus shows us that the defilement and corruption of our souls arises from within us. He shows us that our hearts are polluted, defiled, corrupt, and depraved. We are all by nature corrupt at heart, in need of God's free, saving grace, and Christ's precious blood atonement.

The Pharisees of old, like the religionists of our day, taught that holiness, righteousness, and godliness depended upon abstaining from certain meats and drinks and carefully observing religious ceremonies of washing and purification. Our Saviour overthrows this doctrine by declaring three things.

It is not what you put in your body that defiles you, but what comes out of your heart (Romans 14:17).

Material things cannot defile your soul by using them. And material ceremonies cannot cleanse your soul by enduring them. Carnal things can neither corrupt nor cleanse the soul. If we would worship and serve God, we must have something more than a separated life and a form of godliness. We must have a heart that is clean and upright before God, a clean heart and a right spirit. Such a heart is the gift of God's grace, the work of his Spirit in the new birth.

All sin and defilement originates in and springs from the heart. It is not our environment that corrupts us, nor our company, nor our education, but our hearts.

Listen to this list, "From within, out of the heart of men, proceed evil thoughts, adulteries, fornications, murders, thefts, covetousness, wickedness, deceit, lasciviousness, an evil eye, blasphemy, pride, foolishness". What a catalogue! What must that heart be out of which so many evils pour forth! If these are the bees, what must the hive be? "Evil thoughts", evil devising such as the Pharisees displayed, come from the heart. "Murders" begin not with the dagger, but with malice in the soul. "Adulteries" and "fornications" are committed in the heart, before they are performed by the body. The heart is the cage from which every unclean bird flies forth into the world. "Thefts" are born in the covetousness of the heart.

No man steals what he does not first covet. "False witness", lying and slander, is venom in the heart that is spewed out of the mouth. "Blasphemies" are the enmity of the heart expressed by the vile speech of the tongue. All these, and all other evils, ooze from the vile cesspool inside fallen man called, "the heart".

"All these evil things come from within, and defile the man". It is the corruption of the heart that makes fallen man unfit for communion with God, not failure to pour water on your hands before you eat, or failure to observe religious duties. The heart of man is abominable before God. The evils gushing from the heart make fallen man loathsome and revolting before God and expose all to shame and ruin. It is only the blood of Christ that can cleanse us from the pollution and guilt of our corrupt hearts and save us from the wrath of God, which we so fully deserve. Yet, those who know nothing of the corruption of their hearts, know nothing of God's saving grace, know nothing of repentance and faith in Christ, are horrified when they see one who worships God in Spirit and in truth neglecting the religious traditions by which their blind leaders lead them into hell.

God looks on the heart; but we prefer outward things, because we are able to perform them and they call attention to us.

Few are able to grasp such elementary, but vital truths, because they are turned away from the simplicity that is in Christ by self-righteous, works religion. There is a vast difference between physical and spiritual defilement. What we eat and drink does not touch the soul. It passes through the body; but it does not reach our hearts. Material things cannot defile a person. That which is eaten is material substance, and cannot make anyone spiritually or morally unclean. That fact is so obvious that no one would ever imagine otherwise, were it not for the man made dogmas of false religion.

The only hope for your soul and mine is that God might be pleased to save us from ourselves. I have no hope but Christ. He alone is all my Wisdom, Righteousness, Sanctification, and Redemption. May God make him yours.

"And when he had called all the people unto him, he said unto them, Hearken unto me every one of you, and understand: There is nothing from without a man, that entering into him can defile him: but the things which come out of him, those are they that defile the man. If any man have ears to hear, let him hear. And when he was entered into the house from the people, his disciples asked him concerning the parable. And he saith unto them, Are ye so without understanding also? Do ye not perceive, that whatsoever thing from without entereth into the man, it cannot defile him; Because it entereth not into his heart, but into the belly, and goeth out into the draught, purging all meats? And he said, That which cometh out of the man, that defileth the man. For from within, out of the heart of men, proceed evil thoughts, adulteries, fornications, murders, Thefts, covetousness, wickedness, deceit, lasciviousness, an evil eye, blasphemy, pride, foolishness: All these evil things come from within, and defile the man".

(Mark 7:14-23)

Chapter 28

Total Depravity

All human religion, like the religion of the Pharisees, operates on the assumption that the defilement and corruption of a person's soul comes from without, from the things we come into contact with in this world. The creed of such religion is, "Touch not, taste not, handle not" (Colossians 2:21). But in this passage the Lord Jesus shows us that the defilement and corruption of our souls arises from within us. He shows us that our hearts are polluted, defiled, corrupt, and depraved. As we go through these verses together, I want to call your attention to three things.

The Dullness Of Our Minds

First, we have before us a clear demonstration of the dullness of our minds (vv. 14, 16, 18). The simple fact is fallen man has absolutely no spiritual understanding. He is not just slow to understand the things of God. He is incapable of understanding. Our Lord called for the multitudes to "Hearken unto him and understand". Then he said to his disciples, "Are ye so without understanding also?"

The natural man is totally void of spiritual discernment. Until a person is born again by God the Holy Spirit, he cannot understand anything spiritual. The language of holy scripture is crystal clear, "The natural man receiveth not the things of the Spirit of God: for they are foolishness unto him: neither can he know them, because they are spiritually discerned" (John 3:3; Romans 3:11; 1 Corinthians 2:14).

The corruption of the human nature is a universal corruption. It affects every man's heart, his will, his emotions, and his conscience; and it affects his mind as well, his reasoning, his memory, and his understanding. Those who are smart and even brilliant in other things, until they are taught of God, are without understanding in spiritual matters. Worldly men of brilliance often stumble over the simplest things revealed in the gospel. They see no beauty of revelation, spiritual wisdom, or depth of meaning in the clearest statements of gospel truth. To the worldly wise man, those things which hold the believer's mind in rapturous wonder are foolishness. He listens, if he listens at all, to the preaching of the gospel like a man listening to someone talk in a foreign language, catching a word here and there, but missing the drift of the conversation. He hears but he does not and cannot understand the things of God. The Holy Spirit tells us that the world by wisdom knows not God (1 Corinthians 1:21).[4]

Sovereign election, to the worldling, seems unfair. Divine predestination, to the unbeliever, appears to be fatalism. The doctrine of the Trinity appears to the brilliant infidel an impossible riddle. The incarnation and virgin birth of Christ to the worldly mind appear to be both needless and impossible. Substitutionary redemption and penal satisfaction to unbelievers are barbaric concepts. Imputed righteousness to self-righteous worldlings is utter nonsense. Salvation by grace alone is foolishness to men and women who have no idea what grace is (1 Corinthians 1:18-31).

Even those who are born again and taught of God are often slow to understand the things of God. I know that Christ's sheep hear his voice and follow him. I know that all who are born again have the mind of Christ and, being taught of God, discern all things spiritual. However, so long as we live in this world, our discernment and understanding is at best partial and tainted.

Certainly that was the case with the Lord's earliest disciples. Looking at it from this distance, our Lord's teaching here seems so very simple that we wonder how anyone could miss it. But "his disciples asked him concerning the parable". They said, "What did you mean by that parable?" And the Master replied, "Are ye so without understanding also?"

---

[4] Let me give you an example. Thomas Jefferson was one of America's most brilliant and distinguished forefathers. Like most of our nation's earliest statesmen, he was a Deist. (A Deist is one who believes in a god on purely rational grounds, without any revelation or inspired authority. Deists believe that a god created the world and established certain laws of nature, but has nothing else to do with the world he created). Jefferson seems to have been brilliant with regard to almost all things natural. But he was totally ignorant of all things spiritual. This is what Thomas Jefferson had to say about the God of the Bible:

"I can never join Calvin in addressing 'his God'. He was indeed an atheist, which I can never be; or rather his religion was demonism. If ever a man worshipped a false god, he did. The being described in his five points is not the God whom you and I acknowledge and adore, the Creator and benevolent Governor of the world, but a demon of malignant spirit."

Jefferson stands as a glaring display of that which God the Holy Spirit declares. "The natural man understandeth not the things of the Spirit of God, for they are foolishness unto him: neither can he know them, for they are spiritually discerned"!

Let us pray continually for the teaching of God the Holy Spirit, that we might understand the scriptures and the things of God. Without the teaching of the Spirit, the most brilliant mind is confused by the simplest of truths. In reading the Word of God, as we hear the preaching of the gospel, and as we seek to know the ways of God, the direct intervention and illumination of the Spirit is vital. We must always approach the things of God with a humble, childlike, teachable spirit, praying with David, "Teach me thy statutes" (Psalm 119:64).

The Defilement Of Our Nature
Second, our Lord here sets before us the defilement of our nature. "There is nothing from without a man, that entering into him can defile him: but the things which come out of him, those are they that defile the man. If any man have ears to hear, let him hear" (vv. 15, 16). Asceticism is not Christianity. Separationism is not spirituality. Moral and spiritual purity does not depend upon washing or not washing our hands, touching or not touching things, eating or not eating them. Moral, spiritual purity certainly cannot be obtained by the most diligent practice of religious ritualism and ceremonialism.

That which enters our bodies by the mouth, or enters our minds by the eye or the ear is not that which defiles us, but our own hearts. All evil speech springs from our evil hearts. All corrupt behaviour arises from our corrupt hearts. It is the heart that defiles the body, not the body that defiles the heart. The evil of our hearts is that which defiles the mind and conscience, the faculties of the soul, and the members of the body, making fallen man abominable in the sight of God, exposing him to wrath and judgment.

Every man, woman and child in this world carries in his inmost being a cesspool of wickedness. None of us need bad company to corrupt us. We are bad company! We have in us the root and beginning of all moral and spiritual wickedness. The beginning of all evil is within us all. We ought to always bear this in mind, especially when training and educating our children.

It is not wise, in my opinion, to shelter our children and raise them in isolation from the world. To do so is to teach them, by implication, that they are better than others, that they are not so depraved as others. When they do wrong, we should never blame their companions or their environment. Foolishness is bound up in the heart of every child; and the rod of correction must be used to drive it from him. Do not misunderstand me. Though we should not live as religious hermits, we should not keep company with evil doers, and should not allow our children to do so (Psalm 26:5; 1 Corinthians 5:11; 15:3). But it is not bad company that corrupts. The corruption is within. "It is," John Gill wrote, "sin in the heart, and what proceeds from it; as all evil thoughts, wicked words, and impure actions; which denominate a man filthy and unclean, and expose him to the abhorrence of God".

Let us train our sons and daughters in the way they should go, ever reminding them of their own personal depravity and need of Christ, diligently praying for them. The only hope any of us have, the only hope our children have of being made righteous and of being accepted with God is Christ. We must be washed in his blood, robed in his righteousness, born of his Spirit.

Corrupt and sinful as we all are in nature, we are all utterly self-righteous by nature. That is the reason we are all so naturally inclined to embrace the practices of legalistic Pharisees, so quick to look upon those who do not observe ascetic religious traditions as wicked, and ourselves as righteous. Knowing this, and knowing that his doctrine would be received by none except those who are given grace to receive it, our Saviour says, "If any man have ears to hear, let him hear". If God the Holy Spirit gives us such spiritual discernment, let us ever give him thanks and praise for his grace.

The Depravity Of Our Hearts

In verses 20-23, we are given a clear description of the depravity of our hearts. "And he said, That which cometh out of the man, that defileth the man. For from within, out of the heart of men, proceed evil thoughts, adulteries, fornications, murders, thefts, covetousness, wickedness, deceit, lasciviousness, an evil eye, blasphemy, pride, foolishness: All these evil things come from within, and defile the man".

These words describe us all. Our Lord is not here speaking only of the profligate, the base, and the disreputable, but also of the high, the mighty, and the respectable. These words describe every human being, without exception. The seeds of evil may lie hidden within us, covered by the pretence of piety and restrained by society; but they are at the very core of our beings. We are all unclean things! In our "inward part is every wickedness" (Psalm 5:9), and nothing good (Isaiah 1:2-6; Romans 3:10-18).

All "evil thoughts" concerning the triune God, his sovereignty and his salvation, and all "evil thoughts" of our fellow creatures proceed from our depraved hearts. All wicked imaginations, carnal reasonings and lusts, and malicious imaginations rise from, and are devised, and forged in the corrupt heart of man. All "adulteries", all unlawful intercourse in thought and deed, between married people, rise from the heart of fallen men and women. All "fornications", sexual evil, pornography, paedophilia, incest, homosexuality, perversions and idolatry of all kinds are evils residing in every heart by nature.

All "murders", including the hatred and malice from which murder springs, and slanders by which men assassinate one another's name and character, are deeds of the heart, before they are committed by the hand. All "thefts", by force or by fraud, arise from the heart. All "covetousness", greed, envy and extortion, an insatiable desire after the things of the world, springs from the heart. All "wickedness", every act of iniquity, every transgression of God's holy law, every sinful thought and deed, doing harm to others, every evil thing comes from the heart. All "deceit", guile, hypocrisy, subtlety, and craftiness are evil traits of the heart, not learned practices.

All "lasciviousness", licentiousness, the lack of contentment, and filth of mind are the lusts of the heart of fallen man. The "evil eye" refers to man's rejoicing at the miseries of others. It includes sorcery and witchcraft. All "blasphemy", evil speech regarding God or men, comes from the heart. All "pride", the root of all evil, be it pride of race or pride of place, springs from the evil heart of wickedness, that resides in every human being. All "foolishness", senseless, rash, reckless behaviour, springs from the proud, egotistical heart of man, who thinks of none but himself.

"All these evil things come from within, and defile the man". That being so, how humble we should be! "Behold, I was shapen in iniquity, and in sin did my mother conceive me" (Psalm 51:5). "For I know that in me (that is, in my flesh,) dwelleth no good thing: for to will is present with me; but how to perform that which is good I find not" (Romans 7:18).

"Know ye not that the unrighteous shall not inherit the kingdom of God? Be not deceived: neither fornicators, nor idolaters, nor adulterers, nor effeminate, nor abusers of themselves with mankind, Nor thieves, nor covetous, nor drunkards, nor revilers, nor extortioners, shall inherit the kingdom of God. And such were some of you: but ye are washed, but ye are sanctified, but ye are justified in the name of the Lord Jesus, and by the Spirit of our God ... What? know ye not that your body is the temple of the Holy Ghost which is in you, which ye have of God, and ye are not your own? For ye are bought with a price: therefore glorify God in your body, and in your spirit, which are God's" (1 Corinthians 6:9-11, 19, 20).

How thankful we ought to be for God's free grace, Christ's blood atonement and imputed righteousness. How thankful we ought to be for God's immutable mercy! How thankful we ought to be for God's unspeakable gift, Christ our Saviour! It is by God's grace alone that we are in Christ, "who of God is made unto us wisdom, and righteousness, and sanctification, and redemption: That, according as it is written, He that glorieth, let him glory in the Lord" (1 Corinthians 1:30, 31).

"And from thence he arose, and went into the borders of Tyre and Sidon, and entered into an house, and would have no man know it: but he could not be hid. For a certain woman, whose young daughter had an unclean spirit, heard of him, and came and fell at his feet: The woman was a Greek, a Syrophenician by nation; and she besought him that he would cast forth the devil out of her daughter. But Jesus said unto her, Let the children first be filled: for it is not meet to take the children's bread, and to cast it unto the dogs. And she answered and said unto him, Yes, Lord: yet the dogs under the table eat of the children's crumbs. And he said unto her, For this saying go thy way; the devil is gone out of thy daughter. And when she was come to her house, she found the devil gone out, and her daughter laid upon the bed".

(Mark 7:24-30)

Chapter 29

Mercy Needed, Mercy Sought, Mercy Given

Here Mark gives us his inspired history of this poor woman, her great need, the mercy she obtained of the Lord Jesus, and his high commendation of her faith. It is the same story Matthew gives us in Matthew 15:21-28. But both Matthew and Mark give specific details the other was not inspired by the Spirit of God to relate. It will be helpful to read Matthew's account as well.

"Then Jesus went thence, and departed into the coasts of Tyre and Sidon. And, behold, a woman of Canaan came out of the same coasts, and cried unto him, saying, Have mercy on me, O Lord, thou Son of David; my daughter is grievously vexed with a devil. But he answered her not a word. And his disciples came and besought him, saying, Send her away; for she crieth after us. But he answered and said, I am not sent but unto the lost sheep of the house of Israel. Then came she and worshipped him, saying, Lord, help me. But he answered and said, It is not meet to take the children's bread, and to cast it to dogs. And she said, Truth, Lord: yet the dogs eat of the crumbs which fall from their masters' table. Then Jesus answered and said unto her, O woman, great is thy faith: be it unto thee even as thou wilt. And her daughter was made whole from that very hour".

Matthew tells us that this woman was of Canaan. She was a Gentile. Mark adds that she was a Syrophenician, that is, she belonged to that part of Phoenicia that bordered Syria. She came seeking Christ. Who taught her about the Lord Jesus? How did she come to know that he was the Christ, the Son of David? We are not told what instrument God used to teach her; but it is obvious that God himself was her Teacher. God the Holy Spirit had given her faith in Christ.

"And all thy children shall be taught of the LORD; and great shall be the peace of thy children" (Isaiah 54:13). "All that the Father giveth me shall come to me; and him that cometh to me I will in no wise cast out. For I came down from heaven, not to do mine own will, but the will of him that sent me. And this is the Father's will which hath sent me, that of all which he hath given me I should lose nothing, but should raise it up again at the last day. And this is the will of him that sent me, that every one which seeth the Son, and believeth on him, may have everlasting life: and I will raise him up at the last day" (John 6:37-40).

Taking the accounts of Matthew and Mark together, I see many gospel lessons clearly set before us in the story of this Syrophenician woman. Man's unbelief never thwarts or even hinders the purpose of God. "Then Jesus went thence, and departed into the coasts of Tyre and Sidon" (Matthew 15:21).

It is written, "For what if some did not believe? shall their unbelief make the faith of God without effect? God forbid: yea, let God be true, but every man a liar; as it is written, That thou mightest be justified in thy sayings, and mightest overcome when thou art judged" (Romans 3:3, 4). The Pharisees would not hear him or receive his Word. Their pride, self-righteousness, and religious traditions kept them out of the kingdom of God. Therefore, in judicial reprobation, our Lord left them; but his leaving them was that he might enter into the coasts of Tyre and Sidon and there bestow his grace upon a chosen Gentile woman. Before ever a sinner will come to Christ seeking mercy, the Lord Jesus Christ must come to that sinner in mercy.

We do not read this story aright if all we see is a needy soul coming to Christ. Certainly, we must not neglect that; but this Syrophenician woman could never have come to Christ for mercy if Christ had not come to her in mercy. She sought the Lord; but he came to seek her first. It is not the lost sheep who seeks and finds the Shepherd, but the Shepherd who seeks and finds his one lost sheep. If we love him it is because he first loved us (1 John 4:19). And if we seek him, it is because he first sought us.

"And it shall come to pass, that before they call, I will answer; and while they are yet speaking, I will hear" (Isaiah 65:24). Our Lord passed by the crowds, the congested cities, the people of renown. He came to the outskirts of nowhere to show mercy to a nobody.

Grace Always Comes To The Most Unlikely

I get a little uneasy when I hear men talk about being able to tell who is going to be saved. Anyone would have thought, "If the Lord is going to do any great work or perform any great miracle, he will pick someone important, someone respected, someone other people will look up to." But that simply is not the case. The Son of God comes to a Greek, a Canaanite, a Syrophenician woman, a woman with no promise from God, no covenant rights with God, no relationship to God, and nothing to offer God; but she was "a certain woman" loved and chosen by God as the special object of his special grace.

When the Lord God intends to be gracious to a sinner, he always causes that sinner, like this poor woman, to "hear of him", to hear the gospel of his free and sovereign grace in Christ. "For a certain woman, whose young daughter had an unclean spirit, heard of him, and came and fell at his feet" (v. 25).

As already stated, we do not know who the instrument was by whom this woman was taught of God; but we do know that an instrument was used. The scriptures tell us it is the will, pleasure, and purpose of God to use gospel preaching, by one means or another, to save sinners, give them faith in Christ, and teach them (Romans 1:15, 16; 10:13-17; 1 Corinthians 1:18-29; Ephesians 1:13; 4:8-16; 1 Timothy 4:12-16; James 1:18; 1 Peter 1:23-25).

We preach the gospel with a sense of urgency, knowing that sinners cannot believe on Christ until Christ is preached to them. Yet, we preach with confidence of success, knowing that our labour is not in vain in the Lord (1 Corinthians 15:58). God's Word will not return to him void. It will accomplish his will and prosper in the thing it is sent to accomplish (Isaiah 55:11). Every chosen, redeemed sinner must be called by the Holy Spirit through the preaching of the gospel.

True prayer arises from a heartfelt need of mercy, grace, and divine intervention. "And, behold, a woman of Canaan came out of the same coasts, and cried unto him, saying, Have mercy on me, O Lord, thou son of David; my daughter is grievously vexed with a devil" (Matthew 15:22).

"The woman was a Greek, a Syrophenician by nation; and she besought him that he would cast forth the devil out of her daughter" (v. 26).

Such is the pride, self-sufficiency, and arrogance of our hearts that we will never come down until God brings us down. We will never beg for mercy until we need mercy. We will not seek grace until we need grace. We will not come to Christ until we have to have him.

This woman came to the Lord Jesus because her daughter was "grievously vexed with a devil". Her only hope was the Son of God who was manifested to destroy the works of the devil (1 John 3:8). How blessed it is to have such a Saviour to whom we may turn in times of distress and trouble (Hebrews 4:16). May God the Holy Spirit give us such faith in Christ as this woman had, that we may spread our sorrows before him and seek grace to help in every time of need.

This woman wanted just one thing from the Lord, mercy! She cried, "Have mercy on me, O Lord"! What a comprehensive prayer that is. If he will have mercy, we need no more. The ground upon which she hoped for mercy was the fact that the man Jesus is the "Son of David", Immanuel, God with us, God in our nature, God and man in one person. She sought mercy from Christ because he is the Christ.

Thousands of the Jews saw him daily, who knew him not; but this woman who was a Gentile knew him, believed him, came to him, and sought mercy from him. Obviously, none but God could have taught her; and the teaching of God infallibly brought her to Christ. So it has ever been; and so it shall ever be (John 6:45, 46).

The Place Of Mercy Is At His Feet

Look at Mark's description of this woman's behaviour. "For a certain woman, whose young daughter had an unclean spirit, heard of him, and came and fell at his feet: The woman was a Greek, a Syrophenician by nation; and she besought him that he would cast forth the devil out of her daughter" (vv. 25, 26).

She was in trouble and had a desperate need. She heard about Christ. She came to the Son of God. She fell at his feet. If we would worship Christ and obtain mercy from him, we must be found, like this needy soul, "at his feet" (Mark 5:22; Luke 7:2; John 11:32; Revelation 1:17). This is the place of mercy, the place of humility, the place of reverence, the place of worship, the place of love, the place of obedience, the place of blessing, the place of honour, the place of peace, and the place of contentment.

True Faith Always Bows To Christ

Faith does not rebel against Christ's words or his deeds. Faith bows, and acknowledges Christ's place, dominion, and rights as Lord.

"But he answered her not a word. And his disciples came and besought him, saying, Send her away; for she crieth after us. But he answered and said, I am not sent but unto the lost sheep of the house of Israel. Then came she and worshipped him, saying, Lord, help me. But he answered and said, It is not meet to take the children's bread, and cast it to dogs. And she said, Truth, Lord: yet the dogs eat of the crumbs which fall from their masters' table" (Matthew 15:23-27).

"But Jesus said unto her, Let the children first be filled: for it is not meet to take the children's bread, and to cast it unto the dogs. And she answered and said unto him, Yes, Lord: yet the dogs under the table eat of the children's crumbs" (vv. 27, 28).

The Lord Jesus ignored her; but she considered that his right and waited for him to acknowledge her. For her benefit and ours, the Master spoke to her plainly about the purpose of God in election and the distinguishing character of his grace; and she worshipped him (Matthew 15:24, 25). The Lord described her in the most humbling terms, calling her a dog; but she took the ground he gave her, and begged his mercy and help, even if it were just the crumbs others despised.

Faith Honours Christ And Christ Honours Faith

"Then Jesus answered and said unto her, O woman, great is thy faith: be it unto thee even as thou wilt. And her daughter was made whole from that very hour" (Matthew 15:28).

"Be it unto thee even as thou wilt". Robert Hawker suggested that it is "as if Jesus threw the reins of government into her hand." Does he not say as much to all true faith? "Thus saith the LORD, the Holy One of Israel, and his Maker, Ask me of things to come concerning my sons, and concerning the work of my hands command ye me" (Isaiah 45:11).

When Christ enters into the house of man's soul and takes possession of it, he drives the devil out by the power of his grace. We are told that when this woman came into her house, "she found the devil gone out".

Let me show you one more thing. I readily admit that I'm stretching the text, using it now in a strictly allegorical, spiritual way; but I am not stretching the scriptures. What I have to say in the last place is the teaching of scripture, and a blessed teaching it is. Here is a sweet dessert indeed. In Mark 7:30 we read, "And her daughter laid upon the bed". Consider this lesson:

When Christ Saves Sinners He Always Puts Them To Bed

Isaiah tells us of those who lay in a bed of religious deceit, a bed of free will, works religion, in which no rest is to be found. The bed of your works is too short to stretch out on it; and the covering of your self-righteousness is too narrow to wrap up in (Isaiah 28:20).

Here is a bed you can stretch out on; Christ's blood atonement! Here is a covering you can wrap up in; Christ's perfect righteousness! But the only way you will ever stretch out on this bed and wrap up in this cover is if Christ himself gives you rest. Therefore, he graciously bids weary, helpless, guilty sinners to come to him for mercy and grace.

"Come unto me, all ye that labour and are heavy laden, and I will give you rest. Take my yoke upon you, and learn of me; for I am meek and lowly in heart: and ye shall find rest unto your souls. For my yoke is easy, and my burden is light" (Matthew 11:28-30).

May God the Holy Spirit lay to our hearts the wonders of God's free grace in Christ that are displayed in the inspired records Matthew and Mark have given us of this woman.

We see the sovereignty of God's grace in this chosen vessel, called from the coasts of Tyre and Sidon. Christ has his elect in all nations, who must be gathered to him. They shall come from north, south, east and west. They shall come willingly in the day of his power (Psalm 110:3).

Often our God uses great afflictions and troubles to sweetly force his own to seek his mercy, just as he did in the case of this woman (Psalm 107). How we ought to thank him for those trials of life by which our Saviour sweetly causes us, under the influence of his grace, to seek him!

In order to enhance his blessing in our estimation and to improve our faith, the mercy we desperately need is sometimes withheld for a season, just as it was with this woman. By graciously forcing us to wait at his feet, our Saviour renews our strength (Isaiah 40:27-31).

When the Lord was about to perform his wondrous mercy for this woman, he first forced her to take her proper place of humility before him, calling her a dog, to which she replied, "Truth, Lord". She acknowledged that she was altogether unworthy of children's bread. A proper view of Christ's greatness, grace, and glory always causes sinners to have a proper view of themselves. Christ alone is exalted where Christ is known in the blessed experience of his grace (Psalm 115:1).

All who have experienced God's mercy in Christ can gladly sing with Augustus Toplady:

> A debtor to mercy alone—
> Of covenant mercy I sing;
> Nor fear, with thy righteousness on,
> My person and off'ring to bring.
> The terrors of law and of God,
> With me can have nothing to do;
> My Saviour's obedience and blood,
> Hide all my transgressions from view.
>
> The work which his goodness began,
> The arm of his strength will complete;
> His promise is Yea and Amen,
> And never was forfeited yet;
> Things future, nor things that are now,
> Not all things below nor above,
> Can make Him His purpose forego,
> Or sever my soul from His love.
>
> My name from the palm of his hands,
> Eternity will not erase;
> Impressed on his heart it remains,
> In marks of indelible grace.
> Yes, I to the end shall endure,
> As sure as the earnest is giv'n—
> More happy, but not more secure,
> The glorified spirits in heav'n.

Mercy Needed, Mercy Sought, Mercy Given

"And again, departing from the coasts of Tyre and Sidon, he came unto the sea of Galilee, through the midst of the coasts of Decapolis. And they bring unto him one that was deaf, and had an impediment in his speech; and they beseech him to put his hand upon him. And he took him aside from the multitude, and put his fingers into his ears, and he spit, and touched his tongue; And looking up to heaven, he sighed, and saith unto him, Ephphatha, that is, Be opened. And straightway his ears were opened, and the string of his tongue was loosed, and he spake plain. And he charged them that they should tell no man: but the more he charged them, so much the more a great deal they published it; And were beyond measure astonished, saying, He hath done all things well: he maketh both the deaf to hear, and the dumb to speak".

(Mark 7:31-37)

Chapter 30

"Ephphatha"

We have before us the story of the remarkable cure wrought by our Lord Jesus Christ upon a man who was a deaf mute. It is a story told only by Mark.

"Departing from the coasts of Tyre and Sidon, he came unto the sea of Galilee, through the midst of the coasts of Decapolis". How quickly the Son of God passes by! While he is present there is hope. When he is gone there is none! He came into the coasts of Tyre and Sidon. While he was there one lone Canaanite woman seized the opportunity. One lone woman came to the Master and obtained mercy. Now, he was gone! Mercy was gone! Grace was gone! The Son of God passed through the coasts of Tyre and Sidon, but did not stay long. What a warning! He came there to show mercy to that chosen sinner. Indeed, he showed mercy to every sinner who sought him for it. Then he left as quickly as he had come. Well might we cry with Fanny Crosby:

> Pass me not, O gentle Saviour! Hear my humble cry,
> While on others Thou art calling, do not pass me by!

Our Lord Jesus, while he walked on this earth, never stayed in one place for very long. When he had cured the Canaanite woman's daughter, he had done what he came there to do. Then he went through the coasts of Decapolis; he came again unto the sea of Galilee, where he had so often performed miracles of mercy and taught sinners the way of life.

As our Lord's departure from the coasts of Tyre and Sidon is a warning, his return unto Galilee is most hopeful and encouraging. The Son of God is often found in the same place and often performs his wonders among the same people. I cannot tell you how that inspires me as a member of a local church where the Lord Jesus has constantly manifested his presence for twenty-eight years. As I try to prepare my heart for worship, Sunday after Sunday and Tuesday after Tuesday, I come to the house of God with the prayer and hope, with the reverent expectation that Christ will meet with us again, that he will show himself again, that he will speak again, that he will again stretch forth his mighty arm of grace for the saving of chosen, redeemed sinners, that he might again embrace me in his arms, smother me with his love, and revive me with his Spirit!

A Very Sad Condition

The healing of this deaf mute by the Son of God is a tremendous picture of our Lord's power and of his grace. In verse 32 we see a man in a very sad condition. "And they bring unto him one that was deaf, and had an impediment in his speech; and they beseech him to put his hand upon him".

We are not told who these people were that brought this poor deaf-mute to the Lord Jesus. We do not need to know. But someone had heard about Christ. Perhaps they had personally seen or experienced the Master's miraculous healing, saving power. Whatever the case, they knew who Christ was, where he was, what he could do, and how desperately this poor soul needed the Saviour. So they brought him to the Lord Jesus, knowing that if he would just lay his hand on him, the deaf-mute would be healed. "Gracious souls", Robert Hawker observed, "who know the Lord, do well to bring to Jesus those who know him not. He that hath unstopped your ears, and opened your lips, can do the same by others." John Gill wrote, concerning those who brought this man to Christ:

> As the friends and relations of this man, having a great opinion of Christ, and a persuasion of his ability to relieve and cure him, bring him unto him, that he might put his hands upon him; so do such who know Christ themselves, and have felt the power of his grace upon their own souls, bring their deaf and dumb, their relations in a state of nature, under the means of grace; being very desirous that Christ would make bare, and put forth his mighty arm of grace, and lay hold upon them, and work a good work in them, and give them ears to hear his voice, and a tongue to speak his praise.

Notice how the Holy Spirit directed Mark to choose his words, "and they beseech him to put his hand upon him." That is to be commended. They firmly believed that Christ could heal this poor man by merely laying his hands upon him. Yet, they made a big mistake, as we shall see. They dared to presume to tell the Son of God how to heal him! We must never do so. We must never presume to prescribe to God how to do his work, or even presume that he must always work his wonders the same way. Every child of God discovers the same grace, by the same means; but we all have differing experiences of grace. This man's experience was truly singular. He knew the grace and power of God like no one else in the world!

This poor, needy creature is a good picture of all men by nature, representing unregenerate sinners, who are deaf to the voice of both the law of God and the gospel. All who are yet without life and faith in Christ are very much like this man.

He does not hear what God says by way of wrath and condemnation in his holy law. The unregenerate do not hear the command of the law. He will not and cannot obey the precepts of the law. And he is not moved by the menacing curse, condemnation, and terrible wrath and justice of the law. God says, "The soul that sinneth it shall die". But that does not bother him. He is deaf. He is not at all affected and disturbed with such things. You might as well be talking to stones, when talking to unregenerate souls about the things of God. Indeed, you are talking to stones. Until God graciously takes away the stony heart, none can hear.

Unregenerate souls stop their ears to the melodic sound of the gospel. The sweet sound of Jesus Christ and Him crucified, they utterly despise. They consider it contemptuous, bothersome and irksome. They are deaf to all the instructions, directions, cautions, and exhortations of God's Word, his servants, their dearest relations and their best friends.

Not only are all men by nature spiritually deaf, they are deaf-mutes. Try as they might they cannot speak the language of Canaan. It is a strange language to them. They cannot speak it; and they cannot understand it when others speak it. Things of Christ sound like meaningless babble about nothing to them. And, having no true experience of the grace of God in their souls, they simply cannot speak of what they do not know. Robert Hawker says:

> Nothing becomes more striking, in proof of a spiritual deafness and dumbness, than a poor unawakened sinner. He is like the deaf adder, which stoppeth her ears at the voice of the charmer; charm he never so wisely; for all the melody of mercy in the gospel of Christ, nor all the harsh sounds of condemnation in the law of God, can affect his mind, And as he hears of nothing, either to allure, or to alarm, so no cry for salvation ever passeth his lips.

I think it is also proper to say that this poor deaf-mute is a picture of sinners newly awakened by the Spirit of God. When a person is first born again, we ought not expect him or her to walk and talk like an aged saint. Babes in Christ usually behave as such, though they may think they are very strong, mature, and knowledgeable. Children often think that way. And those who are under the first workings of the Spirit of God upon their souls are often as it were, tongue tied. Through fear or bashfulness, or temptations of Satan, they fear to speak; or with great difficulty are brought to speak of what God has done for them. When they do it is in a lisping, stammering way.

A Very Singular Cure

"And he took him aside from the multitude, and put his fingers into his ears, and he spit, and touched his tongue; And looking up to heaven, he sighed, and saith unto him, Ephphatha, that is, Be opened. And straightway his ears were opened, and the string of his tongue was loosed, and he spake plain" (vv. 33-35).

This mighty miracle performed by our Saviour was a clear demonstration of his sovereign power over creation and over all the elements of nature in creation. But, if all we see in this miracle is the fact that a deaf-mute was miraculously cured by the power of God, if all we see here is a picture of physical healing, we have missed the point altogether. There are precious, spiritual truths revealed here, lessons about God's saving power, mercy, and grace in Christ toward helpless sinners.

The Holy Spirit intends for us to see here that the Son of God has power to heal the spiritually deaf. He can give the most hard-hearted, spiritually deaf sinner a hearing ear and make him delight in hearing the very gospel he once despised. As he can heal spiritually deaf sinners, he can also untie the tongue of those who are spiritually mute. Jesus Christ can cause the most obstinate rebel to call upon him in faith. He can put a new song of grace in the heart and in the mouth of the vilest transgressor. And he can make the basest blasphemer a preacher of the gospel.

When the Son of God comes in saving power, nothing is impossible. We believe in and preach irresistible grace, grace that cannot be resisted. When God has a will to save, the sinner he comes to save has no will to resist. "Thy people shall be willing in the day of thy power, in the beauties of holiness from the womb of the morning: thou hast the dew of thy youth" (Psalm 110:3). Let no sinner regard himself as being beyond the reach of God's omnipotent arm. Let us never consider anyone beyond hope. Jesus Christ, our all glorious Saviour, is that One who is Mighty to save. He that healed the deaf-mute still lives.

I remind you again that our all glorious Saviour is not limited to any one way of doing things. The peculiar means employed by the Son of God in healing this man may have many hidden lessons that I do not see, but this is the most obvious thing about it. I know that God saves chosen sinners by the appointed means of grace, as he has declared in scripture. "Faith cometh by hearing, and hearing by the Word of God". Still, sometimes God works one way and sometimes another. Sometimes he works through the Word preached publicly. Sometimes he works by the Word spoken privately. Sometimes he is pleased to use the oral exposition of the Word, and sometimes the written exposition. Sometimes he uses great adversities and afflictions to bring sinners to himself. Sometimes he uses the gentle, loving persuasion of a friend or relative to arrest the attention of the chosen. But of this you may be sure: God almighty will not perform his wonders of grace like a trained seal in obedience to our whims and plans! As soon as we begin to think this is the way the Son of God works, by laying his hands on the needy soul, he uses something as despised by us as spit, and gives no account of his matters.

Look at the details of what the Lord Jesus did here and glean the spiritual truths set before us in this wonder of mercy. He took him aside, separating him from everyone else. When the Lord Jesus comes to save, he separates his people, like sheep singled out of a flock by the shepherd, from the rest of the world. He allures his chosen into the wilderness that he may speak to their hearts, that he may speak grace to the soul. He calls his elect out of the world, out of Babylon, and brings them to himself.

The Master put his fingers into the deaf man's ears, as if to say, "I alone, who made the ear, can give the hearing ear to whom I will by the finger of my grace." He puts his finger into the ears of his redeemed and opens them to hear "the joyful sound". He spat and touched the man's tongue, as if to say, "Only that which comes forth out of me entering into you can loosen your tongue and cause you to know and show forth my praise." Hawker says, "He truly toucheth our tongues with the spittle of his mouth, when he looseneth our lips to speak his praise." What a humbling, but necessary picture!

The Lord Jesus looked up to heaven, as One who is the Servant of God on a mission from God, doing the will of God, teaching us that all grace and power, all good and perfect gifts, indeed, all things are of God. Then, he sighed. No doubt this is a picture of our Saviour's compassion, pity, and mercy for needy souls. It was a sigh for this man, but for many others as well.

Next, he looked at the deaf-mute himself and spoke a single word of sovereign power and authority, "Ephphatha"! The word means, "Be opened"! Immediately, the man's ears were opened and his tongue was loosed, so that he spoke plainly. Those whose ears are opened and whose tongues are loosed by Christ speak plainly and clearly of what they have seen and heard, of what they have experienced and been taught by the grace of God. They can give a ready answer to any man who asks the reason of their hope. Mr Spurgeon once told a story illustrating this beautifully.

Once there was a poor man, a huckster called Jack, who used to go through country villages selling his goods. This poor creature, while going round on his journeys, heard some women singing a little chorus. It went:

'I'm a poor sinner, and nothing at all,
But Jesus Christ is my all in all.'

Jack said to himself, 'That sure suits me.' So he started to hum the tune to himself, as he walked along. By God's grace, in time, the words of the little chorus worked their way into the poor man's heart.

After some time he was converted and began to attend church regularly. Finally, he made up his mind to publicly confess his faith in Christ and join the church. So he went to see the pastor. The pastor asked him, 'What can you say for yourself?' 'Not much,' Jack replied, 'only this':

> 'I'm a poor sinner, and nothing at all,
> But Jesus Christ is my all in all.'

'You must tell me more than that,' the pastor said. 'No, I can't,' Jack answered, 'for that is all I know. That's my confession of faith.' 'Well,' the pastor said, 'I cannot refuse you church fellowship, but you will have to come before the elders and deacons. They will see you and judge you.'

At the appointed time the poor huckster met with the elders and deacons. They wanted to see if they could find some fault with him. Being asked to stand and state his experience, Jack simply said:

> 'I'm a poor sinner, and nothing at all,
> But Jesus Christ is my all in all.'

One of the old men asked, 'Is that all you have to say?' 'Yes, that's all,' he answered. The pastor said, 'You may ask him some questions, if you wish.' So another man spoke up. 'Brother Jack, Do you have many doubts and fears?' 'No,' Jack answered, 'I can never doubt that I am a poor sinner and nothing at all, for I know that I am. And I can never doubt that Jesus Christ is my all in all, for he says he is. How can I doubt that?'

Then another man said, 'But sometimes I lose my evidences and my graces, and then I get very sad.' 'Oh,' Jack said, 'I can never lose anything, for, in the first place, I am a poor sinner and nothing at all. No one can rob me if I am nothing. And in the second place, Jesus Christ is my all in all. And who can rob him? He is in heaven. I never get richer or poorer, for I am always nothing, but I always have everything.'

'But, my dear brother, Jack,' another man asked, 'Don't you sometimes doubt whether you are a child of God?' 'Well,' he said, 'I don't quite understand your question. But I can tell you I never doubt but that I am a poor sinner and nothing at all and that Jesus Christ is my all in all.'

They were astonished at Jack's simple, constant composure. They had a world of doubts and fears. When they asked him why he never doubted, he just said, 'I cannot doubt but that I am a poor sinner, and nothing at all, for I know that, and feel it every day. And why should I doubt that Jesus Christ is my all in all? for he says he is.'

'Oh,' one of the men said, 'I have my ups and downs.' 'I don't,' Jack replied. 'I can never go up, for in myself I am a poor sinner and nothing at all; and I cannot go down, for Jesus Christ is my all in all.'

The deacons and elders kept trying to shake the simple man from his simple faith. 'Why,' said one brother, 'I sometimes feel so full of grace, I feel so advanced in sanctification, that I begin to be very happy.' 'I never do,' Jack replied. 'I am a poor sinner and nothing at all.' 'Then, I go down again, and think I am not saved, because I am not as sanctified as I used to be,' the brother continued. 'I never doubt my salvation,' Jack said, 'because Jesus Christ is my all in all, and he never alters.'

They admitted Jack into the church, and he continued all the days of his life with this simple confession:

> 'I'm a poor sinner, and nothing at all,
> But Jesus Christ is my all in all.'

That was all his experience, and you could not get him beyond it. For the rest of his days on earth, the poor huckster was called 'Happy Jack', because of his happiness in faith. Happy Jack's simple story is beautifully instructive. It sets forth a picture of plain, simple, clear faith in Christ. It exemplifies adherence to Paul's admonition in Colossians 2:6. 'As ye have therefore received Christ Jesus the Lord, so walk ye in him.'

A Very Satisfying Confession

"And he charged them that they should tell no man: but the more he charged them, so much the more a great deal they published it; And were beyond measure astonished, saying, He hath done all things well: he maketh both the deaf to hear, and the dumb to speak" (vv. 36, 37).

The Lord charged them to tell no man what he had done. Perhaps he did so because he sought not the praise of men, perhaps so that he might try these people, to see if they were truly grateful for his grace. Whatever the case, this deaf-mute was not about to keep his mouth shut! He went everywhere confessing Christ who had wrought such wonders in him. He who is God our Saviour "maketh both the deaf to hear and the dumb to speak"!

"He hath done all things well". No doubt these poor souls no more knew the full meaning of their words when they spoke them than we do in repeating them; but what a help is here for our souls. "He hath done all things well"! Let us remember this when we think about the past, as we consider the present, and as we anticipate the future. In that great and glorious eternal day awaiting us, we will fully see and gladly confess "He hath done all things well"! In that great day we will understand the why and wherefore of all things. We will wonder at our past blindness and marvel that we could ever have doubted our Saviour's love or called into question his faithfulness.

"And were beyond measure astonished, saying, He hath done all things well: he maketh both the deaf to hear, and the dumb to speak".

(Mark 7:37)

Chapter 31

"He Hath Done All Things Well"

Try to picture the scene. Our Lord Jesus has just come to Decapolis from the coasts of Tyre and Sidon, where he had healed the Syrophenician's daughter, who was vexed with an unclean spirit. Here he continued his acts of mercy, healing one who was both deaf and suffered from a speech impediment.

His fame was so great that he simply could not be hidden. There is a huge crowd before him. He had caused the lame to walk, the deaf to hear, and the dumb to speak. He who cast out devils, opened the eyes of the blind, and raised the dead by the mere word of his power stood before the astonished crowd, who in their amazement said, "He hath done all things well". If these men and women who had seen our Saviour's miracles were astonished and cried out, "He hath done all things well", how much more astonished we ought to be who have tasted and experienced his grace! How much more we ought to confess to God our Saviour, to the angels before his throne, to wondering worlds, and to one another, "He hath done all things well"!

My Testimony
Looking over all the days of my life and everything I have experienced these 57 years, I lift my heart to heaven and say, "He hath done all things well"! Like you, I have had a few trials and heartaches, a little pain and sorrow, a little hurt and bitterness. And, I am ashamed to confess, I have caused much more than I've felt. But God my Saviour has been so kind to me, that were I to die this day, you can write these words on my gravestone. "'He hath done all things well!' Here lies a man who was for 57 years the benefactor of unceasing, special divine care. And 'My Jesus hath done all things well.'"

> Sinners redeemed, with wonder tell,
> Christ Jesus has done all things well!
> By His great sin-atoning blood,
> Believing, we have peace with God.
>
> That One who bought us with His blood
> Now reigns on high, the Son of God!
> This fact our every fear should quell—
> Christ Jesus has done all things well!

A Question

Can you not testify the same? "He hath done all things well"! Does your own life's experience not verify this? If you are one of God's elect, I know it does. Yes, from first to last, from the day of our birth to this very hour, from the earliest pangs of sin's conviction to the blessed thrill of sin's forgiveness, from the cradle to the grave, from earth to heaven, this will be our testimony regarding all the way our ever-gracious God has led us through this wilderness and every step along the way, "He hath done all things well"!

In providence and in grace, in every truth revealed in his Word, in every token of his love, in every stroke of his rod, in every sunbeam of his goodness, in every cloud that has darkened our skies, in every sweet morsel he has put into our lives, in every bitter thing he has mixed into our cup, in all that has been mysterious, confusing, painful, and humiliating, in all that he has given, and in all that he has taken away, this is the sum of it all. "He hath done all things well"! This is, must be, and shall be our grateful acknowledgment through time and eternity. "He hath done all things well"!

Our great God and Saviour who loved us, chose us, redeemed us and saved us by his grace, who has kept us in all our ways, has done all things well! He who is our God is too wise to err, too strong to fail, and too good to do wrong. He cannot do wrong. Study his universe, all the history of it; study his creation, his providence, his judgments, and his grace; view them in every light; examine them in their most minute detail, as you would the petal of a flower, or the wing of an insect; study all with the microscope of faith, and this will be your glad testimony to his praise, "He hath done all things well"! This is David's testimony; and it is ours. "Thou hast dealt well with thy servant, O LORD, according unto thy word. Teach me good judgment and knowledge: for I have believed thy commandments. Before I was afflicted I went astray: but now have I kept thy word. Thou art good, and doest good; teach me thy statutes" (Psalm 119:65-68).

I could never find better words to sum up my life's experience than those. God my Saviour has dealt with me. What an awesome thought! All the days of my life my God has dealt with me. All the days of my life the Angel of the Lord has pitched his tent around me and dealt with me (Psalm 34:7). Not only that, he has dealt well with me! Truly, "Thou hast dealt well with thy servant". In fact he has dealt so well with me that these words do not begin to start telling my astonishment at how well he has dealt with my soul.

The word David uses for "well" is one of those magnificent little words that is bursting with meaning. It means, most favourably, most kindly, most graciously, most lovingly, most pleasurably, most sweetly, most prosperously, most finely, most joyfully, and most merrily.

Particularly, these last 41 years since he saved me by his grace, my God has dealt well with me as his servant. Of course, he has dealt with me as his son, as his spouse, and as his friend. But, like David, I take particular delight in saying he has dealt well with me as his servant (Ephesians 3:8; 1 Corinthians 1:26-29), in his appointing and calling me to be his servant, in providing for me as his servant, in his protection of his servant, and in the reward he gives to his servant.

He has dealt well with me all the days of my life according to his Word. "Thou hast dealt well with thy servant, O LORD, according unto thy word". According to his word of predestination, according to his inspired, written Word of promise, according to his word of grace, and according to Christ his Word, truly, "He hath done all things well"! Let me elaborate just a little.

Let every redeemed sinner who serves God with a willing heart acknowledge the Lord's unfailing goodness to him. Truly, he has dealt well with all his servants, according to his Word. In addition to the immeasurable riches of his grace to us in Christ, our great God has constantly loaded our days with goodness in providence! He promised, "There shall no evil happen to the just". And no evil has ever befallen one of God's elect. Much that we experience appears to be evil at the time. We may, in our unbelief, even look upon it as evil. But God has proved himself faithful. Looking back upon the things we thought were most evil at the time we experienced them, we now can say, "I thank God that happened. I praise him for that experience. By it good has come to me and good has come to a brother here and a sister there."

It is good to acknowledge the good when we see it; but it is far better and far more honouring to God to acknowledge the goodness of his providence when nothing good can be seen, except by the eye of faith. When I can look up to my Father, with tears burning my cheeks and sorrow crushing my heart, and say with confident faith, "Thou hast dealt well with thy servant", then I will have proved the reality of my faith.

Child of God, whatever your God has done or allowed to be done for you, with you, or to you, he has done you good. The same is true of me. So let us, with glad hearts, acknowledge now what we will acknowledge when all things are set in their true light. "Thou hast dealt well with thy servant, O Lord, according unto thy word".

> Let us His praise and wonders tell,
> Sing! For our God's done all things well!
> Through Jesus' sin-atoning blood,
> Sinners are reconciled to God.
> In grace and providence, as well,
> The Triune God does all things well!

The Father, Son, and Holy Ghost,
The Triune God in whom we trust,
Has promised, and He's proved it good,
That He works all things for our good.
In grace and providence, as well,
The Triune God does all things well!

Let sinners loved of God and bought,
Who by free grace have been sought out,
Love Him who has made us His choice.
In joyful praise, lift up your voice!
In grace and providence, as well,
The Triune God does all things well!

In Eternity

He has done all things well from eternity. When we think of all that our Saviour did for us as our Surety in old eternity (if I can use such language), before the world was, our hearts gladly confess, "He hath done all things well"! In the covenant of grace, when he took upon himself all responsibility for our souls and espoused our cause as our great Surety, "He hath done all things well"! He drew nigh to God on our behalf. His delights were with us. His heart was upon us. He pledged himself to redeem and save us. He gave himself as the Lamb of God to redeem us. And the Father accepted us and blessed us with all spiritual blessings in him, trusting him as our Surety (Ephesians 1:3-12).

In His Incarnation

In the fulness of time, when God sent forth his Son, made of a woman, made under the law, to redeem them that were under the law, when the Son of God came down here and took on him the seed of Abraham, "He hath done all things well"!

As a Man, the Lord Jesus Christ lived on earth in perfect righteousness, not for himself, but for us, that he might bring in everlasting righteousness of infinite worth on our behalf, that he might be "The Lord our Righteousness". "Of him are ye in Christ Jesus, who of God is made unto us righteousness". "He hath made him to be sin for us, who knew no sin, that we might be made the righteousness of God in him".

Look back upon your past sins, look upon your present infirmities, and look upon your future errors, and, while you weep the tears of repentance, rejoice that there is no fear of condemnation, for Christ is our Righteousness.

Child of God, today you stand before God robed in the garments of Christ. With unspeakable joy, I assert that in Christ we are as holy as our Holy Redeemer. We have a better righteousness than Adam had in the garden. Christ's righteousness is compared to fine linen clean and white; and if we wear it, then we are without spot. In this robe we are worthy to sit at the wedding feast of the great King. In the parable of the prodigal son this is called "the best robe". It is a better robe than Adam had in the Garden. It is a better robe than the angels have. And it is a robe that shall never be worn out.

Not only is Christ our righteousness for justification, he is our righteousness for sanctification, too (1 Corinthians 1:30; Hebrews 10:10-14). Ralph Erskine said, "If you would have righteousness, you must have it in and from Christ. He has to give you both an imputed righteousness for justifying you; and an imparted righteousness for sanctifying you." Just as the fallen, unrighteous nature of Adam was imparted to all men by natural birth, the holy, righteous nature of Christ is imparted to all God's elect in the new birth. The righteousness of Christ is imputed to us for justification; and the righteousness of Christ is imparted to us in regeneration by the irresistible power and effectual grace of God the Holy Spirit (1 Peter 3:10-12; 1 John 3:7-9).

J. C. Philpot once said:

> If once I catch by the eye of faith this glorious truth, that Jesus Christ is of God made unto me 'righteousness' the moment I see that by the eye of faith, a measure of imparted righteousness flows into my heart. The soul then receives internally what Christ has done externally. In a word, when Christ is received as 'wisdom, righteousness, sanctification, and redemption,' he becomes all these in vital manifestation.

Because we were justified by Christ's imputed righteousness at the cross, we are sanctified by his imparted righteousness in the new birth. "I will greatly rejoice in the Lord, my soul shall be joyful in my God; for he hath clothed me with the garments of salvation, he hath covered me with the robe of righteousness" (Isaiah 61:10).

It is only in Christ that God is well pleased. He declares, "This is my beloved Son in whom I am well pleased", not *with* whom, but *in* whom I am pleased, satisfied, delighted. And in Christ, God is well pleased with us. It is only through the merits and mediation of Christ our Righteousness that God accepts us in Christ as "a living Sacrifice", holy and acceptable to God, and accepts the sacrifices we bring to him by Christ, that living Sacrifice

(Romans 12:1; 1 Peter 2:5). The only claim that we have to the heavenly inheritance is Christ our righteousness; but we need no other claim. In him we have been made worthy of heaven's glory, worthy "to be partakers of the inheritance of the saints in light" (Colossians 1:12).

In Redemption
But he did not stop there. The life of Christ in perfect obedience to the Father would be of no benefit to our souls without atonement. His righteousness could never have been ours had he not also redeemed us with his precious blood. Therefore, "in due time Christ died for the ungodly". And in his great, wondrous work of redemption, "He hath done all things well"! When the Lord Jesus was made sin for us, that we might be made the righteousness of God in him, he laid down his life for us, and in so doing made complete satisfaction for our sins to God's holy law and offended justice. And now, the Lord God comes to chosen, redeemed sinners in grace as "a just God and a Saviour". Justice is satisfied. Sin has been put away. The curse of the law is gone forever. And we are free (Romans 8:1-4, 32-34; Galatians 3:13; 1 Peter 1:18-20; 3:18; Isaiah 12:1).

In Grace
Reflect upon this fact, too. "He hath done all things well" in the mighty operations of his saving grace. In Holy Spirit conviction, in effectual calling, in conversion, in the forgiveness of our sins, and in preserving our souls, "He hath done all things well" (Psalms 32:1-5; 34:1-4, 6; 116:1-7).

> I spurned his grace, I broke his laws,
> And yet he undertook my cause,
> To save my sinful soul from hell,
> My Jesus hath done all things well.

In Love
How our hearts rejoice to know and acknowledge, "He hath done all things well" in every display of his great love for us.

"That Christ may dwell in your hearts by faith; that ye, being rooted and grounded in love, May be able to comprehend with all saints what is the breadth, and length, and depth, and height; And to know the love of Christ, which passeth knowledge, that ye might be filled with all the fulness of God" (Ephesians 3:17-19).

"But God commendeth his love toward us, in that, while we were yet sinners, Christ died for us. Much more then, being now justified by his blood, we shall be saved from wrath through him. For if, when we were enemies, we were reconciled to God by the death of his Son, much more, being reconciled, we shall be saved by his life" (Romans 5:8-10).

"Behold, what manner of love the Father hath bestowed upon us, that we should be called the sons of God: therefore the world knoweth us not, because it knew him not" (1 John 3:1).

"Hereby perceive we the love of God, because he laid down his life for us: and we ought to lay down our lives for the brethren" (1 John 3:16).

"In this was manifested the love of God toward us, because that God sent his only begotten Son into the world, that we might live through him. Herein is love, not that we loved God, but that he loved us, and sent his Son to be the propitiation for our sins" (1 John 4:9, 10).

"We love him, because he first loved us" (1 John 4:19).

In Providence
"I will sing unto the Lord, because he hath dealt bountifully with me" (Psalm 13:6) "Return unto thy rest, O my soul; for the Lord hath dealt bountifully with thee" (Psalm 116:7). "We know that all things work together for good to them that love God, to them who are the called according to his purpose" (Romans 8:28).

What a good God and Saviour we have! What a text this is! Our biographies, the stories of our lives, expound it far better than any book. The Lord has dealt bountifully with us. He who gave us his darling Son has with him freely given us all things.

He has given us his Spirit and he conveys to us all spiritual blessings in Christ. Our God deals with us like the good and gracious God he is. He lays open all his infinite fulness to us. "And of his fulness have all we received, and grace for grace".

Is not your life a verification of these things? Mine is. Truly, in all the affairs of providence, "He hath done all things well"! And that which he has done, he is doing and shall forever continue to do, until he has finished doing all that he purposed to do in eternity. Then, we shall look back upon all things and say, "He hath done all things well"!

In that great day, when our mansions are prepared, our bodies raised from the dead, and we are perfectly conformed to the image of our Lord and Saviour in resurrection glory, when we hear him say, "Come, inherit the kingdom prepared for you from the foundation of the world", oh, with what rapture, gratitude, rejoicing, and love shall we shout, "HE HATH DONE ALL THINGS WELL"!

261

Samuel Medley wrote:

O for a heart prepared to sing,
To God, my Saviour and my King:
With all the saints I'll join to tell,
My Jesus hath done all things well.

All worlds his glorious power confess,
His wisdom all his works confess,
But O his love what tongue can tell!
My Jesus hath done all things well.

How sovereign, wonderful, and free,
Is all His love to sinful me!
He plucked me as a brand from hell—
My Jesus hath done all things well.

And since my soul has known His love,
What mercies He has made me prove,
Mercies which all my praise excel—
My Jesus will do all things well.

Soon I shall pass this vale of death,
And in his arms shall lose my breath,
Yet, then my happy soul shall tell,
My Jesus hath done all things well.

And when to that bright world I rise,
And join the anthems in the skies,
Among the rest, this note shall swell,
My Jesus hath done all things well.

"He Hath Done All Things Well"

In light of these facts, can you imagine what must be waiting for us on the other side, in that land where there is no darkness, no weeping, no sorrow, no pain, and no sin, in that blessed place called "Heaven", where "the former things are passed away"?

We read of a place that's called heaven.
It's made for the pure and the free.
These truths in God's Word He hath given—
How beautiful heaven must be!

In heaven no drooping nor pining,
No wishing for elsewhere to be.
God's light is forever there shining—
How beautiful heaven must be!

Pure waters of life there are flowing;
And all who will drink may be free.
Rare jewels of splendour are glowing—
How beautiful heaven must be!

The angels so sweetly are singing
Up there by the beautiful sea.
Sweet chords from their gold harps are ringing.
How beautiful heaven must be!

How beautiful heaven must be!
Sweet home of the happy and free,
Fair heaven of rest for the weary,
How beautiful heaven must be!

"In those days the multitude being very great, and having nothing to eat, Jesus called his disciples unto him, and saith unto them, I have compassion on the multitude, because they have now been with me three days, and have nothing to eat: And if I send them away fasting to their own houses, they will faint by the way: for divers of them came from far. And his disciples answered him, From whence can a man satisfy these men with bread here in the wilderness? And he asked them, How many loaves have ye? And they said, Seven. And he commanded the people to sit down on the ground: and he took the seven loaves, and gave thanks, and brake, and gave to his disciples to set before them; and they did set them before the people. And they had a few small fishes: and he blessed, and commanded to set them also before them. So they did eat, and were filled: and they took up of the broken meat that was left seven baskets. And they that had eaten were about four thousand: and he sent them away".

(Mark 8:1-9)

Chapter 32

Satisfaction Found In The Wilderness

Once again our Saviour is seen here miraculously feeding a hungry multitude in the wilderness. Here he fed four thousand men with just seven loaves of bread and a few pieces of fish. A similar miracle is recorded in Mark 6 and this same miracle was recorded by Matthew in Matthew 15.

The Son of God knew (and knows) the heart of man. He knew that cavilling sceptics would arise in every age who would deny his miraculous works, works that displayed his divinity with undeniable clarity. Therefore, he repeated this great miracle in a very public manner, before thousands of witnesses. He has fixed it so that the only way you can read the Bible and still go to hell in unbelief is by jumping over walls of stumbling blocks. Yet, men far prefer to explain away the very existence of God by the most ludicrous arguments imaginable, than believe the Word of God, trust a crucified Substitute, and bow to a sovereign Lord.

Satisfaction For Our Souls

"And his disciples answered him, From whence can a man satisfy these men with bread here in the wilderness?" (v. 4) In this wilderness we call life, in this world of sin, sorrow and suffering, and in the world to come, in that great wilderness called eternity, there is no satisfaction to be found for our immortal souls, except that satisfaction which is found in the Lord Jesus Christ, the Bread of Life.

Let me find nothing satisfying until I find Christ in it. I know that nothing can be dissatisfying, no matter how unpleasant and painful it is in itself, if I can see Christ in it. A conscious awareness of his presence sweetens every earthly bitterness. The love-tokens of his favour increases every joy. The sweet savour of his blessed name is as ointment poured forth, a spikenard very precious to perfume the lives of all who trust him. May God be pleased to make Christ the satisfaction of your heart and soul and of mine forever. Let us find satisfaction in nothing except our Saviour! He alone leads his chosen to "fountains of living water" and feeds us with the "bread of life". He makes his flesh to be meat indeed and his blood to be drink indeed, and he promises, that feeding upon him, we shall never hunger or thirst after the unsatisfying things of time and sense again (Revelation 7:17; John 6:51; 4:15).

False Faith

"The multitude was very great" (v. 1). There is, in the multitudes who followed our Saviour, though they never knew his grace, a clear demonstration of that false faith, by which multitudes deceive themselves. These vast multitudes followed our Master because of the loaves and fishes. They had either seen or heard about his miraculous powers and bountiful provisions.

Like these multitudes, many today take up a profession of faith and follow Christ in this world, sometimes for many years, who never know him. Some do so because they imagine they have seen a supernatural vision, or miracle. Some do so because they have been convinced of the historic facts of our Lord's earthly accomplishments. Some simply continue in the religious traditions in which they have been reared. Many take up a profession of religion for purely carnal, covetous reasons. Many more do so at a time of emotional crisis. But the solemn reality is that the vast majority of all those who profess faith in Christ prove in time that they never knew Christ.

True, saving faith is much, much more than a religious experience, a doctrinal position and a form of godliness. True faith essentially involves three things.

Knowledge
You cannot trust Christ if you do not know who he is and what he has done.

Assent
We must agree with God's testimony concerning his Son.

Commitment
We must bow to the Son of God as our Lord, trusting our souls upon his merit and to his dominion.

Matthew Henry wrote, "True zeal makes nothing of hardships in the way of duty. They that have a full feast for their souls may be content with slender provision for their bodies." However, it is not at all unusual for false piety to produce the same outward zeal. Religion without zeal is certainly false. But outward zeal is no true evidence of inward grace. Grace produces love, kindness, compassion, and care.

Frequently, those who are deceived with a false faith will endure great hardships to keep up their profession. These people underwent a great deal of difficulty in following Christ. They were with him three days, and had nothing to eat. That was hard service. Probably, there were some who brought some food with them from home. But by this time it was all gone. And they were a long way from home in the wilderness. Yet, they continued with Christ, and did not speak of leaving him.

Christ's Compassion

"I have compassion on the multitude, because they have now been with me three days, and have nothing to eat: And if I send them away fasting to their own houses, they will faint by the way: for divers of them came from far" (vv. 2, 3).

Our all glorious Christ is a Saviour full of compassion for needy souls. He has a compassion for those who are in need. As a man, he was the most caring of men. Yet, he has a special, particular concern for those that are reduced to need because of their zeal and devotion to him. He said, "I have compassion on the multitude". John Gill observed,

> Christ is a compassionate Saviour both of the bodies and souls of men: he had compassion on the souls of this multitude, and therefore had been teaching them sound doctrine and he had compassion on the bodies of many of them, and had healed them of their diseases; and his bowels yearned towards them all.

Those whom the proud Pharisees looked upon with disdain, the Son of God looked upon with pity and tenderness. We ought to do the same. Our Lord knew that the vast majority of those before him were hypocrites. Yet, he was moved with compassion toward them. He felt tenderly toward them. Thus, by example, he teaches us to love our enemies and to do good to those who hate us. I fear any form of religion that makes people hard, callous, unkind, and uncaring. Whatever it is, it is not the religion of Christ.

Yet, we must never fail to observe that our Lord's primary concern here and in all things is for his elect among the mixed multitude. While the multitudes often have a temporal benefit from his mercy, his mercy is designed for his elect. Paul tells us that he is the Saviour of all men, but that he is specially, particularly, and distinctly the Saviour of his elect. With that in mind, he said, "They have been with me three days, and have nothing to eat".

Our Master will see that we lack nothing by following him. Whatever losses we may incur, whatever hardships we may endure, whatever sacrifices we may be compelled to make because of our faith in, love for, and devotion to him will be taken care of by our Master. We shall lose nothing in this world and nothing in the world to come. He has promised, "Them that honour me I will honour" (1 Samuel 2:30), and "They that seek the LORD shall not want any good thing" (Psalm 34:10).

The Lord Jesus said, "If I send them away fasting to their own houses, they will faint by the way". He knows and considers our frame. If we seek to glorify him, we shall be fed by him. He considered that many of these men came from afar, that they were a long way from home. He would not send them home fasting. It is not his way to send those away empty who look to him for bread.

Grace Sufficient
"And his disciples answered him, From whence can a man satisfy these men with bread here in the wilderness?" (v. 4) Here we are reminded of the terrible weakness of our faith. Like these poor disciples, we quickly forget the wondrous things we have seen and experienced; and, forgetting them, our hearts are filled with foul unbelief. How weak we are! Yet, Our Lord's all-sufficiency and grace is made perfect in our weakness. That is what the Master tells us in 2 Corinthians 12:9. "My grace is sufficient for thee: for my strength is made perfect in weakness".

Our unbelief and sin is often the black backdrop against which the diamonds of our Lord's mercy, love, and grace shine forth most brilliantly. Our unfaithfulness makes his faithfulness all the more radiant.

I do not suggest for a moment, "Let us sin that grace may abound". But I am saying that our faults and failings, the sins and unbelief of God's elect are graciously overruled by our great and glorious Saviour to make his grace shine forth most brightly in us forever.

These disciples could not imagine how so many men should be satisfied with bread in the wilderness, though they had seen it before. That therefore which they considered impossible, must have appeared all the more glorious when it was done.

The fact is, our blessed Saviour usually intervenes at the time of utmost extremity. Christ's time to act for the relief of his people is when things are brought to the last extremity. He made provision for these men when they were at the point of fainting (v. 3). When they were reduced to absolute dependence upon him, he stepped in for their salvation. That is always the time when mercy comes. When we are completely helpless, he steps in to deliver us from trouble. When we are at our wits end he steps in graciously to save.

Grace Inexhaustible

Our Saviour's storehouse of grace is inexhaustible. He performed virtually the same miracle twice before, and seems to have done so with a specific purpose in mind. He wanted to show that he is ever gracious and infinitely bountiful in grace and power. He is still the same today. His throne is a throne of grace. He invites us to come, as often as we have need, that we may obtain mercy and find grace to help in time of need (Hebrews 4:16).

Notice this, too. In the first miracle he took five loaves and two small fish and used them to feed five thousand men. Here he takes seven loaves and a few small pieces of fish to feed four thousand. Why? I think he intends for us to understand three things specifically. It is our responsibility to use everything God puts in our hands for the work he gives us opportunity to do for the souls of men and the glory of his name.

If the work we are doing is God's work, it matters not whether we appear to have much or little. It is all the same to him. What we have is utterly insignificant. Our greatest assets and abilities are just as insignificant in the work of God's kingdom as our greatest needs and liabilities. With our great God and Saviour nothing is impossible.

In our Father's house there is bread enough and to spare. "So they did eat, and were filled: and they took up of the broken meat that was left seven baskets" (v. 8). They all had a full meal. Not one left the scene desiring more. As John Trapp wrote, "They did eat to satiety, as men use to do at feasts, where the tables seemed to sweat with variety". And, spiritually, there is such a fulness in Christ, which he communicates to all who come to him, that from it we receive, and "grace for grace" (John 1:16). Those who live upon Christ shall always have bread enough and to spare and should never fear being brought to need. "I have been young, and now am old; yet have I not seen the righteous forsaken, nor his seed begging bread", neither for their bodies or their souls. "For he satisfieth the longing soul, and filleth the hungry soul with goodness" (Psalms 37:25; 107:9).

"And straightway he entered into a ship with his disciples, and came into the parts of Dalmanutha. And the Pharisees came forth, and began to question with him, seeking of him a sign from heaven, tempting him. And he sighed deeply in his spirit, and saith, Why doth this generation seek after a sign? verily I say unto you, There shall no sign be given unto this generation. And he left them, and entering into the ship again departed to the other side. Now the disciples had forgotten to take bread, neither had they in the ship with them more than one loaf. And he charged them, saying, Take heed, beware of the leaven of the Pharisees, and of the leaven of Herod. And they reasoned among themselves, saying, It is because we have no bread. And when Jesus knew it, he saith unto them, Why reason ye, because ye have no bread? perceive ye not yet, neither understand? have ye your heart yet hardened? Having eyes, see ye not? and having ears, hear ye not? and do ye not remember? When I brake the five loaves among five thousand, how many baskets full of fragments took ye up? They say unto him, Twelve. And when the seven among four thousand, how many baskets full of fragments took ye up? And they said, Seven. And he said unto them, How is it that ye do not understand?"

(Mark 8:10-21)

Chapter 33

Watch Out For The Leaven!

We have before us a very solemn portion of scripture. The Lord Jesus came into a place called "Dalmanutha"[5] preaching the gospel. We are told that he came there by ship. What a blessed opportunity the people of that region were given! The Son of God came into their midst with his disciples with the gospel of free grace and salvation. But the opportunity and privilege afforded them in God's good providence was despised. Not one person in that place seems to have availed himself of the privilege set before him. Instead, our Master was confronted by a group of self-righteous religionists who wanted to argue doctrine with him.

Because of their folly, the Holy Spirit tells us that the Lord Jesus turned around, got back into the ship with his disciples, and sailed away. What a solemn passage of scripture this is. May God the Holy Spirit be our Teacher and open it to us, and open our understanding to it. May he be pleased to effectually instruct our hearts and use his Word to convey to us the grace and knowledge of our Lord Jesus Christ.

The Pharisees
"And straightway he entered into a ship with his disciples, and came into the parts of Dalmanutha. And the Pharisees came forth, and began to question with him, seeking of him a sign from heaven, tempting him. And he sighed deeply in his spirit, and saith, Why doth this generation seek after a sign? verily I say unto you, There shall no sign be given unto this generation. And he left them, and entering into the ship again departed to the other side" (vv. 10-13).

When the Lord Jesus saw these Pharisees and heard their religious cavilling, "he sighed deeply in his spirit". What a sweet testimony this is of

---

[5] Matthew says, "he came into the coasts of Magdala" (Matthew 15:39); but there is no conflict between Matthew and Mark. Dalmanutha was a place within Magdala, just as Danville is a city within Boyle County, Kentucky.

our Saviour's humanity. Our great Saviour, as he walked through this world, was a man subject to all the sorrows, griefs, and passions we experience, except sin. He who rules the universe and makes intercession in heaven as our Great High Priest is God in human flesh, a man touched with the feeling of our infirmities (Hebrews 2:14-17; 4:14-16).

Yet, it cannot be imagined that our Lord's sighing was any indication of frustration on his part, or that he both willed the salvation of these Pharisees and willed it not! He spoke plainly when he called them a generation of vipers who could not believe and could not escape the damnation of hell (Matthew 23:1-33).

Though, as a man, his heart was grieved by their unbelief (as ours should be), our Saviour fully acquiesced in his Father's sovereign will (Matthew 11:25-27). May God give us grace to imitate him, ever bowing to his sovereign and absolute will of predestination; yet, having hearts full of tenderness, even toward the most obstinate, self-righteous, and unbelieving sinners. And let us ever seek grace from God the Holy Spirit to magnify and rejoice in our heavenly Father's distinguishing grace. Did he not make us to differ, we would all be just like these Pharisees; and we would all perish with them (1 Corinthians 4:7; 2 Thessalonians 2:13, 14).

Though our Lord Jesus "sighed deeply in his spirit", because of their unbelief and hardness of heart, he shows us plainly that nothing is more disgusting and contemptuous to him than smug, religious hypocrisy and self-righteousness. These Pharisees, presuming themselves to be righteous, had no need for the grace proclaimed by the Son of God and the redemption he had come to accomplish. To them the gospel of grace was an affront. Who needs grace, when you are righteous? Notice four things here.

These men came to the Master not to learn, but to ask carping questions of no profit.

"They Began To Question Him"

They did not ask questions to learn, but to discuss and debate, to show how much they knew. We are warned again and again to avoid such people (1 Timothy 6:3, 4; 2 Timothy 2:23; Titus 3:9). There are many who are ever learning, but never come to the knowledge of the truth. They play religious games, trifling with the Word of God, with less reverence than our modern Supreme Court does the Constitution of the United States. They think they are smart, spiritual giants; but they are really spiritual morons and pigmies. Our Lord refused to answer their questions. He would not stoop to debating with them about holy things. The sooner we learn to follow his example, the better.

They Came To The Lord Jesus Seeking A Sign

Paul told us later, "The Jews (lost religious people) require after a sign. The Gentiles (lost irreligious people) seek after wisdom". Both groups reject the authority of God and his Word. Both pretend that they would believe, if you could give them either a sign from heaven or intellectual proof. But they deceive themselves.

The Lord Jesus refused to give these religious zealots a sign. He said, "There shall no sign be given to this generation". Many signs had already been given on earth, signs that could be easily investigated; but they would not receive them. There was a public sign from heaven at his baptism in the descent of the dove and the voice of God being audibly heard (Matthew 3:16, 17). If they had attended John the Baptist's ministry, as they ought to have done and could have done, they might themselves have seen the sign. Our Lord's miracles of mercy were all performed in the most public manner. Not one of them was ever disputed by anyone. But those whose faith is built on signs and miracles never have enough signs. We see this in the fact that afterward, when the Lord of glory was nailed to the cross, these same men were still demanding a sign. They said, "Let him come down from the cross, and we will believe him". Matthew Henry correctly observed,

> Thus obstinate infidelity will still have something to say, though ever so unreasonable. They demanded this sign, tempting him; not in hopes that he would give it them, that they might be satisfied, but in hopes that he would not, that they might imagine themselves to have a pretence for their infidelity.

Nothing is more contemptuous than religious infidelity and hypocrisy. The scriptures tell us here that, "He sighed deeply in his Spirit". Here is the God of glory sighing, sighing deeply in his spirit, groaning as one in painful vexation of soul. Then he said, "Why doth this generation seek after a sign?" That generation so unworthy to have the gospel brought to it wanted a sign! That generation that so greedily swallowed the traditions of the elders, without the confirmation of any sign at all, wanted a sign! That generation, which, by the calculating of the times set and revealed in the Old Testament, might easily have perceived that the time of the Messiah had come, wanted a sign! That generation, which had seen such great wonders and miracles, as were given to none before or since, wanted a sign! What an absurdity! But religious men, without life before God, are always absurd beyond imagination in their objections to divine revelation.

God has spoken in his Word. It is the height of presumption to demand signs and proofs from the Almighty. "Shall a man teach God knowledge?" Our Lord denied the demand of these pompous Pharisees. With disgust and contempt he said, "No, I will not give you a sign"!

Then, he left them. "And he left them, and entering into the ship again departed to the other side" (v. 13).

Oh, what a solemn word that is. "He left them"! He left them in the darkness of their own light! He left them in the corruption of their own self-righteousness! He left them in the ignorance of their own brilliance! He left them forever!

If God Almighty is kind enough, good enough, merciful enough to speak to you by his Word, by the gospel of his grace, and you are fool enough to spit in his face, despise his grace and favour, and refuse to believe the record he has given of his dear Son, the time will come when he will leave you alone. And if God ever leaves you to yourself, you will be left to yourself forever!

"Turn you at my reproof: behold, I will pour out my spirit unto you, I will make known my words unto you. Because I have called, and ye refused; I have stretched out my hand, and no man regarded; But ye have set at nought all my counsel, and would none of my reproof: I also will laugh at your calamity; I will mock when your fear cometh; When your fear cometh as desolation, and your destruction cometh as a whirlwind; when distress and anguish cometh upon you. Then shall they call upon me, but I will not answer; they shall seek me early, but they shall not find me: For that they hated knowledge, and did not choose the fear of the LORD: They would none of my counsel: they despised all my reproof. Therefore shall they eat of the fruit of their own way, and be filled with their own devices. For the turning away of the simple shall slay them, and the prosperity of fools shall destroy them. But whoso hearkeneth unto me shall dwell safely, and shall be quiet from fear of evil" (Proverbs 1:23-33).

"He, that being often reproved hardeneth his neck, shall suddenly be destroyed, and that without remedy" (Proverbs 29:1).

The Leaven Of The Pharisees
Our gracious Lord warns us once more to beware of the leaven of the Pharisees and of Herod. "And he charged them, saying, Take heed, beware of the leaven of the Pharisees, and of the leaven of Herod" (v. 15). "Take heed, beware", lest you partake of "the leaven of the Pharisees", lest you embrace the tradition of the elders, to which they are so wedded, lest you be proud, hypocritical ritualists like the Pharisees.

Watch Out For The Leaven!

This was not an isolated warning. It is given to us numerous times. Matthew adds, "and of the Sadducee". Mark adds, "and of Herod". The Pharisees were religious conservatives. The Sadducees were religious liberals. Herod was an infidel. Our Lord warns us to ever beware of the leaven of these three groups. We are not left to guess what our Lord means by this warning.

The leaven of the Pharisees and Sadducees is the leaven of false doctrine. False doctrine is any doctrine, liberal or conservative, Catholic or Protestant, Jewish or Muslim, any doctrine that makes salvation dependent upon you. The Pharisees and Sadducees were two distinct, doctrinally different religious sects among the Jews. The Pharisees were self-righteous religious ritualists and conservative, theological purists, a form of religion which appeals to many. The Pharisees' religion would appeal to most of the people we know. The Sadducees were self-righteous religious liberals, just as ritualistic as the Pharisees, but theological liberals, the smug intellectuals who were tolerant of anything except the dogmatism of the gospel. The Sadducees' religion is the religion of people who think they are smarter than God and more diverse thinking than hell.

Herod and those like him were self-serving, self-righteous worldlings, self-serving materialists, infidels who believed nothing and stood for nothing except that which would advantage themselves. They were pragmatists.

Our Lord warns us to beware of the leaven of false doctrine, because "a little leaven leaveneth the whole lump". That statement is used twice in the New Testament. Both times the one making the statement is the apostle Paul. We find this statement first in 1 Corinthians 5:6. "Your glorying is not good. Know ye not that a little leaven leaveneth the whole lump?" The leaven here refers to sin. The Spirit of God is warning us that like a little yeast in a large lump of dough will gradually spread through the whole lump, so the tolerance of any sin is disastrous. We must never be satisfied with anything less than perfection. Our goal must always be to "sin not" (1 John 2:1).

Paul tells us the very same thing about false doctrine in Galatians 5:9. "A little leaven leaveneth the whole lump". If we tolerate anything, be it a work, an experience, a feeling, or even a decision, if we tolerate anything, be it ever so small, as a condition we must meet in order to be saved, we cut ourselves off from Christ and from the grace of God in him (Galatians 5:1-4). Salvation, from election to glorification and everything between, is the work of God's free and sovereign grace in Christ. The voice of the world, the whole world, the Pharisees, the Sadducees, and the Herods, constantly says, "That's too strict. That's too dogmatic. That's too bigoted." But remember, "A little leaven leaveneth the whole lump".

False doctrine, like leaven in the dough, always begins with something small, almost undetectable. It moves through and permeates with great subtlety, but with deadly efficacy. The same thing is true of sin and worldliness. The deceitfulness of riches, the care of this world, and the lusts of other things, like leaven in the lump, begins with such small, insignificant compromises that they are hardly detectable until their work is done.

Spiritual Weakness
This passage also demonstrates the fact that as long as we are in this world we will have a sinful, fleshly dullness to all things spiritual. Read verses 14 and 16-21, and understand that the strongest believers in this world are terribly weak and full of unbelief.

"Now the disciples had forgotten to take bread, neither had they in the ship with them more than one loaf ... And they reasoned among themselves, saying, It is because we have no bread. And when Jesus knew it, he saith unto them, Why reason ye, because ye have no bread? perceive ye not yet, neither understand? have ye your heart yet hardened? Having eyes, see ye not? and having ears, hear ye not? and do ye not remember? When I brake the five loaves among five thousand, how many baskets full of fragments took ye up? They say unto him, Twelve. And when the seven among four thousand, how many baskets full of fragments took ye up? And they said, Seven. And he said unto them, How is it that ye do not understand?"

The most godly of God's saints in this world are only sinners still. The most learned and well instructed of God's people are still dull of understanding. Abraham sometimes trembles. Lot, the righteous man, sometimes makes sinful choices. Job, the perfect man who fears God and eschews evil, will on some occasions curse the day of his birth. Noah, that man who found grace in the eyes of the Lord, may be found in a drunken stupor. Moses, the meekest man who ever lived, will strike out at God himself with his rod in a fit of anger. David, the man after God's own heart, will, when left to himself, commit adultery and then murder to protect his image. Bold Peter will wither before a maiden, curse, and deny the Master he loves above everything. The Apostle Paul and his companion Barnabas, loyal, faithful friends; loyal, faithful servants of God, will, when weak and in the flesh, part company and never walk together again in this world.

Like the Lord's disciples here, we are often overwhelmed with present cares and distrusts, because we do not understand and remember what we have known and seen of the power and goodness of our all glorious Saviour.

Matthew Henry wrote, "When we thus forget the works of God, and distrust him, we should chide ourselves severely for it, as Christ doth his

276

disciples here; 'Am I thus without understanding? How is it that my heart is thus hardened?'"

Why does our God so plainly set before us such weaknesses, sins, unbelief, and dullness of understanding in the lives of his beloved people? Here are seven obvious reasons for such revelations:

1. We must be constantly reminded that salvation is God's work alone.
2. We must be constantly reminded not to think too highly of ourselves.
3. We need to learn to be tender, patient, forbearing with and forgiving of one another.
4. We constantly need to be reminded that Christ alone gives us acceptance with God.
5. We must ever be reminded that it is he alone who keeps us in life, and in grace, and in faith.
6. While we live in this world, we must never imagine that we have arrived at anything close to perfection.
7. Yet, we must also be constantly reminded that though we are sin and do sin, we have an Advocate with the Father, an ever-living, ever-faithful High Priest (1 John 2:1, 2).

"And he cometh to Bethsaida; and they bring a blind man unto him, and besought him to touch him. And he took the blind man by the hand, and led him out of the town; and when he had spit on his eyes, and put his hands upon him, he asked him if he saw ought. And he looked up, and said, I see men as trees, walking. After that he put his hands again upon his eyes, and made him look up: and he was restored, and saw every man clearly. And he sent him away to his house, saying, Neither go into the town, nor tell it to any in the town".

(Mark 8:22-26)

Chapter 34

"He Saw Every Man Clearly"

This is another of the miracles related by none of the other Evangelists. Mark alone was inspired to tell us about the healing of this blind man at Bethsaida.

None of our Lord's miracles were accidental or mere representations of his supernatural power over physical things. Every miracle performed by the Master was designed to teach us spiritual, gospel truths, particularly truths about the workings of his grace in his elect. On this occasion, we see a blind man who was healed gradually, by degrees. This is the only time in the New Testament that happened. So, we might properly expect that it is, in itself, highly significant and instructive. The healing of this blind man is a picture of the way God saves chosen, redeemed sinners by the almighty power and grace of his Holy Spirit. As our Lord Jesus took this poor blind man by the hand, he takes chosen sinners by his hand and leads them to himself, giving them light and grace and life by his omnipotent mercy.

Brought By Friends

"And he cometh to Bethsaida". Bethsaida was a fishing village, the home of Andrew, Peter, and Philip (John 1:44). The Lord Jesus came here on an errand of mercy. In verse 13 we read that our Saviour left the Pharisees. What solemn words we read there, "And he left them"! Having left them in judgment, he came to Bethsaida on an errand of mercy, seeking one of his lost sheep for whom the "time of love had come", a poor blind man who must now receive his sight. "And they bring a blind man unto him, and besought him to touch him". Here is a blind man brought to the Lord Jesus Christ by his friends. Mark tells us three simple, but important things in this verse.

First, we are told that the man was blind. In that fact, he is representative of all men in their natural, unregenerate state. Whether religious or irreligious, educated or uneducated, all human beings are spiritually blind. This poor man did not have so much as one faint, glimmering ray of light, until the Lord Jesus touched him. So it is with every man by nature. Those who are without Christ, who alone is Light, live in darkness. They have no sight. They cannot see themselves. They cannot see the kingdom of God, or the things of God. They are blind. That is the condition of all men naturally. It is not that there is a lack of light, but a lack of sight. "There is none that understandeth, there is none that seeketh after God" (Romans 3:11). "The natural man receiveth not the things of the Spirit of God: for they are foolishness unto him: neither can he know them, because they are spiritually discerned" (1 Corinthians 2:14). Fallen man is poor, miserable, wretched, and naked; but he cannot see it, because he is blind. Though the Son of God stands before him, he cannot see him, because he is blind. Though God's salvation is displayed before his very eyes, he cannot see it, because having eyes, he sees not. He is blind.

Second, Mark tells us that this poor blind man's friends brought him to the Master. We are not told that this blind man believed anything or expected anything from the Lord at all. He seems to have come to the place where the Master was simply because his friends persuaded him to do so. What a blessed man he was to have such friends! He did not know Christ, but his friends did. He did not believe Christ, but his friends did. He would never have come to Christ, but his friends brought him.

Third, having done all that they could do, this blind man's friends "besought the Lord Jesus to touch him". They could not heal him, but they knew Christ could. This blind man, it appears, did not have sense enough to pray for himself. So his friends prayed for him. Blessed is the man who has such friends! Blessed is the man who is such a friend!

Divine Separation

Then in verse 23 we see our Saviour performing his operation of grace upon this man in a most unusual way. We have no other picture like this in all the Word of God. He performs his work gradually and in private. Surely this is intended to teach us some things we need to learn and remember. This is what the Son of God does for sinners in the saving operations of his grace, when he turns them from darkness to light. "And he took the blind man by the hand, and led him out of the town; and when he had spit on his eyes, and put his hands upon him, he asked him if he saw ought".

The Master "took the blind man by the hand". Can you imagine how elated, how thrilled, how excited this man's friends were when they saw the Master stretch out that arm which they knew was the arm of omnipotence in mercy, love, and grace to their friend? That was in itself an act of great condescension. But here is a far greater act of condescension. One day the Lord Jesus took me by the hand! He took me in his hand as my Surety in eternity. Taking me in his hand, he separated me from all the rest of the human race by sovereign election and particular redemption. Then, at the appointed time of his love, the God of all grace stooped to take me by the hand in effectual calling.

If he takes a sinner into his hand he will open his blind eyes. If he takes you by the hand he will never let you go. If he takes you by the hand you are perfectly safe. No man can pluck you out of his hand. If he takes you by the hand in time, he took you in his hand before time began. When the Lord thus takes sinners, he "becomes", as John Gill wrote, "their guide and leader. A better, and safer guide they cannot have. He brings them by a way they know not, and leads them in paths they had not known before; makes darkness light before them, and crooked things straight, and does not forsake them".

Next, he "led him out of the town". As Hosea allured Gomer and brought her into the wilderness, that he might speak comfortably to her, so the Lord Jesus graciously brings the chosen sinner away to himself alone, that he might speak comfortably to his beloved in the time of love. He led this poor blind man out of the town, because he was not interested in the town, but in this one man. He did not want the applause of the people of Bethsaida, but the heart of this sinner. The people of Bethsaida, because of unbelief, were unworthy even to witness the wondrous works of Christ (Matthew 11:21). So "he took the blind man by the hand, and led him out of the town". When the Son of God saves his people, he calls them out of the world. He bids us come unto him without the camp: outside the camp of human religion, the camp of worldly ambition, the camp of sin's dominion. Outside the camp unto him!

A Despised Means
The next thing our Saviour did, if he had allowed anyone to see it, would have been looked upon as an utterly despicable, contemptible, and foolish thing. "And when he had spit on his eyes". Why did our Lord do that? Some suggest it may have been a common medical practice, doctors believing there was healing, medicinal power in saliva. By this reasoning, our Lord used the medical practices of the day to heal the man, adding to it his divine power. Needless to say, I do not agree. The Son of God did not employ falsehood to perform his work. However, our all-wise Saviour did choose (and still chooses) to use a terribly despicable means to perform his work of grace upon this poor blind man. God has chosen the foolishness of preaching to save his elect. The spit from the Saviour's lips represents the eye salve of the gospel with which the Son of God anoints the eyes of the blind (Revelation 3:18). After spitting on the man's eyes, the Lord Jesus "put his hands upon him". The touch of his hand is the symbol of his omnipotent grace, without which the means of grace, the preaching of the gospel, is utterly useless.

A Sovereign Saviour
What we have before us is a picture of our Lord's sovereignty in the exercise of his grace. God will not be put in a box. He never limits himself and cannot

be limited by men. He heals some gradually and others immediately, some with spit and others without any spit. All saved sinners trust the same Saviour, experience the same grace and believe the same gospel. But we do not all experience grace the same way. This will come as a shock to some; but God does not deal with us all the same way. In fact, we are told in the New Testament of five blind men who were healed by our Saviour (Matthew 9:27-30; Mark 10:46-52; Luke 18:35-43; John 9:1-7). Three were healed by his mere word, without his touch. One was healed by the Saviour spitting in his eyes and touching them. And another was healed by our Saviour spitting on the ground, making clay, and anointing his eyes with the clay. In all five cases there were certain things that were done differently.

Trees Walking

The Lord Jesus required a confession from this blind man. "He asked him if he saw aught". Remember, this man had not expressed any faith in the Son of God. He had not even acknowledged his blindness and need of cure. Now the Master requires him to acknowledge both his infirmity and the power of God he had experienced. There is no salvation apart from a personal confession of faith in the Lord Jesus Christ (Romans 10:1-10; 1 John 1:9). Secret disciples are always suspect disciples. No one can be looked upon, treated as, or think of himself as a child of God until Christ is confessed. Our Saviour requires and deserves that we confess him before men.

After he touched the blind man's eyes, the Saviour asked him if he could see anything. He "looked up, and said, I see men as trees, walking" (v. 24). He could see, but not very clearly. So it is with us. When the Lord God saves a sinner, he is immediately translated from darkness to light. Every saved sinner sees the kingdom of God; but we do not immediately see everything in the kingdom of God.

The light of God's grace often comes gradually. Christ, who is the Light of the world and came preaching the recovering of sight to the blind (Luke 4:18), gave what he proclaimed and compelled the man who had received his sight to tell what had happened to him. This blind man confessed exactly what he knew and had experienced, no more and no less. He was not delivered from his blindness all at once, but by degrees. He saw a little, but not much; and what he did see he did not see clearly. He did not pretend to see what he did not see.

This blind man received his sight gradually. The work was as truly gracious, miraculous, and glorious as the healing of Bartimaeus, the healing of the woman with the issue of blood, and the healing of the leper. But it was less spectacular. However, it is not a miracle to be despised and ignored because it was gradually performed. Our Lord hereby shows us that his works of grace in the lives of chosen sinners are sometimes gradual. Men and women usually come to light and understanding in spiritual things gradually. J. C. Ryle, made three very simple, but profoundly instructive comments about this man's experience and the lessons it is intended to convey. He said, "We are all naturally blind and ignorant in the matters which concern our souls. Conversion is an illumination, a change from darkness to light, from blindness to seeing the kingdom of God. Few converted people see things distinctly at first."

While we are rightfully insistent that there is no saving faith, no conversion, no true salvation apart from the knowledge of Christ (John 17:3) in his true character, as he is revealed in the gospel, we readily acknowledge that saving knowledge is but limited knowledge while we live in this world. Be sure you understand this. Light is light; but it usually comes to our sin blinded souls by degrees. We all see spiritual things gradually. First we see the sinfulness of our deeds, then the sinfulness of our hearts. First we see the suitableness and ability of Christ to redeem and save, then his willingness to save us. We see the fact of forgiveness, then the experience of forgiveness. We see the good news of the gospel, then the great truths of the gospel.

When God first saved me, I knew whom I believed; but I did not know much about him. I knew that the Lord Jesus Christ is my God and Saviour; but I did not know much about eternal Sonship and the distinction of persons in the Holy Trinity. I was convinced of my sin; but I did not know the difference between iniquity, transgression, and sin. I was convinced that Christ had brought in everlasting righteousness for me, and that I had no righteousness but him; but I knew nothing about imputation and forensic righteousness. I was convinced that judgment was finished by the judgment of my sin in Christ my Substitute; but I did not know a thing about justification. I knew that it was God who had saved me, that "Salvation is of the Lord;" but I didn't know a thing about the decrees of God. If you had asked me about lapsarianism, I would probably have said, "I don't know anything about Lapland". If someone had asked me about election, I would most likely have said, "I'm not old enough to vote". I knew my Saviour; but I really knew very little about how he had saved me. I could say with the blind man our Lord healed in John 9, "Once I was blind, but now I see. Yet, I did not see much. All I saw was "men as trees walking".

Yet, the Son of God never does his work partially. This man's healing was soon completed. Once he has begun his work of grace in a man's soul, he never stops working until he says, "It is finished". "He which hath begun a good work in you will perform it until the day of Jesus Christ" (Philippians 1:6).

The healing of this blind man gives us a picture of both the present and future condition of God's saints. As long as we live in this world we see as through a glass darkly. We are like men travelling by night. We see what the light before us reveals; but we see very little around us. We see many things here that we simply do not understand, particularly in matters of providence. There are many things in the Word of God as well, which we simply do not understand. We are at best able to perceive spiritual things, like this man, as trees walking, so long as we live in his world. But the time will soon come when we shall see all things clearly. When the Lord Jesus comes again, our spiritual eyesight will be greatly improved!

The Second Touch
"After that he put his hands again upon his eyes, and made him look up: and he was restored, and saw every man clearly" (v. 25). When the Master touched this man's eyes a second time and made him look up, he was restored and "saw every man clearly". It is written, "The path of the just is as the shining light, that shineth more and more unto the perfect day" (Proverbs 4:18). So it is with us. Our shining light increases, and shines more and more unto the perfect day. Yet, in this world, the light we have is far from perfect, even among those who see the most and see most clearly. There are things you do not yet know, and things you know, about which you know very little. If we are truthful we must acknowledge, that we "see through a glass darkly".

After reading this passage in one of our evening worship services several years ago, Bro. Rex Bartley said, "When Christ heals a sinner, restores his sight, and makes him look up to him, he sees every man clearly." Then he named four men spoken of in holy scripture, and said, "When a sinner is taught of God, he sees these four men clearly."

When a sinner is taught of God he sees the first man Adam clearly, as both a representative man representing all the human race (1 Corinthians 15:45) and a typical man typifying our Lord Jesus Christ (Romans 5:12-21).

Every saved sinner sees the second man, Christ our Lord, clearly. The first man, Adam, was made in the image and likeness of the second Man, the Lord Jesus Christ. He is the God-man, our Mediator, our divine Surety, Jehovah's righteous Servant, our sin-atoning Substitute, the Lord our Righteousness (1 Corinthians 1:30, 31). "In him dwelleth all the fulness of the Godhead bodily. And ye are complete in him, which is the head of all principality and power" (Colossians 2:9, 10).

Then, the scriptures speak of the natural man, that is man in his lost, ruined condition, without Christ. All who are taught of God see the natural man clearly. The natural man is dead in trespasses and in sins, without Christ, an alien from the commonwealth of Israel, a stranger to the covenant of promise, having no hope, without God in this perishing world.

There is another man set before us in the Book of God; and all who are taught of God see him clearly, too. The Holy Spirit calls him "the new man" (2 Corinthians 5:17; Ephesians 4:24; Colossians 3:10). This new man is that holy thing in you called, "Christ in you, the hope of glory", that is "born of God", "his seed" that remaineth in you, "the spirit", "the divine nature". John tells us "he cannot sin, because he is born of God". The new man "created in righteousness and true holiness". The new man in you, "the spirit", is warring with the old man, the natural man, "the flesh". The new man delights in the law of God (Galatians 5:16-25). This new man is a new creature in Christ (2 Corinthians 5:17; Ephesians 2:13-15; Colossians 3:10, 11).

We see "every man clearly", but not perfectly. Soon, that will change. Soon, we shall see face to face and know even as we are known. How clearly will all things be seen in the new Jerusalem. There will be no need of the light of the sun or the moon of gospel ordinances there; but Christ, the Lamb, will be the everlasting light of that City, in which the nations of them that are saved shall walk! Then, when we see our Saviour face to face, and not until then, will we see all things perfectly.

Tell It Not
There is one more thing I want you to see in this passage. It may seem strange, and it should. In verse 26 the Lord Jesus Christ, our God who "delighteth in mercy", performs an act of judgment. That, too, is his work; but it is "his strange work". "And he sent him away to his house, saying, Neither go into the town, nor tell it to any in the town". Our Saviour told this man to go home, commanding him not to go back to Bethsaida and not to tell anyone in that town what the God of all grace had done for him. Why?

The Lord Jesus had done many wonderful works among the inhabitants of Bethsaida; but they did not believe him. They would not hear him and would not believe him, so he left them to themselves. As Matthew Henry observed, "Bethsaida, in the day of her visitation, would not know the things that belonged to her peace, and now they are hid from her eyes. They will not see, and therefore shall not see". This is horrible to consider; but it is his just judgment upon men who will not receive his Word (Proverbs 1:23-33). What wrath our God heaps on those who refuse to believe him! He orders his servants to preach no more to them. He allows none to tell them of the good news of life and salvation by him. He even commands his prophets not to pray for them. And even if they try to do otherwise, they simply cannot. As soon as our Lord had healed this man, he took his disciples and left town (v. 27), but not until he had healed the man he came to Bethsaida to heal.

"And Jesus went out, and his disciples, into the towns of Caesarea Philippi: and by the way he asked his disciples, saying unto them, Whom do men say that I am? And they answered, John the Baptist: but some say, Elias; and others, One of the prophets. And he saith unto them, But whom say ye that I am? And Peter answereth and saith unto him, Thou art the Christ. And he charged them that they should tell no man of him. And he began to teach them, that the Son of man must suffer many things, and be rejected of the elders, and of the chief priests, and scribes, and be killed, and after three days rise again. And he spake that saying openly. And Peter took him, and began to rebuke him. But when he had turned about and looked on his disciples, he rebuked Peter, saying, Get thee behind me, Satan: for thou savourest not the things that be of God, but the things that be of men".

(Mark 8:27-33)

Chapter 35

Get Thee Behind Me, Satan

Mark has informed us of the doctrine Christ preached and the miracles he performed. Whenever we think of our Lord's miracles, we must never associate them in our minds with the self-proclaimed miracle workers of our day. Our Lord's miracles were numerous, well-attested, wrought in many different places, performed before countless eye witnesses who knew the people who were healed, raised from the dead and fed by his power. They were so well established as facts, that no one, not a single person familiar with his life and ministry, not a single one of his enemies and accusers ever even questioned their validity.

Having spoken so much of these things, the Holy Spirit would now have us pause to consider what they mean. Those wondrous works which our Lord would not allow his disciples to publish in the streets of Israel were recorded for us in the Book of God for our learning and admonition. These things were not written by the finger of God for our amusement, or for debate. "But these are written, that ye might believe that Jesus is the Christ, the Son of God; and that believing ye might have life through his name" (John 20:31).

We have before us a conversation which took place between our Lord Jesus and his disciples as they were walking towards Caesarea Philippi. We read in verse twenty-seven that "Jesus went out, and his disciples, into the towns of Caesarea Philippi: and by the way he asked his disciples, saying unto them, Whom do men say that I am?" There is something for us to learn even from this thing, which seems to have been just casually observed by Mark. We ought to take advantage of every opportunity to do good. Let us never behave as pretentious, religious hypocrites, who cannot talk about anything but religion, or as people who try to button hole everyone they meet. Yet, we ought to do what we can to do good to men's souls and to help one another, ever watching for opportunities to speak a word in season.

Knowledge And Faith
Many confuse doctrinal knowledge with saving faith. They vainly imagine that knowing the facts revealed in the gospel is knowing Christ, that having a good opinion of Christ is to know Christ. Multitudes have a very high and good opinion of Christ and his doctrine who do not know him. That fact is evident in verses 27 and 28.

"And Jesus went out, and his disciples, into the towns of Caesarea Philippi: and by the way he asked his disciples, saying unto them, Whom do men say that I am? And they answered, John the Baptist: but some say, Elias; and others, One of the prophets".

There was among the Jews a great variety of opinions about Christ. Almost everyone thought he was a very good man, a godly man, even a great man. Most considered him a great prophet, perhaps even a resurrected prophet. They compared him to John the Baptist, Elijah and Jeremiah. Almost to a man the Jews thought he was a great prophet who had come back from the dead. No one, at this time, considered him a deceiver or a wicked man. Only the Scribes and Pharisees spoke evil of him, and they did so only because of envy. Multitudes knew much about the Saviour and approved of what they knew. Yet, very few knew him.

Things are pretty much the same today. Christ and his gospel are just as commonly misunderstood and unknown today, among religious people as they were among the Jews two thousand years ago. Almost everyone knows the name of Christ. Many of our relatives and neighbours go to church and acknowledge that Jesus came into the world to save sinners, that he died on the cross, was buried, and rose again the third day. In remembrance and honour of him, they set aside special holy days, build huge buildings, and engage in great enterprises. Yet, there are very few who know him. Vague ideas about Christ are common. Few people know who he is, what he did, or why he did it. Those who know the Son of God are very few.

Many there are who move beyond vagueness, and have very clear, even an orthodox knowledge of gospel doctrine and of the historic facts revealed in the gospel. They readily confess that Jesus Christ is the incarnate God, that he is God the eternal Son. They understand and defend the doctrines of substitution, redemption, justification, sanctification, and regeneration. They can accurately describe Christ's resurrection, ascension and exaltation, his priestly intercession at the Father's right hand as our Advocate, and the promise of his second coming. Yet, they obviously do not know him.

Those who know the Son of God by faith appear to be very few. Yet, apart from knowing him there is no salvation. Without the knowledge of him, there is no eternal life. Until you know him, you are dead in trespasses and in sins (John 17:3); and if we would know him we must be born again (John 3:5-7).

Three hundred years ago, the heretic Robert Sandeman insisted that to teach (as the scriptures demand) that in regeneration the heaven born soul is made partaker of the divine nature and that this new, righteous nature imparted to God's elect by grace is vital to salvation, is to teach men to look for righteousness in themselves, rather than in Christ. Like his successors today, Sandeman insisted that the new birth is nothing more than giving assent to doctrinal facts. Another heretic, Alexander Campbell, founder of the Arminian, works-denomination, *The Church of Christ*, foolishly wrote, "Sandeman was like a giant among dwarfs." Heed Paul's warning. "Beware, lest any man spoil you through philosophy and vain deceit". Any man who denies the necessity of the Spirit's work in us, teaching that faith in Christ is nothing but learning doctrine, is a heretic to be marked and avoided.

The new birth is more than a change of mind. It is more than the mere acquirement of religious knowledge. Anyone who is familiar with the Word of God knows that all men and women have some awareness of God, of sin, of life, of death, of judgment and of eternity (Romans 1:18-20; 2:14, 15). Man is by nature a very religious creature (John 5:39, 40). And unsaved religious people often recognize and believe some true facts about God and Christ and salvation (John 3:2). But the quickening, regenerating work of God the Holy Spirit is much, much more than embracing facts about God and salvation. As John Owen wrote,

> Of all the poison which at this day is diffused in the minds of men, corrupting them from the mystery of the gospel, there is no part that is more pernicious than this one perverse imagination, that to 'believe in Christ' is nothing at all but to believe the doctrine of the gospel!'

In the new birth Christ is revealed in the chosen sinner (Galatians 1:15, 16). God the Holy Spirit gives impotent, dead sinners eternal life (John 3:5-8; Ephesians 2:1-5). And the life he imparts is Christ himself (Colossians 1:27; 2 Peter 1:4). Revealing Christ in the heart, he convicts and convinces sinners of sin, righteousness and judgment (John 16:8-15; 1 Corinthians 2:7-10; Zechariah 10:12), and effectually draws sinners to Christ and makes them willing to come (John 6:44, 45; Psalm 110:3).

Saving Knowledge
Allow me to pointedly apply these things to the present day. In 2 Corinthians 5:14 Paul declares that all who are born of God are constrained, motivated, and ruled by the love of Christ. The love of Christ rules in our hearts, he tells us in verse 15, because we have been born again. We have been born again because Christ died for us. His death as our Substitute obtained and guaranteed our new birth. And, being born of God, we live, not unto ourselves, but unto Christ, who died for us and rose again. Then, in verse 16, the inspired writer tells us that our knowledge of Christ is not a carnal

apprehension of the intellect, but the gift and revelation of God the Holy Spirit. "Wherefore henceforth know we no man after the flesh: yea, though we have known Christ after the flesh, yet now henceforth know we him no more".

Be sure you understand what the Spirit of God tells us here. Our knowledge of Christ is not a carnal apprehension of the intellect, but the gift and revelation of God the Holy Spirit. Being born again by the omnipotent grace and irresistible mercy of God the Holy Spirit, all who are taught of God, know Christ after the Spirit, and not after the flesh.

Will worshipping Arminians have long taught that faith in Christ is nothing but an act of the will; mental assent to the historic facts of the gospel. When I was a seven year old boy, I was conned into a profession of faith by will-worshipping fundamentalists, who told me that salvation would be mine if I would simply believe "God's plan of salvation". Giving assent to what I was told, a "soul-winner" put his arms around me, with tears in his eyes, and announced, "Praise the Lord, son, you're saved! You are born again". But I didn't know God from a gourd.

Such deception is common among fundamentalists. But today there are some who claim to believe the gospel, or what we refer to as the doctrines of grace, who teach the same heresy, utterly denying the gospel of God's free and sovereign grace in Christ. Theirs is a much more subtle and dangerous heresy.

They tell us that faith in Christ is nothing but agreement with "God's testimony". They laugh at what the apostle Paul calls "the mystery of the faith", asserting that there is nothing mysterious about it. Being too deceptive to openly assert what their doctrine is, they continue to use terms like "regeneration", "the new birth", "effectual calling", "the new nature", "the new man", and "Christ in you".

Yet, everything they teach denies the work of God the Holy Spirit in chosen redeemed sinners, teaching that salvation is arrived at by acquired knowledge, not by divine regeneration, by an act of the will, not by the revelation of grace. This philosophy of vain deceit denies the necessity of the new birth, denies that the believer is given a new nature by the Spirit of God, denies that righteousness is imparted to us, and that we are made partakers of the divine nature in regeneration. These modern-day Gnostics speak of God's saving grace as nothing more than a "principle" (an accepted philosophical rule).

They look upon those of us who believe God's revelation of himself in his Word and trust Christ as their Wisdom, as well as their Righteousness, Sanctification, and Redemption, as poor, ignorant people, without spiritual understanding. One such deceiver has described what the scriptures call a

God given light shining "in our hearts, to give the light of the knowledge of the glory of God in the face of Jesus Christ" as "a mystical, religious experience that takes place in ecstatic ignorance"!

Deceivers are never honest men! The liberals of the mid-1900s, at first, were not manly enough to openly state that they did not believe in blood atonement, regeneration, and the resurrection. They made it a point to use such words frequently. But, with their "enlightened" understanding, they gave those clearly defined biblical terms new definitions.

Carnal Knowledge

That is exactly what is happening in our day. Many, who talk much about faith in Christ and imagine that no one possesses it except those who bow to their shrines, openly assert that, "Mental assent itself is equal to faith". That is Gnosticism in its very essence. That is free-willism of the most deceptive form. It is the assertion that salvation is nothing but a man's decision to agree with irrefutable facts!

That which they have arrived at by their imaginary "brilliance of intellect" the Holy Spirit calls knowing "Christ after the flesh", by mere carnal reason. They are people with religious knowledge, who are totally void of grace and spiritual life, groping in the darkness of their invented light.

Most people presume that knowledge is the basis of faith; but the scriptures assert exactly the opposite. Hebrews 11:3 declares, "Through faith we understand". Through faith we see, perceive and comprehend all things spiritual. And this faith, which gives spiritual understanding, is the result of the new birth, without which no man can see the kingdom of God (John 3:5-7). Faith in Christ is the basis of spiritual knowledge and understanding. Spiritual knowledge is the result of faith in Christ. As I have heard Pastor Henry Mahan say so many times, "You don't get to Christ by doctrine. You get to doctrine by Christ." Saving knowledge is not what you know, but who (John 17:3).

Believe And Confess

"And he saith unto them, But whom say ye that I am? And Peter answereth and saith unto him, Thou art the Christ. And he charged them that they should tell no man of him" (vv. 29, 30).

All true Christians know, believe and confess that Jesus of Nazareth is the Christ, the Son of the living God. Matthew Henry put it like this, "To be a Christian is to sincerely believe that Jesus is the Christ."

The confession of faith in Christ that Peter here gave was remarkable. He made this confession when the Lord Jesus was in a very poor earthly condition, without honour, without power, without majesty, without wealth, without influence. It was a confession made in opposition to the opinions and thoughts of the world in which he lived. All the Jewish world, civil and ecclesiastical, refused to acknowledge him as the Christ, and the entire Gentile world laughed at him as a Jewish zealot.

Yet, Peter boldly confessed, "Thou art the Christ". His faith was not shaken by opposition. His confidence did not waver before popular opinion. Peter believed that Jesus of Nazareth is indeed the Christ, the promised Messiah, the Prophet like Moses, the Priest like Melchizedek, the King like David. He believed and confessed the Man Christ Jesus to be God the Son!

Erring and unstable as his faith sometimes was, Peter was a man of strong, exemplary faith. He believed the record God had given of his Son and boldly confessed his Master and his faith in him. Obviously, there was much that he did not know, much that had not yet been plainly revealed; but Peter was loyal to the core and confessed Christ unhesitatingly.

Let us follow this faithful disciple's example. Christ and his doctrine have never been popular, especially in the religious world. We must be prepared to confess him, though, if necessary, we are compelled to do so outside the camp of the religious world (Acts 2:36; 4:11, 12; Hebrews 13:7-12). All true Christians know, believe and confess that Jesus of Nazareth is the Christ, the Son of the living God.

We should not overlook the fact that Mark, by divine inspiration, omitted the words that Matthew was inspired to include, "That thou art Peter, and upon this rock I will build my church" (Matthew 16:18). Had Mark esteemed Peter as the foundation rock upon which the church is built, as papists assert, he would certainly have included those words of our Lord. Indeed, had any of the Apostles thought that our Lord was referring to Peter as the rock, surely we would have some indication of it in the New Testament.

The fact is, Matthew, Mark, Peter, and all the writers of the New Testament understood clearly that our Saviour's words, "upon this rock I will build my church", had reference to himself as the Foundation Stone upon which we are built. That fact is so evidently stated in holy scripture that the delusion of papists is obviously a wilful delusion (Psalm 118:22; Isaiah 28:16; Matthew 21:42; Mark 12:10; Luke 20:17; Acts 4:11, 12; 1 Corinthians 3:11; 1 Peter 2:7).

Must Suffer

"And he began to teach them, that the Son of man must suffer many things, and be rejected of the elders, and of the chief priests, and scribes, and be killed, and after three days rise again" (v. 31). Our Lord spoke these things openly. He did not preach in code. He did not wrap his message in ambiguous words. When he began to teach his disciples, he used plain, clear speech. Every true prophet does the same.

Here the Lord Jesus made a full declaration of his own coming death and resurrection as our Substitute. Can you imagine how strange this must have sounded in the ears of these disciples, these men who knew he was the Christ, but who were yet looking for him, at any moment, to establish a great Jewish empire over the world in which he would sit as King forever? Yet, he now declares that he must suffer many things, that he must be rejected of the elders, the chief priests, and the scribes, that he must be killed, and that he must rise again in three days.

Why did our Lord use the term "must"? Why must these things be done? What was the great necessity that demanded the suffering and death of God's dear Son? Was it because some force greater than he would compel him to endure these things? Was he saying that he would not be able to prevail over his enemies? Of course not! Was he saying he must endure these things to set a good example of love, self-denial and self-sacrifice? Nonsense! Our Master said that these things must come to pass because they were decreed by the Father, declared in the Old Testament scriptures, demanded by the law and justice of God for the salvation of his elect, and greatly desired by Christ himself. He said, "With desire have I desired to eat this supper with you."

It was necessary for Christ to suffer and die on the cross, under the wrath of God, to save his people. He did not have to save us; but if he would save us, he could not save in any other way. Justice demanded satisfaction (Proverbs 16:6; 17:15; Romans 4:5; 1 Peter 3:18). Since it was the design, purpose, and pleasure of the Almighty to bring chosen sinners into eternal glory and happiness as the sons of God by Christ, it was necessary for Christ, the Son of God, to suffer all that the law and justice of God required for the punishment of sin, dying under the wrath of God as our Substitute.

I do not suggest that the sin-atoning death of Christ, by which justice has been satisfied, procures the love of God for us. It does not. The death of Christ is the fruit of God's love, not the cause of it. But I am saying that it is the death of Christ and the satisfaction of justice by his death that opens the way into the embraces of God's arms. We could never have been reconciled to God without the shedding of Christ's blood.

Our Saviour said, "As Moses lifted up the serpent in the wilderness, even so must the Son of man be lifted up: That whosoever believeth in him should not perish, but have eternal life" (John 3:14, 15). He came into this world with a commission, on a mission of mercy, under the bondage of his own voluntary suretiship engagements, which he assumed for us as the Surety of the everlasting covenant. His death upon the cursed tree was no accident. It was not something that came to pass because of man's free will, or because

293

the Jews would not let him be their king! The Lord Jesus died at Calvary because he must die at Calvary! Why? What necessity was there for the death of the Son of God upon the cursed tree? Why must this Holy One be made sin for us? Why must this Saviour be put to death? Here are four reasons why he had to die the painful, shameful, cursed death of the cross at Jerusalem.

(1) The Lord Jesus Christ had die at Jerusalem as he did because God the Father purposed it from eternity (Acts 2:23). (2) Our dear Saviour had to die at Jerusalem, in order to fulfil his covenant engagements for us. Our Lord Jesus Christ voluntarily assumed all responsibility for our souls in the covenant of grace; but once he assumed that responsibility, he must fulfil it. He was honour bound to do so (Genesis 43:8, 9; John 10:18; Acts 13:29). (3) The Son of God must die as he did because the scriptures must be fulfilled (Psalm 22; 40; 69; Isaiah 53). (4) It was absolutely necessary for the Lord Jesus Christ to die as he did upon the cursed tree, lifted up from the earth, in order for the holy Lord God to save us from our sins (Romans 3:24-26; John 3:14-17). If God would save us from our sins, he could only do it this way, righteousness must be maintained, sin must be punished, justice must be satisfied, forgiveness must be legitimate, and love must be blameless. If the holy, just and true God, would be the Saviour of sinners, it must be by the satisfaction of justice and justice could be satisfied in no other way. Now the God of grace declares himself to be "a just God and a Saviour" and bids sinners look to him in his Son and live forever (Isaiah 45:20-25).

Peter's Great Error
"And he spake that saying openly. And Peter took him, and began to rebuke him. But when he had turned about and looked on his disciples, he rebuked Peter, saying, Get thee behind me, Satan: for thou savourest not the things that be of God, but the things that be of men" (vv. 32, 33).

As often as I read this passage, I pause, as I hear our Saviour rebuke his servant Peter, and try to remind myself that there is in every true child of God a strange mixture of flesh and Spirit, grace and infirmity, strength and weakness, faith and unbelief, knowledge and great ignorance, the old man and the new.

I can almost see Peter. No doubt, he acted out of love and zeal for his Lord. It is as though, he took the Master by the arm and said, "Now don't you fret about these scribes, elders, and chief priests. We're not about to let anything happen to you". But his love and zeal were misguided passions of carnal reason and ignorance. He attempted to stand in the Lord's way and, in doing so, drew down upon himself the sharpest rebuke that ever fell from our Saviour's lips upon one of his disciples. John Gill explained,

Peter might more especially be concerned at this free and open account Christ gave of his sufferings and death, because he had just now acquainted him, that he should have the keys of the kingdom of heaven; by which he might understand some high post in the temporal kingdom of the Messiah he expected; and immediately to hear of his sufferings and death, damped his spirits, and destroyed his hopes, and threw him into such difficulties he was not able to remove; and therefore he takes Christ aside, and very warmly expostulates with him about what he had said, and chides him for it, and entreats him that he would not think, or talk of such like things.

And John Trapp wrote:

Peter having made a notable profession of his faith, and being therefore much commended by Christ, presently takes occasion to fall from the true holiness of faith to the sauciness of presumption, in advising his Master to decline the cross.

When he did, the Lord Jesus said to this man who had just declared, "Thou art the Christ, the Son of the Living God", "Get thee behind me, Satan: for thou savourest not the things that be of God, but the things that be of men". He called this disciple, one of his chosen Apostles, "Satan", because the devil himself had taken advantage of Peter's weakness and ignorance, and acting through his flesh inspired Peter to contradict and dispute his God and Saviour, dissuading him from suffering and dying for the salvation of his people, urging him not to pursue his purpose and fulfil his work as Jehovah's Righteous Servant and his eternal engagements as the Surety of the covenant. Though he was a true believer, a heaven-born soul, and a faithful servant of Christ, Peter was still a sinful man, just like you and me. When he spoke as he did here to the Saviour, he spoke as a carnal man, savouring the things of men, not the things of God. May God the Holy Spirit teach us the things these two verses are obviously intended to teach us. May he give us grace never to forget them.

The best of God's saints are but poor, fallible, sinful creatures. As long as we are in this world, our highest attainments of knowledge are ignorance. Let no child of God entertain high thoughts about himself. Let us be charitable and gracious toward our erring brethren (Galatians 6:1).

"And when he had called the people unto him with his disciples also, he said unto them, Whosoever will come after me, let him deny himself, and take up his cross, and follow me. For whosoever will save his life shall lose it; but whosoever shall lose his life for my sake and the gospel's, the same shall save it. For what shall it profit a man, if he shall gain the whole world, and lose his own soul? Or what shall a man give in exchange for his soul? Whosoever therefore shall be ashamed of me and of my words in this adulterous and sinful generation; of him also shall the Son of man be ashamed, when he cometh in the glory of his Father with the holy angels".

(Mark 8:34-38)

Chapter 36

Truths Of Deepest Importance

The words of our Lord Jesus Christ in these five verses of scripture are solemn and weighty words. They separate the precious from the vile. They are a winnowing fan in the Master's hand, by which he distinguishes wheat from the chaff. These are words which ought to be read often, prayed over much, and mediated upon continually. These few words define true Christianity more distinctly than all the volumes of theology and apologetics written by men. Robert Hawker observed:

> A single soul is of more value than the whole world; and for this plain reason: The time is coming, when the whole world and all that is in it will be destroyed; but the soul of every individual must live, either in happiness or misery, forever. Reader, pause over the subject, and calculate, if possible, the value of a single soul. The creation of it called forth the council of the whole persons of the Godhead. The redemption of it cost Christ his blood. The regeneration of it was the work of God the Holy Ghost. The everlasting happiness of it engageth the services of angels and of men continually. Angels rejoice in heaven in the recovery of every sinner. Hell rageth in the event of their salvation. The soul hath a capability of grace here, and glory forever. And therefore what a loss, incalculably great, must it be, that a being of such qualities, and so formed, should be exposed to everlasting destruction.

Coming To Christ
Throughout the scriptures faith is portrayed as a matter of coming to Christ. To believe on the Son of God is to come to him. To come to him is to believe on him. We come to him by following after him, as disciples follow after their Master. Our all glorious Christ says, "Whosoever will come after me, let him deny himself" (v. 34).

Coming to Christ is the result of a deliberate, purposeful choice. It is an act of the will. Our Master says, "whosoever will". Let us never alter his

Word. I know that faith is a gift of God. I know that none will ever come to Christ unless God the Holy Spirit graciously, effectually causes them to come. Yet, it is certain that any who come to him, come to him because they want him and choose him. God does not save sinners by knocking them in the head and dragging them to Christ. He saves sinners by causing them to want Christ more than life itself.

Faith in Christ is not a matter of conscription, but a voluntary act. The soldiers in Christ's army are not drafted, forced soldiers, but volunteers. It is written, "Thy people shall be willing in the day of thy power" (Psalm 110:3). "Blessed is the man whom thou choosest, and causest to approach unto thee, that he may dwell in thy courts" (Psalm 65:4).

Coming to Christ is an act of the heart, a spiritual, not a carnal thing. No one has ever come to Christ by walking a church aisle, kneeling at an altar, saying a prayer someone taught them to repeat, or signing a decision card. If you would come to Christ, you must do so without moving a muscle. You must come to him in your heart.

Faith is a heart work (Romans 10:8-10). True faith is the wilful, deliberate, voluntary confidence of my heart in the power and grace of the Lord Jesus Christ. It is trusting the merits of his blood and righteousness as my only acceptance before God. Faith in Christ involves the willing surrender of my heart to him as my Lord. It is the bowing and submission of my heart to him as my Lord (Luke 14:25-33).

Coming to Christ is a continual thing. Our Saviour does not speak of coming to him as a one-time thing, as a single act, but as a constant, continual, lifelong thing. Faith in Christ is not an event in life, but a way of life. "If so be ye have tasted that the Lord is gracious. To whom coming, as unto a living stone, disallowed indeed of men, but chosen of God, and precious" (1 Peter 2:3, 4).

Not only are sinners bidden to come to Christ, we are commanded to come (1 John 3:23). The warrant of faith is not my feeling, my emotion, my meeting certain prescribed conditions, but God's Word. If the Son of God says for me to come to him, then I may come to him!

Any sinner in all the world who will come to Christ may come to Christ. Our Master uses that blessed world of universal application and uses it frequently "Whosoever". I am so thankful he said, "Whosoever will", rather than, "if Don Fortner will". Had he said that, I would have concluded he must have meant some other Don Fortner. But I cannot doubt that "whosoever" includes me!

"Come unto me, all ye that labour and are heavy laden, and I will give you rest. Take my yoke upon you, and learn of me; for I am meek and lowly in heart: and ye shall find rest unto your souls. For my yoke is easy, and my burden is light" (Matthew 11:28-30). "He that believeth on the Son hath everlasting life: and he that believeth not the Son shall not see life; but the wrath of God abideth on him" (John 3:36). "And the Spirit and the bride say, Come. And let him that heareth say, Come. And let him that is athirst come. And whosoever will, let him take the water of life freely" (Revelation 22:17).

Carrying The Cross Of Christ

The first aspect of faith is coming to Christ. The second is carrying his cross. This is not an optional thing. Here, and throughout the Word of God, our Master tells us plainly that if we would follow him, if we would be his disciples, if we would be saved, self-denial is an absolute necessity. "And when he had called the people unto him with his disciples also, he said unto them, Whosoever will come after me, let him deny himself, and take up his cross, and follow me" (v. 34).

Again, this is a matter of personal, deliberate choice. Carrying your cross for Christ is not enduring providential hardships with patience, but deliberately choosing a course that is sure to bring trouble upon you, because trouble lies in the path of following Christ.

Salvation is by grace alone, through faith alone, in Christ alone. We are not saved by what we do, but by what God does and has done. We are saved by grace alone (Ephesians 2:8-10). Yet, if we are saved by the grace of God, we must through much tribulation enter into the kingdom of God; and we must deny self. J. C. Ryle was correct when he wrote, "A religion which costs nothing is worth nothing. It will do us no good in the life that now is. It will lead to no salvation in the life to come." If I am saved by the grace of God, I take up my cross and follow my Master. I must take up the cross of his doctrine, the cross of his will, and the cross of his honour. Our Saviour's words here are as plain as the noonday sun. If I choose not to bear his cross on this earth, I shall never wear his crown in heaven.

Our Master teaches us that true, saving faith involves deliberate and persevering self-denial and consecration. Matthew Henry wrote, "The first lesson in Christ's school is self-denial." Those who deny themselves here for Christ shall enjoy themselves in Christ forever. Grace is free; but it is not cheap. Faith in Christ involves the total surrender of myself to him, to his dominion as my Lord and Saviour, my Priest and King. That is what it is to take up your cross and follow Christ.

Christianity, true Christianity, true saving faith involves a total surrender to Christ the Lord. Either you will be a servant under the dominion of King Jesus, voluntarily giving up all to his claims, or you will go to hell. You may not have to give up anything in actuality. But surrender to Christ must be just as real and complete in your heart as if you had actually given up everything, even down to life itself. Our Lord Jesus Christ requires total and unreserved surrender to himself. Christ will be Lord of all, or he will not be Lord at all. Is Jesus Christ, the Son of God, your Lord? Think well before you answer. Is he truly your Lord?

But we must never imagine that this is a matter dealt with only in the initial experience of grace and in the initial act of faith. Here our Lord Jesus addresses these words to men who had been his faithful disciples for a long time. How graciously he warns us and teaches us to guard against the terrible tendency of our sinful flesh to rebel against his rule and his will. How much evil we bring upon ourselves by our carnal misapprehensions! We are all, like Peter (v. 33), inclined to judge things by our emotions, personal desires, and carnal reason. We must not. Rather, we must seek grace to know and bow to the will of God our Saviour in all things. Oh, for grace to savour the things which are of God, and not those which are of men!

Consecration To Christ

Faith is coming to Christ, carrying the cross of Christ, and consecration to Christ. "For whosoever will save his life shall lose it; but whosoever shall lose his life for my sake and the gospel's, the same shall save it. For what shall it profit a man, if he shall gain the whole world, and lose his own soul? Or what shall a man give in exchange for his soul?" (vv. 35-37).

If I would save my life, I must lose it to Christ. I repeat myself deliberately. Salvation is neither more nor less than surrender to the rule and reign of Jesus Christ as my Lord and King.

"And there went great multitudes with him: and he turned, and said unto them, If any man come to me, and hate not his father, and mother, and wife, and children, and brethren, and sisters, yea, and his own life also, he cannot be my disciple. And whosoever doth not bear his cross, and come after me, cannot be my disciple. For which of you, intending to build a tower, sitteth not down first, and counteth the cost, whether he have sufficient to finish it? Lest haply, after he hath laid the foundation, and is not able to finish it, all that behold it begin to mock him, Saying, This man began to build, and was not able to finish. Or what king, going to make war against another king, sitteth not down first, and consulteth whether he be able with ten thousand to meet him that cometh against him with twenty thousand? Or else, while the other is yet a great way off, he sendeth an ambassage, and desireth conditions of peace. So likewise, whosoever he be of you that forsaketh not all that he hath, he cannot be my disciple" (Luke 14:25-33).

Faith in Christ is giving over the rule of your life to Christ; but that is no great sacrifice at all. "For what shall it profit a man, if he shall gain the whole world, and lose his own soul? Or what shall a man give in exchange for his

300

soul?" That question is so well known and so often repeated that I fear that few take it to heart. It ought to sound in our ears like a trumpet, whenever we are tempted to neglect our eternal interests. Each of us has an immortal soul, a soul that will live forever, either in the bliss of eternal life or in the torment of eternal death. There is nothing the world can offer, nothing money can buy, nothing a man can give, nothing to be named in comparison with our souls. We live in a world where everything is temporal. We are going to a world where everything is eternal. Let us count nothing here more valuable than we shall when we have to leave it forever!

It is a very easy thing for you to lose your soul. You can murder it, by loving and clinging to the world. You can poison it with the deadly wine of false, freewill works religion. You can starve it, by neglecting God's ordained means of grace, the preaching of the gospel, by keeping from it the bread of life, by the neglect of prayer, the neglect of worship and the neglect of his Word. There are many ways to hell. Whichever way you choose is a matter for which you alone are responsible. But there is only one way to life eternal. Christ is that Way.

Confessing Christ

Faith in Christ involves coming to Christ, carrying the cross of Christ, consecration to Christ, and confessing Christ. "Whosoever therefore shall be ashamed of me and of my words in this adulterous and sinful generation; of him also shall the Son of man be ashamed, when he cometh in the glory of his Father with the holy angels" (v. 38).

Who is capable of being ashamed of Christ and his words? None among the sons of men can be compared to him. We do not have to guess what it is to be ashamed of Christ. It is to refuse to confess him, to refuse to identify ourselves with him. Every son and daughter of Adam show themselves ashamed of him and his gospel who refuse to seek salvation in his name, trusting him alone as Saviour and Lord. All who seek to add their own works to his righteousness and his precious blood for acceptance with God prove themselves ashamed of him. To refuse to trust the Lord Jesus Christ is to deny him. That is what it is to be ashamed of him.

If you are ashamed of Christ's doctrine, you are ashamed of him (Romans 1:16, 17). If you are ashamed of Christ's ordinances, you are ashamed of him. If you are ashamed of Christ's people, ashamed to identify yourself with them, you are ashamed of him. If you are ashamed of Christ in this adulterous and sinful generation, he will be ashamed of you when he comes in the glory of his Father with his holy angels to judge the world.

301

"And he said unto them, Verily I say unto you, That there be some of them that stand here, which shall not taste of death, till they have seen the kingdom of God come with power. And after six days Jesus taketh with him Peter, and James, and John, and leadeth them up into an high mountain apart by themselves: and he was transfigured before them. And his raiment became shining, exceeding white as snow; so as no fuller on earth can white them. And there appeared unto them Elias with Moses: and they were talking with Jesus. And Peter answered and said to Jesus, Master, it is good for us to be here: and let us make three tabernacles; one for thee, and one for Moses, and one for Elias. For he wist not what to say; for they were sore afraid. And there was a cloud that overshadowed them: and a voice came out of the cloud, saying, This is my beloved Son: hear him. And suddenly, when they had looked round about, they saw no man any more, save Jesus only with themselves. And as they came down from the mountain, he charged them that they should tell no man what things they had seen, till the Son of man were risen from the dead. And they kept that saying with themselves, questioning one with another what the rising from the dead should mean. And they asked him, saying, Why say the scribes that Elias must first come? And he answered and told them, Elias verily cometh first, and restoreth all things; and how it is written of the Son of man, that he must suffer many things, and be set at nought. But I say unto you, That Elias is indeed come, and they have done unto him whatsoever they listed, as it is written of him".

(Mark 9:1-13)

302

Chapter 37

Lessons From The Transfiguration

We must never fail to consider the context in which something is revealed in holy scripture. In Mark 9 we are given a description of our Lord's transfiguration before Peter, James, and John. It is a passage full of instruction and inspiration. But we are sure to miss much if we do not remember that this story follows, by divine arrangement, our Lord's comments in Mark 8 about his own suffering and death, and his teaching that if we would be his disciples we must deny ourselves, take up our cross, lose our lives in his dominion, and follow him even unto death.

Now, lest we grow weary in well doing, lest we be tempted to lay down the cross, lest we think self-denial is too demanding, our Lord follows those strong, demanding words with the promise of his kingdom and a sight of his own glory in that kingdom, even giving us a foretaste of the glory awaiting us when our warfare here is ended. When we are tempted to give up the fight and turn from the battle, we ought to seek a fresh vision of Christ's great glory and of the glory promised to us in him. May God the Holy Spirit enable us to see and hear those things which Peter, James, and John saw and heard when they were with the Lord in the holy mount.

Taste Of Death
"And he said unto them, Verily I say unto you, That there be some of them that stand here, which shall not taste of death, till they have seen the kingdom of God come with power" (v. 1). What a blessed thing it is to read those words "taste of death"! God's elect only "taste of death". The wicked are swallowed by it. They are "killed with death" (Revelation 2:23). Believers shall never die (John 11:26). Actually, for the believer death is not death at all, but the beginning of life. The death of a believer's body is the liberation of his soul; and as soon as our souls are freed from this body of sin and death we shall enter heaven. This is the doctrine of God's Word (Isaiah 57:1, 2). When the righteous perish from the earth, they live in uprightness forever. Those who have been made righteous by the grace of God, being made the righteousness of God in Christ, when they die are taken away from evil. They enter into a world of peace. They rest in their beds, their bodies in the grave

and their souls in the arms of Christ. And they live in the uprightness of glorified spirits forever.

As soon as the believer dies he is carried by the angels of God into heaven, "Abraham's bosom" (Luke 16:22-25), the place of endless comfort. At death every repentant sinner is taken to be with Christ in paradise (Luke 23:43). Paradise is heaven, the garden of God (Revelation 2:7). It is that place of assured blessedness promised to sinners who seek the mercy of God in Christ. Our Saviour said to the dying thief, "Today", immediately, "shalt thou", assuredly, "be with me", in endless company, "in paradise", heavenly glory. Death for the believer is infinite, immeasurable, immediate gain (Philippians 1:21-23). Believers, upon leaving this world, lose nothing but sin and sorrow and gain everything good and glorious.

What is the state of the saints' life between death and the resurrection? I will not say more than God has revealed; but we are assured that God's saints are not floating around in the sky sleeping! They have gone to a specific place called Heaven where Christ is. There they are assembled as a glorified Church (Hebrews 12:22, 23). And their souls exist in a recognizable form, just as surely as Lazarus, Moses, and Elijah exists in a recognized form (Luke 16:23; Mark 9:4). Do God's saints have a body between death and the resurrection? A physical body? No. A spiritual body, a heavenly form, a house for their souls? Most definitely! Read 2 Corinthians 5:1. Every believer as soon as he leaves this body of flesh enters into heaven with Christ. It is this assurance that makes death a desirable thing for the believer to taste.

The Coming Of The Kingdom
"And he said unto them, Verily I say unto you, That there be some of them that stand here, which shall not taste of death, till they have seen the kingdom of God come with power" (v. 1).

The disciples were terribly perplexed by our Lord's declaration described in verse thirty-one of chapter eight that he must be rejected and killed. I do not doubt that they were very concerned about the demands of true discipleship described in the last few verses of that chapter. Here the Lord Jesus promised them that he is indeed God's Messiah and that the kingdom of God was at hand, so very near at hand that some of them would still be living upon the earth when it came. Our Lord plainly told his disciples that his kingdom was about to be established. He was not talking about a literal, earthly, millennial kingdom to be established in Israel at some distant time in the future. He was talking about something that was about to happen at the time.

It is a great mistake to miss the teaching of scripture regarding the spiritual, present nature of Christ's kingdom. We do not look for some future time when the Lord Jesus will establish a carnal millennial kingdom on earth. We who believe are the Israel of God. God's church is his kingdom, the true Zion. Believers are the children of Abraham. This kingdom began when Christ entered into his glory. All the fanciful nonsense about a secret rapture, a future, literal seven-year tribulation period, a 1000-year Jewish kingdom, the return of Jewish sacrifices, etc. is nothing but human invention, tradition, and religious escapism. When Christ comes the second time, it will not be in secret, it will not be to give the Jews a second chance to receive him, or to rebuild the Jewish priesthood and temple services! When the Son of God comes again, it will be with power and great glory for the ultimate salvation of his people and the destruction of his foes. The Word of God never speaks of Christ coming secretly, or of a secret rapture of the church (2 Thessalonians 1:6-10).

In this opening verse of Mark 9 our Lord Jesus tells us three things specifically about his kingdom. First, the Saviour declared that the kingdom of God would come, and would come so as to be seen. The kingdom of the Messiah was to be set up in the world by the utter destruction of the Jewish nation, both physically and spiritually. In Genesis 49:10 we are told that the sceptre of power and the lawgiver would depart from Judah when Shiloh was come. Here Shiloh declares, I have come and the sceptre of power as well as the lawgiver shall now depart from Judah. In Romans chapters 9 to 11 the Holy Spirit explains that it was necessary for God to destroy the Jewish nation and send blindness to that one nation, so that he might send the gospel into all the world and gather his elect out of every nation, kindred, tribe, and tongue. Matthew Henry correctly observed, "This was the restoring of the kingdom of God among men, which had been in a manner lost by the woeful degeneracy both of Jews and Gentiles."

Second, our Master asserted that his kingdom would come with power, power to make its own way and overcome all the opposition that might stand in its way. It came with power when the Holy Spirit was poured out upon it on the day of Pentecost. It came with power when God sent the Roman armies under the command of Titus through Jerusalem in 70 AD. It came with power when the gospel was brought to chosen, redeemed sinners among the Gentiles, breaking the chains of sin, idolatry, and superstition. And the kingdom of God still comes with power every time the Holy Spirit conquers a rebel sinner's heart by the gospel.

Third, our Lord Jesus asserted that some who stood with them on the earth at that time would continue to live until he had fulfilled his purpose in coming to the earth in human flesh and returned to glory and poured out his Spirit as the ascended, enthroned King of Zion (Acts 2:36, 37). There were some standing there, that did not taste of death, until they saw it. This is virtually the same thing he said in Matthew 24:34. These very same disciples, though they saw and understood very little at this time, he promised would see the kingdom of God, when the others could not discern it to be the kingdom of God, for it comes not with observation. The only people in all the world who can see and enter into this kingdom are those who are born of God (John 3:3-7).

Having made this promise, a promise which seemed altogether unbelievable, six days later our Saviour took Peter, James, and John up into a high mountain and showed them some things which they later looked back upon as convincing proofs of his kingdom and glory.

The Transfiguration

In verses 2-10 we see where Mark describes the Saviour's transfiguration. Though there was an interval of six days, it seems clear that Mark was inspired by the Holy Spirit to give his account of the transfiguration as a prophetic vision of that which our Saviour declared in verse one. It is given here as a representation of the coming of the kingdom of God and of Christ's exaltation and glory as our King. Though they were commanded to say nothing about it at the time, both Peter and John gave very clear accounts of what they had seen later (2 Peter 1:16; 1 John 1:1-3). Mark 9:2-10 is a picture of the glory our great and glorious Saviour now has as our exalted Mediator and King.

The days of his sorrow and humiliation are over forever. Our Lord Jesus is crowned with glory now. When the scripture says here that he was transfigured before these disciples, the word "transfigured" is translated from the word from which we get our word metamorphosis. It means that he changed before their very eyes.

In this way, our Lord showed his disciples the glory awaiting him when he had finished his work of redemption. I am not guessing about this. Peter, James, and John, as they watched this heard those Old Testament giants Moses and Elijah talking to him about the death he was to accomplish at Jerusalem (Luke 9:29-31). Our blessed Lord and Saviour's transfiguration "testified beforehand of the sufferings of Christ and the glory that should follow" (1 Peter 1:11).

This vision of Christ's transfiguration was also a gracious pledge of glorious things which are in store for God's elect (Colossians 3:1-4). Though reviled and persecuted in this world, though despised and hated for the gospel's sake, there is a day coming when we shall be clothed with majesty, honour, and glory forever (Ephesians 2:7).

I must not pass this opportunity to point out the fact that Moses and Elijah knew each other, and were known by these disciples, though they lived hundreds of years apart and the disciples had never seen them or even a picture of them before. I am often asked, "Will we know one another in heaven?" Obviously, the answer is, "Yes". As soon as these bodies close their eyes in death, believers enter into "an house not made with hands, eternal in the heavens". In that house we will know and converse with one another, as well as with Christ himself. And the primary subject of conversation in heaven will be the death accomplished at Jerusalem by our most glorious Christ.

This vision of our Lord's transfiguration is also a picture of the fact that Moses and Elijah, the law and the prophets, find their fulfilment in the substitutionary sacrifice of our Lord Jesus Christ at Calvary. The law was not given to be nothing more than a code of ethics. It was given to point to Christ. The prophets were not written merely to foretell future events. The books of the prophets were written to proclaim the coming of Christ and to verify his claim as the Christ when he did come.

What great comfort and consolation a sight and apprehension of glory gives to troubled believers! When Peter, speaking for himself, as well as James and John, said, Lord, let us stay right here forever, there is much in the statement which is reprehensible. It showed a terrible slowness to hear the Word of God and great ignorance on his part. The Lord Jesus had just told him a few days earlier that he must be killed at Jerusalem. It showed a very regrettable forgetfulness of his brethren and selfishness on his part. It certainly showed the folly of popping off about things of which we are ignorant. Yet, if I had been there, indeed, if I could be there now, I think I would want the same thing Peter wanted. I would say, "Let's stay right here on this mountain. I don't ever again want to go back down to where I was."

Be that as it may, it will do our hearts good to look forward, and try to get some apprehension of the indescribable pleasure and glory awaiting us when we meet our Saviour to part no more. What shall we say when we are made partakers of his glory? What emotions will flood our souls when we enter into his holy company and know that we shall go out no more? What shall it be to enter into his glory? Peter had a foretaste of these things. I suspect that when we experience them we will say with one heart and one voice, "It is good for us to be here".

Further, the transfiguration gives us another of those plain, clear declarations of our great Saviour's eternal Godhead. While they were with the Saviour in the mount, with Moses and Elijah standing in front of them, the Lord God spoke from heaven and said, "This is my beloved Son". Moses, Elijah, Peter, James, and John were all like us, sinners saved by grace, the sons of God by adoption and grace. Jesus Christ is distinctly God the Son, the Son of God by nature. The man Christ Jesus is himself God! He is God manifest in the flesh. His name is Immanuel, God with us. None but God could redeem us. None but God could put away our sins. None but God could save us by his grace.

And in this vision we are clearly and distinctly taught that all power and authority are in the Lord Jesus Christ, our Saviour and King. That same Voice which spoke from heaven at our Master's baptism and declared our Saviour to be God the Son, spoke again at his transfiguration. On both occasions the Voice was the same. On both occasions, the Father owned the Son as the Son. But here two very important words are added. "Hear him"! In the Church and Kingdom of God there is no voice of authority but his voice. He is our Teacher. If we would be wise, we must learn of him. He is the Light of the world. If we would walk in the light, we must follow him. He is the Head of the church. If we would be members of his body, we must be joined to him. He alone is the Saviour of men. If we would be saved, we must look to him. Blessed, eternally blessed are all those sinners who upon this earth are graciously taught of God and learn by his grace to look to Christ and "hear him" (John 10:27, 28).

Elijah Must Come

The disciples, as they came down off the mountain after seeing the Lord Jesus transfigured before them, after seeing and hearing Moses and Elijah, after hearing God the Father speak from heaven, were specifically told to tell no one about the things they had seen until the Lord Jesus was risen from the dead. Hearing that, they seemed to forget everything else and returned to their usual questions and debates about what the Lord meant. This time, they debated about what he meant by rising from the dead. They still did not believe that the Lord Jesus was really going to die (vv. 9, 10). They were, indeed, coming down!

"And they asked him, saying, Why say the scribes that Elias must first come? And he answered and told them, Elias verily cometh first, and restoreth all things; and how it is written of the Son of man, that he must suffer many things, and be set at nought. But I say unto you, That Elias is indeed come, and they have done unto him whatsoever they listed, as it is written of him" (vv. 11-13).

We must never attempt to interpret the Word of God carnally. The Pharisees believed and taught, as many do today, that before Christ comes in his glory and establishes his kingdom Elijah must literally come to the earth again. The disciples were familiar with and confused by the influence of the Pharisees.

The prophecy of Malachi certainly tells us that Messiah's coming must be preceded and introduced by the coming of Elijah.

"Behold, I will send you Elijah the prophet before the coming of the great and dreadful day of the LORD: And he shall turn the heart of the fathers to the children, and the heart of the children to their fathers, lest I come and smite the earth with a curse" (Malachi 4:5, 6).

But we know Malachi's prophecy did not refer to Elijah literally coming back to the earth, because the Lord Jesus tells us plainly in verse 13 that Malachi's prophecy was fulfilled in the ministry of John the Baptist. John the Baptist came not in the body of Elijah, but in the spirit and power of Elijah. That was the meaning of Malachi's message. Let us never attempt to interpret the Word of God carnally. And we should always beware of the influence of false religion. There is no hindrance to the understanding of the Word of God like the prejudice of false religion. Seldom, very seldom is the majority, or the historical opinion of things right. These disciples misunderstood Malachi's words, because they allowed themselves to be influenced by the carnal doctrine of the Pharisees.

"And when he came to his disciples, he saw a great multitude about them, and the scribes questioning with them. And straightway all the people, when they beheld him, were greatly amazed, and running to him saluted him. And he asked the scribes, What question ye with them? And one of the multitude answered and said, Master, I have brought unto thee my son, which hath a dumb spirit; And wheresoever he taketh him, he teareth him: and he foameth, and gnasheth with his teeth, and pineth away: and I spake to thy disciples that they should cast him out; and they could not. He answereth him, and saith, O faithless generation, how long shall I be with you? how long shall I suffer you? bring him unto me. And they brought him unto him: and when he saw him, straightway the spirit tare him; and he fell on the ground, and wallowed foaming. And he asked his father, How long is it ago since this came unto him? And he said, Of a child. And ofttimes it hath cast him into the fire, and into the waters, to destroy him: but if thou canst do any thing, have compassion on us, and help us. Jesus said unto him, If thou canst believe, all things are possible to him that believeth. And straightway the father of the child cried out, and said with tears, Lord, I believe; help thou mine unbelief. When Jesus saw that the people came running together, he rebuked the foul spirit, saying unto him, Thou dumb and deaf spirit, I charge thee, come out of him, and enter no more into him. And the spirit cried, and rent him sore, and came out of him: and he was as one dead; insomuch that many said, He is dead. But Jesus took him by the hand, and lifted him up; and he arose. And when he was come into the house, his disciples asked him privately, Why could not we cast him out? And he said unto them, This kind can come forth by nothing, but by prayer and fasting".

(Mark 9:14-29)

Chapter 38

A Welcome Intrusion

When our Lord Jesus came down off the mount of transfiguration, he found his disciples being harassed by the scribes, apparently because they were not able to perform the miracle of casting out the demon which possessed a young man who was brought to them. When the Lord Jesus saw what was going on, he immediately stepped in to defend the nine disciples who were baffled by their inability to perform this miracle and baffled by the learned scribes who were disputing with them. He asked the scribes why they were disputing with (questioning) his disciples. But, before the scribes said anything, before any of the disciples said anything, a man butted into the conversation.

Normally, in polite society, such an intrusion is looked upon as rudeness and is disdained. However, this man's intrusion was most welcome because it was the intrusion of a desperate, loving father for his demon possessed son. This poor man cared nothing for the dispute between the scribes and our Master's disciples. His son was possessed of the devil! His son was pining away under satanic influence. His son was perishing and he was helpless. Therefore, he came directly, as soon as he had opportunity, to the only One who could help. He brought his son to the Son of God, seeking mercy, grace, and life for his son by the power of our great and glorious Saviour.

Mountain-top Experiences
The first thing I see in this passage is the fact that mountain-top experiences seldom last very long. The contrast between this paragraph and the one preceding it is striking and must not be overlooked. We move from the mount of transfiguration to the valley of sorrow, from the vision of Christ's glory to a sad, sad history of Satan's power and influence in the life of one young man.

Peter, James, and John had been in the blessed company of Moses and Elijah. They had just heard God the Father speaking from heaven. They had just seen the Son of God transfigured before their eyes. Now they come into the scene of conflict, pain, weakness, and misery. Here is a boy in agony, tormented by the devil. Here is a father with a broken heart, in deep distress. Here is a band of weak disciples baffled by Satan's power and unable to help. That is a fairly vivid picture of every Christian's life in this world. Mountain-top experiences are delightful, blessed times; but we must not expect them too often or expect too many of them. Most of the believer's life is spent in conflict with the world, the flesh, and the devil. Our blessed visions of glory, those sweet foretastes of heaven, those seasons spent on the holy mount with the Lord are to be seized and enjoyed when God gives them. But that is the exception, not the norm. When we are in the valley, let us try always to remember that the Lord Jesus comes to his disciples in the valley, just as he does in the mountain. He always comes, manifesting himself to us at precisely the right time. And the sorrows and conflicts of our valleys are as much by divine arrangement as the joys of our mountain-tops.

Utterly Dependent

We are also reminded by this story that we are utterly and entirely dependent upon our Lord Jesus Christ. This is brought out very clearly in these verses. Like Moses when he came down from Mt Sinai, our Lord found his disciples in a state of complete confusion. They were under the assault of a malicious group of scribes. The occasion of this was the fact that they had attempted to cast the demon out of this man's son without success. These are the same men who had, just a short time earlier, done many miracles and cast out many devils. Yet, before this man and his son, they were utterly helpless.

These disciples learned by humble experience a very needful lesson. It is a lesson we must learn, a lesson that must be burned into our hearts. You will find it in the words of our Lord Jesus Christ to his chosen disciples in John 15:5. He said, "Without me ye can do nothing". This is a lesson contrary to our flesh and bitter. But it is a lesson demonstrated over and over again in scripture. We must not forget it.

If the Lord leaves us to ourselves, we have no strength to do anything or in any way resist the devil. The experience of Noah, Abraham, Lot, David, and Peter are written in bold letters to remind us of this fact. May God the Holy Spirit teach us daily that we are weak, weakness itself, and utterly helpless without the wisdom, presence, and grace of Christ, which he alone can give us.

Satan's Power

This story is also recorded upon the pages of holy scripture to teach us and warn us of the horror of satanic power. Let no one imagine that Satan is a fictional force of evil. Let none laugh and think that Satan is just a religious boogie man conjured up by crotchety old men to scare little children. In this inspired narrative we hear a father describe the power and influence of Satan over his son as a foul spirit and a destructive spirit. The demon that controlled this young man was a deaf and dumb spirit. And the demon possessing this child possessed his heart as well as his body as a lunatic spirit (Matthew 17:15). Matthew describes his condition as a form of epilepsy, which causes fainting and dumbness, which John Gill identifies as, "a delirium of the heart".

This demon took possession of this young man as a mere child. This is a matter of deepest importance. We must labour to do good to our children and to serve the interests of their souls, even from their earliest years. If Satan begins early to destroy them, we must begin early to save them. We must, to the best of our ability, control who has influence over them, choosing their friends and companions, instruct them in the scriptures and the blessed gospel of Christ, and pray for them.

Weak Faith, But True Faith

We also see in this passage another of the numerous examples given in scripture of the dual nature of the believer. Who can read this paragraph and fail to see that faith and unbelief, righteousness and sin are found in the same person? The father of this child said, "Lord, I believe, help thou mine unbelief". He believed. Yet, he had some doubts. He brought his child with hope. Yet, he was fearful. He seems to express this honestly (v. 22). He said to Christ, "If thou canst do anything, have compassion on us and help us".

You may think, "That's not much faith". You would be right in your thinking if you did. But it was enough. He took his son home completely freed of the demon's power. He had faith as a grain of mustard seed; but it was true, God-given faith. None of God's people in this world are perfect, not even in a single area. It is not our faith, neither its strength, nor its quality, nor its quantity that matters, but Christ, the Object of our faith.

Though this man's faith was weak, it was true. It was the gift of God in him. He shows us by example that though our faith may be weak, we have cause, as Robert Hawker observed, "to bless God, for the smallest degree of faith than for all the riches of the world". Faith brought him to Christ. His faith caused him to confess his conscious weakness of faith before the omnipotent One who had given him faith. And his faith obtained the mercy he needed. Do you have such faith, even as a grain of mustard seed? If so, bless God for it. Faith in Christ is the evidence of our union with Christ and of our salvation by him (Acts 10:43; 13:48; Hebrews 11:1, 2). Let us desire and pray for greater faith, while we cherish the smallest measure of faith, by which our calling and election are proved and made sure to our souls.

313

Christ's Dominion

We are taught here, by vivid example the totality of Christ's dominion. There are many who foolishly imagine that Satan and the demons of hell are rivals to God, that they are somehow out of control. Nothing could be further from the truth. The devil is God's devil. He is under God's control. God uses him to accomplish his own purposes. And when he gets done with him, he will destroy him.

Do you see this? Our Lord Jesus Christ exercises total dominion over Satan and his agents at all times. He speaks with almighty, sovereign authority, and Satan and his demons immediately, implicitly, and totally obey his voice. Satan is strong, malicious, and busy. We are no match for him. But the Lord Jesus Christ is yet able to save to the uttermost all who come unto God by him. He saves his elect from Satan's power. Satan can never snatch us from our Saviour's almighty, omnipotent hands. And, soon the God of peace will bruise Satan under our heels (Romans 16:20).

Believing Parents

No doubt, this story is recorded upon the pages of Inspiration to remind us again of the privileges and responsibilities of believing parents. We cannot save our children. We cannot change their nature. We cannot give them life and faith in Christ. Many believing men and women have raised a house full of rebels. Let none of us arrogantly and ignorantly imagine that because children are wicked something must be amiss with the parents. Such talk betrays the pride and stupidity of a man who has never raised a family!

Yet, there are some things we can and must do for our children. We can do for our sons and daughters what this man did for his son. He brought his son to the Saviour, to the place where Christ was to be found. We can and must bring our children with us to the house of God. He brought the Saviour to his Son by fervent prayer. He acknowledged his son's condition to the Lord Jesus. He told the Lord Jesus plainly that his son, the child he dearly loved, was deaf and dumb, a lunatic, wicked to the core of his being, and dying. He added that he had always been like that from his youth.

His son's desperate need was his need. His prayer was not, "Have compassion on him, and help him". His prayer was, "Have compassion on us, and help us"!

His son did not believe God; but he believed God for his son. He could not believe instead of his son as a proxy. There is no such thing as proxy faith. But he did believe for his son. This man understood that foolishness is bound in the heart of every child. The rod of correction must be used to drive it from him; but only the grace of God can effectually deliver a sinner from the foolishness that is in him and from the power of Satan that rules him.

God's Operations
This passage of scripture is also an instructive, beautiful picture of God's mighty operations of grace. Whenever God saves a sinner, there are certain things you can expect to see, and certain things you can expect to happen. I do not suggest by any means that all who are saved have the same experiences; but every believer's experience is similar. Death is death. Life is life. Grace is grace. And salvation is salvation. This is how God performs it. This is how the Lord God performs his mighty operations of grace in us.

First, when God saves a sinner, there is a divine call. The Master said, "Bring him unto me" (v. 19). So it is with all to whom God is gracious. He commands them to come to Christ and commands all creation to bring them to him, saying, "Bring my sons from far, and my daughters from the ends of the earth" (Isaiah 43:6).

Whenever the Lord Jesus calls sinners to himself, as they are coming to him, there is usually a satanic throw (v. 20). When the Saviour calls the sinner to himself, Satan is now in a rage because he knows his time is short (Revelation 12:12).

Third, when the Lord comes to give eternal life, there is a hopeful slaughter. He kills before he makes alive. He brings us down before he lifts us up. That is vividly set before us in verses 25 and 26.

"When Jesus saw that the people came running together, he rebuked the foul spirit, saying unto him, Thou dumb and deaf spirit, I charge thee, come out of him, and enter no more into him. And the spirit cried, and rent him sore, and came out of him: and he was as one dead; insomuch that many said, He is dead".

Then, blessed be his name, when the Lord Jesus comes in saving power, there is a resurrection from the dead. "Jesus took him by the hand, and lifted him up; and he arose" (v. 27). The new birth is a resurrection from spiritual death to life eternal by the power and operation of God's omnipotent mercy (John 5:25; Ephesians 2:1-5; Revelation 20:6).

"And they departed thence, and passed through Galilee; and he would not that any man should know it. For he taught his disciples, and said unto them, The Son of man is delivered into the hands of men, and they shall kill him; and after that he is killed, he shall rise the third day. But they understood not that saying, and were afraid to ask him. And he came to Capernaum: and being in the house he asked them, What was it that ye disputed among yourselves by the way? But they held their peace: for by the way they had disputed among themselves, who should be the greatest. And he sat down, and called the twelve, and saith unto them, If any man desire to be first, the same shall be last of all, and servant of all. And he took a child, and set him in the midst of them: and when he had taken him in his arms, he said unto them, Whosoever shall receive one of such children in my name, receiveth me: and whosoever shall receive me, receiveth not me, but him that sent me".

(Mark 9:30-37)

Chapter 39

Matters Of Tremendous Importance

The Greatest Of All Doctrines

"And they departed thence, and passed through Galilee; and he would not that any man should know it. For he taught his disciples, and said unto them, The Son of man is delivered into the hands of men, and they shall kill him; and after that he is killed, he shall rise the third day. But they understood not that saying, and were afraid to ask him" (vv. 30-32).

The doctrine taught in these verses is the blessed gospel doctrine of substitutionary atonement, the satisfaction of divine justice for our sins by the blood sacrifice of our Lord Jesus Christ as the sinner's Substitute. This is the doctrine of the Bible. It is the universal theme and message of holy scripture. This is the doctrine God's servants are sent to preach. This is the message by which the holy Lord God reveals himself to chosen sinners in saving mercy. This is the message by which God's saints are edified, encouraged, instructed, challenged, and reproved.

In verse 30 we are given a display of divine sovereignty. We are told that the Lord Jesus, when he was passing through Galilee again, "would not that any man should know it. For he taught his disciples". The Master taught the gospel doctrine concerning his sin-atoning death to his chosen disciples alone. God hides the gospel from some and reveals it to others, according to his own sovereign will and pleasure (Matthew 11:25-27).

The Galileans had seen many mighty displays of our Saviour's person, power, and grace. Yet, they believed not. Therefore, he refused to make himself known to them. That fact is most solemn. I do not find in the Bible a single example of the Son of God crossing a sinner's path repeatedly. Those who despise him despise life and court destruction. Christ was present, but unknown by the people of Galilee! How often that is the case! Be warned. If you refuse to believe the gospel that has been preached to you, that gospel which is the power of God unto salvation to everyone that believeth, the gospel itself will be your eternal tormentor in hell (Proverbs 1:23-33). It is written, "He, that being often reproved hardeneth his neck, shall suddenly be destroyed, and that without remedy" (Proverbs 29:1).

The glorious sovereignty of our God is also displayed in the sufferings and death of his dear Son. Our Saviour here declares, "The Son of Man is delivered into the hands of men". He spoke of it as a matter already done, because it was done from eternity by the determinate counsel and foreknowledge of God the Father. Nothing about the death of Christ was accidental. This was the reason why God created the universe. The Son of God came here in time to fulfil what he agreed upon in eternity as our Surety. This was the mission upon which he was sent into the world (Matthew 1:21; 20:28).

The immense importance of Christ's sin-atoning sacrifice apparently was not yet understood by the disciples. Though he spoke often about it, their religious prejudices and preconceived ideas about what Messiah would do blinded their minds to his doctrine. Do not let those things blind your mind to this glorious, gospel doctrine. Substitution is the sum and substance of the gospel (2 Corinthians 5:21; Galatians 3:13; Romans 5:6-8).

Substitution is the only remedy for sin. The substitutionary sacrifice of Christ is the only hope for sinners. It is the revelation of the glory of God (2 Corinthians 4:6) and the joy of redeemed sinners (2 Corinthians 9:15; 1 John 4:9, 10, 19). The substitutionary sacrifice of our dear Saviour is the motive for all worship, devotion, and service to Christ (2 Corinthians 8:9; 1 Corinthians 6:19, 20), and the rallying point of all true believers (Colossians 3:11).

When the Lord Jesus announced that after his death upon the cursed tree he would rise from the dead in three days, he was asserting that by his one great sacrifice for the sins of his people he would completely satisfy the justice of God for us and would thereby forever put away our sins. Whenever we think about this, the greatest of all doctrines, think of it under these terms: Sovereignty, Substitution, Satisfaction, and Success.

The Greatest Of All Deceivers

"And he came to Capernaum: and being in the house he asked them, What was it that ye disputed among yourselves by the way? But they held their peace: for by the way they had disputed among themselves, who should be the greatest" (vv. 33, 34).

What a strange, what a sad, sad thing this is to see! The Lord Jesus has just told these disciples the greatest of all truths, and they are fussing about who shall be the greatest in the kingdom of heaven! These simple fishermen, chosen, redeemed, and called by pure grace, are arguing with each other about something that is both in direct opposition to grace and in direct opposition to the teachings of scripture. These brethren were divided because each had a secret longing for preference and pre-eminence!

The sad fact is we are all proud, self-righteous Pharisees by nature. We all think far more highly of ourselves than we ought. We all think we deserve better treatment than we get. We are all easily deceived by this, the greatest of all deceivers, pride. The scriptures warn us constantly about this thing called pride. There is nothing we more abhor in others and more carefully nurture in ourselves than pride.

Pride is a very old sin. It was pride that destroyed Lucifer. It was pride that destroyed Adam and drove him from the garden. It was pride that ruined our race. And it is pride that keeps sinners from the Saviour.

Pride is a very blinding sin. These disciples could not understand the glorious gospel doctrine of substitutionary redemption because their minds were occupied with their own visions of grandeur about themselves in the kingdom of heaven!

Pride is a very subtle sin. Where it is the strongest, it is the least detected. It rules multitudes without notice, often wearing the garb of humility. "The pride of thine heart hath deceived thee".

Pride is a soul-robbing sin. How often men and women miss God's blessings, especially under the ministry of the Word, because they secretly nurture their own pride. These disciples missed the blessing of Christ's teachings because of their silly pride.

Pride is the great dividing sin. "Only by pride cometh contention: but with the well advised is wisdom" (Proverbs 13:10). "He that is of a proud heart stirreth up strife: but he that putteth his trust in the LORD shall be made fat" (Proverbs 28:25). In fact, the cause of all strife, contention, and division between brethren is pride. All hurt feelings are just injured pride. All gossip, the love of talking about people, is pride. Someone once said, "Great minds discuss great ideas and principles. Little minds talk about people". If that is so, we appear to be living in a world full of mental pigmies.

Pride is a soul-ruining sin. "Pride goeth before destruction, and an haughty spirit before a fall" (Proverbs 16:18). "A man's pride shall bring him low: but honour shall uphold the humble in spirit" (Proverbs 29:23). Pride keeps sinners from repentance. Pride keeps people from trusting Christ. Pride robs us of peace, personally and with one another. Pride destroys brotherly love. Pride builds fences. Pride promotes self and seeks to pull others down. Pride makes people malicious, uncaring about the feelings of others, self-centred, unforgiving, unbending, unyielding, critical, and volatile.

Ever beware of pride. Nothing is more deceitful. Nothing is more disruptive. Nothing is more unbecoming men and women who belong to the Son of God.

The Greatest Of All Deeds
"And he sat down, and called the twelve, and saith unto them, If any man desire to be first, the same shall be last of all, and servant of all. And he took

a child, and set him in the midst of them: and when he had taken him in his arms, he said unto them, Whosoever shall receive one of such children in my name, receiveth me: and whosoever shall receive me, receiveth not me, but him that sent me" (vv. 35-37).

"And he sat down, and called the twelve, and saith unto them, If any man desire to be first, the same shall be last of all, and servant of all". This is our Lord's standard of true greatness. The world says, "Greatness is ruling over others". The Son of God says, "Greatness is serving others". David was a great man, not because he was a mighty king, but because he served his generation by the will of God as their king. Let us not seek honour, attention, and power, but humility, love, and our place of service in Christ's kingdom.

Far too often, I fear, men confuse carnal ambition for a call to the ministry. Many want to preach because that is the place, they think, of pre-eminence. God's servants are men who labour in the Word, addict themselves to the service of men's souls, and seek to serve Christ by faithfully serving the souls of his people. There is a difference.

Empty boasts of orthodoxy are useless. The mere love of good preaching and religious activity is a mockery. If our religion does not translate into serving one another, our religion is a delusion (James 1:25-27).

People who are willing to be last of all, least of all, and servants of all for Christ's sake are always few. But these are the people who do good, who break down prejudices, who build the kingdom of God.

Just to make sure that we do not miss the meaning of his instruction, our Lord illustrates what he is talking about in verses 36 and 37. "And he took a child, and set him in the midst of them: and when he had taken him in his arms, he said unto them, Whosoever shall receive one of such children in my name, receiveth me: and whosoever shall receive me, receiveth not me, but him that sent me".

Believers are often compared to little children, because children are easily taught, are not easily offended, forgive quickly, and are very trusting. Usually, unless taught otherwise, children are willing to share whatever they have with others.

Anything done for or to one of God's children is considered as being done for him or to him. Do we really believe that? If we did, we would be more thoughtful and caring about one another, and we would be far more guarded in our attitudes toward one another. This is true godliness. These are the things the Bible calls "good works". Children of God, love one another!

Jesus! and shall it ever be,
A mortal man ashamed of Thee?
Ashamed of Thee, whom angels praise,
Whose glories shine through endless days?

Ashamed of Jesus? Sooner far,
Let evening blush to own a star.
He sheds the beams of light divine,
O'er this benighted soul of mine.

Ashamed of Jesus? Just as soon,
Let midnight be ashamed of noon.
'Tis midnight with my soul till He,
Bright Morning Star, bids darkness flee.

Ashamed of Jesus, that dear Friend,
On whom my hopes of heaven depend?
No; when I blush, be this my shame,
That I no more revere His name.

Ashamed of Jesus? Yes, I may,
When I've no guilt to wash away,
No tears to wipe, no joys to crave,
No fears to quell, no soul to save.

Till then, nor is the boasting vain,
Till then I boast a Saviour slain.
And oh, may this my portion be,
That Christ is not ashamed of me!

Joseph Grigg

"And John answered him, saying, Master, we saw one casting out devils in thy name, and he followeth not us: and we forbad him, because he followeth not us. But Jesus said, Forbid him not: for there is no man which shall do a miracle in my name, that can lightly speak evil of me. For he that is not against us is on our part. For whosoever shall give you a cup of water to drink in my name, because ye belong to Christ, verily I say unto you, he shall not lose his reward. And whosoever shall offend one of these little ones that believe in me, it is better for him that a millstone were hanged about his neck, and he were cast into the sea. And if thy hand offend thee, cut it off: it is better for thee to enter into life maimed, than having two hands to go into hell, into the fire that never shall be quenched: Where their worm dieth not, and the fire is not quenched. And if thy foot offend thee, cut it off: it is better for thee to enter halt into life, than having two feet to be cast into hell, into the fire that never shall be quenched: Where their worm dieth not, and the fire is not quenched. And if thine eye offend thee, pluck it out: it is better for thee to enter into the kingdom of God with one eye, than having two eyes to be cast into hell fire: Where their worm dieth not, and the fire is not quenched. For every one shall be salted with fire, and every sacrifice shall be salted with salt. Salt is good: but if the salt have lost his saltness, wherewith will ye season it? Have salt in yourselves, and have peace one with another".

(Mark 9:38-50)

Chapter 40

The Salt Of Hell And The Salt Of Grace

Blessed are they to whom God by his Spirit gives grace to "discern between the righteous and the wicked, between him that serveth God and him that serveth him not" (Malachi 3:18). Our Saviour's language here is decisive. "He that is not against us is on our part". No one can be neutral. Either we serve Christ, or we are opposed to Christ. There is no middle ground. It was said of Solomon, "Happy are thy men, happy are these thy servants, which stand continually before thee, and that hear thy wisdom" (1 Kings 10:8). How much more must it be said of Christ our great King, "Happy are thy men, happy are these thy servants, which stand continually before thee, and that hear thy wisdom"!

Other Brethren
The first thing to be learned from this passage is the fact that all who truly serve the Lord Jesus Christ are brethren (vv. 38-42). How sad it is for brethren to isolate themselves from one another! And for brethren to oppose one another is utterly inexcusable. Yet, that is precisely what we see the Apostle John doing here. He said to the Lord Jesus, "Master, we saw one casting out devils in thy name, and he followeth not us: and we forbad him, because he followeth not us". The man was doing good. He was casting out devils in the name of Christ. But he was not numbered among the Lord's disciples. He was not a member of their little band. He was fighting the same war, but with a different battalion. That did not sit well with John. Therefore he rebuked the man.

John's rebuke of this man did not sit well with the Lord Jesus. He said to John, "Forbid him not: for there is no man which shall do a miracle in my name, that can lightly speak evil of me. For he that is not against us is on our part".

It was an offence to John to see a man casting out devils in the name of Christ who was not numbered among his apostles, who was unknown to the Lord's known disciples, and was not identified with them. It seemed strange to him that a man was casting out devils in the name of Christ, doing the same work they were doing, who was not associated in any way with the apostles of Christ. Perhaps this man was a disciple of John the Baptist.

Perhaps not. We are not told. However, we are told that our Lord Jesus rebuked John for rebuking him. There is a reason for that.

The sad fact is, we are all so proud that we are all prone to think that nothing good can be done unless it is done by us, or by one of those with whom we are identified.

We must never be tolerant toward those who oppose the gospel of God's free and sovereign grace in Christ. Let men call us bigots and slander us as narrow-minded sectarians, if they must. Our responsibility is clear with regard to every form of false religion, every form of freewill, works religion. Our God says to all who would follow him, "Come out from among them, and be ye separate, saith the Lord, and touch not the unclean thing; and I will receive you" (2 Corinthians 6:17; Revelation 18:4; Isaiah 48:20; 52:11, 12; Jeremiah 50:8, 45; Galatians 1:6-9; 1 John 4:1; 2 John 9-11).

I say to all who embrace as brethren those who oppose our God and the gospel of his grace, "Shouldest thou help the ungodly, and love them that hate the Lord?" (2 Chronicles 19:2). There is absolutely no place for compromise with regard to the gospel of God's free and sovereign grace in Christ. That is the cursed way of Balaam. We must never yield to it. Those who do not believe and preach the gospel of our Lord Jesus Christ are not with us, but against us. They are not the servants of Christ, but the servants of Satan. They do not do good to the souls of men, but ruin them. With regard to such men, the Lord Jesus Christ spoke very plainly in Matthew 12:30. "He that is not with me is against me; and he that gathereth not with me scattereth abroad".

But here in Mark our Lord Jesus teaches us to bend over backwards and always to be lenient with those who preach the gospel, but, for some reason, do not identify themselves with us. Sometimes faithful men are divided. There came a time when Paul and Barnabas, both faithful men, had to part company.

That is a sad fact, but a fact nonetheless. Similarly, as was the case in Elijah's day, so it is today. God still has his thousands who have not bowed the knee to Baal. Many of them are simply not known to one another. But if they preach the same message we preach and serve the same Master we serve, they are our brethren. Even if they act out of envy, jealousy, and strife, if they preach the gospel of Christ, let us never be found fighting against them.

There are two relevant passages we should look at which will help us in understanding our Master's proverbial statement here in Mark (Numbers 11:27-29; Philippians 1:15-18).

"And there ran a young man and told Moses, and said, Eldad and Medad do prophesy in the camp. And Joshua the son of Nun, the servant of Moses, one of his young men, answered and said, My lord Moses, forbid them. And Moses said unto him, Enviest thou for my sake? would God that all the LORD'S people were prophets, and that the LORD would put his spirit upon them"! (Numbers 11:27-29).

"Some indeed preach Christ even of envy and strife; and some also of good will: The one preach Christ of contention, not sincerely, supposing to add affliction to my bonds: But the other of love, knowing that I am set for the defence of the gospel. What then? notwithstanding, every way, whether in pretence, or in truth, Christ is preached; and I therein do rejoice, yea, and will rejoice" (Philippians 1:15-18).

Let us never be found opposing Christ (vv. 41, 42). Those who serve Christ in any way, no matter how insignificant it may seem to be, shall be honoured by Christ. "For whosoever shall give you a cup of water to drink in my name, because ye belong to Christ, verily I say unto you, he shall not lose his reward". It is better that a person had never been born than that he be found persecuting and opposing the Lord's children. "And whosoever shall offend one of these little ones that believe in me, it is better for him that a millstone were hanged about his neck, and he were cast into the sea".

With those things in mind, let us learn always to be lenient and tolerant toward those who profess to be our brothers and sisters in Christ. We simply do not know who belongs to Christ and who does not. We do not have the ability to discern between sheep and goats, or tares and wheat. Remember, "He that is not against us is on our part".

Self-denial

Immediately following this, our Lord Jesus shows us the necessity of rigorous self-denial. In verses 43-48 our Saviour tells us plainly that we must willingly give up anything and everything, which stands between us and him. The hand and foot which are to be cut off, and the eye that is to be plucked out, if they offend, if they keep us from following Christ, they are idols which we must destroy with our own hands. Though it is as dear to me as my right eye, my right hand, or my right foot, anything that stands between me and Christ, anything that keeps my soul from him, is to be cut off, no matter how painful and costly (Luke 14:26, 27, 33). If we would follow Christ, we must go to the cemetery and bury our idols, the sooner the better.

At first sight, our Lord's teaching in this regard may seem to be hard and rough. But there is a reason for it. Compliance is absolutely essential. If we do not tear every idol from its pedestal in our hearts, the idol we most cherish is sure to drag us down to hell. If we would follow Christ, if we would be his disciples, we must consecrate ourselves to him day by day with deliberate, unyielding determination (Galatians 5:24; 1 Corinthians 9:27).

Hell's Reality
The third thing plainly revealed in this passage of scripture is the reality of everlasting hell (vv. 43-49). I do not know what hell is, or where it is. I do not know what the fires of hell are, or what the blackness and darkness of hell are. But I do know this the Lord Jesus Christ, the Son of God, warns us repeatedly of a place of torment reserved for the damned, a place where the worm never dies and the fire is not quenched.

These are awful expressions. They call for meditation more than exposition. Ponder them. Consider them. Reflect upon them. Think about them. It matters not whether you regard the language as figurative or literal. If the worm and the fire are literal the prospect is intensely horrible. If the worm that never dies and the fire that is never quenched are figures they are figures of real things.

There is a real place of eternal torment called hell. In hell, the gnawing worm of a guilty conscience never dies or is, to any degree, silenced. In hell the fire of God's wrath is never quenched. The torments of the damned can never satisfy the wrath and justice of the holy Lord God for sin. Therefore, our Lord makes reference to the sacrifices of the Old Testament in which God required every sacrifice to be salted with salt. In verse 49 he says, "For every one shall be salted with fire, and every sacrifice shall be salted with salt".

If you die in your sins, if you perish without Christ, you will be cast into hell to suffer the everlasting, indescribable horror of the wrath of God. There the worm of your tormenting conscience will relentlessly gnaw at your soul. There the fires of God's wrath will burn forever. As salt preserves meat from corruption, the fire of hell is such that it preserves the damned from being consumed.

Here, our Lord Jesus tells us that the fires of God's wrath in hell will do the same thing that salt does to the flesh of slaughtered animals. As the salt preserves the flesh from putrefaction and corruption, so the fire of hell, while burning, torturing, and tormenting the damned, will preserve their bodies and souls in their being forever.

In other words, the very fire that burns will keep them from being consumed. Their souls shall never die. Their bodies will not consume away. They will lose none of their powers, faculties, or senses. Rather, they shall all be intensified! That is what our Lord means by men being salted with fire and the fire being unquenchable!

In hell there will be no mercy, no blood atonement, no grace, no Christ, and no hope!

Salt Of Grace

In verse 50 our Lord Jesus speaks about the salt of grace and peace. "Salt is good: but if the salt have lost his saltness, wherewith will ye season it? Have salt in yourselves, and have peace one with another". Let us make certain that we have the salt of God's grace in us, that salt of grace which will preserve us and sanctify us in Christ. Do not be satisfied with a mere profession of faith. Make sure you believe on the Lord Jesus Christ. Do not be satisfied with a religious experience. Be sure you have the salt of God's grace (2 Corinthians 13:5).

And let the children of God have peace with one another. In the Old Testament the covenant of peace is called the covenant of salt (Numbers 18:19; 25:12). Here our Lord Jesus takes opportunity to admonish his disciples, who had just been disputing about who should be greatest, to promote and maintain peace among themselves. It is the unity of the Spirit in the bond of peace which is the strength and preserving quality of God's church in this world. If we would truly promote peace, we must always season our speech with the salt of grace (Colossians 4:6; Ephesians 4:29; Romans 12:18; 14:19; 2 Corinthians 13:11).

"And he arose from thence, and cometh into the coasts of Judaea by the farther side of Jordan: and the people resort unto him again; and, as he was wont, he taught them again. And the Pharisees came to him, and asked him, Is it lawful for a man to put away his wife? tempting him. And he answered and said unto them, What did Moses command you? And they said, Moses suffered to write a bill of divorcement, and to put her away. And Jesus answered and said unto them, For the hardness of your heart he wrote you this precept. But from the beginning of the creation God made them male and female. For this cause shall a man leave his father and mother, and cleave to his wife; And they twain shall be one flesh: so then they are no more twain, but one flesh. What therefore God hath joined together, let not man put asunder. And in the house his disciples asked him again of the same matter. And he saith unto them, Whosoever shall put away his wife, and marry another, committeth adultery against her. And if a woman shall put away her husband, and be married to another, she committeth adultery. And they brought young children to him, that he should touch them: and his disciples rebuked those that brought them. But when Jesus saw it, he was much displeased, and said unto them, Suffer the little children to come unto me, and forbid them not: for of such is the kingdom of God. Verily I say unto you, Whosoever shall not receive the kingdom of God as a little child, he shall not enter therein. And he took them up in his arms, put his hands upon them, and blessed them".

(Mark 10:1-16)

Chapter 41

The Master Teaches About Marriage And Children

It is the ploy of unregenerate religious men to attempt to trick God's servants and his people into saying things they can use against them. Crafty followers of the Serpent, in a pretence of sincerity, try to ask leading questions, which will cause us to give answers they can turn against us. You do not have to experience their craftiness many times before you are able to hear the hiss of the Serpent in their speech. When we meet with such people, the best way to send them slithering back into their own slime is simply not to answer them. I learned long ago if you get into a spitting contest with a skunk, even if you win the contest, you are sure to end up smelling like a skunk.

Here in Mark 10 our Saviour had just such an experience with the Pharisees. They posed their question about divorce in such a way as to try to get him to speak against Moses and the law so that they might pretend to have a basis upon which to accuse him of being an antinomian, against the law. Our Master was too wise for them. Rather than answer in his own words, he answered them from the Word of God. The things taught in these verses are of utmost importance. May God the Holy Spirit teach us that which he inspired Mark to record in this passage.

Christ's Example

"And he arose from thence, and cometh into the coasts of Judaea by the farther side of Jordan: and the people resort unto him again; and, as he was wont, he taught them again" (v. 1). Our Lord Jesus Christ was an exemplary, faithful, fervent preacher of the gospel. How faithful, patient, and persevering our Lord Jesus was as a preacher. "Unwearied in all his services", wrote Robert Hawker, "with zeal to his Father's glory, and his people's happiness, the sun watched his path by day, and the stars witnessed to his communion by night." In all things he was the example of what we ought to be. But his exemplary conduct as a preacher and the demands it places upon those who follow him in the work of the ministry are often overlooked.

Wherever our Saviour went, he was always about his Father's business. From the opening day of his public ministry, to his last breath upon the cross, our Lord Jesus Christ laboured for the good of men's souls for the glory of God. He lost no opportunity. We do not read in the entire history of his earthly ministry that he spent a solitary day in idleness. He "sowed beside all waters" (Isaiah 32:20). "In the morning he sowed his seed, and in the evening withheld not his hand" (Ecclesiastes 11:6). He was untiringly, unceasingly fervent and faithful. When he came to the farther side of Jordan and the people gathered around him, he did "as he was wont. He taught them".

Those men who devote their lives to the labour of the gospel ministry are often urged, by well meaning friends and people who love them, to slow down, not to take the work so seriously, and to preserve their energies. Let none heed such counsel. When we open the Book of God and see the kind of preacher the Son of God was, we should pray, Saviour, give grace to your servant to follow your example. It is far better to burn out than to rust out!

I am sure one reason why our Master was always "wont" to preach and teach the gospel was the fact that he knew the urgency of his work. No one else understood this. His mother did not. His friends did not. No one else understood the urgency of his mission. He knew time was short. The Lord Jesus was always ready to preach the gospel, even though the vast majority of those to whom he preached refused to believe his message. His miracles were popular, but not his doctrine. For the most part, his words fell upon deaf ears, unheeded and ignored. Those who did not ignore him despised him.

Once in John 6 he preached to the great multitude who saw the miracle of the loaves and fishes, many of whom ate the bread and the fish. But when he preached to them the message of God's free and sovereign grace, they were offended and walked away. In that passage our Lord Jesus proclaimed that the only way a sinner can please God is by faith in his Son (v. 29), that Moses spoke of him (vv. 32-35), that the only way any sinner would ever believe on him unto life everlasting is by the effectual work of God's irresistible grace (vv. 36-40, 44, 45, 63-65), that the singular object of faith is his obedience and death as the sinners' Substitute (vv. 53-58), and that salvation is according to God's sovereign election (vv. 64, 70). When they heard these things, the multitude turned and walked away.

That which is required of all who would, like the Lord Jesus Christ, serve God is faithfulness (1 Corinthians 4:1, 2). We are not to give up our labours because we do not see the results we desire. We are not to relax our efforts because we see no fruit from them. It is our duty to do what we have opportunity and ability to do. The results are up to our Master. It is not to the good and successful servant that the Master will say, "well done", but to the "good and faithful servant" (Matthew 25:21). Not all of God's servants are reapers. Some plough, others sow, water, or reap; but it is God who gives the increase. In this, as in all other spiritual matters, we must judge nothing by what we see. Every faithful servant of God is a successful servant of God.

Marriage And Divorce

"And the Pharisees came to him, and asked him, Is it lawful for a man to put away his wife? tempting him. And he answered and said unto them, What did Moses command you? And they said, Moses suffered to write a bill of divorcement, and to put her away. And Jesus answered and said unto them, For the hardness of your heart he wrote you this precept. But from the beginning of the creation God made them male and female. For this cause shall a man leave his father and mother, and cleave to his wife; And they twain shall be one flesh: so then they are no more twain, but one flesh. What therefore God hath joined together, let not man put asunder. And in the house his disciples asked him again of the same matter. And he saith unto them, Whosoever shall put away his wife, and marry another, committeth adultery against her. And if a woman shall put away her husband, and be married to another, she committeth adultery" (vv. 2-12).

Let us carefully note that our Lord's teaching with regard to the dignity and permanence of marriage is crystal clear. In these verses our Lord Jesus Christ first answers the question put to him by the Pharisees publicly and then answers the question put to him by his disciples privately. It matters not what men teach upon this subject. This is our Master's teaching about marriage, divorce, and remarriage. Two other passages that are very important in understanding what our Saviour taught on this subject are Matthew 5:31, 32 and Matthew 19:3-9.

"It hath been said, Whosoever shall put away his wife, let him give her a writing of divorcement: But I say unto you, That whosoever shall put away his wife, saving for the cause of fornication, causeth her to commit adultery: and whosoever shall marry her that is divorced committeth adultery" (Matthew 5:31, 32).

"The Pharisees also came unto him, tempting him, and saying unto him, Is it lawful for a man to put away his wife for every cause? And he answered and said unto them, Have ye not read, that he which made them at the beginning made them male and female, And said, For this cause shall a man leave father and mother, and shall cleave to his wife: and they twain shall be one flesh? Wherefore they are no more twain, but one flesh. What therefore God hath joined together, let not man put asunder. They say unto him, Why did Moses then command to give a writing of divorcement, and to put her away? He saith unto them, Moses because of the hardness of your hearts suffered you to put away your wives: but from the beginning it was not so. And I say unto you, Whosoever shall put away his wife, except it be for fornication, and shall marry another, committeth adultery: and whoso marrieth her which is put away doth commit adultery" (Matthew 19:3-9).

These three passages of scripture show us what the Lord Jesus Christ taught about the dignity and permanence of marriage. Other aspects of the privileges and responsibilities of men and women in marriage are found in Romans 7:1-4, 1 Corinthians 7, and Ephesians 5. I have no interest in debating with anyone about these issues. I do not, for a moment, think that I am going to change the thinking of godless people about the dignity, importance, and permanence of marriage. I am addressing myself to you who revere God and his Word, to you who seek to honour him and do his will. The things I have to say are for you. I hope you will all read these lines with careful attention.

Our Lord teaches us that marriage is for life. The marriage union of a husband and wife is never to be dissolved. It cannot be broken, except for very specific, serious reasons. The importance of our Lord's teaching cannot be overstated. The well-being of nations, the happiness of men and women, the moral strength of society, and the welfare of God's church in this world depends upon the strength of families. Family strength, family values, and family wholeness depend upon a proper understanding of and respect for the teaching of God's Word about marriage. During the days of our Lord's earthly ministry, when the Roman Empire was at its zenith, moral decadence was much the same as it is in western society today. Divorces were common. Marriages were dissolved, even among the Jews, for frivolous and trifling reasons. Mark did not record the Pharisees question quite the same way Matthew did. Matthew 19:3 tells us that the Pharisees asked the Lord Jesus, "Is it lawful for a man to put away his wife for every cause?"

It is true, because of the hardness of men's hearts, to prevent them from abusing and even killing their wives, Moses did permit them to divorce their wives, but not "for every cause" (Deuteronomy 24:1-4). Yet, by long tradition and laxity, that which Moses permitted, men and women commonly practised. Marriage had become, as it is today, a whimsical thing, regarded by most as a bothersome burden.

The disciples' comment in Matthew 19:10 will give us some idea of just how bad things were. "His disciples say unto him, If the case of the man be so with his wife, it is not good to marry". When they heard the Lord Jesus say, "No you cannot put away your wives for every cause", they as good as said, "If a man cannot get rid of his wife whenever he wants to, he would be better off not to marry". When men and women abandon God's law and look contemptuously upon marriage, they produce a generation of children without conscience (Malachi 2:14-16).

Marriage is a relationship of greater importance and greater influence than any other earthly relationship. It was established by God in the garden for the happiness and well being of man before sin entered into the world (Genesis

2:18-25). Marriage was chosen by God to be typical of the relationship which exists between Christ and his church (Ephesians 5:25-33). Marriage is a relationship superior even to the relationship of parents and children (Ephesians 5:31). It involves commitment and devotion. A man ought to be committed to his wife, like Christ is committed to his church. A woman ought to be committed to her husband, like true believers are to Christ.

Marriage involves sacrifice and self-denial. Husbands are to sacrifice themselves to their wives and families, just as Christ sacrificed himself for us. Wives are to sacrifice themselves to their husbands, just as believers sacrifice themselves to Christ. Marriage involves love. Husband are to love their wives, even as Christ also loved the church and gave himself for it. Wives are to reverence and obey their husbands, as the church reverences and obeys Christ in love. Love is giving, never taking. Love is yielding, not demanding. Love is unconditional, not qualified.

Marriage necessarily involves the dissolution of all other relationships and a blessed isolation to and with one another. Again, it is a blessed isolation to and with one another, like the isolation of Christ to and with his church. It is a growing isolation, like the isolation of the church to Christ.

In a word, our Lord Jesus teaches us that this blessed relationship of marriage is a life-long union. J. C. Ryle wrote: "He refers to the original institution of marriage at the creation, as the union of one man and one woman. He quotes and endorses the solemn words used at the marriage of Adam and Eve, as words of perpetual significance: 'A man shall leave his father and mother, and shall cleave to his wife: and they twain shall be one flesh.' He adds a solemn comment to these words: 'What God hath joined together, let not man put asunder.' And, finally, in reply to the inquiry of his disciples, He declares that divorce followed by remarriage, except for the cause of unfaithfulness, is a breach of the seventh commandment."

These days, very few people enter into marriage with the determination "This is forever, no matter what". Multitudes write out prenuptial agreements in anticipation of divorce. Many do not even bother with having a wedding ceremony. They just shack up like wild animals until someone more attractive comes along. "From the beginning it was not so". "What God hath joined together, let no man put asunder". All who violate God's Word in this matter are guilty of adultery and cause those abandoned to do the same.

This lifelong marriage union can be dissolved lawfully, biblically, only for extreme reasons. Though Mark omits it, in Matthew 5:32 and in Matthew 19:9 our Lord cites fornication as the singular basis for divorce. The word "fornication" is the word from which we get our word "pornography". It refers to all sexual perversion. As used in relation to marriage, it speaks of any form of sexual infidelity. Our Lord does not teach that men and women ought to get a divorce if one or the other commits an act of sexual infidelity. We ought to forgive! However, he does teach us that in such cases the marriage union may be dissolved. It is permitted because of the hardness of men's hearts. The apostle Paul, writing by divine inspiration, also allows that abandonment also dissolves the marriage union (1 Corinthians 7:15). In such cases the person abandoned, or the person against whom the infidelity was committed is free to marry again in the Lord (Deuteronomy 24:1-4).

What about those who have already experienced divorce and remarriage? How do we deal with those believers, or those who are converted by the grace of God, who are already divorced, or who are already divorced and remarried? We are to deal with them as we are to deal with any other redeemed, forgiven sinner, as redeemed, forgiven sinners, just like the rest of us. If they are believers, if they are washed in the blood of the Lamb, they are forgiven of all sin, free from all condemnation, and are new creatures in Christ (Romans 8:1).[6]

Here are three words of instruction that will benefit all who heed them: 1. When you marry, marry only in the Lord. 2. Do not expect too much from your husband or wife. Marriage is the union of two sinners who need constant forgiveness, not the union of two angels. 3. Seek, with constant earnestness, one another's spiritual good.

Our Example
As in all things, the example to be followed is Christ himself. Our blessed Saviour refuses to put away his wife, the church. He who inspired the Apostle Paul to write, "Husbands, love your wives, and be not bitter against them" (Colossians 3:19), has never been and can never be bitter against his wife. He who teaches every husband to love his wife as his own body, ever nourishing and cherishing her (Ephesians 5:28, 29), so loves, nourishes, and cherishes his wife as his own body.

Robert Hawker, commenting on this passage, wrote,

> As no man ever hated his own flesh; even though covered with sores and wounds, so Jesus loved his Church, though leprous and unclean. Oh, precious, precious Lord Jesus!

---

[6] 1 Timothy 3:2 has nothing to do with divorce and remarriage. In that passage Paul is dealing with the matter of polygamy, which had to be dealt with in receiving Gentile converts into the churches. It would be insanely ludicrous to tell a converted man who had many wives and children by them before God saved him (as do many of our African brethren) that he must choose one woman and her children and throw out the rest. That would be barbaric. However, a man with more than one wife cannot be pastor of a church. That is the teaching of 1 Timothy 3:2.

How blessed it is to hear the Lord God of Israel say that, "he hateth putting away" (Malachi 2:14-16). Let all who worship and serve him hate it as well. How we will praise and give thanks to him in eternity when, after all the treacherous departures of his church, in all her spiritual adulteries, the Lord Jesus presents her "to himself a glorious church, not having spot, or wrinkle, or any such thing; but that it should be holy and without blemish" (Ephesians 5:27; Revelation 19:5-9).

Little Children
"And they brought young children to him, that he should touch them: and his disciples rebuked those that brought them. But when Jesus saw it, he was much displeased, and said unto them, Suffer the little children to come unto me, and forbid them not: for of such is the kingdom of God. Verily I say unto you, Whosoever shall not receive the kingdom of God as a little child, he shall not enter therein. And he took them up in his arms, put his hands upon them, and blessed them" (vv. 13-16).

These little children were brought to our Lord just like other sick and diseased, that he might lay his hands on them and bless them. There is no more and no less in the text than that. It is ludicrous beyond imagination to suggest as J. C. Ryle and others have, "to teach how much encouragement there is to bring young children to be baptized". There is not a word in this passage about whose children these were, not a word about baptism, much less sprinkling! There is nothing about baby dedication services. Our Saviour teaches us that all who enter into his kingdom must do so as little children. These verses are given to us by the Spirit of God to teach us three things.

If we would do our children good, we must bring them to Christ. The text simply tells us that these people brought their children to the Saviour, just as they did their sick, that he might lay his hands upon them. Let us do that for our children, and we have done the very best we can for them. Bring them to Christ in prayer. Ask that he may lay his hand upon them, the hand of his saving grace. And leave them in his hands.

The Lord Jesus humbled himself to serve the needs of little children. What a tender-hearted man he is! How accessible to sinners! If we would be saved, we must come to the Lord Jesus Christ as little children. Like children, we must be brought to the Saviour by one stronger than ourselves, by God the Holy Spirit. We must be made as inoffensive and dependent upon him as a little child. When we think of what a preacher should be, let us look to Christ. He is the pattern. When we think of marriage, let our hearts be drawn first and foremost to Christ. Be married to him! Those who are first married to him make the best husbands and wives. When you see a child, embrace it, care for it, take time for it, and ask God to make you as such before him.

"And when he was gone forth into the way, there came one running, and kneeled to him, and asked him, Good Master, what shall I do that I may inherit eternal life? And Jesus said unto him, Why callest thou me good? there is none good but one, that is, God. Thou knowest the commandments, Do not commit adultery, Do not kill, Do not steal, Do not bear false witness, Defraud not, Honour thy father and mother. And he answered and said unto him, Master, all these have I observed from my youth. Then Jesus beholding him loved him, and said unto him, One thing thou lackest: go thy way, sell whatsoever thou hast, and give to the poor, and thou shalt have treasure in heaven: and come, take up the cross, and follow me. And he was sad at that saying, and went away grieved: for he had great possessions. And Jesus looked round about, and saith unto his disciples, How hardly shall they that have riches enter into the kingdom of God! And the disciples were astonished at his words. But Jesus answereth again, and saith unto them, Children, how hard is it for them that trust in riches to enter into the kingdom of God! It is easier for a camel to go through the eye of a needle, than for a rich man to enter into the kingdom of God. And they were astonished out of measure, saying among themselves, Who then can be saved? And Jesus looking upon them saith, With men it is impossible, but not with God: for with God all things are possible".

(Mark 10:17-27)

Chapter 42

"Jesus Beholding Him Loved Him"

We have before us the story of the rich young ruler. It is recorded three times in the New Testament. Matthew, Mark and Luke were inspired by God the Holy Spirit to write it out in detail for our learning. The threefold repetition of the simple facts recorded in this story is intended to make us aware that the lessons taught here are of immense importance. May God the Holy Spirit inscribe upon our hearts those things, which he would have us to learn from this story. Were it not for the grace of God, we would all make the same choice this rich young ruler made and perish with the world.

Three Common Delusions
"And when he was gone forth into the way, there came one running, and kneeled to him, and asked him, Good Master, what shall I do that I may inherit eternal life? And Jesus said unto him, Why callest thou me good? there is none good but one, that is, God. Thou knowest the commandments, Do not commit adultery, Do not kill, Do not steal, Do not bear false witness, Defraud not, Honour thy father and mother. And he answered and said unto him, Master, all these have I observed from my youth" (vv. 17-20).

There are many things about this young man, which, at first sight, appear to be commendable. He was earnest and zealous. He came running to Christ. He was reverent and respectful. He kneeled to the Saviour in a respectful, reverent, if not worshipful, manner. He was thoughtful of his soul and eternity. And, at least in his outward behaviour, he was a very moral man. Any mother or father looking for a young man for their daughter to date and perhaps marry, if this rich young ruler were around, would urge her to set her hat for him. But this rich, moral, zealous, religious man was deluded by his own self-righteousness and pride. His delusion was the common delusion of all men since the fall of Adam. It was a threefold delusion.

First, he thought salvation could be obtained by something he could do. This is the delusion of all lost men, in all ages, the delusion of all human religion, and the delusion of antichrist. All men think that salvation comes as the result of something they do. Few deny grace altogether, or deny that God has something to do with salvation. This young man acknowledged that eternal life is the inheritance and gift of grace; but he still thought it was to be obtained by something he could do.

Being ignorant of God's righteousness, he went about to establish his own righteousness. And anyone who seeks to establish righteousness for himself will not and cannot submit to the righteousness of God in Christ (Romans 9:31-10:4). "It is not of him that willeth, nor of him that runneth, but of God that showeth mercy" (Romans 9:16). "Salvation is of the Lord" (Jonah 2:9). "By the works of the law shall no flesh be justified" (Galatians 2:16). To every self-righteous person who asks, "What must I do?", I answer in the words of James Procter:

> Nothing, either great or small,
> Nothing, sinner, no;
> Jesus did it, did it all,
> Long, long ago!
>
> When He, from His lofty throne,
> Stooped to do and die,
> Everything was fully done.
> Hearken to His cry—
>
> "It is finished"! Yes, indeed,
> Finished every jot:
> Sinner, this is all you need.
> Tell me, Is it not?
>
> Weary, working, plodding one,
> Why toil you so?
> Cease your doing, all was done,
> Long, long ago!
>
> Till to Jesus' work you cling,
> By a simple faith,
> Doing is a deadly thing.
> Doing ends in death.
>
> Cast your deadly doing down,
> Down at Jesus' feet!
> Stand in Him, in Him alone,
> Gloriously complete!

This man's second delusion was that he thought the law of God only had to do with outward behaviour. When you read verses 19 and 20, do not be so foolish and ignorant as numerous learned theologians, and imagine that the Lord Jesus was teaching that there really are two ways of salvation, that a man can either be saved by grace or by works.

That is not the case at all. Our Lord is well aware that there is but one way of salvation (John 14:6). This man asked what he could do, and the Master told him what he must do. If you want to be saved by your works, all you have to do is keep the law *perfectly!* "For as many as are of the works of the law are under the curse: for it is written, Cursed is every one that continueth not in all things which are written in the book of the law to do them" (Galatians 3:10).

Our Lord's purpose was not to teach salvation by legal obedience, but the impossibility of it, and to expose this man's sin to himself. Painful as it is to experience, no one will ever be saved until he is made to see himself as he really is, a vile, hell-bent, corrupt, ungodly wretch. The first work of grace in our soul is to make us feel our need of it!

This self-righteous Pharisee was, like all lost religious people, totally ignorant of the spiritual nature of God's law. He thought the law reached no further than outward deeds. He never took into consideration the fact that the Lord looketh on the heart.

He thought that adultery was intercourse, not lust, that murder was killing someone, not anger, stealing was taking something that belongs to another, not covetousness, that bearing false witness was openly lying about someone, not insinuating or thinking evil, that fraud was taking another person's property, not wanting it, that parental honour was saying "Ma'am" and "Sir", not reverencing his parents' name, honouring their wishes, and taking care of them in their old age.

His third delusion was that he thought he had actually obeyed God's law and thus was worthy of God's acceptance in and of himself. "And he answered and said unto him, Master, all these have I observed from my youth".

I never cease to be amazed by the fact that even the most base, profligate, sensual men and women of this world are really very proud and think so very highly of themselves that they brazenly presume they are good enough for God!

That is really the root of all unbelief. Everyone in his own humble opinion is too good to need the grace of God and the blood and righteousness of his dear Son. May God the Holy Spirit continually teach us who and what we are and who Christ is, lest we perish in our proud delusions of self-righteousness.

Christ's Compassion

Next we are told that our dear Saviour beheld this man and loved him "Then Jesus beholding him loved him" (v. 21). Mark saw a remarkable display of tenderness, love, and compassion in the Lord Jesus toward this young man.

It is sickening to read the comments of many on this text. The Arminians rush to tell us, "There, you see, God loves even those who are not saved, even those who go to hell. The love of God is universal".

The Calvinists, imagining that God's love must be protected and that Arminian fools are worthy of being answered, run to the Greek language and find some far out, outlandish usage of the word "loved" (agape) to prove that the word does not really mean love at all.

Take this blessed text just as it stands, learn what it teaches, and rejoice in the great love of Christ for sinners! There are two things to be observed here.

First, the Lord Jesus beheld this man. He beheld everything about him. He beheld his present condition. He beheld his heart. And he beheld what he had done and would do for him.

Second, the Son of God loved this man. I have no doubt at all that though this man at first chose the world over Christ (just as I did), he was later converted by God's free grace. I say that because God the Holy Spirit inspired Mark to tell us that, "Jesus beholding him loved him".

Here are four sweet, indisputable facts revealed in holy scripture about the love of God our Saviour:

1. Those who are loved of Christ are loved by him from eternity (Jeremiah 31:3).

2. Those who are loved by the Son of God are loved by him immutably (Malachi 3:6).

3. Those who are loved by the Lord Jesus are loved by him unto the end (John 13:1).

4. Those who are loved of God are saved by his free and sovereign grace; he has mercy upon those for whom he has compassion (Romans 9:15; Jeremiah 31:3).

These four sweet facts of divine revelation tells us that this young man who was loved by the Saviour from eternity, and loved by him in his rebellion, was saved by him at the appointed time of love.

Sin Exposed

The Lord Jesus so loved this man that he graciously uncovered his sin, pulled the covering off his heart, and in verses 21 and 22 discovered his inward, hidden corruption.

"Then Jesus beholding him loved him, and said unto him, One thing thou lackest: go thy way, sell whatsoever thou hast, and give to the poor, and thou shalt have treasure in heaven: and come, take up the cross, and follow me. And he was sad at that saying, and went away grieved: for he had great possessions".

The Lord Jesus met this man at his point of rebellion. He always does. Sooner or later, he will meet you at your point of rebellion and demand surrender. This young man's reigning sin was an overwhelming affection for the things of this world. His riches were his idol. His heart was set upon and trusted in his wealth. John Gill wrote:

"He was so far from keeping all the commandments, that he had not kept the first; 'thou shalt have no other gods before me'. There was more than one thing wanting in him, but Christ takes notice of this as the first; and there was no need to mention any other. This touched him sensibly, and fully tried, and sufficiently exposed the vanity of his boasted perfection ... Finding that he must part with two things his heart was set upon, his idol of self-righteousness, and his mammon of unrighteousness; the bladder of his pride was pricked, and his vanity and self-conceit were exposed ... which were sadly mortifying, and exceedingly disagreeable to him".

What is your point of rebellion? That is where you must do business with God. Did you ever notice how often those two words, "one thing", are used in scripture? They are very instructive. David desired "one thing", that he might dwell in the house of the Lord forever (Psalm 27:4). Mary chose the "one thing" needful, to sit at Jesus' feet and hear his words (Luke 10:42). The man born blind, who was healed by the Master, said, "One thing I know, that, whereas I was blind, now I see" (John 9:25). Paul said, "One thing I do: forgetting those things which are behind, and reaching forth unto those things which are before, I press toward the mark, for the prize of the high calling of God in Christ Jesus" (Philippians 3:13, 14).

But this proud, self-righteous young rich man was lost, because "one thing" was lacking. Though he felt much, did much, thought much, and believed much, the one thing lacking was faith in Christ.

A Blessed Revelation

As this rich man walked away, clinging to his riches, the Lord Jesus made a statement to his disciples, which disturbed them greatly and opened the way for him to instruct them and us with a blessed revelation.

"And Jesus looked round about, and saith unto his disciples, How hardly shall they that have riches enter into the kingdom of God! And the disciples were astonished at his words. But Jesus answereth again, and saith unto them, Children, how hard is it for them that trust in riches to enter into the kingdom of God! It is easier for a camel to go through the eye of a needle, than for a rich man to enter into the kingdom of God. And they were astonished out of measure, saying among themselves, Who then can be saved? And Jesus looking upon them saith, With men it is impossible, but not with God: for with God all things are possible" (vv. 23-27).

Commenting on these verses, Robert Hawker wrote:

> The concluding part of this passage is uncommonly beautiful and interesting. While Jesus in strong figures represents the total impossibility of the mere efforts of nature, rising above nature, he sets forth the ease and blessedness with which his redeemed, through his grace, will attain his kingdom. A huge camel might as soon pass through the eye of a needle, as for a rich man; rich in his own fancied goodness, swollen and bloated with his own Pharisaical righteousness, but never regenerated by grace, to enter into the kingdom of God. While on the other hand, every one of Christ's regenerated family, poor in spirit, rich in faith, and heirs of the kingdom, and who give proofs of the triumphs of grace over nature, leaving all for Christ, will enter with a full tide of glory into Christ's kingdom being saved, not by works of righteousness which they have done, but according to rich, free and sovereign mercy, by the washing of regeneration and renewing of the Holy Ghost, shed upon them abundantly through Jesus Christ our Lord (Titus 3:5, 6).

There are in verses 23-27 three very important truths, which very few understand, and fewer still lay to heart. The most deceitful, dangerous thing in this world is riches, the love of money, the love of the world. With men, salvation is an utter impossibility. With God, all things are possible.

So great, so magnanimous, so good is the grace of God that he can strip and empty the most self-sufficient Pharisee and bring him through the needle's eye of faith in Christ into his kingdom. God almighty can save even the richest man in the world. The man who thinks himself spiritually rich and loves himself is no more beyond the reach of omnipotent mercy than the most promiscuous harlot. The man who loves the world, trusts in his riches, and therefore despises the things of God is not beyond the power of free grace. If, indeed, salvation is by grace alone (and it is!), there is no case or circumstance, which should cause us to despair.

John Newton once said, "When I get to heaven, I am sure that three things will simply astonish me. I am sure very many will be there whom I never expected to be there. I am sure that many will not be there whom I fully expected would be there. But the most astonishing thing of all will be the fact that old John Newton will be there". Later, just before his death, Newton said, "I am an old man. I cannot remember much. But I do remember two things: I am a great sinner; and Jesus Christ is a great Saviour".

"Then Peter began to say unto him, Lo, we have left all, and have followed thee. And Jesus answered and said, Verily I say unto you, There is no man that hath left house, or brethren, or sisters, or father, or mother, or wife, or children, or lands, for my sake, and the gospel's, But he shall receive an hundredfold now in this time, houses, and brethren, and sisters, and mothers, and children, and lands, with persecutions; and in the world to come eternal life. But many that are first shall be last; and the last first. And they were in the way going up to Jerusalem; and Jesus went before them: and they were amazed; and as they followed, they were afraid. And he took again the twelve, and began to tell them what things should happen unto him, Saying, Behold, we go up to Jerusalem; and the Son of man shall be delivered unto the chief priests, and unto the scribes; and they shall condemn him to death, and shall deliver him to the Gentiles: And they shall mock him, and shall scourge him, and shall spit upon him, and shall kill him: and the third day he shall rise again".

(Mark 10:28-34)

Chapter 43

Our Saviour's Amazing Doctrine

That which our Lord Jesus Christ taught not only astonished the public, it also amazed his disciples. Truly, those things our Lord taught, his doctrine concerning his grace, his salvation, and his sin-atoning sacrifice are amazing things to consider.

A Glorious Promise
The very first thing that catches our attention as we read this brief paragraph is the fact that our Saviour's response to Peter was not a word of rebuke but a glorious promise.

"Then Peter began to say unto him, Lo, we have left all, and have followed thee. And Jesus answered and said, Verily I say unto you, There is no man that hath left house, or brethren, or sisters, or father, or mother, or wife, or children, or lands, for my sake, and the gospel's, But he shall receive an hundredfold now in this time, houses, and brethren, and sisters, and mothers, and children, and lands, with persecutions; and in the world to come eternal life" (vv. 28-30).

Peter's statement in verse twenty-eight was an honest, true statement. He might be blamed for the reason he made this statement. He might be blamed for the apparent expectation he had of the Lord rewarding him, as though he had earned a reward from the Lord of Glory. Matthew tells us that this statement was followed by a very foolish question. "What shall we have therefore?" (Matthew 19:27).

Yet, when all is said and done, if our faith in Christ does not involve the kind of self-denying devotion and consecration to Christ that Peter here expresses, our faith is an empty, vain delusion. "Then Peter began to say unto him, Lo, we have left all, and have followed thee". True faith forsakes all and follows Christ. True faith is the unqualified, unreserved surrender of myself, my life, my all to the dominion and rule of the Lord Jesus Christ as my Lord, my Master, and my King. This is what the story of the rich young ruler in the preceding paragraph teaches. If salvation can be gained simply by believing the right things, that man would not have gone away sorrowful. Salvation involves leaving all for Christ's sake and the gospel's.

Our Saviour graciously seized the thought suggested by Peter's carnal question to assure us that having left all to follow him, his disciples have lost nothing, and gained indescribably more than any of us can ever imagine.

"And Jesus answered and said, verily I say unto you, There is no man that hath left house, or brethren, or sisters, or father, or mother, or wife, or children, or lands, for my sake, and the gospel's, but he shall receive an hundredfold now in this time, houses, and brethren, and sisters, and mothers, and children, and lands, with persecutions; and in the world to come eternal life" (vv. 29, 30).

Few promises can be found in the Book of God more comprehensive than this. I know of none that hold before us such great encouragements for life in this world, as well as in the world to come. Let every faithful, but faint hearted follower of Christ mark this promise, read it often, meditate upon it daily, and find in this cluster of grapes wine to make his heart merry. Let all who endure hardness and persecution for Christ's sake and the gospel's study this promise well and drink often from this deep well. It speaks of this life and of the life to come.

Child of God, whatever it is that following Christ costs you, you shall receive in this life one hundredfold! As Israel lacked nothing all the while they roamed about in the wilderness, as the disciples lacked nothing while they walked with the Son of God on this earth, so our Saviour declares that the obedience of faith will never cause us to be in want, but shall only enrich us a hundredfold in this world.

Not only does the Son of God promise us pardon, peace, redemption, and reconciliation through his blood and his grace, he promises us that we shall have, even here upon the earth, comforts and joys more than sufficient to make up for that which we have left for him. Child of God, bear me witness. Is this not so?

Have you not found in the communion of God's saints new friends, new relationships, and new companions more loving, more faithful, more lasting, more valuable, and more numerous than you ever had before? That may seem impossible to any who do not know our God, his grace, or his people; but every believer in this world will say, "Amen", to what our Lord here asserts. Our God supplies all our need "according to his riches in glory by Christ Jesus" (Philippians 4:19).

In addition to all this our Saviour promises all who follow him eternal life in the world to come. "The Lord will give grace and glory"! He gives grace here and he will give glory hereafter. As soon as we put off these earthly tabernacles, we will enter into the glorious rest of the sons of God (2 Corinthians 5:1-9). In the last day, in the resurrection morning, we shall be given honour, joy, and glory surpassing our highest, most reverent expectation (1 Corinthians 2:9). Our light affliction here shall redound to our Saviour's greater honour and our greater joy in eternity (2 Corinthians 4:17, 18). We shall dwell forever with the Son of God in a world where sin and sorrow, sickness and death, Satan and temptations, parting and weeping shall be no more! Child of God, take heart. Time is short. Our sorrows shall soon be no more. Our end is sure. Weeping may endure for the night; but joy will come in the morning!

A Solemn Warning

"But many that are first shall be last; and the last first" (v. 31). Here is a solemn warning. Our Master saw the self-conceit which defiled his disciples, and frankly warned them all to be watchful over their souls. If this warning was needed by Peter, James, and John, how much more it is needed by you and me. Let us take heed to these words and learn what they mean.

Without question, this warning was applicable to the twelve Apostles to whom it was first given. There was one standing among them who was more highly esteemed and trusted than all the others, who was a devil and would soon be in hell. His name was Judas. He was the first, in his own eyes and in the eyes of the twelve; but now he is the last.

There was another who was not among them. In fact, he was just a young man, a young Pharisee, being trained at the feet of Gamaliel, a zealous religionist, learning to hate Christ, his gospel, and his people. Any who knew him would say, "This young man is the last man who would be numbered among the disciples of Christ" but God had purposed otherwise. The young Pharisee's name was Saul of Tarsus. Soon, he would be elevated to the most prominent position in the kingdom of God.

This warning explains the entire history of the Church of God in this world. There was a time when Asia Minor, Greece, and Northern Africa were flourishing with the light of the gospel; but now their light has been tuned into darkness. Today, in this land, which was once darkness, God has established the light of his grace again. Let us take heed lest we as a people are again engrossed in utter darkness.

This warning is a warning which ought to sound as an alarm in the ears of us all. How many there are known to us all who seemed to run well for a season. They stood out in the crowd. They seemed to be head and shoulders above the rest of us. They were so zealous, so committed, so knowledgeable, so confident, so sure about everything. They were the first. But now where are they? They are gone. They are the last. The love of the world got one. The deceitfulness of riches got another. A bad marriage got another. A flattering woman took another. False doctrine destroyed another.

Let us pray for grace to run our race to the end. It is not enough to begin well. We must persevere. We must continue in the faith. We must end well. God give us grace to begin with Christ, stay with Christ, and end with Christ!

A Faithful Surety

In verses 32-34 we see that our Lord Jesus Christ is indeed a faithful Surety. Calmly and deliberately, our Saviour told his disciples why he was going to Jerusalem and all that he must there suffer and do as our great Surety, Substitute, and Saviour.

"And they were in the way going up to Jerusalem; and Jesus went before them: and they were amazed; and as they followed, they were afraid. And he took again the twelve, and began to tell them what things should happen unto him, Saying, Behold, we go up to Jerusalem; and the Son of man shall be delivered unto the chief priests, and unto the scribes; and they shall condemn him to death, and shall deliver him to the Gentiles: And they shall mock him, and shall scourge him, and shall spit upon him, and shall kill him: and the third day he shall rise again".

The Son of God went up to Jerusalem willingly, purposefully, and deliberately to die there as our covenant Surety.

"The Lord GOD hath opened mine ear, and I was not rebellious, neither turned away back. I gave my back to the smiters, and my cheeks to them that plucked off the hair: I hid not my face from shame and spitting. For the Lord GOD will help me; therefore shall I not be confounded: therefore have I set my face like a flint, and I know that I shall not be ashamed" (Isaiah 50:5-7).

"And other sheep I have, which are not of this fold: them also I must bring, and they shall hear my voice; and there shall be one fold, and one shepherd. Therefore doth my Father love me, because I lay down my life, that I might take it again. No man taketh it from me, but I lay it down of myself. I have power to lay it down, and I have power to take it again. This commandment have I received of my Father" (John 10:16-18).

He went to Jerusalem to suffer and die at the hands of wicked men on the cursed tree by the determinate counsel and foreknowledge of God. The Lord of glory went to Calvary to make satisfaction to the law and justice of God for the sins of his people, that he might put away our sins and save us by the sacrifice of himself.

On the third day, after his death as our Substitute, the Lord Jesus Christ publicly declared that he had fully satisfied the justice of God and put away all the sins of his people, which were made his and imputed to him, by rising from the dead.

And he who has satisfied the whole of God's law and justice for his people will, without fail save those people for whom he has made satisfaction. He who was able to satisfy the law and justice of God and rise from the dead is able to save to the uttermost every sinner who comes to God by him. If the Lord Jesus Christ so willingly suffered all the hell of God's wrath for us, it is but a most reasonable thing that we should devote ourselves to him. May God the Holy Spirit give us grace to do so.

"And James and John, the sons of Zebedee, come unto him, saying, Master, we would that thou shouldest do for us whatsoever we shall desire. And he said unto them, What would ye that I should do for you? They said unto him, Grant unto us that we may sit, one on thy right hand, and the other on thy left hand, in thy glory. But Jesus said unto them, Ye know not what ye ask: can ye drink of the cup that I drink of? and be baptized with the baptism that I am baptized with? And they said unto him, We can. And Jesus said unto them, Ye shall indeed drink of the cup that I drink of; and with the baptism that I am baptized withal shall ye be baptized: But to sit on my right hand and on my left hand is not mine to give; but it shall be given to them for whom it is prepared. And when the ten heard it, they began to be much displeased with James and John. But Jesus called them to him, and saith unto them, Ye know that they which are accounted to rule over the Gentiles exercise lordship over them; and their great ones exercise authority upon them. But so shall it not be among you: but whosoever will be great among you, shall be your minister: And whosoever of you will be the chiefest, shall be servant of all. For even the Son of man came not to be ministered unto, but to minister, and to give his life a ransom for many".

(Mark 10:35-45)

Chapter 44

Five Great Things

We have before us a very sad, sad picture. Our Lord Jesus has just taught his disciples again that he was going to Jerusalem to suffer and die according to the will of God as our Substitute. Once he had satisfied the wrath and justice of God for us, he promised that he would rise from the dead on the third day.

One would think the disciples would have been so overcome by such teaching that they could hardly think of anything else, much less talk about anything else. But that was not the case. James and John, two of the Lord's most intimate disciples, had something else altogether on their minds. These two brothers asked the Master that he would grant to them the place of highest honour and greatness in his kingdom!

This sad story is recorded here by divine inspiration for our learning and admonition. May God the Holy Spirit be our Teacher as we study it together. If there is anything plainly revealed and taught in these verses of Inspiration it is the fact that the best, noblest, and most highly honoured of God's saints in this world are sinners still, in constant need of grace and forgiveness by the blood of Christ.

A Great Problem
The Holy Spirit holds up these disciples to set before us a very great problem, a problem with which we all struggle all the time. The problem of which I speak is pride; ungodly, disgusting, shameful, sinful, foolish pride.

"And James and John, the sons of Zebedee, come unto him, saying, Master, we would that thou shouldest do for us whatsoever we shall desire. And he said unto them, What would ye that I should do for you? They said unto him, Grant unto us that we may sit, one on thy right hand, and the other on thy left hand, in thy glory. But Jesus said unto them, Ye know not what ye ask: can ye drink of the cup that I drink of? and be baptized with the baptism that I am baptized with? And they said unto him, We can ... And when the ten heard it, they began to be much displeased with James and John" (vv. 35-41).

James and John were true believers. They were born of God. They truly loved the Lord Jesus Christ. But they were terribly ignorant of some very important, basic things, ignorant of some very basic gospel truths. Their ignorance was overshadowed only by their pride. These two brothers asked the Lord to give them the place of pre-eminence in his kingdom! They presumed that they could personally suffer and endure all that the Lord Jesus would have to suffer and endure as the Lamb of God! And they sought a position of superiority over their brethren!

Here are two of the Apostles of Christ seeking great things for themselves. But we must not be too severe in our judgment of them. Their pride was only a fair representation of the pride of our own hearts. It is the pride of our hearts that this passage of scripture is intended to expose and check. Let me point out two or three things in these verses.

First, let us all learn this fact: genuine believers are often ignorant of things which seem elementary to others. Though our Lord plainly instructed them, though they were themselves chosen Apostles, James and John simply did not understand the spiritual nature of Christ's kingdom, or the necessity of his substitutionary sacrifice and sin-atoning death. Mary Magdalene understood those things, but they did not, at least not at this time. They truly trusted Christ. They were men whose sins the Lord Jesus had forgiven, men into whose hands he had placed the keys of his kingdom; but they had a lot, an awful lot to learn!

Many assert dogmatically that a person cannot be saved without a specific measure of doctrinal knowledge and understanding. The measure by which they make such judgments is always their own "knowledge and understanding". What arrogance! What foolishness! The issue is not what we know, but who. Salvation is not in knowing doctrines and facts. Salvation is knowing a Person, the Lord Jesus Christ.

Second, we see here that God's saints in this world are sinners still. That includes you and me. We are a people with a vile, sinful, hellish, ungodly nature called "flesh"; and "that which is born of the flesh is flesh"! We are such wretched sinners that we must constantly watch over our souls and guard against pride, self-esteem, and self-confidence. These things are so deeply rooted and ingrained in us that we are seldom truly aware of their presence.

The other disciples were as guilty as James and John. They were displeased with James and John, not because they asked for this place of honour, but because they did not ask first. They were upset because James and John wanted to be exalted above them!

It is not at all unusual for those who truly have come out of the world, taken up the cross, forsaken all, and follow Christ to become envious, jealous, and offended if a brother or sister is promoted above them. We are so proud and fickle that we get our feelings hurt if someone mentions two or three names in public, but fails to mention ours! Such pride is horribly shameful. It causes strife and division. It ought not to be. But it certainly is not unusual.

The fact is, the greatest problem we face, the most dangerous enemy we have to deal with is our own stinking pride. Pride is the oldest of all sins, the most universal, and the most destructive. We all love power, pre-eminence, prestige, position, and property, because we are all terribly proud. It is our pride that causes us to crave attention and to become upset with those who get it instead of us. Pride inspired Lucifer's fall (Isaiah 14:12-14). Pride brought one third of the heavenly angels down to hell (Jude 6). Pride seduced Eve. Pride destroyed Adam. And it is always pride that causes strife and division among the sons and daughters of Adam (Psalm 10:2). What is it that divides, separates, and distinguishes men and women from one another according to race, rank, and riches? Pride! What is it that divides brethren? Pride! What is it that splits up families? Pride! What is it that causes war? Pride!

Yes, even among God's saints, our greatest problems, difficulties, injuries, and troubles are the result of pride. Thomas Hooker once said, "Pride is a vice that cleaveth so fast unto the hearts of men that if we were to strip ourselves of all faults one by one, we would undoubtedly find it the very last and hardest to put off".

Of all those things named in the Bible which God hates, pride is number one (Proverbs 6:17). It is our pride that makes us weak and vulnerable to temptations. It is pride that keeps sinners from seeking the Lord (Psalm 10:4). Let us pray, day by day, that our God may deliver us from the pride of our hearts.

When our Lord asked James and John if they could endure the baptism he had to endure and drink the cup he had to drink, they did not hesitate to say, "We can". Did you ever notice in the Word of God that the recorded falls of God's saints are usually at the very point where they were strongest, not at their weakest point, but at their strongest? Look at Job. What man was ever so patient as Job? Yet, I know of none more impatient. Moses was the meekest of men. Yet, his rash anger kept him out of the promised land. Samson was the strongest man who ever lived. Yet, he was conquered by a woman. Saul never had a friend so loyal as David. Yet, David killed his friend Uriah. Solomon was the wisest of men; but he was also, undoubtedly, one of the most foolish.

My point is this: We must never be so proud as to trust in our own strength. God's strength is made perfect in our weakness, not in our strength. Therefore, Paul said, "When I am weak, then am I strong". When we foolishly imagine in the pride of our hearts that we are strong, then we are most weak. When we think we are strong, we think we do not need Christ!

A Great Promise
In spite of their ignorance, pride, and sin, the Lord Jesus gave his disciples a great promise.

"Jesus said unto them, Ye shall indeed drink of the cup that I drink of; and with the baptism that I am baptized withal shall ye be baptized: But to sit on my right hand and on my left hand is not mine to give; but it shall be given to them for whom it is prepared" (vv. 39, 40).

When the Lord Jesus said to James and John, "Ye shall indeed drink of the cup that I drink of; and with the baptism that I am baptized withal shall ye be baptized", perhaps there is some sense in which our Lord was saying, "You, too, shall be persecuted and required to suffer much" but that is not all that is contained in these two verses. The Saviour said that they would drink the very same cup he drank and would be baptized with the very same baptism with which he was baptized.

Certainly, our Saviour was here assuring them and us that all the horror of God's indescribable wrath, which he was about to endure as our Substitute, he would endure voluntarily. He compares his sufferings and death as a baptism, an immersion. He was wholly immersed in the overwhelming wrath of the infinite God for us, in our place, as our Substitute. But by referring to his sufferings as a baptism, he is telling us that they were not forced upon him by the hand of another. Baptism is not something forced upon a man. It is a voluntary act. Yet, it is something done to him by another. The Son of God was voluntarily baptized in the wrath of God by his Father's own hand. It is written, "It pleased the Lord to bruise him".

Our all-glorious Christ also refers to his sin-atoning sacrifice and the wrath he experienced and endured as our Substitute as a cup. A cup is something taken voluntarily. The Lord of Glory willingly took the cup of wrath, when he was made to be sin for us. Voluntarily, with one tremendous draught of love, he drank damnation dry for us! He so loved us that he took the cup of God's wrath as our Substitute as willingly as a thirsty man takes a cup of water!

Still, there is more. The Lord Jesus here promised these sinful, errant disciples that they would indeed be baptized with his baptism and drink his cup. I can only think of one way that is possible. The only way on this earth you and I can be baptized with his baptism and drink his cup is representatively, in him as our Surety and Substitute; and that is exactly what took place at Calvary.

Let every redeemed sinner sing with the psalmist, "What shall I render unto the LORD for all his benefits toward me? I will take the cup of salvation, and call upon the name of the LORD" (Psalm 116:12, 13).

This is exactly what is symbolized and pictured in the ordinances of the gospel. We in our baptism, our immersion, have confessed that we were crucified with Christ at Calvary, buried with him, and raised with him representatively. As we take the bread and wine of the Lord's Supper, we symbolically take the Bread of Life and the Cup of Salvation, symbolically eating and drinking the body and blood of our Lord and Saviour in blessed remembrance of him.

Then, in verse 40 the Lord Jesus assures us that there is a kingdom of glory, a kingdom of heaven, already prepared by our heavenly Father for his elect, which shall be given to those for whom it was prepared. Eternal life, the heavenly glory, is a kingdom prepared by God the Father from the foundation of the world, not for everyone, but for his elect. All for whom that kingdom was prepared shall possess it at last in all its fulness and glory. They shall possess it in its entirety by the gift of God's free grace in Christ, by the merits of his blood and righteousness.

A Great Precept
"But Jesus called them to him, and saith unto them, Ye know that they which are accounted to rule over the Gentiles exercise lordship over them; and their great ones exercise authority upon them. But so shall it not be among you: but whosoever will be great among you, shall be your minister: And whosoever of you will be the chiefest, shall be servant of all" (vv. 42-44).

Here is a great precept. Oh, may the Spirit of God give us grace to follow it. A life of self-denying kindness and service to others is the secret of true greatness. In the kingdom of God he is truly great who lives for, seeks, and promotes the temporal, spiritual, and eternal welfare of others. J. C. Ryle wrote:

"True greatness consists, not in receiving, but in giving, not in the selfish absorption of good things, but in imparting good to others, not in being served, but in serving, not in sitting still and being ministered to, but in going about and ministering to others".

If I want true greatness in the kingdom of God, I must find that place in God's kingdom where I am needed and can be most useful, and there be a minister, a servant. The word translated "minister" is the same word that is commonly translated "deacon". It refers to a person who does menial labour, house cleaning, serving tables, gardening, etc. It is the least recognized, but often the most needed, and certainly the most basic service.

If I really want to be a truly admirable person in the church and kingdom of God, I must make myself the servant of all, a slave to the people of God. Those who are truly great and admirable in the family of God are those men and women who devote themselves as willing slaves in humble, self-denying, self-abasing, self-sacrificing service to God's elect. They willingly serve the Lord's people for Christ's sake. They are people who have learned that "it (really) is more blessed to give than to receive" (Acts 20:35).

Truly great people are those who enrich the lives of others. They are the very few men and women of whom it can be truthfully said, "The world is a better place because of them than it would otherwise be."

Perhaps you think, "That is just too much to expect from anyone. It is unreasonable to expect anyone to stoop so low." You are right, unless that person is interested in striving to be like Christ. Look at verse 45.

A Great Pattern

"For even the Son of man came not to be ministered unto, but to minister, and to give his life a ransom for many". Here, the Lord Jesus Christ, the Son of God, who loved us and gave himself for us, uses himself as a great pattern and example for us to follow. Our Saviour's message here is very simple and clear. He is saying, "Strive to be like me." It is written, "He that saith he abideth in him ought himself also so to walk, even as he walked" (1 John 2:6).

Did the Lord Jesus live in this world as the servant of God, to do the will of God (Hebrews 10:5-10)? If I would be like him, I must seek to live in this world as the servant of the Most High God, doing the will of God (Philippians 2:1-9). Did the Son of God live in this world as the servant of men (John 13:4, 5, 12-17)?

If I would walk in his steps, I must endeavour to spend my life and energy serving the temporal needs, spiritual needs, emotional needs, and eternal needs of others.

> Lord, help me to live from day to day,
> In such a self-forgetful way,
> That even when I kneel to pray,
> My prayer shall be for others.
>
> Help me in all the work I do,
> To ever be sincere and true,
> And know that all I'd do for You,
> Must needs be done for others.

> Saviour, help me in all I do,
> To magnify and copy You,
> That I may ever live like You,
> Help me to live for others.

A Great Purchase

Here is the greatest thing of all, the great purchase of our souls, by the sacrifice of God's dear Son. "The Son of man came not to be ministered unto, but to minister, and to give his life a ransom for many" (v. 45). Not only has the Lord Jesus given us a noble example of self-denying love and service by his obedience to God the Father for us, he has by his great, sin-atoning sacrifice and substitutionary death purchased and ransomed us from the curse of God's Holy law by his precious blood (Romans 8:1-4, 33, 34; Galatians 3:13). He has delivered us from the slavery of sin by his blood applied in saving grace (Romans 6:18) into the glorious liberty of the sons of God, redeeming us to himself as his own peculiar people (Titus 2:14). Let us never forget that the ransom price by which we have been redeemed is his precious blood (Ephesians 1:7; 1 Peter 1:18-20; Revelation 5:9).

That precious blood, the ransom price, was paid for "many", and paid for them in particular, as the objects of his special love and saving purpose. The "many" for whom the Lord Jesus Christ paid this great ransom price are clearly identified in the Book of God as the many God has ordained unto eternal life (Acts 13:48), the many the Father gave to the Son in the covenant of grace before the worlds were made (John 6:37-40), the many for whom the Lord Jesus makes intercession (John 17:9, 20), the many who are called by his Spirit's effectual, irresistible grace (Revelation 19:9), the many who are saved by his mercy (John 1:12, 13), the many to whom he gives the gift of faith (Ephesians 2:8), and the many for whom his Father has prepared and to whom he shall give the kingdom of Glory (v. 40).

"And they came to Jericho: and as he went out of Jericho with his disciples and a great number of people, blind Bartimaeus, the son of Timaeus, sat by the highway side begging. And when he heard that it was Jesus of Nazareth, he began to cry out, and say, Jesus, thou Son of David, have mercy on me. And many charged him that he should hold his peace: but he cried the more a great deal, Thou Son of David, have mercy on me. And Jesus stood still, and commanded him to be called. And they call the blind man, saying unto him, Be of good comfort, rise; he calleth thee. And he, casting away his garment, rose, and came to Jesus. And Jesus answered and said unto him, What wilt thou that I should do unto thee? The blind man said unto him, Lord, that I might receive my sight. And Jesus said unto him, Go thy way; thy faith hath made thee whole. And immediately he received his sight, and followed Jesus in the way".

(Mark 10:46-52)

Chapter 45

"Jesus Stood Still"

In the tenth chapter of Joshua, at the command of a man, "the sun stood still"! We are told, "There was no day like that before it or after it, that the Lord hearkened unto the voice of a man" (Joshua 10:14). Here is something even more remarkable than that. Here is a man who caused the God who made the sun to stand still!

As he was coming up out of Jericho on his way to Jerusalem to redeem his people, our Lord Jesus heard a poor, blind beggar crying for mercy. At the sound of his cry, we are told, "Jesus stood still"! What a wonderful, amazing picture we have before us! Here is the omnipotent God stopped in his tracks, held fast by the cry of a needy soul for his mercy.

He was on his way to Jerusalem to accomplish the redemption of his people, to fulfil the will of God. Nothing could stop him. Nothing could cause him to pause. Nothing could detour him from his work. Neither Herod, nor Satan, nor the Pharisees, nor his disciples, not even his own mother could stop our Saviour or cause him to pause in his path, as he went about to do his Father's business. But one solitary, helpless soul, one blind beggar crying for mercy, looking to him for help, believing him, crying to him, stopped the Son of God in his tracks. At the cry of a needy sinner for mercy, "Jesus stood still"! The Son of God will never ignore the cry or refuse the faith of a sinner seeking mercy. The Lord Jesus Christ is constrained by his very mission to seek and save the lost (John 6:37). What a joyful picture this piece of our Redeemer's earthly history gives us! Let us turn aside from the trifles of this world to see this great sight. There are lessons to be learned here that are of more value than gold.

An Unexpected Believer
Bartimaeus was an unexpected believer. None of the Lord's disciples expected to see this man exercising faith in Christ. But faith is frequently found where it is least expected. There were great multitudes who followed the Lord Jesus as he walked along and taught the people, some for loaves and some for love, some out of curiosity and some out of conviction, some for greed and some for grace. But there were few, very few who believed on Christ. Many who saw his miracles yet believed him not. But here is a blind

man, a man who never saw any of our Lord's miracles, a man who knew the Saviour only by hear-say, by the testimony of others, who believed him.

What a picture Bartimaeus is of us! His father, Timaeus, whose name means "an honour" or "honourable", was, like our father Adam, an honourable man. Bartimaeus was the blind son of an honourable man, who had been reduced to abject poverty, begging for bread. The Son of God came to "give light to them that sit in darkness and the shadow of death" (Isaiah 35:5; 42:6, 7; 49:9; 61:1; Luke 4:18). Robert Hawker rightly observed, "Such is every man's state, though he waiteth on the highway of ordinances till Jesus pass by; and the Spirit of Jesus put a cry in his heart for spiritual light and understanding."

Bartimaeus simply heard other men and women talking about the Saviour. We read that he began to cry after the Saviour, "When he heard". He simply heard others talking about the Redeemer and the wondrous works of mercy he had performed. Blessed gossip! Perhaps he heard how the Master had healed a blind man on his way into Jericho (Luke 18:35-43). Without question, he had heard who Christ is. He called him by his name, "Jesus". He addressed him as "Lord". And he acknowledged him as the Messiah God had promised, calling him the "Son of David". He heard about the Lord's mighty miracles of mercy. He heard that "Jesus passed by". And he knew he might never pass his way again.

Hearing these things, Bartimaeus believed the Son of God. His faith puts us to shame. We have books of evidence, libraries of theology, volumes of biographies, yet, how little there is of this childlike confidence and faith in Christ. Even among true believers, simple, confident, unhesitating faith is found where we least expect it. The humble soul believes God and walks in peace, while the learned, well-read theologian is harassed with doubts and questions. This faith is the gift and operation of God the Holy Spirit. Who but God the Spirit could have convinced Bartimaeus of these things? No one but God the Spirit could have put such a cry in his heart, a cry that none could stifle, until the mercy needed had been granted.

Available Means

Bartimaeus availed himself of the means he was given that he might obtain mercy. And if we hope for mercy, we must avail ourselves of every means of good to our souls. Yes, God is sovereign. Salvation is of the Lord. Every chosen, redeemed sinner shall be saved. I am fully aware of those blessed facts of divine revelation, and rejoice to proclaim them. Yet, the scriptures make it clear that every man is responsible for his own soul. We are responsible to use the means of grace God gives us.

When this blind man heard that "Jesus passed by", he was found "sitting by the highway side", crying for mercy. He took up a hopeful position "by the highway side". There he would be likely to hear any good news that might be spread. There he was most likely to meet with and be seen by the compassionate. Though he was blind, he was not deaf. And he used what he had to obtain the good he needed.

Bartimaeus employed the means given him to obtain alms to relieve his physical needs. But the Lord God has ordained specific means of grace, which he is pleased to use for the salvation of his elect and the good of our souls. To despise them is to despise his grace. To neglect them is to neglect his grace. To use them is to be in the path of mercy (Matthew 18:20). Do not forsake the house of God, where he meets with his people (Hebrews 10:25). Do not forsake the reading of holy scripture, which are able to make you wise unto salvation (2 Timothy 3:15). Do not abandon the preaching of the gospel. It is God's pleasure to save sinners by the instrumentality of gospel preaching (1 Corinthians 1:18-23; Romans 10:17). Do not forsake private prayer. Though God promises covenant mercy to his chosen, he declares, "I will yet for this be enquired of by the house of Israel, to do it for them" (Ezekiel 36:37).

Discouragements Overcome

"And many charged him that he should hold his peace: but he cried the more a great deal, Thou son of David, have mercy on me" (v. 48).

What discouragements Bartimaeus had to endure and overcome. He exemplifies the fact that "the kingdom of heaven suffereth violence, and the violent take it by force" (Matthew 11:12). As soon as a sinner is brought into serious concern for his soul's everlasting welfare, enemies of Christ and his soul try to stifle all conviction and crush the infant desire for mercy, grace, and salvation. Even before Christ has been formed in the heart as their hope of glory, some of God's elect are sharply tried by the foolish counsel of those around them and by the accusations of Satan.

Those very people who should have encouraged Bartimaeus' faith greatly discouraged him. They charged him to hold his peace, suggesting that he was too poor, too dirty, too blind, too worthless to obtain the mercy Christ bestows! But Bartimaeus needed mercy. He knew that Christ could give him the mercy he needed. He knew that he might never get this opportunity again. Consequently, the opposition he met with was hardly noticed by him.

Christ's Call

"And Jesus stood still, and commanded him to be called. And they call the blind man, saying unto him, Be of good comfort, rise; he calleth thee" (v.

49). How the Son of God loves needy sinners! Our Saviour's love for this poor, needy soul is to be seen in everything he did for him. The Lord Jesus graciously blinded the eyes of his body for a season, that he might open the eyes of his soul forever. In time the Son of God sent someone to tell this man about his greatness and glory. The Lord Jesus Christ passed his way in mercy, love, and grace. He heard the man's prayer. He commanded him to be called. Then he personally called Bartimaeus. What a call his call was! What a cause for comfort! The disciples said, "Be of good comfort ... He calleth thee"! And when he did, the Lord Jesus spoke a word of grace to him. "Jesus said unto him, Go thy way; thy faith hath made thee whole". What a word of grace! The grace poured into his lips as this poor sinner's Surety in eternity now poured from his lips into the chosen sinner's heart! Then, he went on to Jerusalem to redeem him!

Faith Obtains Mercy

Faith always gets what it seeks. Mercy! Look what this man did when the Saviour called him. He arose, cast off his garment, and came to Christ. Such are the sweet results of Christ's effectual call. The poor sinner is enabled, by the same grace that calls him, to cast away everything of his own, all the filthy rags of his own righteousness, and come to Christ, just as he is, poor, and blind, and wretched, and needy, and receive all from Christ. "Immediately he received his sight". And as soon as the sinner comes to Christ, he receives his sight. When the Master told him to go his way, Bartimaeus "followed Jesus in the way". Christ, who is THE WAY, became his way. So it is with all who are called by grace. They follow Christ in the way of faith, in the way of his doctrine, in the way of his ordinances, in the way of his worship, in the way of his example.

"Jesus Stood Still"

"And when they came nigh to Jerusalem, unto Bethphage and Bethany, at the mount of Olives, he sendeth forth two of his disciples, And saith unto them, Go your way into the village over against you: and as soon as ye be entered into it, ye shall find a colt tied, whereon never man sat; loose him, and bring him. And if any man say unto you, Why do ye this? say ye that the Lord hath need of him; and straightway he will send him hither. And they went their way, and found the colt tied by the door without in a place where two ways met; and they loose him. And certain of them that stood there said unto them, What do ye, loosing the colt? And they said unto them even as Jesus had commanded: and they let them go. And they brought the colt to Jesus, and cast their garments on him; and he sat upon him. And many spread their garments in the way: and others cut down branches off the trees, and strawed them in the way. And they that went before, and they that followed, cried, saying, Hosanna; Blessed is he that cometh in the name of the Lord: Blessed be the kingdom of our father David, that cometh in the name of the Lord: Hosanna in the highest."

(Mark 11:1-10)

Chapter 46

Christ Our King

This event in the earthly life and ministry of our Saviour is one of just a few that are recorded in detail by Matthew, Mark, Luke, and John. It is the only event in our Saviour's earthly life and ministry that he seems to have deliberately made a matter of great, public display. Surely, that which is here revealed is a matter of great importance. Several things recorded here are obvious facts. It is obvious that the Bible is, indeed, the Word of God, the inspired, inerrant Word of the living God (2 Timothy 3:16; 2 Peter 1:21). Matthew tells us that all this was done that the prophecy of Zechariah 9:9 might be fulfilled. "Rejoice greatly, O daughter of Zion; shout, O daughter of Jerusalem: behold, thy King cometh unto thee: he is just, and having salvation; lowly, and riding upon an ass, and upon a colt the foal of an ass".

It is equally obvious that our great Saviour, the Lord Jesus Christ, is the omniscient, all-knowing God. He told his disciples exactly where they would find the ass and her colt and exactly what would happen when they found them. He did not come to Jerusalem to be made a King. He came into Jerusalem triumphantly as the King. He was going by way of the cross to receive his kingdom. But he was King already. The ass and her colt and the men who owned them belonged to him. All were his servants. All did his bidding.

Our Lord Jesus Christ is, always was, and always shall be King over everyone and everything by virtue of the fact that he is God. The one true and living God is King everywhere. He always has his way and does his will. Here we see the Lord Jesus ascending up to Jerusalem as our mediatorial King to take possession of his kingdom, the kingdom and dominion given to him as the God-man by his Father as the reward of his obedience to God as our Mediator (Romans 14:9; John 17:2; Philippians 2:9-11). The Lord Jesus Christ, our Redeemer and Saviour, is the King of Glory and the King of the universe. In this passage Mark shows us four things about Christ our King.

The King's Power

The Lord Jesus displayed the universality of his power and dominion as the sovereign God and King, as the absolute Ruler of all things, by sending his disciples to fetch an ass's colt, on which no man had ever even attempted to ride, to carry him into Jerusalem (vv. 1-6).

"And when they came nigh to Jerusalem, unto Bethphage and Bethany, at the mount of Olives, he sendeth forth two of his disciples, And saith unto them, Go your way into the village over against you: and as soon as ye be entered into it, ye shall find a colt tied, whereon never man sat; loose him, and bring him. And if any man say unto you, Why do ye this? say ye that the Lord hath need of him; and straightway he will send him hither. And they went their way, and found the colt tied by the door without in a place where two ways met; and they loose him. And certain of them that stood there said unto them, What do ye, loosing the colt? And they said unto them even as Jesus had commanded: and they let them go".

There are many things in these first six verses, which might properly demand our attention, but my purpose now is to show you the totality of Christ's sovereign power as our God and King. Here we see clear, evident displays of that sovereign power. Our Saviour has complete and absolute power over all the affairs of providence. It was he who put the ass and her colt where he wanted them, when he wanted them there. Our great God and Saviour has complete and absolute power over the wills of all men.

We have no way of knowing whether the man who owned the ass and her colt was a believer or an unbeliever. But there is no indication that he either knew the Lord or had any advance knowledge that the Master wanted his colt. Yet, he willingly sent his colt away with two strangers because the Lord Jesus so inclined his will. And he who is our great Lord and King has complete and absolute power over all animals and all creation. Who ever heard tell of a man riding an ass's colt the first time it was attempted? Yet, the Son of God has such power over the animal kingdom that this untamed ass's colt rides him through the streets as quietly as any gentle old mare a man ever rode.

Such a God, such a Saviour and King has power to save whom he will. He is God mighty to save! We can safely trust to this great, omnipotent God and King the present and eternal welfare of our lives. Everything that may be needed to carry this great King through the world, everything that may be needed to preach his gospel wherever he wants it preached, whenever he wants it preached, will be provided with ease by the King himself.

The servants of such a God and King beg for nothing! We do not serve a pigmy king or a pigmy god. We serve the omnipotent, sovereign God, the King of glory, who rules all things, owns all things, and disposes of all things as he will. You will not find the servants of this great King bowing and scraping before men, or begging men to help them do what God has sent them to do. The ambassadors of this King act like they are the ambassadors of this King!

The King's Poverty

"And they brought the colt to Jesus, and cast their garments on him; and he sat upon him" (v. 7). Here is an indication of the great poverty in which our Lord Jesus Christ, the great King voluntarily lived all the days of his life on this earth. The Lord Jesus did not ride into Jerusalem on a white stallion with a diamond studded saddle. He did not fly into town on a private jet. He did not come in a pope-mobile, wearing a white dress and funny looking hat with an entourage of effeminate looking men wearing red capes rubbing good luck beads. The Son of God rode into Jerusalem exactly as he chose to live in this world in utter poverty, though he was in need of absolutely nothing. He rode into town on a borrowed colt, not even a borrowed horse's colt, a borrowed ass's colt, without a saddle, sitting on someone else's clothes.

"For ye know the grace of our Lord Jesus Christ, that, though he was rich, yet for your sakes he became poor, that ye through his poverty might be rich" (2 Corinthians 8:9). When he was born, he was laid in a borrowed manger. When he crossed the Sea of Galilee, it was in a borrowed boat. When he rode into Jerusalem, it was on a borrowed ass's colt. When he looked for a saddle, he was given borrowed coats. When he died, he was buried in a borrowed tomb.

In the person of our Saviour, while he lived upon this earth, there was a marvellous, mysterious, blessed union of humanity and divinity, weakness and power, poverty and riches. He who fed thousands with a few loaves of bread and two sardines was often hungry. He who healed the sick was often weary. He who cast out devils with his word was himself tempted of the devil. He who raised the dead died for sinners!

What divine, God-like power our Lord displayed in bending the wills of the multitude to escort him into Jerusalem! Yet, what human, man-like weakness he showed in riding into town on his inauguration day on a borrowed ass's colt!

What are we to learn from this? The Lord Jesus Christ is a sympathizing High Priest who is touched with the feeling of our infirmities, as well as a God mighty to save.

Learn this, too. There is no shame in poverty. There is great shame, or should be, in those characteristics of life and behaviour that lead to poverty: drunkenness, profligacy, extravagance, dishonesty, and laziness. But honest, hard working men and women who are poor are just as honourable as honest, hard working men and women who are rich. And they ought to be treated just as respectfully.

As our Saviour proved the sincerity of his love for us by giving himself for us, giving himself to the utmost poverty when he was made sin for us, let us prove the sincerity of our love for him by our giving (2 Corinthians 8:7-9).

The King's Parade

Normally, our Lord Jesus sought seclusion. He often withdrew from the crowd. When men sought to take him by force and make him a king, because his hour was not yet come, he withdrew himself. He was often in the wilderness, in the mountain, or in the desert place. He never sought the public eye, the applause of men, or even the attention of men. In fact, the only time we see the Lord Jesus deliberately calling public attention to himself is here, when he rode into Jerusalem as the King to whom the city belonged.

What a stir there was on that day. I doubt there was a house in the city, or even an inn, in which the events of the day were not discussed well into the night, as well they should have been. Never before or since did any city in this world behold such a parade as this. Yet, there were very few who had even the slightest idea what the events of the day meant. Do you? Do you understand the significance of the things recorded here?

"And many spread their garments in the way: and others cut down branches off the trees, and strowed them in the way. And they that went before, and they that followed, cried, saying, Hosanna; Blessed is he that cometh in the name of the Lord: Blessed be the kingdom of our father David, that cometh in the name of the Lord: Hosanna in the highest. And Jesus entered into Jerusalem, and into the temple: and when he had looked round about upon all things, and now the eventide was come, he went out unto Bethany with the twelve" (vv. 8-11).

Our Lord deliberately overruled everything and everyone to draw attention to himself as he rode into Jerusalem at the annual Feast of Passover to die as our Substitute, as the true Paschal Lamb. He fixed it so that every eye was upon him. The scribes, the Pharisees, the Romans and all the people were made aware of his entrance. He wanted everyone to witness what he was doing.

He publicly presented himself as the Christ, the Messiah, the King of Glory, of whom the Old Testament spoke. There is no question about this. Those who sang his praise used the very words of a messianic psalm to laud him. He was about to enter into his kingdom and glory (Psalm 24). His kingdom is not like any other. His is a spiritual, not a carnal, material kingdom. His coming into Jerusalem was the coming of the true and spiritual "kingdom of our father David".

When he came into the temple, our Lord Jesus, this man of Nazareth, came to announce himself as God almighty, the everlasting Son, to whom the house of God belongs, and by whose word it is ruled. In verses 15-17, when our Lord Jesus drove the religious thieves out of the temple, he called the house of God his own house. Christ alone is the King and Lawgiver in his house and kingdom, the church. He alone is the Head of his Church. His Word alone is our doctrine book, rule book, and ordinance book!

The Son of God drew all this attention to himself on this occasion, because he intends for us to know and understand the unspeakable importance and pre-eminence of his sin-atoning death as the Lamb of God.

It was not by accident, but by special divine arrangement, that he came to Jerusalem at this time. The true Paschal Lamb had come to the holy city to make atonement for sin by the sacrifice of himself. And our Saviour would have us to know that this is the most important of all events in history, the most important of all his works, and the most important of all things taught in holy scripture. Apart from and without this, everything else is altogether meaningless. Thank God for his incarnation and birth. Treasure up his gracious sayings. Seek to imitate his holy life of serving one another. Cherish his blessed intercession and priesthood. Look for his blessed second coming. But that one mighty, mysterious work, to which our Lord Jesus called the attention of his disciples, to which he calls the attention of the world, to which he especially calls the attention of his elect, the crowning act of God himself, is his death upon the cursed tree as our blessed Substitute.

God give us grace to prize it more dearly, to preach it more fully, to think of it more reverently, and to stand in unceasing amazement and ever increasing love before him who loved us and gave himself for us! It is not the birth of Christ that gives us life, but his death. It is not the example of Christ that inspires our devotion, but his death. It is not the second coming of Christ that gives us hope, but his death. Our Master gave us no ordinances to remember or celebrate his birth, or his life, but he gave us two to celebrate his death.

The King's Praise

"And they that went before, and they that followed, cried, saying, Hosanna; Blessed is he that cometh in the name of the Lord: Blessed be the kingdom of our father David, that cometh in the name of the Lord: Hosanna in the highest" (vv. 9, 10).

This is almost a direct quote from Psalm 118:25, 26 (compare Psalm 24:7-10). "Save now, I beseech thee, O Lord: O Lord, I beseech thee, send now prosperity. Blessed be he that cometh in the name of the Lord: we have blessed you out of the house of the Lord". Here is a prayer of faith. "Hosanna! Save now I beseech Thee, O Lord! O Lord, I beseech Thee, send now prosperity"! Here is an ascription of praise. "Blessed is he that cometh in the name of the Lord"! Here is a benediction of grace. "Blessed be the kingdom of our father David, that cometh in the name of the Lord ... We have blessed you out of the house of the Lord".

"And Jesus entered into Jerusalem, and into the temple: and when he had looked round about upon all things, and now the eventide was come, he went out unto Bethany with the twelve. And on the morrow, when they were come from Bethany, he was hungry: And seeing a fig tree afar off having leaves, he came, if haply he might find any thing thereon: and when he came to it, he found nothing but leaves; for the time of figs was not yet. And Jesus answered and said unto it, No man eat fruit of thee hereafter for ever. And his disciples heard it. And they come to Jerusalem: and Jesus went into the temple, and began to cast out them that sold and bought in the temple, and overthrew the tables of the moneychangers, and the seats of them that sold doves; And would not suffer that any man should carry any vessel through the temple. And he taught, saying unto them, Is it not written, My house shall be called of all nations the house of prayer? but ye have made it a den of thieves. And the scribes and chief priests heard it, and sought how they might destroy him: for they feared him, because all the people was astonished at his doctrine. And when even was come, he went out of the city".

(Mark 11:11-19)

Chapter 47

"Nothing But Leaves"

In this passage of scripture the Holy Spirit uses a cursed fig tree and the corrupt religion of the Jews to teach us very important spiritual lessons.

Sinners' Friend

"And Jesus entered into Jerusalem, and into the temple: and when he had looked round about upon all things, and now the eventide was come, he went out unto Bethany with the twelve" (v. 11). The first thing Mark shows us here is that the Lord Jesus Christ, the sinners' Friend, is just the Saviour and friend we need.

The Lord Jesus loved to visit Bethany. After riding into Jerusalem on an ass's colt and being publicly announced as Messiah the King, our Saviour left the city with his disciples and walked out to Bethany. What a blessed town that was. It was about two miles out of Jerusalem. And it seems that the Master never missed an opportunity to go there. There was an elect family in Bethany, the special objects of Christ's mercy, love, and grace. Martha, Mary, and Lazarus lived there. No doubt the Lord Jesus often spent a night with that chosen family. O blessed, indescribably blessed, eternally blessed is that home where the Son of God and his disciples are at home! Blessed is that home that entertains, feeds, and gives rest to the Lord Jesus Christ.

Perhaps you ask, "How can anyone do that today?" Let me remind you once more that the blessed Book of God teaches us that that which is done and for the Lord's children is done to and for him; and that which is done against the Lord's people is done against him. Wherever there is an open door, a room, a chair, a plate, a bed, a welcome sign for God's saints, the Son of God is present to bless.

Bethany was a blessed place, because Martha, Mary, and Lazarus, this elect family, lived there. As God's elect are the salt of the earth, this family was the salt of Bethany. Bethany means "House of Sheep", and it was that. Bethany means "House of Obedience", and it was that. Bethany means "House of Affliction", and it was that, too. Sheep, obedience, and affliction are always found in the same place.

"And on the morrow, when they were come from Bethany, he was hungry" (v. 12). With those words we are reminded that the Lord Jesus Christ really is both God and man. In verse seventeen, he speaks of the temple in Jerusalem, the house of God, and calls it, "My house". Thus, he plainly declares his divinity. He could not have stated it more precisely and clearly if he had said, "I, the man standing before you, Jesus of Nazareth, am the almighty God".

Yet, this great God really did assume our nature. He took into union with himself humanity. We read that, "He was hungry". While he lived upon this earth, our blessed Lord Jesus had a nature exactly like ours, sin alone excepted. He wept. He rejoiced. He felt pain. He felt gladness. He got tired and needed rest. He got thirsty and needed to drink. He got hungry and needed to eat.

These are wonderful, amazing things upon which we should frequently meditate. He who is the eternal God, the Creator and Sustainer of all things; he who feeds every sparrow and clothes every lily; he who holds every beast of the field, every bird in the sky, and every fish in the sea in the palm of his hand; he from whom all things came and to whom all things go, when he came to save his people from their sins, was hungry!

God the Son condescended to become a man. He condescended to every weakness of humanity. He who thought it not robbery to be equal with God took upon himself the form of a servant and humbled himself! No wonder Paul speaks of "the unsearchable riches of Christ"!

Yet, his stooping to humanity and to all the infirmities of humanity is only the beginning of the story. This man who is God, though he knew no sin, though he was holy, harmless, undefiled, and separate from sinners, was willingly made sin for us, that we might be made the righteousness of God in him (2 Corinthians 5:21; 8:9). Jesus Christ is God mighty to save. He is a man like us, able to suffer, bleed, and die. He is the God-man, who has redeemed us by a sacrifice of infinite merit. And, though he is now exalted to heaven's highest glory, this great Saviour is still a man, God in human flesh!

He who sits upon the throne of the universe, he who occupies the throne of grace is a man touched with the feeling of our infirmities. He knows the experiences of our humanity, all of them! He knows what pain, weakness, weariness, and hunger are. He knows the feeling of abandonment, isolation, betrayal, and slander. He knows what it is to visit the sick room of one who is dearly beloved. He knows what it is to stand by the graveside and weep. When we speak to the Lord Jesus Christ about these things, he knows what we are talking about. The Lord Jesus Christ is no stranger to trouble and sorrow.

"Surely", J. C. Ryle observed, "this is just the Saviour and Friend that poor, aching, groaning human nature requires".

What a Friend we have in Jesus,
All our sins and griefs to bear!
What a privilege to carry,
Everything to God in prayer!

Fruitless Religion

The next thing taught in these verses is that nothing in all the world is so disgusting to the Son of God and so surely damning to our souls as fruitless religion.

"And seeing a fig tree afar off having leaves, he came, if haply he might find any thing thereon: and when he came to it, he found nothing but leaves; for the time of figs was not yet. And Jesus answered and said unto it, No man eat fruit of thee hereafter for ever. And his disciples heard it". (vv. 13, 14)

As our Lord and his disciples walked along, they saw this fig tree. It stood out from all the others because, though the time of figs had not yet come, this fig tree was in full foliage. The other trees were just beginning to shoot forth their buds; but this one was large, spreading its full foliage of leaves, and waving in the wind, as if to say, "Look at me"! But when our Lord walked with his disciples over to the tree to gather some figs, he found "nothing but leaves", and immediately pronounced a curse upon the tree, and by sun up the next morning, it had withered in death from its roots (v. 20).

Without question, this event is full of spiritual meaning. It is a parable as full of instruction for our souls as any of our Lord's spoken parables. Without a doubt, this barren, cursed, withered fig tree represents apostate Judaism. The Jews, the Scribes, the Pharisees, the Sadducees, all were rich in leaves. They possessed more leaves than anyone. Ceremony, creed, history, doctrine, show, tradition, and reputation they had in great abundance. And they did not mind calling attention to their beautiful leaves. But they were utterly destitute of faith toward God. They had no fruit. Therefore, that nation and their religion has been specifically cursed of God and forever abandoned (Matthew 23:38)

This barren fig tree represents every apostate church and religious denomination in the world. I am talking now about churches which claim to be Christian, which claim to believe in and defend the Book, the blood, and the blessed hope, Churches which wear the name of Christ, but have departed from the doctrine of Christ. If I could get their attention, I would say to every man, woman, and child in such churches, "Escape for your life! Flee from Babylon. Get out of Sodom. The curse of God is in that place you think is the house of God". The greatest missionary field in the world today is the professed church of God. Where can you find a church today where the Word of God is faithfully preached, the glory of God is paramount, the will of God rules, and the gospel of Christ is proclaimed?

Robert Hawker wrote of such:

> Deceiving by the appearance of large full leaves of a profession without fruit, in the end (they) will be found dried up from the roots, with the curse of a broken law falling everlastingly upon them, untaken away by Christ.

Above all else, this barren fig tree represents religious hypocrisy: carnal, half-hearted, hypocritical professors of Christianity. All who are content with a name that they live, though they are dead, should see their faces in this mirror! Their fine, showy, impressive leaves, those things that impress them so much with themselves, mean nothing to God almighty. They stink in his nostrils! Their religion is their damning delusion! They may have great experiences, but no experience of grace. They may have a rich history, but no holiness. They may enjoy religious excitement and displays of emotion; but they possess neither righteousness nor expiation. Their doctrine may be precise; but it is precisely dead. Their religion may be rich in ceremonial tradition; but it is poor in comfort and truth. It is useless religion, because it is fruitless religion. It does not produce faith in Christ, hope in Christ, or love for Christ. J. C. Ryle said:

> A sure way to go to hell is by living and dying without any religion at all. You may live like a beast, prayerless, godless, graceless and faithless. This is a sure way to go to hell.
>
> Another way to go to hell is by taking up some kind of useless religion. You can live and die contenting yourself with a false christianity and rest on a groundless hope. This is probably the most common way to hell that there is today. There are many ways to hell, but only one way to heaven.
>
> A religion is useless in which Jesus Christ is not the principle object. Most people today know nothing about Christ. Their religion is a few vague notions and empty expressions. They say, 'I am no worse than others. I go to church when it is convenient. I really don't do anybody any harm. I hope God will be merciful to me.' But He won't! God shows no mercy apart from his Son.

Let us each one make our calling and election sure. Baptism, Church membership, religious ceremony, doctrinal orthodoxy, and deep religious emotions are not synonyms for Christianity! They are just leaves, nothing but leaves. They will no more cover the nakedness of our souls from God's all-seeing eye in the day of judgment than Adam's fig leaves covered his nakedness in the garden. Christianity is faith in Christ alone!

"Examine yourselves, whether ye be in the faith; prove your own selves. Know ye not your own selves, how that Jesus Christ is in you, except ye be reprobates?" (2 Corinthians 13:5). If Christ is in you, if Christ is in me, if he is dwelling in us by his Holy Spirit, if he is the life that is in us, he brings forth fruit, even the fruit of the Spirit in us (Galatians 5:22, 23).

I would rather stand before God in the day of judgment guilty of any crime known to man than stand before that bar of his august majesty guilty of self-righteousness and hypocrisy! If you die without Christ, your religion will sink your soul into the lowest hell! Your religion will be your greatest curse! The Son of God has pronounced his curse upon the barren fig tree and barren, fig-leaf religion!

The House Of God
Here is the third thing taught in this passage. When we come to the house of God, we ought to behave as people who have come to the house of God.

"And they come to Jerusalem: and Jesus went into the temple, and began to cast out them that sold and bought in the temple, and overthrew the tables of the moneychangers, and the seats of them that sold doves; And would not suffer that any man should carry any vessel through the temple. And he taught, saying unto them, Is it not written, My house shall be called of all nations the house of prayer? but ye have made it a den of thieves. And the scribes and chief priests heard it, and sought how they might destroy him: for they feared him, because all the people was astonished at his doctrine. And when even was come, he went out of the city" (vv. 15-19).

The temple in Jerusalem was typical and representative of the Church, which really is the house of God (1 Timothy 3:15). When the Bible speaks of the Church and House of God, it is talking about the assembled body of believers, gathered in one place for public worship. When we come together in the name of Christ, the Son of God meets with us (Matthew 18:20), the Spirit of God dwells within us, and we are the Temple of God (1 Corinthians 3:16).

Let us attach no idolatrous superstition to any building or material place. The building in which we meet is not the church. The church just meets there. The auditorium is not a holy sanctuary. It is just a room in which the holy

Word of God is preached. The pulpit is not a holy desk. It is just a pulpit in which a faithful man stands to preach the holy Word.

The lessons taught in this passage of scripture, with regard to the church, the temple, the house of the living God, are obvious. The church is God's house. It does not belong to you and me. It is not our church. It belongs to Christ. It is his church. That means that Christ alone makes the rules, enforces the rules, and exercises rule. The only Ruler in Zion is the Son of God. His Word is our only creed. His revealed will is our rule of life. His glory is our guiding principle.

The function and business of the house of God is prayer, the worship of God our Saviour in songs of praise and the preaching of the gospel. It is utterly abhorrent that anyone should make the house of God a place of trade, commerce, and entertainment. When we come into the church, the house, the temple of the living God, we should always behave ourselves reverently (Ecclesiastes 5:1, 2; James 1:19-22).

Everything we say and do, when we come to worship God, ought to reflect reverence for our great God and Saviour. We certainly ought never to be less precise, punctual, and reverent than Aaron and his sons were required to be. When they came to the house of God, they paid real close attention to things. It is nothing less than a lack of reverence for God that causes people to rush into the house of God at the last minute, or even worse, late! It is nothing less than a lack of reverence for God that causes people to come into God's house with a flippant attitude, ignoring the solemnity of such a privilege and responsibility! It is nothing less than a lack of reverence for God that causes people to come to the house of God dressed like they were going to the beach or a ball game!

David Pledger rightly observed:

> Even our dress should and will be governed by our thoughts about God. I know that God looks on the heart and we surely do not think to impress him by our dress, but we will show respect. A worship service is not to be like a sporting event. We do not have rules, and we never want to say anything that would keep one from coming to hear the gospel. Yet, I'm of the old school and believe that we should wear modest and appropriate attire, and I prefer that women wear dresses. We live in a time when everyone wants to be casual, but there is nothing casual about the worship of God Almighty. I would not wear blue jeans to a friend's funeral if I had something better. Out of respect for my friend I would wear my best, and why would I show less respect when

coming to worship the living God? May God help us to always dress in a way that honours God wearing the type of attire that shows our love and respect for our great God and Saviour Jesus Christ.

Let us ever be aware of the fact that the Son of God takes notice of the things that go on in his house. Profanity, irreverence, and indifference are an affront to him. Let us take heed, when we come to God's house, that we do not offer the sacrifice of fools. When we start getting ready to go to church, let us try to remember whose house it is and why we are going there. Beware of empty religious formality! When you come to God's house, bring your heart with you. Don't leave it in the world. Leave your business, your money, your politics and carnal levity at home. "Let us beware", Ryle cautioned, "of allowing any buying and selling in our hearts, in the midst of our religious assemblies. The Lord still lives who cast out buyers and sellers from the temple, and when He sees such conduct He is much displeased".

"And in the morning, as they passed by, they saw the fig tree dried up from the roots. And Peter calling to remembrance saith unto him, Master, behold, the fig tree which thou cursedst is withered away. And Jesus answering saith unto them, Have faith in God. For verily I say unto you, That whosoever shall say unto this mountain, Be thou removed, and be thou cast into the sea; and shall not doubt in his heart, but shall believe that those things which he saith shall come to pass; he shall have whatsoever he saith. Therefore I say unto you, What things soever ye desire, when ye pray, believe that ye receive them, and ye shall have them. And when ye stand praying, forgive, if ye have ought against any: that your Father also which is in heaven may forgive you your trespasses. But if ye do not forgive, neither will your Father which is in heaven forgive your trespasses".

(Mark 11:20-26)

Chapter 48

"Have Faith In God"

The fig tree the Lord Jesus cursed dried up from its roots. No doubt its roots died as soon as it was cursed; but the disciples did not see until the next morning, as they passed by and saw its tender branches and leaves withered. Let every eternity bound soul be warned. He who smites the earth with the rod of his mouth and caused the fig tree to wither with his word shall slay the wicked with the breath of his lips (Job 4:9; Isaiah 11:4). This fig tree was useless when green and flourishing with life, because it bore no fruit; but, when it was withered, it was used of God to arouse his servant Peter and made opportunity for the Master to give us the important instructions here set before us about faith in God. We should never forget that all things were made by him and for him (Colossians 1:16; Romans 11:36), that all things were made for his glory (Proverbs 16:4), and that he uses all things for the benefit of his elect (Romans 8:28). Here, the Lord Jesus used the useless fig tree to teach us about faith in God. Faith, true faith in God, is that which distinguishes true believers from mere religious hypocrites. May God the Holy Spirit teach us that which our Lord Jesus here taught his disciples, that we may "have faith in God".

Essential Faith
"And Jesus answering saith unto them, Have faith in God. For verily I say unto you, That whosoever shall say unto this mountain, Be thou removed, and be thou cast into the sea; and shall not doubt in his heart, but shall believe that those things which he saith shall come to pass; he shall have whatsoever he saith" (vv. 22, 23).

When the Master said to Peter, "Have faith in God", he was reminding him and us of the lesson of the barren fig tree. Faith in God is essential. Peter appears to have been surprised that the fig tree, which was cursed yesterday, was withered today. But the Lord Jesus here declares that all men shall likewise perish without true faith in God. It is not just faith that is essential. Everyone has faith in something. That which is essential is true faith in the one true and living God, the glorious, triune, eternal, sovereign, holy Lord God who has revealed himself in the person and work of the Lord Jesus Christ through the scriptures.

Believers are people who live by faith in Christ, who is God our Saviour. It is written, three times in holy scripture, "The just shall live by faith" (Romans 1:17; Galatians 3:11; Hebrews 10:38). Faith is more than an isolated act. It is more than a creed, a confession, or a ceremony. Faith is the believer's heart attitude of confidence in the Lord God. This faith in God is the gift of God to chosen, redeemed, called sinners. It is the very root and essence of true Christianity.

Initially, it is trusting Christ alone as our Lord and Saviour (1 Corinthians 1:30). But true faith is something more than trusting Christ to save me. It is trusting Christ to rule me, protect me, provide for me, and do all things needful for me, according to his own infinite wisdom, goodness, and grace for all time and all eternity.

If we would know the true meaning and value of faith, we should often read and meditate upon Hebrews chapter eleven. It was by faith that the elders obtained a good report. "He that cometh to God must believe that he is, and that he is the Rewarder of them that diligently seek him".

Our Lord used a proverbial saying in verse 24 to describe the great power of faith in God. This proverbial statement about removing mountains must be interpreted cautiously and soberly in this day of religious nuts, who have been taught by health, wealth, prosperity hucksters that if you want a million dollars, just trust the Lord for it; and show that you trust him by sending me all your money. Our Lord's statement here is not a blanket promise that God will do anything we take a notion for him to do, as long as we have enough faith, or believe perfectly, without a doubt in our hearts.

What he is telling us is this. True faith in our God enables believers to overcome great obstacles, accomplish great things, and triumph over great difficulties. Do you want to grow in the grace and knowledge of your Lord Jesus Christ? Do you want to be a strong, valiant believer? Do you desire to grow in spiritual maturity? If you do, pray for more faith and jealously guard that faith God has given you. Nurture it with the Bread of Life in the house of God, water it with prayer, and exercise it with consecration to Christ.

We must never imagine that true faith is perfect faith. The fact is no one on this earth has perfect faith. With regard to the salvation of our souls, the smallest measure of faith in Christ, because it is the fruit and gift of God the Holy Spirit, proves our saving union with Christ. A drop of water in the morning dew is as truly water as all the rivers of the world. It is the same in nature and in quality, though not in quantity. The same thing is true regarding faith. I say that specifically for the comfort and encouragement of God's saints who are weak in faith and continually cry to him to increase their faith (Luke 17:5).

To those poor souls who are cast down because of the weakness of their faith, the Spirit of God declares, "Unto you it is given in the behalf of Christ, not only to believe on him, but also to suffer for his sake" (Philippians 1:29). Faith itself is the gift of God; and the measure of faith we are enabled to exercise is the gift of God, according as God deals "to every man the measure of faith" (Romans 12:3). Wherever this grace of faith in Christ is given, it proves the possessor of it to be a heaven born soul, elect of God, for only those who were ordained to eternal life believe (Acts 13:48).

Robert Hawker rightly observed:

> As to the act of being justified by faith, it is plain from the whole tenor of scripture that while it is blessed to have strong and lively acting of faith on the person, work, and righteousness of God our Saviour, yet the babe in Christ, as well as the strong man in the Lord, is as truly justified, because it is Christ which justifieth, and not the strength of our faith in Christ which contributes thereto. By him, (saith Paul) that is, by Christ, all that believe, whether slender faith or strong faith, all that believe, are justified from all things (Acts 13:39).

Our Lord's word to his disciples in verse 23 is sweet and precious. Faith in God, trusting the rich mercies of God in Christ, will remove all sin and all difficulties. He compares our sins and all the obstacles and difficulties in this world arising from sin to a mountain. He perhaps pointed to the Mount of Olives and said, "Whosoever shall say unto this mountain, Be thou removed, and be thou cast into the sea; and shall not doubt in his heart, but shall believe that those things which he saith shall come to pass; he shall have whatsoever he saith". By faith in Christ, we cast the mountains of our sins into the sea of God's forgetfulness, where God has cast them. As soon as we trust him, they are gone. And, as soon as we take any mountain of trouble in the hand of faith and lay it upon the broad shoulders of God our Saviour who cares for us, the troublesome weight of care is gone. With the faith he gives, as with God who gives it, nothing shall be impossible (Matthew 17:20; Luke 1:37). Blessed are they who rest the whole weight of all things upon their faithful, covenant God and Father, who walk by faith and not by sight. "He that believeth shall not make haste" (Isaiah 28:16).

Praying Faith
"Therefore I say unto you, What things soever ye desire, when ye pray, believe that ye receive them, and ye shall have them" (v. 24). Here our

Saviour teaches us that faith, true faith, inspires earnest prayer. Prayer is not, as many ignorantly presume, a blank cheque waiting for you to fill in the amount you want. Prayer is a spiritual exercise, involving spiritual matters. I do not mean that prayer has nothing to do with carnal things. It has everything to do with the believer's carnal things. But to the believer, his carnal things are spiritual matters turned over to the Master. So when our Lord here tells us that when we pray in faith, we have whatever it is that we desire, he is simply re-enforcing what he taught in the model prayer, by which he taught us to pray (Matthew 6:9-13).

I do not pretend to know much about prayer; but I do know that the things our Saviour taught us to pray for in Matthew 6 are the things for which we commonly pray. In all our petitions before God, these are, essentially, the things we truly want, the desires of our hearts. And, if these are the things we really want from God, when we pray, we shall have whatsoever we desire.

We want the honour of God's name "Our Father which art in heaven, Hallowed be thy name." We desire the establishment of God's kingdom, i.e. the salvation of his elect, "Thy kingdom come." We want the will of God our Father. "Thy will be done in earth, as it is in heaven". We trust our God to supply the daily provision for our needs. "Give us this day our daily bread." We desire God's forgiveness of our sins. "And forgive us our debts, as we forgive our debtors." We want our God to protect us from temptation, sin and Satan. "And lead us not into temptation, but deliver us from evil." We seek grace from our God to personally give praise, honour, and glory to him. "For thine is the kingdom, and the power, and the glory, for ever. Amen."

Are these the things that concern your soul? Are these the matters dearest to your heart? Are these things you ardently crave from God? "Believe that ye receive them, and ye shall have them". They are as sure as if you already possessed them, for it is written, "The desire of the righteous shall be satisfied" (Proverbs 10:24).

Forgiving Faith
"And when ye stand praying, forgive, if ye have ought against any: that your Father also which is in heaven may forgive you your trespasses. But if ye do not forgive, neither will your Father which is in heaven forgive your trespasses" (vv. 25, 26).

That faith which is wrought of God in the hearts of sinners, that faith in Christ by which we obtain the forgiveness of sins is a forgiving faith. The connecting link between the necessity of faith and the spirit of forgiveness is prayer. First our Lord taught us that faith is essential to both life and prayer. Here, he teaches us that we do not have true faith and cannot truly pray, if we have not been given a forgiving spirit from God the Holy Spirit.

382

Worship and prayer are works of the heart. Commonly, when we think of prayer, we think of kneeling. Here our Lord speaks of standing to pray. This is not accidental. When we worship God, in public or in private, our physical position and posture is totally insignificant. The only thing required in this regard is that we do nothing to call attention to ourselves, that we make no pretentious show of piety or humility. The standing that matters is standing before God, presenting ourselves to our God in prayer.

The one thing that does matter in all aspects of worship and prayer, the one fruit of grace and faith, without which we cannot worship or pray, is that brotherly love which is manifest in a spirit of forgiveness. Our Lord, of course, is not telling us that we win God's forgiveness by forgiving one another. But he is telling us that if we have not learned to forgive one another, we have not yet experienced or known God's forgiveness.

It is not enough that our prayers be earnest, fervent, and sincere. It is not enough that we pray in Christ's name. Our prayers must have one more ingredient, or they are worthless. They must rise to the throne of God from a forgiving heart.

We do not seek mercy, if we refuse to extend mercy. We cannot seek forgiveness from God if we do not forgive one another. We must have the heart of a brother if we call God our Father and Christ our Brother. We only flatter ourselves with a delusion if we think we have the Spirit of adoption, but harbour ill feelings, cherish resentment, and deny forgiveness to one another.

What a heart-searching matter this is. Not all are gifted to sing, preach, or even speak a word for Christ. But all who truly know what forgiveness is forgive the offences of others. Our Saviour went to great lengths to teach us this repeatedly. May he give us grace to lay it to heart.

The nearest approach we can make to being like Christ in this world is to bear injuries, forbear offences, and forgive one another. God's free forgiveness of our sins is our highest privilege and greatest joy, and our only title to heaven and eternal life in the world to come. Let us, therefore, be merciful, kind, tender-hearted, and forgiving in the few days we have in this world, where forgiveness is needed. God's saints will need no one's forgiveness in heaven; but we all need much forgiveness here. "Be ye kind one to another, tenderhearted, forgiving one another, even as God for Christ's sake hath forgiven you. Be ye therefore followers of God, as dear children; And walk in love, as Christ also hath loved us, and hath given himself for us an offering and a sacrifice to God for a sweetsmelling savour" (Ephesians 4:32-5:2).

"And they come again to Jerusalem: and as he was walking in the temple, there come to him the chief priests, and the scribes, and the elders, And say unto him, By what authority doest thou these things? and who gave thee this authority to do these things? And Jesus answered and said unto them, I will also ask of you one question, and answer me, and I will tell you by what authority I do these things. The baptism of John, was it from heaven, or of men? answer me. And they reasoned with themselves, saying, If we shall say, From heaven; he will say, Why then did ye not believe him? But if we shall say, Of men; they feared the people: for all men counted John, that he was a prophet indeed. And they answered and said unto Jesus, We cannot tell. And Jesus answering saith unto them, Neither do I tell you by what authority I do these things".

(Mark 11:27-33)

Chapter 49

Three Spiritual Evils

In this passage of scripture we see our Lord Jesus Christ walking in the temple with his disciples, teaching and preaching the gospel. As he walked back and forth through the house of God, a multitude gathered around and listened intently to his every word.

The event recorded here took place the day after our Lord cursed the barren fig tree and drove the money changers from the temple, two days after his entrance into Jerusalem. In the crowd listening to our Saviour's doctrine were those chief priests, scribes, and elders who were determined to destroy the Master, his doctrine and his people.

Once more, they thought they had a perfect opportunity to discredit him. The Lord Jesus had come into Jerusalem accepting the praises of men as the Messiah, the Christ of God. He entered the house of God, drove out the money-changers, and set things in order as the Master of the house. On top of all that, he called the house of God his house. Thus declaring himself to be God! As he taught the gospel of God in the house of God, contrary to the accepted traditions and customs of the Jews, these great, respected, scholarly infidels, who were the religious leaders of the Jewish world, asked the Lord Jesus the source of his authority.

When the religious, spiritual leaders of a church, denomination, nation, or age do not know God, when spiritual leaders are really infidels, those who blindly follow their blind guides do so to the eternal peril of their souls, and to the eternal peril of all who are under their influence. Three spiritual evils stand out in these verses as glaring beacons to warn us.

The Evil Of Spiritual Ignorance
You may think, "Pastor, how can you say that spiritual ignorance is an evil? Can a person be faulted for his ignorance in the things of God?" Yes, a person can and should be, indeed shall be, held accountable by God for that which he could have known and should have known had he simply walked in the light God gave him. Do you understand the implications of what I have just stated? Not only will God Almighty hold people accountable at the day of judgment for everything they have heard and despised concerning the gospel of his dear Son, he will hold them accountable for everything they could have heard had they chosen to do so!

Any man who speaks to, teaches, leads and preaches to others in the name of God must have a firm, well grounded, God given assurance concerning the things of God. Leading and instructing eternity bound men and women in the name of God puts a man under a tremendous weight of responsibility. Knowing what I do of God's character, his Word, and the seriousness of this business, I would not dare speak or write another word, or continue another day in the work of the ministry, if I were not absolutely confident of both the call of God and the message God has sent me to declare.

I say to any man, old or young, who is just chomping at the bit to be a preacher, before you assume this work, "Be certain that you know God and the gospel of his grace. Be certain that God has called you and sent you to the work. Be certain that you have a message from God. Be certain that you faithfully perform the work and faithfully proclaim God's message". Pastors, teachers, missionaries and religious leaders stand as watchmen over the souls under their care. That makes them responsible before God for those they teach (Ezekiel 3:17-21; 33:1-16).

You may be thinking, "What does all that have to do with Mark 11:27-33? These chief priests, scribes, and elders stand before us as glaring examples of the fact that those who hold highest place in the religious world are often totally ignorant of the things of God. These men were not peons. They were the most highly trained, specialized religious scholars, selected from an elite group of elite men.

They were not just priests; they were the chief priests. They were not just teachers; they were the scribes. They were not just elders; they were *the* elders. They were regarded by the religious world of their day as the very source and fountain of all spiritual knowledge. They were, for the most part, direct descendants of Aaron; and they could prove it. Their doctrine had the full weight and force of mainstream, historic Jewish tradition; and they could prove it. But these great, highly respected, well-trained religious leaders did not know God from a box of rocks!

Spiritually, they were blind. They had memorized, categorized and compartmentalized the scriptures; but they had absolutely no understanding of the message of God's word. They could tell you everything you could want to know about God and his Son, the Christ, the Messiah, but one thing. They could not tell you who he is! They did not see him standing in their midst! All true, saving, spiritual knowledge comes by divine revelation. I wonder if we will ever learn this. In spiritual matters nothing matters except spiritual matters. Worldly praise, academic scholarship, historic approval, celebrated fame, religious order and tradition are all meaningless. We know nothing until God, by his Spirit, causes the light of the glory of God in the face of Jesus Christ to shine in our hearts. Christ must be revealed in us!

Once that happens, once Christ is revealed in a person, he is unceasingly taught of God and convinced of three things. These three things are the most important truths we ever consider. They are indescribably deep. We can never fully learn them. Yet, if we are taught of God, we will never cease to learn them, as long as we live in this world. When God the Holy Spirit comes upon a sinner in the mighty, saving operations of his grace, he convinces the chosen, redeemed sinner of sin, of righteousness, and of judgment (John 16:8-11; Romans 8:1-4; 10:4; 2 Corinthians 5:21).

Every person taught of God is convinced of sin, his own sin and the sin of his fallen, depraved race. Those who are born of God are convinced of righteousness accomplished, given to and bestowed upon sinners by the obedience of the Lord Jesus Christ as the sinner's Substitute. All who are saved by the grace of God are convinced that there is no possibility of judgment, or condemnation for those for whom Christ died. Any preacher or religious teacher who is not convinced of these things does not know God, and must not be heard.

As you care for your soul and for the souls of your families and all who may be influenced by you, try the spirits to see whether they be of God (1 John 4:1-3). Spiritual ignorance, ignorance of Christ and his gospel, among preachers, teachers, and religious leaders is an inexcusable evil, by which multitudes are being led to hell. When blind men are led by blind men, both fall into the ditch.

The Evil Of Spiritual Arrogance
Here is a group of men, pretending that they are doing God's service, daring to challenge the incarnate God himself about his authority, moved by nothing but envy, jealousy, arrogance and pride. They were not even slightly motivated by the glory of God. Their only concern was their own position and power! They said, "By what authority doest thou these things?"

They could not refute his doctrine. They could not make any charge of wickedness stick to him. They could not deny the power of God displayed in his works. The only thing left was to challenge his right to do the things he did in the name of God. They were asking, "By what authority do you preach? Who ordained you? What right do you have to curse a fig tree, created by God? How dare you come into the house of God and set things in order, without consulting us?"

Nothing makes a lost religious man more arrogant, insecure, envious, and malicious than the sight of another man doing the will of God, preaching the truth of God he refuses to preach, Consecrated to the glory of God, while he is consecrated to nothing but himself, secure in the place God has put him and in doing the work God has given him, while he knows nothing but insecurity. When he sees God's servant at rest in the will of God, when he cannot find a moment's rest in his soul, his envy turns to arrogance; and arrogance is always malicious (Psalms 10:2; 73:6; 119:69, 78, 85; 140:5; Proverbs 8:13; 13:10; 28:25).

It is spiritual arrogance, especially among religious leaders, which keeps men from bowing to the truth of God, when plainly confronted with it; and the embarrassment of having that wickedness exposed in their own hearts makes those, who appear to be sugary sweet into raging persecutors. It was the spiritual arrogance of these men that dragged them down to hell.

Everyone acknowledged that John the Baptist was a prophet of God; but these fine men were not about to sit at the feet of such an unacceptable teacher. He had no theological training and no religious credentials. John the Baptist did not appear to be a learned man, and certainly did not look or act like the priests, scribes and Pharisees. All he had was the truth of God, the power of God and the presence of God!

Because they would not hear God's servant, they could not believe God's Son. The Lord Jesus declared and displayed in undeniable ways that he is the Christ, the Messiah. He both claimed to be and proved himself to be God. But they refused to believe him. Because they refused to hear God's messenger and refused to believe God's Son, they despised God's ordinance, believer's baptism, refusing to confess that righteousness comes only by the obedience of Christ unto death, which believer's baptism symbolizes (Matthew 3:15).

The Evil Of Spiritual Dishonesty
Spiritual ignorance always leads to spiritual arrogance; and spiritual ignorance and arrogance always produce religious or spiritual dishonesty. Those who are, by their wilful unbelief, prejudiced against the truth of God, in the attempt to justify themselves will, without hesitation, lie and act in dishonesty to their own consciences. Like these chief priests, scribes and elders, they will display this dishonest behaviour in the name of honouring God and in the house of God. There is nothing dishonest men will not do to save face before men. Our Lord did not ask these men a hard, perplexing question. He just asked them whether John's ministry was of God or of men.

"And Jesus answered and said unto them, I will also ask of you one question, and answer me, and I will tell you by what authority I do these things. The baptism of John, was it from heaven, or of men? answer me" (vv. 29-30). These men did not even think about giving a plain, honest, straight-forward answer. Immediately, they put their heads together, not to find out the truth, but to figure out how to save face (vv. 31-33).

Rather than speak the truth, they told a direct and obvious lie. They said, "We cannot tell". Multitudes today behave exactly like these men. Rather than simply bowing to Christ, they lie to themselves, lie to those who minister to their souls, and lie to God. They attempt to justify themselves in their unbelief and soothe their consciences by saying, "I want to believe, but I just cannot understand the doctrines of the gospel". Who cannot understand satisfaction and substitution? They say, "I am really trying to believe, but I just can't". Who cannot fall, if he is willing to fall? They say, "I really want to be a Christian and serve the Lord, but not right now". The simple fact is, they are lying. When a person says, "I cannot believe on Christ", the real truth is he will not believe. That is exactly what God the Holy Spirit teaches throughout the Book of God.

Man's real problem is that he loves darkness rather than light (John 3:19), and has no desire to change. Therefore, he refuses to come to the Light. If they were willing to live up to the light God has already given them, if they were willing to act upon the knowledge they already have, they would soon know the doctrine of Christ, come to Christ, and walk in the light with Christ (John 7:17). Man's problem is that he is so full of hatred toward God that he would rather call God a liar (1 John 5:10) and go to hell than admit that he is himself a liar. Yes, I am fully aware that no man has the ability to trust Christ, and faith in Christ is the gift of God. No lost, ruined, helpless sinner can believe on the Lord Jesus Christ, except he be born again. But unbelief is not man's misfortune; it is his fault and his sin (Proverbs 1:23-33; 29:1). In John 6:37-45, when our Lord reproved the unbelief of men, he laid the blame squarely at the feet of those who "believe not", while at the same time declaring that none can believe on him except God give them faith.

"All that the Father giveth me shall come to me; and him that cometh to me I will in no wise cast out. For I came down from heaven, not to do mine own will, but the will of him that sent me. And this is the Father's will which hath sent me, that of all which he hath given me I should lose nothing, but should raise it up again at the last day. And this is the will of him that sent me, that every one which seeth the Son, and believeth on him, may have everlasting life: and I will raise him up at the last day ... No man can come to me, except the Father which hath sent me draw him: and I will raise him up at the last day. It is written in the prophets, And they shall be all taught of God. Every man therefore that hath heard, and hath learned of the Father, cometh unto me".

With these wonderful, instructive words, the Lord Jesus Christ teaches four things, four great gospel truths that need to be proclaimed everywhere: No one can come to him. Anyone may come to him. There are some who must and shall come to him. All who come to him have everlasting life.

"And he began to speak unto them by parables. A certain man planted a vineyard, and set an hedge about it, and digged a place for the winefat, and built a tower, and let it out to husbandmen, and went into a far country. And at the season he sent to the husbandmen a servant, that he might receive from the husbandmen of the fruit of the vineyard. And they caught him, and beat him, and sent him away empty. And again he sent unto them another servant; and at him they cast stones, and wounded him in the head, and sent him away shamefully handled. And again he sent another; and him they killed, and many others; beating some, and killing some. Having yet therefore one son, his wellbeloved, he sent him also last unto them, saying, They will reverence my son. But those husbandmen said among themselves, This is the heir; come, let us kill him, and the inheritance shall be ours. And they took him, and killed him, and cast him out of the vineyard. What shall therefore the lord of the vineyard do? he will come and destroy the husbandmen, and will give the vineyard unto others. And have ye not read this scripture; The stone which the builders rejected is become the head of the corner: This was the Lord's doing, and it is marvellous in our eyes? And they sought to lay hold on him, but feared the people: for they knew that he had spoken the parable against them: and they left him, and went their way".

(Mark 12:1-12)

390

Chapter 50

"This Was The Lord's Doing, And It Is Marvellous In Our Eyes"

This is clearly an historical parable. We are told in verse twelve that the chief priests, scribes and elders of the Jews "knew that the Lord Jesus had spoken the parable against them".

The history of the Jewish nation, from the time that the Lord brought them out of Egypt until the time of their destruction in 70 AD, is set before us in these twelve verses. Under the emblem of a vineyard and husbandmen (vinedressers), our Master tells us the story of God's dealings with that nation, both in great mercy and in great judgment.

This parable is recorded here in the Book of God to stand as a beacon to warn us lest we, who have received and experienced far greater mercies than the Jews ever did, should also at last be dashed in pieces upon the rocks of God's righteous retribution and judgment.

A National Warning

The things I am about to write may appear to many to be out of place in a commentary; but it is my purpose ever to apply the scriptures as personally as possible to those who hear my voice or read what I write. Therefore, I make no apology for writing as I do. Rather, I urge you to read the following with great care.

Without question, there is a warning for us as a nation in this parable. The United States of America is a nation which has been blessed of God, perhaps unlike any other, with great providential mercies. We have enjoyed prosperity as no other nation in the world. We have lived in the lap of luxury, freedom and safety. There has never been a nation more blessed than ours has been historically with the gospel. God has sent prophet after prophet, generation after generation, through the length and breadth of this land. Israel had peculiar privileges indeed; but their providential blessings were nothing compared to ours.

But, like Israel of old, throughout our history we have provoked the Lord to jealousy. It seems to me, both as I read history and from the experience of my own brief lifetime, that the more greatly and signally the Lord has showered his mercies upon us, the more blatantly we have turned from him.

Truly, we must acknowledge as did the psalmist, "He hath not dealt with us after our sins; nor rewarded us according to our iniquities". Like the Jews of old, we have mocked the messengers of God, despised his words and misused his prophets (2 Chronicles 36:16).

I am astonished that God has not destroyed our nation before now. Our streets run red with blood, blood shed by unrestrained, undisciplined children. This generation of children and young people has educated barbarians for parents. Parents these days are more like brute beasts and crawling reptiles that lay their eggs, bury them in the sands of the world and forget them. Parents who refuse to train and discipline their children, who refuse to mould their characters for good, are nothing more than breeding beasts. My apologies to the beasts!

Indeed, it is customary these days for men and women, boys and girls simply to breed like dogs, first with one and then another. Common adultery has brought about an utter disregard for marriage, law and order. Fornication is smiled at as a light thing. It is as common for girls to have babies out of wedlock as it is for dogs to scratch fleas. Homosexuality is not only tolerated, it is accepted, taught and shamelessly promoted in the classrooms of our schools!

As it has been throughout history when nations have abandoned God for their lusts, abandoned his way for pleasure, abandoned law and order in the name of freedom, human life has become so cheap in our society that abortion is more common than getting your teeth cleaned. Unborn infants are regarded as unwanted fat to be sucked away as desired. A man may easily get a longer prison sentence for killing your dog than for raping your wife or killing you!

It is astounding to me that God has not swept us away into oblivion. Yet, the fact that he has not yet destroyed us gives me hope. Maybe our great, gracious and glorious God will once more in wrath remember mercy! Maybe he yet has in store for our land such a great spiritual deliverance out of Babylon as he granted to the Jewish nation from their physical Babylonian captivity! Maybe!

A Greater Evil
Having said all that, as horrible as things are on the streets of our cities, in the classrooms of our schools, and among our political leaders, bad as the social fabric of our land is, there is a worse problem. Indeed, this worse problem is the root cause of the other problems we have to deal with everyday. The problem I speak of is this: The churches, preachers, teachers and spiritual

leaders of our land, those who profess to be God's servants, those who are responsible to teach us God's Word and God's ways, have long since abandoned the Word and truth of God. If you will read the first chapter of Romans, you will see that the moral decline of any people begins with spiritual decline, idolatry and apostasy from the Revelation of God in holy scripture.

This parable of the vineyard certainly speaks historically of the nation of Israel. It is, without question, a warning to us as a nation and a warning to other nations like ours in this apostate age who are reaping the consequences of forsaking God and his Word. But it is primarily a warning to local churches, a warning to those who are now so greatly blessed in these dark, dark days with the privilege of sitting in the house of God, under the ministry of faithful gospel preaching. This is what God the Holy Spirit intends for us to learn from this parable: "Be not highminded, but fear: For if God spared not the natural branches, take heed lest he also spare not thee" (Romans 11:20, 21). There are seven important lessons in this parable.

God's church in this world is his vineyard. "And he began to speak unto them by parables. A certain man planted a vineyard, and set an hedge about it, and digged a place for the winefat, and built a tower, and let it out to husbandmen, and went into a far country" (v. 1). There certainly are applications of this parable to be made to the church universal; but it speaks principally of the church local, local assemblies of men and women who profess to be followers of Christ and his gospel. Every true gospel church is a vineyard of God's planting. The local church is God's vineyard. It belongs to the Lord. He separated a piece of ground (a place) for it. He planted it. He has hedged it about. And the local church, the place where you gather with God's elect, worship the Lord Jesus Christ, hear the gospel of his grace, and have Christ revealed to you through his Word, is the greatest blessing you have in this world.

The Lord God has let out this vineyard to us as his husbandmen (v. 1). There is no greater privilege in this world and no greater responsibility under heaven than this: The Lord God has given us the treasure of the gospel, trusting to our hands the message of his grace, that we might be in this age "the pillar and ground of the truth", holding forth the light of the gospel in a world of darkness (1 Timothy 3:15, 16).

At the appointed season, the Lord God looks for and rightfully expects to find fruit from the husbandmen of his vineyard. "And at the season he sent to the husbandmen a servant, that he might receive from the husbandmen of the fruit of the vineyard"(v. 2). The rent he requires of us is very reasonable. All he demands from us is that we reverence his Son (v. 6). God simply requires that we worship his Son. That worship is more than attending worship services two or three times a week. The worship of Christ involves faith in him and faithfulness to him as stewards in his house (1 Corinthians 4:1, 2; 2 Corinthians 4:1-7).

In verses 2 to 8 our Saviour teaches us that as men and women deal with, and treat God's faithful servants, so they deal with and treat God's Son.

"And at the season he sent to the husbandmen a servant, that he might receive from the husbandmen of the fruit of the vineyard. And they caught him, and beat him, and sent him away empty. And again he sent unto them another servant; and at him they cast stones, and wounded him in the head, and sent him away shamefully handled. And again he sent another; and him they killed, and many others; beating some, and killing some. Having yet therefore one son, his wellbeloved, he sent him also last unto them, saying, They will reverence my son. But those husbandmen said among themselves, This is the heir; come, let us kill him, and the inheritance shall be ours. And they took him, and killed him, and cast him out of the vineyard".

Lost religious men and women love religion, religious duties, religious activity, religious ceremonies, religious history and religious tradition, but utterly despise God, his Son, and his gospel, and would (if they could) cast God's Son off his throne, out of his Kingdom, and kill him. "But those husbandmen said among themselves, This is the heir; come, let us kill him, and the inheritance shall be ours ... And they sought to lay hold on him, but feared the people: for they knew that he had spoken the parable against them: and they left him, and went their way" (v. 7, 12). The reason preachers, teachers, churches and religious leaders despise and cast Christ and his Word out is obvious. They want the vineyard for themselves. The Pharisees did what they did during our Lord's earthly ministry, and at last crucified the Son of God for only one reason. They wanted to preserve their position of power and influence over the people (John 11:47-54). That is the reason, the only reason, preachers and religious leaders like Diotrephes despise Christ, his gospel and his servants in every age (3 John 9; Psalm 2:1-12).

If we despise the privileges and opportunities God has given us, he will both take away those great privileges and make those things which might have been the means of our everlasting salvation and make them the very basis of our everlasting ruin. "What shall therefore the lord of the vineyard do? He will come and destroy the husbandmen, and will give the vineyard unto others. And have ye not read this scripture; The stone which the builders rejected is become the head of the corner" (vv. 9, 10). Present privileges are no guarantee of future privileges. The Lord Jesus warns us that he will remove the candlestick that is despised (Revelation 2:5). If the preaching of the gospel is not a savour of life unto you, it will be to you a savour of death (2 Corinthians 2:14-16).

God's purpose is not hindered. "And have ye not read this scripture; The stone which the builders rejected is become the head of the corner: This was the Lord's doing, and it is marvellous in our eyes?" (vv. 10, 11). Though many do despise God's grace and thus heap destruction upon themselves, when he takes the gospel from one people, he gives it to another and the purpose of God is not thwarted or even hindered. Christ is still exalted and his people shall be saved (Romans 3:3; 11:26, 33-36).

"Give ear, O Shepherd of Israel, thou that leadest Joseph like a flock; thou that dwellest between the cherubims, shine forth. Before Ephraim and Benjamin and Manasseh stir up thy strength, and come and save us. Turn us again, O God, and cause thy face to shine; and we shall be saved. O LORD God of hosts, how long wilt thou be angry against the prayer of thy people? Thou feedest them with the bread of tears; and givest them tears to drink in great measure. Thou makest us a strife unto our neighbours: and our enemies laugh among themselves. Turn us again, O God of hosts, and cause thy face to shine; and we shall be saved. Thou hast brought a vine out of Egypt: thou hast cast out the heathen, and planted it. Thou preparedst room before it, and didst cause it to take deep root, and it filled the land. The hills were covered with the shadow of it, and the boughs thereof were like the goodly cedars. She sent out her boughs unto the sea, and her branches unto the river. Why hast thou then broken down her hedges, so that all they which pass by the way do pluck her? The boar out of the wood doth waste it, and the wild beast of the field doth devour it. Return, we beseech thee, O God of hosts: look down from heaven, and behold, and visit this vine; And the vineyard which thy right hand hath planted, and the branch that thou madest strong for thyself. It is burned with fire, it is cut down: they perish at the rebuke of thy countenance. Let thy hand be upon the man of thy right hand, upon the son of man whom thou madest strong for thyself. So will not we go back from thee: quicken us, and we will call upon thy name. Turn us again, O LORD God of hosts, cause thy face to shine; and we shall be saved" (Psalm 80:1-19).

"And they send unto him certain of the Pharisees and of the Herodians, to catch him in his words. And when they were come, they say unto him, Master, we know that thou art true, and carest for no man: for thou regardest not the person of men, but teachest the way of God in truth: Is it lawful to give tribute to Caesar, or not? Shall we give, or shall we not give? But he, knowing their hypocrisy, said unto them, Why tempt ye me? bring me a penny, that I may see it. And they brought it. And he saith unto them, Whose is this image and superscription? And they said unto him, Caesar's. And Jesus answering said unto them, Render to Caesar the things that are Caesar's, and to God the things that are God's. And they marvelled at him".

(Mark 12:13-17)

Chapter 51

"Knowing Their Hypocrisy"

Our Saviour declared, in Psalm 35:16, "With hypocritical mockers in feasts, they gnashed upon me with their teeth". Here we see those prophetic words fulfilled. The scriptures declare that we who follow Christ are and must be crucified unto the world. That man or woman who believes on the Son of God is and must be dead to the world. Henry Mahan once said:

> 'How is the believer dead to the world when he lives in the world, works a regular job, raises a family, and owns property in the world?', a young student asked his Bible teacher. The teacher sent him out to the gravesite of a friend with instructions to criticize the dead friend, harass him, and find fault, and then praise him with glowing terms and brag on him to excess. Upon his return, the teacher asked, 'What did your friend say when you criticized him?' 'Nothing.' 'How did he react when you praised him?' 'It made no difference to him; he is dead!' 'That is what it means to be dead to this world,' said the teacher. Its applause means nothing and its hatred means nothing. We neither admire the people of this world nor do we fear them. The riches of this world are but the fancy of fools, and the honours of this world mean little or nothing; for to be a child of God is the highest calling. The religious traditions and ceremonies of the world have no attraction nor meaning when Christ is all! That which was once important to us we now consider loss for the excellency of the knowledge of Christ, our Lord. This spiritual life in Christ cannot be explained; it must be experienced.

No one so thoroughly and constantly exemplified this deadness to the world as he who came to do the will of God and always did the Father's will perfectly. Our Lord Jesus Christ was dead to both the flatteries and the abuses of the world; and if we would follow him and do his will we must be as well. We see a clear example of the Saviour's deadness to the world in his dealings with the Pharisees and the Herodians in this passage.

Truth From Lying Lips

The very first thing that strikes me, as I read this passage is the fact that God often causes the truth to be spoken from lying lips. In his great sovereignty, our God often causes the enemies of the gospel to proclaim the truth, though they despise it. These hypocritical religious leaders came to our Redeemer for the purpose of laying a snare before him, to catch him in his words. When they did they declared as clearly as any prophet or apostle three great truths about his character, both as God and as the God-man.

In verse 14 they said:

"Thou art true".

"Thou carest for no man: for thou regardest not the person of men".

"Thou teachest the way of God in truth".

In John 11, God the Holy Spirit forced a false prophet, Caiaphas the high priest, to declare the gospel of our Redeemer's substitutionary death in the room of his elect as clearly as the Apostle Paul declared it in 2 Corinthians 5:17-21. Speaking by the Spirit of God, Caiaphas said, "It is expedient for us that one man should die for the people, that the whole nation perish not" (John 11:50, 51).

In fact, in the case of the dying thief (Luke 23:39-43), it appears that the Lord God used the truth spoken by unbelieving men as the means by which he gave faith to the chosen object of his grace. My reason for stating this is to show that the means of grace is not always obvious. We know that "faith cometh by hearing, and hearing by the word of God" (Romans 10:17). We know that sinners are "born-again, not of corruptible seed, but of incorruptible, by the word of God, which liveth and abideth for ever ... And this is the word which by the gospel is preached unto you" (1 Peter 1:23-25). But many point to the dying thief and say, "That man was saved without hearing the gospel". Was he?

No! Let me remind you of the things he heard, as he hung upon the cross. I do not know what he heard, or did not hear beforehand. But as he hung by his dying Saviour, he heard and saw the gospel as clearly as anyone ever could. He heard the crucified Christ hailed as "the King of Israel" (Matthew 27:42). He heard that the man hanging beside him had claimed to be the Son of God. "He said, I am the Son of God" (Matthew 27:43). He heard the chief priests and scribes say, "He saved others; himself he cannot save" (Mark 15:31). He read Pilate's testimony, "This is Jesus of Nazareth, the King of the Jews" (Luke 23:38; John 19:19). And he saw the Lamb of God dying as a Substitute in the place of a guilty man (Barabbas), who was released from death because he died in his place.

Mutual Enemies Unite
The next thing we see in these verses is the fact that lost men and women who are mutual enemies, people who utterly despise one another, will unite in opposition to Christ and his gospel. The Pharisees were religious fundamentalists, superstitious ceremonialists and self-righteous moralists. Religion was their life. They lived to go to church and do religious stuff. The Herodians were mere worldlings. They had absolutely no use for religion. They cared no more for the honour of God (his name, his will, his glory) than for the life of a maggot.

Yet, when the Lord Jesus Christ came preaching the gospel, the Pharisees and the Herodians were united like blood kin in the common cause of opposing him. Both the religious crowd and the worldly crowd despised the gospel of God's free and sovereign grace in Christ, as Christ himself preached it and personified it.

That is the way it has always been. That is the way it is now. And that is the way it will always be, as long as the world stands, until Christ makes all things new. The cross of Christ is an offence to unregenerate men, both religious and irreligious (Galatians 5:11; 1 Corinthians 1:17-24).

All lost men hate God and the gospel of Christ. All despise those things revealed in the gospel. There are no exceptions. God's sovereignty offends man's pride and sense of self-determination. Fallen man desperately wants some credit for the salvation of his soul. Man is repulsed by the Bible doctrine of election because he thinks it is unfair for God to be gracious to whom he will be gracious. The teaching of holy scripture that man is totally depraved offends man's sense of self-worth and his love of his own imaginary righteousness.

The Bible's teaching about Christ's limited atonement, the effectual redemption of God's elect by the death of Christ, enrages men who think God owes sinners salvation, or at the very least, that he owes men a "chance" to be saved. The fact that salvation comes by the revelation of God the Holy Spirit in irresistible grace offends man's love of wisdom. When faced with the plain declaration of the gospel, men who despise one another, always unite in opposition to it.

Bold Hypocrisy
These Pharisees and Herodians stand before us as glaring examples of the brazen boldness of hypocrisy. No one is more confident, bold, or arrogant than the hypocrite. He never openly shows his true colours. In order to cover his hypocrisy he has a bold, brazen, outward pretence of sincerity. Do you see that in verses 13 and 14?

"And they send unto him certain of the Pharisees and of the Herodians, to catch him in his words. And when they were come, they say unto him, Master, we know that thou art true, and carest for no man: for thou regardest not the person of men, but teachest the way of God in truth: Is it lawful to give tribute to Caesar, or not?"

When they could not find anything in his own doctrine or conduct for which to kill him, these proud hypocrites thought they could out-smart the Son of God and trick him into saying something with which to accuse him. They began by flattering him as a man who was true, sincere, faithful and honest, unmoved, unimpressed and uninfluenced by men, and beyond the reach of bribery and intimidation. None are more subtle and deceiving than religious people who hate God.

But the Lord Jesus was much more than a mere man. He was and is the omniscient God before whom all things are naked and open. He knew their hypocrisy and caught them in their own trap.

"And they come to Jerusalem: and Jesus went into the temple, and began to cast out them that sold and bought in the temple, and overthrew the tables of the moneychangers, and the seats of them that sold doves; And would not suffer that any man should carry any vessel through the temple. And he taught, saying unto them, Is it not written, My house shall be called of all nations the house of prayer? but ye have made it a den of thieves" (vv. 15-17).

Political Controversies
There is no greater, more effective snare, by which both God's people and his servants are apt to be ensnared than overmuch concern about the cares and controversies of civil government. As I write this, the United States is in the middle of a presidential election. How sad it is to see so many who are citizens of another world embroiled in heated political controversy.

"Fret not thyself because of evildoers, neither be thou envious against the workers of iniquity. For they shall soon be cut down like the grass, and wither as the green herb. Trust in the LORD, and do good; so shalt thou dwell in the land, and verily thou shalt be fed. Delight thyself also in the LORD; and he shall give thee the desires of thine heart. Commit thy way unto the LORD; trust also in him; and he shall bring it to pass" (Psalm 37:1-5).

Our Lord would not allow himself to be drawn into the trap of political wrangling and worldly strife. We cannot be too careful about these things. We must not allow ourselves to be overly concerned about the things of this world. I do not say that we are to have no concern about civil matters, or that we should not vote in political elections. Not at all. Believers should be the best of citizens; and good citizens act responsibly for the welfare of their nation. But the politics of this world, its pleasures, its treasures and its opinions should be of little concern to those who are crucified to the world.

Yet, faith in Christ and obedience to him is never a justification for any of us neglecting our God given responsibilities in this world. Our Lord Jesus commands us to render unto Caesar the things that are Caesar's and unto God the things that are God's. That simply means that it is the responsibility of all men to both worship God and to be responsible, productive citizens in this world. The fact is, those who truly do worship God are the very best, most responsible, dependable, productive citizens in every generation.

Marvelling Not Believing

Learn this too, marvelling at Christ's doctrine is not believing on the Son of God. Many marvel at Christ and his doctrine who never believe. The last sentence of verse 17 reads, "And they marvelled at him". The same thing often happens today. Frequently, men and women are impressed with a system of doctrine, the abilities of a preacher, a church, or a group of people. They attach themselves to preachers, churches, doctrines and causes, but not to Christ. They marvel for a while, but never come to trust the Son of God.

Salvation is something more than being impressed with and marvelling at Christ. Salvation is knowing him and trusting him. I am not interested in impressing you. I want you to know Christ. Without him, you are without life, without forgiveness, without righteousness, without God, without hope. Why will you perish? Why will you die? Come to Christ and live forever. God help you now to come to him. The Lord Jesus Christ himself bids you come and promises to receive you, save you, and keep you, if you come to him.

"Then come unto him the Sadducees, which say there is no resurrection; and they asked him, saying, Master, Moses wrote unto us, If a man's brother die, and leave his wife behind him, and leave no children, that his brother should take his wife, and raise up seed unto his brother. Now there were seven brethren: and the first took a wife, and dying left no seed. And the second took her, and died, neither left he any seed: and the third likewise. And the seven had her, and left no seed: last of all the woman died also. In the resurrection therefore, when they shall rise, whose wife shall she be of them? for the seven had her to wife. And Jesus answering said unto them, Do ye not therefore err, because ye know not the scriptures, neither the power of God? For when they shall rise from the dead, they neither marry, nor are given in marriage; but are as the angels which are in heaven. And as touching the dead, that they rise: have ye not read in the book of Moses, how in the bush God spake unto him, saying, I am the God of Abraham, and the God of Isaac, and the God of Jacob? He is not the God of the dead, but the God of the living: ye therefore do greatly err".

(Mark 12:18-27)

Chapter 52

"The God Of The Living"

Earlier in the day the Pharisees and Herodians tried to catch him in his words. Here the Sadducees try to do the same thing.

The Sadducees were the smallest, but by far the most wealthy and influential of the Jewish sects. They were the aristocrats of Judaism, and for the most part controlled the priesthood and the temple. Though that was the case, the Sadducees were not commonly respected by the people. They, supposing themselves to be smarter than God, denied the resurrection. They were the most liberal sect of the Jews. They were religious; but their religion was the religion of infidelity. It was their infidelity regarding the resurrection of the dead which made the Sadducees and Pharisees bitter enemies, much like the liberals and the conservatives of any religious denomination today.

When the Lord Jesus came to Jerusalem, exerting his rightful claims and sovereign power as the Son of God, Messiah, he drove the money changers from the temple, and began to disrupt the religious order, demanding that God be worshipped as God in his house. Then the Pharisees and Sadducees, and all the other religious groups, joined forces against him.

"How could this happen?" you might ask. How could religious people with such strong doctrinal and ceremonial differences at once unite in opposition to the Son of God? The answer is obvious. They really believed the same thing essentially. The Pharisees, the Herodians, the Sadducees, the Essenes, the Zealots, and the Scribes all held to the idolatrous, pagan notion that salvation was in some way dependent upon and determined by man's will, works, and worth. Whereas, the Lord Jesus plainly declared that salvation is the work of God's free and sovereign grace alone.

God's church and God's servants today must not expect things to be any different. Those who despise the gospel of God's free and sovereign grace in Christ, though they may be bitter enemies, will unite like beloved brethren to oppose the gospel of Christ. We must always expect and be prepared for the assaults and deceitful slanders of infidels, Arminians and workmongers who wear the badge of Christianity. As the Pharisees, Sadducees and Scribes in this chapter united in their opposition to Christ, the whole religious world unites and speaks as one voice in its opposition to the gospel of Christ today.

As we consider the ludicrous question of the Sadducees and the answer our Master gave them, four things stand out as matters of great importance.

Religious Infidelity
First, these Sadducees stand before us as glaring examples of religious infidelity. The vast majority of people in this world who profess the name of Christianity, including the most powerful and most influential religious leaders of it, are real infidels. Their religion is a matter of convenience, not conviction. It is, for the most part, a religion which holds the Word of God, the truth of God, the gospel of God, the will of God and the glory of God in utter contempt, just like these Sadducees.

These Sadducees laughed at the doctrine of the resurrection. They were the "freethinkers" of their day. They thought themselves too educated, too enlightened to believe such sentiments. The question they posed to the Lord Jesus illustrates their arrogance. "Then come unto him the Sadducees, which say there is no resurrection; and they asked him, saying, Master, Moses wrote unto us, If a man's brother die, and leave his wife behind him, and leave no children, that his brother should take his wife, and raise up seed unto his brother. Now there were seven brethren: and the first took a wife, and dying left no seed. And the second took her, and died, neither left he any seed: and the third likewise. And the seven had her, and left no seed: last of all the woman died also. In the resurrection therefore, when they shall rise, whose wife shall she be of them? for the seven had her to wife" (vv. 18-23).

The Sadducees' pretended to reverence the Lord Jesus, calling him, "Master". They pretended to respect Moses and reverence the Word of God, referring to that which "Moses wrote". And they pretended to have a genuine concern for the teaching of holy scripture, asking the Lord Jesus, if seven brothers were married to the same woman, "In the resurrection whose wife shall she be?"

They presented their question as though it were a factual thing, as though they were really interested in knowing the answer. Any statistician will tell you that you would have a far greater chance of winning the lottery than of this actually happening. The only thing these men were interested in was raising a question, which they were confident the Master could not answer.

We will be wise to mark the things recorded here and learn from them not to allow modern religious infidels to entrap us. When carping religious infidels want to argue with you, just ignore them. Give them plain statements of scripture, and leave them alone. If you get into a hissing contest with a snake, you are going to lose. Such people always try to press difficult and abstruse points of doctrine. They always act dishonestly and they always deserve contempt.

Yet, it is delightful to see that our blessed Saviour causes even the wrath of men to serve his glory and his people (Psalm 76:10). With that as his purpose, he graciously seized the opportunity to the comfort of his elect, both by establishing the doctrine of the resurrection and by declaring that in the resurrection all earthly relationships will be dissolved. In the resurrection body, in immortality, we will have no need of those things that are necessary to sustain our mortal bodies on earth, or to gratify the needs of mortality. And there will be nothing to divide the affections of one from another. We shall be perfectly one in Christ (John 17:22, 23).

Spiritual Ignorance
Second, our Saviour shows us that people may be very religious and very highly educated, as the Sadducees were, and still be completely engulfed in spiritual darkness and ignorance. "And Jesus answering said unto them, Do ye not therefore err, because ye know not the scriptures, neither the power of God?" (v. 24). Those men did not believe in the resurrection of the dead because they did not know the teaching of holy scripture and did not know the power of God.

I do not doubt for a moment that they knew the letter of the scriptures. No doubt, they could quote huge passages of the Bible from memory. I do not doubt that they were very keenly aware of the historic events and chronological order of things recorded in the scriptures. They knew the history of Israel, and even knew what the prophecies of the Old Testament said. But they had absolutely no knowledge of the meaning and message of holy scripture. Their understanding was nothing but the understanding of carnal reason and religious tradition.

Do you understand the message of scripture? The Book of God is all about Christ. The message of the Bible is the gospel of Christ (Luke 24:27, 32, 44, 45; John 5:39; 1 Peter 1:23-25). Spiritual knowledge is not merely doctrinal knowledge, creedal knowledge, logical knowledge, and factual knowledge. Spiritual knowledge is the revealed knowledge of a person, and that Person is the Lord Jesus Christ.

The resurrection is more than a doctrine. It is a person (John 11:25). You cannot know the Person without knowing the doctrine; but you certainly may know the doctrine without knowing the Person. Christ is our resurrection and our life. He is our Resurrection and Life representatively in redemption (Ephesians 2:4-6). He is our Resurrection and our Life experimentally in regeneration (John 5:25; Revelation 20:6; Colossians 3:1-3). And the Lord Jesus Christ is our Resurrection and our Life prospectively in the last day (Colossians 3:4).

The truth of God, the gospel of his grace, is much more than doctrinal, historical facts. Christ himself is the gospel. The gospel is a Person (John 14:6). Without question, this Person is revealed and made known to us and in us in the context of revealed, doctrinal truth. But life and salvation comes by knowing God himself in the person of our all glorious Saviour, the Lord Jesus Christ the Son of God (John 17:3). Salvation is not merely knowing about Christ. Salvation is knowing Christ as my God, my Surety, my Substitute, my King, my Priest, my Prophet and my Saviour!

The Power Of God
Spiritual ignorance, doctrinal error, and heresy of every kind, according to this statement by our Saviour, must be traced to ignorance of the power of God. I take that to mean three things. These three things you will find throughout the scriptures are what is meant by the power of God.

1. Spiritual ignorance arises from and must be traced to an utter ignorance of God's sovereignty, his absolute authority as God.

2. Spiritual ignorance arises from and must be traced to an utter ignorance of God's omnipotence, his absolute, almighty ability to do all his pleasure.

3. Spiritual ignorance arises from and must be traced to an utter ignorance of God's gospel, which is the power of God unto salvation.

The Sadducees did not believe in the resurrection, because they were ignorant of God's sovereignty, his omnipotence and his gospel. All heresy, all spiritual ignorance must be attributed to these things. All false religion, all free will, works religion denies the sovereignty of God's will and purpose in election and predestination. It denies the omnipotence of his power and grace in redemption, regeneration and effectual calling. It denies the gospel's good news of redemption accomplished by the blood of his dear Son. Those who have never *felt* the power of God in the experience of grace cannot *know* the power of God, and are therefore completely ignorant of all the works of God.

The Resurrection Life
"For when they shall rise from the dead, they neither marry, nor are given in marriage; but are as the angels, which are in heaven" (v. 25). There will be a resurrection of the dead. When our Lord Jesus comes again, there will be a resurrection of the just and of the unjust. The scriptures universally declare it (Exodus 3:6; Job 19:25, 26; Psalms 16:9, 10; 49:15; 73:24; Hosea 6:1, 2; Daniel 12:2; John 5:29; 1 Corinthians 15:35-58; 1 Thessalonians 4:13-18). And the fact of the resurrection is inscribed upon every man's heart and conscience by the finger of God in creation. Anyone who denies the resurrection is a liar. He lies against his own conscience.

"The God Of The Living"

In the resurrection God's saints shall be as the angels of God. The Lord Jesus declares, "For when they shall rise from the dead, they neither marry, nor are given in marriage; but are as the angels, which are in heaven". In the resurrection we will be free of all carnal distinctions, weaknesses, cares, needs, and passions. There will be no need for marriage and procreation, because there will be no more sickness, sorrow, bereavement or death! We will possess the constant knowledge and assurance of God's approval, enjoy uninterrupted assurance of complete security with Christ and have perfect communion with our Redeemer. Like the heavenly angels, we will always be engaged in the gratifying service of our great God. Worshipping him! Celebrating his works! Doing his will! We will have unbroken, everlasting rest! Like those celestial spirits above, we will gaze upon our Saviour. As "they do always behold the face of God", we "shall see his face"!

Then our Saviour tells us the meaning of his words to Moses in Exodus 3, when he spoke to Moses out of the burning bush. "And as touching the dead, that they rise: have ye not read in the book of Moses, how in the bush God spake unto him, saying, I am the God of Abraham, and the God of Isaac, and the God of Jacob? He is not the God of the dead, but the God of the living: ye therefore do greatly err" (vv. 26, 27). It was Christ himself who appeared to Moses in the bush (Acts 7:30), declaring himself to be the eternal, self-existent "I AM" (Exodus 3:14; John 8:58). When he spoke to Moses he was saying, "I am the God of the living". He who is our God is the God of the living. Remember, it was Christ our Mediator who spoke those words to Moses. Our Saviour is telling us he is the God of the living (Romans 14:9).

Abraham, Isaac, and Jacob represent all God's elect. They were chosen of God as heirs of a covenant made on their behalf. They believed God and lived in communion with God. But, they did not enjoy the fulfilment of God's promises until they left this vale of tears. Their bodies are in the grave but they live still, as God promised (Hebrews 11:13-16). So it is with all God's saints who have left this world. They are not dead, but living.

The Lord's words to Moses, he tells us, refer to the resurrection. His covenant promises and engagements for Abraham, Isaac and Jacob, and for all his elect, involve the complete recovery of his people, body and soul, from the ruin of the fall of our father Adam. The fulfilment of God's covenant promises depend upon the resurrection of our bodies, and, thus, assures us of it. All who were redeemed by his blood were raised from the dead with Christ representatively, and are made partakers of the first resurrection in the new birth (Revelation 20:6); and they shall be made partakers of "the resurrection of life", when the Lord Jesus Christ comes again to be glorified in his saints (Romans 8:21-23; 1 Corinthians 15:51-58; 1 Thessalonians 4:13-18), because he is "the God of the living"!

"And one of the scribes came, and having heard them reasoning together, and perceiving that he had answered them well, asked him, Which is the first commandment of all? And Jesus answered him, The first of all the commandments is, Hear, O Israel; The Lord our God is one Lord: And thou shalt love the Lord thy God with all thy heart, and with all thy soul, and with all thy mind, and with all thy strength: this is the first commandment. And the second is like, namely this, Thou shalt love thy neighbour as thyself. There is none other commandment greater than these. And the scribe said unto him, Well, Master, thou hast said the truth: for there is one God; and there is none other but he: And to love him with all the heart, and with all the understanding, and with all the soul, and with all the strength, and to love his neighbour as himself, is more than all whole burnt offerings and sacrifices. And when Jesus saw that he answered discreetly, he said unto him, Thou art not far from the kingdom of God. And no man after that durst ask him any question".

(Mark 12:28-34)

Chapter 53

So Near Home, Yet Lost

No doubt this scribe came to the Lord Jesus with the same malicious intent as the others. The Pharisees, Herodians and Sadducees had come to the Master with the specific determination to "catch him in his words" (v. 13). But as he listened to the Saviour's conversation with the Sadducees, he realized that everything the Lord Jesus said made perfectly good sense. He perceived "that he had answered them well", that is with purpose and understanding.

The Question
This scribe asked the Lord Jesus, "Which is the first commandment of all?" No doubt he had often debated that question with others. Religious people love to debate intricate points of doctrine, striving about words to no profit (2 Timothy 2:14). They imagine that they know much, though they know nothing. And their debate is but the outward display of their inward lust for recognition and praise (Romans 1:29). The religion of the self-righteous is all about themselves. They exercise their religion only "for strife and debate, and to smite with the fist of wickedness" (Isaiah 58:4).

Be warned. Nothing spiritual is ever gained by religious wrangling. We all love debate, because we all love to impress others with our knowledge; but it is always carnal and sinful. Debate is not witnessing. It is only debate, the display of carnal pride. It is never for the glory of God or the good of immortal souls. Therefore, we are admonished to "avoid foolish questions, and genealogies, and contentions, and strivings about the law; for they are unprofitable and vain" (Titus 3:9). Witnessing is not showing people what you know, but telling them "how great things the Lord hath done for thee, and hath had compassion on thee" (Mark 5:19).

The Master's Answer
Wicked as this man's motives were, we have reason to give thanks to God that he asked it. Otherwise, we might never have been given the instruction of infinite wisdom given by the Lord Jesus in verses 29-31. Here, again, we see our God overruling evil for good (Psalm 76:10). He makes even the most

malicious designs of wicked men beneficial to his elect, and uses them for his own praise. "Out of the eater came forth meat" (Judges 14:14).

This scribe asked the Master, "Which is the first commandment of all?" He probably expected to receive some instruction about the observance of some outward ceremony, or some very costly duty. Instead, the Lord Jesus seized the opportunity to declare the supremacy of the triune God and that which he both requires and deserves of his creatures.

First, the Saviour sets before this scribe the great supremacy of our God in the trinity of his sacred persons: Father, Son and Holy Spirit. "The first of all the commandments is, Hear, O Israel; The Lord our God is one Lord" (v. 29). In verses 29 and 30 our Saviour quotes a portion of scripture with which the scribe had to have been very familiar (Deuteronomy 6:4, 5), and asserts that this is the matter of utmost priority. "Hear, O Israel; The Lord our God is one Lord"! That is the first thing God commands, that we recognize and worship him alone as God. He who is our God, the covenant God of his people, is alone God.

This sentence is bursting with meaning. First, the Lord, Jehovah, the triune God, is one Jehovah (1 John 5:7). Second, he is the God of Israel in a special, distinct way. He is God over all; but he has made himself our God. "Blessed is the nation whose God is the LORD; and the people whom he hath chosen for his own inheritance" (Psalm 33:12).

I am not sure why, but Mark never uses the word "law" in his gospel narrative. But in verse 30, quoting Deuteronomy 6:5, the Lord Jesus declares that the whole commandment of God, that is all the law of God, directs us to and requires faith in Christ, who is Jehovah the Son. We know that this is the meaning of our Saviour's words here because that is what the Holy Spirit declares in 1 John 3:23. "And this is his commandment, That we should believe on the name of his Son Jesus Christ, and love one another, as he gave us commandment".

The law of God has but one purpose. It is designed to shut us up to Christ alone as our God and Saviour, and to faith in him as our God and Saviour (Galatians 3:19-25). And that faith that is given to and wrought in sinners by the grace of God is "faith which worketh by love" (Galatians 5:6). The law of God demands that we love both God and our fellow man perfectly. Read the Master's words just as they stand.

"And Jesus answered him, The first of all the commandments is, Hear, O Israel; The Lord our God is one Lord: And thou shalt love the Lord thy God with all thy heart, and with all thy soul, and with all thy mind, and with all thy strength: this is the first commandment. And the second is like, namely this, Thou shalt love thy neighbour as thyself. There is none other commandment greater than these".

God does not simply command us to love him sincerely. He commands us to love him perfectly in all his character as God with all our heart, soul, mind and strength. And he demands that we love our neighbours as we love ourselves. Though all hate God by nature (Romans 8:7), there is no question that every heaven born soul loves God in all his character as God; and every ransomed sinner loves his brother. But none would ever dare presume to assert that he loves God with all his heart, soul, mind and strength, or that he loves his brother as he loves himself.

Yet, by faith in Christ, we establish and fulfil the law (Romans 3:31; 8:1-4). God gives what he requires; and believing on the Lord Jesus Christ we offer to God that which he requires, perfection (Leviticus 22:21).

As our Representative, covenant Surety and Substitute, the Lord Jesus Christ lived the full age of a man, loving God and his neighbour, perfecting, fulfilling all righteousness, a righteousness of infinite merit and efficacy, for God's elect. Then he died under the penalty of our sins, being made sin for us, satisfying God's offended justice for the redemption of our souls that we might be made the righteousness of God in him (2 Corinthians 5:21; Galatians 3:13).

When he accomplished this great work, we were one with him and in him, so really and truly one with him and in him that when he obeyed we obeyed, and when he died we died. Therefore he is called "The Lord our Righteousness" and we are called "The Lord our Righteousness" (Jeremiah 23:6; 33:16).

Far Off, In Or Near

In 1859, a Welsh ship called *The Royal Charter* safely sailed around the world, navigating treacherous waters in every part of the globe. The ship docked briefly at Queenstown, Ireland, on October 26, and one of the sailors telegraphed his wife, telling her that he would be home in a few hours. You can imagine her excitement. She had not seen or heard from her husband in months. With joy and anticipation, she hurriedly prepared supper, set the table, and got all spruced up. Excitedly, she sat in the parlour, waiting for her husband to walk through the door. Instead, a messenger appeared at the door who told her that as the ship approached its homeport, it was smashed to pieces in Moelfre Bay, on the coast of Wales, and her husband was drowned!

As soon as her pastor, William Taylor, heard what had happened, he hurried over to minister to this shocked and grieving widow. He said later, "Never can I forget the grief, so stricken and tearful, with which she wrung my hand." As that lady held her pastor's hands, these are the words with which she expressed her grief "So near home, and yet lost! So near home, and yet lost! So near home, and yet lost!"

411

That is precisely where our Saviour said this scribe was, near the kingdom of God but not in it, near home but lost. He said, "Thou art not far from the kingdom of God".

"And the scribe said unto him, Well, Master, thou hast said the truth: for there is one God; and there is none other but he: And to love him with all the heart, and with all the understanding, and with all the soul, and with all the strength, and to love his neighbour as himself, is more than all whole burnt offerings and sacrifices. And when Jesus saw that he answered discreetly, he said unto him, Thou art not far from the kingdom of God. And no man after that durst ask him any question" (vv. 32-34).

It is possible for a person to be very near the kingdom of God and not be in it. It is possible for a sinner to perish upon the doorsteps of mercy, "not far from the kingdom of God". There are many to whom the Saviour's words to this scribe apply, "Thou art not far from the kingdom of God". This scribe was a man of far greater knowledge than most. He saw things most of the scribes and Pharisees could not see. His knowledge was such that our Lord said to him, "Thou art not far from the kingdom of God". Yet, he was lost. He was near, but not in the kingdom. Be warned. You may have great knowledge of truths and never know him who is the Truth. Salvation is not knowing about Christ. Salvation is knowing Christ (John 17:3).

The kingdom of God is that kingdom of grace in which all are voluntary, loyal subjects, under the rule of Christ. It is a spiritual kingdom, governed by Christ through the power of his Spirit and the Word of his grace. The kingdom of God is the church and family of God in this world.

Some are in the kingdom of God. Some are far off from the kingdom of God. And some are near, but not in the kingdom of God. Those who are in the kingdom of God are sinners who have been quickened, regenerated and made alive by the Spirit of God (v. 27; Ephesians 2:1; Revelation 20:6). They have been brought to the obedience of faith by the Spirit of God (Romans 16:25, 26). They have been adopted into the family of God (Ephesians 1:4-6; 1 John 1:9). They are led, ruled, governed and directed in life by the Spirit of God (Romans 8:9, 14). If you are in the kingdom of God, you are in it because God, by a work of his almighty grace, has put you in it. He "hath delivered us from the power of darkness, and hath translated us into the kingdom of his dear Son" (Colossians 1:13).

Most are far off from the kingdom of God. They have no interest in the things of God, no interest in their souls, no interest in Christ, and no interest in the gospel of his grace. Like a brute beast, they live only for time and only for the physical, sensual pleasures of life. But there are some of who, like this scribe, are "not far from the kingdom of God". What did the Saviour see in this man that he did not see in the Pharisees, Herodians and Sadducees who had come before him? Why did he say he was not far from the kingdom of God? The Lord saw standing before him a man of sincerity and truthfulness. This scribe was something more than a religionist. He was no hypocrite. He sincerely studied the law of God, saw something of the supremacy of God and tried to order his life by the law of God. Like the Jews Paul spoke of, he had a zeal for God, but not according to knowledge (Romans 10:1-4).

This man seems to have understood something of the spiritual nature of the law. He saw that the law had more to do with the glory of God and the inward principle of love for God and man than it did with mere outward deeds. He saw that the worship of God was inward, not outward, spiritual, not ceremonial. He saw more than the papist, who makes worship nothing but ceremonies. He saw more than the doctrinalist, who puts head knowledge above heart experience. And he saw more than the legalist, who puts outward morality above love and kindness.

The Lord Jesus saw in this scribe a teachable spirit. What a rare thing that is! Here was a man who was willing to have his doctrine, his religion and his opinions examined and corrected by the Word of God. This man appeared to be in a very hopeful condition. He saw the unity, the breadth and the spirituality of the law. And he appears to have realized something of his own inability to keep the law. He knew that God required what he could not give. There is reason to have hope for a man who knows that much. Few do!

Are you like this scribe? Do you, like the five foolish virgins, have the lamp of religion? If you do, do not be content. They perished with the lamp of religion. You must have the oil of grace. Like the rich young ruler, this scribe had much, but he lacked the one thing needful. He lacked faith in Christ. He was near, but not in the kingdom. Do not be content to live and die in such a position. If you die near, but not in the kingdom of God, eternal damnation will be your portion forever. The borderland is a place of danger. If you are satisfied with being "not far from the kingdom of God", you will in the end be shut out forever (Luke 13:23-30). If you do not enter in by Christ into the kingdom of God, either you will go back into hopeless apostasy (Hebrews 10:25-31; 2 Peter 2:1, 2, 20-22; 1 John 2:19), or you will become content without Christ, indifferent, and gospel hardened.

The borderland of religion without Christ is the most dangerous place to be! If you die without Christ, you will be lost. "So near home, and yet lost"! God has opened the way by which sinners may enter the kingdom (Hebrews 10:19-23, Mark 16:16). The only Door by which sinners enter into the kingdom of God is Christ (John 10:9). We must enter in by his blood and his righteousness. Will you enter into the kingdom of God; or will you die "not far from the kingdom of God"? God help you to enter in, for Christ's sake.

"And Jesus answered and said, while he taught in the temple, How say the scribes that Christ is the Son of David? For David himself said by the Holy Ghost, The LORD said to my Lord, Sit thou on my right hand, till I make thine enemies thy footstool. David therefore himself calleth him Lord; and whence is he then his son? And the common people heard him gladly. And he said unto them in his doctrine, Beware of the scribes, which love to go in long clothing, and love salutations in the marketplaces, And the chief seats in the synagogues, and the uppermost rooms at feasts: Which devour widows' houses, and for a pretence make long prayers: these shall receive greater damnation".

(Mark 12:35-40)

Chapter 54

Temple Teachings

Our Master is sitting in the temple, in the house of God at Jerusalem, teaching the people and preaching the gospel. He told his disciples and his enemies in no uncertain terms of God's certain, impending judgment upon the Jews, and displayed that it would be a matter of righteousness and justice (vv. 1-12). Perceiving that he was talking about them, the Scribes, Pharisees and Sadducees got so mad that they wanted to kill him on the spot; but they feared the people.

As the Lord Jesus continued to teach, these men put their heads together and decided that they would try to trick him into saying something erroneous. So they came to him, first the Pharisees and Herodians, then the Sadducees, then a Scribe, with leading questions, trick questions, questions which were designed for strife and division, not for edification (vv. 13-34). One of these men, the Scribe (vv. 28-34), was obviously moved and impressed by our Lord's doctrine. By the time he came with his appointed question, he appeared to be genuinely concerned to hear and understand the things of God. The Son of God said to him, "Thou art not far from the kingdom of God".

In this last section of the chapter our Saviour draws from the scenes before him in the temple and teaches us about the message of holy scripture, the wickedness and utter repugnancy of hypocrisy and self-righteousness, and the simplicity, devotion and blessedness of true faith.

A Question About Scripture

And Jesus answered and said, while he taught in the temple, How say the scribes that Christ is the son of David? For David himself said by the Holy Ghost, The LORD said to my Lord, Sit thou on my right hand, till I make thine enemies thy footstool. David therefore himself calleth him Lord; and whence is he then his son? And the common people heard him gladly" (vv. 35-37).

Here is a question very different from those that had been raised by the Saviour's religious critics in the previous verses. The questions of religionists gender strife. Here is a question that unites the souls of men. The questions of religious know-alls are always about trivial, insignificant matters. Here is a question of vital importance.

The question which our Lord here propounds is about the Christ of God and the meaning and message of holy scripture. What a blessed thing it would be if all discussions among those who wear the name of Christianity, if all religious and theological conversations, if all preaching and religious instruction were less about trifles and more about these weighty matters. These are the things that concern our souls, the glory of God and the salvation he bestows. Let us look at this question and learn the Master's doctrine.

The message of the Old Testament scriptures as well as the New is the Person and work of the Lord Jesus Christ. The passage here quoted by our Saviour is Psalm 110:1. This is a messianic psalm. It was and still is regarded as such by almost all who expound the Word of God. It is a psalm full of instruction about the Christ of God, the Messiah. Look at the first four verses of that psalm.

"The LORD said unto my Lord, Sit thou at my right hand, until I make thine enemies thy footstool" (v. 1). That is a promise and prophecy of Christ's exaltation, which is the result of the sure and certain victory he would accomplish at Calvary (Hebrews 1:1-3; 10:10-14).

"The LORD shall send the rod of thy strength out of Zion: rule thou in the midst of thine enemies" (v. 2). Here the Psalmist declares that the risen Christ must and shall have all power over all flesh, that he might give eternal life to all his covenant people (John 17:2).

"Thy people shall be willing in the day of thy power, in the beauties of holiness from the womb of the morning: thou hast the dew of thy youth" (v. 3). With those words, David asserts the glorious efficacy of God's saving grace in Christ and the strict justice and holiness of his operations of grace.

"The LORD hath sworn, and will not repent, Thou art a priest for ever after the order of Melchizedek" (v. 4). Blessed be His name, our great and glorious Redeemer is a Priest forever after the order of Melchizedek. He is the only Priest there is and the only Priest we need!

Our Lord's obvious intention here was to show us that the one subject about which David and all the writers of Old Testament scriptures were inspired to write was Christ. He is the singular message of God's Book (John 5:39; Luke 24:27, 44-47; Acts 10:43). We should always remember this when we read and study the Word of God, especially the Old Testament. All the types, prophecies, promises and laws of the Old Testament were intended to teach us about Christ.

We must never undervalue the Old Testament. I hear people talk about the "Old Bible" and the "New". That is wrong. We do not have two words from God, but one. We do not have two revelations from the Lord, just one. The Old Testament is the New Testament concealed. The New Testament is the Old Testament revealed. Let us treasure, study, believe and seek to understand all the Word of God.

The key to understanding the Word of God is Christ. Jesus Christ is the Foundation, the Centre, and the Mainspring of all Divine Truth. This is what the Master himself said: "Search the scriptures; for in them ye think ye have eternal life: and they are they which testify of me". If we would avoid error in interpreting and applying the scriptures, we must understand that everything in the Bible speaks of and relates to Christ. Divorce any doctrine from Christ and that doctrine becomes heresy. Divorce any precept from Christ and that precept becomes self-righteous legality.

Look at verses 35 and 36 again. Here are five profound facts, stated with the utmost simplicity. That which is written in the Book of God is written by divine inspiration. "David himself said by the Holy Ghost" (v. 36). God's promised Messiah, the King, our Redeemer and Saviour is and must be the Son of David. He is not "a" son of David, but "the" Son of David, the Son promised when God said his Son would sit upon his throne forever, the Son of whom Solomon was only a type. All the scribes, Pharisees, and even the Sadducees understood this (v. 35).

This Messiah, the Son of David, though he is a man, is himself God Almighty, the sovereign Lord of the universe! This Man who is David's Son is also David's Lord! Christ, the Messiah, God in human flesh, having finished the work he was sent here to do, now sits upon David's throne, the throne of grace, at the right hand of the Majesty on High. There he exercises total dominion over all flesh, to give eternal life to his chosen, redeemed people.

He must reign until all his enemies are made his footstool! We read in verse 37, "And the common people heard him gladly"! They still do! How happy they must have been to hear the Word of God opened, read and explained in language they could understand by someone who knew what he was talking about. How refreshing it is to hear about the Person of whom the Book speaks, rather than hearing men fuss about things nobody understands!

A Warning About Self-Righteousness

Read verses 38-40, and learn this. Nothing in all the world is more obnoxious, odious, and repugnant to God than self-righteousness, hypocrisy and the outward show of religion.

"And he said unto them in his doctrine, Beware of the scribes, which love to go in long clothing, and love salutations in the marketplaces, And the chief seats in the synagogues, and the uppermost rooms at feasts: Which devour widows' houses, and for a pretence make long prayers: these shall receive greater damnation".

If you read the four gospels carefully, you cannot avoid observing that this wickedness of self-righteousness, hypocrisy and the outward show of religion was and is manifest in men in every walk of religion: conservative and liberal, orthodox and heterodox, Bible thumpers and Bible mockers. It was the common sin of the Pharisees and the Sadducees, Herod and the Scribes, the Herodians and the Zealots. The same is true today.

The word "Beware" was a word seldom used by our Lord. When he did use it, he used it only to give warnings of utmost importance. Here are five passages in which the Son of God warns us to beware. In all five passages the warning is about religious people, specifically religious leaders.

"Beware of false prophets, which come to you in sheep's clothing, but inwardly they are ravening wolves" (Matthew 7:15).

"Behold, I send you forth as sheep in the midst of wolves: be ye therefore wise as serpents, and harmless as doves. But beware of men: for they will deliver you up to the councils, and they will scourge you in their synagogues" (Matthew 10:16, 17).

"Then Jesus said unto them, Take heed and beware of the leaven of the Pharisees and of the Sadducees. And they reasoned among themselves, saying, It is because we have taken no bread. Which when Jesus perceived, he said unto them, O ye of little faith, why reason ye among yourselves, because ye have brought no bread? Do ye not yet understand, neither remember the five loaves of the five thousand, and how many baskets ye took up? Neither the seven loaves of the four thousand, and how many baskets ye took up? How is it that ye do not understand that I spake it not to you concerning bread, that ye should beware of the leaven of the Pharisees and of the Sadducees? Then understood they how that he bade them not beware of the leaven of bread, but of the doctrine of the Pharisees and of the Sadducees" (Matthew 16:6-12).

"In the mean time, when there were gathered together an innumerable multitude of people, insomuch that they trode one upon another, he began to say unto his disciples first of all, Beware ye of the leaven of the Pharisees, which is hypocrisy" (Luke 12:1).

"And he said unto them, Take heed, and beware of covetousness: for a man's life consisteth not in the abundance of the things which he possesseth" (Luke 12:15).

In Mark 12:38-40 our Saviour specifically warns us to beware of those people who teach, by word or by practice, to make an outward show of godliness, seeking the praise and approval of men. The things he mentions are things designed to impress men. Over the years I have often heard people excuse doing these things in the name of being a testimony to others. But they are really designed to draw attention and applause to ourselves. They are here strictly forbidden by the Son of God.

He tells us that we are not to dress in a way that calls attention to ourselves as religious people. We are not to use or encourage others to use religious titles of distinction. We are not to make any outward display of religion. Specifically, he tells us not to pray in restaurants (market places) before we eat a meal. We are not to seek honour from or among men, desiring the place of prominence. When we do pray before others, in the house of God, or in private gatherings with our families, or with other believers, we are not to pray in a manner that calls attention to ourselves.

In a word, we are not to be pretentious hypocrites, calling attention to ourselves, making an outward show of religion (Matthew 6:1-18). Our Saviour warns us to beware of those religious leaders who practice such things and teach you to practice them, because they devour widows' houses in the name of God. You can mark it down: everything they do is in some way or another motivated and governed by the love of honour and the love of money. Beware of the tendencies of your flesh to pretence, hypocrisy, self-righteousness and a carnal show of religion, because these things are natural to, approved of and promoted by all men. Beware of following such men, because if you do, you shall with them "receive greater condemnation".

Let us ever pray for grace to avoid hypocrisy, pretence, and a religious show. May God give us grace to be honest, thorough and sincere before him and before men.

"And Jesus sat over against the treasury, and beheld how the people cast money into the treasury: and many that were rich cast in much. And there came a certain poor widow, and she threw in two mites, which make a farthing. And he called unto him his disciples, and saith unto them, Verily I say unto you, That this poor widow hath cast more in, than all they which have cast into the treasury: For all they did cast in of their abundance; but she of her want did cast in all that she had, even all her living".

(Mark 12:41-44)

Chapter 55

Lessons From A Certain Poor Widow

Why do you go to work every day? What is your purpose in working? It does not matter what kind of work you do. We live in a society that honours and praises professionals, whose jobs require a college education. Doctors, lawyers, politicians and executives are usually the people who have influence in society, before whom others bow and scrape like grovelling dogs. What a pity!

It is altogether proper that we give honour to whom honour is due; but we ought never to look upon one person with contempt and another with adulation, simply because of their different social status. It does not matter in the least where you work, or what kind of work you do. All honest labour is honourable labour. I do not care whether you work for minimum wages by the hour or whether you make a million dollars a week. If your labour is honest labour, it is honourable labour.

Motives For Work
My question has nothing to do with the kind of work you do. I want you to consider only one thing: Why do you do it? What is your reason for working? In the Word of God, I find three things, and only three things, which should motivate believers in their labour. These three motives are very clear. There is nothing profound or mysterious about them. I hope you will be surprised by the fact that among these three motives for working, and working hard, there is not a word written about gaining riches, getting more stuff, or increasing our social rank. Are you interested in Bible motives for work? Here they are:

The Glory Of God
When we go about our daily employment, whatever it is, let us seek to honour our God in the work we do (1 Corinthians 10:31; Ephesians 6:5, 6; Colossians 3:22-24).

The Needs Of Our Families
It is the responsibility of every man to provide for his family. That provision reaches beyond physical things. We are also responsible to provide for our families spiritually. Every man is responsible to serve God as a prophet, priest and king in his own house (1 Timothy 5:8).

The Privilege Of Giving
We ought to be motivated every day, as we do the work the Lord has given us to do, to do that work (whatever it is) to the best of our ability for the glory of God and the good of our families. But there is a third reason for working, a third noble, biblical principle which ought to be a high priority and motive to every child of God in his daily employment. We ought to work that we might enjoy the high honour and privilege of giving (Ephesians 4:28).

If we belong to Christ, if we are his servants, we ought to make the business of giving, open handed, open hearted, generous giving, a high priority in our lives. There are many, many great examples of this kind of giving in the Word of God (2 Samuel 24:24; Mark 14:3-9; 2 Corinthians 8:9; Philippians 4:15-19). I urge you to read those passages carefully before proceeding.

There are few events in the earthly life of Christ more commonly overlooked than the giving of this poor widow, described in Mark 12:41-44, and our Redeemer's commendation of it. Few of the words of the Son of God are more commonly unnoticed than these.

Our Lord Jesus saw "many that were rich cast in much". Without question, those who have more should give more. That is seldom the case; but it should be. Usually, the wealthiest people really give the least. And when they do give a little something somewhere, they have lots of strings attached and a bag of instructions!

Then, our Master noticed "a certain poor widow, and she threw in two mites, which make a farthing. And he called unto him his disciples, and saith unto them, Verily I say unto you, That this poor widow hath cast more in, than all they which have cast into the treasury: For all they did cast in of their abundance; but she of her want did cast in all that she had, even all her living". I call your attention to four things in this story. May God the Holy Spirit graciously and effectually teach us the things here revealed in his Word.

The Observer
"And Jesus sat over against the treasury, and beheld how the people cast money into the treasury: and many that were rich cast in much". The first thing evident in this passage is the divinity of our Lord Jesus Christ. There is

no indication that our Master was informed by anyone about the wealth of the rich or the poverty of this woman. Yet, he who is the omniscient God knew everything about everyone before him. He knew how much each possessed, how much each gave, why they gave it and what the circumstances of their lives were. I stress this fact because I want us ever to remember that he who gave his all to redeem and save us is himself the almighty, omniscient God. He who is God gave himself for us![7]

"For ye know the grace of our Lord Jesus Christ, that, though he was rich, yet for your sakes he became poor, that ye through his poverty might be rich" (2 Corinthians 8:9).

"Let this mind be in you, which was also in Christ Jesus: Who, being in the form of God, thought it not robbery to be equal with God: But made himself of no reputation, and took upon him the form of a servant, and was made in the likeness of men: And being found in fashion as a man, he humbled himself, and became obedient unto death, even the death of the cross" (Philippians 2:5-8).

That Man who loved us and gave himself for us is himself our God. "Thanks be unto God for his unspeakable gift"!

"He beheld how the people cast money into the treasury". He did not merely observe the fact that they gave, he observed "how" they gave. He observed what they gave and why they gave it. We should ever be aware of this fact. Our God knows and observes all things. He looks beyond what we do and observes why we do it. All things are naked and open before the eyes of him with whom we have to do. He weighs not what we give, but how we give.

The Givers

"And Jesus sat over against the treasury, and beheld how the people cast money into the treasury: and many that were rich cast in much. And there came a certain poor widow, and she threw in two mites, which make a farthing" (vv. 41, 42).

There are many in this world who are rich, very rich in material things, even rich in religious tradition, ceremony and activity, who are poor, utterly destitute before God. And there are many very poor people in this world who are rich, indescribably and eternally rich toward God, rich in Christ.

Learn what that means. Riches, luxury, ease of life and earthly exaltation are no indication of God's favour; and poverty, afflictions and earthly

---

[7] The fact of Christ's divinity assures us of the certain efficacy of his work. If he is God, he cannot fail. If he can fail, for any reason, to accomplish what he desires or tries to accomplish, then he is not God!

sorrows are no indication of God's disfavour (Psalm 73). Those who have Christ have all; and those who are without Christ have nothing. Without Christ, they are without God, without promise, without grace, without mercy, without hope!

The Gifts

In the temple worship of the Old Testament, in addition to the tithe required by the law, those who were so inclined brought their voluntary gifts (freewill offerings) and put them in an offering box, here called the treasury. These offerings were used in the maintenance of the temple and God's appointed priests, and to supply the priests with those things necessary for the service of the temple and the worship of God. Though the worship of God had degenerated to nothing but religious ritualism, during the days of our Lord's earthly ministry, it was customary for people, when they entered the temple, to put some money in the box. Many, we are told, who were rich cast in much. But our Saviour calls our attention to a certain, poor widow. She had only two mites to her name. And those two mites is what she put into the collection box.

"And he called unto him his disciples, and saith unto them, Verily I say unto you, That this poor widow hath cast more in, than all they which have cast into the treasury: For all they did cast in of their abundance; but she of her want did cast in all that she had, even all her living" (vv. 43, 44).

Anyone who observed such an act as this, were this story not recorded upon the pages of Inspiration, would declare that it was an inexcusable act of misplaced zeal. It would be condemned by all as an unnecessary, useless act of presumption. It would appear that her gift was unnecessary, because God did not require it. It might be thought useless, because her two mites were materially insignificant. It might be considered presumptuous, because, when she had given all she had, she had not exercised any wisdom or prudence with regard to her future needs. But the Son of God not only approved of what she did, he called his disciples' attention to her gift, and said, "Men, this is what the Bible calls giving"!

Though she gave only two mites, our Saviour commends her gift as something both great and good. It was a great act, because it involved great sacrifice. And it was a good gift, because she gave as unto the Lord, for the glory of God, to the utmost stretch of her ability.

This poor woman's gift in itself was small, insignificant, even contemptible in the eyes of men; but it was highly valued and esteemed by the Son of God! All that was given by the wealthy was given out of their abundance. It was just the overflow, the excess, what they had left over after buying all they wanted, throwing away all they wanted and saving all they wanted. They gave a portion, but only a portion of what they had. She gave all. They gave out of their wealth. She gave out of her poverty. They gave and had much remaining. She gave everything she had, all her daily sustenance.

As John Gill observed:

> She did cast in all that she had, even all her living; her whole substance, all that she had in the world; what was to have bought her food, for that day. She left herself nothing, but gave away all, and trusted to providence for immediate supply.

They gave out of a sense of duty. She gave because she wanted to give. They gave to be seen of men. She gave because she loved the Lord. They gave to get glory to themselves. She gave to the glory of God. They gave what they did not need. She gave what she very much needed. They gave their spare change. She gave everything. I have heard men and women speak with a pretended modesty of giving their "two mites;" but we have not given our "two mites" until, like this blessed woman, we have given our all.

The Lesson

We find the lesson of this story in 2 Corinthians 9:7. "Every man according as he purposeth in his heart, so let him give; not grudgingly, or of necessity: for God loveth a cheerful giver". God loves a cheerful giver.

Such giving as that which this poor widow exemplified arises from love, not law. Believers give, not by legal constraint, but by grace, not by force of law, but by the force of gratitude. Believers understand what the world can never understand. Why do believers give as they do? Because we recognize that Christ gave his all for us, and we understand that everything we have has been given to us (1 Corinthians 4:7). Believers love Christ, his gospel, and his people. Believers understand that it really is more blessed to give than to receive.

There is an abundance of instruction in the New Testament about Christian giving. All of 1 Corinthians chapter 9, 2 Corinthians chapter 8, and 2 Corinthians chapter 9 are taken up with this subject. But there are no commands to the people of God anywhere in the New Testament about how much we are to give, when we are to give, or where we are to give. Tithing and all systems like it are things altogether foreign to the New Testament. Like all other acts of worship, giving is an act of grace. It must be free and voluntary. But there are some plain, simple guidelines laid down in the New Testament for us to follow.

Christian giving must be motivated by love and gratitude towards Christ (2 Corinthians 8:8, 9). Love needs no law. It is a law unto itself. It is the most powerful and most generous of all motives.

Our gifts must arise from willing hearts (2 Corinthians 8:12). If that which we give arises from a willing heart, if it is given freely and cheerfully, it is accepted of God. The Lord is not concerned with the amount of our gifts, be it great or small; he looks to the motive behind them.

We should give to the work of the gospel in proportion to our blessings from the Lord (1 Corinthians 16:2). We are expected to give generously in accordance with our own ability.

All of God's people should give ("everyone", 1 Corinthians 16:2; "every man", 2 Corinthians 9:7). Men and women, rich and poor, old and young all who are saved by the grace of God are expected to give for the support of God's church and kingdom.

We should be both liberal and sacrificial in our giving (2 Corinthians 9:5, 6). We have not really given anything until we have taken that which we need, want and have use for and given it to the Lord.

Our gifts must be voluntary (2 Corinthians 9:7).

We are to give as unto the Lord (Matthew 6:1-5). We give, not to be seen of men, but for the honour of Christ, hoping for nothing in return.

This kind of giving is well-pleasing to God (Philippians 4:18; Hebrews 13:16).

This is the teaching of the New Testament about the matter of giving. First, give yourself to Christ. Give purposefully, in proportion as the Lord has prospered you. Give secretly, unto the Lord. Give cheerfully, with "a willing mind". Give generously. Give regularly. And give for the glory of God, as unto the Lord. "Upon the first day of the week let every one of you lay by him in store, as God hath prospered him". As every ransomed sinner does so, every need of God's church will be supplied by the free generosity of his people.

"What have we to cast into the Lord's treasury?" Robert Hawker asked. Then he wrote, "Indeed, and in truth, nothing but what we have first received. We have two mites: soul and body; and these are both the Lord's: Oh, for grace to give both these; and Jesus looking on; Jesus disposing to the act, and Jesus accepting all to his glory (1 Corinthians 6:19, 20)".

"Remember the words of the Lord Jesus, how he said, It is more blessed to give than to receive" (Acts 20:35). It really is! May God the Holy Spirit graciously teach us all to abound in this grace also, for Christ's sake.

Lessons From A Certain Poor Widow

"And as he went out of the temple, one of his disciples saith unto him, Master, see what manner of stones and what buildings are here! And Jesus answering said unto him, Seest thou these great buildings? there shall not be left one stone upon another, that shall not be thrown down. And as he sat upon the mount of Olives over against the temple, Peter and James and John and Andrew asked him privately, Tell us, when shall these things be? and what shall be the sign when all these things shall be fulfilled? And Jesus answering them began to say, Take heed lest any man deceive you: For many shall come in my name, saying, I am Christ; and shall deceive many. And when ye shall hear of wars and rumours of wars, be ye not troubled: for such things must needs be; but the end shall not be yet. For nation shall rise against nation, and kingdom against kingdom: and there shall be earthquakes in divers places, and there shall be famines and troubles: these are the beginnings of sorrows".

(Mark 13:1-8)

Chapter 56

"The Beginnings Of Sorrows"

Our daily newspapers are filled with stories of misery, woe and sorrow. Sicknesses, diseases, wars, famines, earthquakes, pestilence, floods, hurricanes, tornadoes and the like, ravage the earth. Add to these things the robberies, rapes and murders that are reported every day, and you cannot help asking yourself this question: If God almighty is truly good and he absolutely rules the universe in total sovereignty, if God really is in absolute, total control of everything, how can these things be?

Would a good God allow such things as this? If God is in total control of all things, how can we explain fathers raping their own daughters, mothers murdering their own children, sons slaughtering their parents, grandparents, brothers and sisters, and schoolboys murdering their classmates?

There is absolutely no question that God is good, perfectly good, and that he is in absolute, total control of all things at all times. "Our God is in the heavens. He hath done whatsoever He hath pleased"! Not only does he allow these things, he brings them to pass. These things are not accidents. They are the work of God's hands. He says, "I form the light and create darkness: I make peace and create evil: I the Lord do all these things"!

This world of sorrow and woe is a world full of sin; and a holy, good God must and shall punish sin. The sorrows of this world are God's judgments upon this world. Yet, all the misery, woe, trouble and sorrow we see here are just "the beginnings of sorrows". The troubles, woes and sorrows of life in this world, no matter how severe, no matter how relentless they may be, are but "the beginnings of sorrows".

These things are just the forerunners of that great and terrible day when God shall judge all men in strict justice. They are just the forerunners of wrath to warn us of the infinite, indescribable, eternal wrath that shall be relentlessly poured out upon your soul in hell, upon all who perish under the wrath of God.

If you are not in too big a hurry to go to hell, pay attention to what you have just read. Paul said, "Knowing the terror of the Lord, we persuade men". If you are yet without Christ, I pray that God the Holy Spirit will be pleased to persuade you by his Word and by his omnipotent mercy to flee to Christ, to be reconciled to God. The wrath of God is upon you. The Lord Jesus Christ is your only hope.

Unless God saves you by his almighty, free grace in Christ, you will soon be in hell. O sinner, trust Christ now. Come, plunge into that fountain drawn from Immanuel's veins. Wash your soul in the blood of Christ. Lay hold upon eternal life. Cast yourself down at the throne of grace and sue for mercy. Trust Christ, and live forever! It is written, "Believe on the Lord Jesus Christ, and thou shalt be saved". Will you now trust the Son of God? May God give you faith in his dear Son. Oh, I pray that he will make you willing in the day of his power! Mark 13 is all about the judgment of God upon men and women who despise his grace.

The Destruction Of The Temple

"And as he went out of the temple, one of his disciples saith unto him, Master, see what manner of stones and what buildings are here! And Jesus answering said unto him, Seest thou these great buildings? there shall not be left one stone upon another, that shall not be thrown down. And as he sat upon the mount of Olives over against the temple, Peter and James and John and Andrew asked him privately, Tell us, when shall these things be? and what shall be the sign when all these things shall be fulfilled?" (vv. 1-4).

This thirteenth chapter of Mark is full of judgment. It speaks of the destruction of the temple at Jerusalem, the destruction of the Jewish church state and of the civil government of the Jewish nation, which was consummated in 70 AD, just forty years after our Lord was crucified. This is exactly according to the prophecy given in Genesis 49:10.

When our Saviour "went out of the temple", he went out never to return to it. What solemn thoughts that should awaken in our minds.

Robert Hawker wrote:

> When the Lord departs, woe to that land, woe to that house or family, where the Lord's gracious presence is not. No sooner had Lot departed from Sodom than the next account is the destruction of it (Genesis 19:22-24). And who shall say how much the Christless owe in being saved from instant ruin, both in nations, and cities, and families, from the seed of Christ living in the midst of them.

It seems obvious to me that this passage also speaks of the glorious second advent of our Lord Jesus Christ, when he shall come in flaming fire taking vengeance on his adversaries.

While no man knows the day or hour of Christ's second advent, or even the approximate time when the end will come, we are assured throughout the scriptures that Christ shall come again. Trusting his Word, his providence and his grace, it is enough for us to live in anticipation of that great day, waiting for the promise of his coming. It is far better for us not to know the time when he shall appear. If we knew when he would appear, we would be irresponsible and neglect our daily responsibilities in this world, just as people have always done when they thought they knew when he was coming. It is best for us to live in the anticipation of faith, waiting for the Lord from heaven, believing that he will do as he said.

"Let not your heart be troubled: ye believe in God, believe also in me. In my Father's house are many mansions: if it were not so, I would have told you. I go to prepare a place for you. And if I go and prepare a place for you, I will come again, and receive you unto myself; that where I am, there ye may be also" (John 14:1-3).

Yet, it is a serious mistake to read such passages as the one now before us as merely referring to prophetic things, as though they had no immediate message for us. You will notice that our Lord hardly even answered the disciples' question about when these things would be and what would be the sign of their fulfilment. Reading the entire chapter, you cannot miss the fact that our Lord deliberately seized this opportunity, not to answer those questions about prophetic things, but to warn and teach them and us about present dangers and responsibilities. We see this clearly in the opening verses of the chapter.

When they walked out of the temple, the disciples' looked over that splendid piece of architecture, the centre and glory of the Jews' religion, with great pride, and said, "Master, see what manner of stones and what buildings are here! And Jesus answering said unto him, Seest thou these great buildings? there shall not be left one stone upon another, that shall not be thrown down".

What does the Holy Spirit intend for us to learn from this statement and our Lord's reply to it? Obviously, he intends for us to learn more than the mere fact that our Lord here declared he would come in judgment against the Jews and destroy their temple.

The very first thing that seems obvious to me is this: Every mere form of godliness, religion, worship and ceremony, without the power of godliness, is an abomination to God.

The Jews' religion was rich in tradition, rich in outward appearance, rich in respectability and rich in history. But they had forsaken the Word of God and the worship of God. They had a form of religion that impressed everyone but God. They had a form of godliness, but denied the power thereof. They had a name that they lived, but they were dead. Our Master said to them, "Ye are they which justify yourselves before men; but God knoweth your hearts: for that which is highly esteemed among men is abomination in the sight of God" (Luke 16:15).

"This know also, that in the last days perilous times shall come. For men shall be lovers of their own selves, covetous, boasters, proud, blasphemers, disobedient to parents, unthankful, unholy, Without natural affection, trucebreakers, false accusers, incontinent, fierce, despisers of those that are good, Traitors, heady, highminded, lovers of pleasures more than lovers of God; Having a form of godliness, but denying the power thereof: from such turn away" (2 Timothy 3:1-5).

The power of godliness is the gospel of Christ (Romans 1:16). Every form of religion that denies the gospel of Christ is an abomination to God. We are strictly commanded, as we care for our souls and care for the glory of God, to turn away from it (Revelation 18:4).

Next, we will do well to remember that we are all too much inclined to judge things by the outward appearance. We are too much like little children, who are much more excited about a field of dandelions than a field of corn. We are too much impressed with stately, ornate buildings, stained glass, marble floors and religious images and icons. Those things that appeal to our senses more easily attract us than that which meets the needs of our hearts and souls.

That which is essential to the worship of God is not physical, but spiritual. The gospel of God's grace, the revelation of his glory, the presence of his Spirit, and the knowledge of his Son are the things that are of singular importance! If we have these things, all is well. If we are lacking these things, our religion is vanity, and worse than vanity. Without these things, our religion is useless and damning, and God will soon destroy it.

Let us learn from our Lord's words here that the true glory of a church is not buildings, creeds, rituals and history, but the knowledge of and faith in the Lord Jesus Christ. Yet, we must not run to the absurd extreme of being indifferent about that building which is set aside for the worship of God.

"Let all things be done decently and in order" (1 Corinthians 14:40). It is no shame for a congregation to meet in a barn or under a tree, if they can do no better. But it is abhorrent for people who live in beautiful, richly furnished homes to be content for the house of God to be a run down shack. The buildings in which God's people meet to worship him are erected for and dedicated to the worship of our God. We ought to care for them and treat them as the house of God. We certainly ought to take as much interest in the appearance of God's house as we would of our own houses.

The Deception Of The World
"And Jesus answering them began to say, Take heed lest any man deceive you: For many shall come in my name, saying, I am Christ; and shall deceive many" (vv. 5, 6).

This solemn warning is repeated frequently throughout the New Testament There have been many throughout history who have come claiming to be the Christ, the Messiah. Every time such a blasphemer arises a few fools follow them. But never do they deceive many. Our Lord is here warning us of something more subtle than a man openly claiming that he is the Christ. His warning is against those by whom the nations of the world are deceived. He is talking about that strong delusion, which God himself sends upon those who will not receive the love of the truth.

"And then shall that Wicked be revealed, whom the Lord shall consume with the spirit of his mouth, and shall destroy with the brightness of his coming: Even him, whose coming is after the working of Satan with all power and signs and lying wonders, And with all deceivableness of unrighteousness in them that perish; because they received not the love of the truth, that they might be saved. And for this cause God shall send them strong delusion, that they should believe a lie: That they all might be damned who believed not the truth, but had pleasure in unrighteousness" (2 Thessalonians 2:8-12).

There are many false prophets who preach a false Christ, by whom men and women are deceived, deluded, and damned: the false christs of liberals, cults and papists, and the false Christ of Arminian, freewill, works religion. There are many false christs, many antichrists, by whom the souls of men are deceived and damned. I want to be as charitable, kind and gracious as I can; but charity, kindness and grace will not allow me to be silent while immortal souls are deceived and God's glory is trampled beneath the feet of men. If you trust a false Christ, you cannot be saved any more than you could be saved by trusting a tadpole. We are called of God to trust, love, follow and obey the true Christ and him only. Salvation is promised to none but those who trust the true Christ. Therefore, we are warned, "Take heed that no man deceive you". We must take heed to the teachings of holy scripture, lest we be deceived by some false Christ.

O let Thy Word for ever be,
My counsel and delight.
And may I still new wonders see,
Through faith's increasing light.

433

The Christ of scripture is himself almighty God incarnate in human flesh, who alone is the Saviour of the world. He is the Surety of an elect, covenant people (Hebrews 7:22). He is the Substitute who has satisfied divine justice for and effectually redeemed his people by the sacrifice of himself (Isaiah 53:10; 2 Corinthians 5:21; Galatians 3:13; Ephesians 1:7; Hebrews 9:12). He is the Saviour who saves his people from their sins (Matthew 1:21). He is the Sovereign who sits upon the throne of universal dominion (John 17:2).

What should our attitude be toward those who preach Christ in all the fulness of his grace and glory as our all-sufficient Saviour? Isaiah declares, "How beautiful upon the mountains are the feet of him that bringeth good tidings, that publisheth peace; that bringeth good tidings of good, that publisheth salvation; that saith unto Zion, Thy God reigneth"! (Isaiah 52:7).

What should our attitude be toward those false prophets who preach a false Christ and deceive the souls of men? The scriptures are equally clear in answering that question. "As we said before, so say I now again, If any man preach any other gospel unto you than that ye have received, let him be accursed" (Galatians 1:9). "I would they were even cut off which trouble you" (Galatians 5:12). "If there come any unto you, and bring not this doctrine, receive him not into your house, neither bid him God speed: For he that biddeth him God speed is partaker of his evil deeds" (2 John 10, 11).

The Displays Of God's Judgment

"And when ye shall hear of wars and rumours of wars, be ye not troubled: for such things must needs be; but the end shall not be yet. For nation shall rise against nation, and kingdom against kingdom: and there shall be earthquakes in divers places, and there shall be famines and troubles: these are the beginnings of sorrows" (vv. 7, 8).

Now, I pointedly address any who read these lines who are yet without Christ. How often God has spoken to you by the displays of his judgments upon others and by the displays of his wrath and judgment against you! Time and again he has made you see clear, manifest, undeniable tokens of his wrath in this world. Time and again he has brushed your soul with the fires of hell. What misery, what trouble, what woe, what ruin your sin has brought upon you!

Yet, you turn a deaf ear to the voice of God's providence! You try, with all your power, to silence the torments of your guilty conscience. You try your best not to hear the Word of God. Oh, how I pray that God will not allow you to have your way!

I warn you again, the troubles you see and the troubles you experience in this world are just "the beginnings of sorrows"! There is a day coming when the holy Lord God will judge all men by that Man whom he has appointed.

When that day comes, if you are found out of Christ, if you are found among those whose names are not written in the book of life, you shall perish forever in hell! No mind can imagine, no tongue can describe the horror of sorrow which shall torment your soul forever in hell!

"And I saw a great white throne, and him that sat on it, from whose face the earth and the heaven fled away; and there was found no place for them. And I saw the dead, small and great, stand before God; and the books were opened: and another book was opened, which is the book of life: and the dead were judged out of those things which were written in the books, according to their works. And the sea gave up the dead which were in it; and death and hell delivered up the dead which were in them: and they were judged every man according to their works. And death and hell were cast into the lake of fire. This is the second death. And whosoever was not found written in the book of life was cast into the lake of fire" (Revelation 20:11-15).

I set before you life and death, eternal life and eternal death. Why will you die? Why will you choose death, when life can be had so freely? Christ is willing to save all who trust him. He is able to save all who trust him. Christ will save all who trust him. Indeed, he has saved all who trust him. Come, O Spirit of God. Breathe upon the poor, helpless, slain sinner, for Christ's sake. Cause the dead to hear the voice of the Son of God and live.

"But take heed to yourselves: for they shall deliver you up to councils; and in the synagogues ye shall be beaten: and ye shall be brought before rulers and kings for my sake, for a testimony against them. And the gospel must first be published among all nations. But when they shall lead you, and deliver you up, take no thought beforehand what ye shall speak, neither do ye premeditate: but whatsoever shall be given you in that hour, that speak ye: for it is not ye that speak, but the Holy Ghost. Now the brother shall betray the brother to death, and the father the son; and children shall rise up against their parents, and shall cause them to be put to death. And ye shall be hated of all men for my name's sake: but he that shall endure unto the end, the same shall be saved".

(Mark 13:9-13)

Chapter 57

"Take Heed To Yourselves"

As our Lord Jesus warns us of the trials, troubles and persecutions we must face while we live in this world, he admonishes us, saying, "Take heed to yourselves". Our Saviour here reminds us both of the troubles we must expect in this world and the consolations God has given us in anticipation of them, lest we be overcome by them. Let us ever beware of these things and take heed to ourselves. We must through much tribulation enter into the kingdom of God.

Troubles Sure

Many have the dreamy-eyed idea that faith in Christ puts an end to earthly trouble. Nothing can be further from the truth. There are many troubles that are sure to follow faith in Christ. It is written, "Man is born to trouble as the sparks fly upward" (Job 5:7). Trouble, sorrow, heartache and pain are the things assured to all men because of sin. It is the common lot and portion of Adam's fallen race. Where there is sin there is sorrow. These are the thorns and thistles of our hearts.

Yet, there are specific troubles to which all true believers are and must be exposed in this world. These are our lot and portion as long as we are in this body of flesh. The believer's life is a chequered history of great sorrow and great joy. All the prophecies dealing with the church of God on the earth between Christ's first and second advent assert this plainly. Certainly, none can doubt that our Lord asserts this in Mark 13:9-13. Our Master tells us plainly, "In the world you shall have tribulation". In Philippians 1:29 the Holy Spirit tells us, "Unto you it is given in the behalf of Christ, not only to believe on him, but also to suffer for his sake". As long as we live in this body of sin, every believer has his divinely appointed miseries and his divinely appointed mercies. We will all have our nights of darkness and days of brightness, our trials and our triumphs, our falls and our restorations, our sorrows and our joys. Our heavenly Father has so ordained it.

There is no question about the fact of our many problems and troubles in this world. But we are often surprised by their sources, though we should not be. Our Lord also told us plainly what the sources of our woes would be. We must always expect trouble from people of the world, especially lost religious people (vv. 9, 11, 13).

Never look for help or favour from "rulers and kings". Our way of life, the gospel we believe and the God we worship is a constant annoyance to this world. These things will never bring us favour with men. Our gospel constantly exposes their sin, their idolatry and their condemnation. Those who dream that politicians and civil magistrates will one day help the cause of Christ as they once did, have misread both the Word of God and history.

Many there are who have been persecuted, imprisoned, beaten and burned at the stake for absolutely no reason, except their adherence to the gospel of Christ. Trouble from the world is not too surprising. But there is another source of trouble plainly stated in this passage, a source that every believer will experience, which almost always shocks us. If we are faithful to Christ and the gospel of God's free and sovereign grace in him, we must expect trouble from our families, too. "The brother shall betray the brother to death, and the father the son; and children shall rise up against their parents, and shall cause them to be put to death" (v. 12).

Do not be surprised, my brother, my sister, when those to whom you are most devoted, even father and mother, brother and sister, son and daughter, husband or wife, speak evil of you, hold you in contempt and treat you as an enemy. We must not be surprised if those whose hearts are enmity against our God are also enmity against us. Cain will always persecute Abel. Esau will ever despise Jacob. The seed of the serpent will always persecute the seed of the woman.

We will be wise to remember these things and lay them to heart. We must, if we would follow Christ, "count the cost" of being his disciples. I know that we are living in days of great freedom. Physical persecution, at least in free societies, is not a fear to God's church today. But persecution is still sure to follow true faith in and faithfulness to the Son of God. You can bank on it. Believers still suffer in their livelihoods for the gospel's sake. God's children must still endure scorn, slander, laughter, ridicule, isolation and petty hostilities for their faith in Christ, even from their families. "The offence of the cross" has not ceased. It is still true that "the natural man receiveth not the things of the Spirit of God". Those who are "born after the flesh" still persecute those who are "born after the Spirit". Let us never forget or doubt this word from our God and Saviour. It is as true as the declaration that Christ died for our sins. "Ye shall be hated of all men for my name's sake".

Add to these things the fact that many of God's people in this world live with indescribable bodily infirmities, sorrows, bereavements and losses, and domestic troubles. Yet, there is another source of great trouble. Indeed, the greatest source of our trouble in this world is this third source. We must, as long as we live in this world, expect to have an unceasing warfare in our souls between the flesh and the Spirit, between the old man and the new (Romans 7:14-23; Galatians 5:16, 17). Let me illustrate what I am saying by asking you to consider a few questions. Be honest with yourself. These are things which trouble me greatly. I am sure they trouble you, too.

Before God saved you, did you ever imagine that a believer, a sinner redeemed by the blood of Christ, robed in his righteousness, saved by God's free grace, living in the prospect of heavenly glory, a person truly born of God, one who truly believes and loves the Lord Jesus Christ, could have so much difficulty with inward lusts as you do? Could find it so difficult to read the Word of God as you do? Could be so indifferent to the things of God as you are? Could have such a hard time praying as you do? Could love the world so much and love Christ so little as you do?

No wonder our Lord said, "take heed to yourselves"! We who know ourselves to be such sinners have great reason constantly to give thanks to God that salvation is by grace alone (1 Corinthians 15:10). Let us ever give thanks for him who is our unceasing, all-prevailing Advocate with the Father (1 John 2:1, 2).

God's Promises
Our blessed God and Saviour holds before us in his Word an immeasurable, rich range of promises to encourage, comfort and inspire us in the midst of the many problems and trials we have in this world. Here are two sweet cordials with which we may encourage our own hearts and one another.

First and foremost, we are assured that God's purpose of grace in Christ shall be fulfilled. Look at verse ten. Right in the middle of this list of woes, our Saviour interjects this blessed word of promise. "And the gospel must first be preached among all nations". He seems to be saying, these things are all necessary for the accomplishment of God's purpose of grace toward his elect. This is how I am going to bring about the fulness of my kingdom and the glory of my name. There is a people in this world, loved and chosen of God, redeemed by the blood of Christ, who must and shall be saved by God's irresistible grace. God's appointed means of grace and salvation is the preaching of the gospel (Romans 1:16, 17; 10:17; 1 Corinthians 1:18-23). Therefore the gospel must be preached among all nations.

Let men and devils, kingdoms, empires and nations do what they will, God's purpose of grace cannot be thwarted. Those specks of dust, though they swell and burn with rage against our God, his Christ and his gospel, are as surely under God's control and as surely used by him to fulfil his purpose of grace toward his elect as the angels of heaven. The Word of God is not bound and cannot be bound (Isaiah 55:11; 2 Timothy 2:9).

Second, our Lord Jesus here assures us that when special help is needed special help will be given. "But when they shall lead you, and deliver you up, take no thought beforehand what ye shall speak, neither do ye premeditate: but whatsoever shall be given you in that hour, that speak ye: for it is not ye that speak, but the Holy Ghost" (v. 11).

Many pervert our Lord's words here and use them as an excuse for laziness and being unprepared for the pulpit ministry. Such an attitude toward preaching the gospel is utter foolishness! God's servants labour in the Word and doctrine of Christ, studying diligently, praying earnestly, as they seek God's message for his people. Faithful men never step into the pulpit unprepared!

Our Lord's promise in verse 11 has nothing to do with preaching. It is talking about persecution. Our Master here promises that as he gave words of wisdom to his apostles before their persecutors, so he will give us words of wisdom to answer our persecutors as needed, or else he will give us wisdom and grace not to answer them at all (1 Corinthians 10:13; Isaiah 43:1-5; 2 Corinthians 12:9; Romans 16:20).

Salvation Promised

Tribulations shall come. But our Saviour holds out a word of promise to those who endure to the end, to those who will not forsake the gospel, who will not, for any reason, receive the mark of the beast. "And ye shall be hated of all men for my name's sake: but he that shall endure unto the end, the same shall be saved" (v. 13).

Let it be clearly understood that perseverance is a matter of personal responsibility. We must hold on our way. We must cleave to Christ. We must take heed to ourselves, lest we wind up like those who perished in the wilderness. Demas, Diotrephes, Judas and Lot's wife stand upon the pages of holy scripture like blazing beacons to warn us.

Having put our hands to the plough, we must not look back. We must not drop out of the race. We must resolutely take up our cross every day and follow Christ.

Yet, perseverance for God's elect is a matter of absolute certainty. Our names are written in the book of life. We have been predestinated to everlasting salvation. Our Surety, Christ Jesus, has already obtained the purchased possession for us. We have the pledge of heavenly glory within us. We are sealed unto eternal life. We are kept by the power of God's grace in Christ. We have our Saviour's promise. "They shall never perish"! In fact, the Book of God declares that all God's elect were glorified with Christ before the world began (Romans 8:30) and that we were risen and seated at the right hand of the Majesty on high with our blessed Substitute when he took his seat in heaven (Ephesians 2:6).

All who persevere unto the end shall reap a rich harvest of grace. "The same shall be saved"! We may sow in tears; but we shall reap with joy. We may pass through much tribulation; but we shall pass through it into the kingdom of God. Our light affliction, which is but for a moment, shall work for us a far more exceeding and eternal weight of glory! When those who hate our God, despise our gospel and persecute us are cast into hell, we shall enter into life everlasting with Christ (Revelation 19:1-8; 21:1-5).

"But when ye shall see the abomination of desolation, spoken of by Daniel the prophet, standing where it ought not, (let him that readeth understand,) then let them that be in Judaea flee to the mountains: And let him that is on the housetop not go down into the house, neither enter therein, to take any thing out of his house: And let him that is in the field not turn back again for to take up his garment. But woe to them that are with child, and to them that give suck in those days! And pray ye that your flight be not in the winter. For in those days shall be affliction, such as was not from the beginning of the creation which God created unto this time, neither shall be. And except that the Lord had shortened those days, no flesh should be saved: but for the elect's sake, whom he hath chosen, he hath shortened the days. And then if any man shall say to you, Lo, here is Christ; or, lo, he is there; believe him not: For false christs and false prophets shall rise, and shall shew signs and wonders, to seduce, if it were possible, even the elect. But take ye heed: behold, I have foretold you all things".

(Mark 13:14-23)

Chapter 58

"The Abomination Of Desolation"

In this paragraph our Lord Jesus both warns us of a time of great spiritual darkness, deception and trouble, which must come upon the earth, and assures us of the infallible security of God's elect in the midst of it. As we look at these verses of holy scripture, may God the Holy Spirit inscribe upon our hearts the things here taught. Let me direct your attention to three things revealed in our text.

A Time Of Great Deception

"But when ye shall see the abomination of desolation, spoken of by Daniel the prophet, standing where it ought not, (let him that readeth understand,) then let them that be in Judaea flee to the mountains" (v. 14).

In this thirteenth chapter of Mark the Lord Jesus warns us over and over again of a time of terrible spiritual darkness, delusion, deception and danger that must sweep across the earth before he comes again. Without question, the warnings given in verses 14 to 18 had a specific reference to the judgment of God which fell upon Jerusalem in 70 AD.

When the armies of Rome destroyed Jerusalem, when God sent Titus into that once holy city, which had become an abominable house of devils, when swine's blood was offered up in the most holy place, when the temple was levelled, when the sceptre of civil government departed from Judah, God's judgment upon the nation was manifest and obvious to everyone except the nation of Israel. The Jews were scattered to the four corners of the earth.

However, our Lord specifically directs our attention to Daniel's prophecy (Daniel 9:20-27). In that prophecy, though Daniel speaks of the abomination of desolation, he was also assured by Gabriel, "thou art greatly beloved". Daniel had been praying for God to show mercy and exercise forgiveness. He had been praying that the Lord God would in wrath remember mercy toward his holy city and his chosen people.

In verses 24-27 Daniel is given a vision, by which he was assured of both God's justice and his mercy. In strict justice the Lord God declared that he would destroy the physical nation of Israel and the physical city of Jerusalem. At the same time, he assured his prophet that he would accomplish the everlasting salvation of his elect, his people, his holy city, his royal priesthood.

"And whiles I was speaking, and praying, and confessing my sin and the sin of my people Israel, and presenting my supplication before the LORD my God for the holy mountain of my God; Yea, whiles I was speaking in prayer, even the man Gabriel, whom I had seen in the vision at the beginning, being caused to fly swiftly, touched me about the time of the evening oblation. And he informed me, and talked with me, and said, O Daniel, I am now come forth to give thee skill and understanding. At the beginning of thy supplications the commandment came forth, and I am come to shew thee; for thou art greatly beloved: therefore understand the matter, and consider the vision. Seventy weeks are determined upon thy people and upon thy holy city, to finish the transgression, and to make an end of sins, and to make reconciliation for iniquity, and to bring in everlasting righteousness, and to seal up the vision and prophecy, and to anoint the most Holy. Know therefore and understand, that from the going forth of the commandment to restore and to build Jerusalem unto the Messiah the Prince shall be seven weeks, and threescore and two weeks: the street shall be built again, and the wall, even in troublous times. And after threescore and two weeks shall Messiah be cut off, but not for himself: and the people of the prince that shall come shall destroy the city and the sanctuary; and the end thereof shall be with a flood, and unto the end of the war desolations are determined. And he shall confirm the covenant with many for one week: and in the midst of the week he shall cause the sacrifice and the oblation to cease, and for the overspreading of abominations he shall make it desolate, even until the consummation, and that determined shall be poured upon the desolate" (Daniel 9:20-27).

Seventy Weeks

I will leave it to others to debate and argue about the 70 weeks and the time span they cover. I am not very interested in that. But I am interested in the things here promised.

In these verses we are given a clear, prophetic declaration of two things: redemption and wrath, deliverance and damnation, mercy and justice. Daniel's prophecy is a profound declaration of Christ's great work of redemption, by which he satisfied the justice of God and put away the sins of his people. In fact, there are eight things promised here. All of them depended upon and have been effectually accomplished by, the sin-atoning death and glorious exaltation of our Lord Jesus Christ.

In verse 26 we are told that the Lord Jesus Christ, the Messiah, must be cut off, slaughtered, not for himself, but for his people. "And after threescore and two weeks shall Messiah be cut off, but not for himself: and the people of the prince that shall come shall destroy the city and the sanctuary; and the end thereof shall be with a flood, and unto the end of the war desolations are determined".

In verse 27 we are told that after he was cut off out of the land of the living, our Lord Jesus Christ would confirm the everlasting covenant of grace to many. "And he shall confirm the covenant with many for one week: and in the midst of the week he shall cause the sacrifice and the oblation to cease, and for the overspreading of abominations he shall make it desolate, even until the consummation, and that determined shall be poured upon the desolate".

Our blessed Saviour confirmed the covenant with his blood (Hebrews 13:20). When he did, when he died as our Substitute, our dear Redeemer caused the sacrifices and oblations of the Old Covenant to cease forever (Hebrews 10:1-22). Though this was done in the most public, conspicuous manner when the Romans destroyed Jerusalem and the temple, pouring swine's blood upon the altar, the oblations ceased when Christ died!

Our Lord Jesus confirmed the covenant at the appointed time "one week". At the specific time God ordained from eternity, in due time, when the fulness of time was come, Christ the Messiah confirmed the covenant with many. He confirmed the covenant with his blood. If you will read verse 24 again, you will see some of the things confirmed to us, confirmed to God's elect by the blood of the everlasting covenant.

"Seventy weeks are determined upon thy people and upon thy holy city, to finish the transgression, and to make an end of sins, and to make reconciliation for iniquity, and to bring in everlasting righteousness, and to seal up the vision and prophecy, and to anoint the most Holy".

The Lord Jesus Christ, by his obedience unto death as our covenant Surety and sin-atoning Substitute, finished the transgression of his people. Transgression is the breach of the law. The Son of God erased our breaches of God's holy law.

He made an end of sins, all the sins of his people. When he was made sin for us, he put away our sins by the sacrifice of himself.

Our all-glorious Christ made "reconciliation for iniquity". Iniquity speaks of failure, inequity, missing the mark. Everything we messed up, Christ fixed!

Thus, by his obedience unto death, the God-man brought in everlasting righteousness for all the Father gave him to save before the world began.

John Kent wrote:

> 'Twixt Jesus and the chosen race,
> Subsists a bond of sovereign grace,
> That hell, with its infernal train,
> Shall ne'er dissolve nor rend in vain.
>
> Hail! sacred union, firm and strong,
> How great the grace, how sweet the song,
> That worms of earth should ever be,
> One with incarnate Deity!
>
> One in the tomb, one when He rose,
> One when He triumphed o'er His foes,
> One when in heaven He took His seat,
> While seraphs sang all hell's defeat.
>
> This sacred tie forbids their fears,
> For all He is or has is theirs;
> With Him, their Head, they stand or fall,
> Their Life, their Surety, and their All.

Thus, the Lord Jesus Christ sealed the vision of the Old Testament prophets (Hebrews 1:1-3). He completely fulfilled the vision of Old Testament prophecy.

Having finished everything he came here to do, our great Redeemer has been anointed as the King of kings and Lord of lords with the oil of gladness. He is the "Most Holy"!

These are the blessed things spoken of by Daniel; but our Lord directs our attention also to Daniel's prophecy of wrath and judgment. Look at Daniel chapter 9 especially verses 26 and 27 again, and you will see that Daniel spoke by divine inspiration about God's wrath and judgment upon those who refuse to bow to and trust his Son.

We will not read the verses again; but the "overspreading of abominations", by which the Lord God made Jerusalem and all Israel spiritually desolate, by which he destroyed the city, the sanctuary and the nation in the flood of his wrath, was not accidental, but precisely what God had purposed. Daniel was specifically told that these "desolations are determined".

Horrible as that act of divine judgment was, it was nothing compared to the abomination of desolation which the Lord God has sent upon this reprobate age in which we live. The things which happened in Jerusalem 2000 years ago only foreshadowed the judgment of God which has fallen upon this generation. Read the first chapter of Romans, and you will discover that ours is not a generation ripe *for* the judgment of God. This is a generation *under* the judgment of God. I can think of no age, no generation, no circumstance under which the warning of verse seventeen is more appropriate than it is in this day of apostate, freewill, works religion. "But woe to them that are with child, and to them that give suck in those days"!

Just as the Jews fled for fear of their lives from Titus and the Roman armies who engulfed Jerusalem, you and I will be wise to flee the abominations of Arminian, freewill, works religion, lest we be forever damned with Babylon (Revelation 18:4; 2 Corinthians 6:14-18). Let nothing, neither house, nor property, nor clothes, not even family, hold you in Babylon.

"But when ye shall see the abomination of desolation, spoken of by Daniel the prophet, standing where it ought not, (let him that readeth understand,) then let them that be in Judaea flee to the mountains: And let him that is on the housetop not go down into the house, neither enter therein, to take any thing out of his house: And let him that is in the field not turn back again for to take up his garment. But woe to them that are with child, and to them that give suck in those days! And pray ye that your flight be not in the winter. For in those days shall be affliction, such as was not from the beginning of the creation which God created unto this time, neither shall be" (vv. 14-19).

The danger, the trouble, the affliction spoken of here is far more serious than physical persecution. This peril is a peril of soul. It is altogether spiritual!

"For in those days shall be affliction, such as was not from the beginning of the creation which God created unto this time, neither shall be. And except that the Lord had shortened those days, no flesh should be saved: but for the elect's sake, whom he hath chosen, he hath shortened the days. And then if any man shall say to you, Lo, here is Christ; or, lo, he is there; believe him not: For false christs and false prophets shall rise, and shall shew signs and wonders, to seduce, if it were possible, even the elect. But take ye heed: behold, I have foretold you all things" (vv. 19-23).

"And then shall that Wicked be revealed, whom the Lord shall consume with the spirit of his mouth, and shall destroy with the brightness of his coming: Even him, whose coming is after the working of Satan with all power and signs and lying wonders, And with all deceivableness of unrighteousness in them that perish; because they received not the love of the truth, that they might be saved. And for this cause God shall send them strong delusion, that they should believe a lie: That they all might be damned who believed not the truth, but had pleasure in unrighteousness" (2 Thessalonians 2:8-12).

False prophets abound everywhere. False prophets are those preachers, teachers and religious leaders who point sinners to a false Christ, a false Saviour. That is, a redeemer who did not redeem, a saviour who cannot save, a king who cannot rule, a priest who cannot prevail. They seduce unsuspecting multitudes by satanic power with signs and wonders, imitating and pretending to be the apostles of Christ.

I have deliberately spent the bulk of my time on the first point of our study, because it leads to and takes in the last two things I want you to see. The second point in this passage is:

A Matter Of Great Responsibility

Our Master's command is, "Flee to the mountains"! It is our responsibility to use the means and the good sense God has given us both to provide for and protect our physical well-being and our spiritual well-being. If you care for your soul and the souls of your family and those under your influence, you will diligently use the means God has given you for your souls' eternal welfare.

Those who profess to believe God, while they idly sit still and do nothing, show more contempt for God than conviction from him. Their faith is fanaticism. Their profession is a pretence. They may bluster; but they do not believe! Their loud sounds are just lip service. Because he believed God, when Hezekiah said, "The Lord is with us to fight our battles", he also built up the walls of the city and made swords and shields (2 Chronicles 32:5). Paul had a word directly from heaven assuring him that no man on board his ship would perish. Yet, he knew they would perish if they did not throw over all their cargo and stay on the ship (Acts 27:31).

If you want God's salvation, put yourself under the sound of the gospel. Addict yourself to the Word of God. Use God's appointed means of grace! If you want your family saved, get them under the sound of the gospel. Addict yourself and your family to the worship of God. Use God's appointed means of grace!

A Reason For Great Praise

Here is the reason given by our Lord himself for great praise and thanksgiving to God. Election! "And except that the Lord had shortened those days, no flesh should be saved: but for the elect's sake, whom he hath chosen, he hath shortened the days" (v. 20). "For false Christs and false prophets shall rise, and shall show signs and wonders, to seduce, if it were possible, even the elect" (v. 22). Let every saved sinner give thanks to God for his free, sovereign, eternal, electing love.

There is a people in this world called "the elect" who must and shall be saved. Everything God does in this world he does "for the elect's sake". Every sinner who trusts the Lord Jesus Christ is numbered among "the elect". God's elect shall not be deceived by the false prophets and false Christs of the world. And it is only because of God's election that we are not deceived by the abomination of desolation called freewill, works religion. Thank God for electing love, mercy and grace!

"We are bound to give thanks alway to God for you, brethren beloved of the Lord, because God hath from the beginning chosen you to salvation through sanctification of the Spirit and belief of the truth: Whereunto he called you by our gospel, to the obtaining of the glory of our Lord Jesus Christ" (2 Thessalonians 2:13, 14).

"But in those days, after that tribulation, the sun shall be darkened, and the moon shall not give her light, and the stars of heaven shall fall, and the powers that are in heaven shall be shaken. And then shall they see the Son of man coming in the clouds with great power and glory. And then shall he send his angels, and shall gather together his elect from the four winds, from the uttermost part of the earth to the uttermost part of heaven. Now learn a parable of the fig tree; When her branch is yet tender, and putteth forth leaves, ye know that summer is near: So ye in like manner, when ye shall see these things come to pass, know that it is nigh, even at the doors. Verily I say unto you, that this generation shall not pass, till all these things be done. Heaven and earth shall pass away: but my words shall not pass away".

(Mark 13:24-31)

Chapter 59

The Lord Is Coming!

The historians tell us that the early saints used to greet one another with these words, "He is risen;" and upon parting they would say, "The Lord is coming". Thus they constantly encouraged one another in the faith and constantly reminded one another of both the accomplishment of redemption by Christ and the certainty of resurrection glory with Christ.

Before he left this world, our Lord Jesus assured his disciples that, just as surely as he arose from the grave, he would come again to raise his saints from their graves and translate all his elect in resurrection glory to heaven. That is the subject of Mark 13:24-31. Without question, this is a prophecy of our Lord's coming in judgment to destroy Jerusalem, the temple, and the nation of Israel, but it cannot and should not be limited to that. It is also a prophecy of our Saviour's second coming. As we read this passage it should always stir our hearts with expectation and desire for the Lord's coming. May God give us grace ever to live on the tip-toe of faith in the blessed expectation of Christ's glorious Second Advent. The Lord Jesus Christ is coming again.

The Glory Of Christ's Coming
"But in those days, after that tribulation, the sun shall be darkened, and the moon shall not give her light, and the stars of heaven shall fall, and the powers that are in heaven shall be shaken. And then shall they see the Son of man coming in the clouds with great power and glory" (vv. 24-26).

In the ninth chapter of the Book of Hebrews (vv. 24-28) we are told that the Son of God appeared once to put away our sins by the sacrifice of himself. Christ came here to die in our place, to put away our sins by his death; and he has effectually performed that which he came here to accomplish. As our great Advocate and High Priest he now appears in the presence of God for us, making intercession for his elect according to the will of God (1 John 2:1, 2). Our great God and Saviour shall, at the appointed time, appear again on this earth to consummate his great work of saving his people from their sins.

As our Saviour describes his second advent here in Mark 13, it is obvious that when he comes again, it will not be a secret thing. At his glorious second advent, he will appear with power and great glory. That is the language of holy scripture.

"And to you who are troubled rest with us, when the Lord Jesus shall be revealed from heaven with his mighty angels, in flaming fire taking vengeance on them that know not God, and that obey not the gospel of our Lord Jesus Christ: Who shall be punished with everlasting destruction from the presence of the Lord, and from the glory of his power; When he shall come to be glorified in his saints, and to be admired in all them that believe (because our testimony among you was believed) in that day" (2 Thessalonians 1:7-10).

"Behold, he cometh with clouds; and every eye shall see him, and they also which pierced him: and all kindreds of the earth shall wail because of him. Even so, Amen" (Revelation 1:7). Our Lord speaks about the sun being turned into darkness, the moon refusing to give light, the falling of stars and the shaking of powers in the heavens. Such words conveys the idea of a great convulsion, a climactic dismantling of creation by the finger of God.

The language used is very much like the language with which Peter was inspired of God to describe the coming of Christ. "The day of the Lord will come as a thief in the night; in the which the heavens shall pass away with a great noise, and the elements shall melt with fervent heat, the earth also and the works that are therein shall be burned up" (2 Peter 3:10).

The Order Of Events
In other words, that which shall immediately precede the glorious appearing of Christ will be the conflagration of the universe. The order of events at the second coming seems to be as follows. These things are not written in concrete. I would not argue in defence of them for even a second. However, this is what appears to me to be likely. I have formed this order by carefully comparing scripture with scripture. Whatever the order of events may indeed be, it will not take long to accomplish the whole thing. When the Son of God rises from his throne and says, "Behold, I make all things new", it will all be done quickly.

> Our blessed Christ will come in the clouds of heaven.
> He will raise up the bodies of saints which sleep in the earth.
> Those who are living in faith when he comes shall be caught up to meet the Lord in the air.
> He will destroy the present creation and all his enemies with it, and make all things new.

Then we shall come with him to the earth. We shall come with him into a new heavens and a new earth.

Then will come the resurrection of the dead and the great white throne judgment.

After these things *eternal life with Christ in glory*!

Radically Different

Christ's second advent will be radically different from his first. Our Saviour came the first time in humiliation, an infant, born of a poor woman, laid in a manger at Bethlehem, unnoticed, unhonoured, unknown. He is coming the second time in power and great glory, in royal dignity, with all the armies of heaven surrounding him, to be seen, recognized, known, acknowledged and feared by all people, nations, tribes and tongues.

Christ Jesus came the first time to suffer, to bear the sins of his people, to be made a curse, to be despised, rejected, unjustly condemned and slain. He is coming the second time as the reigning, almighty Monarch of the universe to put down every foe, put an end to all rebellion, to take possession of all the kingdoms of this world, to judge the world, to destroy his enemies, to make all things new and to be eternally admired by redeemed sinners.

We would all be wise to lay these things to heart and meditate upon them regularly. These facts are filled with comfort for every believer. Our great King, our all glorious Christ, will soon be here again! We shall, with him, inherit all things. We will soon exchange the cross for a crown. We shall enter into everlasting honour, joy, bliss and life.

For all who believe not, the facts revealed in the Book of God about the second coming of Christ ought to be terrifying. Indeed, if any dare think upon them, I know they are terrifying to their souls. The Christ they despise, reject, and mock will soon call them before his holy bar of judgment. That God-man, whose gospel they trample beneath their feet, will soon hold them accountable. In that day they shall receive of the Lord's hand their exact, just due for all their sins. Hell will be their everlasting portion.

The Gathering Of God's Elect

In verse twenty-seven, our Master tells us plainly that the first order of business and the primary purpose of his great second advent shall be the gathering of his elect. Throughout the Word of God we are distinctly and constantly taught that our God does all things for the elect's sake. "And then shall he send his angels, and shall gather together his elect from the four winds, from the uttermost part of the earth to the uttermost part of heaven".

Just as God's servants, as the angels of God, are sent out by the preaching of the gospel to gather his elect into his kingdom from the four corners of the earth, so at the end of time those heavenly spirits created to minister to the chosen shall be sent forth to fetch them out of the earth and gather them, all of them, even their dust and ashes, unto Christ in glory! As the angels carried Lazarus into Abraham's bosom, so they shall carry all God's elect into heaven's bosom to be with Christ!

As stated above, the gathering out of God's elect will immediately precede the Lord's judgment of the earth. Our safety shall be taken care of, when the Lord consumes the earth with the fiery brightness of his coming. Nothing shall be done to destroy the earth until all God's elect are beyond the reach of harm. Not one drop of rain fell until Noah was safe in the ark. Fire and brimstone could not fall upon Sodom until Lot was safely secluded in Zoar. And God's wrath will not consume his enemies in the earth until he has taken his saints out of the earth.

Blessed be our God, there is a great gathering day coming! We who believe ought to look forward to that great day with unmingled joy, without the slightest dread or fear (2 Thessalonians 2:1). What a gathering "our gathering together unto him" shall be! It will be a gracious gathering, a righteous gathering, a loving gathering and a permanent gathering of all the family of God!

The Parable Of The Fig Tree

"Now learn a parable of the fig tree; When her branch is yet tender, and putteth forth leaves, ye know that summer is near: So ye in like manner, when ye shall see these things come to pass, know that it is nigh, even at the doors. Verily I say unto you, that this generation shall not pass, till all these things be done" (vv. 28-30). Our Lord sternly reproved the Pharisees because they could not "discern the signs of the times" (Matthew 16:3). They could not see that the sceptre was passing away from Judah. They did not see that Daniel's seventy weeks were fulfilled. Let us beware of such blindness. It is a blindness caused by spiritual lethargy and an overmuch fondness for this world. This parable of the fig tree is not a deep, mysterious, secretive thing. In this parable our Master tells us plainly that when we see the things spoken of in this context, (when we see the abomination of desolation spoken of by Daniel the prophet), his glorious second advent is at hand.

The abomination of desolation spoken of by Daniel is the revelation, to God's saints, not to the world, of antichrist i.e. Arminian, free will, works religion. It is that which Paul speaks of in 2 Thessalonians 2, the loosing of Satan to deceive the nations of the world (Revelation 20:1-8).

The Lord Is Coming!

The lesson of the parable of the fig tree is just this: While we must never even guess at, or try to figure out the time of Christ's coming, increasing darkness, ungodliness, apostasy and idolatry ought to cause every believer to live on the tip-toe of faith, looking expectantly for Christ's appearing.

The rising infidelity, increasing acceptance of popery, Islam, Judaism and mysticism, the worldwide will-worship of this apostate age, the lawlessness, the anarchy, the contempt of authority, the acceptance of sexual promiscuity, (fornication, adultery, homosexuality), and the general calling of evil good and good evil ought to be glaring beacons in our eyes and trumpets in our ears telling us, "This is the end! Judgment has begun. The end is near. The Lord is coming".

The more we see these things coming to pass the more reason we have to look up in hope. Our redemption draws nigh! We must therefore watch, be sober, keep our garments white and unspotted from the world (Revelation 16:15). Armageddon is here. The judgment of the great whore is at hand. The Lord is coming!

The Certainty Of God's Word

In verse 31 our Lord seems to have anticipated our tendency toward scepticism and unbelief, and therefore warns us emphatically against it. "Heaven and earth shall pass away: but my words shall not pass away".

We must never allow ourselves to give any credibility to any questioning of God's Word. Let us never dare imagine that any word of prophecy is improbable, or unlikely simply because it seems contrary to nature, or experience, or our judgment. Let us never be found among those arrogant fools who imagine that they are smarter than God. We must never find ourselves agreeing with those scoffers who, walking after their own lusts, say, "Where is the promise of his coming?" (2 Peter 3:3, 4). Christ is coming again. Rejoice!

"But I would not have you to be ignorant, brethren, concerning them which are asleep, that ye sorrow not, even as others which have no hope. For if we believe that Jesus died and rose again, even so them also which sleep in Jesus will God bring with him. For this we say unto you by the word of the Lord, that we which are alive and remain unto the coming of the Lord shall not prevent them which are asleep. For the Lord himself shall descend from heaven with a shout, with the voice of the archangel, and with the trump of God: and the dead in Christ shall rise first: Then we which are alive and remain shall be caught up together with them in the clouds, to meet the Lord in the air: and so shall we ever be with the Lord. Wherefore comfort one another with these words" (1 Thessalonians 4:13-18).

"Heaven and earth shall pass away: but my words shall not pass away. But of that day and that hour knoweth no man, no, not the angels which are in heaven, neither the Son, but the Father. Take ye heed, watch and pray: for ye know not when the time is. For the Son of man is as a man taking a far journey, who left his house, and gave authority to his servants, and to every man his work, and commanded the porter to watch. Watch ye therefore: for ye know not when the master of the house cometh, at even, or at midnight, or at the cockcrowing, or in the morning: Lest coming suddenly he find you sleeping. And what I say unto you I say unto all, Watch".

(Mark 13:31-37)

Chapter 60

No One Knows

Soon you and I must meet the thrice holy God face to face in judgment. Soon we will cross over that river that will carry us out of this changing, temporal world of time and sense into that world in which all things are unchanging and eternal. Soon you and I are going to meet God.

Like Amos the prophet, I urge you, "Prepare to meet thy God"! When Paul knew that the time of his departure was at hand, he said, "I am now ready". Are you? Are you ready? Are you prepared to meet God?

Soon we must meet God in judgment, but no one knows when. Therefore, our Lord gives us a word of constant, pressing urgency as he concludes his discourse in Mark 13. He calls us to watchfulness. We should always be on the lookout for Christ's second coming. Every redeemed soul, in whom God the Holy Spirit has performed the saving operations of his grace, is always ready for his Lord's return and ready to meet God. Yet, it is most blessed to be, as Robert Hawker put it, "in an actual state of waiting, looking, longing for and hastening to the Lord's coming ... Think what a blessed privilege this is, and beg of the Lord Jesus to be so found at his coming (2 Peter 3:12)".

A Promise

Our Saviour makes a promise we would be wise to lay to heart. "Heaven and earth shall pass away: but my words shall not pass away". All creation and all things connected with this present creation, all things involved in the curse, all things affected by and infected with sin shall pass away. This present heaven and earth shall soon be dissolved, burnt up with the fire of God's holy wrath (Mark 13:24, 25; 2 Peter 3:10-14; 2 Corinthians 4:18).

We live in a world in which everything is temporal and passing away. We are all going to a world in which everything is permanent and eternal. The bliss of heaven is eternal. The torments of the damned in hell are everlasting. Our state in that unseen world of eternity depends entirely upon our relationship to the Son of God, the Lord Jesus Christ, in this world of time.

If you are washed in Christ's blood and robed in his righteousness now, you will be clean and holy forever. If you trust Christ as your Saviour now, he will be your Saviour forever. If you are one with Christ now, you shall be one with Christ in eternity. If you love Christ and are loved of Christ now, you shall love Christ and be loved of Christ forever.

If you meet Christ in judgment as an unbeliever, you will be an unbeliever forever. If you are unclean when you leave this world, you will be unclean forever. If you are a rebel when you draw your last breath, you will be a rebel forever. If you are cursed and damned when you go out to meet God in judgment, you will be cursed of God, hated by God, and damned by God forever!

Our only hope for eternal life is the free, sovereign, saving grace of God in Christ, the sinners' Substitute.

> There is a fountain filled with blood,
> Drawn from Immanuel's veins;
> And sinners plunged beneath that flood,
> Lose all their guilty stains.
>
> The dying thief rejoiced to see,
> That fountain in his day;
> And there may I, though vile as he,
> Wash all my sins away.
>
> E'er since by faith I saw the stream,
> Christ's flowing wounds supply,
> Redeeming love has been my theme,
> And shall be 'til I die!

"Heaven and earth shall pass away: but my words shall not pass away". God's Word is immutable, absolute, certain and unalterable. That statement applies to God's written Word of Inspiration, the holy scriptures, and to every word of decree, doctrine, grace, promise and judgment revealed in holy scripture (Isaiah 40:8; 46:9-11; 55:11; Psalm 119:89). He who is the omniscient, holy, perfect, omnipotent, unchangeable God never needs to alter his Word. God's Word is never yea and nay, but always yea and amen.

A Problem
In verse 32 the Lord Jesus makes a declaration, which presents a problem to many. "But of that day and that hour knoweth no man, no, not the angels which are in heaven, neither the Son, but the Father".

Here is the problem: If the Lord Jesus Christ is himself God the Son, equal in all things and one with the Father and the Spirit, as the scriptures universally assert that he is and the doctrine of the Trinity demands, if he is God all-wise, all-knowing, omniscient, before whom darkness is light, from whom nothing can be hid, How can he be ignorant of the day and hour of his second advent?

The answer is both simple and obvious, when we compare scripture with scripture. In fact, the imagined problem is no problem at all, but merely a demonstration of the fact that our Lord Jesus Christ is exactly who and what he claims to be both God and man as truly and completely God as if he were not man, and as truly and completely man as if he were not God.

As a man, our Saviour was no more omniscient than he was omnipotent or omnipresent. When he hungered, it was not God who hungered, but man. When he thirsted, it was not God who thirsted, but man.

In the four gospels he sometimes speaks of himself as a man (as here), and sometimes he speaks of himself as God, in order to show us that he is fully both. As God, he said to his disciples, "Our friend, Lazarus, sleepeth", though no one had informed him of Lazarus' death. Yet, when he came to Bethany, he asked as a man, "Where have ye laid him?"

The same thing is true in Mark 13:32. Obviously, as the Son of God, he knew and always has known the precise second of his second advent. But as the Son of man, he was altogether ignorant of it. He who is our Redeemer must be both God and man in one glorious person.

No One
In this day of prophecy mania our Lord's words here need to be emphasized and remembered. He tells us in the plainest terms possible that no one knows when the Lord Jesus Christ shall appear in his glorious Second Advent. The language of scripture in this regard is crystal clear (Acts 1:4-11).

No one knows, or even has a hint of an idea, when the Lord Jesus will come again to this world. The event is certain; but no one knows the time. Not only do the scriptures tell us this emphatically, we have a glaring proof of the fact in our Saviour's own words. If the perfect, holy man Christ Jesus, that man who knew the Book of God like no other man, did not know it, if he did not figure out the day or hour of his appearing, no other man is about to do so!

And no one knows when Christ is coming to take him out of this world to meet God in judgment. I find it utterly amazing that we so blatantly ignore this fact. David said, "There is but a step between me and death". We all say we realize that; but very few people seem to live like they realize it. "There is but a step between me and death"! God has, from eternity, fixed the moment and the means by which he will take each of us out of this world. When our time is up, we shall be taken. And as soon as God takes us out of this world, we are going to stand before him in judgment.

I know there is a Day of Judgment at the end of time. Following the general resurrection, there will be a general judgment (John 5:28, 29; Revelation 20:11-15). But the scriptures plainly speak of us meeting God in judgment as soon as we draw our last breath (2 Corinthians 5:10, 11; Hebrews 9:27). "How wilt thou do in the swelling of Jordan?" (Jeremiah 12:5).

A Parable

In verses 34 and 35 our Master puts forth a parable, in which he explains our present position and responsibility as his servants in this world.

"For the Son of man is as a man taking a far journey, who left his house, and gave authority to his servants, and to every man his work, and commanded the porter to watch. Watch ye therefore: for ye know not when the master of the house cometh, at even, or at midnight, or at the cockcrowing, or in the morning".

There are several things in this parable which we ought to lay to heart. The church of Christ is his house: he alone is the Master of his house. The Lord Jesus left his church, his house, under the care, authority and rule of his servants. His servants are men counted worthy by him to preach the gospel and to rule his house with the authority of his Word (Acts 20:28; Hebrews 13:7, 17; 1 Peter 5:1-3; 1 Thessalonians 5:12, 13).

The Lord Jesus has appointed to each of his own a specific work to do. "He gave to every man his work". Our Master has not abandoned his house: he is coming back to it; and his coming will be sudden, without warning. Let us live in the blessed anticipation of his arrival, watching for his appearance, praying for his grace and working in his house for the good of his house and the glory of his great name.

The Post

The Master has assigned a post to each of his own in this world.

"Take ye heed, watch and pray: for ye know not when the time is ... Watch ye therefore: for ye know not when the master of the house cometh, at even, or at midnight, or at the cockcrowing, or in the morning: Lest coming suddenly he find you sleeping. And what I say unto you I say unto all, Watch" (vv. 33, 35-37).

Ever be watchful of your own soul. Ever stir yourself up to renewed consecration to Christ. When the Master comes, I pray that he will not find me sleeping at my post. One of the old, old writers said, "Be doing something, that the devil may always find you engaged". When John Calvin's health was failing him and his friends urged him to rest more and do less work to preserve his health, he responded "Would you want my Master to find me idle?" Let us not be found sleeping at our post, but watching, praying and working.

"After two days was the feast of the passover, and of unleavened bread: and the chief priests and the scribes sought how they might take him by craft, and put him to death. But they said, Not on the feast day, lest there be an uproar of the people. And being in Bethany in the house of Simon the leper, as he sat at meat, there came a woman having an alabaster box of ointment of spikenard very precious; and she brake the box, and poured it on his head. And there were some that had indignation within themselves, and said, Why was this waste of the ointment made? For it might have been sold for more than three hundred pence, and have been given to the poor. And they murmured against her. And Jesus said, Let her alone; why trouble ye her? she hath wrought a good work on me. For ye have the poor with you always, and whensoever ye will ye may do them good: but me ye have not always. She hath done what she could: she is come aforehand to anoint my body to the burying. Verily I say unto you, Wheresoever this gospel shall be preached throughout the whole world, this also that she hath done shall be spoken of for a memorial of her".

(Mark 14:1-9)

Chapter 61

A God To Trust And An Example To Follow

In this chapter Mark begins to describe those things which our Lord Jesus Christ suffered as the Lamb of God. Up to this point, he has spoken of our Saviour as our Prophet, teaching us the things of God. Now, he begins to describe the Lord of glory as our great High Priest. Mark has shown us the miracles and sayings of the Master. Now, he begins to describe his vicarious sacrifice.

God Our Saviour
The scriptures set forth a stark contrast between the God of the Bible and the gods of men (Isaiah 45, 46, 47). The gods of men, those idols invented by men, the gods of this religious age no more resemble the God of the Bible than a gnat resembles an angel. The gods of religion want to do things, desire to do things, and try to do things, but are unable to accomplish them because of the works of the devil and the wills of men.

The God of the Bible, the only true God, he who is our God and Saviour never wants to do, desires to do, or tries to do anything except what he does. He is a God in whom we can be confident, a God who can be trusted implicitly, because he always has his way and does as he will.

In these first two verses of Mark 14 we have a very clear example of God's total sovereignty and omnipotent power to accomplish his will. He who truly is God over all and blessed forever always has his way. Here we see our great God disappointing the plans and designs of wicked men, overruling their wills and decisions to accomplish his own eternal purpose of grace in predestination.

"After two days was the feast of the passover, and of unleavened bread: and the chief priests and the scribes sought how they might take him by craft, and put him to death. But they said, Not on the feast day, lest there be an uproar of the people".

Our Lord's enemies did not want his death to be a public spectacle. Repeatedly, they tried to stone him to death, throw him off a cliff, or in some other way murder him without the common people being aware of what they had done. Notice the words of our text – Therefore, "the chief priests and the scribes sought how they might take him by craft, and put him to death". But that was not what God had purposed. Therefore, in his wise and adorable providence, he simply overruled their schemes. God defeated their counsel and performed his own.

It was the purpose of God from eternity that the Lord Jesus Christ must be lifted up upon the cursed tree and crucified as a cursed man as our Substitute. There was no other way possible for God to be both just and the Justifier of chosen sinners except by his own dear Son dying in our room and stead as our substitute. His justice must be satisfied. Else, he could not forgive sin. Christ alone, the God-man Mediator, could satisfy the justice of God for us. Yet, in order to fulfil the scriptures, our Saviour must die "according to the scriptures". You will recall that our Saviour often said, with reference to his sin-atoning death at Calvary, "The scriptures must be fulfilled" (v. 49).

In other words, the Lord Jesus must be betrayed by his own familiar friend for thirty pieces of silver, crucified by the hands of Gentiles at the insistence of the Jews, without a single bone in his body being broken, yet having his heart pierced. He must be numbered with transgressors in his death, mocked, beaten, spit upon, and stripped in public humiliation. And the soldiers who crucified him must cast lots to see which one would get his garment.

All these things were prophesied in the Old Testament scriptures. But "the chief priests and scribes sought how they might take him by craft and put him to death". That presented no problem to God Almighty! His counsel stood firm. His purpose was fulfilled. God's will always prevails. These men thought they would put an end to Christ's kingdom by killing him; but they were actually instruments in God's hands for the erection and building of his kingdom. When they did, with vile hearts, have the Lord Jesus crucified, they thought they would vilify him and make him a laughing stock; but God used them to make his name glorious. The Jews thought they would scare his disciples into silence by killing our Master; but God used their wicked deeds to embolden his disciples in preaching the gospel.

Sovereignty And Responsibility
Understand these two things plainly revealed in holy scripture: first, the Lord our God is in absolute control of this world (Psalm 76:10); and second every person is so completely responsible for the evil he performs that they shall give account of every idle word they speak (Matthew 12:36).

Though it was necessary that Christ our Passover be sacrificed for us, and though wicked men did no more in the crucifying of the Lord of Life and

Glory than God had before ordained must be done (Acts 2:22, 23; 4:27, 28), the deed itself and the malice with which it was performed was all their own. The opening verses of this chapter give us an awful representation of this fact, displaying the baseness of the depraved hearts of fallen men. "The chief priests and scribes", while engaged in the most solemn religious ceremonies, while pretending to worship God, sought to take the Son of God "by craft and put him to death"!

This God, and this God alone, who is in absolute, total control of the entire universe, we can and should trust with implicit confidence in all things and with all things. The Word of God, the promises of God, the prophecies of holy scripture are all utterly meaningless, unless our God is the God who rules everything, whose will is always performed, whose purpose stands fast, whose thoughts are irresistible!

Here is the basis of our faith and the foundation of our comfort. We live in a world of woe. We are often tossed to and fro in this world, confused and perplexed by many things. Let us ever rest ourselves in our God. "All things are of God". All things are ordered by our heavenly Father for our good. All things are arranged by God's infinite wisdom and omnipotent arm for his glory.

Look yonder to Calvary and laugh at those will-worshippers, who vainly imagine that the events of this world are ordered not by the will of Almighty God, but by the wills of puny men! We often hear preachers and others say, "God will never interfere with the will of man". This passage shows otherwise. It was the will of these men that Christ be put to death secretly. But God willed that he be publicly crucified in due time for the ungodly. God would not allow these wicked men to kill his Son when they wanted to, the way they wanted to, or in the place they wanted. However, he did permit them to kill his Son exactly according to the malice of their hearts. Yet, he used their sinful malice to accomplish his purpose of grace in the redemption of his people, exactly as he had purposed from eternity (Acts 13:28-30).

If the god you trust can be controlled, hindered, or even influenced by you, by Satan, or by all the powers of earth and hell combined, the god you trust is no God at all, and you are an idolater. Our God is not a spectator or even a competitor in this world. He is the Ruler of it. Salvation is knowing him, the only true and living God as he is revealed in the Lord Jesus Christ his Son, the God-man, our Saviour (John 17:3). He who is our God is the God we can trust.

An Example to Follow

In verses 3-9 we are given an example to follow. Here, Mark records, by divine inspiration, the story of a woman coming into the house of Simon the leper and anointing the Lord Jesus for his burial. It is an event recorded in all four of the gospel narratives (Matthew 26; Mark 14; Luke 7; and John 12). Comparing scripture with scripture, I cannot avoid the conclusion that this woman was Mary, the sister of Martha and Lazarus, and that she is the same woman often referred to as Mary Magdalene, out of whom the Lord Jesus had cast seven devils (Mark 16:9; Luke 8:2).

Mary was a remarkable woman. Modest and unassuming, she said very little. In fact, as far as I can determine, there is only one sentence written in the scriptures which was spoken by Mary. It is found in John 11:32. Yet, it is obvious that Mary was a woman of great wisdom, devotion, and faith, a woman who truly loved the Lord Jesus Christ. The Word of God presents Mary to us as an example of faith, devotion, and love on four different occasions.

We see Mary sitting at the Lord's feet, absorbing every word which fell from his lips (Luke 10:39).

We see her falling at the Master's feet in humble, submissive faith (John 11:32). As a broken-hearted woman might run into the arms of her husband for comfort, Mary ran to the Lord Jesus, fell at his feet, and sought comfort in him in her time of great sorrow.

We see Mary early in the morning of the resurrection at the tomb where our Lord's body had been buried (Matthew 28:1-9). She was the first one to hear the good news of the resurrection. She was the first one to see the risen Christ. This woman was the first one to proclaim the resurrection.

Here in Mark 14, we see Mary in the house of Simon the leper breaking an alabaster box of ointment of spikenard very precious", anointing the Lord Jesus for his burial (Mark 14:3-9).

This picture of this dear woman is perhaps the most instructive of the four. Our Lord himself declares, "She hath wrought a good work on me ... She hath done what she could. Verily I say unto you, Wheresoever this gospel shall be preached throughout the whole world, this also that she hath done shall be spoken of for a memorial of her". Truly, this woman sets before us a remarkable example to follow.

This good work, which was performed by Mary, might be most reasonably expected from any believer. Like you and me, Mary had experienced the grace of God in Christ. This work which she performed was only the spontaneous response of gratitude and love for the grace of God she had experienced. It was but her reasonable service (Romans 12:1, 2). Mary had been given faith in Christ. The Lord Jesus revealed himself to her and gave her the gift of faith. He chose her and graciously caused her to choose him. The demons who tormented her and held her captive were driven from her; and the Son of God established his throne in her heart. Her sins, which were many, were all forgiven her. The Lord graciously revealed to her the mysteries of the gospel. Mary alone seems to have known and understood how the Lord Jesus would accomplish redemption by his death as our Substitute. With all these things in her heart, Mary came to Simon's house to anoint her Lord in anticipation of his death and resurrection.

They Murmured

Mary's loving devotion and sacrificial zeal drew a very unexpected response from those who witnessed it.

"And being in Bethany in the house of Simon the leper, as he sat at meat, there came a woman having an alabaster box of ointment of spikenard very precious; and she brake the box, and poured it on his head. And there were some that had indignation within themselves, and said, Why was this waste of the ointment made? For it might have been sold for more than three hundred pence, and have been given to the poor. And they murmured against her" (vv. 3-5).

Mary must have been shocked by the comments she heard. She only wanted in some modest, but public way to honour her Lord. For her good work Mary was severely censored by Judas, the church treasurer (John 12:4-6). All the disciples followed Judas' wicked lead and became indignant at what they considered was Mary's waste (Matthew 26:8).

If you are committed to Christ, if you are inclined to do something for him, just for his honour and his glory, for the interests of his kingdom, for the furtherance of his gospel, simply because you love him, simply out of a deep sense of overwhelming gratitude, do not expect the approval of either the world, or religious hypocrites, or even true believers. The fact is, those who serve the Lord Jesus with the most ardent, self-sacrificing devotion are often ridiculed and criticized by those who ought to imitate their example.

Whole-hearted devotion exposes and condemns half-hearted religion. It stirs up the wrath of those whose hearts are cold and indifferent. Real consecration to Christ is sure to be criticized and mocked by those who know nothing about it. Though her actions were criticized and condemned by others, even by her friends, the Lord Jesus approved of, highly esteemed, and commended both Mary and her work.

"And Jesus said, Let her alone; why trouble ye her? she hath wrought a good work on me. For ye have the poor with you always, and whensoever ye will ye may do them good: but me ye have not always. She hath done what she could: she is come aforehand to anoint my body to the burying. Verily I say unto you, Wheresoever this gospel shall be preached throughout the whole world, this also that she hath done shall be spoken of for a memorial of her" (vv. 6-9).

Because the Lord Jesus was pleased with Mary, she seems oblivious to what anyone else had to say about the matter. She did it just for him. They really did not matter. Her faith in, love for, and devotion to the Son of God gave her courage and strength.

If I am conscious that I am sincerely doing something as unto the Lord, for the glory of his name, the interests of his kingdom, and the furtherance of his gospel, the opinions of men, their approval and their disapproval, are really of no consequence to me. As David said to his half-hearted brothers, I say, "Is there not a cause?" We must not allow the opinions of men to be the rule of our actions (John 2:5; Galatians 1:16).

A Good Work
Here the Holy Spirit shows us what a good work is. Our Saviour said of Mary, "She hath wrought a good work on me". This woman is held before us as a noble example to follow. Our Lord holds her up as an example of what we should be and do as his servants in this world. Here are seven things about what this dear lady did, by which her work shows itself to be indeed a good work done for Christ.

1. It was a work done for the glory of Christ alone. She was wrapped up in, absorbed with, and consumed by the Lord Jesus Christ. She cherished him. This perfume was meant for no one but him. She had no regard for herself, the consequences of her actions, what she might lose, or what she might gain. She wanted nothing but to honour Christ.

2. This was an act of pure love. This is exactly what Luke's narrative of this event teaches us (Luke 7:36-52). The one thing that motivated this woman to do what she did was love for Christ (1 John 4:19; 2 Corinthians 5:14). When our hearts and lives are ruled by love for Christ, they are well ruled.

3. This was a work requiring considerable cost, self-denial, and sacrifice. If you read the accounts of Mark and John, you will find that this ointment was worth nearly a year's wages (300 pence, compare Matthew 20:9-13).

4. This great sacrifice was the result of thoughtful, deliberate preparation. This was something she had been planning for some time. She had been saving this rich, costly perfume specifically to use it for Christ's honour at the appropriate opportunity (John 12:2).

5. This woman's sacrifice was made silently. She said nothing; she drew as little attention to herself as she possibly

could. She said nothing about what she would like to do, what she planned to do, what she was doing, or what she had done. She just did what she could.

6. This was the response of a believing heart to the sacrifice of her Lord. This woman appears to have been the only one of the Lord's disciples who clearly understood at the time how he must accomplish our redemption by his death as our Substitute.

7. This was an act of faith. She anointed him for his burial, but she did so in anticipation of his resurrection (Isaiah 53:10-12). The primary object of embalming was and is a belief in the resurrection of the dead.

I see in this incident a blessed foretaste of the honour that shall be given to God's elect on the Day of Judgment. In that great and glorious day no honour done to Christ shall be forgotten. The speeches of orators, the feats of warriors, the deeds of the greatest politicians, the trophies of athletes, the poetry and literature and art produced by men, all shall be forgotten; but this work, and the least work of any and every believing man and woman, even the giving of a cup of cold water in Christ's name shall be remembered and honoured before men by God himself! So let us do what we can for our Redeemer and his honour as he gives us opportunity (1 Corinthians 6:19, 20; 10:31; Romans 12:1, 2; 1 Corinthians 15:58).

"And being in Bethany in the house of Simon the leper, as he sat at meat, there came a woman having an alabaster box of ointment of spikenard very precious; and she brake the box, and poured it on his head. And there were some that had indignation within themselves, and said, Why was this waste of the ointment made? For it might have been sold for more than three hundred pence, and have been given to the poor. And they murmured against her. And Jesus said, Let her alone; why trouble ye her? She hath wrought a good work on me. For ye have the poor with you always, and whensoever ye will ye may do them good: but me ye have not always. She hath done what she could: she is come aforehand to anoint my body to the burying. Verily I say unto you, Wheresoever this gospel shall be preached throughout the whole world, this also that she hath done shall be spoken of for a memorial of her".

(Mark 14:3-9)

Chapter 62

A Good Work Done For Christ

Let us dwell a little longer on the account of the woman coming into the house of Simon the leper and anointing the Lord Jesus for his burial. As we have seen, it is an event recorded in all four of the gospel narratives (Matthew 26; Mark 14; Luke 7; and John 12). Passing over the negative attitudes and wicked conduct of Judas and the Lord's disciples, I want us only to observe what this woman did, why she did it, and what the Lord Jesus said about her and her work. This was the Master's commentary on this dear woman and what she did. "She hath wrought a good work on me ... She hath done what she could. She is come aforehand to anoint my body to the burying. Verily I say unto you, Wheresoever this gospel shall be preached throughout the whole world, this also that she hath done shall be spoken of for a memorial of her" (vv. 6, 8, 9). May God the Holy Spirit be our Teacher as we seek to learn from him the lessons set before us in this portion of his Word.

A Scripture Fulfilled

"And being in Bethany in the house of Simon the leper, as he sat at meat, there came a woman having an alabaster box of ointment of spikenard very precious; and she brake the box, and poured it on his head" (v. 3).

This act performed upon the Lord Jesus was an act of singular respect and honour. It showed great humility on the part of this woman. More importantly, it was a literal fulfilment of the Song of Solomon (1:12) "While the king sitteth at his table, my spikenard sendeth forth the smell thereof".

What this woman did for the honour of Christ, every gospel preacher must do every time he stands to preach the gospel. The Word of God is like a sacred chest containing precious spikenard, the rich, fragrant spikenard of Christ crucified. As this dear women broke open her box of spikenard, it is the privilege and responsibility of the gospel preacher to break open the Word of God, that the sweet, sweet aroma of Christ may fill his house. The gospel of Christ is as ointment poured forth. The sweet savour of the knowledge of Christ is diffused in the house of God when Christ is preached.

Let every ransomed sinner anoint the Son of God spiritually, by faith in him, giving him the honour he so richly deserves. Anoint him as your sovereign King, with the kiss of allegiance. Anoint him as your glorious Saviour with the kiss of repentance. Anoint him as your Beloved with the kiss of affection.

A Sinner Forgiven
When we read Luke's account of this event, we find that Luke was inspired to give a few details that Mark was inspired to omit; and those details help us to understand the reason for this woman's actions.

"And one of the Pharisees desired him that he would eat with him. And he went into the Pharisee's house, and sat down to meat. And, behold, a woman in the city, which was a sinner, when she knew that Jesus sat at meat in the Pharisee's house, brought an alabaster box of ointment, And stood at his feet behind him weeping, and began to wash his feet with tears, and did wipe them with the hairs of her head, and kissed his feet, and anointed them with the ointment. Now when the Pharisee which had bidden him saw it, he spake within himself, saying, This man, if he were a prophet, would have known who and what manner of woman this is that toucheth him: for she is a sinner" (Luke 7:36-39).

This woman was Mary Magdalene, mentioned in the next chapter, out of whom the Lord had cast seven devils. Though most theologians and commentators disagree, I am convinced that all four accounts of our Lord being anointed by a woman are of the same event, performed by the same woman. Try to picture the scene here.

Here is a woman who had been a notorious sinner, once possessed of seven devils. But she had been the object of God's saving grace. The Lord Jesus had forgiven her of all her sins, robed her in his righteousness, and told her plainly that he would soon die as her Substitute and rise again. Now, here she stands, looking at him, listening to him, loving him.

As she stood at his feet behind him, she remembered what she was and who she was. She remembered who he is and what he had done for her. She knew that the time of his death was at hand. Her heart broke with gratitude and love for Christ. She wanted to honour him. So she washed his feet with her tears and wiped them with the hairs of her head. A woman's hair is her glory (1 Corinthians 11:15). She untied her glory as she knelt at the Saviour's feet, and wiped his feet with that which was her glory. Then, she kissed his feet, and kissed the incessantly. The Saviour said, "This woman, since the time I came in, hath not ceased to kiss my feet" (Luke 7:45). And she anointed him. She poured the ointment on his head. When she did, it ran down his beard, over his body, down to his feet.

A Simple Faith

"She hath done what she could: she is come aforehand to anoint my body to the burying" (v. 8).

Faith is simply trusting Christ, taking God at his Word, believing him. That faith which stands in the word of man is not faith at all. True faith stands in the Word of God alone. Our Lord Jesus told his disciples that he must die and rise again. Mary simply believed him, and came as a penitent sinner to anoint him for his burial. Where does your faith stand? What is the basis of your faith? Is it your feeling? Your experience? Or, is it the Word of God? Faith believes the Word of God (1 John 5:7-12).

The basis of our faith is the Word of God, and the Word of God alone. I fully agree with Martin Luther who wrote:

> Feelings come and feelings go,
> And feelings are deceiving.
> My warrant is the Word of God;
> Naught else is worth believing!

With David, I say, "My soul fainteth for thy salvation: but I hope in thy word". "Thou art my hiding place and my shield: I hope in thy word". "Remember the word unto thy servant, upon which thou hast caused me to hope". "I wait for the LORD, my soul doth wait, and in his word do I hope" (Psalms 119:81, 114, 49; 130:5). Our feelings are no basis for hope. Our hope is in that which God has caused to be written in holy scripture. If I have "a good hope through grace", I ought to be able to turn to some text, or fact, or doctrine of God's Word as the source and basis of it. Our confidence must arise from something that God has said in his Word, that we have received and believed with our hearts. "The heart is deceitful above all things" (Jeremiah 17:9). "He that trusteth in his own heart is a fool" (Proverbs 28:26). Good feelings are deceiving, unless we can point to "Thus saith the Lord" as the basis of our hope. Our hope is found in, arises from, and is based upon the Book of God. "For whatsoever things were written aforetime were written for our learning, that we through patience and comfort of the scriptures might have hope" (Romans 15:4). The Book of God was written specifically to give believing sinners an assured hope of grace, salvation and eternal life in Christ (1 John 5:1-3).

The basis of hope is the Word of God. And that which is revealed in the Word of God which gives us hope is the Person and work of the Lord Jesus Christ, our Substitute (Romans 8:34, 35; 2 Corinthians 5:17-21). Christ is the Foundation upon which we are built. "Christ is our Hope" (1 Timothy 1:1).

We "hope in our Lord Jesus Christ" (1 Thessalonians 1:3). "The LORD is my portion, saith my soul; therefore will I hope in him" (Lamentations 3:24). Our hope is in Christ, our Covenant Surety, our blessed, sin-atoning Redeemer, our Righteousness, and our Advocate and High Priest in heaven. "I know whom I have believed, and am persuaded that he is able to keep that which I have committed unto him against that day" (2 Timothy 1:12).

The basis of our hope is the Word of God. That which is revealed in this Book that gives us hope is the Person and work of the Lord Jesus Christ. And I want you to see that the good hope of grace and salvation that God gives to his elect is something that is felt in us, felt inwardly in our hearts. The Apostle Paul speaks of God's saints as people "rejoicing in hope" (Romans 12:12). We read in Romans 5:5, "Hope maketh not ashamed, because the love of God is shed abroad in our hearts by the Holy Ghost which is given unto us".

A Service Found

Mary wanted to honour the Lord Jesus. She wanted to serve him. She wanted everyone around her to understand how gracious he had been to her, how much she owed him, how great, how glorious he is. But how could she do it. She was a woman. Modesty and obedience to God would not allow her to preach. She could not become a pastor, a deacon, a missionary, or an evangelist. But Mary was not one of our modern, mouthy, obnoxious domineering women. This woman, rather than being repulsed by her proper place in the kingdom of God, used it most honourably. She found a place where she could serve her Lord. She found a way to do something for Christ. She could not do what others could do. But she could do what she could do, and she did. Look at what our Lord says of her in verse 8. "She hath done what she could".

What an honourable thing! Blessed is that person who does what he or she can for Christ! Mary did what she had opportunity to do. She did what she had the God-given ability to do. And she did what she could when it had to be done. Had she not done this thing now, she could never have done it at all. "Whatsoever thy hand findeth to do, do it with thy might; for there is no work, nor device, nor knowledge, nor wisdom, in the grave, whither thou goest" (Ecclesiastes 9:10). "Whether therefore ye eat, or drink, or whatsoever ye do, do all to the glory of God" (1 Corinthians 10:31). "And whatsoever ye do, do it heartily, as to the Lord, and not unto men" (Colossians 3:23).

Because she did what she could, the Lord Jesus said of this woman, "She hath wrought a good work on me". Oh, for grace to do what I can for Christ! If we would just do what we could, we would do a good work for our Master.

Let me show you several things in summary which are obvious about this great thing Mary did for the Lord Jesus, several things that make her work a good work.

Mary did what she did for the glory of Christ alone. All that perfume, all that sweet aroma, all that precious spikenard was meant for Christ alone!

This was an act of pure love. Love never counts the cost. Love never weighs the consequence. Love never considers a loss a loss when the cost is incurred for the one who is loved.

This was a work requiring considerable sacrifice and self-denial. Three hundred pence was a year's wages (Matthew 20:9-13).

Though it was a spontaneous act of love, this sacrifice and anointing required thoughtful, deliberate preparation. Our Master tells us (John 12:7) that Mary had specifically kept this precious ointment for this occasion.

Mary did this thing without calling any attention to herself. Spurgeon said, "Silent acts of love have musical voices in the ears of Jesus. Sound no trumpet before thee, or Jesus will take warning and be gone."

This was the response of Mary's heart to the sacrifice of her Saviour, her Lord, her Redeemer. She believed what she heard the Lord speak (John 3:14-16) and understood that the price of her soul's ransom was his life's precious blood!

This great sacrifice was a work of faith. She knew that the Lord Jesus was about to die as her Substitute; but she believed that he would rise from the dead. Therefore, she anointed him for his burial in anticipation of his resurrection (Isaiah 53:10-12).

It appears that everything Mary owned in this world was in that little box of precious spikenard she had saved. With happy, willing, grateful heart, she poured it all out on the Saviour. Even so, if we would honour the Lord Jesus Christ, he must be honoured with all we have (Romans 12:1, 2). Those who have been forgiven much love much.

A Singular Fame

"Verily I say unto you, Wheresoever this gospel shall be preached throughout the whole world, this also that she hath done shall be spoken of for a memorial of her" (v. 9).

Mary lost nothing. Her oil was not wasted. Her labour was not spent in vain. She got by it that good name which Solomon says is "better than precious ointment". You can count on this: those who honour Christ, Christ will honour (1 Samuel 2:30). "Whether therefore ye eat, or drink, or whatsoever ye do, do all to the glory of God" (1 Corinthians 10:31).

475

"And Judas Iscariot, one of the twelve, went unto the chief priests, to betray him unto them. And when they heard it, they were glad, and promised to give him money. And he sought how he might conveniently betray him. And the first day of unleavened bread, when they killed the passover, his disciples said unto him, Where wilt thou that we go and prepare that thou mayest eat the passover? And he sendeth forth two of his disciples, and saith unto them, Go ye into the city, and there shall meet you a man bearing a pitcher of water: follow him. And wheresoever he shall go in, say ye to the goodman of the house, The Master saith, Where is the guestchamber, where I shall eat the passover with my disciples? And he will shew you a large upper room furnished and prepared: there make ready for us. And his disciples went forth, and came into the city, and found as he had said unto them: and they made ready the passover".

(Mark 14:10-16)

Chapter 63

"Furnished And Prepared"

In Mark 14 we have come to that solemn evening which preceded the most significant event in history. We should always read the things recorded here with great care, asking God the Holy Spirit to be our Teacher, asking him to inscribe the lessons in these verses upon our hearts with the finger of omnipotent grace.

From eternity, before the worlds were made, the Lord God ordained the sacrificial, sin-atoning death of his darling Son at Calvary. He predestined the time, place, and means of his Son's death as well as its sure accomplishments. God sent forth his Son to be the propitiation for our sins, to satisfy his justice for the sins of his people, to put away our sins, so that he might be both just and the Justifier of all who believe on the Lord Jesus Christ. The holy, just, and true God demands satisfaction for sin. Satisfaction could be made only by the sacrifice of his dear Son. Therefore, as it is written, "When the fulness of time was come, God sent forth his Son, made of a woman, made under the law, to redeem them that were under the law, that we might receive the adoption of sons".

The Lord Jesus lived as our representative for thirty-three years in perfect righteousness. He worked out a perfect righteousness for us. But his obedience in life alone could never save anyone. Justice must be satisfied. Our debt had to be paid. Our sins must be punished to the full satisfaction of divine justice. Therefore, "In due time Christ died for the ungodly".

The time had come for the observance of the passover. Therefore, the Master sent two of his disciples to Jerusalem in preparation for this ordinance of divine worship. What are the lessons set before us in this passage of inspiration by God the Holy Spirit?

False Faith

First, Judas is held before us as a glaring example of false faith. There are many in the visible church of God like Judas, many profess faith in Christ who do not possess faith in Christ.

"And Judas Iscariot, one of the twelve, went unto the chief priests, to betray him unto them. And when they heard it, they were glad, and promised to give him money. And he sought how he might conveniently betray him" (vv. 10, 11).

Like Judas, many men and women feel much, experience much, and do much in religion in the name of Christ, whose faith is but a false faith, a satanic delusion. It is impossible to imagine a greater, more glaring example of this fact than Judas Iscariot. J. C. Ryle rightly observed, "If ever there was a man who at one time looked like a true disciple of Christ, and bade fair to reach heaven, that man was Judas." Judas was personally chosen by Christ himself to be an apostle. He was a close companion of the Son of God for three years. He was an eye-witness to the mighty works and miracles of the Lord Jesus throughout his earthly ministry. Judas was a fellow-labourer with Peter, James, and John for three years. He was doctrinally orthodox, as doctrinally orthodox as the rest of those men who were personally taught the gospel by the lips of the Lord Jesus. He was sent forth with the others to preach the gospel and perform miracles in the name of Christ. Judas was highly regarded by all the other apostles, so highly regarded that he was made the group treasurer, so highly regarded that even when the Lord Jesus said "One of you shall betray me", not one of them suspected Judas! Yet Judas was apostate, a child of the devil all along. He departed from the faith completely. He betrayed the Son of God with the kiss of a friend!

If we compare Mark's account with what we are told in John 13:27 of Satan entering into Judas, it seems obvious that Mary's act of pouring her ointment out upon her Saviour's head caused such rage in Judas that it became the incentive that moved him to perform his vile deed. How often that grace the Lord gives his chosen stirs the malice of the reprobate (Acts 7:54). Judas must have gone from Bethany into Jerusalem, immediately after the Lord's commendation of Mary for her good work. Remember, the chief priests were in council at Jerusalem when this took place (v. 1). Once Judas made his deal with the chief priests, to cover his diabolical purpose, he returned to the disciples and sat with them at the supper.

How can we account for the conduct of this man? Was he once saved and then lost at last? No! Those who speak like that know nothing of the grace of God. When God saves, he saves forever (Ecclesiastes 3:14). He gives eternal life; and those to whom he gives eternal life shall never perish (John 10:28).

Judas was a tare sown among the wheat, a goat among the Lord's sheep, a wolf in sheep's clothing. He had the garments of religion, but not the garment of salvation. He had the doctrine of Christ, but not Christ. He had the religion of Christ, but not redemption. Though he professed to be a disciple of Christ, Judas was a covetous man. "The love of money" was the cause of his fall.

Covetousness was his ruin. That same grovelling covetousness which enslaved Balaam and turned Gehazi into a leper brought Judas to utter apostasy and to hell. The Holy Spirit tells us plainly that "He was a thief" (John 12:6). Judas stands before us as a glaring commentary on 1 Timothy 6:10. "The love of money is the root of all evil"!

Do not be content with anything short of the true grace of God in Christ. Great knowledge, great gifts, great experiences, great privileges, an outwardly holy life, church membership, power in prayer, preaching, and witnessing are all useless things, if we are not converted. We must be born again, made righteousness, and converted by the grace of God.

"Beware of covetousness"! Covetousness is a sin that eats like a cancer. It is the most heart-hardening of all idolatries. If we indulge this lust of the flesh, there is no end to the wickedness into which it will lead us. May God give us grace to be content with such things as we have (Hebrews 13:5). Money is not the one thing needful. Christ is!

How do we account for Judas' behaviour? Judas was a sinner, a fallen child of Adam, apt to be taken captive by Satan at his will. Who can comprehend the enormity of the fall? Let all who have experienced God's rich mercy in Christ ever give thanks to him for his precious, free, distinguishing grace (John 13:18; 1 Corinthians 4:7).

Christ Is God
Second, we have before us another of those many displays of the fact that the man Christ Jesus really is himself God.

"And the first day of unleavened bread, when they killed the passover, his disciples said unto him, Where wilt thou that we go and prepare that thou mayest eat the passover? And he sendeth forth two of his disciples, and saith unto them, Go ye into the city, and there shall meet you a man bearing a pitcher of water: follow him. And wheresoever he shall go in, say ye to the goodman of the house, The Master saith, Where is the guestchamber, where I shall eat the passover with my disciples? And he will show you a large upper room furnished and prepared: there make ready for us. His disciples went forth, and came into the city, and found as he had said unto them: and they made ready the passover" (vv. 12-16).

Throughout his earthly ministry, the Lord Jesus Christ claimed that he is God. The scriptures everywhere assert that he is God. In fact, if he is not God, he was not a good man, but a liar and an impostor; and we are yet in our sins. He who is our Saviour and Redeemer must also be our God. Only one who is both God and man could put away sin.

Frequently, this man, Jesus of Nazareth, demonstrated in the clearest manner possible the attributes of divinity, by which he enforced his claims.

Discovering Christ In The Gospel Of Mark

Who but the omnipotent God could raise the dead with nothing but the words of his mouth, the touch of his hand, or the will of his heart? Who but the Creator God could multiply a few loaves and fishes to feed thousands so completely that none wanted another bite and twelve baskets of fragments remained? Who but the all-knowing, omniscient God could have known that his disciples, upon entering Jerusalem, would find a man carrying a pitcher into a specific house, with a room large enough for him and his disciples to keep the passover together?

Preparation For Worship
Third, we have before us an example of the fact that the worship of God requires preparation and sacrifice. In order to keep the feast of the passover and worship God, our Lord and his disciples must go to Jerusalem. There it was common practice for people to prepare and rent out rooms to the multitudes who came in from outside the city.

Our Lord and his disciples did not live in luxury. They purposefully avoided anything like a show of wealth. However, when it came to worshipping God, keeping the feast of the passover, no ordinary place would do. He sent his disciples ahead of time to find the finest, most well-prepared, well-furnished place in town. One of the old writers suggested that the words "furnished and prepared", mean that the room was beautifully adorned and laid with carpets. Once the disciples found this large upper room, beautifully adorned and laid with carpets, they were commanded "There make ready for us". Robert Hawker reminds us that the keeping of the passover required considerable preparation. He wrote:

> By the disciples' making ready the Passover, I should apprehend they bought a lamb to celebrate this feast; and as the law enjoined, they must have carried it to the court of the temple for slaughter, and there burnt the fat upon the altar, sprinkling the blood upon it, before they brought it home to the house where it was to be eaten. And I should apprehend also, that the roasting it whole, and the bitter herbs, and bread and wine, were all included in what is said of the disciples' making ready before that Jesus came in the evening to sit down with the twelve. See Exodus 12 throughout. Deuteronomy 16:1-8.

In all this we have a vivid portrayal of something woefully neglected in our day *preparation for worship*! How little thought is given to the seriousness of public worship and our need to prepare ourselves for the worship of God! This is a matter about which much needs to be said.

480

As the passover had to be kept at Jerusalem, if we would worship God, we must come to the place where he has established his worship. I know that God is Spirit, and we worship him in Spirit. But I also know that we must worship him in truth. We cannot worship God in falsehood. We cannot worship God apart from the ministry of his Word in the assembly of his saints, where he has established his Word and his worship.

God detests profaneness, irreverence and carelessness in his presence. We cannot and will not worship him without preparation (Ecclesiastes 5:1, 2; James 1:19-21). When we come together with God's saints for public worship, we should remember that we are coming into the house of God to hear from and worship God Almighty in all the splendour, beauty and glory of his holy being. We must see that we give him the reverence of our hearts.

Let us ever come to God's house prepared to worship. We should prepare our hearts, our bodies and our minds to worship God. This may mean cutting out some weekend recreation, or curtailing our hours of work in order to get enough rest so that we do not come to the house of God tired and sleepy. If people stay up late on Saturday night, sleep late on Sunday morning, and rush into the house of God without thought or preparation of heart, they are not likely to worship God. More often than not, their minds will wander in a thousand directions until, weary from lack of rest, they go to sleep. God deserves better!

We ought to come to the house of God, the seat of public worship, promptly. Men and women have a thousand excuses for being late for worship services, but these same people get to work every day on time, get their children dressed, fed and off to school on time, and get to an appointment at the doctor's on time. Why do people persistently come to the house of God late? I will tell you, it is because they do not consider the worship of God to be a matter of great importance. If our souls, the gospel of Christ, the worship of Christ and the glory of Christ are important to us, we will arrange to come to the house of God with promptness.

Would you be late for an appointment with the President of the United States, the Queen of England, or any dignitary? Tardiness for such an appointment would be embarrassing to you and intolerable before your royal host. Dare we treat the King of heaven with less regard?

We should always come praying for grace to worship. We should seek grace from the Lord to worship in the Spirit. We are to pray for God to speak to our hearts through his Word, in the prayers that are offered and by the songs that are sung. We are to pray for those who lead the congregation in worship, that they may be led of the Spirit, and for the man who preaches the gospel, that he may preach in power. We should pray for ourselves and our brethren, that we may see, hear, worship and obey the Lord Jesus Christ.

We should always come to the house of God for prayer and praise. We must be prepared to worship when we come. We are to put the cares of the world, as much as possible, out of our minds, and sit before the throne of God with humility, wonder, attention and reverence. No disturbances or distractions of any kind are to be tolerated. It is unthinkable that men and women who hold God in reverence would run in and out, talk, allow their children to play, or disrupt the worship of God with crying babies, while the Word of God is being read, the praise of God is being sung, the message of God is being delivered, or the throne of God is being supplicated!

The keeping of the passover involved considerable personal sacrifice; and we can never worship God without personal sacrifice. Read Malachi 1 and understand this: God almighty will not be worshipped with our leftovers! He deserves the best of our time, our attention and our property. If we bring less, we need not expect the God of Glory to receive it!

Christ Our Passover
Fourth, let us rejoice to remember that "Christ our Passover is sacrificed for us" That fact is stated in 1 Corinthians 5:7; and it is beautifully illustrated here. It was no accident that our Lord Jesus Christ was crucified on the very day that the paschal lamb was sacrificed. This was not a fluke, a matter of lucky timing, or the result of blind fate or chance!

This came to pass as it did by the hand of God. He predestinated it in eternity and arranged it in providence. It was thus arranged because God would make it manifest that the Lord Jesus Christ, the Lamb of God slain from the foundation of the world, is the true Passover, of whom the Old Testament paschal lamb was but a type, picture, and prophecy. Indeed, all the laws, ordinances, and sacrifices of Old Testament worship pointed to Christ, were fulfilled by Christ, and have been forever abolished by Christ as a way, means, or grounds of worship.

The passover was a reminder of deliverance from bondage, darkness, and tyranny, according to the promise of God made with a covenant head long before the bondage ever began. The passover was a reminder of special, particular redemption by the life's blood and violent death of an innocent lamb. The passover was a reminder of blood sprinkled, applied to every house in Israel, by the commandment of God.

In Exodus 12:23 we read, "For the Lord will pass through to smite the Egyptians; and when he seeth the blood upon the lintel, and on the two side posts, the Lord will pass over the door, and will not suffer the destroyer to come in unto your houses to smite you". Most of the commentators I have consulted give the impression that as the destroyer went through the land of Goshen, whenever he saw the blood of the lamb applied to the door posts and lintel of a house, he simply skipped by that house. But the words "pass over" mean something else. They mean "jump, or leap against". In other words, when the blood was applied to the house, the Lord God himself, Jehovah (God who saves), jumped against the door of that house to protect it from the destroyer! What a picture! Child of God, try to grasp this, He who is himself the mighty God has jumped over your door and stands between you and the destroyer!

None were safe on the night of the Passover, except those who personally ate the slain lamb. And so it is with regard to the crucified Lamb of God, our Lord Jesus Christ. None are safe, except those who eat his flesh and drink his blood. None are safe, except those who personally trust the Son of God.

"Then Jesus said unto them, Verily, verily, I say unto you, Except ye eat the flesh of the Son of man, and drink his blood, ye have no life in you. Whoso eateth my flesh, and drinketh my blood, hath eternal life; and I will raise him up at the last day. For my flesh is meat indeed, and my blood is drink indeed. He that eateth my flesh, and drinketh my blood, dwelleth in me, and I in him. As the living Father hath sent me, and I live by the Father: so he that eateth me, even he shall live by me. This is that bread which came down from heaven: not as your fathers did eat manna, and are dead: he that eateth of this bread shall live for ever" (John 6:53-58).

All for whom the paschal lamb was slain had the blood applied by the Father's hand, ate of the lamb personally, and came out of Egypt by God's almighty, stretched out arm, at exactly the time God had ordained. That is a very clear and precise picture of our redemption by Christ. It is a threefold redemption: redemption by divine purpose, redemption by divine purchase, and redemption by divine power.

"And in the evening he cometh with the twelve. And as they sat and did eat, Jesus said, Verily I say unto you, One of you which eateth with me shall betray me. And they began to be sorrowful, and to say unto him one by one, Is it I? and another said, Is it I? And he answered and said unto them, It is one of the twelve, that dippeth with me in the dish. The Son of man indeed goeth, as it is written of him: but woe to that man by whom the Son of man is betrayed! good were it for that man if he had never been born. And as they did eat, Jesus took bread, and blessed, and brake it, and gave to them, and said, Take, eat: this is my body. And he took the cup, and when he had given thanks, he gave it to them: and they all drank of it. And he said unto them, This is my blood of the new testament, which is shed for many. Verily I say unto you, I will drink no more of the fruit of the vine, until that day that I drink it new in the kingdom of God".

(Mark 14:17-25)

Chapter 64

Lessons From The Last Supper

In the verses before us we have Mark's inspired account of the last supper our Saviour ate with his disciples the night before he was crucified. No doubt, we have all wondered what that last meal must have been like. What solemnity, what anxiety, what fears must have filled the disciples' hearts! What love, what grace, what compassion dropped from the Saviour's every word and gesture! What demonic hypocrisy, what cold hatred, what spiritual hardness possessed the betrayer! What reverence the picture before us in this passage of scripture demands! May God the Holy Spirit teach us the things revealed in this portion of holy writ.

A Question To Face
As the Lord Jesus and his disciples sat together at the passover table, the Master announced that one of them would betray him. When he did, they all asked, "Is it I?" (vv. 17-20).

"And in the evening he cometh with the twelve. And as they sat and did eat, Jesus said, Verily I say unto you, One of you which eateth with me shall betray me. And they began to be sorrowful, and to say unto him one by one, Is it I? and another said, Is it I? And he answered and said unto them, It is one of the twelve, that dippeth with me in the dish".

Matthew informs us that, after hearing all the others ask, "Lord, is it I? ... Judas, which betrayed him, answered and said, Master, is it I?" (Matthew 26:21-25).

Judas is held before us throughout the gospels as a beacon, warning us to beware of religion without Christ. Judas was a man whose heart was as hard as it was hypocritical, as stony as it was sinful, and as proud as it was base. His religion gave him a cloak for his wickedness. His barren familiarity with the things of God made him twofold more the child of hell than he was before. But do not forget, this hellish man appeared to be very pious to all who observed him. Even after he agreed to betray the Son of God with a kiss, he kept up the appearances of sincerity. Judas convinced all the disciples that he was a true believer, one truly devoted to the Saviour. None were even slightly suspicious of him. To the very end they all thought Judas was alright. Perhaps Judas even convinced himself that he was genuine. He knew he had done wrong; but he may not have known he was a lost man, a child of hell, the son of perdition. The scripture says, "Then Judas, which betrayed him, answered and said, Master, is it I? He said unto him, Thou hast said".

The betrayer's heart was hard beyond imagination. He had just returned from his meeting with the chief priests, with whom he arranged to betray the Son of God with a kiss. Yet, he took his place with the other apostles at the table, pretending to be one of them, pretending to be a true worshipper of God, utterly devoted to Christ. What obduracy of heart hypocrisy produces!

Matthew tells us that the other disciples asked, "Lord, is it I?" But Judas did not call him "Lord". Judas called him "Master", saying, "Master, is it I?" The word "Master" is a title implying a closeness and affection that is not conveyed by the more reverential title "Lord". While asking the question merely to give the appearance of sincerity, Judas chose the word "Master", rather than "Lord", because he wanted to show his love for and allegiance to the one he was arranging to betray!

Judas' behaviour should convince us to examine ourselves continually and honestly. I do not know how to deal with the matters of examination and assurance as they ought to be dealt with; but I do know that faith in Christ is neither proud presumption nor dread despair. Assurance is neither a fleshly familiarity with God, nor a slavish fear of God. The believer's hope lies somewhere between that carnal security that says, "Once saved always saved", and that blind, stoic fatalism that says "If I'm one of the elect, I'll be saved, if not I won't".

In the Word of God we are constantly hedged in on two sides. On the one side, we have the many promises of God, lest we despair. But on the other side are countless warnings, lest we presume. On the one side, we see sinful men and women kept by the power of grace, assuring us of immutable grace. On the other side, we see apostate after apostate, warning us that we must endure to the end if we would be saved. Therefore we are to examine ourselves and make our calling and election sure (2 Corinthians 13:5; 2 Peter 1:2-11).

A Conflict Resolved
"The Son of man indeed goeth, as it is written of him: but woe to that man by whom the Son of man is betrayed! good were it for that man if he had never been born" (v. 21; Matthew 26:24; Luke 22:22). The question is often asked, "Did Judas have a choice in this matter?" The scriptures clearly state that our Lord Jesus died according to the purpose and decree of God. The scriptures

manifestly prophesied Judas' betrayal of the Lord Jesus. Surely, then, he cannot be blamed and held accountable for what he did. Such reasoning may suit our puny brains; but such reasoning is entirely wrong. Whether we can understand it or not, we must bow to the Word of God. These two are facts plainly revealed in holy scripture: (1) God almighty is totally sovereign and always does exactly what he will (Isaiah 14:26, 27; 46:9, 10; Ephesians 1:11); and (2) every man is totally responsible for his own sin. While the actions of wicked men and women never thwart, but only fulfil the purposes of God, God does not compel, coerce, entice, or tempt any man to evil (James 1:13-18). Reprobation and judgment are always presented to us in the Word of God as matters of justice and divine retribution. Salvation, grace, and eternal life are always presented as the sovereign prerogative and gift of God (Romans 6:23).

The Lord Jesus Christ died for our sins according to the will, decree and Word of God (1 Corinthians 15:1-3). He died according to the purpose of God revealed in the Word, according to the promises of God throughout the Word, according to the prophecies of God in the Word, and according to the pictures of grace in the Word. And one of the means used by our God to accomplish his purpose of grace in redemption was Judas' wilful betrayal of the Lord Jesus (Acts 2:23).

A Picture Of Redemption

"And as they did eat, Jesus took bread, and blessed, and brake it, and gave to them, and said, Take, eat: this is my body. And he took the cup, and when he had given thanks, he gave it to them: and they all drank of it. And he said unto them, This is my blood of the new testament, which is shed for many" (vv. 22-24).

The Lord Jesus did not bless the bread and wine in the sense of consecrating them, making them holy, or changing their substance. He blessed them in exactly the same way we bless them, or bless a meal, in the sense of giving thanks to God for them.

The breaking of the bread and distribution of the wine, by the Lord Jesus was expressly intended to convey the spiritual lessons of his body being broken and his blood shed. Peace and pardon come to sinners in and through the offering of the body of Jesus Christ once for all his people.

The unleavened bread represented our Redeemer's holy humanity, his body, which was especially prepared by God the Holy Spirit in the womb of the virgin Mary to put away our sins (Hebrews 10:1-5). It was a body without sin, in which righteousness was established by our Lord's obedience, and the body sacrificed for us.

The cup of wine represented the blood of the Lord Jesus Christ by which we are redeemed (Hebrews 9:22). It is the blood of the new covenant, the blood by which all the blessings of the covenant of grace flow to chosen sinners (Hebrews 9:11-16; 13:20). The blood of our Lord Jesus Christ is infinitely meritorious, effectual, sin-atoning, precious blood. All the blessings of the covenant were set forth and sealed in his blood. And we are specifically told by Christ himself that his precious blood was shed not for all, but for many. It was not shed for those who are forever lost in hell. It was shed for God's elect, those who were actually redeemed by his blood when he died to redeem them. The words Joseph Irons penned 200 years ago on this subject accurately describe the common delusion of our day.

> The common delusion of the day in which we live is to think of and speak of Christ as if He were merely a Saviour who had done all he could to save all mankind, but after all, had left it quite uncertain whether any will be eventually saved; whereas, his official character (Prophet, Priest, King, Messiah, Redeemer, Mediator, Covenant Head, Surety, Lord), and consequent covenant engagements, render the salvation of all his church a matter of infallible certainty.

Eating the bread and drinking the wine is a picture of that God given faith by which we personally receive Christ for ourselves (John 6:51-58). All who eat and drink the flesh and blood of the Son of God live forever. It is written, "Believe in the Lord Jesus Christ, and thou shalt be saved"!

An Ordinance To Keep

"And as they did eat, Jesus took bread, and blessed, and brake it, and gave to them, and said, Take, eat: this is my body. And he took the cup, and when he had given thanks, he gave it to them: and they all drank of it. And he said unto them, This is my blood of the new testament, which is shed for many. Verily I say unto you, I will drink no more of the fruit of the vine, until that day that I drink it new in the kingdom of God" (vv. 22-25).

The institution of the Lord's Supper as soon as the paschal feast was finished, as Robert Hawker observes, "intimates the superseding of the one, in the establishment of the other". We are not left to guess about this. The apostle Paul, writing by divine inspiration, tells us that our Saviour here established the blessed ordinance of the Lord's Supper (1 Corinthians 11:23-29).

The Lord's Supper is not a sacrament, a means by which we obtain grace. It is an ordinance by which we celebrate grace bestowed upon us through the precious blood of Christ. Justin Martyr wrote, "The Lord's Supper is food made up all of thanksgiving". As often as we come together to observe the Lord's Supper, let every believer examine himself, and then eat the bread and drink the wine in faith, "Discerning the Lord's body", understanding what Christ accomplished for us by his incarnation and death as our Substitute. Let us eat the bread and drink the wine with humility, gratitude, love and hope, "looking for the mercy of our Lord Jesus Christ unto eternal life" (Jude 21). There is a day coming when we shall drink new wine with our Saviour in the kingdom of God.

"And when they had sung an hymn, they went out into the mount of Olives. And Jesus saith unto them, All ye shall be offended because of me this night: for it is written, I will smite the shepherd, and the sheep shall be scattered. But after that I am risen, I will go before you into Galilee. But Peter said unto him, Although all shall be offended, yet will not I. And Jesus saith unto him, Verily I say unto thee, That this day, even in this night, before the cock crow twice, thou shalt deny me thrice. But he spake the more vehemently, If I should die with thee, I will not deny thee in any wise. Likewise also said they all".

(Mark 14:26-31)

Chapter 65

A Great Saviour For Great Sinners

Truly, the Lord Jesus Christ shows himself the great Saviour of great sinners in these six verses of Inspiration. Christ's greatness as Saviour is set before us in three things: the people he saves, the punishment he suffered, the perseverance of his love.

The People He Saves
Our blessed Saviour knew exactly what he was getting when he saved us. That shows his greatness as our Saviour. My sin often astonishes me; but it never astonishes him. The Lord Jesus knew when he chose me, long before he saved me, what a vile, fickle sinner I would be. He knew before he saved me that I would constantly be in need of his grace and his forgiveness. Just in case you are wondering, he knew the same about you.

We see this clearly exemplified in this passage. Our Lord knew the weaknesses, sins, and infirmities of his disciples. He told them plainly what they were going to do. Their pride was offended when they heard it. None of them really believed they were capable of such evil. He said, "All ye shall be offended because of me this night". He told Peter, specifically, "Verily I say unto thee, That this day, even in this night, before the cock crow twice, thou shalt deny me thrice". Yet, our Saviour's knowledge of what poor disciples they would be did not prevent him from choosing these men to be his disciples, even his apostles. And his knowledge of what poor disciples we would be did not prevent him from choosing us. The Lord Jesus loved us and chose us, though he knew we would never choose him and would never love him in return, except he create that love in us and cause us by his grace to choose him. Our Saviour loved us, though he knew that our love for him, as long as we live in this world, will be an alloyed love at best. The Son of God chose us, as he did these disciples, to be his intimate friends and companions, though he knew beforehand what great evil we would do.

With such a charitable, gracious, forbearing Saviour, you and I ought to be charitable, forbearing, and gracious with one another. We ought never conclude that a person has no grace, or does not know Christ, because we perceive that he or she has many weaknesses and much corruption. We are all weak, sinful, fallen and falling creatures. Our only hope is grace. Our only salvation is Christ. As such, we ought to pity one another. God the Holy Spirit puts it this way, "And be ye kind one to another, tenderhearted, forgiving one another, even as God for Christ's sake hath forgiven you. Be ye therefore followers of God, as dear children" (Ephesians 4:32-5:1). Our Saviour's greatness is to be seen in the people he saves.

"For ye see your calling, brethren, how that not many wise men after the flesh, not many mighty, not many noble, are called: But God hath chosen the foolish things of the world to confound the wise; and God hath chosen the weak things of the world to confound the things which are mighty; And base things of the world, and things which are despised, hath God chosen, yea, and things which are not, to bring to nought things that are: That no flesh should glory in his presence. But of him are ye in Christ Jesus, who of God is made unto us wisdom, and righteousness, and sanctification, and redemption: That, according as it is written, He that glorieth, let him glory in the Lord" (1 Corinthians 1:26-31).

The Punishment He Suffered

Next, our Saviour's greatness is displayed in the punishment he suffered as our Substitute. "And Jesus saith unto them, All ye shall be offended because of me this night: for it is written, I will smite the shepherd, and the sheep shall be scattered" (v. 27). In making that statement the Lord Jesus was quoting Zechariah 13:7. "Awake, O sword, against my shepherd, and against the man that is my fellow, saith the LORD of hosts: smite the shepherd, and the sheep shall be scattered: and I will turn mine hand upon the little ones".

In order to redeem and save us the Son of God assumed our nature, became one of us. bore our sins in his own body on the tree, was made sin for us, and voluntarily suffered all the infinite fulness of God's holy wrath to the full satisfaction of his justice as our Substitute. Look at this verse line by line.

"Awake, O sword, against my Shepherd". The Lord Jesus Christ is Jehovah's Shepherd. These are the words of God the Father concerning his Son as our Mediator. He calls the God-man "My Shepherd", because he was chosen, appointed, called, and trusted by God the Father as the Shepherd of his sheep in the covenant of grace before the world began. He is the One on whom the Father has laid the iniquity of his sheep. And he is the one responsible and accountable for the sheep.

Those words, "Awake, O sword", speak of the violent death of our Lord Jesus Christ and of the glittering sword of divine justice, which was drawn out against him, when he was made sin for us. That sword, once unsheathed in Jehovah's angry hands of omnipotent wrath, was never sheathed again, until it was sheathed forever in Immanuel's heart!

The sword of justice is here called to "awake", because it appeared to sleep, and to have been asleep for a very long time. It had been a long, long time since sin first entered into the world by our father Adam. It had been a very long time since the Son of God, our ever-blessed Christ, stepped forward and became our Surety, pledging himself in eternity to satisfy the justice of God for us. It had been a long time since the promise was first given that the Son of God would be stricken, smitten of God, and afflicted as our Substitute.

"Awake, O sword, against my Shepherd, against the man that is my fellow, saith the Lord of hosts". He who is our Redeemer is and must be a man; and this man, who is our Substitute and Saviour, is and must be Jehovah's fellow God incarnate! "Smite the Shepherd"! The order was given by God himself to the sword of his justice to smite his darling Son to death. The Lord Jesus Christ was delivered to death and slain by the hand of God, according to the decree of God, at the command of God, for the glory of God.

Next, we hear the God of Glory who slew his Son for us declare, "and the sheep shall be scattered". This is the part of Zechariah's prophecy that our Lord Jesus applied to his disciples, when he said, "All ye shall be offended because of me this night". "Then saith Jesus unto them, All ye shall be offended because of me this night: for it is written, I will smite the shepherd, and the sheep of the flock shall be scattered abroad ... But all this was done, that the scriptures of the prophets might be fulfilled. Then all the disciples forsook him, and fled" (Matthew 26:31, 56).

"Awake, O sword, against my Shepherd, against the man that is my fellow, saith the Lord of hosts: smite the shepherd, and the sheep shall be scattered". I am so thankful that the text does not end there. The Lord God goes on to say something else, something great and glorious! "And I will turn mine hand upon the little ones". These "little ones" are the sheep who were scattered, the straying, scattered sheep, the disciples of Christ who forsook him. Yet, the text in Zechariah clearly speaks of more than just those sheep. It speaks of the certain salvation of all the Lord's sheep. Zechariah's prophecy asserts emphatically that all those sheep for whom the Shepherd was smitten at Calvary shall be saved.

"Awake, O sword, against my shepherd, and against the man that is my fellow, saith the LORD of hosts: smite the shepherd, and the sheep shall be scattered: and I will turn mine hand upon the little ones. And it shall come to pass, that in all the land, saith the LORD, two parts therein shall be cut off and die; but the third shall be left therein. And I will bring the third part through the fire, and will refine them as silver is refined, and will try them as gold is tried: they shall call on my name, and I will hear them: I will say, It is my people: and they shall say, The LORD is my God" (Zechariah 13:7-9).

There is a remnant according to the election of grace (here called a third part of the earth), which shall be saved because Christ died for them. The Lord God says, "I will turn mine hand upon the little ones", not his hand of wrath and justice, but his hand of mercy, grace, and power.

The Perseverance Of His Love
We see our Saviour's greatness in the perseverance of his love, too. Let me remind you of the perseverance of his love, mercy and grace to his erring, fallen, sinful people. What great comfort there is for our souls in this! The Lord Jesus does not cast off or forsake his people because of their faults, failures, and sins. He knows what we are. "He remembereth our frame. He knoweth that we are dust". Like a loving husband who has taken a wife, takes her forever, and never dreams of putting her away because he later finds fault in her, so Christ took us, knowing our deformity, to be his bride forever.

Yes, the Lord Jesus chose us, redeemed us, called us, and took us for his bride, knowing full well what he was getting! He is a merciful and compassionate High Priest. It is the glory of our Lord Jesus Christ to pass over iniquity, transgression, and sin. "It is the glory of God to conceal a thing" (Proverbs 25:2).

Our Lord Jesus knew what we were before he saved us; yet he saved us. He knew what we would be after he saved us; yet he saved us. He cannot be induced for any reason, by anything, or at any time to cast us away now! He says, "I will never leave the nor forsake thee". He is our unchanging, unchangeable God, "Jesus Christ, the same, yesterday, and today, and for ever"!

A Great Thief
What a great thief unbelief is! Our Lord Jesus spoke to his disciples often and plainly about his death and his resurrection. He said, in verse 28, "But after that I am risen, I will go before you into Galilee". He could not have been clearer. Yet, his words seem to have just passed over their heads altogether. Not one of the disciples laid them up in his heart or remembered them. When he was betrayed, they all forsook him. When he was crucified, they were almost driven to despair. When he was raised from the dead, and they were told about it by credible witnesses, none of them were quick to believe it.

Only in eternity will we know how much we have robbed ourselves by our unbelief. Our unbelief robs God of his glory; and robs us of more peace, joy, and contentment than we can imagine. Like Hagar's well in the wilderness, we have the truths and promises of our God right before our eyes in his Word; but we do not see them, because of unbelief (Genesis 21:19). What anxiety, what sorrows we might avoid if we simply believed God!

Great Sinners

"But Peter said unto him, Although all shall be offended, yet will not I. And Jesus saith unto him, Verily I say unto thee, That this day, even in this night, before the cock crow twice, thou shalt deny me thrice. But he spake the more vehemently, If I should die with thee, I will not deny thee in any wise. Likewise also said they all" (vv. 29-31).

What great and horrible sinners we are! There is in all of us an enormous measure of pride that must be abased, a huge portion of self-confidence that must be destroyed, and a hideous mass of self-righteousness that must be slain. Peter simply could not believe what the Lord Jesus said. He argued in defence of himself. He was highly offended and insulted that the Lord should even think he might forsake him. He said, "If I should die with thee, I will not deny thee". But Peter was not alone in his arrogance. The other disciples were of the same high opinion about themselves. "Likewise said they all".

Peter told the truth. He was truly willing to die with his Lord, and eventually did. But Peter, as well as the others, was unaware of the great evil still in him which had to be exposed and dealt with. In just twelve hours, all these men forsook the Master. Their bold, proud claims were forgotten. Their promises of fidelity were swept away. Their imagined strength withered. Their great faith failed. Yet, even in this, we see the overruling hand of our God in goodness, grace, and providence. Had Peter not trembled before the maid and denied his Lord here, he could never have preached so boldly as he did at Pentecost or confessed Christ so fearlessly as he did in Acts 4. Had Peter and these disciples, our brethren, not forsaken the Lord Jesus, we could never have known the goodness, love, and faithfulness of our great God and Saviour in his immutability toward his fallen saints as it is here revealed.

Though redeemed by the precious blood of Christ, justified, forgiven of all sin, regenerated and kept by the grace of God, we are still such great sinners, that there is no sin into which the most eminent saint will not run, except God hold us by his grace. "Pride goeth before destruction, and an haughty spirit before a fall" (Proverbs 16:18). Wisely does Solomon counsel us, "He that trusteth in his own heart is a fool" (Proverbs 28:26).

"Wherefore let him that thinketh he standeth take heed lest he fall. There hath no temptation taken you but such as is common to man: but God is faithful, who will not suffer you to be tempted above that ye are able; but will with the temptation also make a way to escape, that ye may be able to bear it" (1 Corinthians 10:12, 13).

What great reason we have to ever give thanks to our God that salvation is by grace alone, without works!

"And they came to a place which was named Gethsemane: and he saith to his disciples, Sit ye here, while I shall pray. And he taketh with him Peter and James and John, and began to be sore amazed, and to be very heavy; And saith unto them, My soul is exceeding sorrowful unto death: tarry ye here, and watch. And he went forward a little, and fell on the ground, and prayed that, if it were possible, the hour might pass from him. And he said, Abba, Father, all things are possible unto thee; take away this cup from me: nevertheless not what I will, but what thou wilt. And he cometh, and findeth them sleeping, and saith unto Peter, Simon, sleepest thou? couldest not thou watch one hour? Watch ye and pray, lest ye enter into temptation. The spirit truly is ready, but the flesh is weak. And again he went away, and prayed, and spake the same words. And when he returned, he found them asleep again, (for their eyes were heavy,) neither wist they what to answer him. And he cometh the third time, and saith unto them, Sleep on now, and take your rest: it is enough, the hour is come; behold, the Son of man is betrayed into the hands of sinners. Rise up, let us go; lo, he that betrayeth me is at hand".

(Mark 14:32-42)

Chapter 66

Gethsemane

We come now with the Son of God into his favourite place of prayer, the garden of Gethsemane. The word "Gethsemane" means "olive press". What a fitting place Gethsemane was for the events which transpired on this dark, dark night. Here, the Lord of glory wept in agony of soul, prayed with a heavy, broken heart, and began to have his soul crushed in anticipation of being made sin for us. So heavy was the burden of his heart that the pores of his flesh poured with a bloody sweat!

I never read this passage and its parallels in Matthew, Luke, and John without a great sense of utter ignorance and inability. How can a mortal man of sinful flesh comprehend what our Master experienced in Gethsemane? It is simply impossible. You can imagine how utterly insufficient I feel in attempting to explain, to any degree, the meaning of this passage. This portion of holy scripture contains things which the wisest of faithful, godly men cannot explain. As we look at our Saviour and his disciples as they are set before us in this passage, I will direct your attention to those things that are obvious.

The Cause Of Sorrow
"And they came to a place which was named Gethsemane: and he saith to his disciples, Sit ye here, while I shall pray. And he taketh with him Peter and James and John, and began to be sore amazed, and to be very heavy; And saith unto them, My soul is exceeding sorrowful unto death: tarry ye here, and watch. And he went forward a little, and fell on the ground, and prayed that, if it were possible, the hour might pass from him. And he said, Abba, Father, all things are possible unto thee; take away this cup from me: nevertheless not what I will, but what thou wilt" (vv. 32-36).

What was the cause of this great heaviness and sorrow? What was it that crushed our Master's heart? What so greatly disturbed him? Certainly, it was not the fear of physical pain, the fear of death, or even the fear of dying on the cross. That which crushed our Saviour's heart was the anticipation of being made sin for us. The heavy, heavy burden that crushed his very soul was the enormous load of sin and guilt, the sin and guilt of all God's elect which was about to be made his.

Our Saviour's great sorrow was caused by his anticipation of being made sin for us. "It was", wrote J. C. Ryle, "a sense of the unutterable weight of our sins and transgressions which were then specially laid upon him." He who knew no sin was about to be made sin for us! He who is the only man who really knows what sin is, the only man who sees sin as God sees sin, was about to become sin! He who is the holy, harmless, undefiled Lamb of God was about to be made sin, about to be made a curse for us! The holy Son of God was about to be made sin and forsaken by his Father!

Our Lord Jesus Christ, the Son of God, "began to be sore amazed", to be in great consternation and astonishment, at the sight of all the sins of his people coming upon him; at the black storm of wrath that was gathering thick over him; at the sword of justice which was brandished against him, and at the curse of his own righteous law which, like thunderbolts of vengeance from heaven, was directed at him. No wonder the verse closes by telling us that in consideration of these things our Saviour began "to be very heavy"! That which crushed our Saviour's very heart and soul was the very thing for which he had come into the world: The prospect of what he must endure as our Substitute.

The Lord Jesus Christ, the incarnate God, our Mediator and Surety, died in our place, in the place of God's elect, as our Substitute. By his own blood, when he was made sin for us, when he was slain in our stead, he satisfied the justice of God for us, magnified his holy law, made it honourable, and purchased for us the complete, everlasting forgiveness of all our sins. He died, the Just for the unjust, that he might bring us to God. Christ died at Calvary so that God might be both just and the Justifier of all who believe. It is written, "By mercy and truth iniquity is purged" (Proverbs 16:7; Romans 3:19-28; Ephesians 1:7).

Since the Lord Jesus Christ died as the sinners' Substitute, since he has met and fully satisfied the justice of God for us, believing sinners have no reason ever to fear condemnation by God, accusation before God, or separation from God (Romans 8:1-4, 31-39). Let every believing sinner ever rejoice and give thanks to the Lord Jesus Christ. Since Christ died for me, I cannot die! If you are in Christ, if you believe on the Son of God, there is no possibility of condemnation for you. No sin shall ever be laid to your charge. You cannot be separated from the love of God in Christ.

It was the enormous load of our sin and our guilt that crushed our Saviour's heart in Gethsemane (Isaiah 53:4-6), a load of sin and guilt that would have crushed us in hell forever; but a load that can never come upon us now, because Christ died in our place!

Let us never look lightly upon sin. What a horrible, monstrous, ignominious thing it must be! Nothing so displays the exceeding sinfulness of sin as the death of our Lord Jesus Christ at Calvary. When the holy Lord God found sin on his own darling Son, he poured out all the fury of his holy wrath and unmitigated justice upon him, he forsook him, and he killed him without mercy! If God finds sin on you, he will do the same thing to you, forever!

The Saviour's Prayer
"And saith unto them, My soul is exceeding sorrowful unto death: tarry ye here, and watch. And he went forward a little, and fell on the ground, and prayed that, if it were possible, the hour might pass from him. And he said, Abba, Father, all things are possible unto thee; take away this cup from me: nevertheless not what I will, but what thou wilt" (vv. 34-36).

In his time of great heaviness, sorrow and distress, we find our Lord Jesus in prayer. What an example he sets before us. The first one to whom we should turn in every time of trouble is our heavenly Father. Our God should be the first to hear the words of our complaints. He may or may not relieve our trouble; but it is good for our souls for us to unburden our hearts at the throne of grace. There, and only there, will we discover the all-sufficiency of his grace. "Let us therefore come boldly unto the throne of grace, that we may obtain mercy, and find grace to help in time of need" (Hebrews 4:16). "Is any among you afflicted? let him pray" (James 5:13).

But what was our Lord praying for in the garden of Gethsemane? Let us never entertain idle curiosity about the things of God, especially when discussing the heart-wrenching agony of soul endured by the Son of God to save us. Still, this agony of soul which the Lord Jesus endured for us is recorded in all four Gospel narratives. Matthew and Mark both tell us that our Saviour uttered this prayer in much the same words three times. Luke adds the details about his bloody sweat and an angel coming to minister to him.

"And he went a little farther, and fell on his face, and prayed, saying, O my Father, if it be possible, let this cup pass from me: nevertheless not as I will, but as thou wilt. And he cometh unto the disciples, and findeth them asleep, and saith unto Peter, What, could ye not watch with me one hour? Watch and pray, that ye enter not into temptation: the spirit indeed is willing, but the flesh is weak. He went away again the second time, and prayed, saying, O my Father, if this cup may not pass away from me, except I drink it, thy will be done" (Matthew 26:39-42).

"And he was withdrawn from them about a stone's cast, and kneeled down, and prayed, Saying, Father, if thou be willing, remove this cup from me: nevertheless not my will, but thine, be done. And there appeared an angel unto him from heaven, strengthening him. And being in an agony he prayed more earnestly: and his sweat was as it were great drops of blood falling down to the ground" (Luke 22:41-44).

While the apostle John does not specifically deal with our Lord's prayer in Gethsemane, he does give us a hint at the meaning of his prayer. In John 12 we see our Saviour in a similar position and experience six days before the betrayal in Gethsemane

"And Jesus answered them, saying, The hour is come, that the Son of man should be glorified. Verily, verily, I say unto you, Except a corn of wheat fall into the ground and die, it abideth alone: but if it die, it bringeth forth much fruit. He that loveth his life shall lose it; and he that hateth his life in this world shall keep it unto life eternal. If any man serve me, let him follow me; and where I am, there shall also my servant be: if any man serve me, him will my Father honour. Now is my soul troubled; and what shall I say? Father, save me from this hour: but for this cause came I unto this hour. Father, glorify thy name. Then came there a voice from heaven, saying, I have both glorified it, and will glorify it again. The people therefore, that stood by, and heard it, said that it thundered: others said, An angel spake to him. Jesus answered and said, This voice came not because of me, but for your sakes. Now is the judgment of this world: now shall the prince of this world be cast out. And I, if I be lifted up from the earth, will draw all men unto me. This he said, signifying what death he should die" (John 12:23-33).

Here we see our Saviour in great agony of soul. His agony was clearly related to his death at Calvary. Yet, he set his face steadfastly toward the cross without flinching. While he certainly has his death at Calvary in mind, our Lord Jesus, obviously, was not asking that he might be kept from that appointment for which he came into this world. He had come to this place on purpose, that he might be betrayed by Judas, arrested, and hanged upon the cursed tree by the hands of wicked men to fulfil the will of his Father as our covenant Surety (Hebrews 10:1-10).

If the Lord Jesus was not praying to be saved from dying in our place as our sin-atoning Substitute, what was he praying for his Father to do here? Our dear Saviour was here, once more, under the assault of hell. Satan was making his last effort to keep him from fulfilling his Father's purpose of grace in redemption. He was doing everything he could to keep the Seed of the woman from crushing his head.

I have no doubt at all that our Saviour, being overwhelmed with the prospect of being made sin, in this state of soul agony, was as a man fearful of dying before he had finished his work, before he reached the cross. He was fearful of dying in the garden of Gethsemane. There is no other event in his humiliation to which the words of Hebrews 5:7 might reference. "Who in the days of his flesh, when he had offered up prayers and supplications with strong crying and tears unto him that was able to save him from death, and was heard in that he feared".

We must never forget that our Lord Jesus is both God and man in one glorious person. As God he could never know fear. Yet, he could not be a man tempted in all points like as we are if he did not know fear. These two, distinct natures in Christ, the divine and the human, are obvious throughout the gospel narratives, especially in those passages dealing with his temptations, sufferings, and death. Here in Gethsemane we see the man Christ Jesus begging for relief from this great trial of agony. Yet, his submission and resignation to the Father's will is submission and resignation to his own will as God.

"The hour" from which our Lord prayed for release was not the hour for which he had come into the world, but this hour in the Garden. "The cup" which he prayed might pass from him was not the cup of his Father's wrath. That cup Jehovah's Servant took with determinate purpose and resolve. The cup he wanted to pass from him was the fear of dying in the Garden before he could take the cup of his Father's wrath and drink it for us.

Christ's Example
What a remarkable example our Saviour set before us of submission to the will of God. "And he said, Abba, Father, all things are possible unto thee; take away this cup from me: nevertheless not what I will, but what thou wilt" (v. 36).

"For even hereunto were ye called: because Christ also suffered for us, leaving us an example, that ye should follow his steps: Who did no sin, neither was guile found in his mouth: Who, when he was reviled, reviled not again; when he suffered, he threatened not; but committed himself to him that judgeth righteously: Who his own self bare our sins in his own body on the tree, that we, being dead to sins, should live unto righteousness: by whose stripes ye were healed" (1 Peter 2:21-24).

This is the highest measure of practical godliness and holiness. Let men brag and boast to themselves and before others as they may about their imaginary godly deeds. The surrender of my will to God's will in all things is godliness: to bear patiently whatever my Father sends, to desire only what God has purposed, to want nothing but what God wills, to prefer pain to pleasure, if that is my Father's will, to willingly be as passive before God as wet clay in the potter's hands. That is godliness.

Nothing can make us happier in this world than submission to the will of God. Nothing brings us so much heartache and misery in this world as having our own way. May God give us grace to willingly submit to his will. Submit to his eternal will of predestination and his performed will in providence, and learn to live in peace. Like Eli of old, regarding all matters, may God the Holy Spirit teach us to say humbly, "It is the Lord, let him do what seemeth him good". Submit to his revealed will in scripture, and walk in obedience to him.

Horrid Indifference
"And he cometh, and findeth them sleeping, and saith unto Peter, Simon, sleepest thou? couldest not thou watch one hour? Watch ye and pray, lest ye enter into temptation. The spirit truly is ready, but the flesh is weak. And again he went away, and prayed, and spake the same words. And when he returned, he found them asleep again, (for their eyes were heavy,) neither wist they what to answer him" (vv. 37-40).

What fickle, sinful creatures the very best of God's saints are in this world! We have a painful illustration of this fact in the slothful indifference of Peter, James, and John. But we have an even more painful illustration of it in ourselves. How horribly we sleep when we ought to pray, ignore our Lord when he is near, and quickly let slip those things we ought to hold fast! Again, we see clearly that God's people, all who are born of God, so long as they live in this world, are people with two diametrically opposite, warring natures (Romans 7:14-23; Galatians 5:17; Psalm 73). The spirit is ready and willing, it truly is; but the flesh is sinful and weak.

Therefore, we must ever watch and pray. We must always be on guard, as soldiers in hostile, enemy territory, knowing that there is a malicious traitor within. We must fight the battles daily. We must wage warfare against our flesh daily. Our rest is yet to come.

"Now we exhort you, brethren, warn them that are unruly, comfort the feebleminded, support the weak, be patient toward all men. See that none render evil for evil unto any man; but ever follow that which is good, both among yourselves, and to all men. Rejoice evermore. Pray without ceasing. In every thing give thanks: for this is the will of God in Christ Jesus concerning you. Quench not the Spirit. Despise not prophesyings. Prove all things; hold fast that which is good. Abstain from all appearance of evil. And the very God of peace sanctify you wholly; and I pray God your whole spirit and soul and body be preserved blameless unto the coming of our Lord Jesus Christ. Faithful is he that calleth you, who also will do it" (1 Thessalonians 5:14-24).

Sleep On
"And he cometh the third time, and saith unto them, Sleep on now, and take your rest: it is enough, the hour is come; behold, the Son of man is betrayed

into the hands of sinners. Rise up, let us go; lo, he that betrayeth me is at hand" (vv. 41, 42).

What reason we have to give thanks to our dear Saviour for his steadfast resolve as our Surety. How we ought to admire and love him! "He cometh the third time, and saith unto them, Sleep on now, and take your rest: it is enough". These words, "It is enough", are related only by Mark. Did the Lord Jesus here speak as though the work of our redemption was already done? It certainly appears that he did. The word "enough" carries the idea of a debt paid in full. Our Lord is not now chastising his sleeping disciples, but speaking for their comfort and ours. He is saying, "It is done, the work is complete, I have finished the work of my obedience". "The hour is come". The appointed hour of his death, the appointed hour of redemption had come. "Rise up, let us go". The blessed Saviour says here, "I must finish the work my Father gave me to do for you. I must go yonder to die in your place".

Nothing could keep our Saviour from Calvary. Nothing could keep him from dying for us. Nothing could prevent him from accomplishing that death at Jerusalem for which he had come into this world. And, blessed be his name, nothing can keep him from saving those whom he redeemed with his own precious blood at Calvary! Let us ever find and take our rest in him (Matthew 11:28-30).

"And immediately, while he yet spake, cometh Judas, one of the twelve, and with him a great multitude with swords and staves, from the chief priests and the scribes and the elders. And he that betrayed him had given them a token, saying, Whomsoever I shall kiss, that same is he; take him, and lead him away safely. And as soon as he was come, he goeth straightway to him, and saith, Master, master; and kissed him. And they laid their hands on him, and took him. And one of them that stood by drew a sword, and smote a servant of the high priest, and cut off his ear. And Jesus answered and said unto them, Are ye come out, as against a thief, with swords and with staves to take me? I was daily with you in the temple teaching, and ye took me not: but the scriptures must be fulfilled. And they all forsook him, and fled. And there followed him a certain young man, having a linen cloth cast about his naked body; and the young men laid hold on him: And he left the linen cloth, and fled from them naked".

(Mark 14:43-52)

Chapter 67

The Betrayal

The agonies of Gethsemane are over. The temptations our Lord endured there, from the assaults of the prince of darkness, are finished. In verse 42 the Lord Jesus called Peter, James, and John, rousing them from their sleep, and hurried them to follow him, as he went forth in holy zeal to meet the betrayer and the band of soldiers following him, to finish his work. Let us never fail to remember that in the totality of his work as our Substitute our Lord Jesus Christ did what he did for us as Jehovah's voluntary Servant (Psalm 40:6-8; John 10:16-18).

Robert Hawker wrote,

> He had said before to Judas at the table, that thou doest do quickly. But no man at the table knew for what intent Jesus said this unto him (John 13:27, 28). But we may learn from it, that it showed the promptness of Christ's heart to the work. And though he knew the sorrows which it must induce, yet, for the joy that was set before him, he endured the cross, despising the shame. Yea, Jesus called the time, the hour of his glory. And as soon as the traitor had left the company, Jesus declared that he was now glorified (see John 13:31, 32).

I request you never to lose sight of those two grand points, in the sufferings and death of the Lord Jesus. The one is: the infinite dignity of his person, God and Man in one. The other is the free-will offering of the Lord. Behold him under these views coming forth from the garden to meet the traitor, and crying out, Rise up! let us go! lo! he that betrayeth me is at hand".

With those things in mind, let us look into this passage of holy scripture dealing with our Saviour's arrest in the garden, and ask God the Holy Spirit to inscribe its lessons upon our hearts. I direct your attention to five things in these verses.

The Enemies Of God
This passage opens by identifying the enemies of God. We should always be aware of who our Lord's enemies are and where they are found. His enemies are the same in all ages; and they are found in the same places. We need to be able to recognize them, because our Lord's enemies are our enemies. Notice how they are identified for us in verse 43.

> "Judas, one of the twelve".
> The Roman soldiers "a great multitude with swords and staves".
> "The chief priests, and the scribes, and the elders".

Our Lords enemies and ours are ever to be found among the people of the world. That is no surprise. We expect the world to oppose Christ, the gospel of his grace, and us, as we preach it. If we preach the gospel, insisting that men have no righteousness of their own, declaring that the only righteousness is the righteousness of God in Christ, we expect the world's opposition. The offence of the cross has not ceased (Matthew 5:10-12).

We have come to expect opposition and persecution from religionists as well. The lost religious people of this world, being duped, deceived, lied to, and instigated by their leaders, their chief priests, their scribes, and their elders, being ignorant of Christ and the gospel of God's free and sovereign grace in him, are historically the most incessant persecutors of God's saints in the world.

History demonstrates the fact that the politicians of the world become persecutors of believers only when instigated (as here) by God-hating religionists, who are too good in their own eyes to need grace, a sin-atoning Substitute, and imputed righteousness. No one hates grace like lost religionists! There is no missionary field in the world more needy or more hostile today than the professed church of this reprobate age.

We expect to find our enemies in the world, and even in the religious world around us. But, often the Lord's enemies and ours are wolves in sheep's clothing and, like "Judas, one of the twelve", are found in the house of his friends (Psalms 41:9; 55:12, 13). Our Lord warned us repeatedly, as did his apostles throughout the New Testament, that our most dangerous foes are those whom we least suspect, those who are, by profession, our brothers, sisters, and friends. These warnings are given not to make us suspicious and wary of one another, but to prepare us for the shock and pain of betrayal (Matthew 10:24-26).

The Kingdom Of God

Second, we must never expect the people of this world, neither the politicians, nor the educators, nor the religionists of this world, to understand the nature of the kingdom of God. In fact, our Lord's own disciples did not grasp what he taught in this regard at the time.

This bloodthirsty mob came out against the Lord Jesus, as if they were hunting for a wild, murdering revolutionary, with swords and clubs. When they did, one of the Lord's disciples drew out a sword and cut off the high priest's servant's ear. John tells us that that bold, zealous, but mistaken disciple was Peter. But the Lord Jesus stopped the conflict by healing the man's ear, as Luke tells us.

The chief priests and scribes clung tenaciously to the errant idea that Messiah's kingdom would be a worldly, political, Zionist kingdom. They expected that this man who claimed to be the Messiah would defend his kingdom with the sword. They came prepared for a blood-letting conflict.

Our Lord later told Pilate plainly that his kingdom is not of this world. This is a lesson which still needs to be taught, and taught often (John 18:36). The kingdom of God is not, has never been, and can never be built, promoted, and propagated by the arm of the flesh. The cause of truth does not need political, legislative, or carnal force to maintain it. "The weapons of our warfare are not carnal, but mighty through God to the pulling down of strong holds" (2 Corinthians 10:4). It is written, "Not by might, nor by power, but by my spirit, saith the Lord of hosts" (Zechariah 4:6).

Papacy, Mohammedanism, Hinduism, and Judaism must have the sword to survive. The kingdom of God stands not by the sword, but in spite of it. False religion depends upon and survives by every carnal means imaginable: programs, puppet shows, entertainment, bake sales, tricks, gimmicks, rituals, and ceremonies. Whatever it takes to be successful is what is done!

It is a sad fact that pastors, local churches and religious denominations and organizations in the United States (both liberal and conservative) commonly engage in political debate. We cannot protect or expand the cause of Christ by political and social activism, no matter how great or sincere the efforts. Ours is a spiritual battle waged against worldly ideologies and dogmas arrayed against God. The only way we can triumph over them is by the gospel.

The church and kingdom of God, the gospel of his grace stands by the power of God the Holy Spirit, by the Sword of the Spirit, the Word of God, and the effectual operations of his grace in the hearts of men by the Word (Hebrews 4:12). The Lord God has not left us here to be political activists, but to be evangelists. It is not ours to seek to reform the nation. Our only business is the glory of God in the salvation of sinners.

If we would do God's work, in God's name, for God's glory, it must be done in God's way. The church and kingdom of God can only be built by the preaching of the gospel. Our needs for that work are supplied by the generous giving of God's people, as they are directed by the Spirit of God.

The Word Of God

Everything that happened to our Saviour, everything he suffered at the hands of ungodly, reprobate men, from Gethsemane to Calvary, was written hundreds of years before in the Word of God. These men, by their wicked deeds, not only fulfilled the scriptures, they stand as unanswerable arguments for the infallible, inerrant, verbal inspiration of the Word of God.

"And Jesus answered and said unto them, Are ye come out, as against a thief, with swords and with staves to take me? I was daily with you in the temple teaching, and ye took me not: but the scriptures must be fulfilled" (vv. 48, 49).

"Men and brethren, children of the stock of Abraham, and whosoever among you feareth God, to you is the word of this salvation sent. For they that dwell at Jerusalem, and their rulers, because they knew him not, nor yet the voices of the prophets which are read every sabbath day, they have fulfilled them in condemning him. And though they found no cause of death in him, yet desired they Pilate that he should be slain. And when they had fulfilled all that was written of him, they took him down from the tree, and laid him in a sepulchre" (Acts 13:26-29).

The rage of his enemies, the betrayal of Judas, the price of the betrayal (thirty pieces of silver!), the forsaking of his friends, our Lord's being dealt with as a malefactor, numbered with the transgressors, the piercing of his hands and feet, the parting of his raiment, all were precisely foretold in the Word of God. Psalm 22 and Isaiah 53 were precisely fulfilled, exactly as they were written. How can we account for these things?

"All scripture is given by inspiration of God, and is profitable for doctrine, for reproof, for correction, for instruction in righteousness: That the man of God may be perfect, throughly furnished unto all good works" (2 Timothy 3:16, 17).

"We have also a more sure word of prophecy; whereunto ye do well that ye take heed, as unto a light that shineth in a dark place, until the day dawn, and the day star arise in your hearts: Knowing this first, that no prophecy of the scripture is of any private interpretation. For the prophecy came not in old time by the will of man: but holy men of God spake as they were moved by the Holy Ghost" (2 Peter 1:19-21).

Everything that took place in the sufferings of the Son of God was ordered and ordained by God, written in his Word, and brought to pass by his hand for the ransom of our souls, to make atonement for our sin. Those armed men Judas brought with him to take the Master; Judas, the chief priests, the scribes, the elders, the Jews, Herod, and Pilate, were but the hands of God, unconscious instruments of his sovereignty, by which he accomplished his purpose!

"Arise, O LORD, disappoint him, cast him down: deliver my soul from the wicked, which is thy sword: From men which are thy hand, O LORD, from men of the world, which have their portion in this life, and whose belly thou fillest with thy hid treasure: they are full of children, and leave the rest of their substance to their babes" (Psalm 17:13, 14).

Children of God, here is rest for our souls, a soft, soft pillow for our aching heads. Everything and everyone in this world is ruled by the wisdom, grace, and goodness of our omnipotent God! The course of this world is usually contrary to our desires. The church of God seems always to be struggling to survive. The wickedness of men appears to abound on every hand. The inconsistencies of our brethren often hurt and disturb us. Our own sins and inconsistencies disappoint and disturb many, and cause us great distress. But he who is our God and heavenly Father knows exactly what he is doing. And he always does only that which is absolutely best. He is simply fulfilling his purpose, working out his plan, accomplishing his predestination, fulfilling his Word. Read the 2nd Psalm and rejoice.

On the resurrection morning, when all things are made manifest, our Lord will show that even in the most distressing times and circumstances, he was simply fulfilling his wise and holy will.

The People Of God

Again and again, the Holy Spirit reminds us of the faults and failures, fickleness and falls, sins and shortcomings of the people of God in this world. "And they all forsook him, and fled" (v. 50). Noah's drunkenness, Abraham's fear, Lot's choice, David's adultery and murder, Peter's fall, and the abandonment of our Lord by all his disciples in the garden are things recorded for our learning. They are written to teach us and remind us that all flesh is grass and salvation is of the Lord. Our only righteousness is that which God has given us in Christ. If we are kept in grace, we are kept and preserved by grace alone. We must never place any confidence in ourselves.

With these faithful, faithful men, faith gave way to fear. Overwhelmed by their circumstances, they all forsook their Saviour and fled. We ought to be humbled before the Lord, knowing that our flesh is just like theirs, weak and prone to any and every sin. How charitable we should be to our erring, fallen, inconsistent brothers and sisters. We ought to be most thankful to our God for his faithful, preserving grace. We should ever be mindful of and give praise to our God for such a sympathizing High Priest as our Lord Jesus Christ who is touched with the feeling of our infirmities.

If there is one trial more difficult to bear than any other, I think it must be disappointment, betrayal, or abandonment by one who is close and trusted as a friend, companion, or loved one. But there is one faithful Friend who never disappoints his friends; and his compassions fail not!

The Gospel Of God

"And there followed him a certain young man, having a linen cloth cast about his naked body; and the young men laid hold on him: And he left the linen cloth, and fled from them naked" (vv. 51, 52).

We are not told who this young man was. That may be because no one knew his name. It seems that he was awakened in the middle of the night by all the commotion going on around him. He seems to have simply wrapped a sheet around himself to step outside and see what was happening. As he followed the crowd, trying to see, the soldiers grabbed him. So furious was the bloodthirsty mob that they were ready to arrest and kill anyone even suspected of being a follower of Jesus. Realizing the danger he had unwittingly stepped into, this young man "fled from them naked", leaving his sheet behind.

Why is this, seemingly insignificant, event written in the Book of God? I know it is written for our learning, that we might through the patience and comfort of the scriptures have hope (Romans 15:4). But what are we to learn from this event? It seems to me that this young man is held before us here as a portrayal of the gospel itself, a picture of a sinner redeemed by the blood of Christ. He seems to be a providential antitype of what took place on the day of atonement and at the ceremonial cleansing of the leper (Leviticus 16:22; 14:7).

When the leper was cleansed, one bird was killed and the other bird, being dipped in the dead bird's blood, was set free. One the day of atonement one goat was slain and the other set free. Even so, in the gospel we learn that our Lord Jesus Christ, the Lamb of God, was slain for us, and we are set free, just as he was taken in the garden and this young man fled away to freedom.

I have no idea whether that is why this event is recorded; but I do know by the glorious experience of grace that the allegory is true! The law of God and hell itself held me in its grip; but when it took my Substitute, I fled away to freedom. The law stripped me naked. Fearing for my life, I left my filthy rags of self-righteousness in its teeth, and fled away naked to Christ.

The Betrayal

The great hymn writer Augustus Toplady knew something of the sinner's spiritual nakedness and need for the robe of Christ's righteousness when he wrote,

Rock of Ages cleft for me,
Let me hide myself in Thee;
Let the water and the blood,
From Thy riven side which flowed,
Be of sin the double cure,
Cleanse me from its guilt and power.

Not the labours of my hands,
Can fulfil Thy law's demands;
Could my zeal no respite know,
Could my tears forever flow,
All for sin could not atone;
Thou must save, and Thou alone.

Nothing in my hand I bring,
Simply to Thy cross I cling;
Naked, come to Thee for dress;
Helpless, look to Thee for grace;
Foul, I to the fountain fly;
Wash me, Saviour, or I die.

While I draw this fleeting breath,
When my eyelids close in death,
When I soar through tracts unknown,
See Thee on Thy judgment throne;
Rock of Ages, cleft for me,
Let me hide myself in Thee.

"And they led Jesus away to the high priest: and with him were assembled all the chief priests and the elders and the scribes. And Peter followed him afar off, even into the palace of the high priest: and he sat with the servants, and warmed himself at the fire. And the chief priests and all the council sought for witness against Jesus to put him to death; and found none. For many bare false witness against him, but their witness agreed not together. And there arose certain, and bare false witness against him, saying, We heard him say, I will destroy this temple that is made with hands, and within three days I will build another made without hands. But neither so did their witness agree together. And the high priest stood up in the midst, and asked Jesus, saying, Answerest thou nothing? what is it which these witness against thee? But he held his peace, and answered nothing. Again the high priest asked him, and said unto him, Art thou the Christ, the Son of the Blessed? And Jesus said, I am: and ye shall see the Son of man sitting on the right hand of power, and coming in the clouds of heaven. Then the high priest rent his clothes, and saith, What need we any further witnesses? Ye have heard the blasphemy: what think ye? And they all condemned him to be guilty of death. And some began to spit on him, and to cover his face, and to buffet him, and to say unto him, Prophesy: and the servants did strike him with the palms of their hands".

(Mark 14:53-65)

Chapter 68

"They Led Jesus Away"

Solomon tells us that one evil he had seen under the sun is "when folly is set in great dignity, and the rich sit in low place" (Ecclesiastes 10:5, 6). No words can more accurately describe the scene before us in Mark 14:53-65. Here is the Son of God, our Lord Jesus Christ, "in whom are hid all the treasures of wisdom and knowledge", arraigned as a common criminal before "all the chief priests, and the elders, and the scribes". In these verses of holy scripture the Holy Spirit inspired Mark to record an astounding piece of history for our comfort and edification in the knowledge of Christ.

Here all the religious and political leaders of the Jews were gathered in complete agreement for the express purpose of murdering the Christ of God. These trusted, upstanding leaders of the nation deliberately sought false witnesses to condemn to death the holy Son of God. Here puny, petty, sinful men dared sit in judgment over the very God who made them, calling God himself to give an account to them, judging him who will one day come again to this earth to judge them and all the world!

In this passage of scripture, in this inspired, historical narrative, we see "folly sitting in great dignity and the rich sitting in low place". Though he was rich, yet for our sakes, the Lord Jesus Christ became poor, that we through his poverty might be made rich.

Peter's Great Folly

Great falls are usually preceded by smaller inconsistencies. We know that God's saints in this world are sinners still. We need nothing more than a moment's reflection upon our own hearts to convince us of that fact. Loved from eternity, chosen by grace, redeemed by the precious blood of Christ, called by his Spirit, robed in his righteousness and kept by the power of his grace we are. Yet, we live in this body of flesh. We are sinners still.

Therefore, we are warned repeatedly to watch, and pray, and beware. If we would honour the Lord our God in this world, if we would live in this world for the glory of Christ, we must beware of the sin that is in us. We must pray for grace to keep us from the evil that is in us. And we must watch over our souls with great care, resisting the world the flesh and the devil.

We all know these things. Yet, we all commonly act as though they are unnecessary. Peter stands before us as a glaring example of just how foolishly we often act, refusing to take heed to our Master's word and refusing to beware of ourselves. "And Peter followed him afar off, even into the palace of the high priest: and he sat with the servants, and warmed himself at the fire" (v. 54).

The Lord Jesus warned Peter plainly that Satan desired to have him, that he might sift him as wheat. He told Peter that he was about to both forsake him and deny him. But Peter did not believe he could do such things.

Even after forsaking the Lord Jesus in the garden, Peter rushed headlong into greater temptation. He saw no danger within or without. Yet, there were plenty of warnings, numerous red flags, which should have kept Peter from his dreadful, inexcusable act of denying Christ. The Lord Jesus told Peter that Satan was after him. Peter's rashness and pride, once exposed by the Master, should have humbled him. Fleeing from the Lord Jesus in the garden in fear, forsaking him in the hour of trouble, should have made him aware of his weakness. But now, just before his denial of his Saviour, we see Peter following Christ afar off, sitting in the company of the Lord's malicious enemies, as one of them, warming himself by their fire!

Lot would never have wound up living in Sodom had he not made his first choice of the well watered plains to the south based upon his lust after the things of the world. In his old age, I am sure, as Bro. Lot thought about his wife, his daughters, and his sons-in-law in hell, as he looked over an ill-spent life full of wasted opportunities, he must have rued the day when strife over cattle separated him from Abraham! David would never have taken Bathsheba, he would never have murdered his faithful servant, Uriah, had he not lingered in the palace in ease, when there was a battle to be fought for the glory of God. Peter would not have been tempted to deny the Lord Jesus as he did, if he had not followed the Lord afar off into the palace of the high priest, sat down with the Lord's enemies, and warmed himself by their fire. Let us ever take heed to ourselves, lest we fall into temptation by our own inconsistencies and indiscretions. Let us ever pray that we may not be led into temptation, but that the Lord would ever deliver us from evil.

"My son, attend to my words; incline thine ear unto my sayings. Let them not depart from thine eyes; keep them in the midst of thine heart. For they are life unto those that find them, and health to all their flesh. Keep thy heart with all diligence; for out of it are the issues of life. Put away from thee a froward mouth, and perverse lips put far from thee. Let thine eyes look right on, and let thine eyelids look straight before thee. Ponder the path of thy feet, and let all thy ways be established. Turn not to the right hand nor to the left: remove thy foot from evil" (Proverbs 4:20-27).

"Keep yourselves in the love of God, looking for the mercy of our Lord Jesus Christ unto eternal life" (Jude 21). We must ever beware of our own sinfulness, depravity, and weakness. May God give us grace ever to trust Christ and seek his glory. Ever resist temptation. Always strive against sin. Crucify the flesh. Say no to ungodliness. Do not ever be afraid of being too particular or too strict with yourself. Once we give in to petty inconsistencies, once we begin to indulge the flesh, we are paving the road to shame.

Christ's Great Humiliation

Our Lord Jesus Christ willingly endured indescribably great shame and humiliation that he might be our great Saviour. Mark records our Saviour's arrest, the false accusations made against him, the venomous spit of men's throats upon his face, the angry beatings our Lord endured, the cruel buffeting, the haughty slaps of rage, and the taunting jeers and mockery Immanuel endured before the high priests and the assembly of the chief priests and elders of Israel. These things are not easily endured. We would never voluntarily subject ourselves to such things. But the Son of God, our Saviour, willingly took our shame, as well as the sin that caused it, that he might redeem us and save us from our sins (Isaiah 53:4-7; 2 Corinthians 8:9; Philippians 2:5-11; Hebrews 2:10).

Robert Hawker wrote, "Every minute circumstance merits our closest regard. Perhaps there is not the smallest indignity offered to the person of the Lord Jesus, but had a mystical meaning". As soon as he was arrested, the Lamb of God was led away to the high priest, because the law of God required that the sacrifice be brought before the priest for inspection before it was offered upon God's altar (Leviticus 17:5).

Our Great God

Our holy Redeemer was accused of plotting to destroy the temple, refusing to pay tribute to Caesar, and blasphemy against God. These and many other charges were brought forward; but no witnesses could be found, or even hired, to substantiate them. But when the high priest asked him pointedly, "Art thou the Christ, the Son of the Blessed?" and the Lord Jesus told him plainly that he is, asserting his eternal divinity and Godhead, "all condemned him to be guilty of death".

He who is our great Saviour is the Christ, the Son of the Blessed. The man Christ Jesus is our great God and Saviour. The high priest asked our Lord this solemn question: "Art thou the Christ the Son of the blessed?" And our Lord Jesus gave him an immediate, unmistakable answer. "And Jesus said, I am: and ye shall see the Son of man sitting on the right hand of power, and coming in the clouds of heaven" (v. 62).

Our Master was dealing with an arrogant, self-righteous, know-it-all rebel. When he answered this great religious leader, he did not gratify his imaginary brilliance or show the least respect for his position. He offered no proof for his assertion, though there was an abundance of proof at hand. He simply stated the fact of who he was and is, demanding that this sinner make an immediate decision.

Look at our Lord's statement carefully, and hear it clearly. He said to this Caiaphas, the high priest of Israel, "I AM"! That is no small statement! The Lord Jesus could have used any word he desired. He could have simply said, "Yes", or "That is who I am" or "The scriptures testify that I am". Instead, he chose to answer this rebel in such a way that he must either bow to him, or demand his execution. He took the very name of God unto himself! This man said to the high priest, the elders and the scribes, "I AM THE I AM"!

Then he said, "You shall see me, the Son of man, sitting as God on the right hand of power"! That is the meaning of the next part of the sentence. To sit on the right hand of power is to sit upon the throne of God! In other words the Lord Jesus said to Caiaphas, "Just in case you did not get my meaning, I am telling you that this man standing in front of you is God almighty".

He came into this world as a man to save his people from their sins. Caiaphas was about to have him executed, precisely because he was determined to die upon the cursed tree as our Substitute. When he finished his work of redemption, he went back to glory and took his seat upon the throne of God, the throne of grace. Now, there is a man in Glory who is touched with the feeling of our infirmities, a man who is himself our great God! He rules the universe for us. He intercedes for us. He will save us.

Our Lord Jesus said to Caiaphas, "You will soon see me come again in the clouds of heaven to sit in judgment over you"! "And Jesus said, I am: and ye shall see the Son of man sitting on the right hand of power, and coming in the clouds of heaven". What a stern warning this is! There is a judgment to come. One day soon, you and I will stand before the great white throne, before the tribunal of the holy Lord God.

Man's Great Offence
Man's unbelief is a wilful, deliberate choice and decided declaration that God is a liar, that Jesus Christ deserved to be put to death, and that the Word of God is a horrible, hellish hoax devised to delude and deceive the souls of men. Like Caiaphas, sinners are confronted with the claims of the Christ of God. We must either bow to his claims or perish under the wrath of God. As we preach the gospel, we call for a decision from all who hear. "Will you, or will you not trust the Son of God? Bow to him you will, sooner or later; but will you bow to him now and seek his mercy whose wrath you cannot bear?"

If the rebel says, "No", his unbelief is not a matter of ignorance or indifference. He is saying, "God is a liar, Jesus Christ was an impostor who deserved to be put to death, and the Bible is a hellish hoax upon the souls of men". That is what Caiaphas did; and that's what every unbeliever does. Unbelief is nothing less than spitting upon the face of the Son of God; but men will not forever spit upon the Christ of God and get by (1 John 5:10-12; Proverbs 1:23-33).

"And as Peter was beneath in the palace, there cometh one of the maids of the high priest: And when she saw Peter warming himself, she looked upon him, and said, And thou also wast with Jesus of Nazareth. But he denied, saying, I know not, neither understand I what thou sayest. And he went out into the porch; and the cock crew. And a maid saw him again, and began to say to them that stood by, This is one of them. And he denied it again. And a little after, they that stood by said again to Peter, Surely thou art one of them: for thou art a Galilaean, and thy speech agreeth thereto. But he began to curse and to swear, saying, I know not this man of whom ye speak. And the second time the cock crew. And Peter called to mind the word that Jesus said unto him, Before the cock crow twice, thou shalt deny me thrice. And when he thought thereon, he wept".

(Mark 14:66-72)

Chapter 69

Peter's Fall And Restoration

The verses before us record the painful, but very instructive, story of Peter's terrible denial of the Lord Jesus. This sad story is recorded in detail in all four gospel narratives. Yet, neither Matthew, Mark, Luke, nor John make any excuse for or defence of their friend, Peter. They all wrote their histories, not as mere men writing about men, but as instruments of divine inspiration. This story of Peter's fall was written by the inspiration of God the Holy Spirit for our learning and admonition. May the Spirit of God, who gave us this story four times, now inscribe its lessons upon our hearts by his almighty grace, for Christ's sake.

Try to picture the scene and the events which transpired on that cold, bitter night. It was a solemn, solemn night. Our Lord Jesus himself called it, "the judgment (crisis) of this world". The disciples had just observed the last passover meal of the legal dispensation and the first communion service of the gospel age. The Lord Jesus told them plainly of his certain, imminent betrayal and death. Peter, James and John had spent the night with the Son of God in Gethsemane. On that sacred evening, our Saviour preached that marvellous sermon that is recorded in John 14, 15 and 16. It was on this night, earlier in the evening, that our Master, our great High Priest, offered that great prayer for us recorded in John 17. The soldiers came, like a mob of lynch men, into the garden to arrest the Lord of glory, led by his own familiar friend, Judas Iscariot. Judas betrayed him with a kiss. And Peter denied the Lord Jesus, denied him again, and denied him a third time, cursing.

Why is this record given four times in the New Testament? Surely the Holy Spirit means us to give it special attention. There at least three reasons why this sad tale is told in such detail by all four gospel writers.

Peter's denial of the Lord Jesus must have greatly increased the pain and sufferings of our tender-hearted Saviour. The Holy Spirit would set before us in a most emphatic way the greatness of our Saviour's saving power, the majesty of his unconditional grace, and the immutability of his faithfulness.

The divine Comforter knew that we would all be subject to these same temptations. This fourfold record of Peter's fall is intended to be a startling, instructive lesson for us concerning the frailty of the best of men, and especially a startling reminder of our own frailty.

The Word of God does not tell us very much even about the very best of men who lived in Bible times. The histories of God's saints in scripture are very scanty. Yet, the Word of God very particularly records the faults and falls of the most eminent saints. It seems that the Holy Spirit's purpose is to remind us incessantly that "all flesh is grass"! The best of men are only men at best. And he incessantly reminds us that "Salvation is of the Lord"! Peter was not the infallible bishop of Rome, as the papists pretend. He was just a frail, fallible, fickle, sinful man. At least one thing the pope has in common with Peter is his denial of Christ. Peter's fall seems to say to us all, "You, too, are weak. You, too, will fall, if left to yourself. Do not ever trust yourself. Trust Christ entirely. Lean on him incessantly. Do not rely upon your great experiences or the imaginary strength and firmness of your faith. Satan has desired to have you that he may sift you as wheat. Christ alone can hold you up. Christ alone can keep you." We must ever watch and pray! We must each diligently watch over our own souls and prayerfully seek the Lord's preserving grace, if we would live for the honour of his name.

I want to live for the honour of Christ. I want to honour and magnify him in my living, as well as in my preaching and writing. I know that you who love him want the same thing. My heart shudders, my soul trembles at the thought of bringing reproach upon the name of him who loved me and gave himself for me. Yet, I know this: Unless Christ himself preserves me from the evil that is in me, and preserves you from the evil that is in you, we will, most certainly, profane his name.

The Circumstances Of Peter's Fall

How did such a great man come to commit such a grievous evil? This portion of holy scripture is not talking about a lost man, but a saint, a child of God, redeemed by blood, justified in Christ, saved by grace, and sanctified by the Spirit. Peter was a faithful giant among faithful giants. Few before him and few after him could stand shoulder to shoulder with him. He was a man strong in faith, firm in conviction, bold in preaching and unrelenting in his zeal for Christ.

This man was eminent even among the apostles, a leader among leaders, an example among examples. But this man, great as he was, was just a man. Like you and me, he was a man whose heart, by nature, was full of sin, whose flesh was weak. On that dark, dark night in the High Priest's palace, this man's evil heart broke out in a horrible display of ungodliness, in an act as evil and vile as any in human history. The godly apostle Peter blasphemously denied the Son of God with foul oaths!

How can we account for this thing? As we look at the circumstances of Peter's fall, I remind you, there were no extenuating circumstances to excuse or even mitigate his guilt. Indeed, everything recorded in the inspired gospel records aggravates his offence. Peter's fall was very strange because he was one of the Lord Jesus' most highly favoured and most highly honoured disciples. The greater our privileges and the higher our honours, the greater our responsibilities are and the more horrible our offences.

The Lord had done so much for Peter. He was one of the very first to whom the Son of God made himself known while he was in the world, one of the first to be saved by the power of his Word (John 1:40-42). Peter was in the inner circle of the Master's intimate friends. He seems to have been the chief spokesman for the early church. Peter's fall is especially sad because he was plainly and faithfully warned of his great danger (Luke 22:31-34). Our Lord Jesus told Peter in the plainest language possible exactly what was going to happen to him. He even gave him the details. Peter was told of the danger to which he was about to be exposed. Satan desired to have him. His faith would be fiercely attacked. Therefore, he must watch and pray that he enter not into temptation. But Peter walked headlong into danger. He rejected the light God had given him. He ignored the revelation of God's Word.

Peter's guilt is aggravated by the fact that it came so soon after he had confidently declared his loyalty to Christ (Matthew 26:31-35; Luke 22:33). Just a few short hours after proudly and confidently boasting of his love for Christ, Peter cursed and denied him three times. How fickle we are!

Peter's fall did not come at once, but by degrees. He followed the Lord afar off. Then, he sat in the seat of scorners, seeking the comfort and warmth their fire provided. Next, he denied the Lord Jesus by degrees. At first, he pretended not to understand the maiden's words. Then, he denied that he knew the man. He denied his own confession of faith and, by implication if not outright, denied the Saviour's divinity, (compare Matthew 16:18 and John 6:69). At last, he took the profane language of base, ungodly men to prove that he was no follower of the holy Lamb of God. There are many, many ways by which men and women deny the Lord Jesus Christ; but usually the falls of God's saints are not sudden. Normally, great falls are preceded by much smaller inconsistencies.

It takes very little to make a great saint fall into great sin, if God leaves him to himself. Peter's trial was nothing but the word of a weak young woman, who said, "Thou also wast with Jesus of Nazareth". Here is another very great aggravation of Peter's sin: All this was done very close to the place where his Lord and Master was at that time suffering for him, bearing his reproach! The Lord Jesus Christ was standing right in front of Peter, hearing every word! What was the reason for Peter's fall? How can we account for this? How did this man, so great, so unique in so many ways, come to commit such a horrible offence? Peter was too proud of himself, too confident of his own strength. He was overcome by the fear of man; in this case, by the fear of a woman who had no obvious power against him. He neglected watchfulness over his own heart and soul (Proverbs 4:23). I suspect that, like mother Eve, Peter had begun to doubt the Saviour's word.

The Means Of Peter's Recovery

Peter fell but he did not perish. His faith weakened; but it did not die. He sinned; but he was not cast off or forsaken. He denied the Lord; but the Lord did not deny him. Peter belonged to Christ; and Christ can never lose one of his own. The good Shepherd can never lose one of his sheep. Peter fell, but Christ graciously raised him up. The righteous fall seven times a day; but the Lord raises them up (Proverbs 24:16). How did the Lord Jesus restore his fallen servant? I see four things the Lord used to restore his fallen child.

First, he used a work of providence. "The cock crew"! God has many ways of reaching a man's conscience. He can make asses speak as easily as prophets and roosters to crow on cue.

Second, he used a work of grace. "The Lord turned and looked on Peter" (Luke 22:61). What a look! The Lord Jesus turned to Peter. Peter did not turn to the Lord. He looked upon Peter, not in anger and disgust, but in mercy, love and grace! That look was a look of tenderness, compassion and faithfulness. With that look, the Lord spoke silently, but effectually, to the heart of his fallen son.

He seems to have said, "I have loved thee with an everlasting love. Ye have not chosen me; but I have chosen you. I gave unto you eternal life; and you shall never perish. I will never leave thee nor forsake thee. I, even I, am he that blotteth out thy transgressions. Fear not, for I have redeemed thee. In me thy righteousness is found. I am thy strength. I am the Lord, I change not; therefore ye sons of Jacob are not consumed. Greater love hath no man than this, that a man lay down his life for his friends. Return unto me, return unto me; and I will pardon. Let not your heart be troubled: ye believe in God, believe also in me".

Third, he used a work of the word. "Peter called to mind the word that Jesus said unto him" (v. 72). At the appointed time, the Word of God graciously and effectually brought Peter to repentance.

Fourth, Peter was restored by a work of our blessed Advocate, the Lord Jesus, who told him even before his fall, "I have prayed for thee" (Luke 22:32). As a great High Priest and Intercessor, the Lord Jesus Christ prayed for Peter's preservation in faith and restoration by grace, even before he fell! That same great High Priest is our Advocate on high. He intercedes for us now, and has interceded for us from eternity (1 John 2:1, 2).

The Signs Of Peter's Restoration
The Lord's works for and upon Peter were effectual. They accomplished their intended design. And Peter was graciously restored by the very Saviour he so vehemently denied. His trial and fall were not accidents. Satan ran God's child through his rough sifter; but he lost nothing in the process except chaff. Peter came out of this thing a much better man than he was before (Acts 2 and 4). Even this tragic affair was under the control of God's sovereign providence and according to his purpose of grace.

Let us ever remember that the devil is God's devil. That fiend of hell is the unwilling, unwitting vassal of the Almighty (Isaiah 14:12-27). The dragon of hell is as much included in all things working together for good to God's elect as the angels of light (Romans 8:28). Immediately after the Lord looked upon him, Peter went out of the place (Luke 22:62). Once fire was restored in his soul, he no longer needed the warmth of that fire which the Lord's enemies had kindled. He immediately forsook those who had turned his heart from his Lord. As he left the high priest's house, Peter wept bitterly (v. 72; Luke 22:62). Convulsive weeping overcame him. He could not stand himself. His very heart was crushed within him. Oh, blessed is that man whose heart is broken before God. Christ Jesus heals the broken-hearted! "The sacrifices of God are a broken spirit: a broken and contrite heart, O God, thou wilt not despise"! Do you know anything about repentance?

The Lessons For Us Today
What are we to learn from this tragic event in Peter's life? How can we benefit from it? What lessons are taught by this man's fall and restoration? Certainly, these things are recorded by the Spirit of God to teach us something about ourselves. We must never be presumptuous about ourselves. We are all very much like Peter in his weakness. We are all fickle, sinful wretches by nature. There is no evil in this world of which we are not capable (1 Corinthians 10:12; 4:7). May God the Holy Spirit teach us and give us grace never to be severe with our erring brethren.

Peter's fall and restoration is an emphatic declaration that "Salvation is of the Lord". It is altogether the work of God's free grace in Christ. It is unconditional, immutable and indestructible! What blessed security our souls have in Christ! Nothing can sever us from our Saviour! "Keep yourselves in the love of God". Trust Christ alone. Live always at the cross. Cling to your crucified Saviour tenaciously. As often as you fall, return to him. He will receive you. He will forgive you. He will be gracious to you. He will forget the wrong you have done!

"And straightway in the morning the chief priests held a consultation with the elders and scribes and the whole council, and bound Jesus, and carried him away, and delivered him to Pilate. And Pilate asked him, Art thou the King of the Jews? And he answering said unto him, Thou sayest it. And the chief priests accused him of many things: but he answered nothing. And Pilate asked him again, saying, Answerest thou nothing? behold how many things they witness against thee. But Jesus yet answered nothing; so that Pilate marvelled. Now at that feast he released unto them one prisoner, whomsoever they desired. And there was one named Barabbas, which lay bound with them that had made insurrection with him, who had committed murder in the insurrection. And the multitude crying aloud began to desire him to do as he had ever done unto them. But Pilate answered them, saying, Will ye that I release unto you the King of the Jews? For he knew that the chief priests had delivered him for envy. But the chief priests moved the people, that he should rather release Barabbas unto them. And Pilate answered and said again unto them, What will ye then that I shall do unto him whom ye call the King of the Jews? And they cried out again, Crucify him. Then Pilate said unto them, Why, what evil hath he done? And they cried out the more exceedingly, Crucify him. And so Pilate, willing to content the people, released Barabbas unto them, and delivered Jesus, when he had scourged him, to be crucified".

(Mark 15:1-15)

Chapter 70

Barabbas: A Picture Of Substitution

Mark 15 describes the slaying of "the Lamb of God, which taketh away the sin of the world". Whenever we think about the death of our Lord Jesus Christ upon the cross, we ought to always remember three things.

The death of Christ upon the cursed tree was a substitutionary sacrifice. The Lord Jesus Christ did not suffer for any crimes of his own. He did not die because of his own sins. He was not cut off from the land of the living for his own transgressions. The Lord of Glory died upon the cross for our sins, for the transgressions of his people, for the iniquities of God's elect, which were imputed to him, when he was made to be sin for us (Isaiah 53:4-6, 8; Daniel 9:26; 2 Corinthians 5:21; 1 Peter 3:18)

The substitutionary sacrifice and death of our Lord Jesus Christ is the focal point, the essence, and the message of all the Word of God. The law was given at Sinai to show us our need of a substitute. All the sacrifices, rites, rituals, and ceremonies of the Old Testament scriptures, all the priests, priestly garments, and priestly functions, all the deliverances of Israel from the hands of their enemies, all the services of the tabernacle and the temple, all the psalms, all the prophets, and all the historical narratives, the manna, the rock, the brazen serpent, the pillars of fire and cloud, everything in the Old Testament and in the New was written by inspiration of God the Holy Spirit to reveal Christ, to show us our great, glorious, almighty Substitute (Luke 24:27, 44, 45; 1 Peter 1:23-25; John 20:30, 31).

The cross of Christ, the doctrine of substitution, is both the revelation of the glory of God and the glory of the gospel (2 Corinthians 4:4-6; Galatians 6:14). The death of Christ upon the cross, the sacrifice of God's Lamb as our sin-atonement, is the life of our souls. Had the Lord Jesus Christ not died in our stead, the justice of God could never have been satisfied and we would all have perished in our sins forever.

When the apostle Paul thought of these things, he said, "Thanks be unto God for his unspeakable gift"! May God the Holy Spirit so graciously flood our hearts and souls with the knowledge of our crucified Substitute that we may ever have our hearts and minds fixed upon our blessed Saviour and his great sacrifice of himself for us, and have the apostle's words reverberating in our souls. "Thanks be unto God for his unspeakable gift"!

A Fulfilment Of Prophecy

"And straightway in the morning the chief priests held a consultation with the elders and scribes and the whole council, and bound Jesus, and carried him away, and delivered him to Pilate" (v. 1). Why did these chief priests, scribes and elders carry the Lord Jesus to Pilate, the Roman governor of Judea? Why did they not just stone him to death themselves? The reason is obvious. They had no legal, civil authority to do so. They should have known that the time of the Messiah was upon them, because Jacob's prophecy in Genesis 49:10 had been fulfilled.

Moreover, they must themselves also fulfil the scriptures in their deeds; and the scriptures required that our Redeemer be crucified in a publicly shameful way, not merely stoned to death, as Jewish law would have required (Deuteronomy 21:22, 23). His body, according to the Old Testament scriptures, had to be pierced and not a bone of it broken (Zechariah 12:10; John 19:36; Exodus 12:46; Numbers 9:12; 1 Corinthians 5:7). Though they were so blinded by their unbelief that they could not see it, the Lord's enemies were themselves simply fulfilling the purpose of God to the very letter of holy scripture, even in their rage against his dear Son (Acts 4:27, 28; 13:28, 29).

How comforting it is to know that wicked men are never out of God's control. They only do what his hand and purpose have from eternity determined must be done for the salvation of our souls. When Satan roars, when scoffers scoff, when mockers mock, when deceivers deceive, they only perform that which was long ago written in the scriptures (2 Peter 2:3). Man, in the folly of his rebellion and unbelief, and Satan himself, even the demons of hell, all are but the unwitting vassals of the Almighty, our heavenly Father, to serve his purpose of grace toward us.

They "bound Jesus". If the Lord Jesus would set us free, he must be bound. As Isaac and the legal sacrifices were bound and laid upon the altar (Genesis 22:9; Leviticus 4:10, Psalm 118:27), so the Son of God, when he was about to be made sin for us, was bound as a criminal, and was bound to the cursed tree for us.

An Example Of Patience

When the holy Son of God stood before Pilate's bar, he was falsely accused of many evils. The trumped up charges against him were all false. Yet, when he was accused, "he answered nothing". What an example he set before us of patience and humility, bowing to the providence and purpose of God.

"And Pilate asked him, Art thou the King of the Jews? And he answering said unto him, Thou sayest it. And the chief priests accused him of many things: but he answered nothing. And Pilate asked him again, saying,

Answerest thou nothing? behold how many things they witness against thee. But Jesus yet answered nothing; so that Pilate marvelled" (vv. 2-5).

We can do nothing more dishonouring to our God and contrary to our faith than grumble and murmur against him when he sends trouble our way. And we never more glorify our God and exemplify the character of Christ than when we bear afflictions, false accusations, and injustices patiently (Isaiah 53:7; Hebrews 12:1-3; 1 Peter 2:20-24; Psalm 39:1).

An Abuse Of Power
"And so Pilate, willing to content the people, released Barabbas unto them, and delivered Jesus, when he had scourged him, to be crucified" (v. 15).

Do not be fooled by the political manoeuvrings of this Roman governor. Pilate knew the chief priests and scribes had delivered the Lord Jesus to him out of envy (v. 10). He made some feeble attempts to release him to soothe his own conscience; but, in the shameful behaviour typical of politicians and political appointees, Pontius Pilate was "willing to content the people", even if it meant sacrificing his own conscience and the life of an innocent man to do it!

I mention this, not to stir up more anger and greater disgust toward our president, congressmen, and senators. They manage very well on their own. I mention it that we may take a higher road than the rest of the world. Men in high places, without the knowledge of Christ, without even a hint of moral integrity, are to be pitied. They have nothing to restrain them from yielding to every temptation to great evil, except the prayers of God's saints. Let us, therefore, pray for them, as the Word of God tells us (1 Timothy 2:1, 2).

A Portrait Of Depravity
"But the chief priests moved the people, that he should rather release Barabbas unto them. And Pilate answered and said again unto them, What will ye then that I shall do unto him whom ye call the King of the Jews? And they cried out again, Crucify him. Then Pilate said unto them, Why, what evil hath he done? And they cried out the more exceedingly, Crucify him" (vv. 11-14).

In these days of universal compromise and ecumenical religion everyone is trying to remove every possible point of offence, take away all guilt and blame, and fix things up so that everybody is saved, and all their works, no matter how vile, if not saintly, are at least excusable. Historians are re-writing history everyday to suit the trends of modern thinking. Theologians are re-writing the Bible to mould it to the opinions of men. But all the re-arranging of things by men will never alter facts.

Here is a fact: while Pilate and his soldiers (pagan Gentiles) were the ones who executed the Lord Jesus Christ, the Jews (the religious people, the people who claimed to be God's servants) were them who cried, "Crucify him! Crucify him! Let his blood be upon us and our children"!

We marvel at their act. They acted against evidence plainly presented. When they had opportunity given them in the eleventh hour to back away from their rash demands, they stayed their course to the everlasting ruin of their souls, the souls of their children, and of their children's children.

Even when it meant the release of a known, notorious murderer among their wives and children, they stayed with their decision. They could not be persuaded to change course or alter their decision concerning Barabbas, or Jesus, by any moral pressure or sane reasoning. Blindness was never more blind! Folly was never more foolish! Madness was never more mad! How can this be explained?

The only thing on this earth that can explain such behaviour is the fact that all men are totally depraved. The heart of man is deceitful above all things and desperately wicked. The carnal mind is enmity against God. It is not possible for any man to do anything good, or even to make a good, or even reasonable, decision apart from divine intervention.

Let us not be found following the example of these lost, religious rebels. Let us not choose Barabbas over Christ. Let us not choose wickedness and despise righteousness. Let us not choose the world and reject Christ. Yet, that is exactly what we will do, unless God intervenes and stops us from fulfilling the madness of our own hearts' lusts.

A Picture Of Substitution

"Now at that feast he released unto them one prisoner, whomsoever they desired. And there was one named Barabbas, which lay bound with them that had made insurrection with him, who had committed murder in the insurrection. And the multitude crying aloud began to desire him to do as he had ever done unto them. But Pilate answered them, saying, Will ye that I release unto you the King of the Jews? For he knew that the chief priests had delivered him for envy. But the chief priests moved the people, that he should rather release Barabbas unto them. And Pilate answered and said again unto them, What will ye then that I shall do unto him whom ye call the King of the Jews? And they cried out again, Crucify him. Then Pilate said unto them, Why, what evil hath he done? And they cried out the more exceedingly, Crucify him. And so Pilate, willing to content the people, released Barabbas unto them, and delivered Jesus, when he had scourged him, to be crucified" (vv. 6-15).

What a beautiful picture we have here of the gospel. Barabbas, the guilty man, was set free. The Lord Jesus Christ, the holy, innocent Lamb of God, died in his place. A great sinner went free because a great Substitute took his place. Barabbas was spared because Christ died in his place. That is, in its very essence and glory, the gospel of God. It can be summed up in one word, *substitution* (Romans 3:21-26; 5:6-8; 8:1-4, 32-34; 2 Corinthians 5:20, 21).

"And so Pilate, willing to content the people, released Barabbas unto them, and delivered Jesus, when he had scourged him, to be crucified. And the soldiers led him away into the hall, called Praetorium; and they call together the whole band. And they clothed him with purple, and platted a crown of thorns, and put it about his head, And began to salute him, Hail, King of the Jews! And they smote him on the head with a reed, and did spit upon him, and bowing their knees worshipped him. And when they had mocked him, they took off the purple from him, and put his own clothes on him, and led him out to crucify him. And they compel one Simon a Cyrenian, who passed by, coming out of the country, the father of Alexander and Rufus, to bear his cross. And they bring him unto the place Golgotha, which is, being interpreted, The place of a skull. And they gave him to drink wine mingled with myrrh: but he received it not. And when they had crucified him, they parted his garments, casting lots upon them, what every man should take. And it was the third hour, and they crucified him. And the superscription of his accusation was written over, THE KING OF THE JEWS. And with him they crucify two thieves; the one on his right hand, and the other on his left. And the scripture was fulfilled, which saith, And he was numbered with the transgressors. And they that passed by railed on him, wagging their heads, and saying, Ah, thou that destroyest the temple, and buildest it in three days, Save thyself, and come down from the cross. Likewise also the chief priests mocking said among themselves with the scribes, He saved others; himself he cannot save. Let Christ the King of Israel descend now from the cross, that we may see and believe. And they that were crucified with him reviled him. And when the sixth hour was come, there was darkness over the whole land until the ninth hour. And at the ninth hour Jesus cried with a loud voice, saying, Eloi, Eloi, lama sabachthani? which is, being interpreted, My God, my God, why hast thou forsaken me? And some of them that stood by, when they heard it, said, Behold, he calleth Elias. And one ran and filled a spunge full of vinegar, and put it on a reed, and gave him to drink, saying, Let alone; let us see whether Elias will come to take him down. And Jesus cried with a loud voice, and gave up the ghost. And the veil of the temple was rent in twain from the top to the bottom. And when the centurion, which stood over against him, saw that he so cried out, and gave up the ghost, he said, Truly this man was the Son of God".

(Mark 15:15-39)

Chapter 71

"He Saved Others: Himself He Cannot Save"

If the Lord God wants Balaam to hear his word, he can speak as easily through Balaam's ass as he can through a man or an angel. And, sometimes, in his infinite sovereignty, the Lord God uses lost, unregenerate, spiritually ignorant men to proclaim gospel truth as plainly and as powerfully as any inspired prophet. Those men remain as ignorant of the gospel as ever. Yet, they become voices by which God declares his truth. Numerous examples of this fact are given in the Book of God (John 11:47-52; Numbers 23:19-21; 1 Samuel 26:25). In the passage now before us the Spirit of God gives several more examples of God speaking glorious, gospel truths by men, who themselves knew nothing of the things they spoke. Repeatedly, those who mocked the Master in their jeers spoke plainly, declaring that the man hanging on the cursed tree between two thieves was and is "The King", and most distinctly "The King of Israel". Then, in verse 39 the centurion said, "Truly, this man was the Son of God"!

This is a matter of tremendous importance. The one through whom God speaks is nothing; but the message God speaks, the gospel of Christ, is the power of God unto salvation! Pastor Scott Richardson once said, "A preacher is a nobody trying to tell everybody about somebody who can save anybody".

"Likewise also the chief priests mocking said among themselves with the scribes, He saved others; himself he cannot save" (v. 31). In the angry, blood thirsty, jeering mob we hear the lost religious leaders of the day joining in the hellish revelry. Though they spoke with a hatred for the Son of God, these chief priests and scribes spoke the plain truth of the gospel most clearly. "He saved others; himself he cannot save".

Because the Lord Jesus Christ came here to save his people from their sins, because he came to save us from the wrath of God, he could not save himself from being made sin for us, he could not save himself from the wrath of God. This is the very essence of the gospel. See that you understand it clearly. The holy Lord God could not save sinners apart from the satisfaction of his law and justice by the obedience and death of his own dear Son as our

Substitute. God is sovereign. He did not have to save anyone but, having chosen to save some, he cannot save any except in a manner that honours his law and justice (Job 33:23, 24; Romans 3:23-26). If righteousness could come by another way, Christ died in vain (Galatians 3:21).

Mark 15:15-39 sets before us the most wondrous, most glorious event in the history of the universe. Indeed, this is the reason why God created the world in the first place. We have before us the suffering and death of the Lord Jesus Christ as the sinners' Substitute. Here the infinite love of God for sinners is set forth magnificently.

The sufferings described here would be astonishing, shocking to behold under any circumstances. Should we see any man endure such horror and grief, our hearts would be sick, deeply moved with compassion. But the man before us here is the eternal Son of God! I am astounded, amazed, lost in wonder as I read these words of Inspiration.

Here is something even more astounding. All that the Lord Jesus Christ endured, when he was made sin for us, he willingly, voluntarily endured. Even when he was made sin, it was by his own will that it came to pass. He willingly took upon himself our sins. He willingly went to the cross. He willingly died the shameful, ignominious death of the cross. He willingly became the object of his Father's holy wrath and indignation. The Lord Jesus Christ willingly took the cup of wrath and, with one tremendous draught of love, drank damnation dry for us. Why? Simply because he loved us! He loved us.

Here is "The love of Christ that passeth knowledge" (Ephesians 3:19). "God commendeth his love toward us in that while we were yet sinners, Christ died for us" (Romans 5:8). "Herein is love, not that we loved God, but that he loved us, and sent his Son to be the propitiation for our sins" (1 John 4:10). "Hereby perceive we the love of God, because he laid down his life for us" (1 John 3:16).

I want us to simply observe from the passage before us the things our Lord Jesus suffered, when he was made sin for chosen sinners. I want us to follow our Redeemer, step by step, from his condemnation to his death. There is deep meaning, spiritual instruction, and great consolation in everything our Substitute endured when he suffered the wrath of God in our place.

As we dwell upon these things, let us not forget, not even for a moment, that our sins and the salvation of our souls were the cause of all his agony. It was our hell that he endured! It was our death that he died. Child of God, the Holy Spirit here shows us the accomplishments of our great Surety and Substitute as he offered himself to God to make atonement for our sins (2 Corinthians 5:21; 1 Peter 2:24; 3:18).

Christ Condemned

"And so Pilate, willing to content the people, released Barabbas unto them, and delivered Jesus, when he had scourged him, to be crucified" (v. 15). Here we see the Son of God delivered into the hands of Roman soldiers, condemned to death, to be crucified as a common criminal. Here is that One before whom, one day soon, the whole world must stand in judgment. The great Judge, who shall summon all men before the great white throne in the last day, is here judged of men, sentenced to death and delivered up to be executed by the hands of wicked men.

Do you ask why? It was that he might deliver us from judgment, the pit of destruction, and the sentence of eternal death in hell. The Lord Jesus was made sin, judged guilty, and put to death for his people, so that believing sinners might never be judged for sin, so that he might present all the hosts of God's elect before the presence of his glory, holy, unblameable, and unreproveable in his sight (Romans 4:8; 8:1, 33, 34).

Cruel Mockery

"And the soldiers led him away into the hall, called Praetorium; and they call together the whole band. And they clothed him with purple, and platted a crown of thorns, and put it about his head, And began to salute him, Hail, King of the Jews! And they smote him on the head with a reed, and did spit upon him, and bowing their knees worshipped him. And when they had mocked him, they took off the purple from him, and put his own clothes on him, and led him out to crucify him" (vv. 16-20).

"And they that passed by railed on him, wagging their heads, and saying, Ah, thou that destroyest the temple, and buildest it in three days, Save thyself, and come down from the cross. Likewise also the chief priests mocking said among themselves with the scribes, He saved others; himself he cannot save. Let Christ the King of Israel descend now from the cross, that we may see and believe. And they that were crucified with him reviled him" (vv. 29-32).

Jesus Christ the Righteous is here mocked, jeered, insulted and made a laughing stock before all the world. They clothed him with a purple cloth, put a crown of thorns on his head, and mockingly worshipped him. They cried, "Hail! King"! Then they beat him, spit on him, and laughed him to scorn. As they led him away to crucify him, he became the song of drunkards. Harlots and "holy" men, pimps and priests, sots and scribes joined in hellish revelry as they nailed him to the tree and watched him die. Even the two thieves who were crucified with him found relief from their torture by joining in the scorn. The Son of God was made to be utterly contemptible before men. He was made to be "the filth of the world and the offscouring of all things".

Do you ask why? It was that we who are truly the filth of the world and off-scouring of all things, we who are in truth vile and contemptible might have glory, honour, and eternal life by the merit of his blood, that we might stand before God without one spot of sin or wrinkle of infirmity in perfect holiness. He wore a crown of thorns, that we might wear a crown of glory forever. He bore the spit of man, that men might bear the kiss of God forever. He sunk in humiliation, that we might rise in triumph.

Stripped Naked

"And when they had crucified him, they parted his garments, casting lots upon them, what every man should take" (v. 24). The Lord Jesus was stripped naked before men, exposed in open shame to all his enemies.

Do you ask why? It was that we, who have no righteousness before God, might be clothed with his perfect righteousness. It was that we, who are naked and shameful, all defiled with sin, might wear the wedding garments of grace and sit side by side with the angels of God unashamed. It was that we might forever wear the white robe of his perfect righteousness, the garments of salvation, clean and white, before the great white throne of our God.

Numbered With Sinners

"And with him they crucify two thieves; the one on his right hand, and the other on his left. And the scripture was fulfilled, which saith, And he was numbered with the transgressors" (vv. 27, 28). The Holy One of God was reckoned a transgressor and a sinner. He who did no sin, in whose mouth was no guile, was "numbered with the transgressors".

Do you ask why? Why was he numbered with the transgressors? It was because he was made sin for us, that we might be made the righteousness of God in him (2 Corinthians 5:21). The holy Lamb of God was made to be sin so that we, who are altogether unholy, might be made perfectly holy forever! He was pronounced guilty so that we might be pronounced righteous before God!

Forsaken Of God

"And at the ninth hour Jesus cried with a loud voice, saying, Eloi, Eloi, lama sabachthani? which is, being interpreted, My God, my God, why hast thou forsaken me?" (v. 34) The Son of God was forsaken by his Father. Try to grasp this. When our Surety, Jehovah's righteous Servant, was at the height of his obedience, as he was performing the crowning work he was commissioned of God to do, he was abandoned, forsaken by his Father.

Do you ask why? It was because he was made to be sin; and the holy Lord God cannot look upon sin. Why was he forsaken of God? It was that we might hear the Lord God himself declare, "I will never leave thee nor forsake thee"! Christ was forsaken because he was made sin for us. We can never be forsaken because he has taken our sins away!

Made A Curse

"And they bring him unto the place Golgotha, which is, being interpreted, The place of a skull. And they gave him to drink wine mingled with myrrh: but he received it not. And when they had crucified him, they parted his garments, casting lots upon them, what every man should take. And it was the third hour, and they crucified him. And the superscription of his accusation was written over, THE KING OF THE JEWS" (vv. 22-26).

The Lord of Glory was made a curse for us, crucified and hanged as a cursed thing upon Calvary's tree. Death by crucifixion was reserved for only the most vile of felons. This shamefully horrid, ignominious, torturous form of execution was designed to show the utter contemptibility of the one hanging upon the cross. The man hanging on the tree was counted accursed. The Lord Jesus died the cursed death of the cross.

Do you ask why? It was that we who were born accursed might be delivered from the curse of the law and stand forever blessed of God for Christ's sake (Galatians 3:13, 14).

A Voluntary Sacrifice

"And Jesus cried with a loud voice, and gave up the ghost" (v. 37). The Lord Jesus Christ, our Substitute, freely, voluntarily laid down his life; he gave up the ghost, for his people. He said, "I am the good shepherd: the good shepherd giveth his life for the sheep ... As the Father knoweth me, even so know I the Father: and I lay down my life for the sheep. And other sheep I have, which are not of this fold: them also I must bring, and they shall hear my voice; and there shall be one fold, and one shepherd. Therefore doth my Father love me, because I lay down my life, that I might take it again. No man taketh it from me, but I lay it down of myself. I have power to lay it down, and I have power to take it again. This commandment have I received of my Father" (John 10:11, 15-18).

Do you ask why? "In this was manifested the love of God toward us, because that God sent his only begotten Son into the world, that we might live through him. Herein is love, not that we loved God, but that he loved us, and sent his Son to be the propitiation for our sins" (1 John 4:9, 10).

The Rent Veil

"And the veil of the temple was rent in twain from the top to the bottom" (v. 38). By his blood atonement, by his death under the curse of God's holy law, the Son of God ripped open the veil in the temple. When justice was satisfied, when sin was put away, when there was nothing left to separate the holy Lord God from his people, when the law of God was forever silenced, the symbol of separation was ripped apart.

Do you ask why? It was that redeemed sinners might come to God with the full assurance of faith, being accepted in the beloved (Hebrews 10:12-19).

Our Surety's Shame
In all that is here recorded by the inspiration of God the Holy Spirit let us never lose sight of the fact that our Lord Jesus endured all this pain, shame, and ignominy in his death as our Surety. When the Lord God laid our sins upon him, our Saviour's glory was turned into shame (Psalm 4:2; Hosea 4:7). When he was made to bear our sin in his own body, what reproach, what shame, what cruelty he endured for us!

John tells us that Pilate scourged the Saviour twice, once before this (John 19:1) and again here. Though it was forbidden among the Jews that any man be scourged so severely, "lest thy brother should seem vile" (Deuteronomy 25:3; 2 Corinthians 11:24), stripes were laid upon our Saviour with savage cruelty. Christ our Brother was made vile and made to seem vile beyond imagination. Though we made ourselves vile with sin, with his stripes we are healed, made the righteousness of God in him.

Pilate delivered our Saviour into the hands of the soldiers, calling together the whole band, to insult him. They clothed him with purple, crowned him with thorns, spit upon him, beat his head with a reed, mockingly knelt before him, and stripped him of the sham garments of mock royalty. Stripped of his own garments, he was now stripped even of the garments of mockery. What can be more shameful than to be stripped naked before a multitude? Yet, the Lord of Glory endured the shame for us. As in the Garden our first parents made themselves naked to their shame, if he would take away the curse, Christ Jesus must be put to shame.

The crown of thorns added cruelty to mockery. Thorns were chosen to make the mock crown that his head might be wounded as the sinners Surety (Psalm 68:21). The thorns of the curse (Genesis 3:18) pierced his brow who was made a curse for us. Though they knew it not, these tormenters of our blessed Redeemer were, by their cruel actions, fulfilling both the decree of our God and the very words of prophecy. They intended nothing but insult and barbaric cruelty. Yet, they were all the while performing that which God had purposed from eternity; and their united testimony, "He saved others, himself he cannot save", is exactly what the gospel of the grace of God reveals. He who saved us from our sins could not be saved from being made sin. He who saved us from the curse could not be saved from enduring the curse. He who saved us from the wrath of God could not be saved from all the fury of God's holy wrath, when he was made sin for us!

What a deep sense we ought to have of the debt we owe to the Lord Jesus Christ. All that we have, all that we are, all that we hope for must be traced to the doing and dying of the Son of God for us. By his condemnation, we are acquitted. By his being made sin, we are made the righteousness of God. By his sufferings, we get peace. By his shame, we get glory. By his death, we have life! "Thanks be unto God for his unspeakable gift"! What assurance we ought to have of Christ's great love for us! What a reasonable thing it is that we should unceasingly present ourselves a living sacrifice unto our God by Christ Jesus!

"And when the sixth hour was come, there was darkness over the whole land until the ninth hour. And at the ninth hour Jesus cried with a loud voice, saying, Eloi, Eloi, lama sabachthani? which is, being interpreted, My God, my God, why hast thou forsaken me? And some of them that stood by, when they heard it, said, Behold, he calleth Elias. And one ran and filled a spunge full of vinegar, and put it on a reed, and gave him to drink, saying, Let alone; let us see whether Elias will come to take him down. And Jesus cried with a loud voice, and gave up the ghost. And the veil of the temple was rent in twain from the top to the bottom. And when the centurion, which stood over against him, saw that he so cried out, and gave up the ghost, he said, Truly this man was the Son of God".

(Mark 15:33-39)

Chapter 72

What Convinced Him?

What convinced that battle hardened soldier, a man who had probably slaughtered multitudes with steel-hearted coldness, what convinced this Roman centurion that the man he executed on that dark, dark day was the Son of God? Let me show you what he saw on that day of man's infamy, the day of God's glory, when the Son of God suffered the wrath of God in the place of men and women who were the enemies of God.

Let me show you seven extraordinary miracles which took place when the Son of God was made to be sin for us, that we might be made the righteousness of God in him. Here are seven miracles of Calvary. Six of them, if not all seven, were witnessed and carefully observed by the centurion. They convinced him that Jesus of Nazareth, with whose blood he was covered, is himself the Son of God.

The Mid-day Darkness

"And when the sixth hour was come, there was darkness over the whole land until the ninth hour" (v. 33). Matthew, Mark and Luke all tell us of this phenomenal darkness at midday, when the sun was miraculously turned into darkness for three hours. This noon-day darkness was predicted by Amos as an indication of God's judgment upon the Jewish nation for despising and rejecting his Word (Amos 8:9).

Still, ungodly men appear in every age who try to explain away the miraculous things revealed in the Book of God. They tell us that this just could not have happened and did not happen, that it was just an exaggeration on the part of the Lord's disciples, that it was only meant to teach spiritual lessons, or that it was an ordinary solar eclipse. But none of those arguments will stand.

The report was given by divine inspiration and given by honest men. It was at the time of the Jews' passover, which was always held during the full moon. In the 2nd century Tertullian asserted that this extraordinary midnight darkness at midday was reported and recorded by heathen chronologists and historians in the ancient archives of Rome. John Gill, commenting on Matthew 27:45, refers to one Dionysius the Areopagite, who saw this great darkness over the earth in Egypt and wrote, "Either the Divine Being suffers, or suffers with him that suffers, or the frame of the world is dissolving".

Without question, these three hours of darkness, which engulfed the earth from twelve noon until three o'clock in the afternoon, are intended to teach us many things. Let me point out just a few things that are obvious upon the very surface. Certainly, these three hours of darkness are intended to display in the most convincing manner possible God's abhorrence of sin. When God's own Son was made to be sin for us, when God the Son was forsaken by God the Father as our Substitute, God turned out all the lights of heaven to show his abhorrence of sin.

The darkness that covered the earth that day was symbolic of the darkness and blindness of divine judgment upon fallen men. When God takes away the light, men cannot see. When God sent blindness upon the Jews, they kept all their religious ceremonialism, religious books, and religious customs; but they have no light to this day.

And this darkness was emblematic of the darkness engulfing our Saviour's soul when he was made sin and endured the wrath of God for us. It was at the end of these three hours of darkness, at three o'clock in the afternoon that our Saviour cried out, "My God, my God, Why hast thou forsaken me?" This took place just as the Jews were offering up their daily sacrifice at the very time when the paschal lamb was slain. Both of these were eminent types of Christ, the Sun of Righteousness, whose very soul was engulfed in the darkness of God's holy wrath and fierce justice.

Ripped Apart

"And the veil of the temple was rent in twain from the top to the bottom" (v. 38). Both Matthew and Mark were inspired to tell us specifically that the temple's veil was ripped apart from the top to the bottom, not from the bottom to the top. It did not just wear out at this particular time. God almighty ripped it open!

This was not just a heavy curtain; it was a thick, thick veil, separating the holy of holies from the holy place. It was at least 40 cubits (60 ft.) in length! No one was allowed to go behind this veil, except the high priest. He went in only on the day of atonement, and, even then, only with the blood of the paschal lamb. There he sprinkled the blood upon the mercy-seat and made a typical, ceremonial atonement for Israel's sins.

Can you imagine the shock, the horror which must have seized the emptied-handed priest who was in the temple when this happened? For more than four hundred years the Jewish priests had faked the ordinances of God. Five things that were central to the worship of God in the typical dispensation were never found in the temple at Jerusalem after the Babylonian Captivity:

(1) The Ark of the Covenant, (2) The Mercy-seat, (3) The Urim and Thummim Lights and Perfections, (4) The Continually Burning Fire on the Altar, and (5) The Shechinah. All these things find their fulfilment in Christ, who is the great Glory of the House of God. When the veil was rent apart, the exposed hypocrisy of the empty-handed priest in the holy of holies, with no ark and no mercy-seat upon which to sprinkle the blood of the paschal lamb, must have been shocking.

The rending of that veil displayed in the most vivid way possible the complete fulfilment and abolition of the entire Mosaic economy. The law was now totally fulfilled by the Lord Jesus Christ for us. All its types, all its requirements, all its purposes were fulfilled by our Substitute. "Christ is the end of the law" (Romans 10:4). To try to re-establish the law, the priesthood, altars, sacrifices is nothing short of idolatry. It is an attempt to undo the work of Christ and sew up the ripped veil! Such an evil must not be tolerated.

That veil represented the humanity of our Lord Jesus Christ. When the veil was rent, it meant that the true Paschal Lamb had now been offered and accepted by God for the redemption of his people (Hebrews 9:7-12). When he entered into heaven with his own blood, having obtained eternal redemption for his people, the veil was ripped apart. The God-man's precious blood opened the way for sinners to come to God (Hebrews 10:12-22).

The Earth Quaked
Matthew tells us when the veil of the temple was ripped apart, the earth quaked. "And, behold, the veil of the temple was rent in twain from the top to the bottom; and the earth did quake, and the rocks rent" (Matthew 27:51). This earthquake was a token of God anger, wrath and judgment against the nation of Israel because of their evil works (Amos 8:7, 8; Psalm 18:7). It was an emblem of the shaking and removing of Judaism (Hebrews 12:26, 27).

Rent Rocks
Next, we read in Matthew 27:51 that "the rocks rent". This rending of the rocks certainly implies the terrible fury of God's holy wrath. In fact, the Prophet Nahum uses similar expressions to describe God wrath (Nahum 1:5, 6). What a warning God gives to sinners with every token of his displeasure! These were special, miraculous tokens of judgment upon the Jewish nation and of judgment to come. But every time God sends an earthquake, tornado, flood, tidal wave, or hurricane, he is warning you of the fury of his wrath!

But the rending of the rocks may also represent something gracious. It may speak of the conversion of God's elect by the preaching of Christ crucified. As the result of Christ's death, by the merit of his precious, sin-atoning blood, God the Holy Spirit breaks hard, stony-hearted sinners, takes away the heart of stone, and gives them tender hearts of flesh. John the Baptist once said, "God is able of these stones to raise up children unto Abraham" (Matthew 3:9).

Though the hearts of his elect are as hard as an adamant stone (Zechariah 7:12), the Lord God graciously breaks the hard heart with the Saviour's blood and raises up children unto Abraham from Gentile stones (Acts 2:37-42).

Opened Graves

In Matthew 27:52 we read, "And the graves were opened; and many bodies of the saints which slept arose". John Gill wrote, "This was a proof of Christ's power over death and the grave. By dying, he through death destroyed him that had the power of it, and abolished death itself. He became the plague of death and the destruction of the grave, and took into his hands the keys of hell and death."

A Resurrection

Not only were the graves opened, Matthew tells us that after our Lord's resurrection there was a miraculous resurrection of many of God's saints.

"And, behold, the veil of the temple was rent in twain from the top to the bottom; and the earth did quake, and the rocks rent; And the graves were opened; and many bodies of the saints which slept arose, And came out of the graves after his resurrection, and went into the holy city, and appeared unto many" (Matthew 27:51-53).

We are not told who they were, so I will not guess; but many of the saints came out of their graves in resurrection bodies, just after the Lord Jesus did, walked the streets of Jerusalem, and were seen of many. This, too, was predicted in the Old Testament. It was written in Isaiah 26:19, "Thy dead men shall live, together with my dead body shall they arise. Awake and sing, ye that dwell in dust: for thy dew is as the dew of herbs, and the earth shall cast out the dead".

The resurrection of these saints, by virtue of Christ's atonement, was God's declaration that atonement was indeed made (Romans 4:25). And these resurrected saints stand as the pledge of our resurrection.

A Miracle Of Mercy

I do not know whether the centurion witnessed the resurrection of these saints or not; but there is one more miracle he did witness, by which he was convinced that the crucified Substitute was indeed the Son of God. He witnessed that miracle of mercy described in Luke 23:39-43.

"And one of the malefactors which were hanged railed on him, saying, If thou be Christ, save thyself and us. But the other answering rebuked him, saying, Dost not thou fear God, seeing thou art in the same condemnation? And we indeed justly; for we receive the due reward of our deeds: but this man hath done nothing amiss. And he said unto Jesus, Lord, remember me when thou comest into thy kingdom. And Jesus said unto him, Verily I say unto thee, Today shalt thou be with me in paradise".

What a picture that is of God's rich, free, matchless grace in Christ! Here is a condemned criminal against whom no condemnation can stand, a rebel reconciled to God, a thief transformed into a saint, and a sinner saved by free grace to the soul satisfaction of a dying Saviour! This man's conversion is a picture of ours (Ephesians 2:8, 9).

"And many other signs truly did Jesus in the presence of his disciples, which are not written in this book: But these are written, that ye might believe that Jesus is the Christ, the Son of God; and that believing ye might have life through his name" (John 20:30, 31).

> Convinced of this one thing am I,
> And to the mocking crowd,
> With the amazed centurion cry,
> "THIS IS THE SON OF GOD"!

"My God, my God, why hast thou forsaken me?"

(Mark 15:34)

Chapter 73

Why Was He Forsaken?

These are the words of our great Surety, as he hung upon the cursed tree. The more I study, meditate upon, and pray over them, the more convinced I am that it is simply impossible for a mere earthling to expound them. I am certain there is more contained in and expressed by these few, heavy, heavy words from our Saviour's afflicted soul than is contained in all the commentaries and theology books in the world.

These words of agony no tongue can describe, "My God, my God, why hast thou forsaken me?" are the very words of our Lord Jesus Christ when he engaged all the forces of hell and endured the indescribable wrath of almighty God as our Substitute, when he was made to be sin for us. The Lord Jesus Christ, the Son of God, was forsaken by God the Father when he was made sin for us, so that his people might be forever accepted of God by the merits of his precious blood and perfect righteousness.

This cry of the heart broken Lamb of God is first found in Psalm 22:1. That prophetic psalm should be read often, studied with care, and laid up in the memory of our hearts with gratitude and praise. Everything recorded in the 22nd Psalm, if I understand it correctly, was written prophetically, penned by divine inspiration, as the very words spoken by our blessed Saviour when he hung upon the cursed tree, bearing our sins as our Substitute.

C. H. Spurgeon wrote:

> Before us we have a description both of the darkness and of the glory of the cross, the sufferings of Christ and the glory which shall follow. Oh for grace to draw near and see this great sight! We should read reverently, putting off our shoes from off our feet, as Moses did at the burning bush, for if there be holy ground anywhere in scripture it is in this psalm.

Utterly Forsaken

At the apex of his obedience, at the time of his greatest sorrow, in the hour of his greatest need, the Lord Jesus cried out to his Father, "My God, my God, why hast thou forsaken me?" After asking, "My God, my God, why hast thou forsaken me?", our all-glorious Redeemer tells us how utterly forsaken he was, so utterly forsaken that the Father refused to hear the cries of his own darling Son in the hour of his greatest need. "Why art thou so far from helping me, and from the words of my roaring? O my God, I cry in the daytime, but thou hearest not; and in the night season, and am not silent".

I read those words with utter astonishment. I will not attempt to explain what I cannot imagine. But these things are written here for our learning, that we might, through patience and consolation of the scriptures, have hope. And I hang all the hope of my immortal soul upon this fact. When the Lord Jesus Christ was made sin for me, he was utterly forsaken of God and put to death as my Substitute; and by his one great, sin-atoning Sacrifice, he has forever put away my sins. He not only bore our sins in his body on the tree, he bore them away!

The Demands of Justice

Yet, when we read Psalm 22:3, our holy Saviour, when he was made sin for us, answers the cry of his own soul's agony. "But thou art holy, O thou that inhabitest the praises of Israel". Why was the Lord Jesus forsaken by his Father when he was made sin for us? Because the holy Lord God is of purer eyes than to behold iniquity. Our Saviour was forsaken by the Father, when he was made sin for us, because justice demanded it. "Thou art of purer eyes than to behold evil, and canst not look on iniquity" (Habakkuk 1:13).

Here our Saviour, when he was dying under the wrath of God, justified God in his own condemnation, because he was made sin for us. He proclaims the holiness of God in the midst of his agony. He is so pure, so holy, so righteous, so just that he will by no means clear the guilty (Exodus 34:7), even when the guilty One is his own darling Son! Rather than slight his holy character, our Surety must suffer and die, because he was made sin for us.

Made Sin

Our Saviour had no sin of his own. He was born without original sin, being even from birth "that Holy One" (Luke 1:35). Throughout his life he "knew no sin" (2 Corinthians 5:21), "did no sin" (1 Peter 2:22), "and in him is no sin" (1 John 3:5). But on Calvary the holy Lord God "made him sin for us, who knew no sin, that we might be made the righteousness of God in him" (2 Corinthians 5:21). Just as in the incarnation "the Word was made flesh and dwelt among us" (John 1:14), in substitution the Word, who was made flesh, "was made sin for us".

I do not know how God could be made flesh and never cease to be God; but he was. I do not know how the eternal God could die and yet never die; but he did (Acts 20:28). I do not know how all the fulness of the infinite, incomprehensible God can dwell in Christ bodily; but it does (Colossians 2:9). And I do not know how Christ who knew no sin could be made sin, and yet never have sinned; but he was.

These things are mysteries beyond the reach of human comprehension. But they are facts of divine revelation to which we bow with adoration. The hymnwriter Charles H. Gabriel said it this way:

> I stand amazed in the presence,
> Of Jesus the Nazarene.
> And wonder how He could love me,
> A sinner, condemned, unclean.
>
> Oh, how marvellous! oh, how wonderful!
> And my song shall ever be,
> Oh, how marvellous! oh how wonderful!
> Is my Saviour's love for me!
>
> For me it was in the garden,
> He prayed: "Not My will, but Thine".
> He had no tears for His own griefs,
> But sweat drops of blood for mine.
>
> He took my sins and my sorrows,
> He made them His very own.
> He bore the burden to Calvary,
> And suffered, and died alone.

"Mine Iniquities"

"Withhold not thou thy tender mercies from me, O LORD: let thy lovingkindness and thy truth continually preserve me. For innumerable evils have compassed me about: mine iniquities have taken hold upon me, so that I am not able to look up; they are more than the hairs of mine head: therefore my heart faileth me" (Psalm 40:11, 12). Commenting on these verses, John Trapp wrote, "If this be taken of Christ, he is the greatest of sinners by imputation (2 Corinthians 5:20 Isaiah 53:6), for our sins (which here he calleth his) he suffered; and here his bitter agony in the garden is graphically described. Neither is it absurd to say, that as he bore our sins in his own body upon the tree, he was first redeemed by himself, and afterwards we."

Here we are again allowed to hear the agony of our blessed Redeemer's soul when he was made sin for us. Here his language is even more specific in declaring that our sins were made his. Here, again, the Lord Jesus Christ calls our sins his own, because "He hath made him sin for us".

The One Speaking

The One speaking in this Psalm is beyond all doubt our Saviour. We know this because God the Holy Spirit tells us that it is Christ who is speaking here in Hebrews chapter 10. Our Saviour knew that being made sin for us, he would be brought into a horrible pit (Psalm 69:15) and filled with distress. Yet, his love for us was and is so great that in verse 7 he declares his readiness to assume a body, and to accomplish his Father's will in the salvation of his chosen, according to the ancient settlements written in the Volume of the Book, saying, "Lo! I come, I delight to do thy will, O my God". Then in verses 11 and 12 he prays for deliverance from his deep distresses.

This is exactly the same thing we read in John 12:27, 28. "Now is my soul troubled; and what shall I say? Father, save me from this hour: but for this cause came I unto this hour. Father, glorify thy name. Then came there a voice from heaven, saying, I have both glorified it, and will glorify it again".

The Reason

Why was the Son of God brought to such sorrow and grief? Here is the answer. "He made him sin for us, who knew no sin, that we might be made the righteousness of God in him"! Indeed he could never have suffered the painful, shameful, ignominious death of the cross as our Substitute had he not been made sin for us. Justice would never have allowed it. The Lord God declares, "He that justifieth the wicked, and he that condemneth the just, even they both are abomination to the LORD" (Proverbs 17:15; Exodus 23:7).

Worship Him

Hear the Saviour's words in Psalm 40:12, and worship him. "For innumerable evils have compassed me about". He was beset on every side with evil. Countless woes compassed our great Substitute and Sin-bearer. "Our sins", wrote Spurgeon, "were innumerable, and so were his griefs". All the accumulated sins of all his people, for all time, in all parts of the world, were made his! The Blessed One of God, who knew no sin and did no sin, was made sin!

He cried, "Mine iniquities have taken hold upon me, so that I am not able to look up". He had no sin, but our sins were laid on him, and he took them as his own. "He was made sin for us". Again, I quote Spurgeon, "The transfer of sin to the Saviour was real and produced in him as man the horror which forbade him to look into the face of God, bowing him down with crushing anguish and woe intolerable."

What would our sins have done to us eternally if the Friend of sinners had not condescended to take them all upon himself and make them his own? Oh, blessed scripture! "He hath made him sin for us"! Oh, marvellous depth of love that made the perfectly immaculate Lamb of God to stand in the sinner's place, and bear the horror of great trembling which sin must bring upon those who are forever keenly conscious of it in hell!

Broken Heart

"They are more than the hairs of mine head: therefore my heart faileth me". In dark Gethsemane, even as he anticipated being made sin, our Saviour's holy soul shook within him; and his holy heart broke. Anticipating the pains of God's holy fury against sin, his unbending justice and unmitigated wrath beyond imagination, our dear Saviour's soul was so crushed within him that he was sore amazed, and very heavy even unto a sweat of blood. His strength was gone, his spirit sank; he was in agony.

Then, as he hung upon the cursed tree, bearing our sins in his own body, he cried, as we read in Psalm 22:6, 14, 15, "I am a worm, and no man; a reproach of men, and despised of the people ... I am poured out like water, and all my bones are out of joint: my heart is like wax; it is melted in the midst of my bowels. My strength is dried up like a potsherd; and my tongue cleaveth to my jaws; and thou hast brought me into the dust of death". It was the thought and anticipation of being made sin for us, not of simply paying the debt due unto our sins, but of being made sin, that caused his bloody sweat in Gethsemane. It was this fact, the fact that he was made sin for us, that caused him to be forsaken of his Father as he hung upon the cursed tree on Golgotha's hill (Psalm 22:1-3).

Many tell us that these words cannot be the words of God's darling Son. Indeed, some, in their foolish arrogance, assert that it is blasphemy and heresy to declare that these words are the words of our blessed Saviour. In doing so they dare to defy God himself, for it is God the Holy Spirit who in Hebrews 10 tells us that these are our Saviour's words.

Robert Hawker wrote:

These things, so far from being unsuitable to the holy Jesus, are the very things we might reasonably suppose he would speak of, and consequently his holy soul would feel so painful. And when we consider that as our Surety he bore our sins and carried our sorrows, how very reasonable it is to expect that these cries of the Son of God should be at the very time in which he is set forth as a Sacrifice for them.

Foolishness And Perversity

There can be no question that the One speaking in Psalm 69 is our blessed Saviour. Throughout the New Testament, the words of this Psalm are attributed to him (Psalm 69:4; John 15:25; Psalm 69:9; John 2:17; Romans 15:3; Psalm 69:21; Matthew 27:34, 48; Mark 15:36; Luke 23:36; John 19:28, 29; Psalm 69:22, 23; Romans 11:9, 10; Psalm 69:25; Acts 1:16, 20). The opening verses of this Psalm clearly are the words of the Lord Jesus Christ, our Redeemer.

"Save me, O God; for the waters are come in unto my soul. I sink in deep mire, where there is no standing: I am come into deep waters, where the floods overflow me. I am weary of my crying: my throat is dried: mine eyes fail while I wait for my God. They that hate me without a cause are more than the hairs of mine head: they that would destroy me, being mine enemies wrongfully, are mighty: then I restored that which I took not away" (Psalm 69:1-4)

Verse 5 cannot, with any honesty, be attributed to someone else. Hear the cry of him who was made sin for us. "O God, thou knowest my foolishness; and my sins are not hid from thee". The word "foolishness" means "perversity". The word "sins" means, as it is translated in the marginal reference, "guiltiness". Our Saviour owns our perversity as his perversity and our guiltiness as his guiltiness, because it was made his.

The first Adam hid his perversity and guilt. The last Adam owns ours as his own, and does it before God. It is as though he were saying, "Here, lifted up upon the cross I suffer without the gate for my people, as their Substitute, in such a way that I desire that my sins be conspicuous to every creature in heaven, earth, and hell, my sins, the sins of my people, are all now and forever blotted out and washed away by my blood."

What condescension this is! What grace is here revealed! What unparalleled love! What mystery there is here! The Son of God takes to himself our shame! When the Lamb of God was made sin for us, who knew no sin, that we might be made the righteousness of God in him, it behoved him thus to suffer and thus to cry! "O God, thou knowest my foolishness; and my sins are not hid from thee".

Intercession

Yet, in his soul's utmost agony the Son of God remembered and interceded for us, as our great High Priest. "Let not them that wait on thee, O Lord GOD of hosts, be ashamed for my sake: let not those that seek thee be confounded for my sake, O God of Israel" (Psalm 69:6). In answer to his prayer, the gospel promise is, "Whosoever believeth on him shall not be ashamed" (Romans 10:11). "He that believeth on him shall not be confounded" (1 Peter 2:6).

Then, our sin-atoning Saviour again claims our sins, our reproaches, as his own, as if to tell us that our sins were not merely pasted on him, that he was not simply treated as though our sins were his, but that when he made his soul an offering for sin, he was made sin for us. "Because for thy sake I have borne reproach; shame hath covered my face ... Thou hast known my reproach, and my shame, and my dishonour: mine adversaries are all before thee. Reproach hath broken my heart; and I am full of heaviness: and I looked for some to take pity, but there was none; and for comforters, but I found none" (Psalm 69:7, 19, 20).

"Thanks Be Unto God For His Unspeakable Gift"!

Do you understand what you just read? Do you here see Christ as your Surety, your sin-bearer, taking all your guilt and sin, assuming total responsibility for all that you are? Made a curse for you? Do you see him as your Substitute, your Surety, your Saviour? Do you trust him as such? If so, let your soul be ravished by his great love for you. Adore him! Praise him! Praise him!

Because of his infinite, immeasurable love for us, our blessed Saviour became everything we are in such a real way that he owns our sins as his own before his Father and our Father! "Thou knowest my foolishness; and my sins are not hid from thee". Either he was made sin for us, or that which he confessed in these three psalms is not true. There is no in-between ground. Either our Saviour here spoke the truth or he did not. Blessed be his name, his Word is truth! He made our foolishness his foolishness! He made our sin his sin! He made our perversity his perversity! He made our guiltiness his guiltiness!

This is not a slander against our holy Saviour; but the magnifying of his mercy, love and grace towards us. Christ's love for us is so infinitely great that he made our sins his very own. And by the same wondrous, amazing mercy, love and grace, he then makes his holiness and perfect righteousness our very own.

Yes, we who believe are the very righteousness of God in Christ. With Jacob of old, we say with confidence to every accuser, as he did to Laban,

"So shall my righteousness answer for me in time to come" (Genesis 30:33). With Job, we say, "My righteousness I hold fast, and will not let it go: my heart shall not reproach me so long as I live" (Job 27:6). Why? Because Christ is the Lord our Righteousness, because he is made of God unto us both redemption and righteousness, we have assurance of everlasting salvation (Romans 8:1-4, 33-39). Soon, "unto them that look for him shall he appear the second time without sin unto salvation".

Sin And Substitution

What an infinitely evil thing sin must be! It is such a horrid thing that the holy Lord God cannot tolerate it, even when it was found upon his darling Son. Whenever God sees sin, he will punish it without mercy. When the angels fell, God cast them out of heaven and now holds them in chains of darkness until the day of judgment (2 Peter 2:4; Jude 6). When Adam sinned, he was cursed of God and driven from the presence of the Lord (Genesis 3). When God looked upon the wickedness of Noah's generation, he destroyed the whole world in the flood of his wrath (Genesis 6). Upon the twin cities of perversity, Sodom and Gomorrah, God poured out fire and brimstone (Genesis 19). And when God saw sin upon his darling Son, his only-begotten, well-beloved Son, he forsook him! Be warned! If God finds sin on you, he will destroy you forever in hell, without mercy! Flee to Christ, who alone can cleanse you of all sin!

How thorough and complete was Christ's obedience to the Father as our Surety! We could never obey God perfectly. We could never fulfil the demands of the law or the gospel. But Christ met and satisfied perfectly all the demands of God for his elect. This cry, "My God, my God", was made at the zenith of our Lord's obedience. Christ was obedient even unto death. Our salvation was accomplished both by his doing and by his dying. His doing is imputed to us for righteousness (Romans 5:19). His dying made atonement for our sins (Romans 5:11). Even when he was forsaken of God, our Surety remained obedient. This cry is an expression of Christ's perfect faith in God. As a man he believed God and showed us what it is to believe him. Robert Murray M'Cheyne said, "Faith is believing the Word of God, not because we see it to be true, or feel it to be true, but because God said it." We are often unbelieving. But our Surety never doubted God, even when he was forsaken of God! And this cry is an expression of exemplary love and devotion. Here is love and devotion unrivalled! Hanging upon the cursed tree, without one drop of mercy, one smile from heaven, or one comfort for his soul, Christ loved the very God who forsook him!

What an infinite depth of hell our Saviour endured for us! What is hell if it is not being abandoned totally by God? Why was Christ forsaken? He was forsaken because there was no other way for us to be accepted. Justice had to be satisfied. When the Son of God was made to be sin for us, when our sins were imputed to him, God forsook him and poured out upon him all the fulness of his wrath (Lamentations 1:12). God gave him everything our sins deserve. And now, the holy Lord God accepts all who trust his Son, imputes to them his perfect righteousness, and rewards them with eternal glory for Christ's sake, giving them all that he deserves.

Why was he forsaken? Our Lord Jesus was made sin for us that we might be made the righteousness of God in him. He was forsaken of God that we might be forever, immutably accepted of God in him. He was forsaken because he is our Substitute, our real, absolute Substitute before God!

"And when the centurion, which stood over against him, saw that he so cried out, and gave up the ghost, he said, Truly this man was the Son of God. There were also women looking on afar off: among whom was Mary Magdalene, and Mary the mother of James the less and of Joses, and Salome; (Who also, when he was in Galilee, followed him, and ministered unto him;) and many other women which came up with him unto Jerusalem. And now when the even was come, because it was the preparation, that is, the day before the sabbath, Joseph of Arimathaea, an honourable counsellor, which also waited for the kingdom of God, came, and went in boldly unto Pilate, and craved the body of Jesus. And Pilate marvelled if he were already dead: and calling unto him the centurion, he asked him whether he had been any while dead. And when he knew it of the centurion, he gave the body to Joseph. And he bought fine linen, and took him down, and wrapped him in the linen, and laid him in a sepulchre which was hewn out of a rock, and rolled a stone unto the door of the sepulchre. And Mary Magdalene and Mary the mother of Joses beheld where he was laid".

(Mark 15:39-47)

Chapter 74

The Saviour's Burial

The death of the Lord Jesus Christ as the sinner's Substitute, to put away the sins of his people, is the greatest and the most important event in history. The sin-atoning sacrifice of the God-man, the only Mediator between God and men, is the most important fact of Christianity. All the hopes of fallen men hang upon this one event. If what the scriptures say about the death of God's Son is so, then there is hope for sinners. If these things are not so, there is no hope for anyone.

Knowing something of the importance of this fact, we should not be surprised to find that the fact of our Saviour's death is placed beyond the realm of dispute by God's wise and good providence. The Jews of our Lord's time, and countless scoffers since then, have tried to explain away the fact of our Lord's resurrection by asserting that he never really died at all. They would have us believe that he really just passed out, and everyone thought he was dead. What folly! In the verses before us we see that God wisely arranged to verify the fact of Christ's death by three witnesses. The united witness of the Roman centurion, the women who followed the Saviour, and the disciples who buried his dead body place the matter beyond any dispute.

All these people could not have been deceived. They all saw the Lord Jesus Christ throughout the ordeal of his mock trial and crucifixion. They saw him lay down his life by the triumphant act of his own sovereign will as he became obedient unto death for the salvation of our souls. The Lord Jesus Christ, our incarnate God and Saviour, died for our sins according to the scriptures, under the wrath of God, and was buried in the earth.

The Amazed Centurion

The first thing that stands out in this passage is the amazement of the Roman centurion. "And when the centurion, which stood over against him, saw that he so cried out, and gave up the ghost, he said, Truly this man was the Son of God" (v. 39).

This centurion was the Roman soldier who was the head of a band of soldiers, whose task it was to watch the crucified Son of God to make sure no one took him down from the cross or gave him any comfort. Matthew tells us that there were others with him "watching Jesus".

These men were united in their mockery of the Lord Jesus, humiliating him and tormenting him in every way they could. They had all watched the mock trial before Pilate. They had all spit in his face, beat him and tortured him. They had all nailed him to the tree. They all observed his gracious and regal behaviour. They all saw the three hours of darkness. They all heard and felt the earthquake and the opening of the graves. They all heard the Master's seven statements, as he suffered the wrath of God as our Substitute. And they were all terrified and confessed, "Truly this man was the Son of God". Matthew tells us that "the centurion, and they that were with him, watching Jesus, saw the earthquake, and those things that were done, they feared greatly, saying, Truly this was the Son of God" (Matthew 27:54).

The centurion was placed as he was by God's providence to verify to Pilate and to all reasonable people the fact that the Lord Jesus Christ actually did die at Calvary.

"And Pilate marvelled if he were already dead: and calling unto him the centurion, he asked him whether he had been any while dead. And when he knew it of the centurion, he gave the body to Joseph" (vv. 44, 45).

When this man was called to Pilate to verify the fact that the Lord Jesus was indeed dead, I can almost hear his trembling report. "I heard him cry with a loud voice, 'Father, forgive them!' 'My God, my God, Why hast thou forsaken me?' 'Today, thou shalt be with me!' 'It is finished!' 'Father, into thy hands I commit my Spirit.' I watched him do what I never saw any other man do. He breathed out his own life! When we came to break his legs, as you ordered us, he was already dead. Just to make sure, one of my men shoved his spear through his heart; and the strangest thing happened, water mixed with blood came gushing out of his side. Yes, I would say the man is dead". When he got done, the scripture tells us that Pilate "knew it"!

This centurion also shows us a demonstration of the fact that there is a repentance to be repented of. "For godly sorrow worketh repentance to salvation not to be repented of: but the sorrow of the world worketh death" (2 Corinthians 7:10). This man was convicted; but his conviction was a mere legal conviction. He had repentance, sorrow for his deeds; but it was the sorrow of the world, which ends in death, eternal death in hell.

Legal fear, the fear of death, judgment and eternal damnation in hell, is not repentance. That is not Holy Spirit conviction. True repentance, true conviction is more than a sense of guilt and terror. It is a sorrow for sin. It is taking sides with God against yourself. And it is an acknowledgment that you deserve to go to hell; but it is more, much more. True repentance arises from the revelation of Christ in our hearts. It is the blessed persuasion of sins forgiven, righteousness established and judgment finished (Zechariah 12:10; John 16:8-11). There is no salvation without this conviction.

The Faithful Women

"There were also women looking on afar off: among whom was Mary Magdalene, and Mary the mother of James the less and of Joses, and Salome; (Who also, when he was in Galilee, followed him, and ministered unto him;) and many other women which came up with him unto Jerusalem ... And Mary Magdalene and Mary the mother of Joses beheld where he was laid" (vv. 40, 41, 47).

Where was Peter, who boasted that he was willing to go with his Master to judgment and to death? Where were the other disciples, who all said the same thing? The men, all of them, except for John (who was at some distance from the scene), were all gone. But these faithful women were faithful to the end. They had followed the Lord Jesus from Galilee to Jerusalem. When all others forsook him, they stayed with him. They stayed during all the horrors of that infamous day. They followed him right up to the tomb, and were found there on the morning of the resurrection.

John Trapp observed:

> Heavy they were as heart could hold: yet not hindered thereby from doing their duty to Christ. Even sorrow for sin, if it so exceed as to disable us for duty, is a sinful sorrow, and must be sorrowed for.

God often uses the weak to confound the mighty. How often we see this in the workings of God's providence and grace. Here, the Holy Spirit tells us two things about this band of faithful women. In these two things they are set before us as noble examples of faith.

They followed the Lord. Having been converted by his grace and power, believing his word, understanding his doctrine, having experienced his great forgiveness, these women followed the Saviour. That is what faith does. It follows Christ. Faith follows the Lord Jesus because those who are forgiven much love much.

They ministered to the Son of God. These dear ladies were not at all like the feminists of our day. These women were ladies. They knew their place and kept to it with joy. They were not allowed to be teachers and preachers in the Lord's church and kingdom. That is strictly forbidden in holy scripture. But these women were faithful servants of Christ to the end (Luke 8:3).

There is a great work which women can do for the glory of God and the cause of Christ in this world. Happy is that husband and family in which such a wife and mother is found. Happy is that church whose women know their work and faithfully do it, as unto the Lord. Elizabeth, Martha, Mary, Dorcas, Lydia, and Phoebe are all held before us in the Word of God as elect ladies, in whom the grace of God abounded, causing them to gladly serve the Master by serving his people.

A Secret Disciple

And now when the even was come, because it was the preparation, that is, the day before the sabbath, Joseph of Arimathaea, an honourable counsellor, which also waited for the kingdom of God, came, and went in boldly unto Pilate, and craved the body of Jesus. And Pilate marvelled if he were already dead: and calling unto him the centurion, he asked him whether he had been any while dead. And when he knew it of the centurion, he gave the body to Joseph. And he bought fine linen, and took him down, and wrapped him in the linen, and laid him in a sepulchre which was hewn out of a rock, and rolled a stone unto the door of the sepulchre" (vv. 42-46).

I am so very thankful that the Holy Spirit has placed in the records of sacred history the name and works of Joseph of Arimathaea. We know virtually nothing about him except that he was a rich man from Arimathaea. He was a member of the Jews' religious counsel, the Sanhedrim. He buried the Lord Jesus in his own tomb. And he was a believer, one who "waited for the kingdom of God". Joseph was a secret disciple, but still a true disciple (John 19:38).

We know nothing about him until now; and nothing else is said about him in the Word of God after this. But this man was the man of the hour. He was where he needed to be, when he was needed, to do what was needed. Much could and should be said about this man, but I want to show you just three things here.

1. God always raises up men to do what is needed at the time needed. None of the other disciples were around to do what Joseph did. Perhaps no one else could have gotten Pilate's ear as readily as Joseph. But at the time needed, so that the scripture might be fulfilled (Isaiah 53:9), God raised up a rich man to bury the body of his darling Son in his own new tomb.

Let us learn, then, that the purpose of God is never in danger of failure. The will of God is never hindered. The work of God is never overturned. And the cause of God is never in jeopardy.

2. The Lord God always has many more disciples than any of us ever imagine. I am the first to acknowledge that secret disciples are always suspect disciples. But we must never forget the words of the Lord to Elijah (1 Kings

19:18). Our God still has his seven thousand in Israel, who have not bowed the knee to Baal. At the appropriate time, he will bring them out. The Lord still has many hidden ones in the earth. We may not know who they are, or where they are; but he has them.

Much might be said about this man's failures and weaknesses; but Joseph's faith was in many ways most remarkable. He was strong, when all others were weak. He was bold, when everyone else was terrified. The other disciples honoured and confessed Christ, when he was working miracles and influencing multitudes. Joseph believed him, honoured him and identified himself with him when his body was a cold, dead corpse, covered with his own blood and the spit of others.

3. Joseph wrapped the Lord's body in fine linen. This fine linen was an emblem of our Saviour's own holiness and purity; and this linen is set before us in the scriptures as an emblem of Christ's pure, spotless righteousness, which is imputed to his people (Revelation 19:8).

The Honoured Tomb
"And he bought fine linen, and took him down, and wrapped him in the linen, and laid him in a sepulchre which was hewn out of a rock, and rolled a stone unto the door of the sepulchre" (v. 46). The Lord Jesus was numbered with the transgressors. Yet, he made his grave with the rich, exactly as the scriptures had foretold. He is the Saviour of all, both rich and poor. But the fact that his dead body was laid in the tomb must not be passed over lightly. Our Lord Jesus here puts special honour upon the grave.

The fact is we are all going to the tomb. We do not like to think about it; but we are all going to die, sooner or later. The time will soon come when someone will put our bodies in a coffin, drop us in the cold earth, and cover us out of view. Let us remember, this is the place where our Lord once laid. And, as surely as he arose from the tomb, so to shall all who trust him. When Christ died, we died with him. When he was buried, we were buried with him. When he arose, we arose with him.

Consequently, death has no terror. The grave has no sting. As we have confessed in our baptism, we are confident that, though the worms of the earth shall eat our flesh, yet, at the resurrection, in our flesh we shall see our God and our Redeemer.

"And when the sabbath was past, Mary Magdalene, and Mary the mother of James, and Salome, had bought sweet spices, that they might come and anoint him. And very early in the morning the first day of the week, they came unto the sepulchre at the rising of the sun. And they said among themselves, Who shall roll us away the stone from the door of the sepulchre? And when they looked, they saw that the stone was rolled away: for it was very great. And entering into the sepulchre, they saw a young man sitting on the right side, clothed in a long white garment; and they were affrighted. And he saith unto them, Be not affrighted: Ye seek Jesus of Nazareth, which was crucified: he is risen; he is not here: behold the place where they laid him. But go your way, tell his disciples and Peter that he goeth before you into Galilee: there shall ye see him, as he said unto you. And they went out quickly, and fled from the sepulchre; for they trembled and were amazed: neither said they any thing to any man; for they were afraid".

(Mark 16:1-8)

Chapter 75

"When The Sabbath Was Past"

"As God on the first day of the week drew the world out of that abhorred estate of nothing, and brought light out of darkness, so did Christ, on that day, draw his people out of an estate worse than nothing, and 'brought life and immortality to light by the gospel' (2 Timothy 1:10)". That is how John Trapp began his commentary on the passage before us. It is bursting with rich gospel truths and practical spiritual lessons. Here are seven things set before us in this passage. May God the Holy Spirit write them upon our hearts.

The Sabbath Is Past
That is the first thing we read in this chapter. "And when the sabbath was past" (v. 1). Without question, this means that the old, Jewish sabbath was past. It was now, Sunday morning, the dawning of the first day of the week. But it was not accidental that our Lord was raised from the dead on this particular day. The resurrection of Christ from the dead declares that the Old Testament law of sabbath-keeping is past and the day of grace has dawned!

Look at Matthew 28:1. This is a very remarkable verse of scripture. In our Authorized Version it reads, "In the end of the sabbath, as it began to dawn toward the first day of the week, came Mary Magdalene and the other Mary to see the sepulchre". A better translation would be, "And in the end of the sabbath, as it began to dawn toward the sabbath, came Mary". In fact, Young's Literal Translation reads, "And on the eve of the sabbaths, at the dawn, toward the first of the sabbaths, came Mary the Magdalene, and the other Mary, to see the sepulchre". This is what Matthew 28:1 means: When the Lord Jesus Christ died at Calvary and rose again, the old sabbath of the law ended and the new sabbath of grace began.

Christ fulfilled the law for us. "Christ is the end of the law". "Christ hath redeemed us from the curse of the law". In Christ we are "dead to the law". Language could not be clearer. We are not under the law, but under grace. One of the most beautiful pictures of this is found right here in Mark 16:1. Here the Holy Spirit tells us that the sabbath is past. We keep no legal sabbath day, because God strictly forbids it (Colossians 2:16, 17); and we keep no legal Sabbath, because we keep the blessed sabbath of faith. Christ is our Sabbath. We rest in him. You cannot rest in him if you try to keep a legal sabbath; and you cannot labour under the yoke of the law if you rest in him.

Either you are working, or you are resting. You simply cannot do both at the same time.

The sabbath is past, because "the Lord of the sabbath" (Mark 2:28) has rested from his works (Hebrews 4:10). All who come to Christ keep that rest by faith that was symbolized and typified by the legal sabbath of the law (Matthew 11:28-30; Jeremiah 6:16). We rest in him. He is our Sabbath.

"And very early in the morning the first day of the week, they came unto the sepulchre at the rising of the sun" (v. 2). The words translated here "the first day of the week", as in Matthew 28, would be more accurately translated "the first of the sabbath". As the first day of the world was called "the first day" (Genesis 1:5), so the day of our Lord's resurrection is here called "the first of the sabbath". As that day was the beginning of the creation of God, so this day, when "the Sun of Righteousness" arose with healing in his wings (Malachi 4:2), was the beginning of the new creation of grace, the beginning of glorification, and the beginning of everlasting rest for God's elect.

There is no power in all the world like love to make us bold and courageous. A mother's love will cause a timid, little woman to fight a huge, armed man in defence of her child. A husband's love will cause him to leap into death itself to protect his wife. Well did the wise man say, "Love is strong as death ... Many waters cannot quench love, neither can the floods drown it". Yet, God the Holy Spirit here sets before us a love that exceeds the love of a husband for his wife. It even exceeds the love of a mother for her child. Here we see a little band of three women going early in the morning to the tomb of the Lord Jesus to honour him and take care of his dead body.

"And when the sabbath was past, Mary Magdalene, and Mary the mother of James, and Salome, had bought sweet spices, that they might come and anoint him. And very early in the morning the first day of the week, they came unto the sepulchre at the rising of the sun" (vv. 1, 2).

How significant this is. These women came early in the morning, before sun up, to the tomb of a man who had been condemned as a malefactor, one who had been despised and rejected by the entire nation, and was buried, with his tomb sealed, and his body under the guard of specially appointed soldiers. What gave these women such courage, such boldness? These dear ladies had tasted the Lord's pardoning mercy. Their hearts were filled with love for him who died for them. They felt a great sense of gratitude to him. They felt that they owed him a great debt of love, a debt they could never pay. They believed the Lord, and believing him, they loved him. For Christ, they were willing to hazard their own lives, not because he commanded them to do so, but simply because they loved him. They could not do much; but they must do what they could. So they came to the Lord's tomb.

Why do we see so little of this strong love for Christ today? Why is it that we meet with few today who are moved by such strong love for Christ that they are willing to hazard their lives for him? So few who are willing to face any danger, make any sacrifice, and walk into raging storms and roaring fires for Christ's sake? There is only one answer. It is that in this day there seems to be a prevailing, terribly low sense of debt and obligation to the Son of God. A low sense of sin will always produce a low sense of grace. A low sense of debt will always produce a low sense of duty. A low sense of forgiveness will always result in a low sense of love (Luke 7:47).

It is the love of Christ which constrains believers to serve and honour him (2 Corinthians 5:14). It is the love of Christ experienced in the soul that inspires redeemed sinners to devote themselves to their Saviour and to one another. Grace experienced causes gratitude to be exercised. Tasting the love of Christ makes people loyal to Christ. Faith makes men faithful. A sure hope in Christ causes saved sinners to live for the honour of Christ.

Most Of Our Fears Are Needless Fears
As they walked to the tomb that early Sunday morning, these women were filled with fears about things they thought they might face; but all their fears were needless. That which they feared did not come to pass. They expected trouble they never had to face. "And they said among themselves, who shall roll us away the stone from the door of the sepulchre? And when they looked, they saw that the stone was rolled away: for it was very great" (vv. 3, 4).

How much like these fearful women we are! Most of our worrying and anxiety arises from things we fear may happen, but never do happen. We tend to anticipate troubles that never come to pass. We all tend to carry tomorrow's troubles. But, usually, our doubts, and fears, and unbelief prove to be utterly groundless. Our Lord taught us better (Matthew 6:25-34).

How foolish our worrying is! I do not remember ever pacing the floor, worrying about anything that actually came to pass. Let us ever be confident of the Lord's presence, provision and protection. Trust his providence. The lions we fear are on God's chain. The dark giants that terrify us are just shadows of darkness.

Be not dismayed whate'er betide, beneath His wings of love abide.
Through days of toil when heart doth fail,
When dangers fierce your path assail, God will take care of you.

All you may need He will provide, nothing you need will be denied,
No matter what may be the test,
Lean, weary one, upon His breast, God will take care of you.

The Angels Of God Are Our Friends
"And entering into the sepulchre, they saw a young man sitting on the right side, clothed in a long white garment; and they were affrighted. And he saith unto them, Be not affrighted" (vv. 5, 6).

When Mary Magdalene and her friends came into the tomb, they saw an angel in the form of a man, and were frightened by him. But the angel quickly calmed their fears.

This may, at first, seem insignificant. After all, the Lord no longer speaks to men by angels (Hebrews 1:1-3). Angels no longer appear to men in visible form. But there is a day coming when we will again see them, hoards of them all at once. When Christ comes again to judge the world, he will come with his holy angels. But when we see them, God's elect will have no reason to fear these majestic, holy beings.

The scriptures tell us that the angels will gather together God's elect from the four corners of the earth. The angels will gather the wheat into the barn and bind up the tares for the burning. Those whom the angels take shall be carried up to heaven, to glory, to honour, and to immortality. Those whom the angels leave behind shall be left to shame and everlasting contempt. The angels of God rejoice in heaven when Christ gathers in his sheep, one by one (Luke 15). The angels visit our assemblies to learn about redeeming love and saving grace (Ephesians 3:10). The angels of God are ministering spirits sent forth to minister to those who shall be the heirs of salvation (Hebrews 1:14). The angels of God are our friends and companions in the kingdom of Christ (Hebrews 12:22-24).

I am sure we will never know, as long as we live in this mortal state, what great friends the angels of God are to us. But when we rise from our graves, we will see the angels themselves and be embraced by them as friends to our souls. We will spend eternity in the company of those blessed spirits.

The justice of God has been manifestly satisfied by the sacrificial, sin-atoning death of the Lord Jesus Christ, our all-glorious Substitute.

Hear the words of the angel to these women and understand, child of God, that we have nothing to fear, not even from God himself. "And he saith unto them, Be not affrighted: Ye seek Jesus of Nazareth, which was crucified: he is risen; he is not here: behold the place where they laid him" (v. 6).

Our Saviour's name is Jesus, Jehovah who saves. He is Jesus of Nazareth, a real man, just like you and me. This man, who is himself God, was crucified, slain under the curse of God's holy law, bearing our sins in his own body on the tree, and suffering all the just wrath of God against our sins as our Substitute!

That One who bore our sins in his own body on the tree is now risen from the dead, risen because he accomplished our justification, risen because justice is satisfied and the sin he bore in his own body on the tree he has effectually put away forever by the sacrifice of himself! The stone, rolled against his tomb to seal it by the hand of the law, was rolled away by the hand of God; and the Lord God himself declares to every believing sinner, "Fury is not in me" (Isaiah 27:4).

The risen Christ declares that believing sinners have no reason to be afraid of God. On the contrary, by faith in Christ, by the merit of his blood, God himself bids us come to him freely, even boldly, with "full assurance" of acceptance in and with his dear Son (Hebrews 10:18-22).

The Grace Of God Is Immutable

Look at verse seven. Here is immutable grace, immaculate mercy, infinite, indestructible love. "But go your way, tell his disciples and Peter that he goeth before you into Galilee: there shall ye see him, as he said unto you". Tell his disciples who have forsaken him, and Peter who has denied him that he goes before them; and tell them that he will meet them in Galilee, just like he said he would. In a word, tell them that they are all pardoned, that all is forgiven. Because God's grace is free, because he paid their debt, because he put away their sin, there is no breach between him and them!

This is not the way of men! I think that our views of God and his grace are weakest right here: None of us have any idea how exceedingly willing he is to forgive iniquity, transgression, and sin! At this point, we all think that God is such a one as ourselves. What shameful unbelief! We forget that "He delighteth in mercy" (Micah 7:18-20). His forgiveness is free, full and forever.

He who is God our Saviour is faithful and true – a God to be trusted! Read verse 7 again, and you will see this clearly. "But go your way, tell his disciples and Peter that he goeth before you into Galilee: there shall ye see him, as he said unto you". Our Saviour's name is "Faithful and True". What he has promised, he will do. He will go before you, child of God, all the days of your life. He has gone before you into great sorrow, into the tomb, and into heaven! Robert Hawker wrote:

"The first thing the Lord Jesus had respect to, when he arose from the dead, was to send his Angel to comfort his disciples with the assurance of his love, while he informed them of his resurrection. His almighty power, by which he arose from the dead (Romans 1:4), and his altered state made no alteration in his love. He is still the same Jesus, and the same brother as before. Oh! for grace to have this always in remembrance"!

"Now when Jesus was risen early the first day of the week, he appeared first to Mary Magdalene, out of whom he had cast seven devils. And she went and told them that had been with him, as they mourned and wept. And they, when they had heard that he was alive, and had been seen of her, believed not. After that he appeared in another form unto two of them, as they walked, and went into the country. And they went and told it unto the residue: neither believed they them. Afterward he appeared unto the eleven as they sat at meat, and upbraided them with their unbelief and hardness of heart, because they believed not them which had seen him after he was risen".

(Mark 16:9-14)

Chapter 76

"When Jesus Was Risen"

Many years ago, I read about an old woman, a believer, whose age began to take its toll on her, especially on her memory. At one time, she knew much of the Bible by heart. Eventually, only one precious, little portion stayed with her: "I know whom I have believed, and am persuaded that he is able to keep that which I have committed unto him against that day". Soon, part of that slipped from her mind as well. She would be found often quietly repeating what she could of the text. Family and friends would hear her going over it again and again. "That which I have committed unto Him". Just before she slipped out into glory, her children noticed her lips moving, and they bent over to hear what she was saying. She was repeating just one word, "Him, Him, Him." She had lost the whole Bible, but one word. Yet, she had the whole Bible in that one word. "Him". The Book of God is all about "Him". We come together to worship "Him". We must know, trust and love "Him". Oh, may God the Holy Spirit set our hearts on "Him".

This portion of Mark's gospel is about the resurrection of our Lord Jesus Christ; but it is not the Holy Spirit's intention here merely to prove the resurrection, or convince us of the doctrine of the resurrection. These things are written that we might know him who is himself "The Resurrection and the Life". May God give us grace to know him and the power of his resurrection.

An Undeniable Fact

The first thing that strikes me in this paragraph is that the resurrection of our Lord Jesus Christ from the dead is an undeniable fact. That which is, in many ways, the most important and most significant fact revealed in holy scripture is an undeniable, irrefutable fact of history. This is a very important fact. If the literal, bodily resurrection of Christ from the dead could be disproved, everything else in the Bible must crumble to dust. If there is no resurrection, there is no redemption, no atonement. If there is no resurrection, there is no redemption, no forgiveness. If there is no resurrection, there is no redemption, no salvation. If there is no resurrection, there is no redemption, no gospel, no hope, we are yet in our sins; and we are of all men most miserable!

In these six verses the Holy Spirit tells us three of the occasions when the risen Lord appeared to men. Mark mentions only three of Christ's post resurrection appearances, though there were several others. The risen Saviour appeared first to Mary Magdalene, then to the two disciples on the Emmaus road and, third, to the eleven apostles.

This is a great mercy to us. Our Lord Jesus made his resurrection from the dead a thoroughly established, undeniable fact of history. This fact is a matter of great mercy, because, as I have already asserted, everything we believe, everything revealed in the gospel stands or falls with the resurrection of Christ. The resurrection was the crowning proof of Christ's having put away our sins by the sacrifice of himself, the seal of our redemption, the receipt of our justification, and God's public declaration of his Son's exaltation and glory. The scriptures constantly lay great importance upon the resurrection of our Lord Jesus Christ (Romans 1:1-4; 4:25; 8:34; Ephesians 2:4-6; Hebrews 13:20, 21; 1 Peter 1:3).

The multiplied witnesses of our Lord's resurrection are simply irrefutable (Mark 16:9; John 20:16-18; Matthew 28:5-10; Luke 24:34; 1 Corinthians 15:5; Luke 24:31; John 20:6; John 21:1; 1 Corinthians 15:6; 1 Corinthians 15:7; Matthew 28:16, 17; Mark 16:14; 15 Luke 24:44; Acts 1:4; Acts 1:3-8; Luke 24:50; Acts 1:9-12; Acts 9:5; 1 Corinthians 15:8).

Our Lord Jesus Christ has not only died for our sins, he has risen up from the dead and reigns in glory upon the throne of universal monarchy to give life and salvation to those for whom he died. "For to this end Christ both died, and rose, and revived, that he might be Lord both of the dead and living" (Romans 14:9).

An Unqualified Forgiveness
The second thing that strikes me in this passage is the fact that our Lord's forgiveness of sin is an unqualified forgiveness. Certainly this is evident in the heart of every sinner who has experienced it. It is evident in his many gracious displays of grace and forgiveness that are recorded in holy scripture; but there is no better picture of forgiveness than that which we have before us in the Lord's dealings with "Mary Magdalene, out of whom he had cast seven devils".

The Lord Jesus did not first appear to his mother Mary, or to John the Beloved. No. "He appeared first to Mary Magdalene, out of whom he had cast seven devils". This seems to be written here by the finger of God as a remarkable fact, full of instruction.

Here the Holy Spirit shows us by example that which we are taught throughout the scriptures. Salvation is a matter of absolute, free, unconditional grace. Because salvation is, in its entirety, a matter of free grace, in no way conditioned or dependent upon us, and in no way determined by us, all who are saved by grace stand upon an equal footing before God. In Christ there is no difference between saved virgins and saved harlots, saved scholars and saved sots, saved Pharisees and saved prostitutes, or saved princes and saved paupers!

Truly, "God is no respecter of persons". In Christ we are all equal. The last is first and the first is last. All God's elect are forgiven of all sin. We all possess perfect righteousness, the righteousness of Christ. We all have all grace. Christ is all in all who believe. As we read in 1 Corinthians 1:30, 31, "Of him are ye in Christ Jesus, who of God is made unto us wisdom, and righteousness, and sanctification, and redemption: That, according as it is written, He that glorieth, let him glory in the Lord".

The fact that our Lord Jesus appeared first to Mary Magdalene also teaches us that God honours those who honour him (1 Samuel 2:30). Mary had anointed the Lord for his burial in anticipation of his resurrection. Mary was the last one to confess Christ when he was alive and the first to honour him when he died. Mary was the last one at the cross and the first one at the tomb. And Mary was the first one to see the risen Lord.

Our Lord appeared first to Mary to teach us that He is distinctly the Saviour of poor, needy sinners. Christ came into the world to save sinners; and when he saves sinners, he well saves them. He makes great saints out of great sinners. Those who were once filled with seven devils, he fills with "the seven Spirits of God", that is with all the fulness of his Spirit. Those who were once far off, he brings nigh. Those who were the filth and off-scouring of the earth, he makes to be the sons of God. Those who once sat as beggars in the dung heap of fallen humanity, he lifts by his grace and sets them among princes. And our sins and iniquities he remembers no more (Romans 8:1-4; 2 Corinthians 5:17).

An Unparalleled Friend

The third thing that strikes me in this passage is the fact that Our Lord Jesus Christ is an unparalleled friend. Truly, he who is the Friend of publicans and sinners is the "Friend who sticketh closer than a brother"! How manifestly evident this is in our Lord's dealings with his unbelieving, hard-hearted disciples. Three times Mark describes the unbelief of the Lord's disciples, including his own! The Lord appeared first to Mary; but no one believed her report. Then, he appeared to the two disciples on the Emmaus road; but no one believed them either. At last, he appeared to the eleven apostles in person and upbraided them for their unbelief.

How we rejoice to know that God's salvation is an irreversible act of grace (Ecclesiastes 3:14). Our Lord rebukes and chastens his erring children to correct them from the error of their way; but he never forsakes them. Our salvation no more depends on us after conversion than it did before. We are "kept by the power of God through faith" and the faith is itself the gift of God. Yes, we must persevere in faith; and all who are born of God shall; but we persevere only because we are preserved in Christ Jesus!

We are here reminded again that God's saints in this world are sinners still. Frequently the Holy Spirit shows us this by example and by precept; but the surest proof of it is our own painful and bitter experience. There is much sin in the best of saints. There is great weakness in the strongest of God's people. There is great corruption in the most upright. And there is great unbelief in the strongest believer. Our God would make us ever aware of these things, so that we might not despair of ourselves, and that we might be patient with our brethren (1 Corinthians 15:10).

It is ever the glory of our God to bring good out of evil. The terrible, strong doubt and unbelief of these disciples is itself a validation to the truthfulness of their testimony, once they were convinced (Psalm 76:10).

"When Jesus Was Risen"

"And he said unto them, Go ye into all the world, and preach the gospel to every creature. He that believeth and is baptized shall be saved; but he that believeth not shall be damned. And these signs shall follow them that believe; In my name shall they cast out devils; they shall speak with new tongues; They shall take up serpents; and if they drink any deadly thing, it shall not hurt them; they shall lay hands on the sick, and they shall recover".

(Mark 16:15-18)

Chapter 77

The Great Commission

These words are given to us by Inspiration as our Lord's final words to his church, his final words to you and me, as he was leaving this world. Here he tells us what our privileges and responsibilities are as his servants in this world. These are not the privileges and responsibilities of the apostles alone, or of gospel preachers alone. These are the privileges and responsibilities of all God's people, his servants, in this world.

It is the great privilege and responsibility of every child of God to do what he can for the furtherance of the gospel in his generation, to preach the gospel (and see to it that the gospel is preached) to all the world in the generation in which we live for the glory of Christ and the salvation of God's elect.

The Great Commission
"And he said unto them, Go ye into all the world, and preach the gospel to every creature" (v. 15). It is utterly impossible for me to state emphatically enough the importance, the comprehensiveness, and the depth of meaning there is in these words. Our Lord's charge to us in this one sentence is generally called "The Great Commission". This is our commission from our God as long as we live in this world; and it is great!

It is called "the great commission" because there is a great need. Our Lord commands us to go into all the world preaching the gospel, because all are lost without the gospel. In every corner of the earth the sons and daughters of Adam are the same. All are fallen, lost, without Christ, without God, without hope, and utterly ignorant of God, his grace, his Son and his salvation. Civilized or uncivilized, in Africa, China, or Great Britain, Mexico, California, or Kentucky, all who are ignorant of the gospel are in a state of wrath and condemnation.

It is called "the great commission" because we have a great message. Our Lord here commands us to preach the gospel. This is the work of God's church in this world. We must not neglect charity: feeding, clothing and educating the poor. But that is not our commission. Our commission is far more important than that. Our Lord commands us to preach the gospel. To preach the gospel is to declare the redemption accomplishments of the Lord Jesus Christ.

We are to proclaim to eternity bound sinners the full glorious tidings of salvation by Christ's blood and righteousness (Isaiah 49:1-6). The message we are sent to preach is Christ himself, God's Salvation. Christ crucified is all the counsel of God, the whole gospel. He is the one in and by whom all the blessings of redemption and grace flow to his elect (Numbers 6:22-26; Acts 20:27; 2 Corinthians 2:2, 13:14).

Gospel preaching is God's ordained means of grace for chosen sinners. All men and women have a God consciousness. God's wisdom and power are revealed to all in the splendour of his creation. His law is written upon the hearts of all. Yet, Romans chapters one and two plainly tell us that these things are insufficient for man's salvation. All men know something about God by creation. They are responsible to be holy, because God tells them in their consciences that he demands holiness. Yet, they have no ability to comply with the demands of their own consciences. The light of nature and creation can never convert anyone.

God has ordained the salvation of chosen sinners by the means of gospel preaching. Without the gospel none can ever be saved. This is not my opinion. This is exactly what the scriptures say. The Holy Spirit's exact words are these: It is the gospel preached unto us, "By which also ye are saved" (1 Corinthians 15:2). The preaching of the gospel "is the power of God unto salvation", because it is the revelation of "the righteousness of God" (Romans 1:15-17). It is by the foolishness of preaching that God saves his chosen (1 Corinthians 1:21; Ephesians 1:13; 2 Thessalonians 2:13, 14). "Of his own will begat he us with the word of truth, that we should be a kind of firstfruits of his creatures" (James 1:18). The Word of God, preached to sinners by the gospel, is the instrument by which sinners are born again by the Spirit of God (1 Peter 1:23-25).

"Go ye into all the world and preach the gospel to every creature". God will save his elect. There is no question about that. The redeemed of the Lord shall be converted by his grace. That is a matter of absolute certainty. Every chosen redeemed sinner shall, at the appointed time of love, be born again by the Holy Spirit's irresistible grace and power. The elect of God, purchased by the blood of Jesus Christ, shall all be granted the gift of life eternal and faith in the Lord Jesus Christ. But not one shall be saved without the preaching of the gospel.

Without question, our God could have saved his elect without us. He could send angels, or frogs, or rocks to preach to them, or he could regenerate them without the use of means altogether; but he has ordained the salvation of chosen sinners through the use and instrumentality of other chosen sinners! What a privilege he has bestowed upon us!

I've often thought I would love to have Dick Clark and Ed McMaan's job. I don't have any money of my own; but I would sure like to be the man who carried a ten million dollar check to someone's house! Wouldn't you? That would be a great job to have. But you and I have one that is indescribably better. We are the people commissioned of God to carry his salvation to perishing sinners!

"Unto me, who am less than the least of all saints, is this grace given, that I should preach among the Gentiles the unsearchable riches of Christ; And to make all men see what is the fellowship of the mystery, which from the beginning of the world hath been hid in God, who created all things by Jesus Christ: To the intent that now unto the principalities and powers in heavenly places might be known by the church the manifold wisdom of God, According to the eternal purpose which he purposed in Christ Jesus our Lord". (Ephesians 3:8-11)

Let the redeemed of the Lord, sinners saved by God's free grace in Christ, tell sinners everywhere about the Redeemer and about God's free grace to sinners in him. Let us give ourselves relentlessly to this glorious work of preaching the gospel. Let us all do whatever we can to fulfil our commission in this age for the glory of Christ.

The General Call

"He that believeth and is baptized shall be saved; but he that believeth not shall be damned" (v. 16). The effectual, irresistible call of the Spirit always produces faith in Christ. No man can do that. It is the work of God alone. Yet, the effectual call and irresistible grace of God the Holy Spirit comes to elect, redeemed sinners through the general call that is issued to all men in the preaching of the gospel.

This general call is neither more nor less than the preaching of the gospel to all men. We preach the gospel to all people indiscriminately, because we do not know who God's elect are and because our Lord commands us to do so. Our responsibility is determined by the Word of God, not the decree of God. I repeat myself deliberately. This is the means by which God saves his elect. Richard Sibbes once stated, "All good things come by preaching", because he understood that all God's elect have salvation and all its blessings conveyed to them by the gospel.

The gospel we preach carries the promise of grace, salvation and eternal life to all who trust the Lord Jesus Christ. "He that believeth and is baptized shall be saved". The only way any sinner can ever be saved is by believing on the Lord Jesus Christ. And every sinner in the world who believes on the Son of God is saved.

It is our faith in Christ that makes our calling and election sure (Hebrews 11:1-6). Faith in Christ is the one thing needful. "He that believeth not shall be damned".

This is the matter of great concern. Do we have this gift of faith in Christ? Multiplied thousands are washed in the waters of baptism, who are not washed in the blood of Christ! Multiplied thousands attend church every Sunday, who have never yet worshipped the Lord Jesus Christ! Multiplied thousands eat at the Lord's Table, who have never yet tasted the grace of God in Christ. It is not doctrinal orthodoxy that unites our souls with the Son of God, but faith in him.

"He that believeth on the Son of God hath the witness in himself: he that believeth not God hath made him a liar; because he believeth not the record that God gave of his Son. And this is the record, that God hath given to us eternal life, and this life is in his Son. He that hath the Son hath life; and he that hath not the Son of God hath not life. These things have I written unto you that believe on the name of the Son of God; that ye may know that ye have eternal life, and that ye may believe on the name of the Son of God" (1 John 5:10-13).

The gospel gives the promise of grace, salvation and eternal life to all who believe on the Son of God. But in preaching the gospel we also set before eternity bound sinners the warning of certain and eternal wrath for all who refuse to bow to the Son of God, trusting him alone as their Lord and Saviour. "But he that believeth not shall be damned".

How fearful the thought! How awful the words! Yet, they are true and faithful, and must be proclaimed by those who would be true and faithful to the souls of men. God must and will punish sin. He will send you to hell forever, if you refuse to be saved by the merits of his dear Son. "O that men were wise, that they understood this, that they would consider their latter end"!

The Gospel Confession

Look at verse sixteen again, and learn that baptism, the believer's confession of the gospel, the believer's confession of faith in Christ, is not an insignificant matter, but rather a matter of tremendous importance. "He that believeth and is baptized shall be saved; but he that believeth not shall be damned".

Let me be crystal clear. Baptism does not save anyone. Baptism does not wash away sin. Baptism does not convey grace. Baptism does not regenerate. Baptism does not contribute anything to the saving of our souls.

However, believer's baptism and faith in Christ are intimately connected. True, saving faith in Christ and obedience to Christ go hand in hand. Where there is no obedience to Christ, there is no faith in Christ. "Faith without works is dead"!

There are several things which need to be understood about this blessed ordinance of the gospel.

First, baptism follows faith in Christ; it cannot precede faith. Without faith in Christ, baptism is nothing but an empty, meaningless religious ritual. It serves no purpose, except to make the unbelieving ritualist twofold more the child of hell than he was before. Infant baptism not only does not help children, it positively hurts them. It gives them hope without faith, as they grow up believing they are Christians, rather than being faithfully taught that they must be born again.

Second, believer's baptism is an act of obedience to Christ our Lord. As such, it is the answer of a good conscience toward God.

Third, baptism is the means by which believers first confess their faith in Christ publicly. It is a picture of the gospel, a picture of Christ's death, burial and resurrection, and our death, burial and resurrection with him representatively. It is a public identification with Christ, his gospel and his people.

Believer's baptism is a line of separation from the world and its religion. It is a pledge of commitment to Christ. It is a confession of our hope of resurrection with Christ at the last day.

The Gracious Confirmation
Look at the great, gracious, encouraging promises given in verses 17 and 18. Our Lord Jesus knew what great obstacles we would have to overcome, what tremendous difficulties we would have to endure, what battles we would have to fight, and how easily we would be inclined to give up the effort. Therefore, he cheers and encourages us with the promise of divine, supernatural, omnipotent power to attend our labours, power that will be unceasingly confirmed to us.

"And these signs shall follow them that believe; In my name shall they cast out devils; they shall speak with new tongues; They shall take up serpents; and if they drink any deadly thing, it shall not hurt them; they shall lay hands on the sick, and they shall recover".

It must be stated emphatically, in this day of charismatic chaos and confusion, that the age of signs, and tongues, and miracles ended with the apostolic age and the completion of the scriptures.

These things were literally fulfilled in the book of Acts, in the apostolic age, the formation years of the church. But no one has these apostolic gifts today. They were gifts by which the apostles were confirmed as God's messengers, as his inspired spokesmen in the writing of holy scripture (Hebrews 1:1, 2; 2:3, 4).

Having given us the complete Word of God, God no longer speaks by dreams, and visions, and signs, and wonders. There is no need for me to speak in tongues or perform a miracle to convince anyone that my message is of God. All you need to do is compare what I say with God's Word. Since that which is perfect has come (The Book of God!), then that which was in part has been put away. If miracles were every day events, if they were common things, they would not be miracles!

However, just because the age of physical miracles has past, that does not mean that this text has nothing for us. In fact, its spiritual implications are even more delightful and blessed than the physical miracles performed in apostolic times. Our Lord here promises us that, as we go into all the world preaching the gospel, his presence and power will be with us incessantly, and will be manifestly confirmed to us.

It is a great pity that our faith is so weak that we need for our God to confirm his Word to us; but it is a great mercy that our God condescends to our weakness. His eye is always upon us. His arm is always stretched out for us. His power is manifestly confirmed to us (Isaiah 59:19).

The next time you go to the house of God, the next time you are gathered to worship the Lord Jesus, look around and behold "men wondered at". The household of faith is a house of miracles, divine miracles, by which our God confirms the saving power of his grace revealed in the gospel we preach. His people are a people out of whom the Lord has cast seven devils, by the power of his grace.

We are a people who speak with new tongues. Mouths once filled with cursing and bitterness are now filled with mercy and grace! His are a people who are forced every day to take up the serpents of this world and drink the deadly concoctions of the wicked. Yet, we are unhurt by the serpents' bites and the poisons of the ungodly!

We are a people who were sick with the deadly palsy of sin, who have been restored to health by the grace of God, a people who, like Lazarus, have been raised from the dead. God's saints are a people who are literally going through the world, preaching the gospel, and thereby laying hands upon multitudes of sin-sick, impotent folk, dead in trespasses and sins, who are recovered by the grace of God!

Let us take this great commission to heart. Let each believer take it as the Word of God to him personally. Let every gospel church take this as the great commission given by the Son of God to it, as though it were given to that one assembly exclusively.

The Great Commission

"Go ye into all the world, and preach the gospel to every creature. He that believeth and is baptized shall be saved; but he that believeth not shall be damned. And these signs shall follow them that believe; In my name shall they cast out devils; they shall speak with new tongues; They shall take up serpents; and if they drink any deadly thing, it shall not hurt them; they shall lay hands on the sick, and they shall recover".

"So then after the Lord had spoken unto them, he was received up into heaven, and sat on the right hand of God. And they went forth, and preached every where, the Lord working with them, and confirming the word with signs following. Amen".

(Mark 16:19, 20)

Chapter 78

"So Then"

Every word in these two verses is of immense importance. We ought to read them with great care, praying that God the Holy Spirit will both teach us their meaning and seal them to our hearts.

Mark's Conclusion

"So then ... ". That is a good way to wrap things up. Mark is here drawing his gospel narrative to a close. He is wrapping up his message. He is bringing his story to its conclusion. He is saying to us, "This is the conclusion to the story of the earthly life and ministry of the Lord Jesus Christ". What will the conclusion be? How will he finish the story? Read on:

"So then, after the Lord had spoken unto them ... ". Notice how Mark speaks of the Master, the risen Christ. While on the earth, he wore the name of his humiliation, "Jesus". But here Mark speaks of him as "the Lord". That is more than a title of respect. It is a title of respect, which identifies our Lord Jesus Christ as "the Lord", not "a Lord", not one lord among many lords, but "The Lord". Then he proceeds to describe his lordship.

Let us ever speak with reverence when we speak of our God and Saviour. To speak his name lightly, or without the intention of bringing honour to him is to take his name in vain. "Holy and reverend is his name"!

What is Mark referring to when he says, "after the Lord had spoken unto them"? We know, of course, that our Lord Jesus Christ, the Son of God, is the eternal Word in and by whom God reveals himself to men. Without him, apart from him, God cannot be known by man. Man's quest for God, his search after God, is like a blind man groping about in a dark void. No man knows who God is until God is revealed in the Person and work of the God-man, the Lord Jesus Christ (John 1:1-3, 14, 16-18; 2 Corinthians 4:6; Hebrews 1:1-3).

Christ is the living Word of whom the written Word speaks. Jesus Christ is God; and he alone is the Revelation of God. God does not speak to men, nor will he be spoken to by men, except through the Lord Jesus Christ, the God-man, our Mediator.

But Mark is here talking specifically about that which our Lord had spoken just before his ascension and exaltation. He is talking about the Lord's commission to his church to go into all the world and preach the gospel, and the Lord's promise to confirm them as his servants and give success to their labours, as well as his own unceasing companionship unto the end of time. He promised us his presence, his protection and his power forever. We do not have to guess about this. The Holy Spirit tells us plainly that this is what he is referring to here (Acts 1:2, 3).

Christ's Ascension
When our great God and Saviour, the Lord Jesus Christ, had finished everything he came here to do, "he was received up into heaven, and sat down on the right hand of God". How utterly thrilling that is to my soul. He who is my Saviour, he who came here to save me, who shed his blood to redeem me, who gave his Spirit to quicken and preserve me, has been received up into heaven! There's a Man in glory! What does that mean? That means men are welcome in glory! If one man entered into the holy place, perhaps another can. If there is a Man in glory, maybe this man will be found there!

The Lord Jesus "was received up into heaven". He was received there as the God-man, our Mediator, as "the Lord our Righteousness", as our sin-atoning Sacrifice and Substitute, as our Great High Priest and all-prevailing Advocate and as our Forerunner (Luke 24:51; Acts 1:9). When our Lord Jesus Christ was received up into heaven, the angels of God watched him and worshipped him, Satan and the devils were led captive by him, and his Father crowned him.

"He was received up into heaven, and sat on the right hand of God". He sat down because his work was done. He sat down on the right hand of God, the place of supreme dignity and power, because he is the King of Glory (John 17:2; Romans 8:31-34; Hebrews 10:11-14; Psalm 24:1-10).

Child of God, here is a blessed cordial for your heart and soul in this world of sorrow and woe. Christ sits upon the throne of grace, the throne of sovereign, universal power and dominion. He who loved us and gave himself for us is the absolute Monarch of the universe.

Living in this evil world, in this world of trouble, care and heartache, we are often cast down. Living in this world of sin and death, we are decaying; our bodies and minds are wearing away, as they must. We have before us the prospect of death and judgment and eternity. Here is our comfort: We lean back upon him who is our Lord and Saviour, the King of Glory. We cast ourselves upon him. We fall into his omnipotent arms. We are weak, but he is strong. We grow weary and sleep, but he that keepeth Israel neither slumbers nor sleeps. We fall, but he never can. We are dying, but he is Life!

J. C. Ryle wrote, "Blessed indeed is this thought! Our Saviour, though unseen, is a living person. We travel on towards a dwelling where our best Friend is gone to prepare a place for us (John 14:2). The Forerunner has entered in and made all things ready."

Preached Everywhere

Once the Lord Jesus was received up into heaven, "they went forth and preached everywhere". They went because they were sent. "How can they preach, except they be sent?" They preached. That is the business (the only business) of God's church, and that is the business (the only business) of God's servants!

They preached what they knew: the gospel. They preached Christ. Christ is the gospel. As Robert Hawker put it, "Christ in himself is comprehensive of the whole gospel". The words "preach", "preached" and "preaching" are used 37 times in the Book of Acts. Every time, the subject matter preached is Jesus and the Resurrection. Unless Christ is preached, no preaching has been done in the biblical sense of the word.

They preached everywhere. That is the sphere of our labour. To the best of our ability in the generation in which we live it is our responsibility to preach the gospel to all men everywhere.

The Lord's Work

"The Lord working with them"! Imagine that! What a Companion in labour they had! But Christ is more than our co-labourer. We are the tools. He is the Worker. We are hoes and hoses in his hands, by which he tends his garden. He works with us, using us as he sees fit in his vineyard (Romans 12:3; 1 Corinthians 3:5-9).

Would to God we could learn this! It would put an end to all jealousy, envy, strife and division among God's servants. The work is the Lord's. He works with his tools as he sees fit, where he pleases, to accomplish his purpose. And he does it in such a way as to exalt himself and abase man, "that no flesh should glory in his presence". Yet, we could not be more highly honoured, for "we are labourers together with God".

"And they went forth, and preached every where, the Lord working with them, and confirming the word with signs following". Read the Book of Acts, and you will see how this fact is demonstrated time and again. Read the history of God's church in this world, and you will see this scripture emblazoned upon the pages of history.

"The Word of God is not bound". The Word of truth is not preached in vain. In spite of Satan's rage, in spite of persecutions from popes and pagans, politicians and priests, the Word of God has flourished from land to land, from people to people, and from generation to generation. God has caused his little vine, sown in a dry, desert wilderness, to grow into a huge, fruitful tree.

We have seen these words fulfilled for ourselves. Have we not? I ask you, my brothers and sisters in Christ, do you not see the confirmation of God's power and grace upon us to do the work he has sent us to do? The Word of God by his prophet Isaiah (2:3) is fulfilled in our midst every day, even as it was in the apostolic era.

I have been preaching the gospel of Christ for over forty years. In all those years, I have never yet knocked at a door he did not open, come to a raging sea he did not divide before me, met an enemy he did not slay, or have a need he did not supply.

These things were written for our learning, for our comfort, for our encouragement. The Word of God is never preached in vain. Our labour spent in the cause of Christ is never labour spent for nothing. We may never see the result of our work for Christ while we live in this world. If we did, our chests would burst with horrible pride. But in that day when God makes all things manifest, we will see that our labour was not in vain. Let us cast our bread upon the waters, and wait. After many days, it shall return (Psalm 126:6; Isaiah 55:11; 1 Corinthians 15:58).

There is one more word in Mark's gospel that must be understood. Do not overlook it. "Amen". That means, "So be it", or "So it shall be". Here Mark says, "Amen", to all that Christ did. I do too. "Amen", to all that Christ taught. I do too. "Amen", to all that Christ sent us to do. I do too. "Amen", to all that Christ promised to do with us. I do too. I say, "Amen", to the purpose of God in Christ, the revelation of God in Christ, the Word of God revealing Christ, and the work of God by Christ.

Amen

Index Of Bible Verses

Other books by Don Fortner published by Go Publications:

Basic Bible Doctrine

Discovering Christ In All The Scriptures

Discovering Christ In Galatians

Discovering Christ In Hebrews

Discovering Christ In The Gospel Of Matthew

All titles available from Go Publications

www.go-publications.co.uk and www.go-newfocus.co.uk